# Critical acclaim for
# Running MS-DOS®

"*Running MS-DOS* proves how-to books don't have to be pedantic, ugly and full of mistakes. A book even the PC mavens turn to, it is written by a human being for human beings, in a strange and wonderful tongue: English."

*PC Week*

"This book is simply the definitive handbook of PC-DOS and MS-DOS...written for both novices and experienced users."

*BYTE*

"*Running MS-DOS* combines a lucid presentation of MS-DOS commands and functions with sound advice on approaching the basic housekeeping chores that all PC users need to perform. It's presented in a highly readable format that includes plenty of useful examples."

*PC World*

"If you're new to MS-DOS, Van Wolverton's *Running MS-DOS* is essential. This well-written volume has become a classic and is a must-have for serious PC users. If you can only buy one MS-DOS book, buy this one."

*Compute!*

"Excellent guide for computer novices. The tone is informal yet direct. Features are clearly defined and illustrated. Good one-book reference."

*Computer Book Review*

"One of the most popular MS-DOS books is Van Wolverton's *Running MS-DOS.*"

*PC Magazine*

"Describes in clear terms what MS-DOS can do to help you manage your system. The nice thing about this book is that it is written to show how common daily tasks can be made easier with MS-DOS, making the user, rather than the technology, the focus of the tutorials."

*The New York Times*

"An invaluable reference text written in plain English and loaded with practical information and help.... [It includes] one of the most practical and easiest-to-use listings of MS-DOS commands that I've seen. As in the rest of the book, Wolverton's lucid writing style brings a new level of understanding to this important part of MS-DOS."

*Online Today*

"...essential for those who want to get the most out of their PCs."

"*Running MS-DOS* is well organized and clearly written. Van Wolverton goes to great lengths to explain the commands rather than just show you how to use them."

"This is truly the conerstone book for any serious MS-DOS user's library."

"*Running MS-DOS* has become a sort of operating system bible for PC owners....Wolverton's easygoing style and Microsoft's lavish use of illustrations make this one of the best MS-DOS books on the market."

"...clearly guides you through the mazes of computer disk operating systems for any IBM PC or IBM compatible."

"For anyone eager to get the most from any or all of the currently available versions of MS-DOS, *Running MS-DOS* is the book of choice."

"*Running MS-DOS* succeeds where others fail because it begins on a simple level, yet doesn't bore the reader or talk down to the reader. You can learn more from it than any other single volume available—including the instructions which come with your computer and software."

"If you want to learn something about the IBM disk operating system, the best bet is still a tome called *Running MS-DOS*. Wolverton assumes you are a literate adult, and that's about it. The result is a no-nonsense explanation of how an IBM-compatible works, and how to make it work for you."

"If you want to thoroughly understand the operating system that drives IBM and compatible machines, get Van Wolverton's *Running MS-DOS*."

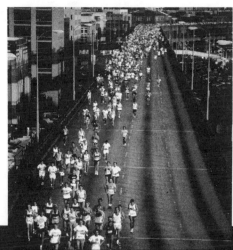

# *RUNNING*

# MS-DOS®

## VERSION 6.2

# Van Wolverton

PUBLISHED BY
Microsoft Press
A Division of Microsoft Corporation
One Microsoft Way
Redmond, Washington 98052-6399

Library of Congress Cataloging-in-Publication Data
Wolverton, Van, 1939–
    Running MS-DOS / Van Wolverton. -- 6th Rev. ed.
      p.  cm.
    Includes index.
    ISBN 1-55615-633-2
    1. MS-DOS (Computer file)    I. Title.
  QA76.76.O63W65   1993
  005.4'469--dc20                                 93-37565
                                                       CIP

Printed and bound in the United States of America.

   4 5 6 7 8 9  AG-M  9 8 7 6 5 4

Distributed to the book trade in Canada by Macmillan of Canada, a division of Canada Publishing
Corporation.

A CIP catalogue record for this book is available from the British Library.

Microsoft Press books are available through booksellers and distributors worldwide. For further
information about international editions, contact your local Microsoft Corporation office, or
contact Microsoft Press International directly at fax (206) 936-7329.

IBM is a registered trademark of International Business Machines Corporation. Microsoft
and MS-DOS are registered trademarks and Windows is a trademark of Microsoft Corporation.
All other trademarks and service marks are the property of their respective owners.

**Acquisitions Editor:** Dean Holmes
**Project Editor:** Maureen Williams Zimmerman
**Manuscript Editor:** Barbara Browne
**Technical Editor:** Dail Magee, Jr.

*For Jeanne,*
*who makes it all worthwhile*

# Contents

## GETTING TO KNOW MS-DOS

## Part II: LEARNING TO USE MS-DOS

## 7   Managing Your Devices           113

## 8   A Tree of Files           135

## 9   Managing Your Hard Disk           169

## Part III: APPENDIXES

# Acknowledgments

It's been more than nine years since the first edition of this book hit the shelves; the world of computers has changed mightily in that time. The person who bought the first edition most likely had an IBM PC with a 4.88-MHz 8088 processor, 64 kilobytes of memory, and two floppy disk drives. Those of you who buy this edition probably have an IBM compatible with a 25-MHz 80486 processor, 2 megabytes of memory, and an 80-megabyte hard disk. And today's machine, although more than ten times more powerful than that 1984 model, costs less.

MS-DOS and this book share astonishing longevity in this quicksilver world of personal computers. The staying power of MS-DOS is due to the remarkable proliferation of IBM and IBM-compatible computers and the usefulness of MS-DOS, for which I thank all those who have labored over the years to put an MS-DOS machine on everyone's desk, especially those at IBM and Microsoft who started things off back in 1981 and have kept the fires burning ever since.

The staying power of this book owes an equal debt to the inspiration and efforts of three remarkable women. My mother, Bee Forsyth Wolverton, has preached the gospel of clear writing as far back as I can remember, reinforcing her message by setting a dauntingly high example. My editor, JoAnne Woodcock, cosseted and cajoled me through four revisions, using her skill, judgment, and patience to improve the book each time; she is without peer. But most of all, Jeanne Elizabeth Wolverton whipped the first edition into shape before anyone else ever saw it, and continues to keep me on the right track; she has been my first editor for more than 30 years, and I'm still learning from her.

Personal thanks to the people of Montana who have made Jeanne and me feel so welcome; it's good to be back.

*Van Wolverton*
*Rubicon*
*Sawmill Gulch Road*
*Alberton, MT 59820*
*November 1993*

# Introduction

It may be tempting to skip these opening words and "get to the meat of it," but please read this introduction anyway. The information included here is both useful and brief.

You may want to know whether this book applies to you. It does if your computer uses MS-DOS. The book itself was written with an IBM personal computer, but it applies equally well to any machine that uses MS-DOS.

You bought this book—or at least took the time to pick it up and glance through it—despite the hefty manual you got with your copy of MS-DOS. Why? What else can a book like this offer? It can offer simplicity. The MS-DOS manual is thorough and complete. It is your official, comprehensive reference guide to MS-DOS, but its goal is really to tell you *about* MS-DOS rather than how to *use* MS-DOS in your everyday work.

This book does not show you how to set up your computer, nor does it describe in detail the pieces of the system, such as the keyboard or the display. These matters should be covered thoroughly in the manuals that came with your computer.

The book assumes neither that you are, nor that you aspire to become, a programmer. It doesn't try to explain how MS-DOS works, and it leaves to the MS-DOS manual the task of explaining some of the more technical features. The book does assume that you have access to an IBM personal computer or one of the many other machines that run MS-DOS, and that you want to put the machine to work. It includes scores of examples, and it is organized by what you want the computer to do, not (as a programmer would expect) by how MS-DOS itself is structured. The examples reflect real-life situations.

You don't have to be a mechanical engineer to drive a car well, but you do need experience. You don't have to be a computer scientist to use MS-DOS well, either, and this book starts you on your way.

## WHAT'S IN THE BOOK AND WHERE

This book covers MS-DOS through version 6.2, as it is used on machines that have a hard disk and either one or two floppy disk drives. Although a hard disk is assumed, the examples are also structured to work on computers that have two floppy disk drives.

Part I, Chapters 1 through 4, describes the pieces of the computer system, defines some terms and concepts, and provides hands-on examples that show you the major capabilities of MS-DOS.

Part II, the bulk of the book, includes Chapters 5 through 17. These chapters show you how to operate your computer system and manage all its parts with the MS-DOS commands.

Chapters 5, 6, and 7 show you how to manage your files, floppy disks, and computer devices such as the printer and the display. Chapter 8 describes the MS-DOS multilevel filing system that allows you to set up a personalized computer file system that matches the way you work. Chapter 9 shows you how to manage the files and directories on a hard disk, and Chapter 10 shows you some ways to protect both the disk and your work from loss or damage.

Chapter 11 takes you through a menu-based program called the Shell (shipped with versions 5 and 6 and available on the supplemental disk to version 6.2) that makes your display visually more interesting and your work with the computer easier in many ways. Chapter 12 describes another menu-based program, the MS-DOS Editor (available in versions 5 and later).

Chapters 13 through 17 describe ways to tailor MS-DOS to your own needs. Chapter 13 shows you how to take control of your system with a special set of commands called filter commands; it also shows you how to use a program named Doskey that can save time and work by recording keystrokes and commands. Chapters 14 through 16 show you how to create your own sets of commands and save them in special files called batch files. Chapter 17 shows you several techniques you can use to make MS-DOS immediately useful in its own right, and it describes ways to help MS-DOS run your computer more efficiently.

Finally, in Part III, Appendix A tells you how to install MS-DOS, Appendix B provides a glossary of commonly used terms, and Appendix C describes the MS-DOS commands, with cross-references to the discussions in the preceding chapters.

If you plan to use your computer for word processing, spreadsheets, database management, games, or any other applications, this book is probably all you'll need. Not only does it show you how to use MS-DOS so you can run your programs, it shows you how to make good use of MS-DOS without additional software.

## ABOUT THE EXAMPLES

The best way to learn how to put MS-DOS to work is to use it. This book, therefore, is devoted primarily to examples. Terms and concepts are defined as you need them and are illustrated with hands-on examples that help you see both what you do and why. Because the book covers different versions of MS-DOS and different types of machines, there are variations in some examples; these alternatives are identified. Unless an example states it is for a particular version or computer setup, the MS-DOS displays shown in this book are the MS-DOS version 6 responses on a computer with one hard disk and one floppy disk drive. If you are using a different version of MS-DOS or a different computer setup, the responses you see may vary somewhat. Do not be concerned.

## What to Type and When

There's an awkward mismatch between a computer and a book that shows you how to use it. The computer is dynamic: It displays messages, moves data back and forth between disks and memory, prints words and pictures, and chirps now and then to announce completion of another task. When you use the computer, you enter into a dialogue: You type something, the computer responds, you type something else, and so on, back and forth, until your work is done.

A book, however, is static. It can show only snapshots of your dialogue with the system, yet it must describe that dialogue well enough so that you can take part in it. In this book, we have to show what you type and how the computer responds. We have to distinguish parts of this dialogue, such as the names of files and messages displayed on the screen, from the surrounding prose. Here are the conventions we've adopted:

- Hands-on examples are shown in different type, on separate lines, just as you would see them on your display. The characters you type are printed in lowercase colored type; MS-DOS usually doesn't care whether you type in uppercase or lowercase, but lowercase seems to be easier. Here is a sample of the conventions for hands-on examples:

  ```
  C:\>format b:
  Insert new floppy disk for drive B:
  and press ENTER when ready  .  .  .
  ```

- Occasionally, similar information occurs in text. In these instances, the interaction between you and MS-DOS is printed in italics to distinguish it from the surrounding text. For example, you may see "Type *n* when MS-DOS displays *Format another (Y/N)?*"

- Many MS-DOS commands include options, or parameters, that allow you to specify a particular disk drive, file, or piece of equipment, or to use a particular form of the command. Options are shown in angle brackets (<>) when they represent a variable entry, such as the name of a file. When they must be entered exactly, they are shown in the form you must use. For example, here are some options of the Format command used in the preceding examples (don't worry about understanding the command at this point):

  **format <drive> /4 /F:<size> /Q**

Now it's time to meet MS-DOS. This book was written to be used alongside the system, so put it beside your keyboard, turn to Chapter 1, and get ready to put MS-DOS to work.

# PART 1

# GETTING TO KNOW MS-DOS

Part I introduces you to the concept of an operating system: what it is, what it does, and why you need it. It then describes the terms and the basic operating principles of MS-DOS. The chapters show you how to start MS-DOS and how to control the system with MS-DOS commands. They give you the foundation for using MS-DOS effectively in your daily work with the computer. The information is primarily tutorial, and many examples are included. Later parts of the book contain detailed reference information that describes the MS-DOS commands and their capabilities.

# What Is MS-DOS?

You've got your computer, and you've probably got one or two programs, such as a word processor or a spreadsheet, to use with it. But what is this thing called MS-DOS? Why do you hear so much about it, and why have hundreds of pages of instructions been written for it?

## MS-DOS IS A PROGRAM

MS-DOS is a program, but it's not just any program. Chances are none of your other programs would work without it because MS-DOS controls every part of the computer system. MS-DOS not only makes it possible for your other programs to work, it also gives you complete control over what your computer does, and how. MS-DOS is the link between you and your computer.

To appreciate the role MS-DOS plays, take a quick look at the pieces of your computer system and what they do.

## HARDWARE MAKES IT POSSIBLE

Your computer equipment, called *hardware*, probably includes a keyboard, display, printer, and one or more disk drives. The purposes of the first three are straightforward: You type instructions at the keyboard, and the system responds by displaying or printing messages and results.

The purpose of a disk drive isn't quite so obvious, but it quickly becomes apparent as you use the system: A disk drive records and plays back information, much as a tape deck records and plays back music. The computer's information is recorded in files on disks; you'll find that disk files are as central to your computer work as paper files are to more traditional office work.

## SOFTWARE MAKES IT HAPPEN

No matter how powerful the hardware, a computer can't do anything without programs, called *software*. There are two major types of software: *system programs*, which control the operation of the computer system, and *application programs*, which perform more obviously useful tasks, such as word processing.

Each program uses the hardware. It must be able to receive instructions from the keyboard, display and print results, read and write files from and to a disk, send and receive data through the computer's communications connections, change the colors on a color display, and so on through all the capabilities of the hardware.

So that each program doesn't have to perform all these functions for itself, a system program called the *operating system* manages the hardware. The operating system allows an application program to concentrate on what it does best, whether it's moving paragraphs about, tracking accounts receivable, or calculating stress in a bridge beam. MS-DOS is an operating system.

# MS-DOS IS A DISK OPERATING SYSTEM

The operating system for IBM and IBM-compatible computers is the Microsoft Disk Operating System—MS-DOS. MS-DOS is called a disk operating system because much of its work involves managing disks and disk files.

## What Does an Operating System Do?

An operating system plays a role something like a symphony conductor. When the score calls for the violins to play, the conductor cues the violins; when the score says the cellos should play more softly, the tympani should stop, or the entire orchestra should pick up the tempo, the conductor so instructs the musicians.

The players in the orchestra and their instruments represent the hardware. The experience and skill of the conductor represent the operating system. The score represents an application program.

When one score is replaced by another—Beethoven's Fifth Symphony is put aside and replaced by Haydn's *Surprise* Symphony, for example—the same musicians use the same instruments, and the same conductor uses the same experience and skills. A different sound, a different mood, perhaps, but the elements are the same.

When one application program is replaced by another—for example, an accounting program is put aside and replaced with a word processor—the same hardware carries out the instructions of the same operating system. A different program, a different purpose, perhaps, but the elements are the same.

MS-DOS coordinates the computer system, just as the conductor coordinates the orchestra. Your application programs run in concert with MS-DOS, trusting it to keep the system humming.

Much of what MS-DOS does, such as how it stores a file on a disk or prints on the printer, is invisible to you. But MS-DOS lets you control the things you care about, such as which program to run, what report to print, or what files to erase. These functions share an important characteristic: They need disks and disk drives.

## Disk Drives

Personal computers use two main types of disk: a flexible disk in a protective plastic jacket, called a *floppy disk*, which you can remove from the drive, and a permanently mounted unit called a *hard disk*. There are two types of floppy disks: 5.25 inches square in a flexible plastic jacket, and 3.5 inches square in a rigid plastic shell.

A hard disk holds much more information than a floppy disk—from 15 to 100 times as much, or even more—and is much faster. Most personal computers have one hard disk and one floppy disk drive. Machines without a hard disk usually have two floppy disk drives.

To distinguish among the types of disk, this book uses *floppy disk* to mean either type of flexible disk, *hard disk* to mean only a permanently mounted disk, and *disk* to refer to both.

## Disk Files

Just as you organize and store your written records in paper files, you organize and store computer information in disk files.

A disk file—usually called a file—is a collection of related information stored on a disk. It could be a letter, an income tax return, or a list of customers. It could also be a program, because the programs you use are stored in files.

Virtually all your computer work revolves around files. Because one of the major functions of MS-DOS is to take care of files, much of this book is devoted to showing you how to create, print, copy, organize, and otherwise manage files.

## Where Is MS-DOS?

When your computer is turned off, MS-DOS is stored on disk. Although it's a special type of program, MS-DOS is still a program, and that means it's stored on disk in a set of files like any other collection of computer information.

If your computer has a hard disk, MS-DOS is probably already on it—placed there, perhaps, by your computer dealer, or by someone else who set up your system. If your computer does not have a hard disk, it must use MS-DOS from floppy disks, so it should have come with a copy of MS-DOS on two or more floppy disks.

## Different Versions of MS-DOS

MS-DOS has been revised a number of times since its release in 1981; the first version was numbered 1.00. MS-DOS is revised to add more capability, to take advantage of more sophisticated hardware, and to correct errors. When you start up your system, MS-DOS may display the version number you are using.

When a new version of MS-DOS appears, a change in the number following the decimal point—6.0 to 6.2, for example—marks a minor change that leaves the new version of MS-DOS substantially the same as the previous version. A change in the number preceding the decimal point marks a major change. Version 6.0, for example, adds several new features that weren't available in version 5.0.

Even though newer versions of MS-DOS have much more capability, they remain compatible with earlier versions. Thus, if you start with version 2.1, you can still use all your knowledge and experience, plus your files and disks, when you move to a newer version of MS-DOS.

For simplicity, this book usually refers to MS-DOS by major version number only—for example, version 6 or version 4, rather than version 6.0 or version 4.01. It also omits references to versions of MS-DOS earlier than version 3, but much of the information applies to these versions too. Remember, version 2 is just as much a part of MS-DOS as version 5. It's simply older and, although it includes many of the features described here, it doesn't provide them all.

## What Is Compatibility?

You've no doubt seen the term *IBM-compatible* in an article or an advertisement. What does compatibility actually mean? Compatibility essentially refers to the ability of one computer to use programs and data created for or stored on another computer. In everyday use, the most meaningful measure of compatibility is the extent to which you can use the same programs, data, and floppy disks in computers of different makes or different models:

- If two systems are totally compatible, they can freely use the same programs and floppy disks. This is the type of compatibility exhibited among different models of IBM Personal Computers and the IBM-compatible machines made by manufacturers other than IBM. On these machines, such full compatibility is made possible in part by MS-DOS: Any computer that can run MS-DOS can run programs designed for MS-DOS, and that computer can (given the proper application programs) freely use floppy disks from any other MS-DOS computer.

- Incompatible systems might use different versions of the same program, but they can't use either programs or floppy disks intended for the other computer. This is typically the situation between IBM and Macintosh computers. An IBM machine can, for example, use the IBM version of Microsoft Word, and the Macintosh can use the Macintosh version of Microsoft Word, but neither computer can use the version intended for the other. Nor can these computers easily exchange floppy disks because neither system can read files stored by the other without special hardware or software.

This book describes how MS-DOS works on all IBM and IBM-compatible machines.

## WHAT CAN YOU DO WITH MS-DOS?

MS-DOS coordinates the operation of the computer for your application programs. That's valuable—essential, really—but MS-DOS has much more to offer. You can use MS-DOS itself, controlling it with instructions called *commands*, to manage your files, control the work flow, and perform useful tasks that might otherwise require additional software.

For example, MS-DOS includes a program that lets you create and revise files of text. Although it's not a word processor, the MS-DOS Editor is fine for short memos and lists. Using it, you can write short documents in less time than it might take using your word processing program.

You can tailor MS-DOS to your specific needs by creating powerful commands made up of other MS-DOS commands, and you can even create your own small applications. For example, this book shows you how to create a simple file manager—a program that lets you search a file for specific information—using nothing but MS-DOS commands.

MS-DOS versions 4 through 6 also include a separate program, called the *Shell*, that lets you choose commands and files from on-screen lists called *menus*. If you want, you can use the Shell for routine work, dispense with it and work directly with MS-DOS, or move freely between MS-DOS and the Shell as your work requires.

Your knowledge of MS-DOS can range from just enough to use a single application program to mastery of the full range of capabilities in the latest version. But no matter how far you go, you needn't learn to program. It's all MS-DOS, and it's all in this book.

## CHAPTER SUMMARY

This quick tour of MS-DOS may have introduced several new terms and concepts. Here are the key points to remember:

- A working computer system needs both hardware (equipment) and software (programs).

- MS-DOS (the Microsoft Disk Operating System) coordinates the operation of all parts of the computer system.

- A file is a collection of related information stored on a disk. Most of your computer work will involve files.

- Besides running your application programs, MS-DOS is valuable in its own right.

The next chapter starts you off at the keyboard.

# Starting MS-DOS

**N**ow that you have been introduced to some of the things MS-DOS does for you, it's time to start your system and do something. Whenever you start your computer, whether it is to use a word processor, an accounting program, or MS-DOS itself, you begin by *loading* MS-DOS into the computer's memory, its workplace. Loading the MS-DOS program and starting it running is sometimes called "booting the system" or "booting the disk." This term is borrowed from the phrase "pulling yourself up by your bootstraps" because MS-DOS essentially pulls itself up by its own bootstraps, loading itself from disk into memory, where it then waits for a command from you.

The examples from here on assume that you have a computer with a hard disk, that your system is set up to use MS-DOS, and that you are familiar with your computer's control switches. If you need to install a more recent version of MS-DOS on your hard disk, refer to Appendix A. (If your computer does not have a hard disk and you're using MS-DOS from floppy disks, have your usual startup disk ready.)

## STARTING THE SYSTEM

When you use MS-DOS from a hard disk, the MS-DOS program must be copied into the computer's memory from the hard disk (usually known to MS-DOS as drive C). All you need to do before starting the system is make sure the latch on drive A (the floppy disk drive) isn't closed; otherwise, the system will try to load the MS-DOS program into the computer's memory from the floppy disk in drive A.

If you're not using a hard disk, the MS-DOS program must be copied into the computer's memory from the floppy disk in drive A. Open the latch of drive A (either the left-hand or the upper floppy disk drive) and put in the floppy disk you use to start MS-DOS—called the *system disk* in this book—with the label up and away from the machine. If you're using a 5.25-inch disk, close the latch.

Turn on the system. The computer seems to do nothing for several seconds, but this is normal. Each time you turn on the power switch, the computer checks its memory and all attached devices to be sure everything is working properly. The system beeps after it has made sure that all is well, the drive lights flash, and the computer begins loading MS-DOS into memory. As soon as the program is loaded, MS-DOS is running and ready to go to work.

## A First Look at MS-DOS

Both MS-DOS and the computers it runs on have evolved in the years since MS-DOS and the IBM PC were introduced. The examples in this book are designed to work correctly with your computer and any release of MS-DOS that supports the commands described, but there are variations in the way computers are set up and in the ways MS-DOS can be organized, installed, and presented to the person who uses it.

One highly visible difference is how MS-DOS looks once it is loaded into memory and ready for you to command. The following sections describe the major variations, one of which should explain what you see on your screen when you start the system.

Many computers today are sold with Microsoft Windows already installed on the hard disk. In some cases, the system is configured so that windows starts automatically each time the computer is turned on. If this is the case, you'll see a screen that looks something like the one shown in Figure 2-1.

**Figure 2-1.**
*The opening (Program Manager) screen of Microsoft Windows.*

Windows requires MS-DOS to run, so you can leave Windows temporarily to use this book. To leave Windows, press the Alt key, then F, then X; when Windows displays a box in the middle of the screen telling you that this will end your Windows session, press Enter.

The screen clears, and now MS-DOS is in control; it displays the following:

```
C:\>_
```

or:

```
C:\DOS>_
```

You're ready to start using MS-DOS. Go on to the heading "The System Prompt."

### Opening with a Startup Menu

If version 6 or later is installed on your machine, when you start it you might see a screen titled *MS-DOS 6 Startup Menu*. Below the title are two or more numbered choices (such a list of choices is called a *menu*); menu choices might include *Normal* or *Start network*. Below the menu is the line *Enter a choice* followed by the number of the default choice. This screen lets you choose different ways of starting your system; you can't hurt anything no matter how you start it, so press Enter to choose the default menu item. (The default might be chosen for you after a few seconds.) After you press Enter, you will see one of the startup variations described in the next four sections.

### Opening with the MS-DOS Shell

If you're using MS-DOS version 4 or later, your system might be set up to start with the MS-DOS Shell. If so, you'll see a display like this one:

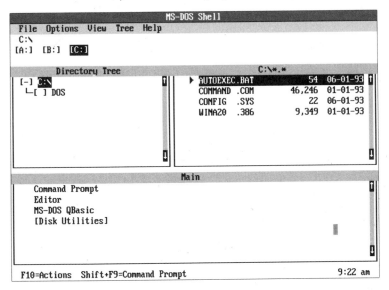

This illustration shows the opening screen of the version 6 Shell as it appears in the form called *text mode*, in which the display is made up of letters, numbers, lines, brackets, and other text characters rather than graphic images such as file folders and arrow-shaped mouse pointers. Your Shell screen might differ in some details.

Chapter 11, "The MS-DOS Shell," shows you how to use the Shell. Because the Shell is optional, however, and because you sometimes leave it to use parts of MS-DOS, the remainder of this chapter—indeed, much of this book—takes you outside the Shell. This should help you become comfortable with MS-DOS itself and should enable users of all versions of MS-DOS to benefit from the examples.

If you see the opening Shell screen, leave the Shell for now by pressing the F3 key. MS-DOS responds by clearing the screen and displaying this:

```
C:\>_
```

or this:

```
C:\DOS>_
```

(If your computer doesn't have a hard disk, you see A:\> instead of C:\>.)

Now you have a direct line to MS-DOS. Go on to the heading "The System Prompt."

## Opening Without Windows or the MS-DOS Shell

On many systems, regardless of the version of MS-DOS you use, MS-DOS starts out by rapidly displaying some brief messages. In version 6.2, for example, the first message you'll see looks something like this:

```
Starting MS-DOS...
```

If you see such a message—or any others that don't require responses from you—you can assume that MS-DOS is settling in properly.

In a startup routine like this, MS-DOS ends by displaying:

```
C:\>_
```

or this:

```
C:\DOS>_
```

or this (if you don't have a hard disk):

```
A:\>_
```

and waits for your command. If your startup ends like this, MS-DOS is ready to go to work. Go on to the heading "The System Prompt."

## Opening with Date and Time Requests

Regardless of the version you use, MS-DOS checks for the correct date and time as part of its standard startup routine. If your computer contains a battery-powered internal clock, MS-DOS checks the clock for the information it needs. If your computer does not have a clock, however, the first thing that MS-DOS does is ask you for the date and time. First, it asks for the date:

```
Current date is Tue 01-01-1980
Enter new date (mm-dd-yy): _
```

If you see this message, press the Enter key for now, even though the date isn't Tuesday, January 1, 1980. MS-DOS requests the time next:

```
Current time is  0:01:30.00a
Enter new time: _
```

Again, just press Enter; you'll see how to set or change both the date and time later in this chapter. MS-DOS should now display a message showing the version you're using, and then end with a display like this:

```
C:\>_
```

or this:

```
C:\DOS>_
```

or this (if you don't have a hard disk):

```
A:\>_
```

Go on to the heading "The System Prompt."

### None of the Above

In the years since MS-DOS appeared, many companies have developed shell programs and more sophisticated software that provide alternative ways to use a computer and manage files and applications. The MS-DOS Shell in versions 4 and later are examples of such programs. Microsoft Windows is another.

If none of the preceding descriptions match what you see when you start your computer, check the documentation that came with your computer, or ask the person who set up your system whether a shell or other special program has been installed and, if so, how you can leave it temporarily to use this book.

## THE SYSTEM PROMPT

The C:\> (or A:\> if you're not using a hard disk) is called the *system prompt* or *command prompt,* because the system program (MS-DOS) is prompting you to type a command. At this point, MS-DOS is at what is often called *command level,* because it's ready and waiting for a command.

The system prompt identifies the *current drive,* the drive where MS-DOS looks for a file. MS-DOS identifies your drives by letter. On a system with one floppy disk drive and one hard disk, the floppy disk drive is identified as both A and B, the hard disk drive as drive C. On a system with two floppy disk drives, the left-hand or upper drive is drive A, the right-hand or lower drive is drive B.

When MS-DOS is loaded from the hard disk (drive C), MS-DOS assumes drive C is the current drive, and the initial system prompt is C:\> or C:\DOS>. If you're not using a hard disk, MS-DOS is loaded from drive A; MS-DOS assumes that drive A is the current drive, and the initial system prompt on your system is A:\>.

This book contains many examples for you to try. With a few exceptions, the examples show the system prompt as C:\> because that is the normal system prompt on a computer with a hard disk and version 6 of MS-DOS. If you're not using a hard disk, proceed with the examples, but bear in mind that where you see C:\> in the book, you will see A:\> on your screen.

# ENTERING MS-DOS COMMANDS

For the first few commands you enter in this session, you need only the standard typewriter keys on the keyboard. Three of those keys, Enter, Backspace, and Up arrow, are shown on the keyboards in Figures 2-2 and 2-3 and are worth separate mention.

**Figure 2-2.**
*The Backspace, Enter, and Up arrow keys on the early PC-compatible keyboards.*

**Figure 2-3.**
*The Backspace, Enter, and Up arrow keys on the enhanced PC-compatible keyboard.*

## The Enter Key

The Enter key is labeled with a bent left arrow (↵), the word *Enter*, or both. Like the return key on a typewriter, it marks the end of a line. In general, MS-DOS doesn't know what you have typed until you press Enter, so remember: End a command by pressing the Enter key.

15

### The Backspace Key

The Backspace key is labeled with a left arrow (←), the word *Backspace,* or both. It erases the last character you typed; use it to correct typing errors.

### The Up Arrow Key

The Up arrow key is labeled with an upward-pointing arrow (↑). It is located on the 8 key in the calculatorlike numeric keypad on all IBM-compatible keyboards and also appears in the set of four "direction" keys to the left of the keypad on enhanced keyboards. The Up arrow key is often used to move a highlight on the screen, but in MS-DOS versions 5 and 6 it also lets you repeat a command, as you'll see in a moment.

## GETTING STARTED

At this point, MS-DOS should be displaying the system prompt, followed by a blinking underline. This underline is the *cursor.* It shows where MS-DOS will display whatever you type next. It also tells you that MS-DOS is waiting for you to type something. It's time to put MS-DOS to work.

The MS-DOS commands you'll try in this chapter are easy to use and remember, so no special preparation is needed. If you have version 5 or later of MS-DOS, however, you have an "extra"—a small program named Doskey that you can load into your computer's memory and use with MS-DOS to make some tasks more efficient. You can try Doskey in this chapter, so if you have version 5 or later, type:

```
C:\>doskey
```

and press the Enter key.

> **NOTE:** *If you're using MS-DOS from floppy disks and see the message* Bad command or file name, *don't worry. The floppy disk in drive A doesn't include the part of MS-DOS needed to carry out your command. Just ignore Doskey for now; you'll soon be able to use it without a second thought.*

### Checking on Your Version of MS-DOS

Some of the examples in this book assume you know which version of MS-DOS you're using. The easiest way to find out about MS-DOS is to ask MS-DOS itself. Whether you know your MS-DOS version or not, try out the Ver (short for *version*) command. Type:

```
C:\>ver
```

and press the Enter key.

MS-DOS responds by displaying a message that identifies the version. The exact wording depends on the computer and version of MS-DOS you have. In Microsoft releases of version 6, for example, the message reads:

```
MS-DOS Version 6.20
```

# KEEPING TRACK OF THE DATE AND TIME

It's important to know which version of MS-DOS you use, but it's more important to know your computer keeps the correct date and time. The computer has an electronic clock that keeps time to the hundredth of a second. MS-DOS uses this clock to keep track of both the time of day and the date.

In some computers, the clock doesn't run when the system is shut off, so each time you start the system MS-DOS sets the date to January 1, 1980 (01-01-1980) and sets the time to midnight (0:00:00.00 or 12:00:00.00a). That's why, on systems without a battery-powered clock of some type, MS-DOS prompts for the correct date and time at startup.

If your system doesn't keep the date and time current, and you just press Enter in response to the date and time prompts when you start the system, MS-DOS assumes that it's midnight on January 1, 1980. Even though you might have been advised (for simplicity) to skip setting the correct date and time earlier in the chapter, it really isn't a good habit to form because MS-DOS marks each disk file you create or change with the current time and date. Such information is useful, so it's a good idea to set the correct date and time—if necessary—each time you start the system.

## Checking or Changing the Date

To check or change the date, you use the MS-DOS Date command. Type:

```
C:\>date
```

and press Enter. MS-DOS responds like this (you probably see a different date):

```
Current date is Mon 08-30-1993
Enter new date (mm-dd-yy): _
```

The cursor now follows the *Enter new date* request. Such a request is called a *prompt*; MS-DOS frequently prompts you to enter information so that you don't have to memorize operating procedures.

To enter the date, you type the numbers that represent the month, day, and year, separated by hyphens, and then you press the Enter key. You don't have to type the day of the week; MS-DOS figures out the day for you.

For this example, set the date to October 16, 1993, by typing the information at the top of the next page (be sure to press Enter after the last number).

```
Current date is Mon 08-30-1993
Enter new date (mm-dd-yy): 10-16-93
```

**NOTE:** *You can also use a slash (/) or a period to separate the numbers. Whichever you use, if you don't do it exactly right (in other words, in a way that MS-DOS recognizes), MS-DOS displays* Invalid date *and prompts you to try again. If you make a mistake or enter the wrong date, don't be alarmed. As you'll soon see, it's easy to fix such errors.*

Check the date again to be sure MS-DOS changed it for you. If you don't have version 5 or later, you repeat your last command by typing it again. Do so now; MS-DOS should respond with its normal date display.

If you have version 5 or later, there's an easier way to repeat a command: Press the Up arrow key once. MS-DOS displays:

```
C:\>date_
```

There's the Date command you just typed. Remember when you entered a Doskey command a few pages ago? Doskey starts a program that keeps track of each command you type in a special area of memory. After you have started Doskey, you can recycle previous commands by pressing the Up or Down arrow key, as you just did.

Press the Enter key, and MS-DOS responds just as if you had typed the Date command:

```
Current date is Sat 10-16-1993
Enter new date (mm-dd-yy): _
```

By pressing just two keys, you have repeated your last MS-DOS command.

You'll correct the date in a moment, but first try the following exercise to see how easily you can fix typing errors.

## Backspacing to Correct Typing Errors

Try out the Backspace key. Type some characters, such as the following, at random, but don't press Enter:

```
Current date is Sat 10-16-1993
Enter new date (mm-dd-yy): w710273_
```

This isn't a valid date. If you were to press Enter now, MS-DOS would display the message *Invalid date* and ask you to try again. Correct your typing "error" by pressing the Backspace key until all the characters are erased and the cursor is back to its original position, just to the right of the colon. The screen looks like it did before:

```
Current date is Sat 10-16-1993
Enter new date (mm-dd-yy): _
```

This time, type the correct date and press Enter—for example:

```
Current date is Sat 10-16-1993
Enter new date (mm-dd-yy): 4-27-93
```

for April 27, 1993.

## Checking or Changing the Time

Just as you can control the date with the Date command, you can check or change the time with the MS-DOS Time command. If your computer has an internal clock/calendar that keeps the date and time current even when the system is turned off, you probably won't have a lot of use for either Date or Time, but they can still come in handy—when the time changes with daylight saving time, for example, or when you want to know what day of the week a certain date falls on.

Once you've seen the Date command, the Time command looks quite familiar. To try it, type:

```
C:\>time
```

MS-DOS displays its version of the time and prompts for a new time:

```
Current time is  8:22:33:55a
Enter new time: _
```

If MS-DOS displays the correct time and you don't want to tamper with it, press Enter without typing a response. If the time is incorrect, or if you feel like experimenting, type the time in the appropriate format for your version of MS-DOS, as described below:

| MS-DOS Version | Time Format | Examples |
|---|---|---|
| 1 through 3 | 24-hour clock | 8:30 (before noon) or 20:30 (after noon) |
| 4 and later | 12-hour or 24-hour clock | 8:30a and 8:30p or 8:30 and 20:30 |

With versions 1 through 3, for example, you would type:

```
Current time is  8:22:33:55a
Enter new time: 13:15
```

to set the time to 1:15 in the afternoon. With versions 4 and later, you could also type:

```
Current time is  8:22:33:55a
Enter new time: 1:15p
```

Versions 4 and later accept either form.

If you've changed to an incorrect time, reset it before continuing: If you have version 5 or later, press the Up arrow key to recall the last command. If you don't have version 5 or later, type *time*. Now type the correct time and press Enter to carry out the command.

## CHANGING THE CURRENT DRIVE

You can change the current drive simply by typing the letter of the new drive, followed by a colon. For example, try changing the current drive to B.

You'll need a floppy disk, so either find one that you have used before or use one of your MS-DOS floppy disks (be careful with it).

If you have one floppy disk drive, insert the floppy disk in the drive with the label up and away from the machine. If you have two floppy disk drives, insert the floppy disk in the drive that does not currently contain your MS-DOS startup disk. Now type:

```
C:\>b:
```

If you have one floppy disk drive, MS-DOS displays the message:

```
Insert diskette for drive B: and press any key when ready
```

The floppy disk is already in the drive, so press a key. MS-DOS responds:

```
B:\>_
```

Now the system prompt is B:\ >, confirming that MS-DOS will look in drive B unless told otherwise.

If you're using a hard disk, change the current drive back to drive C by typing the following:

```
B:\>c:
```

```
C:\>_
```

The system prompt returns to C:\ >.

If you're not using a hard disk, change the current drive back to drive A by typing the following:

```
B:\>a:
```

```
A:\>_
```

The system prompt returns to A:\ >.

## PRINTING WHAT'S ON THE SCREEN

The screen shows you a record of your commands and the responses from MS-DOS; it normally shows a maximum of 25 lines. When all the lines are filled, each additional line causes the entire screen to shift up, or *scroll*, to make room for the new line at the bottom; the top line disappears from view.

Because a copy of what is on the display is often useful, MS-DOS makes it easy to print what's on the screen. Locate the key labeled PrtSc (for *Print Screen*, which is spelled out on some keyboards). Make sure your printer is turned on, hold down the Shift key, and press PrtSc. (This combination is referred to in text as Shift-PrtSc.)

Each line of the screen is printed.

**NOTE:** *If Shift-PrtSc does not produce a printed copy of what's on the screen, you might need to help your printer understand the instruction. With a Hewlett-Packard LaserJet printer, for example, you press the button on the printer labeled* ON LINE, *press the* FORM FEED *button to print the page, then press* ON LINE *again to return the printer to its earlier status. If necessary, check the documentation that came with your printer.*

## CLEARING THE SCREEN

Sometimes, when the screen is filled with commands and responses, you might want to clear it before continuing with your work. You can erase everything on the screen with the Clear Screen (Cls) command. Try it by typing:

```
C:\>cls
```

The screen is cleared, except for the system prompt in the upper left-hand corner.

## TURNING THE SYSTEM OFF

If MS-DOS is displaying the system prompt, all you have to do to shut the system down is turn off the power switch. You can do it anytime, except when the light on a disk drive is on; turning the power off while a drive is in use can cause you to lose the data on the disk. (If you're using an application program and decide to shut the system down, first follow the program's instructions for saving your work and quitting. When the program returns you to the MS-DOS prompt, you can shut down without risking loss of data.)

Some devices attached to your system may have special requirements for shutting down, such as a specific sequence in which they should be turned off. Be sure you know any special instructions for the devices attached to your system.

After you shut the system down, be sure to remove any floppy disks you are using and store them where they will be safe. You can remove your floppy disks before you turn off the power, provided no disk drive is in use.

## CHAPTER SUMMARY

You have completed your first session with MS-DOS. It wasn't very long, but you started the system, entered a few MS-DOS commands, and printed what was on the screen. These are the key points:

- You control MS-DOS by typing commands.

- MS-DOS doesn't know what you have typed until you press the Enter key.

- The Backspace key erases the last character you typed.

- The system prompt tells you that MS-DOS is at the command level, ready to accept a command from you.

- The letter in the system prompt identifies the current drive; you can change the current drive by typing the new drive letter, followed by a colon.

- You can check on your version of MS-DOS with the Ver (for *version*) command.

- The computer keeps track of the date and time. You can also set them with the Date and Time commands.

- In versions 5 and later, Doskey helps you repeat commands quickly and easily.

- Pressing Shift-PrtSc prints the contents of the screen.

- Typing *cls* clears the screen.

# 3

# Getting Your Bearings

**W**hen you venture into new territory—a different part of town, a park, a department store, a building you've never visited—you know where you're starting from, why you're there, and pretty much where you want to go. You took your first steps with MS-DOS in the previous chapter. Now it's time to get your bearings—time to begin learning your way around, moving in the direction of one task or another, and calling a halt if you want or need to.

That's what this chapter is all about. It introduces you to the directory of files that MS-DOS keeps on each disk and shows you how to use the special keys on your keyboard. You use these keys to tell MS-DOS to cancel lines or commands, to freeze the display, and to restart MS-DOS itself. If you have version 5 or 6, you're given a closer look at Doskey, which extends your control over the keyboard and enables you to review and repeat commands you've already used.

To try the examples, start MS-DOS as you normally do, even if your system is already running. Especially with version 6, this will ensure that the examples work as described. If necessary, press F3 to leave the MS-DOS Shell. Don't worry about leaving your computer on while you read the text between examples; MS-DOS is patient.

## THE DIRECTORY

Recall from Chapter 1 that information stored on a disk is stored as a file. For every disk you use, MS-DOS automatically keeps and updates a list of all the files you've saved on the disk. This list is called the *directory*.

If you create and save a new file, MS-DOS adds it to the list for that disk. If you revise an old file, MS-DOS keeps track of that too. The directory eliminates the need for you to keep a separate record of everything you save. You can tell MS-DOS you want to see the directory of a particular disk whenever MS-DOS is displaying the system prompt or, as explained in Chapter 11, when you're using the MS-DOS Shell.

The examples in this chapter give you a look at a directory and show you different ways to display information about your files. But before you begin exploring directories, you should know a little about how MS-DOS saves your files.

Whenever you create a file, you give it a descriptive name, called the *file name*, of up to eight characters. If you want, you can add a suffix, called the *extension*, of up to three more letters. The file name and extension help MS-DOS distinguish one file from another and keep information where it belongs.

Whenever you ask MS-DOS to show you the directory of a disk, MS-DOS lists the files it finds, showing each file name (and extension, if there is one). It also shows you the size of each file, in units called *bytes*, and gives the date and the time the file was created or last changed.

Many people have heard of a byte but aren't quite certain what it is. The easiest way to think of a byte is as the amount of storage required to hold one character in computer memory or on disk. Here are a few familiar items and their sizes, in bytes: the letters *abcd*, 4 bytes, 1 byte per letter; the words *United States*, 13 bytes—blanks count; a double-spaced, typewritten page, 1500 bytes; this book, approximately 1,000,000 bytes.

Depending on the size and type of drives you use (hard disk, floppy disk, or both), a floppy disk can hold from 362,496 to 2,915,328 bytes, and a hard disk can hold anywhere from 20,000,000 to 120,000,000 bytes—even more. For convenience, such large quantities are usually given in kilobytes (KB) or megabytes (MB). One kilobyte equals 1024 bytes, and one megabyte equals 1024 kilobytes, so disk capacity can range from 360 KB to 120 MB or more.

## A Special Kind of Directory

Left to itself, MS-DOS doesn't group files logically as you would, categorizing them by type, content, or any other characteristic. MS-DOS doesn't, for example, keep all program files in one place and all documents in another. To MS-DOS, a file is just a file, and as it keeps track of the files you create, it keeps adding their file names to the disk directory.

The main disk directory cannot simply grow without limit, however, even though a large hard disk can hold thousands of files. To help control growth and give you a way to keep track of similar groups of files, MS-DOS includes commands that let you divide disk storage space into smaller, more manageable areas called *subdirectories*. Subdirectories are the disk equivalent of dividers in a file drawer.

Although you won't be working with subdirectories until later in this book, you do need to know that MS-DOS versions 4 and later normally install themselves automatically, on a hard disk, in a subdirectory named DOS. Earlier versions of MS-DOS, though they did not install themselves, were often placed in a subdirectory by the people who installed them. The tradition of keeping MS-DOS in its own subdirectory is, in fact, so commonplace that this book assumes you have a DOS subdirectory if you use MS-DOS from a hard disk.

If you have a hard disk, you can easily check for a DOS subdirectory. If your system prompt looks like this:

```
C:\DOS>_
```

MS-DOS itself is telling you that you have a DOS subdirectory and it is looking at the subdirectory right now.

If your system prompt looks like this:

```
C:\>_
```

you need to check a little further. Use the Change Directory command, which tells MS-DOS to find and focus its attention on the subdirectory you name. Type:

```
C:\>cd dos
```

If all goes well, MS-DOS turns to your DOS subdirectory, and your system prompt probably changes to C:\DOS>. If MS-DOS cannot find a DOS subdirectory, it responds with the message *Invalid directory* and once again displays the system prompt.

> **NOTE:** *The preceding two examples cover the majority of hard disks equipped with versions 3 through 6 of MS-DOS. If you received the* Invalid directory *message, you can still try the following examples. They'll work just fine, but you should bear in mind that the file names you see might not be the same as those shown in the book.*

Chapter 8, "A Tree of Files," shows you how to create, use, manage, and remove subdirectories. The next part of this chapter shows you how to browse through directories and subdirectories, finding specific files they contain.

## DISPLAYING A DIRECTORY

To display the current directory (the directory MS-DOS uses unless you specify otherwise), you simply type *dir*, the name of the Directory command. Type the command and press Enter (remember, if you don't have a hard disk, your system prompt is A:\>):

```
C:\DOS>dir
```

If you have a hard disk and have displayed the DOS directory, the directory probably scrolled off the screen faster than you could read it. There are several ways to handle that, but one of the simplest uses what's called a *command parameter*. As you'll see in the next chapter, a command parameter lets you refine the action of a command. Here, with the Directory command, you can use a parameter typed as /p to tell MS-DOS to *pause* after displaying a screenful of directory entries. Try it. If your directory listing was too long to fit on one screen, type:

```
C:\DOS>dir /p
```

This time, scrolling stops when the screen is full. Press any key to see the remainder of the directory listing, one screenful at a time. Figure 3-1 shows a sampling of the MS-DOS file names you see on a computer with a hard disk and version 6 of MS-DOS.

```
Volume in drive C is HARD DISK
Volume Serial Number is 1608-5A30
Directory of C:\DOS
.            <DIR>      01-15-93   6:05p
..           <DIR>      01-15-93   6:05p
EGA      SYS     4885  02-01-93  12:00a
FORMAT   COM    33087  02-01-93  12:00a
NLSFUNC  EXE     7052  02-01-93  12:00a
COUNTRY  SYS    17069  02-01-93  12:00a
EGA      CPI    58873  02-01-93  12:00a
HIMEM    SYS    13984  02-01-93  12:00a
KEYB     COM    14986  02-01-93  12:00a
KEYBOARD SYS    34697  02-01-93  12:00a
ANSI     SYS     9029  02-01-93  12:00a
DEBUG    EXE    20634  02-01-93  12:00a
EXPAND   EXE    16885  02-01-93  12:00a
FDISK    EXE    57224  02-01-93  12:00a
MEM      EXE    32198  02-01-93  12:00a
SYS      COM    13440  02-01-93  12:00a
UNFORMAT COM    18560  02-01-93  12:00a
ATTRIB   EXE    15796  02-01-93  12:00a
CHOICE   COM     1733  02-01-93  12:00a
DEFRAG   EXE    70201  02-01-93  12:00a
DEFRAG   HLP    16809  02-01-93  12:00a
```

**Figure 3-1.**
*A sample directory display of version 6 MS-DOS files.*

If you're using floppy disks or a different version of MS-DOS, your directory listing differs—perhaps a little, perhaps a lot. The list might be shorter, for example, or it might show some different names, dates, or times. Regardless, certain names, such as FORMAT, COMMAND, DEBUG, and MODE appear consistently across different versions of MS-DOS. You can check your display for one or two of those names if you want, but the real point of this example is simple: The result of a Directory command is always a list of files stored on the disk.

**NOTE:** *The Directory command is used in examples throughout the book. Unless stated otherwise, the version 6 display is shown.*

The lines at the top of a directory listing give information about the disk itself and are explained in Chapter 6, "Managing Your Floppy Disks." In versions 5 and later, the last two lines of a directory display show the number of files in the directory, the number of bytes of storage they occupy, and—in the last line—the number of bytes of storage remaining on the disk. (In versions before 5, the directory listing ends with a single line that gives the number of files and the number of bytes available for storage.)

Figure 3-2 shows a sample entry from a directory. The file name is DISKCOPY; note that it is eight letters long, the maximum length of an MS-DOS file name. The next item, COM, is the file's extension. The next item tells you the file's size, and the final two entries give the date and time the file was either created or last changed.

DISKCOPY COM     11697    02-01-93    12:00a

| Name | Extension | Size in bytes | Date created or last changed | Time created or last changed |

**Figure 3-2.**
*A sample directory entry.*

## SOME IMPORTANT KEYS

In the examples in the previous chapter, you used the standard typewriter portion of the keyboard to enter commands. Several other keys have important meanings to MS-DOS. Figures 3-3 and 3-4 show where these keys are located on two common versions of the IBM keyboard. If your keyboard does not have the key used in an example, check your system's documentation for equivalent keys.

**Figure 3-3.**
*Special keys on early IBM PC–compatible keyboards.*

**Figure 3-4.**
*Special keys on the enhanced IBM PC–compatible keyboard.*

## Shift

The Shift keys are labeled with an open arrow, the word *Shift*, or both. Like the Shift keys on a typewriter, they have no effect by themselves; they shift the keyboard to uppercase letters and special characters, such as the dollar sign.

## Escape

This key, usually labeled *Esc*, cancels a line you have typed. To see how it works, type several characters (but don't press Enter):

```
C:\DOS>Now is the time
```

To erase this line, you could repeatedly press the Backspace key, but press the Escape key instead:

```
C:\DOS>_
```

If you're using version 5 or later and installed Doskey in Chapter 2, MS-DOS erases the line you typed and moves the cursor back to the system prompt.

If you're using version 4 or earlier, or if you haven't installed Doskey, the result is different:

```
C:\DOS>Now is the time\
```

MS-DOS displays a reverse slash (\) to indicate that the line was canceled and moves the cursor to the next line. MS-DOS doesn't repeat the system prompt, but the cursor indicates it is still ready for you to type a command. Press the Enter key, and MS-DOS displays the system prompt and the cursor on the next line:

```
C:\DOS>_
```

Pressing the Escape key is the quickest way to cancel a line you have typed.

## Control

This key, usually labeled *Ctrl*, has no effect by itself, but it is used like the Shift keys to change the effect of pressing another key. The combination of the Control key and some other key is represented in this book by Ctrl- followed by the other key. Ctrl-Break, for example, means "hold down the Control key, and then press and release the Break key." The Control key combinations are described on the next page.

## Numeric Lock

This key, familiarly known as *Num Lock*, does two things. It switches the effect of the keys in the calculator-style numeric pad at the right side of the keyboard back and forth between cursor movement and numbers. On early PC keyboards, it is also used in combination with the Control key to freeze the display. To test the first function, press Num Lock, and then press the 4 key in the numeric pad several times:

```
C:\DOS>444_
```

The keys produce numbers on the screen. Now press Num Lock again and press the same 4 key you pressed before:

```
C:\DOS>444
```

If you're using version 5 or 6 and installed Doskey, MS-DOS moves the cursor to the left one character so that it is under the last number you typed.

If you're using version 4 or earlier, or if you're using version 5 or 6 and Doskey isn't installed, you'll see the following result:

```
C:\DOS>44_
```

Pressing Num Lock a second time switched the keys to their cursor-movement functions. The 4 key is labeled with a left arrow in addition to the number 4; pressing it moves the cursor left, in the direction of the arrow, and erases a character just as the Backspace key does. Press Num Lock and the same 4 key again:

```
C:\DOS>444_
```

You switched back to numbers. Press Num Lock one more time to switch back to cursor movement, press Esc to cancel the line, and press the Enter key to return to the system prompt:

```
C:\DOS>444\

C:\DOS>_
```

You won't often use the arrow keys for cursor movement with MS-DOS, but many application programs, such as word processors, require frequent cursor movements. If you have version 5 or 6, you'll also use the arrow keys for giving commands to Doskey.

## Break

This key is labeled either *Scroll Lock* and *Break* or *Pause* and *Break*. When labeled *Scroll Lock* and *Break* (as on early PC-compatible keyboards), this key has no effect on MS-DOS by itself, but it is used with the Control key to cancel a command you have entered. If labeled *Pause* and *Break* (as on the enhanced PC-compatible keyboard), this key temporarily halts the display; when used with the Control key, it cancels a command.

## Alternate and Delete

These keys, labeled *Alt* and *Del*, have no effect on MS-DOS by themselves but are used with the Control key to restart MS-DOS.

## Print Screen

This key, labeled *Print Screen, Prnt Scrn, PrtSc,* or some close variation, is used with the Shift and Control keys to print the contents of the screen. You used Shift-PrtSc in the previous chapter; you'll use Ctrl-PrtSc and see the difference in a short while. (If you have an IBM PS/2 keyboard, you don't have to press Shift with PrtSc.)

## Control Key Functions

Figure 3-5 on the following page shows the effects produced by holding down the Control key and pressing another key. You'll probably use these combinations fairly often with MS-DOS, so the next few topics show you examples of each combination. When you are being shown exactly what to type, the names of the keys are separated by hyphens and enclosed in angle brackets to represent pressing a Control key combination. Thus, when you see <Ctrl-Break> in a command, it means "press Ctrl-Break."

Before trying the examples, you should also note that MS-DOS displays the Control key as the symbol ^. MS-DOS does not acknowledge all Control key commands on the screen, but when it does, it uses the symbol ^ in combination with a letter. Control-Break, for example, shows on the screen as ^C and can also be typed by holding down the Control key and typing the letter C.

| | |
|---|---|
| Ctrl-Num Lock or Pause | Halts whatever the system is doing until you press another key. Typically used to freeze the display when information is scrolling by too fast or scrolling off the top of the screen. Can also be typed as Ctrl-S (Ctrl plus the letter S). |
| Ctrl-Break | Cancels whatever the system is doing. Use this when you really don't want the computer to continue what it's doing. Can also be typed as Ctrl-C (Ctrl plus the letter C). |
| Ctrl-PrtSc | Pressing this key combination once causes MS-DOS to start printing every line as it is displayed; pressing Ctrl-PrtSc a second time stops simultaneous displaying and printing. Can also be typed as Ctrl-P (Ctrl plus the letter P). |
| Ctrl-Alt-Del | Restarts MS-DOS. This combination is unique; no other keys can be used to do the same thing. |

**Figure 3-5.**
*Control key combinations.*

### Freezing the Display

As mentioned earlier, MS-DOS lets you temporarily halt the display by pressing the Pause key or, if you have an early PC keyboard, Ctrl-Num Lock. When you do this, the display remains frozen, giving you time to read it. To start the display moving again, you simply press any key.

To test this function, type the following to display the directory. When the entries start appearing on the screen, press Pause or Ctrl-Num Lock to freeze the display:

```
C:\DOS>dir
```

Press any key, and the display resumes. You can press Pause or Ctrl-Num Lock to stop and start the display as many times as you like, so you can view displays that are many screens long.

### Canceling a Command

If you enter a command and then change your mind or realize that you meant to enter some other command, you can cancel the command you entered by pressing Ctrl-Break. To test this function, type the Directory command again. This time, however, press Ctrl-Break when MS-DOS begins to display the directory entries.

Here's an example:

```
C:\DOS>dir

 Volume in drive C is HARD DISK
 Volume Serial Number is 1608-5A30
 Directory of C:\DOS
 .           <DIR>        01-15-93   6:05p
 ..          <DIR>        01-15-93   6:05p
 EGA     SYS      4885 02-01-93   12:00a
 FORMAT  COM     33087 02-01-93   12:00a
 NLSFUNC EXE      7052 02-01-93   12:00a
 COUNTRY SYS     17069 02-01-93   12:00a
 EGA     CPI     58873 02-01-93   12:00a
 HIMEM   SYS     13984 02-01-93   12:00a
 KEYB    COM     14986 02^C

C:\DOS>_
```

Your display probably stopped somewhere else in the directory, but when you press Ctrl-Break, MS-DOS stops what it is doing, displays ^C, and returns to the command level.

### Printing and Displaying Simultaneously

In the previous chapter you printed the contents of the screen by pressing Shift-PrtSc. There's another way to print from the screen: Pressing Ctrl-PrtSc tells MS-DOS to start printing everything it displays. MS-DOS continues to print and display simultaneously until you press Ctrl-PrtSc again.

To test this function, make sure your printer is turned on, press Ctrl-PrtSc, and then enter the Directory command:

```
C:\DOS><Ctrl-PrtSc>dir
```

MS-DOS again displays the directory of the system disk, but this time each line is printed as it is displayed. (If you're using a LaserJet or similar printer, you might have to press Ctrl-P instead.)

The directory is displayed more slowly than when you use the Directory command alone because MS-DOS waits until a line is printed before displaying and printing the next line. You can cancel the Directory command before the complete directory is printed by pressing Ctrl-Break. Remember to press Ctrl-PrtSc as well, to end the simultaneous displaying and printing.

If you want to print something without printing the command that creates the display, type the command, press Ctrl-PrtSc, and then press Enter. For example, when you printed the directory in the preceding example, the Directory command was the first line printed. To avoid printing the command, type:

```
C:\DOS>dir<Ctrl-PrtSc>
```

Now printing begins with the first line of the directory; the Directory command isn't printed. Cancel the command by pressing Ctrl-Break.

Be sure to press Ctrl-PrtSc again to stop printing; otherwise, MS-DOS continues to print everything it displays, even if you go on to an entirely different task.

### Shift-PrtSc versus Ctrl-PrtSc

These two methods of printing from the screen work differently and have different uses. Shift-PrtSc prints everything on the screen and stops. Ctrl-PrtSc, as you just saw, alternates displaying and printing, line by line. If everything you want appears on the screen, use Shift-PrtSc; it's faster. But if you want to print something longer than one screenful, use Ctrl-PrtSc.

Ctrl-PrtSc is better for printing long displays because you press it once to tell MS-DOS to start simultaneous displaying and printing, enter a command— such as the Directory command—to create the display, and then press Ctrl-PrtSc again when you want to stop printing. If you use Shift-PrtSc for printing displays more than one screen long, you have to display the first screen, print it, display the second screen, print it, and so forth until everything you want has been printed.

## Repeating Commands with Doskey

Versions 5 and later of MS-DOS include the Doskey command you learned about in Chapter 2. Doskey makes your work with MS-DOS easier and more efficient by letting you repeat MS-DOS commands you've used recently without retyping them.

To help you minimize keystrokes (and the chance of mistyping a command), Doskey lets you use several special keys, among them the arrow and function keys shown in Figures 3-6 and 3-7.

**Figure 3-6.**
*Keys on the early PC-compatible keyboards that have special meaning to Doskey.*

Figure 3-7.
*Keys on the enhanced PC-compatible keyboard that have special meaning to Doskey.*

**NOTE:** *If you're using MS-DOS version 5 or later from floppy disks and saw the message* Bad command or file name *the last time you tried to start Doskey, you need to insert the floppy disk that contains the DOSKEY file. Now that you're familiar with the Directory command, check your Support disk (and others, if necessary) for this file by typing* dir *or* dir /p. *When you see DOSKEY in the directory list, leave the floppy disk containing the file in drive A.*

The following examples show you some of Doskey's basic features. Recall that you start Doskey simply by typing its name and pressing Enter:

```
C:\DOS>doskey
```

MS-DOS responds:

```
DOSKey installed.
```

As you've seen, Doskey lets you repeat your last MS-DOS command in a simple two-step procedure: Press Up arrow to redisplay the command, and then press Enter to carry it out. But you won't always want to repeat the last command you typed. You might want to repeat one you used several commands ago. Doskey lets you do that, too. To try it, first type the following MS-DOS commands (just press Enter when MS-DOS prompts for the date and time):

```
C:\DOS>date
C:\DOS>time
C:\DOS>ver
C:\DOS>dir
C:\DOS>cls
```

Now you've entered some commands Doskey can help you find and reuse.

Although you probably wouldn't have much trouble remembering five commands, Doskey can help you keep track of dozens. But when you've typed a number of commands, you can't always remember which ones you typed or in what order. Once you've started Doskey, you can simply press the F7 function key to see a list of your previous commands, in sequence. Try it now. Press F7, and Doskey displays:

```
C:\DOS>
1: date
2: time
3: ver
4: dir
5: cls
C:\DOS>_
```

The commands are numbered and in the same order you typed them. Press the Up arrow key. Doskey displays the last command:

```
C:\DOS>cls_
```

Press the Up arrow key again, and Doskey replaces *cls* with *dir*, the next-to-last command. Whenever you press the Up arrow key, Doskey recalls and displays the previous command.

Now try some other keys. Press the Down arrow key. The display changes back to: ·

```
C:\DOS>cls_
```

The Down arrow key does the opposite of the Up arrow key: It tells Doskey to retrieve the next command (as opposed to the previous command) in the list.

You can take bigger leaps through the list, too, with the Page Up and Page Down keys. Press the Page Up key, and the display changes to:

```
C:\DOS>date_
```

Page Up tells Doskey to recall the first command in the current list. And, predictably, when you press the Page Down key, the display changes to:

```
C:\DOS>cls_
```

which is the last command in the current list.

You can also request a specific command by entering its line number. Press the F9 key. Doskey displays:

```
C:\DOS>Line number: _
```

This time, request the Ver command, which is number 3 in the list. Type:

```
C:\DOS>Line number: 3
```

and press Enter, and this appears:

```
C:\DOS>ver_
```

Press Enter. MS-DOS carries out the Ver command and displays the system prompt.

Doskey has many uses for everyone from beginners to advanced users of MS-DOS. These examples showed a few quick ways to use it; later chapters show you how to use Doskey to tailor MS-DOS to the way you work.

## RESTARTING THE SYSTEM

Suppose you find yourself in a situation where your computer is not responding as you think it should, or it complains about something you don't know how to handle, or you decide it would be best to scrap what you're doing and start over from the beginning. You don't have to turn the power switch off and on to restart your system; you can do it by pressing Ctrl-Alt-Del.

Try it. If you are using MS-DOS from floppy disks, check that your normal Startup disk is in drive A. If you have a hard disk, be sure drive A is open.

Now hold down both Ctrl and Alt and press Del.

The screen clears, the drive lights blink, the system beeps, and MS-DOS is loaded just as it was when you turned the power on. Restarting with Ctrl-Alt-Del takes less time, though, because the computer doesn't test all its devices and memory as it does whenever you switch the power off and on. If the MS-DOS Shell appears, press F3 to leave it.

## A SHORT DIVERSION

The system prompt is an economical way for MS-DOS to show you the current drive and directory and to let you know that you can enter a command. But the combination of the current drive and directory and the greater-than sign (>) is only one possible system prompt. The MS-DOS Prompt command lets you change the system prompt to almost anything you want.

For example, you might prefer a more courteous machine. Type the following and press Enter (<space> means press the Spacebar):

```
C:\DOS>prompt May I help you?<space><Enter>
```

Now the system prompt isn't quite so cryptic:

```
May I help you? _
```

Each time MS-DOS returns to the command level, it displays this polite phrase. Try it by pressing the Enter key once or twice to cause MS-DOS to display the system prompt again. Although your new prompt looks quite different from C:\> or C:\DOS> (and actually conveys less information), the meaning is the same: MS-DOS is at the command level, ready for you to enter a command.

To see just how much you can cram into the system prompt, type the following example as a single line (as before, <space> means press the Spacebar). Although the example is shown on two separate lines and won't fit on a single line on screen anyway, don't press the Enter key until you come to <Enter> at the end of the second line:

```
May I help you? prompt The time is<space>$t$_The date is<space>
$d$_The current disk is<space>$n$_Your command:<space><Enter>
```

Now the system prompt is three lines of data followed by a request for a command:

```
The time is 16:26:03.54
The date is Sat 10-16-1993
The current disk is C
Your command: _
```

You would probably quickly tire of all this, but the exercise shows how much flexibility MS-DOS gives you. You don't have to take advantage of it all, but the possibilities are there if you want them.

To return the system prompt to a more normal form, simply type the following Prompt command:

```
The time is 16:26:03.54
The date is Sat 10-16-1993
The current disk is C
Your command: prompt $p$g
```

Your system prompt changes to the familiar C:\> or C:\DOS>.

## CHAPTER SUMMARY

Each disk has a directory that lists the name, extension, and size of each file, and the date and time the file was created or last changed. You can see the directory by typing *dir* and pressing Enter.

- The Escape key cancels a line you have typed.

- Pause or Ctrl-Num Lock freezes the display. Ctrl-S has the same effect.

- Ctrl-Break cancels a command. Ctrl-C has the same effect.

- Ctrl-PrtSc turns simultaneous displaying and printing on and off. Ctrl-P has the same effect.

- Ctrl-Alt-Del restarts MS-DOS.

- The Doskey command helps you display, choose from, and repeat commands you've already used.

Now that you're more familiar with the keyboard, the next chapter gives you a closer look at floppy disks and files.

# 4

# A Look at Files
# and Floppy Disks

he computer's memory is temporary; it is cleared each time you turn off the computer. The only way you can save data permanently is to store the data in a file on a disk. When MS-DOS needs data that is stored in a file, it reads the data from the disk into memory. If you change the data and want to keep the changed version, you must store the revised version on disk before turning off the system.

## TYPES OF FILES

In general, a file contains either a program or data. A *program* is a set of instructions for the computer. *Data* is the text and numbers, such as a project proposal, a table of tax rates, or a list of customers, that the program needs to do your work.

Two types of files are important to your work: text files and command files. They are quite different, so it's important to look more closely at the kind of information these files contain and at how the files are used.

### Text Files

*Text files* are data files that contain characters you can read (everyday letters, numbers, and symbols). Word processing programs store their documents in text files, as does the MS-DOS Editor. Many files you use in your work with the computer—and all the files that you will create and use in this book—are text files.

The definition of a text file may seem self-evident at first, but it actually introduces you to an important characteristic of computer information storage. Your computer keeps information in two very different forms: One is text, the characters contained in text files; the other is machine-readable code, which looks meaningless to most people but is quite meaningful to computers.

### Command Files

*Command files* contain the instructions MS-DOS needs to carry out commands. MS-DOS command files can be programs, such as DISKCOPY.COM, or, as you will see in Chapter 14, "Creating Your Own Commands," they can be a series of commands that you put together to perform a specific task and store in a file.

Not all MS-DOS commands are stored in separate command files, however. Some commands, such as the Directory command, are built into the main body of MS-DOS. When you load MS-DOS into memory, you load these commands with it. When you want to use these commands, MS-DOS has them on tap for immediate use—it does not need to look up a separate command file to carry them out.

These built-in commands are called *permanent*, or *internal*, commands. In contrast, the commands that are kept in command files until they are requested by you are called *temporary*, or *external*, commands. When you use a permanent command, you simply request the command, and MS-DOS carries it out. When you use a temporary command, MS-DOS must load the command file from disk into memory before it can carry out the command.

An application program, such as a word processor, is also stored in a command file; it stores your work, such as documents, in data files.

## HOW FILES ARE NAMED

No matter the type of file, each file must have a file name. Recall that a file name can be up to eight characters long. You can use almost any character on the keyboard when you name your files, but it's a good idea to give your files names, such as BUDGET or SALESRPT, that describe their contents.

To identify a file more completely, a three-character suffix called the file *extension* can be added to the file name; this suffix is separated from the file name by a period. So that you and MS-DOS can tell your files apart, each file on a disk must have either a different name or a different extension; REPORT.JAN and REPORT.FEB, for example, are different files to MS-DOS, even though their file names are the same.

### Specifying the Drive

When you name a file in a command, MS-DOS needs to know which drive contains the disk with the file on it. If you don't specify a drive, MS-DOS looks on the disk in the current drive (the drive letter shown in the system prompt). If the disk containing the file is not in the current drive, you can precede the file name with the letter of the drive and a colon. For example, if you specify the file as *b:report.doc*, MS-DOS looks for it on the disk in drive B.

## PREPARING FOR THE EXAMPLES

The following pages show a number of examples to help you become more comfortable with files and floppy disks. With MS-DOS, as with most other computer applications, doing is often the easiest and most effective way of learning.

If you have a hard disk, make sure the latch on drive A is open, turn on or restart the computer, and go through the startup routine until you see the system prompt (C:\> or C:\DOS>). (If the MS-DOS Shell starts automatically, startup instructions from here on assume that you press F3 to leave the Shell.) You'll be working with files in the DOS subdirectory, so change to it if necessary by typing:

```
C:\>cd \dos
```

Go on to the next heading.

If your system doesn't have a hard disk, start or restart your computer and go through the startup routine until you see the A:\> prompt. The examples use several external MS-DOS commands, beginning with DISKCOPY.COM. Use the Directory command to check your MS-DOS floppy disks for this file, and start with the floppy disk containing DISKCOPY.COM in drive A. Use the Directory command whenever MS-DOS responds *Bad command or file name* because it cannot find the command file it needs for a particular example.

### Don't Worry About Memorizing

You'll use several commands in this chapter, but you needn't remember exactly how to use each one; all the commands are described in more detail in the remaining chapters of the book. The purpose of this chapter is to introduce you to files and floppy disks.

## QUALIFYING A COMMAND

Up to now, most commands you have entered have consisted of a single word or abbreviation, such as *time* or *dir*. Many commands, however, let you add one or more qualifiers to make the action more specific. These qualifiers are called *parameters.*

Some commands require parameters; others allow you to add parameters if you want. The Directory command, for example, does not require parameters, but it lets you tailor a command with specifications such as the name of a particular file you want to see. You'll use some parameters in the following examples; descriptions of commands in later chapters show their parameters, both required and optional.

## DISPLAYING SPECIFIC DIRECTORY ENTRIES

In the previous chapter you used the Directory command to display the directory entries of the files in your DOS subdirectory or on your startup disk. You can display the directory entry of a single file or the directory entries of a set of files by adding a parameter to the Directory command.

### Displaying the Directory Entry of a Single File

To display the directory entry of a specific file, you simply type the file name (and its extension, if there is one) after the command name. For example, the command to copy the contents of one floppy disk to another is called Diskcopy. Its command file is DISKCOPY.COM. To display the directory entry for only DISKCOPY.COM, type the following command. (If you're not using a hard disk, the floppy disk with DISKCOPY.COM should be in drive A; remember that your system prompt is A:\>, not C:\DOS.)

```
C:\DOS>dir diskcopy.com
```

MS-DOS displays only the directory entry of the file you specified (don't worry if you see a different size, date, or time):

```
Volume in drive C is HARD DISK
Volume Serial Number is 1608-5A30
Directory of C:\DOS

DISKCOPY COM      11879 02-01-93  12:00a
        1 file(s)       11879 bytes
                     36333568 bytes free

C:\DOS>
```

If the file you name isn't on the disk, or if you don't type the file name exactly as it is stored, MS-DOS responds *File not found.*

## Displaying the Directory Entries of a Set of Files

What if you remember most of a file name, or the file name but not the extension? MS-DOS helps you out by giving you two wildcard characters, ∗ and ?, that you can substitute for actual characters in a file name. Like wild cards in a poker game, the wildcard characters can represent any other character. They differ only in that ? can substitute for one character, whereas ∗ can substitute for more than one character.

Suppose you remember only that a file's name begins with the letter F. It takes only a moment to check all the files that begin with F.

Use the MS-DOS directory as an example. Type the following command:

```
C:\DOS>dir f*
```

MS-DOS displays the directory entries of all file names that begin with F:

```
Volume in drive C is HARD DISK
Volume Serial Number is 1608-5A30
Directory of C:\DOS

FORMAT   COM      33087 02-01-92    12:00a
FDISK    EXE      57224 02-01-92    12:00a
FASTOPEN EXE      12050 02-01-92    12:00a
FC       EXE      18650 02-01-92    12:00a
FIND     EXE       6770 02-01-92    12:00a
        5 file(s)      127781 bytes
                     36333568 bytes free

C:\DOS>
```

(This listing shows the names of all the MS-DOS files that begin with F. If you're using MS-DOS from floppy disks, your list might differ, but you should see FORMAT.COM or FORMAT.EXE.)

Wildcard characters can simplify the task of keeping track of your files. Chapter 5, "Managing Your Files," includes several examples of using wildcard characters. Now it's time to stop practicing and to create some files of your own.

## PREPARING A FLOPPY DISK FOR USE

Before MS-DOS can store a file on a new floppy disk, it must prepare the floppy disk for use. This preparation, in which MS-DOS writes certain information for its own use on the floppy disk, is called *formatting*. You tell MS-DOS to do this formatting with the Format command. You'll need two formatted floppy disks for the examples in this book. Now is a good time to format them, so get out two blank floppy disks and two blank labels before proceeding. If you've bought floppy disks that have been formatted already, there's really no need to format them again. But go ahead and practice formatting the floppy disks. You'll most likely have to format one sometime.

Type the following:

```
C:\DOS>format b:
```

This command tells MS-DOS to format the floppy disk in drive B.

Formatting a floppy disk effectively deletes any files that may be stored on it, so MS-DOS gives you a chance to make sure you haven't put the wrong floppy disk in the specified drive by displaying a message and then waiting for you to type something:

```
Insert new diskette for drive B:
and press ENTER when ready..._
```

If you discover that you put in the wrong floppy disk, no problem: Just take out the wrong one and put in the right one before you press the Enter key.

If you can't find a floppy disk to format, and you want to cancel the command, no problem again: Don't turn the system off; just press Ctrl-Break.

But you do want to format the floppy disk now. If you have one floppy disk drive, place a blank floppy disk in drive A and close the drive latch if necessary. If you have two floppy disk drives, place a blank floppy disk in drive B and close the latch.

Press Enter. If you have version 5 or later, MS-DOS begins by displaying one or more messages telling you it is checking the disk to see whether it was previously formatted. After these steps, MS-DOS displays a constantly changing message that shows you the progress of formatting the disk:

```
Checking existing disk format.
Saving UNFORMAT information.
Verifying 1.44M

Formatting 1.2M
  8 percent completed.
```

Version 4 of MS-DOS tells you x *percent of disk formatted.* In earlier versions, the message might look like this:

```
Head:    0 Cylinder:    1
```

or it might simply read *Formatting....* In any case, the light on the drive goes on, and MS-DOS begins writing on the floppy disk. When MS-DOS is finished, it tells you *Format complete.* If you have version 4 or later, it then displays the message:

```
Volume label (11 characters, ENTER for none)? _
```

A volume label is a name you give a formatted disk to help identify it and the files it contains. The name can be up to 11 characters long, including blanks, but cannot include certain characters MS-DOS reserves for special uses—characters such as a period (used between a file name and an extension), an asterisk or a question mark (used as wildcard characters), or a forward slash (used when typing command parameters).

You don't have to assign a volume label to a disk, but because MS-DOS displays the volume label at the beginning of any directory listing you request, the few seconds you spend thinking up and typing a volume label when you format a floppy disk can, in the long run, save you time by helping to identify what the disk contains. (If you don't have version 4 or later, you can assign a volume label after formatting with the /V parameter of the Format command; you'll find out about this in Chapter 6, "Managing Your Floppy Disks.")

If MS-DOS is requesting a volume label, assign one to the disk you just formatted. Type a simple but descriptive name, such as:

```
Volume label (11 characters, ENTER for none)? examples 1
```

and press Enter.

MS-DOS then displays some information about the floppy disk, followed by a final message:

```
    1,457,664 bytes total disk space
    1,457,664 bytes available on disk

        512 bytes in each allocation unit
      2,847 allocation units available on disk

Volume Serial Number is 1A2C-13F5

Format another (Y/N)?_
```

The numbers shown are for a 1.44 MB floppy disk. Depending on the type of floppy disk drives you have and the version of MS-DOS you're using, the total disk space in your report might differ—for example, 1,213,952 or 730,112.

The messages about allocation units and the volume serial number are provided by MS-DOS beginning with version 4. Allocation units are groups of bytes used by MS-DOS in storing information; the volume serial number is assigned as part of the formatting procedure. Neither is likely to be significant in your day-to-day use of MS-DOS.

The final message, *Format another (Y/N)?*, means that MS-DOS is now waiting for you to say whether you want to format another floppy disk. Type *y* and press Enter. The message asking you to put the floppy disk in drive B and press Enter is repeated, so go through the same process to format the second floppy disk; name it *examples 2*. When MS-DOS finishes, it asks you again whether you want to format another.

Now type *n* and press Enter. MS-DOS displays the system prompt (C:\DOS>), telling you that the Format command is complete and that MS-DOS is waiting for you to type another command.

You now have two formatted floppy disks. It's time to put one of them to use by creating a file; if you removed the floppy disk you just formatted, put it in your floppy disk drive (drive B if you have two floppy disk drives).

## CREATING A TEXT FILE

An easy way to create a text file is by using the MS-DOS Copy command. As you might guess from its name, the Copy command can be used to make a copy of a file. It can also be used to copy characters from the keyboard into a file.

MS-DOS refers to the parts of your computer, such as the keyboard, display, and printer, as *devices*. To MS-DOS, devices, like files, have names. The keyboard is known to MS-DOS as CON (for CONsole).

You are going to create a file by telling MS-DOS to copy what you type from the keyboard onto the blank floppy disk in drive B.

To create a file named NOTE.DOC on the floppy disk in drive B, type the following example. End each line by pressing Enter; where you see a blank line, press Enter to tell MS-DOS to insert an extra line:

```
C:\DOS>copy con b:note.doc
October 16, 1993

Dear Fred,
Just a note to remind you
that our meeting is at 9.

Jack
```

That's the end of the file. To tell MS-DOS that it's the end of the file, press Ctrl-Z (hold down the Control key and press Z), then press Enter:

```
<Ctrl-Z><Enter>
```

When you press Ctrl-Z, MS-DOS displays ^Z (the ^, remember, represents the Control key). After you press Enter, MS-DOS acknowledges that it copied a file:

```
1 file(s) copied
```

```
C:\DOS>_
```

To verify that the file is there, display the directory of the floppy disk in drive B:

```
C:\DOS>dir b:
```

Sure enough, NOTE.DOC is on the floppy disk:

```
Volume in drive B is EXAMPLES 2
Volume Serial Number is 1839-10EE
Directory of B:\

NOTE     DOC        94 10-16-93    2:03p
         1 file(s)            94 bytes
                    1,457,152 bytes free
```

```
C:\DOS>_
```

This method of creating a text file is quick and convenient and is used in examples throughout the book.

## Displaying a Text File

Because you can read the characters in text files, you'll often want to display a text file on the screen. It's even easier to display one than it is to create it. Just use the MS-DOS Type command. To display your file, type the following:

```
C:\DOS>type b:note.doc
```

MS-DOS displays each line and returns to the command level:

```
October 16, 1993

Dear Fred,
Just a note to remind you
that our meeting is at 9.

Jack
```

```
C:\DOS>_
```

This is the quickest way to see what's in a file; you'll probably use the Type command frequently. Displaying a file isn't always helpful, though, because not all files are text files; they don't all contain readable characters. See for yourself. (If you're using MS-DOS from floppy disks, place the floppy disk with MORE.COM in drive A.) Type:

```
C:\DOS>type more.com
```

Yes, the display is correct. It's hard to tell from that jumble what is in the file because the file contains a program stored in machine code, not text.

## Printing a Text File

One of the main reasons you write documents, of course, is to have a printed copy. You can print your file by copying it to the printer. You've already copied from the keyboard to a disk. Now, copy from the disk to the printer. The printer is known to MS-DOS as PRN. Make certain the printer is turned on, and type the following:

```
C:\DOS>copy b:note.doc prn
```

The file is printed. When you print a file, you'll probably want to position the paper by hand before you enter the command so that the printing will begin where you want it to on the page.

There's an easier way, however, to print a file: the Print command.

**NOTE:** *If you're using MS-DOS from floppy disks, you need the floppy disk containing the file PRINT.COM. Remember, if MS-DOS cannot find a file, it displays the message* Bad command or file name *and waits for you to try again. When necessary, remember to check your MS-DOS disks for appropriate command files. Examples from here on assume that MS-DOS can find the files it needs to carry out your commands.*

To print your file with the Print command, type the following:

```
C:\DOS>print b:note.doc
```

If MS-DOS responds:

```
Name of list device [PRN]: _
```

press the Enter key. MS-DOS displays one or both of the following messages and prints the file you specified:

```
Resident part of PRINT installed

  B:\NOTE.DOC is currently being printed

C:\DOS>_
```

These messages are explained in more detail in Chapter 5, "Managing Your Files."

The Print command makes most printers advance to the next page after printing. Although this file is too short to show it, you can continue to use the system to do other work while the Print command is printing a file.

## Copying a Text File

The Copy command is one of the more versatile MS-DOS commands. You have already used it to create and print a text file. The Copy command also duplicates files.

To copy the file named NOTE.DOC into another file named LETTER.DOC, type:

```
C:\DOS>copy b:note.doc b:letter.doc
```

When you press Enter, MS-DOS copies the file; then it acknowledges that it did so:

```
      1 file(s) copied
```

```
C:\DOS>_
```

Display the directory of the floppy disk in drive B again to verify the copy:

```
C:\DOS>dir b:
```

Now you have two text files:

```
    Volume in drive B is EXAMPLES 2
    Volume Serial Number is 1839-10EE
    Directory of B:\

NOTE      DOC         94 10-16-93  2:03p
LETTER    DOC         94 10-16-93  2:03p
        2 file(s)        188 bytes
                   1,456,640 bytes free
```

```
C:\DOS>_
```

If you wanted, you could make changes to one file and still have a copy of the original version on disk. You'll find the Copy command quite useful when you need several files that differ only slightly or when you have several small files that can be combined in different ways to create other files: often-used paragraphs, for example, that can be recombined in different letters, contracts, or other documents.

## Deleting a Text File

Just as you get rid of paper files, you can get rid of disk files. To delete NOTE.DOC from the floppy disk in drive B, type:

```
C:\DOS>del b:note.doc

C:\DOS>_
```

Now check the directory one more time:

```
C:\DOS>dir b:

 Volume in drive B is EXAMPLES 2
 Volume Serial Number is 1839-10EE
 Directory of B:\

LETTER   DOC          94 10-16-93  2:03p
        1 file(s)            94 bytes
                      1,457,152 bytes free

C:\DOS>_
```

It's gone.

# SOME ADVANCED FEATURES

Several commands and features give you much greater control over the way MS-DOS does its work. You can:

- Sort lines of data—for example, sort alphabetically the list of directory entries produced by the Directory command.

- View a long display one screenful at a time, without having to freeze the display by pressing Pause or Ctrl-Num Lock.

- Tell MS-DOS to send the results, or *output*, of a command to the printer instead of to the display, simply by adding a few characters to the command.

- Search lines of data for a series of characters.

The examples in this section give you a glimpse of these advanced features; the features are described in detail, with many additional examples, in later chapters.

## Sorting Lines of Data

You have probably arranged card files or lists in some sequence, such as alphabetic or numeric order. The Sort command sorts, or arranges, lines of data such as a list of names. To see how this works, sort the lines of the text file LETTER.DOC.

Type the following:

```
C:\DOS>sort < b:letter.doc
```

The less-than symbol (<) tells MS-DOS to send a copy of the file LETTER.DOC to the Sort command, which then displays the lines of the file after rearranging (sorting) them into alphabetic order:

```
Dear Fred,
Jack
Just a note to remind you
October 16, 1993
that our meeting is at 9.

C:\DOS>_
```

Although you probably don't want to sort the lines of your letters, you can put whatever you like in a text file—for example, a list of customers or employees. The Sort command is a powerful addition to your kit of computer tools.

## Viewing a Long Display One Screenful at a Time

When you displayed a directory in Chapter 3, lines might have scrolled off the top of the screen because the display was too long to fit. You saw that you can freeze the display by pressing Pause or Ctrl-Num Lock or by using the /P parameter of the Directory command. There's another way to stop scrolling: The More command displays one screenful, with -- *More* -- at the bottom of the screen, then waits for you to press any key to continue to the next screenful. Display the current directory again, this time using the More command. Type the vertical bar by holding down a Shift key and pressing the key labeled with the ¦ character:

```
C:\DOS>dir ¦ more
```

MS-DOS displays the first screenful, but the last lines aren't displayed yet (notice the -- *More* -- in the last line):

```
 Volume in drive C is HARD DISK
 Volume Serial Number is 1608-5A30
 Directory of C:\DOS
 .            <DIR>      01-15-93     6:05p
 ..           <DIR>      01-15-93     6:05p
 EGA      SYS      4885 02-01-93     12:00a
 FORMAT   COM     33087 02-01-93     12:00a
```

```
NLSFUNC   EXE      7052 02-01-93      12:00a
COUNTRY   SYS     17069 02-01-93      12:00a
EGA       CPI     58873 02-01-93      12:00a
HIMEM     SYS     13984 02-01-93      12:00a
KEYB      COM     14986 02-01-93      12:00a
KEYBOARD  SYS     34697 02-01-93      12:00a
ANSI      SYS      9029 02-01-93      12:00a
DEBUG     EXE     20634 02-01-93      12:00a
EXPAND    EXE     16885 02-01-93      12:00a
FDISK     EXE     57224 02-01-93      12:00a
SYS       COM     13440 02-01-93      12:00a
NFORMAT   COM     18560 02-01-93      12:00a
ATTRIB    EXE     15796 02-01-93      12:00a
CHOICE    COM      1733 02-01-93      12:00a
-- More --
```

To see the rest of the directory, press any key. If MS-DOS once again displays
*-- More --* at the bottom of the screen, press Ctrl-Break to end the command.

The More command displays long output one screenful at a time, giving you
a chance to view it all at your convenience.

**NOTE:** *When you use More and certain other commands that require MS-DOS to*
*manipulate files, you might see directory entries for files with odd names, such as*
*ALCJDEAO, 1106002B, or %PIPE1.$$$. These are temporary files that MS-DOS*
*creates and then erases when it no longer needs them.*

## Sending Command Output to the Printer

In earlier examples, you printed the output of the Directory command by using
the Print Screen key. There's a more direct way to print the output of a command:
Simply follow the command with a greater-than symbol (>) and the name of the
printer, PRN. To print the current directory, make sure the printer is turned on
and type:

```
C:\DOS>dir > prn
```

If you don't want to wait for the whole directory to be printed, cancel the printing
by pressing Ctrl-Break. This same technique can be used to send the output of a
command to some other device or to a file, by substituting the device name or
file name for PRN.

**NOTE:** *If you're using MS-DOS from floppy disks, try using this command to*
*print a list of the command files on each floppy disk. Such lists are useful for*
*reference.*

## Finding a Series of Characters in a File

How many times have you searched through a pile of letters or notes, looking for a particular item or reference? If you have to look through MS-DOS files or the output of MS-DOS commands, the Find command will do the looking for you. For example, suppose you want to see the directory entries of all MS-DOS files with SK in their names. Try the following (the quotation marks tell MS-DOS which letters—known technically as a *character string*, or just *string*—to look for).

(If you don't have a hard disk, check to see which of your MS-DOS floppy disks contains command files with the letters SK in their names.)

Type:

```
C:\DOS>dir | find "SK"
```

MS-DOS displays only the entries with SK in their names (your list might differ):

```
FDISK     EXE     57224 02-01-93  12:00a
CHKDSK    EXE     16216 02-01-93  12:00a
DISKCOMP  COM     10636 02-01-93  12:00a
DISKCOPY  COM     11879 02-01-93  12:00a
DOSKEY    COM      5883 02-01-93  12:00a

C:\DOS>_
```

The Find command is even more useful when you search for a series of characters in a text file. If a file contains a list of names and telephone numbers, for example, you can quickly display one particular entry or all entries that contain a particular series of characters (such as an area code), or you can even display all entries that *don't* contain a particular series of characters. Chapter 13, ''Taking Control of Your System,'' shows you how to create such an automated index of names and telephone numbers with nothing but MS-DOS commands.

## Combining Features

These advanced features of MS-DOS can also be used together in a single command, giving you even more flexibility in controlling MS-DOS. Combining these features makes it possible to do a great deal with just one command. For example, suppose you want to print the directory entries of all files in the current directory whose names include the letter U; further, you want the entries sorted alphabetically. Type the following:

```
C:\DOS>dir | find "U" | sort > prn
```

This whole command translates easily into: Look at the directory, find all files with the letter U in their names, sort those files alphabetically, and send the results to the printer. MS-DOS does as it is told, as shown at the top of the next page.

```
COUNTRY   SYS      17069 02-01-93     12:00a
DEBUG     EXE      20634 02-01-93     12:00a
NLSFUNC   EXE       7052 02-01-93     12:00a
SUBST     EXE      18478 02-01-93     12:00a
UNDELETE  EXE      25916 02-01-93     12:00a
UNFORMAT  COM      18560 02-01-93     12:00a
VIRULIST  CPS      35520 02-01-93     12:00a
WNUNDEL   EXE     129792 02-01-93     12:00a
WNUNDEL   HLP      32329 02-01-93     12:00a
```

(Your list might differ, and you might see the name of a temporary file whose size is 0, but the files should still be sorted alphabetically.)

You may rarely search your directories this carefully, but such combinations make MS-DOS a powerful tool for handling text files.

## CHAPTER SUMMARY

This chapter concludes the portion of the book designed to give you a feel for running MS-DOS, including some of its advanced features. The key points to remember include:

- The computer's memory is cleared each time you turn the system off. To save your work permanently, you must store it in a file on a disk.

- A text file contains ordinary characters you can read.

- A command file contains instructions that MS-DOS uses to carry out a command.

- A file name can be up to eight characters long; you can add an extension of up to three characters, separated from the file name by a period.

- Each file on a disk must have a different name or a different extension.

The remainder of the book shows you how to use MS-DOS to manage your files, disks, and devices; use the MS-DOS text editors; and create your own commands.

# PART II

# LEARNING TO USE MS-DOS

Part II shows you how to use MS-DOS to manage your work with the computer. The chapters in Part II include extensive examples that use real-life situations to illustrate each MS-DOS command, but the information is organized so that you can quickly find a particular topic to refresh your memory.

These chapters present many different features, and much of the material is relevant to all versions of MS-DOS. Chapters 5, 6, and 7 describe managing your files, floppy disks, and devices. Chapter 8 explains a tree-structured file system. Chapter 9 covers the use of a hard disk in detail. Chapter 10 shows you how to safeguard your disks and files against loss or damage. Chapter 11 introduces the MS-DOS Shell. Chapter 12 describes the MS-DOS text editor, and Chapters 13 through 17 show you how to use advanced features.

# 5

# Managing Your Files

**T**he previous chapters defined a file as a named collection of related information stored on a disk and showed you several ways to create, copy, display, print, and otherwise work with your computer files. This chapter describes the MS-DOS filing system in detail, showing you more about how files are named and how you can use MS-DOS to manage your computer files.

> **NOTE:** *A few of the examples in the remaining chapters of this book may look familiar, because they repeat some of the examples in Chapters 2, 3, and 4. This repetition is intentional so that Chapters 5 through 17 present a complete guide to MS-DOS commands. You won't have to refer back to Chapter 2, 3, or 4 for command descriptions.*

## THE MS-DOS FILE COMMANDS

To be useful, a filing system—whether it contains disk files or paper files—must be kept orderly and up to date. Using the MS-DOS file commands, you can manage your disk files much as you manage your paper files. This chapter covers the MS-DOS commands you use most often on a day-to-day basis. It shows you how to:

- Display directory entries in different ways with the Directory command.
- Display a file with the Type command.
- Copy and combine files with the Copy command.
- Send a copy of a file to a device with the Copy command.
- Remove a file from a disk with the Delete command.
- Change the name of a file with the Rename command.
- Compare two files with the Compare command.
- Print a file with the Print command.

## FILE NAMES AND EXTENSIONS

As Chapter 4, ''A Look at Files and Floppy Disks,'' pointed out, files are named so that you (and MS-DOS) can tell them apart; each file on a disk must have a different name. You know that a file name can be up to eight characters long, made up of any letters or numbers; you can also use the following symbols:

        `  ~  !  @  #  $  %  ^  &  (  )  _  -  {  }  \  '

60

You can add a suffix—called an *extension*—to the file name to describe its contents more precisely. The extension can be up to three characters long and can include any of the characters that are valid for the file name. It must be separated from the name by a period. The extension distinguishes one file from another just as the name does: REPORT and REPORT.JAN, for example, are two different files, as are REPORT.JAN and REPORT.FEB. Figure 5-1 shows some valid and invalid file names.

| These File Names Are Valid | These Are Invalid... | Because |
|---|---|---|
| B | 1994BUDGET | Name too long |
| 93BUDGET | BUDGET.1994 | Extension too long |
| BUDGET.93 | .94 | No file name |
| BUDGET.94 | SALES 93.DAT | Blank not allowed |
| BDGT(94) | $1,300.45 | Comma not allowed |

**Figure 5-1.**
*Some valid and invalid file names.*

Try to make file names and extensions as descriptive as possible. A short name might be easy to type, but you can have difficulty remembering what the file contains if you haven't used it for a while. The more descriptive the name, the more easily you can identify the contents of the file.

## Special Names and File Name Extensions

Some names and file name extensions have special meanings to MS-DOS. As you'll see in Chapter 7, "Managing Your Devices," MS-DOS refers to the parts of your computer system by certain reserved names known as *device names*. The keyboard and screen, for example, are named CON, and the system clock is called CLOCK$. You cannot use any of these device names as file names.

Similarly, certain file name extensions have special meanings to MS-DOS. These extensions either are created by MS-DOS or cause MS-DOS to assume the file contains a particular type of program or data. You should avoid giving files any of these extensions. A number of the most important ones are listed in Figure 5-2 on the following page.

Application programs also usually recognize special extensions. For example, Microsoft Word, the Microsoft word processor, uses DOC to identify a document, BAK to identify a backup version of a document, and STY to identify a file that contains a style sheet of print specifications. Again, avoid using extensions that have special meaning for your application programs; these extensions are usually listed in the documentation that comes with each program.

| Name | Meaning to MS-DOS |
|------|-------------------|
| BAS | Short for *Basic*. Contains a program written in the Basic programming language. You run the program while using Basic. |
| BAT | Short for *Batch*. Identifies a text file you create that contains a set of MS-DOS commands that are run when you type the name of the file. |
| COM | Short for *Command*. Identifies a command file that contains a program MS-DOS runs when you type the file name. |
| EXE | Short for *Executable*. Like COM, identifies a command file that contains a program MS-DOS runs when you type the file name. |
| HLP | Short for *Help*. Contains a file of help text displayed by certain programs, including the MS-DOS Shell and the versions 5, 6, and 6.2 Editor and Basic programs. |
| OVL | Short for *Overlay*. Identifies a command file that contains part of a large program. |
| SYS | Short for *System*. Identifies a file that can be used only by MS-DOS. |

**Figure 5-2.**
*Some special MS-DOS file name extensions.*

## Specifying the Drives

You can tell MS-DOS to look for a file in a specific drive by typing the drive letter and a colon before the file name. If you specify a file as *a:report*, for example, MS-DOS looks in drive A for a file named REPORT; if you specify the file as *report*, MS-DOS looks for the file in the current drive.

# PREPARING FOR THE EXAMPLES

If your system isn't running, start it. Place a blank, formatted floppy disk in drive A. Then type the following to change the current drive to A:

```
C:\>a:
```

MS-DOS acknowledges by changing the system prompt:

```
A:\>_
```

Now you're ready to create a set of sample files on this floppy disk. Type the following; where you see ^Z, hold down the Ctrl key and press Z (or press F6), then press Enter:

```
A:\>copy con report.doc
This is a dummy file.
^Z
```

MS-DOS responds:

```
        1 file(s) copied
A:\>_
```

Now that you've created this file, you can use it and the MS-DOS Copy command to create some more. Type the following Copy commands (described in detail later in this chapter) to create some other sample files.

```
A:\>copy report.doc report.bak
        1 file(s) copied

A:\>copy report.doc bank.doc
        1 file(s) copied

A:\>copy report.doc budget.jan
        1 file(s) copied

A:\>copy report.doc budget.feb
        1 file(s) copied

A:\>copy report.doc budget.mar
        1 file(s) copied
```

Now check the directory.

```
A:\>dir
```

It should list six files:

```
        Volume in drive A is EXAMPLES 1
        Volume Serial Number is 1A2C-13F5
        Directory of A:\

        REPORT    DOC         23 10-16-93    9:16a
        REPORT    BAK         23 10-16-93    9:16a
        BANK      DOC         23 10-16-93    9:16a
        BUDGET    JAN         23 10-16-93    9:16a
        BUDGET    FEB         23 10-16-93    9:16a
        BUDGET    MAR         23 10-16-93    9:16a
             6 file(s)          138 bytes
                           1210880 bytes free
```

Remember, the time and date in your list will be different, but the file names and sizes (23 bytes) should be the same.

# WILDCARD CHARACTERS

To make it easier to manage your disk files, most file commands let you use wild-card characters to handle several files at once. That way, when you want to do the same thing to several files—change their names, perhaps, or erase them—you don't have to enter a separate command for each file. You can use wildcard characters to tell MS-DOS you mean a set of files with similar names or extensions. Just as a wild card in a poker game can represent any other card in the deck, a wildcard character can represent any other character in a file name or extension.

There are two wildcard characters, the asterisk (*) and the question mark (?). The following examples use the Directory command to illustrate ways you can use wildcard characters to specify groups of files.

## Using the Asterisk Wildcard Character: *

The asterisk makes it easy to carry out commands on sets of files with similar names or extensions; it can represent up to all eight characters in a file name or up to all three characters in an extension. If you use the asterisk to represent the entire name or extension, you are specifying all file names or all extensions.

The following examples illustrate several ways to use the asterisk character to find selected directory entries. You can use the asterisk with other MS-DOS commands as well.

To specify all files named BUDGET, regardless of extension, type the following:

```
A:\>dir budget.*
```

MS-DOS displays the directory entry of each sample file named BUDGET, regardless of its extension:

```
Volume in drive A is EXAMPLES 1
Volume Serial Number is 1A2C-13F5
Directory of A:\

BUDGET    JAN       23 10-16-93    9:16a
BUDGET    FEB       23 10-16-93    9:16a
BUDGET    MAR       23 10-16-93    9:16a
        3 file(s)         69 bytes
                    1210880 bytes free
```

To specify all file names beginning with B, type the following:

```
A:\>dir b*
```

If you don't specify an extension, the Directory command displays the entry for each file that matches the name, regardless of extension. (It's the equivalent of specifying the extension as *.) There are four such files:

```
Volume in drive A is EXAMPLES 1
Volume Serial Number is 1A2C-13F5
Directory of A:\

BANK      DOC       23 10-16-93    9:16a
BUDGET    JAN       23 10-16-93    9:16a
BUDGET    FEB       23 10-16-93    9:16a
BUDGET    MAR       23 10-16-93    9:16a
        4 file(s)          92 bytes
                      1210880 bytes free
```

To specify all files with the same extension, regardless of name, you replace the name with ∗. For example, to specify each file with the extension DOC, type:

```
A:\>dir *.doc
```

MS-DOS displays just those entries:

```
Volume in drive A is EXAMPLES 1
Volume Serial Number is 1A2C-13F5
Directory of A:\

REPORT    DOC       23 10-16-93    9:16a
BANK      DOC       23 10-16-93    9:16a
        2 file(s)          46 bytes
                      1210880 bytes free
```

## Using the Question Mark Wildcard Character: ?

The question mark replaces only one character in a file name or extension. You'll probably use the asterisk more frequently, using the question mark only when one or two characters vary in the middle of a name or extension.

To see how the question mark works, type the following:

```
A:\>dir budget.?a?
```

This command specifies all files named BUDGET that have extensions beginning with any character, followed by the letter *a*, and ending with any character. MS-DOS displays two entries:

```
Volume in drive A is EXAMPLES 1
Volume Serial Number is 1A2C-13F5
Directory of A:\

BUDGET    JAN       23 10-16-93    9:16a
BUDGET    MAR       23 10-16-93    9:16a
        2 file(s)          46 bytes
                      1210880 bytes free
```

## A Warning About Wildcard Characters

Be careful using wildcard characters with commands that can change files. Suppose you spent several days entering a year's worth of budget data into 12 files named BUDGET.JAN, BUDGET.FEB, BUDGET.MAR, and so on. On the same disk you also have three files you don't need named BUDGET.OLD, BUDGET.TST, and BUDGET.BAD. The disk is getting full, so you decide to delete the three unneeded files. It's 2 A.M., you're tired, and you're in a hurry, so you quickly type *del budget.** and press Enter. You have told MS-DOS to do more than you wanted.

You may realize immediately what you have done, or it may not dawn on you until you try to use one of the 12 good budget files and MS-DOS replies *File not found.* You display the directory; there isn't a single file named BUDGET, because you told MS-DOS to delete them all.

With commands that can change or delete a file, use wildcard characters with extreme caution.

This warning applies even if you have version 5 or later of MS-DOS, which includes a command named Undelete that can help you recover deleted files. Bear this in mind: *Undelete cannot always recover files completely.* As you'll see later in this book, Undelete can be valuable. But don't let it lull you into a false sense of security.

# HELP WHEN YOU NEED IT

> **NOTE:** *If you don't have version 5 or later of MS-DOS, your version of MS-DOS doesn't include the help feature described here. Skip to the heading "Displaying Directory Entries."*

As you work with MS-DOS, you'll find that some commands become so familiar you type them without thinking. Others, which you need less often, will linger in your mind, but you may have to refresh your memory to use them correctly. If you have version 5 or later of MS-DOS, you have a feature called *online help* that you can call on whenever you want help with a command. Online help isn't intended to teach you how to use MS-DOS, but it is a handy guide that can remind you of the form of a command you haven't used in a while.

To see a list of the commands for which you can request help, type *help* and press Enter:

```
A:\>help
```

Versions 6 and 6.2 of MS-DOS respond by displaying three columns of topics enclosed in angle brackets:

```
 File  Search                                                    Help
                      MS-DOS Help: Command Reference
 Use the scroll bars to see more commands. Or, press the PAGE DOWN key. For
 more information about using MS-DOS Help, choose How to Use MS-DOS Help
 from the Help menu, or press F1. To exit MS-DOS Help, press ALT, F, X.

 <ANSI.SYS>              <Fc>                    <Net Start>
 <Append>                <Fcbs>                  <Net Stop>
 <Attrib>                <Fdisk>                 <Net Time>
 <Batch commands>        <Files>                 <Net Use>
 <Break>                 <Find>                  <Net Ver>
 <Buffers>               <For>                   <Net View>
 <Call>                  <Format>                <Nlsfunc>
 <Cd>                    <Goto>                  <Numlock>
 <Chcp>                  <Graphics>              <Path>
 <Chdir>                 <Help>                  <Pause>
 <Chkdsk>                <HIMEM.SYS>             <Power>
 <CHKSTATE.SYS>          <If>                    <POWER.EXE>
 <Choice>                <Include>               <Print>
 <Cls>                   <Install>               <Prompt>
 <Command>               <Interlnk>              <Qbasic>
 <CONFIG.SYS commands>   <INTERLNK.EXE>          <RAMDRIVE.SYS>
 <Copy>                  <International commands> <Rd>
 <Alt+C=Contents> <Alt+N=Next> <Alt+B=Back>              00006:002
```

You can scroll through this list one row at a time with the Up and Down arrow keys, or a screen at a time with the PgUp and PgDn keys. Press Tab to move from one column to the next, and press a letter to move the cursor to the first command that begins with that letter. To display information about any of the commands listed, move the cursor to the command name and press Enter.

For example, you used the Date command in a previous chapter. *Date* is the third entry below *Copy* in the first column; press the Down arrow key until the cursor is under *Date* and press Enter. Now MS-DOS displays the help information about the Date command:

```
 File  Search                                                    Help
                         MS-DOS Help: DATE
 ◄Notes►

                                DATE

 Displays the date and prompts you to change the date if necessary.

 MS-DOS records the current date for each file you create or change; this
 date is listed next to the filename in the directory.

 Syntax

    DATE [mm-dd-yy]

 Parameter

 mm-dd-yy
    Sets the date you specify. Values for day, month, and year must be
    separated by periods (.), hyphens (-), or slash marks (/). The date
    format depends on the COUNTRY setting you are using in your CONFIG.SYS
    file. The following list shows the valid values for the month, day, and
    year portions of the mm-dd-yy parameter.
 <Alt+C=Contents> <Alt+N=Next> <Alt+B=Back>              00001:002
```

In addition to this description of the form of the command (MS-DOS calls this the command's *syntax*), online help also includes notes about how to use the command. Notice that the cursor is on the item *Notes*; press Enter. Now you see the notes about the Date command, and the cursor is on the item *Syntax*. Press Enter again, and once again MS-DOS displays the syntax of the command. Some commands also include examples that you can select just as you selected *Notes* and *Syntax*.

Press the Esc key until you return to the list of commands (the *Contents*). To leave online help, press Alt-F-X. That is, press the Alt key, then press F to display the File menu, and then press X to choose Exit. MS-DOS displays the system prompt.

You can display the help for a specific command directly by typing *help* followed by the name of the command. This has the same effect as typing *help* and then choosing the command from the list. Try it by typing the following:

```
A:\>help date
```

Now MS-DOS displays the syntax screen for the Date command. When you're through with the command information, you can either display the contents list by pressing Alt-C or return to MS-DOS by pressing Alt-F-X. Press Alt-F-X now to return to MS-DOS.

You can display a different sort of help information for a command by typing the name of the command followed by a space and /?. Type the following to see this type of help information for the Date command:

```
A:\>date /?
```

MS-DOS simply displays information about the command you specified and the system prompt; there are no items to choose nor a list of commands:

```
Displays or sets the date.

DATE [mm-dd-yy]

mm-dd-yy    Sets the date you specify.

Type DATE without parameters to display the current date setting
and a prompt for a new one. Press ENTER to keep the same date.
```

If you're using version 5 and type *help*, MS-DOS displays a list of the commands for which you can request help, along with a brief description of what each command does. The list is several screens long; you press any key to move to the next screen. If you're using version 5 and type *help* followed by the name of a command, or the name of a command followed by /?, MS-DOS displays the same information as do versions 6 and 6.2 when you type the name of the command followed by /?, as shown above.

Now on to the MS-DOS file-management commands.

# DISPLAYING DIRECTORY ENTRIES

As you have seen, the Directory (dir) command displays entries from the directory that MS-DOS keeps on each disk. Each entry includes the name and extension of the file, its size in bytes, and the date and time it was created or last updated. You can use the Directory command to display all entries or just the entries of selected files.

In the descriptions of the commands here and throughout the remaining chapters, you are shown the general form of the command—the name of the command and most or all of its parameters—before you try the examples. If a parameter has an exact form, such as /W, the form is shown. If a parameter is something you specify, such as a file name, it is named and shown enclosed in angle brackets—for example, <filename>.

## The Directory Command and Its Parameters

Depending on your version of MS-DOS, the Directory command has either three or seven parameters. All versions allow you to specify a file name and two parameters typed as /W and /P. Versions 5 and later have more parameters, among them one that allows you to display only the file name and extension of the directory entries and another that arranges directory entries by name, extension, size, or date and time.

Written out, the format of the Directory command and these parameters looks like this:

**dir <filename> /W /P /O<sortorder> /B /S**

(Other parameters of the Directory command are described later, and a complete summary appears in Appendix C, "MS-DOS Command Reference.")

If you include <filename>, MS-DOS searches the current directory for the file you specify. You can also:

- Precede <filename> with a drive letter. For example, *dir a:report.doc* tells MS-DOS to look on drive A rather than on the current drive.

- Use wildcard characters to specify a group of files. For example, *dir budget.\** tells MS-DOS to display the entries for all files named *budget* regardless of extension.

- Omit <filename> to tell MS-DOS to display the entries for all files in the current directory. For example, *dir* displays all entries for the current directory in the current drive; *dir b:* displays all entries for the current directory in drive B.

The /W (Wide) parameter tells MS-DOS to display only the file names and extensions in five columns across the screen. This display contains less information than does a complete directory listing because it omits file sizes, dates, and times, but is useful when a directory listing is quite long and you only want to see what files are in the directory.

The /P (Pause) parameter tells MS-DOS to display the entries one screenful at a time; a message at the bottom of the screen tells you to press any key to continue. The /P parameter provides complete file information, including size, date, and time, so it is useful when you want a detailed look at a long directory listing.

The /O<sortorder> parameter in versions 5 and later tells MS-DOS to sort (arrange) a directory listing by name, extension, size, or date and time:

- Typing *dir /on* sorts the files alphabetically by file name.

- Typing *dir /oe* sorts the files alphabetically by extension.

- Typing *dir /os* sorts the files by size, smallest to largest.

- Typing *dir /od* sorts the files by date (earliest to latest) and, within the same date, sorts by the time (morning to evening) the file was created or last changed. You cannot sort by time only; that is, you cannot type *dir /ot* to sort by time but not by date.

The /B (Bare) parameter, in versions 5 and later, tells MS-DOS to display only the names and extensions of the files you specify.

The /S (Subdirectory) parameter, in versions 5 and later, tells MS-DOS to display the files in the directory you specify and in all subdirectories of the directory.

## Examples of Displaying Directory Entries

Because you have already used the Directory command several times, only the options are shown here. First, use the /W parameter to see a wide directory display showing the files on your sample floppy disk. Type:

```
A:\>dir /w
```

MS-DOS arranges just the name and extension of each file in five columns across the screen. If you have version 5 or later, the display looks something like this (only three of the five columns are shown):

```
Volume in drive A is EXAMPLES 1
Volume Serial Number is 1A2C-13F5
Directory of A:\

REPORT.DOC      REPORT.BAK      BANK.DOC    .   .   .
BUDGET.MAR
        6 file(s)         138 bytes
                     1210880 bytes free
```

If you have version 4 or earlier, your display is similar, but doesn't include quite as much detail. Such a display doesn't contain as much information as the standard directory display, but it packs a lot of entries onto the screen. The wide format is particularly handy when all you want is a quick look at the names of the files on a crowded disk.

## Pausing the Directory Display

To display the directory of a disk one screenful at a time, you use the /P option. MS-DOS displays the first screenful of entries, followed by either *Press any key to continue...* or *Strike a key when ready...*, depending on your version of MS-DOS. To see the next screenful, press any key. This option lets you view the entire directory without using Pause or Ctrl-Num Lock to freeze the display periodically.

Your sample disk contains less than one screenful of file names, but you can see the effect by using the /P parameter to list the MS-DOS files on your hard disk. Type the following:

```
A:\>dir c:\dos /p
```

MS-DOS responds by displaying the first screenful of its files and waiting for you to press a key:

```
Volume in drive C is HARD DISK
Volume Serial Number is 1608-5A30
Directory of C:\DOS

.               <DIR>      01-15-93   6:05p
..              <DIR>      01-15-93   6:05p
EGA      SYS      4885 02-01-93  12:00a
FORMAT   COM     33087 02-01-93  12:00a
NLSFUNC  EXE      7052 02-01-93  12:00a
COUNTRY  SYS     17069 02-01-93  12:00a
EGA      CPI     58873 02-01-93  12:00a
HIMEM    SYS     13984 02-01-93  12:00a
KEYB     COM     14986 02-01-93  12:00a
```

```
KEYBOARD SYS      34697 02-01-93   12:00a
ANSI     SYS       9029 02-01-93   12:00a
DEBUG    EXE      20634 02-01-93   12:00a
EXPAND   EXE      16885 02-01-93   12:00a
FDISK    EXE      57224 02-01-93   12:00a
SYS      COM      13440 02-01-93   12:00a
UNFORMAT COM      18560 02-01-93   12:00a
ATTRIB   EXE      15796 02-01-93   12:00a
CHOICE   COM       1733 02-01-93   12:00a
CHKDSK   EXE      12267 02-01-93   12:00a
Press any key to continue . . .
```

Press any key to see the next screenful. Continue pressing the key until MS-DOS displays the system prompt, or press Ctrl-Break to cancel the command.

### Sorting the Directory Display

As described earlier, starting with version 5, MS-DOS added new ways for you to display a directory. Suppose you have a floppy disk full of files with different extensions, and you want to group them to get a better idea of what the floppy disk contains. The /O parameter of the Directory command does the job. If you have version 5 or later, try it. Type:

```
A:\>dir /oe
```

MS-DOS responds:

```
Volume in drive A is EXAMPLES 1
Volume Serial Number is 1A2C-13F5
Directory of A:\

REPORT   BAK        23 10-16-93    9:16a
REPORT   DOC        23 10-16-93    9:16a
BANK     DOC        23 10-16-93    9:16a
BUDGET   FEB        23 10-16-93    9:16a
BUDGET   JAN        23 10-16-93    9:16a
BUDGET   MAR        23 10-16-93    9:16a
        6 file(s)        138 bytes
                    1210880 bytes free
```

The files are arranged alphabetically by extension. Remember that you can also group files by size or by date and time. The latter is particularly useful when you have more than one version of a file and you want to look at the versions in chronological order.

### Listing Only Files

If you simply want to see what files are on a disk, the /B parameter gives you a bare-bones look at its contents. With the sample files, for instance, typing:

```
A:\>dir /b
```

produces this display:

```
REPORT.DOC
REPORT.BAK
BANK.DOC
BUDGET.JAN
BUDGET.FEB
BUDGET.MAR
```

Finally—and this applies to any MS-DOS command—remember that you can type *help* or use the universal */?* parameter to refresh your memory about a command and its parameters.

# DISPLAYING A FILE

Many of the files you use are text files, and there will be times when you want to check the contents of a file but don't need a printed copy. MS-DOS gives you a quick way to see what's in a file: the Type command. (The name Type is a carryover from the days when most computers had only typewriter-like consoles.)

When you use the Type command, MS-DOS displays the file without stopping; if the file is longer than one screenful and you want to read the entire file, freeze the display by pressing Pause or Ctrl-Num Lock.

The Type command has one parameter:

**type <filename>**

<filename> is the name of the file to be displayed. The Type command displays just one file at a time, so you can't use wildcard characters in the file name. If you do use a wildcard character, MS-DOS displays *Invalid filename or file not found* and returns to command level. If the file you name doesn't exist, MS-DOS displays *File not found* and, again, returns to command level.

## An Example of Displaying a File

To display the file named REPORT.DOC on the floppy disk in the current drive, verify that your sample disk is in drive A and type:

```
A:\>type report.doc
```

MS-DOS displays the file:

```
This is a dummy file.
```

You'll probably use the Type command frequently to check your text files.

## MAKING COPIES OF FILES

Just as you sometimes make copies of your paper files, you'll find yourself needing copies of your disk files.

You may want to share a file with a colleague who has a computer, you may want to alter the copy slightly to produce a different version, or you may want to copy a file from your hard disk to a floppy disk you can carry with you. The Copy command can make a copy of a file on the same disk (with a different file name) or on a different disk (with any valid file name).

When used to make copies of files, the Copy command has two major parameters, <file1> and <file2>. The format of the Copy command is:

**copy <file1> <file2>**

<file1> is the name of the file to be copied (the *source* file), and <file2> is the name of the copy to be made (the *target* file). You can use wildcard characters to copy a set of files.

**NOTE:** *Four additional, seldom-used parameters (/A, /B, /V, and /Y) are described in Appendix C, "MS-DOS Command Reference."*

When copying files, if you:

- Specify a <file1> (including the drive letter) that is not on the disk in the current drive and omit <file2>, MS-DOS copies <file1> to the disk in the current drive and gives the copy the same name as the original. Example (if the current drive is C): *copy a:report.mar.*

- Specify only a drive letter as <file2>, the file is copied from the disk in the current drive to the disk in the drive you specify and is given the same name as <file1>. Example: *copy report.feb a:.*

- Specify a <file1> that doesn't exist, MS-DOS responds *File not found,* followed by the name you typed for <file1> and *0 file(s) copied,* and it returns to command level.

- Specify a <file2> that doesn't exist, MS-DOS creates it as a copy of <file1>.

- Specify a <file2> that does exist and you're using version 6 or earlier, MS-DOS replaces its contents with <file1>. This is the same as deleting the existing target file, so be careful not to give the target the same name as an existing file you want to keep.

The following practice session illustrates different ways to copy files; it also describes the type of situation in which you might want to use each form of the command.

## Examples of Copying Files

You want to change a document you already have on disk, but you want to keep the original as well as the changed version. For example, to make a copy of the file REPORT.DOC on the same floppy disk and to name the copy RESULTS, type:

```
A:\>copy report.doc results
```

MS-DOS acknowledges *1 file(s) copied*.

To verify that both files, REPORT.DOC and RESULTS, are on the floppy disk, display the directory by typing:

```
A:\>dir
```

MS-DOS now shows seven files on the floppy disk:

```
Volume in drive A is EXAMPLES 1
Volume Serial Number is 1A2C-13F5
Directory of A:\

REPORT    DOC        23 10-16-93    9:16a
REPORT    BAK        23 10-16-93    9:16a
BANK      DOC        23 10-16-93    9:16a
BUDGET    JAN        23 10-16-93    9:16a
BUDGET    FEB        23 10-16-93    9:16a
BUDGET    MAR        23 10-16-93    9:16a
RESULTS              23 10-16-93    9:16a
         7 file(s)           161 bytes
                         1210368 bytes free
```

Any time you want to verify the results of an example, use the Directory command to see what files are on the floppy disk.

Suppose you want to copy a file from another disk and store it, under the same file name, on the disk in the current drive.

For example, your current drive is drive A. To copy a file from a different drive to the floppy disk in drive A, all you need to specify is the drive letter and name of the source file, because MS-DOS assumes you want to copy the source file to the disk in the current drive and give the target file the same name unless you specify otherwise.

Try it: One of the files in the DOS subdirectory on your hard disk is named README.TXT. To copy it from drive C (the hard disk) to the floppy disk in drive A (the current drive), type the following:

```
A:\>copy c:\dos\readme.txt
```

MS-DOS responds *1 file(s) copied*.

Next, suppose you want to change a file and store the new version under the same file name and on the same disk as the original, but you want to be able to distinguish between the two versions. Simply make a copy of the file on the same disk, with the same file name but a different extension. You can use the asterisk wildcard character to tell MS-DOS to use the same file name. For example, to make a copy of BUDGET.MAR and call it BUDGET.APR, type the following:

```
A:\>copy budget.mar *.apr
```

MS-DOS acknowledges that it copied one file.

You have several files named REPORT stored on disk. Suppose you want to keep the originals but make copies of them all for a new project; to avoid confusion, you want to give the copies a new file name but keep the same extension. For example, to make a copy of each file named REPORT, giving each copy the name FORECAST, type the following:

```
A:\>copy report.* forecast.*
```

MS-DOS displays the name of each source file as it makes the copies:

```
REPORT.DOC
REPORT.BAK
        2 file(s) copied
```

You can copy all the files on a floppy disk by specifying the source file as *.* and specifying the target as just a drive letter. This procedure is not the same as copying the floppy disk with the Diskcopy command; the difference is explained under the heading "Copying a Complete Floppy Disk" in Chapter 6, "Managing Your Floppy Disks."

In addition to the Copy command, MS-DOS versions 3.2 and later include two additional commands for copying files selectively: Replace, which lets you copy only files that already exist on the target disk, and Xcopy, which lets you copy entire subdirectories in addition to files in a directory. Both of these commands are described in Chapter 9, "Managing Your Hard Disk."

## SENDING FILES TO DEVICES

In Chapter 4, "A Look at Files and Floppy Disks," you printed a file by using the Copy command to send a copy of the file to the printer. You can also send a copy of a file to any other output device. If, for example, you copy a file to a communications connection, or *port,* on the computer, the file goes to whatever device is attached to the port—such as a telecommunications line to another computer.

When it is used to send a copy of a file to an output device, the Copy command has two parameters:

**copy <filename> <device>**

<filename> is the name of the file to be sent; <device> is the name of the device to which the file is to be sent.

Be sure <device> exists. If you try to send a file to a device that doesn't exist or isn't ready, MS-DOS might stop running. You won't hurt anything, but you'll have to restart the system.

## An Example of Sending Files to a Device

To send a copy of each sample file with the extension DOC to the printer, make certain your printer is turned on and type:

```
A:\>copy *.doc prn
```

MS-DOS displays the name of each file as it sends the file to the printer:

```
REPORT.DOC
BANK.DOC
FORECAST.DOC
        1 file(s) copied
```

The files are printed with no separation between them. MS-DOS reports only one file copied because, in effect, only one output file was created: the printed copy of the three files.

# COMBINING FILES

Sometimes, it's useful to combine several files. Perhaps you have several short documents, and you decide it would be easier and more convenient to work with a single document that includes all the shorter ones. If you have several sets of files with similar names or extensions, you can combine each set into a new file, creating several new files. The Copy command lets you copy several files into a new file without destroying the original versions.

When it is used to combine files, the Copy command has two parameters:

**copy <source> <target>**

<source> represents the files to be combined. You can use wildcard characters to name the source files to be combined, or you can list several file names, separating them with a plus sign (+). If any file in the list doesn't exist, MS-DOS goes on to the next name without telling you the file doesn't exist.

<target> represents the file that results from combining the source files. If you specify a target, MS-DOS combines the source files into the target file. If you don't specify a target but do specify individual source files, MS-DOS combines all the source files into the first file in the <source> list, changing its contents.

## Examples of Combining Files

Suppose you have two files you want to use as the basis for a single new file, but you want to keep the originals intact. For example, to combine the files BANK.DOC and REPORT.DOC into a new file named BANKRPT.DOC, type:

```
A:\>copy bank.doc+report.doc bankrpt.doc
```

MS-DOS displays the names of the source files as it copies them:

```
BANK.DOC
REPORT.DOC
        1 file(s) copied
```

Again, MS-DOS reports one file copied because the command created only one file.

You can also copy several files into an already existing file. To combine BUDGET.JAN, BUDGET.FEB, and BUDGET.MAR into the first file, BUDGET.JAN, type:

```
A:\>copy budget.jan+budget.feb+budget.mar
```

MS-DOS displays the name of each source file as it copies:

```
BUDGET.JAN
BUDGET.FEB
BUDGET.MAR
        1 file(s) copied
```

Now, suppose you've been keeping monthly budget files. It's the end of the year. You still need separate monthly files for comparison with next year's figures, but right now, you want to work with all the files together. To combine all the files named BUDGET into a file named ANNUAL.BGT, type:

```
A:\>copy budget.* annual.bgt
```

MS-DOS responds:

```
BUDGET.JAN
BUDGET.FEB
BUDGET.MAR
BUDGET.APR
        1 file(s) copied
```

Or, suppose you want to combine pairs of files with the same file names but different extensions. You can combine them under the same file names, with new extensions, and end up with both the original and combined versions.

For example, if you have entered all the examples, among the files on the floppy disk in drive B are REPORT.DOC and REPORT.BAK, FORECAST.DOC and FORECAST.BAK. To combine each pair of files with the same name and the extensions DOC and BAK into a single file with the same name and the extension MIX, type:

```
A:\>copy *.bak+*.doc *.mix
```

MS-DOS displays the names of the files as it copies them:

```
REPORT.BAK
REPORT.DOC
FORECAST.BAK
FORECAST.DOC
        2 file(s) copied
```

This time MS-DOS reports two files copied because the command created two files: REPORT.MIX and FORECAST.MIX.

## Moving Files

The Move command, new to version 6, moves a file from one place to another. Move works much like the Copy command except it doesn't leave a copy of the file in the original location. Because the Move command is most useful in managing directories of files, it is described in Chapter 8, "A Tree of Files," under the heading "Moving Files from One Directory to Another."

# DELETING FILES

Just as you have to clean out a file drawer once in a while, you'll occasionally have to clear your disks of files you no longer need. The Delete command (you can type it either as *del* or as *erase*) deletes one or more files from a disk.

The Delete command has two parameters:

**delete <filename> /P**

<filename> is the name of the file to be deleted. If you use wildcard characters, MS-DOS deletes all files that match <filename>. If the file doesn't exist, MS-DOS displays *File not found* and returns to command level.

/P, in versions 4 and later, tells MS-DOS to prompt you for verification before deleting the file. If you use wildcard characters to delete more than one file, MS-DOS prompts you to verify the deletion of each file.

## Safeguards

When you delete files, MS-DOS assumes you know what you're doing—that you know exactly which files you're eliminating, and that you really don't want them anymore. But being human, you sometimes make mistakes, so you need ways to protect your files.

One good safeguard is the Copy command. MS-DOS doesn't limit the number of times you can copy a file, so you can think of the Copy command as the computer-based equivalent of your photocopy machine. Copy a file, preferably onto a different disk, whenever its value outweighs the minimal time and effort required to copy it.

When you delete files, use the /P parameter, especially if you use wildcard characters to specify a set of files. If you don't use this parameter to tell MS-DOS to prompt for confirmation, the only time it hesitates before carrying out a Delete command is when you type *del* * *. Because this form of the Delete command removes all files in a directory, MS-DOS prompts you *All files in directory will be deleted! Are you sure (Y/N)?*

If your version of MS-DOS doesn't include the /P parameter, double-check the command on the screen before pressing Enter. Verify the drive letter (if necessary), the file name, and the extension you typed. If you used wildcard characters, either be certain you know exactly which files will be deleted or consider using this safety check: Press Esc to cancel the Delete command, and then use the same wildcard characters with a Directory command. The Directory command lists all the files that match the wildcard characters. If the file names you see match the ones you expected to see, you can reenter the original Delete command with confidence.

## Examples of Deleting Files

Cautionary statements aside, Delete itself is one of the easiest MS-DOS commands to use. For example, to delete the file named BUDGET.APR on the floppy disk in the current drive, type:

```
A:\>del budget.apr
```

Press the Enter key, and the file's gone.

Similarly, type the following to delete the MS-DOS file you copied from the hard disk:

```
A:\>del readme.txt
```

The next example deletes all files on the sample floppy disk whose extension is BAK. If you have version 4 or later, use the /P parameter to ask MS-DOS to prompt you for verification. Type the following (omit the /P if you're using an earlier version):

```
A:\>del *.bak /p
```

With the /P parameter, MS-DOS responds by displaying the name of the first file whose extension is BAK and asking you whether to delete it:

```
A:\REPORT.BAK,    Delete (Y/N)?_
```

Type *y* to delete it. Now MS-DOS shows you the name of the next file and again asks:

```
A:\FORECAST.BAK,    Delete (Y/N)?_
```

Type *y* again to delete the file. If you had typed *n* in response to either prompt, MS-DOS would have left the file alone and moved on to the next file (if any) that matched the file name you typed as part of the Delete command. The /P option is thus handy when you want to delete several—but not all—files that have similar names or extensions. The prompt lets you avoid the work of entering a separate command for each file.

But what if your version of MS-DOS doesn't have the /P option? If you typed the Delete command as *del *.bak*, your disk drive became active for a brief time after you pressed the Enter key, and then the system prompt returned to the screen. In that short time, MS-DOS deleted the two sample files whose extension was BAK without telling you the names of the files. This example underscores the need for you to be sure you have typed the correct file name and the correct drive letter or extension (if necessary) whenever you use wildcard characters with the Delete command.

Whether or not you use the /P parameter, be particularly careful when you use the question mark in a file extension. To see why, create two additional test files by typing the following:

```
A:\>copy results *.1
     1 file(s) copied

A:\>copy results *.12
     1 file(s) copied
```

This gives you three files with the same name but different extensions: RESULTS, RESULTS.1, and RESULTS.12. Now type a Directory command, using a single question mark as the extension. Before you press Enter, decide which files you believe MS-DOS will list:

```
A:\>dir results.?
```

MS-DOS lists two files:

```
Volume in drive A is EXAMPLES 1
Volume Serial Number is 1A2C-13F5
Directory of A:\

RESULTS   1         23 10-16-93    9:46a
RESULTS             23 10-16-93    9:46a
        2 file(s)        46 bytes
                    1180160 bytes free
```

If you expected to see only RESULTS.1, the response to this Directory command is a surprise. If you had typed a Delete command instead of a Directory command, the files you see listed are the files MS-DOS would have erased. An unexpected directory listing can be momentarily confusing, but unintentionally deleting files is definitely an unpleasant surprise.

To delete both of the files you just created but leave your original RESULTS file untouched, type the following command:

```
A:\>del results.1?
```

Typing *1* as the first character of the extension ensures that the file RESULTS isn't affected. Note, however, that even though you included a question mark (which takes the place of a single character) after the 1, MS-DOS deleted RESULTS.1 as well as RESULTS.12. Be careful whenever you use wildcard characters with commands that change or delete files.

## CHANGING FILE NAMES

There will be times when you want to change the name of a file. You might simply change your mind, or perhaps you'll have changed the contents of a file so much that you want to give it a name that more closely describes its new contents. For example, if your word processing program automatically makes a backup copy whenever you edit and save a file, the Rename command can be valuable when (as happens) your working copy is inadvertently lost or damaged—perhaps the power fails, you have a problem with the program itself, or you've mangled the file with editing changes and want to start all over from scratch.

The Rename command changes a file's name or extension, or both. You can use wildcard characters to rename a set of files.

You can abbreviate the Rename command as *ren*. It has two parameters:

**rename <oldname> <newname>**

<oldname> is the name of an existing file. If the file doesn't exist, MS-DOS displays *Duplicate file name or file not found* and returns to command level.

<newname> is the name you want to give to the file specified by <oldname>. If there is already a file with the new name, MS-DOS displays *Duplicate file name or file not found* and returns to command level. Two files on the same disk can't have the same name, and MS-DOS would have to erase the existing file to carry out the command, so this built-in safeguard keeps you from inadvertently erasing one file in the process of renaming another.

The Rename command simply changes the name of a file; it doesn't copy a file to a different disk. Both the old name and the new name must refer to a file on the same drive. If you specify a different drive letter with the new name, MS-DOS responds *Invalid parameter.*

## Examples of Changing File Names

To change the name of the file ANNUAL.BGT to FINAL on the disk in the current drive, type:

```
A:\>ren annual.bgt final
```

MS-DOS changes the name and displays the system prompt.

To change the extension of the file BUDGET.MAR from MAR to 003 on the disk in the current drive, you can use the * wildcard character for the new file name. Type the following:

```
A:\>ren budget.mar *.003
```

The file is now named BUDGET.003.

To change the extension DOC to TXT for all files on the disk in the current drive, use the * for both the old and new file names. Type the following:

```
A:\>ren *.doc *.txt
```

Verify this change with the Directory command by typing:

```
A:\>dir *.txt
```

MS-DOS shows four files, all of which used to have the extension DOC:

```
Volume in drive A is EXAMPLES 1
Volume Serial Number is 1A2C-13F5
Directory of A:\

REPORT    TXT        23 10-16-93    9:16a
BANK      TXT        23 10-16-93    9:16a
FORECAST  TXT        23 10-16-93    9:16a
BANKRPT   TXT        47 10-16-93   10:51a
        4 file(s)          116 bytes
                       1181184 bytes free
```

If you use the Directory command now to display the entries of all files with the extension DOC, MS-DOS responds *File not found.*

## COMPARING FILES

Sometimes you'll want to know whether two files are exactly the same. Suppose you have two files named BUDGET on different disks. They're the same length—but are they different budgets or two copies of the same one? You could display or print both files and compare them, but that could take quite a while, and you still might miss some small difference. It's quicker and more accurate to use File Compare (fc).

The File Compare command has two main parameters. See Appendix C, "MS-DOS Command Reference," for a listing of all the parameters.

**fc <file1> <file2>**

<file1> and <file2> are the file names of the files to be compared.

File Compare displays different results depending on the types of files you are comparing. If both files contain only text, File Compare compares the lines of the first file with the lines of the second file. If it finds differences, it displays the last line in each file that matched, the lines that don't match, and the first lines in each file that once again match. File Compare then continues to compare the file until it comes across another unmatching portion, whereupon it displays another set of lines. If File Compare checks 100 lines without finding a match, it displays the message *Resync failed. Files are too different.* (Some versions of MS-DOS display the message ****Files are different***.*)

If one or both of the files you want to compare are nontext files (such as program files) that have the extension EXE, COM, SYS, OBJ, LIB, or BIN, File Compare performs a byte-by-byte comparison. File Compare compares the two files from beginning to end, always checking to see whether the bytes in corresponding positions in the files match. It does not display mismatched lines but lists the characters that differ and how far each is from the beginning of the file. If one file is shorter than the other, File Compare displays the message *FC: FILEx longer than FILEy* at the end of the comparison.

**NOTE:** *MS-DOS versions 3.3 through 5 also include the Compare command. See the Compare entry in Appendix C for more information.*

## Examples of Comparing Files

The following examples show the MS-DOS prompts and responses as they appear in versions 6 and later. If you have an earlier version of MS-DOS, your messages may differ, but the command works as described. Type the commands as shown, but bear in mind that you may not see exactly what is shown here.

To compare REPORT.TXT with BUDGET.FEB, type:

```
A:\>fc report.txt budget.feb
```

The files are identical, so MS-DOS replies as follows:

```
Comparing files REPORT.TXT and BUDGET.FEB
FC: no differences encountered
```

Because all the sample files contain the same words, you'll have to create two different files to see how File Compare notifies you of differences. To create a file named COMPARE1.TXT, type the following:

```
A:\>copy con compare1.txt
This is line 1.
This is line 2.
This is line 3.
This is line 4.
^Z
        1 file(s) copied
```

Now create a file named COMPARE2.TXT that skips line 3 and adds some lines at the end. Type the following:

```
A:\>copy con compare2.txt
This is line 1.
This is line 2.
This is line 4.
This is line 5.
This is line 6.
^Z
        1 file(s) copied
```

Now compare COMPARE1.TXT with COMPARE2.TXT. Type:

```
A:\>fc compare1.txt compare2.txt
```

The File Compare command compares the files and then reports the differences:

```
Comparing files COMPARE1.TXT and COMPARE2.TXT
***** COMPARE1.TXT
This is line 2.
This is line 3.
This is line 4.
***** COMPARE2.TXT
This is line 2.
This is line 4.
*****

***** COMPARE1.TXT
***** COMPARE2.TXT
This is line 5.
This is line 6.
*****
```

As you can see, File Compare found the two mismatching portions of the files. The first section of the display points out the absence of line 3 in

COMPARE2.TXT. The second section lists the two added lines. Because you won't need these two files again, delete them now by typing:

```
A:\>del compare?.txt
```

To see the difference between comparing text files and comparing nontext files, compare two nontext files found in the DOS subdirectory on your hard disk. To compare the files EDIT.COM and HELP.COM, type the following:

```
A:\>fc c:\dos\edit.com c:\dos\help.com
```

MS-DOS quickly displays the differences it finds:

```
Comparing files C:\DOS\EDIT.COM and C:\DOS\HELP.COM
00000196: 45 51
00000197: 44 48
00000198: 43 45
00000199: 4F 4C
0000019A: 4D 50
```

Each line gives the location in the files of the mismatching characters and the values representing the characters. The numbers are combinations of the digits 0 through 9 and the letters A through F. These characters are from the base-16 number system, usually called hexadecimal, in which A through F are used to represent the decimal numbers 10 through 15. If you must know what the differing characters are, or if you must calculate the exact locations, you need a chart of the American Standard Code for Information Interchange (ASCII), which shows how characters are encoded, and you need a guide to hexadecimal arithmetic. The manuals that came with your computer might contain both.

You can use wildcard characters to compare two sets of files with one command. To compare all files with the extension TXT and all files with the same file name but the extension MIX, type the following:

```
A:\>fc *.txt *.mix
```

There are now four files with the extension TXT, but only two (REPORT.MIX and FORECAST.MIX) with the extension MIX. MS-DOS tells you which files it can find and which ones it is unable to compare:

```
Comparing files REPORT.TXT and REPORT.MIX
***** REPORT.TXT
***** REPORT.MIX
This is a dummy file.
*****

Comparing files BANK.TXT and BANK.MIX
FC: cannot open BANK.MIX - No such file or directory
```

```
Comparing files FORECAST.TXT and FORECAST.MIX
***** FORECAST.TXT
***** FORECAST.MIX
This is a dummy file.
*****


Comparing files BANKRPT.TXT and BANKRPT.MIX
FC: cannot open BANKRPT.MIX - No such file or directory
```

# PRINTING FILES

You can print files at the same time you're using the computer to do other things. The Print command keeps a list—called the *print queue*—of files to be printed, and it prints the files in the order in which they appear in the queue. The print queue normally can hold up to 10 files.

In addition to printing files, the Print command lets you change some characteristics of its operation—notably, the size of the print queue and the printer that MS-DOS uses. For a description of these uses of the Print command, see "Changing Operation of the Print Command" later in this chapter.

Because the computer can really do only one thing at a time, MS-DOS prints when nothing else is happening, such as when you pause to think between keystrokes. You'll notice that printing slows and sometimes even stops when something else is going on—especially when MS-DOS is using a disk drive.

You use the Print command to add a file to the print queue, delete a file from the queue, cancel all printing, and display the names of the files in the queue. When used to print a file, the Print command has four parameters:

**print <filename> /P /C /T**

<filename> is the name of the file to be added to or deleted from the print queue. You can enter more than one file name with a Print command; just type the list of file names, separating each from the next with a blank.

/P (Print) tells MS-DOS to add <filename> to the print queue. MS-DOS assumes this parameter if all you specify is <filename>.

/C (Cancel) tells MS-DOS to remove <filename> from the print queue. If the file is being printed, printing stops.

/T (Terminate) stops all printing. If a file is being printed, printing stops and all files are removed from the print queue.

If you enter the Print command with no parameters, MS-DOS displays the list of files in the print queue.

## Examples of Printing a File

The following examples work best with a dot-matrix printer equipped with a tractor feed that uses fanfold paper. If you don't have such a printer, or if you use a network printer, you might prefer to read through these examples rather than try them for yourself. Some examples might not work as described, and several can cause a fast printer to use many sheets of paper.

MS-DOS advances the paper to the next page each time it prints a new file, so check what each example does before you try it. You can then be ready to stop the printing process, and you'll save both time and paper. First, a bit of preparation.

Most of the sample files you created in this chapter consist of a single line and would print too quickly for you to try using all the Print parameters in the following examples. Copy the README.TXT file from the DOS directory on your hard drive to your floppy disk:

```
A:\>copy c:\dos\readme.txt
```

This file is significantly larger than the others on your floppy disk, and will certainly take plenty of time to print.

To print the file README.TXT, type:

```
A:\>print readme.txt
```

The first time you enter the Print command after starting the system, MS-DOS might prompt you for the name of the printer to use:

```
Name of list device [PRN]: _
```

The brackets around PRN mean that MS-DOS will use the device named PRN if you press the Enter key. Unless you have more than one printer attached to your system, or you are using a printer with a serial interface, just press the Enter key. If you have never printed with your printer, press the Enter key.

When you respond to the prompt, MS-DOS loads the Print command file into memory and keeps it there until you either turn the system off or restart MS-DOS. MS-DOS reports that the program is loaded:

```
Resident part of PRINT installed
```

When MS-DOS begins to carry out your Print command, it displays the names and print status of the files in the print queue:

```
A:\README.TXT is currently being printed
```

There is one file in the print queue (README.TXT), and it's now being printed.

When you printed a file in Chapter 4 by copying it to the printer, MS-DOS didn't display the system prompt—and you couldn't use the system—until the file had been printed. This time, the system prompt returned as soon as printing started. As soon as MS-DOS starts printing a file with the Print command, MS-DOS is ready to accept another command from you.

If you decide you don't want to print a file after all, you can remove it from the print queue with the /C parameter; type the following command while README.TXT is being printed:

```
A:\>print readme.txt /c
```

MS-DOS displays a terse acknowledgment of your command:

```
PRINT queue is empty
```

and stops sending lines to your printer, even though your printer will probably continue to operate until it finishes printing the characters it has already received. At that point, the printer stops and advances the paper to a new page. If you check the last line of the printout, you might see a message like this:

```
NOTES ON MS-DOS VERSION 6
=========================

This file provides important information not included in the
Microsoft MS-DOS User's Guide or in MS-
File A:\README.TXT canceled by operator
```

You can put more than one file into the print queue with a single Print command. To tell MS-DOS to print both README.TXT and BUDGET.JAN, type:

```
A:\>print readme.txt budget.jan
```

MS-DOS starts printing README.TXT and displays the print queue:

```
        A:\README.TXT is currently being printed
        A:\BUDGET.JAN is in queue
```

If you want to stop printing, you can remove all files from the print queue with the /T parameter. Type the following, again while README.TXT is being printed:

```
A:\>print /t
```

Again, MS-DOS displays the acknowledgment *PRINT queue is empty*. This time, it prints the message *All files canceled by operator* at the point where it stopped printing and, again, advances the paper and removes all remaining files from the queue.

You can also put several files in the print queue at once by using wildcard characters. To print all the files whose extension is TXT, type:

```
A:\>print *.txt
```

Now MS-DOS tells you that there are five files in the queue (the order might vary), as shown at the top of the next page.

```
A:\REPORT.TXT is currently being printed
A:\BANK.TXT is in queue
A:\README.TXT is in queue
A:\FORECAST.TXT is in queue
A:\BANKRPT.TXT is in queue
```

MS-DOS prints the files in the order shown. Stop all printing again by typing:

```
A:\>print /t
```

Again, MS-DOS stops printing the current file, prints the cancellation message, advances the paper, removes all remaining files from the queue, and acknowledges on the screen *PRINT queue is empty*.

The following example uses several sheets of paper. If you're not using continuous form paper or an automatic sheet feeder, you shouldn't try this example because it might print on the platen of your printer; skip to the heading "Changing Operation of the Print Command."

The print queue normally holds up to 10 files. To fill it, tell MS-DOS to print all the files on the floppy disk in drive A; there are 12 text files, of which MS-DOS puts the first 10 in the queue. Type the following:

```
A:\>print *.*
```

MS-DOS tells you the queue is full and displays the list of files in the queue (again, the order might vary):

```
PRINT queue is full

        A:\REPORT.TXT is currently being printed
        A:\BANK.TXT is in queue
        A:\BUDGET.JAN is in queue
        A:\BUDGET.FEB is in queue
        A:\BUDGET.003 is in queue
        A:\RESULTS is in queue
        A:\README.TXT is in queue
        A:\FORECAST.TXT is in queue
        A:\BANKRPT.TXT is in queue
        A:\FINAL is in queue
```

You really don't need to print all these files. Stop all printing by typing:

```
A:\>print /t
```

MS-DOS empties the queue and alerts you as before:

```
PRINT queue is empty
```

## Changing Operation of the Print Command

MS-DOS initially limits the print queue to 10 files, but you can increase the size of the queue and can also tell MS-DOS to use a printer other than the standard printer, PRN. (More details on printers are in Chapter 7, "Managing Your Devices.")

You can change Print command operations only the first time you use the Print command during a session at your computer; if you try to use these options again before restarting MS-DOS or turning the computer off, MS-DOS displays the message *Invalid switch* and ignores the command.

When used to change the size of the print queue or the name of the printer, the Print command has two parameters:

**print /D:<printer> /Q:<size>**

/D:<printer> tells MS-DOS to use the printer named <printer>. If you omit /D:<printer>, MS-DOS uses the standard printer named PRN.

/Q:<size> tells MS-DOS the number of files the print queue can hold; the minimum number is 4, and the maximum number is 32. If you omit /Q:<size>, the print queue holds 10 files.

If you wanted to increase the size of the print queue to 15 files, you would type *print /q:15* the first time you used the Print command. If you wanted to tell MS-DOS to use the printer named LPT2, you would type *print /d:lpt2*. You can combine these parameters in the same Print command, but you cannot combine them with other parameters unless you are entering the Print command for the first time since starting MS-DOS.

The Print command lets you print text files without losing the use of your system during printing; it can make both you and your system more productive.

Several infrequently used parameters that give you more precise control over how the print program interacts with MS-DOS are described in Appendix C, "MS-DOS Command Reference."

# 6

# Managing Your
# Floppy Disks

**D**isks are the computer's filing cabinets. Managing your computer filing system includes not only keeping track of your files, as described in the previous chapter, but also taking care of your floppy disks. There are many ways to prepare and store information on floppy disks; the concepts underlying floppy disk handling, however, apply to all microcomputers.

Several MS-DOS commands deal with entire floppy disks, not with individual files. For example, you must prepare a new floppy disk for use; this process is called *formatting* (or, less commonly, *initializing*). Or, if you need an exact copy of a floppy disk, you don't copy each file separately; you copy the entire floppy disk with one command.

This chapter suggests ways to handle your floppy disks, briefly describes how MS-DOS stores files on floppy disks, and shows you how to do the following:

- Prepare a floppy disk for use with the Format command.

- Duplicate a floppy disk with the Diskcopy command.

- Compare the contents of two floppy disks with the Diskcomp command.

- Analyze and report on the use of floppy disk storage space with the Check Disk command.

- Assign, change, or delete the volume label (identifying name) of a disk with the Label command.

- Display the volume label of a disk with the Volume command.

The Diskcopy and Diskcomp commands are for floppy disks only. A number of other MS-DOS commands, such as Format, Check Disk, Label, and Volume, are used with both floppy disks and hard disks. Additional commands, such as Backup and Restore, are used exclusively or primarily with hard disks. Depending on which chapter is most appropriate, these disk-management commands are described in this chapter, in Chapter 9, "Managing Your Hard Disk," or in Chapter 10, "Protecting Your Disks and Files."

## HANDLING FLOPPY DISKS

Floppy disks are remarkably durable, especially the 3.5-inch type in a hard plastic shell. The useful life of a floppy disk depends on how often you use it, of course, but even more important is how you treat it. Handle your floppy disks with the same care you use when handling valuable recording tapes or photographs:

- Avoid touching the floppy disk surfaces that show through the openings in the protective jacket. Dirt, fingerprints, or dust can shorten the life of a floppy disk and can damage or destroy the data.

- Keep floppy disks away from magnets and other sources of magnetic influence, such as telephones, electric motors, and televisions.

- Keep food and drinks away from floppy disks. The same goes for cigarettes, cigars, pipes, and ashtrays.

- Don't fold, spindle, or mutilate floppy disks. Don't pile other objects on them.

- Don't write on 5.25-inch floppy disk labels with a pencil, ballpoint pen, or other sharp instrument; use a felt-tipped marker.

- Store your floppy disks in a safe place when you're not using them. Protect them from extreme heat and cold, humidity, and contact with other objects.

Many products are available for storing floppy disks, including plastic boxes, vinyl pockets that fit a three-ring binder, and hanging file folders. All offer good protection; they aren't necessary, but they make it easier for you to organize your floppy disks and store them safely, rather than leaving them scattered around your desk.

Although an office is a mild environment compared to a factory or a shop floor, data on a floppy disk can be damaged by such innocuous objects as a paper clip that has been stored in a magnetic paper-clip holder, a magnetized letter opener, an electric pencil sharpener, or a telephone-answering machine. If you put a letter down on top of a floppy disk lying on your desk, it's all too easy to put a hot coffee cup or a heavy object on the letter without realizing that the floppy disk is underneath.

The safest places for a floppy disk are in the computer and in protective storage. Information and time are two of your most valuable assets. A damaged floppy disk can cost you both, so protect your floppy disks accordingly.

## BACKING UP YOUR FLOPPY DISKS

Even though you treat your floppy disks with care, they can still be mislaid or damaged by accident. Files can be inadvertently changed or erased, and eventually floppy disks simply wear out. Making backup copies of your floppy disks limits the amount of information and time you lose if something goes wrong. The time it takes to make these copies could be one of your better investments.

Unless a floppy disk containing a program is copy protected so that you cannot duplicate the original, make a copy of the program before you ever use it—even if you plan to install the program on your hard disk. Store the original floppy disk in a safe place, and use the copy. If something happens to the copy, make another copy from the original. Always keep the original stored safely.

Your collection of data files will grow as you use application programs such as a word processor or spreadsheet. Back up a floppy disk containing data whenever the value of the information it contains—or the time it would take to recreate it—is greater than the value of a blank floppy disk and the few minutes it takes to make a copy. Keep your backup copies in a safe place, and use your computer with the comforting thought that, should something unforeseen happen, you're protected.

## HOW INFORMATION IS STORED ON A FLOPPY DISK

Information is stored on a floppy disk much as music or video is recorded on tape. A description of how MS-DOS uses a floppy disk helps you understand the commands you use to manage your floppy disks.

### What Is a Floppy Disk?

What we call a floppy disk actually consists of two parts: a disk of thin plastic coated with magnetic material and a protective plastic jacket or hard shell. Figure 6-1 shows a 5.25-inch floppy disk in its flexible jacket, and Figure 6-2 shows both the front and back of a 3.5-inch floppy disk in its hard shell.

**Figure 6-1.**
*A 5.25-inch floppy disk.*

**Figure 6-2.**
*A 3.5-inch floppy disk.*

The dashed lines in Figures 6-1 and 6-2 show how the coated disk lies inside the protective jacket. The magnetic coating itself is visible through the openings in the jacket of a 5.25-inch floppy disk (the dark areas in Figure 6-1). The spring-loaded shutter that normally covers the opening in a 3.5-inch floppy disk is moved aside by the floppy disk drive to provide access to the magnetic coating. The hole in the center of the disk goes around the drive motor, which spins the disk so that data can be written (recorded) or read (played back).

The write-protect notch or slide lets you protect all the files on a floppy disk from being erased or changed. To protect a 5.25-inch floppy disk, cover the write-protect notch with one of the small tabs of tape included with the box of floppy disks. To protect a 3.5-inch floppy disk, move the write-protect slide down (toward the edge of the floppy disk) until the hole through the floppy disk shell is open. To permit files on the floppy disk to be changed or erased, remove the tape or move the slide up until the hole is closed. Protect your MS-DOS floppy disks in this way; protect each of your application program floppy disks, too, unless the application program manual tells you otherwise.

## How Does MS-DOS Keep Track of Files?

Information is recorded on a floppy disk in narrow concentric circles called *tracks;* there are 40 such tracks on a low-density 360-kilobyte (360 KB) floppy disk and 80 tracks on the high-density 5.25-inch and 3.5-inch floppy disks. A track is divided into smaller areas called *sectors,* each of which can hold 512 bytes. Figure 6-3 shows how tracks and sectors are laid out on a floppy disk. For simplicity, the illustration shows only four tracks.

The side, track, and sector numbers of the beginning of a file are stored as part of its directory entry. You don't see this information when you use the Directory command, but MS-DOS can find any sector on a floppy disk by its side, track, and sector numbers, just as you can find any seat in a theater by its section, row, and seat numbers.

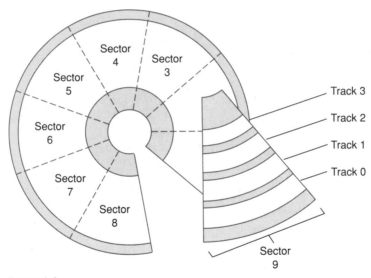

**Figure 6-3.**
*Tracks and sectors on a floppy disk.*

## Floppy Disk Capacity

Tracks on a low-density 5.25-inch floppy disk are numbered 0 through 39 (making 40 in all); sectors are numbered 1 through 9, for a total of 360 sectors (40 tracks times 9 sectors per track) on each side. Each sector holds 512 bytes, so the two sides of a low-density floppy disk have an actual capacity of 368,640 bytes (though not all of it is available for files).

A high-density 5.25-inch floppy disk has 80 tracks (numbered 0 through 79), each of which has 15 sectors, for a total of 1200 sectors per side. A sector still stores 512 bytes, so the two sides of a high-density floppy disk can hold 1,228,800 bytes (1.2 MB).

A 3.5-inch floppy disk has 80 tracks per side. Depending on its capacity, however, it has 9, 18, or 36 sectors per track—still with 512 bytes per sector. The 9-sector floppy disks can hold 737,280 bytes (720 KB); the 18-sector floppy disks can hold 1,474,560 bytes (1.44 MB). The 36-sector floppy disks can hold 2,949,120 bytes, which equals 2.88 MB.

### Volume Label

Any disk can be assigned a name, or *volume label,* to identify its contents. The volume label can be up to 11 characters long, and you can use the same characters allowed in a file name, plus a space. You can assign a volume label when you format a disk or at any time later on. MS-DOS stores the volume label on the disk and displays it when you use the Directory, Check Disk, Label, or Volume command. The volume label is for identification only; you can't use it in a command to specify a disk.

## PREPARING FOR THE EXAMPLES

The examples in this chapter require one floppy disk. If you have version 5 or later of MS-DOS, the Format command is more sophisticated than in earlier versions, so use a new floppy disk that's never been formatted. If you have an earlier version of MS-DOS, use any floppy disk that doesn't contain any files you want to keep (the examples erase any data on the floppy disk). Put the floppy disk in drive A.

## PREPARING A FLOPPY DISK FOR USE

As you've seen, the Format command prepares a floppy disk for use. The floppy disk can be either new or previously formatted. However, formatting means you can no longer use existing files, so don't format a floppy disk that contains files you need.

In carrying out the Format command, MS-DOS normally checks for flaws on the recording surface of the floppy disk and marks any bad sectors so they won't be used. After formatting, MS-DOS displays a message that tells you the maximum number of bytes the floppy disk can hold, how many bytes (if any) are defective, and how many bytes are available for storing files. Beginning with version 4, MS-DOS also tells you how much storage space the floppy disk has in terms of *allocation units* (a term for packages of bytes MS-DOS uses instead of reading from or writing to disk one byte at a time), and it displays the floppy disk's *volume serial number* (a disk identifier MS-DOS assigns during formatting). As mentioned earlier, this information is unlikely to be of any concern to you.

MS-DOS knows the type of floppy disk drive you have and formats the floppy disk accordingly. That is, it can tell whether the drive uses 3.5-inch or 5.25-inch, low-density or high-density floppy disks, and it formats the floppy disk to match the drive's maximum capabilities unless you specify otherwise.

This does not mean, however, that you can simply put any floppy disk in any drive and leave all the details to MS-DOS. It is up to you to provide the appropriate floppy disk for formatting. You cannot expect a half-gallon bucket to hold a gallon of water, nor can you expect MS-DOS to format a 360 KB or 720 KB floppy disk to reliably hold 1.2 MB or 1.44 MB of information.

You can, however, format and use low-density floppy disks in a high-density drive. For example, if you have a high-density 3.5-inch drive and run out of 1.44 MB floppy disks, you can format 720 KB floppy disks in the drive and use them reliably in a 720 KB or a 1.44 MB drive. If you have a 5.25-inch drive, you can format, read, and write 360 KB floppy disks in it. In this case, though, you should expect to use your 360 KB floppy disks only in another high-density drive because a standard 360 KB drive cannot read these floppy disks reliably.

The Format command reserves space on the floppy disk for the directory, thus reducing the amount of storage available for files. Because the size of the directory varies, depending on whether the floppy disk is low or high density, the storage capacity of your floppy disks depends on the type of floppy disk you use. Figure 6-4 shows floppy disk sizes, tracks per side, number of sectors per track, and total disk capacity for standard two-sided floppy disk drives.

| Size | Tracks per Side | Sectors per Track | Total Capacity in Bytes | First Used in MS-DOS Version |
|---|---|---|---|---|
| 3.5-inch | 80 | 36 | 2,949,120 (2.88 MB) | 5.0 |
| 3.5-inch | 80 | 18 | 1,474,560 (1.44 MB) | 3.3 |
| 3.5-inch | 80 | 9 | 737,280 (720 KB) | 3.2 |
| 5.25-inch | 80 | 15 | 1,228,800 (1.2 MB) | 3.0 |
| 5.25-inch | 40 | 9 | 368,640 (360 KB) | 2.0 |

**Figure 6-4.**
*Storage capacity of different floppy disks.*

## Format Command Parameters

When used to prepare a floppy disk, the Format command has the following six main parameters:

**format <drive> /4 /F:<size> /V:<label> /Q /U**

<drive> is the letter, followed by a colon, of the drive that contains the floppy disk to be formatted (such as *b:*). With version 3.1 or earlier, if you omit <drive>, MS-DOS formats the floppy disk in the current drive. If you omit <drive> with later versions, MS-DOS responds either *Drive letter must be specified* or *Required parameter missing* and returns to the system prompt.

/4 formats a 360 KB floppy disk in a high-density 5.25-inch drive.

/F:<size>, in versions 4 and later, formats a floppy disk for the capacity indicated by <size>. You can specify any appropriate floppy disk capacity from 160 KB to 2.88 MB, and you can type <size> in any of the forms shown in Figure 6-5. If you are using version 3.2 or 3.3, two alternative parameters, /N:<sectors> and /T:<tracks>, let you specify floppy disk capacity by giving MS-DOS the number of sectors and tracks to format; examples are given in Appendix C, "MS-DOS Command Reference."

| Disk Capacity | Type in Any of the Following Forms (No Blank Preceding K, KB, M, MB) | | | | | |
|---|---|---|---|---|---|---|
| 360 KB | 360 | 360K | 360KB | | | |
| 720 KB | 720 | 720K | 720KB | | | |
| 1.2 MB | 1200 | 1200K | 1200KB | 1.2 | 1.2M | 1.2MB |
| 1.44 MB | 1440 | 1440K | 1440KB | 1.44 | 1.44M | 1.44MB |
| 2.88 MB* | 2880 | 2880K | 2880KB | 2.88 | 2.88M | 2.88MB |

*Versions 5 and later.

**Figure 6-5.**
*Ways to type <size> as part of the /F:<size> parameter of the Format command in versions 4 and later.*

/V:<label>, in versions 4 and later, assigns the floppy disk the volume label <label>. This parameter speeds formatting by letting you specify the volume label ahead of time and thus skip the usual request for a volume label that MS-DOS otherwise displays at the end of the format procedure. If you have an earlier version of MS-DOS, /V (without <label>) works in reverse, telling MS-DOS to request a volume label at the end of the format procedure.

/Q, in versions 5 and later, tells MS-DOS to perform a quick format. You can perform a quick format only on a previously formatted disk. MS-DOS clears the records on the disk that tell it where files are stored, but it doesn't prepare the disk for use in any other way, nor does it check the disk for bad sectors. A quick format is very fast, and even though it isn't as thorough as a normal format, it does make all of the usable disk space available for storing new files.

/U, also in versions 5 and later, tells MS-DOS to perform an unconditional format—one that clears the disk completely and cannot be reversed with the Unformat command.

> **WARNING:** *If you're not using version 3.2 or later and you type a Format command without specifying a drive letter, MS-DOS formats the disk in the current drive. If the current drive is a floppy disk drive that contains your system disk and you haven't covered the write-protect notch, MS-DOS erases every file on your system floppy disk. If the current drive is a hard disk, formatting erases every file on it—not just the MS-DOS files but every program and data file you have stored. Be certain you know which disk is going to be formatted before you press the Enter key after a Format command.*

## Examples of Preparing a Floppy Disk

Format the floppy disk in drive A, and give it a volume label. If you have version 4 or later, type the following:

```
C:\>format a: /v:dosdisk
```

If you have an earlier version, type:

```
C:\>format a: /v
```

MS-DOS asks you to put the floppy disk in drive A:

```
Insert new diskette for drive A:
and press ENTER when ready..._
```

Make sure the right floppy disk is in the drive, and then press Enter.

If you're using version 5 or later, MS-DOS first displays a message telling you it's checking the existing format (if any) of the disk. Then it begins the formatting and tells the size of the disk it's formatting. Versions 4 and later then report on their progress with a message that *xx percent* of the disk has been formatted.

If you're using version 3.1 or an earlier version, MS-DOS displays *Formatting...* while it formats the disk. If you're using version 3.2 or 3.3, MS-DOS displays *Head: 0 Cylinder: 0* and changes the head and cylinder numbers to show you its progress (*cylinder* is another way of referring to a track).

When MS-DOS has formatted the floppy disk, it displays *Format complete*. If you have version 4 or later, this message is followed by a report on available storage space and, on a separate line, the volume serial number assigned by MS-DOS (which, if you're curious, is based on the current date and time). As you'll see in a moment, MS-DOS has also used the parameter */v:dosdisk* to name the floppy disk DOSDISK. At the end of the report, MS-DOS asks if you want to format another floppy disk:

```
Format another (Y/N)?_
```

Type *n* and press Enter.

If you have an earlier version of MS-DOS, the *Format complete* message is followed by a prompt for the volume label:

```
Volume label (11 characters, ENTER for none)? _
```

Name the floppy disk DOSDISK by typing the following:

```
dosdisk
```

MS-DOS displays the report of available storage on the floppy disk and asks if you want to format another. Reply *n*.

Now display the directory of the disk: It's empty, but you can see the volume label on the first line.

```
C:\>dir a:

 Volume in drive A is DOSDISK
 Volume Serial Number is 2F49-1AFF
 Directory of A:\

File not found
```

(If you don't have version 4 or later, you don't see the volume serial number.)

## COPYING A COMPLETE FLOPPY DISK

The Diskcopy command makes an exact duplicate of any floppy disk. If the target floppy disk isn't formatted, later versions of MS-DOS format it before copying. Diskcopy in earlier versions requires formatted floppy disks. Diskcopy works only with floppy disks of the same size and capacity. For example, you cannot use it to copy from a 360 KB floppy disk to a formatted 1.2 MB, 5.25-inch floppy disk, nor can you use it to copy from a hard disk to any floppy disk.

The Diskcopy command has three parameters:

**diskcopy <source> <target> /V**

<source> is the letter, followed by a colon, of the drive that contains the floppy disk to be copied (such as *a:*).

<target> is the letter, followed by a colon, of the drive that contains the floppy disk that is to receive the copy (such as *b:*). If you have only one floppy disk drive, <source> and <target> can be the same letter (for example, *diskcopy a: a:*).

/V (*verify*) ensures that the floppy disk is copied correctly.

If you omit <target>, MS-DOS copies from the floppy disk in <source> to the floppy disk in the current drive; if you omit <target> and you specify the current drive as <source>, MS-DOS assumes you want to use only the current drive and prompts you to switch floppy disks during the copy. If you don't specify <source> or <target>, MS-DOS assumes you want to use only the current drive and prompts you to switch floppy disks during the copy.

## Examples of Copying a Floppy Disk

This example copies an existing floppy disk, duplicating information from the source floppy disk to the target floppy disk. Use one of your MS-DOS floppy disks as the source. If your MS-DOS floppy disks are not close at hand, use a floppy disk for one of your application programs or use a data floppy disk—the one you used for the examples in Chapter 5, "Managing Your Files," will do. Put the source floppy disk in drive A.

Before proceeding, be sure that your target floppy disk is either unformatted or formatted for the same capacity as the source floppy disk. Remember, Diskcopy works only if the target floppy disk is or can be formatted for the same capacity as the source.

### If You Have One Floppy Disk Drive

Because you have only one floppy disk drive, MS-DOS must use it for both the source and target floppy disks, prompting you to exchange floppy disks as required. Check that the source floppy disk is in the floppy disk drive.

To copy the floppy disk, type:

```
C:\>diskcopy a: a:
```

MS-DOS prompts you to put in the source floppy disk:

```
Insert SOURCE diskette in drive A:

Press any key to continue . . .
```

You put the floppy disk in already, so press any key. MS-DOS tells you how many tracks, sectors, and sides it's copying, then prompts you to put the target floppy disk in the drive:

```
Insert TARGET diskette in drive A:

Press any key to continue . . .
```

Remove the source floppy disk, put in the target floppy disk, and press a key. If the floppy disk is unformatted and your version of MS-DOS formats as it copies, a message tells you what is happening. If you're using version 6 or earlier, MS-DOS will also prompt you to exchange floppy disks until it has finished copying the original. When MS-DOS has finished, it asks if you want to copy another:

```
Copy another diskette (Y/N)? _
```

Reply *n*.

### If You Have Two Floppy Disk Drives

If your system has two disk drives of different types (a 3.5-inch and a 5.25-inch), you can't use both drives because the Diskcopy command only works with identical floppy disks. You can, however, copy a disk by using just one drive; follow the instructions under the preceding heading, "If You Have One Floppy Disk Drive."

If your system has two identical floppy disk drives, your source floppy disk should be in drive A. To copy the source floppy disk in drive A to the target floppy disk in drive B, type:

```
A:\>diskcopy a: b:
```

MS-DOS prompts you to put in the floppy disks. Put the target floppy disk in drive B and press a key. MS-DOS tells you how many tracks, sectors, and sides it's copying, then asks if you want to copy another; reply *n*.

## COMPARING TWO FLOPPY DISKS

Sometimes you'll want to know whether two floppy disks are identical. Diskcomp compares two floppy disks track by track. The Diskcomp command can be used only with floppy disks of the same size and capacity; you cannot use it to compare a hard disk with a floppy disk.

> **NOTE:** *Just because two floppy disks contain the same files, they're not necessarily identical, because the files might be stored in different sectors. If you want to compare all the files on two floppy disks, rather than the floppy disks themselves, use the File Compare (fc) command described in Chapter 5, "Managing Your Files," and specify all files (*.*).*

The Diskcomp command has two parameters:

**diskcomp <drive1> <drive2>**

<drive1> and <drive2> are the drive letters, each followed by a colon, of the drives containing the floppy disks to be compared (such as *a:* and *b:*).

If MS-DOS finds any differences, it displays the side and track of each—for example:

```
Compare error on
side 0, track 33
```

## Examples of Comparing Two Floppy Disks

Follow the instructions under the heading that describes your system.

### If You Have One Floppy Disk Drive

To compare the source floppy disk to the copy you just made, type:

```
C:\>diskcomp a: a:
```

MS-DOS prompts you to put in the first floppy disk:

```
Insert FIRST diskette in drive A:

Press any key to continue . . .
```

Make sure the copy you just made is in the drive, then press a key. You will see something like this:

```
Comparing 40 tracks
9 sectors per track, 2 side(s)
```

MS-DOS prompts you to put in the second floppy disk:

```
Insert SECOND diskette in drive A:
Press any key to continue...
```

Remove the floppy disk, put in the source floppy disk you used for the Diskcopy example, and then press a key. If necessary, MS-DOS continues to prompt you to exchange floppy disks until it finally tells you it's done and asks if you want to compare more floppy disks:

```
Compare OK

Compare another diskette (Y/N) ?_
```

Reply *n*.

### If You Have Two Floppy Disk Drives

If your system has two disk drives of different types (a 3.5-inch and a 5.25-inch), you can't use both drives because the Diskcomp command works only with identical floppy disks. You can, however, compare disks by using just one drive; follow the instructions under the preceding heading, "If You Have One Floppy Disk Drive."

If your system has two identical floppy disk drives, you can compare the floppy disk in drive B (the copy you just made) to the floppy disk in drive A (the floppy disk you used as your source) by typing:

```
C:\>diskcomp a: b:
```

MS-DOS prompts you to put in the floppy disks:

```
Insert FIRST diskette in drive A:

Insert SECOND diskette in drive B:

Press any key to continue . . .
```

The floppy disks are already in the drives, so press a key. MS-DOS reports how many tracks, sectors, and sides it is comparing, then reports the results of the comparison and asks if you want to compare more floppy disks:

```
Comparing 40 tracks
9 sectors per track, 2 side(s)

Compare OK

Compare another diskette (Y/N) ?_
```

Reply *n*.

## CHECKING THE CONDITION OF A DISK

Computers aren't infallible; malfunctions can produce errors in the directory of a disk. Such errors are rare, but the Check Disk (chkdsk) command helps by making sure that all files are recorded properly.

> **NOTE:** *If you're using version 6.2, the ScanDisk program is a better tool for detecting and correcting disk errors. ScanDisk is described in Chapter 9, "Managing Your Hard Disk," under the heading "Checking a Disk for Errors."*

Check Disk analyzes the directory on a disk, comparing the directory entries with the locations and lengths of the files, and reports any errors it finds. The Check Disk report includes the following items:

- The total amount of space on the disk.

- The number of files and directories and how much space they use.

- How much space on the disk remains available for files.

- In versions 4 and later, the size of each allocation unit, the number of such units on the disk, and the number available for storage.

- The size of the computer's memory (up to 640 KB) and how many bytes remain free for use.

You can also ask the command to display the name of each file on the disk and to check whether any files are stored inefficiently.

If possible, MS-DOS stores files in adjacent, or *contiguous*, sectors. As files are deleted and new files are stored, however, they can become fragmented (stored in nonadjacent sectors). A fragmented file isn't a cause for worry; the worst that can happen is that MS-DOS will take slightly longer to read the file. If several files on a floppy disk are fragmented, you can restore them to contiguous sectors by copying all the files to an empty, formatted floppy disk with the Copy command. (Remember, don't use the Diskcopy command because it makes a faithful sector-by-sector copy of the floppy disk, storing the files in exactly the same nonadjacent sectors in which they are stored on the original floppy disk.)

The Check Disk command has four parameters:

**chkdsk <drive> <filename> /V /F**

<drive> is the letter, followed by a colon, of the drive that contains the disk to be checked. If you omit <drive>, MS-DOS checks the disk in the current drive.

<filename> is the name of the file whose storage you want MS-DOS to check. MS-DOS displays a message if the file is stored in noncontiguous sectors. You can use wildcard characters to check a set of files.

/V displays the name of each directory and file on the disk.

/F tells MS-DOS to correct any errors it finds in the directory if you so specify when the error is found.

## Examples of Checking a Disk

Check the floppy disk in drive A by typing:

```
C:\>chkdsk a:
```

Press any key if MS-DOS prompts you to insert a floppy disk in drive A.

MS-DOS displays its report. (The report you see might be different; this example is for a 360 KB floppy disk.)

```
Volume DOSDISK     created on 10-16-1993 12:00a
Volume Serial Number is 1BC6-425F

   362496 bytes total disk space
   350208 bytes in 10 user files
    12288 bytes available on disk

     1024 bytes in each allocation unit
      354 total allocation units on disk
       12 available allocation units on disk

   655360 total bytes memory
   562384 bytes free
```

To check the floppy disk in drive A, and to check whether all files on it are stored in contiguous sectors, type:

```
C:\>chkdsk a:*.*
```

MS-DOS displays the same report as the preceding but adds the following message:

```
All specified file(s) are contiguous
```

If any files were stored in noncontiguous sectors, MS-DOS would display their names and the number of noncontiguous blocks of storage in place of this message.

To check the floppy disk in drive A and, at the same time, display the name of each file on it, type:

```
C:\>chkdsk a: /v
```

MS-DOS displays the name of each file on the floppy disk and then adds its usual report of disk space and memory available. If the list of files scrolls off the top of the screen, remember that, to view it all, you can freeze the display by pressing the Pause key or Ctrl-Num Lock.

> **NOTE:** *If the files on the floppy disk are organized into directories, the /V parameter of the Check Disk command lists the directories, as well as the files they contain. Directories are described in Chapter 8, "A Tree of Files."*

You can combine the Check Disk parameters in one command; for example, *chkdsk a:*.* /v* would check the floppy disk in drive A, check all files on it for fragmentation, and display the names of all files.

If the Check Disk command finds an error in the directory, it displays a message such as *xx lost allocation units found in yy chains. Convert lost chains to files (Y/N)?* Although this message might look confusing, it simply means that Check Disk has found some storage units on the disk that have been used but, because of a program or system problem, aren't linked with any particular files. If you type the Check Disk command with the /F parameter and then type *y* when the *Convert lost chains...* message appears, MS-DOS turns these "lost" units into files with the file name and extension FILE*nnnn*.CHK (where *nnnn* is a number such as 0001). Depending on the type of error that caused these units to be lost, MS-DOS may or may not be able to recover the data in them. When the Check Disk command is complete, you can look at the contents of these files with the MS-DOS Editor and decide whether or not they contain information you want to save. If you don't want to save the information, delete the files to make the storage space available for new files.

## ASSIGNING OR CHANGING A DISK'S VOLUME LABEL

The Label command assigns, changes, or deletes the volume label of a floppy disk or a hard disk. It has two parameters:

**label <drive> <newlabel>**

<drive> is the letter, followed by a colon, of the drive (such as *a:*) that contains the disk whose volume label is to be changed.

<newlabel> is the volume label to be assigned to the disk in <drive>.

If you omit <drive>, MS-DOS assumes you want to change the label of the disk in the current drive. If you omit <newlabel>, MS-DOS prompts you to enter the new label.

### Examples of Changing a Disk's Volume Label

At the beginning of this chapter, you used the /V option of the Format command to assign the volume label DOSDISK to a floppy disk. Sometimes you'll want to change a volume label. You can do so with the Label command. Put your sample floppy disk in drive A, and then type the Label command:

```
C:\>label a:
```

MS-DOS responds with something like this:

```
Volume in drive A is DOSDISK
Volume Serial Number is 2F49-1AFF
Volume label (11 characters, ENTER for none)? _
```

The sample disk isn't really an MS-DOS disk, so change its name to MYDISK by typing:

```
mydisk
```

and press Enter.

If the floppy disk had a volume label and you wanted to delete it, you would reply to the prompt by pressing the Enter key without typing a name. MS-DOS would then ask *Delete current volume label (Y/N)?* You would reply *y* to delete the volume label.

## DISPLAYING A DISK'S VOLUME LABEL

The Volume (vol) command also displays the volume label and volume serial number of a hard disk or a floppy disk but doesn't ask for a new label as the Label command does. If you assign descriptive volume labels to your floppy disks when you format them, you can use the Volume command to make sure that you're using the correct floppy disks. It's faster and easier than checking the directory.

The Volume command has one parameter:

**vol <drive>**

<drive> is the letter, followed by a colon, of the drive (such as *a:*) that contains the floppy disk whose volume label is to be displayed. If you omit <drive>, MS-DOS displays the volume label of the disk in the current drive.

To display the volume label of the floppy disk in drive A, type:

```
C:\>vol a:
```

MS-DOS displays the volume label:

```
Volume in drive A is MYDISK
Volume Serial Number is 2F49-1AFF
```

If the floppy disk had no volume label, MS-DOS would respond *Volume in drive A has no label.*

# 7

# Managing
Your Devices

**D**ata flows into and out of a computer system through pieces of equipment called *devices.* Devices are categorized by whether they handle data coming in (*input*) or going out (*output*) or both. The keyboard, for example, is an input device; the computer gets information from it. A printer is an output device; the computer sends information to it. A disk drive is both an input device and an output device; the computer can either read a file from a disk or write a file onto a disk.

Some devices, such as the keyboard, don't usually need much attention from you because MS-DOS requires no special instructions to operate them. You can, however, fine-tune their performance, as you'll see later in this chapter. Other devices can be operated in different ways and so allow you to tell MS-DOS how you want to use them. For example, modems follow certain rules in transferring information, and some displays allow you to change the number of lines shown on the screen. With MS-DOS, you can set up a modem to work as it should and just as easily alter your display to work as you want.

Displays, keyboards, printers, and the computer's communications channels, called *ports,* can all be used in a variety of ways. This chapter shows you how to do the following with the MS-DOS commands that help you manage your system:

- Check on system memory with the Mem command.

- Clear the screen with the Clear Screen (Cls) command.

- Set the speed at which your keyboard repeats a key that is held down with the Mode command.

- Specify the number of characters and lines on the screen with the Mode command.

- Control the width and line spacing of your printer with the Mode command.

- Define the settings of the communications ports with the Mode command.

- Copy from a device to a file or to another device with the Copy command.

- Enable MS-DOS to print graphics with the Graphics command.

- Change your keyboard layout for use with a different language with the Keyboard (Keyb) command.

# DEVICE NAMES

Just as files have names, so do devices. You can use a device name in many MS-DOS commands just as you would use a file name. MS-DOS assigns all device names, however. You can't name a device yourself. Figure 7-1 shows the devices that make up a typical system, with the names assigned to them by MS-DOS.

CON is short for *Console*. It is both an input device and an output device and refers to both the keyboard (input) and the display (output). Because the keyboard is input only and the display is output only, MS-DOS can tell which one to use by the way you use the name CON in a command.

PRN is short for *Printer*. It is an output device and refers to the parallel printer that MS-DOS uses unless you specify otherwise (much as MS-DOS looks for files on the current drive unless you specify otherwise). You can attach as many as three parallel printers (named LPT1, LPT2, and LPT3) to your computer; PRN usually means LPT1.

AUX is short for *Auxiliary*. It is for both input and output and refers to the communications port that MS-DOS uses unless you instruct otherwise. You can attach devices to one or two communications ports, named COM1 and COM2, with any version of MS-DOS; if you're using version 3.3 or later, you can attach devices to up to four communications ports (COM1 through COM4). Unless you or a program specifies otherwise, MS-DOS assumes that AUX means COM1. On a typical system, COM1 could be used for a modem, and COM2 could be used for a serial printer—or vice versa.

MS-DOS reserves these names for use with devices only; you cannot give any of these names to a file.

**Figure 7-1.**
*MS-DOS device names.*

## PREPARING FOR THE EXAMPLES

> **NOTE:** *Devices on a network are shared resources set up to respond to requests from more than one authorized user. If your computer is part of a network, check with your network administrator before attempting to manipulate or change the settings of shared printers or other devices.*

Devices often need very specific setup instructions and operating parameters. The examples in this chapter work with IBM and IBM-compatible personal computers, displays, and printers. If you're not using one of these machines, you might need to use different instructions to manage your devices. Refer to your documentation for specific information.

When you try the examples, make sure the devices you name are attached to the system and are turned on. You won't hurt anything by entering a command naming a device that isn't present or isn't ready, but the command may cause an error that requires you to restart MS-DOS.

## CHECKING SYSTEM MEMORY WITH THE MEM COMMAND

Even though computer memory isn't a device as you would normally think of the term, it can be both useful and reassuring to know how much memory a system contains, what programs have been loaded into memory, and how much can be used by another program. Beginning with version 4 of MS-DOS, you can use the Mem command to request a report on memory and memory usage. Type:

```
C:\>mem
```

MS-DOS quickly produces a report like this one:

```
Memory Type          Total =  Used  +  Free
-----------------   ------   ------    ------
Conventional          640K      26K     614K
Upper                 147K      53K      94K
Adapter RAM/ROM       237K     237K       0K
Extended (XMS)       3072K    2424K     648K
Expanded (EMS)          0K       0K       0K
-----------------   ------   ------    ------
Total memory         4096K    2740K    1356K

Total under 1 MB      787K      79K     708K

Largest executable program size       614K   (629120 bytes)
Largest free upper memory block        64K   (65552 bytes)
MS-DOS is resident in the high memory area.
```

This is the type of report you see with version 6 on an IBM or compatible computer that has 640 KB of regular, or conventional, memory plus 3.4 MB of extended memory (4 MB total memory).

The upper part of the report—the table—tells how much memory of each type is installed, how much is used, and how much is free:

- Conventional memory is the regular memory used by MS-DOS and application programs. The report shows that 640 KB of memory is installed in the computer; 26 KB is being used and 614 KB is free (available for use by other programs).

- Upper memory is the memory previously (before version 5) available only to devices such as displays but now available to programs. The report shows that the computer has 147 KB of upper memory; 53 KB is being used and 94 KB is free.

- Adapter RAM/ROM is memory installed on printed-circuit cards that operate devices (such as display adapters) attached to the computer. The report shows that the cards installed in the computer have a total of 237 KB of memory, and all of it is being used.

- Extended (XMS) memory is additional memory installed in a computer that can be used by application programs, as well as by MS-DOS. The report shows that 3,072 KB of extended memory is installed in the computer; 2,424 KB is being used and 648 KB is free.

**NOTE:** *Expanded (EMS) memory is another type of additional memory installed in a computer. It also can be used under certain circumstances by both application programs and MS-DOS. Mem reports the amount of expanded memory, if you have any. See Appendix C, "MS-DOS Command Reference," for a full description.*

The middle two lines of the report summarize the total memory figures. Following these lines there are two lines that tell you the largest block of memory available in conventional memory and the largest block of memory available in upper memory. The figures for the largest blocks of conventional and upper memory available will vary with the amount of memory installed in a computer, the version of MS-DOS it runs, and the types of programs being used.

The last line of the report confirms that MS-DOS is loaded in the *high memory area.* (The high memory area, or *HMA,* is a special portion of extended memory.) This information is really quite important: It tells you that MS-DOS has placed a large part of itself outside the computer's 640 KB of conventional memory in order to give application programs more room to work. This ability to use high memory is a significant feature available only in versions 5 and later of MS-DOS. More details on extended memory and high memory are in Chapter 17, "Tailoring Your System."

The Mem command also includes five parameters, most of which cause MS-DOS to produce a more detailed report of memory use. The detailed reports probably won't seem very meaningful unless you're interested in programming or in learning about the inner workings of your computer. The parameters are discussed in Appendix C, "MS-DOS Command Reference."

## CLEARING THE SCREEN

Sometimes you might want to erase distracting clutter from the screen: old directory listings, perhaps, or the display of commands MS-DOS has already completed for you. You can clean things up with the Clear Screen (Cls) command, which erases everything on the screen and then displays the system prompt in the upper left corner.

The Clear Screen command has one form:

**cls**

To test it, type its name:

```
C:\>cls
```

The screen is cleared, except for the system prompt.

## FINE-TUNING THE KEYBOARD

Beginning with version 4 of MS-DOS, you can control how quickly a keystroke repeats when you press and hold a key. To change the way your keyboard operates, you use the Mode command, an all-purpose device-control command that lets you tell MS-DOS how you want to use not only your keyboard but many other parts of your computer system, including your display and printer.

To control your keyboard, the Mode command has three parameters:

**mode con rate=<speed> delay=<pause>**

*con* is the name of the console device (here, the keyboard).

*rate=*<speed> specifies the speed at which MS-DOS is to repeat the keystroke. You can specify any number from 1 through 32.

*delay=*<pause> specifies how long MS-DOS is to wait before starting to repeat the keystroke. You can specify 1 for a 0.25-second delay, 2 for a 0.5-second delay, 3 for a 0.75-second delay, or 4 for a 1-second delay.

You must specify both a rate and a delay. For example, the average keyboard repeats about 20 times per second with a delay of 0.5 second before repeating begins. To see the effect of this version of the Mode command, slow the keyboard repeat rate and delay. Type:

```
C:\>mode con rate=1 delay=4
```

and try holding down the X key to see the result.

If you are a fast typist, impatient with a too-slow keyboard, set the rate to a high value, such as 32, and set the delay to a low number, such as 1. To slow keyboard repetition, lower the rate and, if you want, increase the delay time. To reset the keyboard to its regular repeat rate and delay, type:

```
C:\>mode con rate=20 delay=2
```

## CONTROLLING THE DISPLAY

A number of different displays and display adapters (the printed-circuit cards that operate the display) are used with IBM personal computers and compatible machines. Figure 7-2 describes the most commonly used types of displays and display adapters.

The Mode command has several display-related options. Which one you use depends on the type of display you have and how much you want to see on the screen.

| Short Name | Product Name | Description |
|---|---|---|
| MDA | Monochrome Display Adapter | Text only, medium resolution, one color (usually green on a dark background). |
| CGA | Color/Graphics Adapter | Text and graphics, low resolution, up to 16 colors. |
| Hercules | None (works with monochrome display) | Displays graphics on monochrome display. (Not compatible with CGA. An application program must specifically support the Hercules board, but most major applications do because of its popularity.) |
| EGA | Enhanced Graphics Adapter | Text and graphics, medium resolution, up to 16 colors. |
| MCGA | Multicolor Graphics Array | Text and graphics, low to medium resolution, up to 256 colors. |
| VGA | Video Graphics Array | Text and graphics, medium to high resolution, up to 256 colors. |
| SVGA | Super Video Graphics Array | Text and graphics, medium to very high resolution, up to 256 colors and beyond. |

**Figure 7-2.**
*Common displays and adapters.*

Normally, a computer screen displays 80 columns (characters) across and 25 lines down. If you have an EGA or a VGA display, you can, beginning with version 4, change the size of the characters on your display and the number of lines on the screen. When used in this way, the Mode command has three parameters:

**mode con cols=<columns> lines=<lines>**

*con* is the name of the console device (here, it means the display).

*cols*=<columns> sets the number of characters displayed on each line. <columns> can be either 40 (for extra-large characters) or 80 (for normal-sized characters).

*lines*=<lines> sets the number of lines on the screen. <lines> can be 25, 43, or 50, but not all display adapters can handle all three choices.

To set the screen to display 40 characters per line, type:

```
C:\>mode con cols=40
```

To display 80 characters per line and 43 lines per screen, type:

```
C:\>mode con cols=80 lines=43
```

**NOTE:** *If you try this command and MS-DOS displays the message* Function not supported on this computer, *the command does not work on your computer system. If you see the message* ANSI.SYS must be installed to perform requested function, *you need to add a reference to a program named ANSI.SYS in the startup file named CONFIG.SYS. Chapter 17, "Tailoring Your System," tells you how to do this.*

In all versions of MS-DOS, you can also use another form of the Mode command to control the number of characters per line. When used to control the number of columns, the Mode command has one form:

**mode <characters>**

<characters> is either 40 or 80.

To display 40 columns with this command, type:

```
C:\>mode 40
```

MS-DOS clears the screen and displays the system prompt in large characters in the upper left-hand corner of the screen.

## CONTROLLING THE PRINTER WIDTH AND SPACING

A dot-matrix printer normally prints a maximum of 80 characters per line and 6 lines per inch. It can also print in a smaller type, called *condensed,* that fits 132 characters on a line. This ability to change widths can be useful for printing documents wider than 80 characters. The printer can also print 8 lines per inch, to fit more lines on a page.

**NOTE:** *If you have a laser printer, note that the documentation that came with the printer tells you how to set the printer to work with MS-DOS and how to control the printer's characteristics, such as line and character spacing. The examples here most likely won't work unless your laser printer can emulate an IBM or an Epson dot-matrix printer.*

If your printer is attached to a parallel port, you can use the Mode command to specify the line width (80 or 132) and spacing (6 or 8).

When used to control a dot-matrix printer attached to a parallel port, the Mode command has three parameters, which you type in one of the following two forms. The first form applies to versions 4 and later; the second applies to any version of MS-DOS:

**mode <printer> cols=<width> lines=<spacing>**

or:

**mode <printer> <width>,<spacing>**

<printer> is the name of the printer, followed by a colon (*lpt1:*, *lpt2:*, or *lpt3:*). <width> is either 80 or 132.

<spacing> is either 6 or 8. Notice the comma preceding <spacing> in the second form of the command.

You must always include <printer>. You can omit either <width> or <spacing>, and MS-DOS will leave the current width or spacing unchanged. In the second form of the command, however, if you omit <width> you must still type the comma before <spacing> to tell MS-DOS you omitted <width>.

## Examples of Controlling a Dot-Matrix Printer

The following examples work with a dot-matrix printer connected to the computer's first parallel printer port (LPT1:). If this describes your equipment, be sure your printer is turned on before proceeding with the following examples. If you have a different type of printer or printer setup, you might prefer to read through the examples or skip ahead to the next section, "Controlling the Serial Communications Port."

**NOTE:** *Because different versions of MS-DOS accept different forms of the command, the examples first show the command used with versions 4 and later and then show the command form for earlier versions of MS-DOS.*

To cause a printer attached to LPT1 to print in small type (up to 132 characters per line if the printer can do so), use the appropriate command below.

If you have version 4 or later, type:

```
C:\>mode lpt1: cols=132
```

If you have an earlier version of MS-DOS, type:

```
C:\>mode lpt1: 132
```

MS-DOS replies with a display like this one:

```
LPT1: not rerouted

LPT1: set for 132

No retry on parallel printer time-out
```

The second line of this message, which you see with any version of MS-DOS, tells you that the command worked correctly and your printer is now set for small characters. If you have version 4 or later, the other lines are additional messages telling you that MS-DOS will, indeed, use your parallel printer for output and that, if the printer is busy or turned off, it will not keep trying to send data to it.

To test the new printer setting, print the contents of the screen by pressing Shift-PrtSc. (If you have an IBM PS/2 keyboard, press Print Screen, not Shift-PrtSc.)

To set the spacing of the same printer to 8 lines per inch but leave the width unchanged, use one of the following commands.

If you have version 4 or later, type:

```
C:\>mode lpt1: lines=8
```

If you have an earlier version of MS-DOS, type:

```
C:\>mode lpt1: ,8
```

MS-DOS replies with a message like this:

```
LPT1: not rerouted

Printer lines per inch set

No retry on parallel printer time-out
```

(Again, if you don't have version 4 or later, your message is shorter.)

To see the effect of this setting, print the contents of the screen again by pressing Shift-PrtSc. This time the text is printed both in small type (as set in the previous example) and with closer line spacing.

To restore the printer to normal width and line spacing with version 4 or later, type:

```
C:\>mode lpt1: cols=80 lines=6
```

If you have an earlier version of MS-DOS, type:

```
C:\>mode lpt1: 80,6
```

MS-DOS displays a message similar to those you've already seen:

```
LPT1: not rerouted

LPT1: set for 80

Printer lines per inch set

No retry on parallel printer time-out
```

## CONTROLLING THE SERIAL COMMUNICATIONS PORT

Serial communications is controlled by several characteristics, or *communications parameters*, that define how fast and in what form data is transmitted. Different devices often require different parameter settings. The parameters of your serial port must match those of the device or computer service with which you want to communicate. Before you can use a communications port, you must set these parameters with the Mode command.

The communications parameters you can set include:

- *Baud,* how quickly characters are sent or received.

- *Parity,* the kind of error-checking technique used.

- *Data bits,* the number of electrical signals required to define a character.

- *Stop bits,* the amount of time between electrical signals that marks the end of a character.

A more complete definition of these parameters is beyond the scope of this book. Figure 7-3 on the next page lists the parameters you can set with the Mode command. The documentation of the device or computer service you want to use shows the required setting; compare these settings with the values MS-DOS assumes, shown in Figure 7-3, to see which parameters you must change.

When used to set the parameters of a serial communications port, the Mode command has the following form in versions 4 and later:

**mode <port> baud=<baud> parity=<parity> data=<databits> stop=<stopbits>**

In earlier versions, the command is:

**mode <port> <baud>,<parity>,<databits>,<stopbits>**

<port> is the name of the communications port followed by a colon—
*com1:* through *com4:* (*com1:* or *com2:* if you're using a version earlier than 3.3). The
remaining parameters, separated by commas, are those described in Figure 7-3.

| Name | Valid Settings | How You Specify | Value MS-DOS Assumes |
|------|----------------|-----------------|----------------------|
| Baud | 110, 150, 300, 600, 1200, 2400, 4800, 9600, 19,200* | You can abbreviate to the first two digits (11 for 110, 24 for 2400) | None (you must set a value) |
| Parity | None, Odd, Even, Mark,[†] or Space[†] | N, O, E, M, or S | Even (E) |
| Databits | 5,[†] 6,[†] 7, or 8 | 5, 6, 7, or 8 | 7 |
| Stopbits | 1, 1.5,[†] or 2 | 1, 1.5, or 2 | 2 if baud = 110; 1 otherwise |

\* 19,200 is available from version 3.3 onward and can be used only with a computer capable
of that speed.

[†] Versions 4 and later.

**Figure 7-3.**
*Serial communications parameters.*

You must specify a value for <baud> each time you enter this form of the
Mode command. MS-DOS assumes the values for the other parameters listed in
the last column of Figure 7-3 unless you specifically change them; you needn't
specify these parameters unless the device or service with which you want to communicate requires values different from those that MS-DOS assumes.

If you omit any parameter from the second form of the Mode command
shown above, you must still type the comma that precedes it, to show MS-DOS that
you omitted the parameter.

## Examples of Controlling the Serial Communications Port

These examples show you different uses of the Mode command. Don't enter
them unless you have a serial communications port and you want to change the
settings.

To set the baud rate for COM1 to 1200 (and let MS-DOS assume values for the
other parameters), you would type one of the following commands.

If you have version 4 or later:

```
C:\>mode com1: baud=1200
```

If you have an earlier version of MS-DOS:

```
C:\>mode com1: 1200
```

MS-DOS would reply by reporting the current setting of each parameter:

```
COM1: 1200,e,7,1,-
```

This report shows that <baud> is 1200, <parity> is even, <databits> is 7, and <stopbits> is 1. The hyphen at the end tells you that MS-DOS will not keep trying to send to a device that isn't ready but will stop after a brief time.

To set <baud> for COM1 to 2400, set <parity> to none, leave <databits> set to 7, and set <stopbits> to 2, you would type one of the following commands.

If you have version 4 or later:

```
C:\>mode com1: baud=2400 parity=n stop=2
```

If you have an earlier version of MS-DOS:

```
C:\>mode com1: 2400,n,,2
```

(Note the two commas before the 2, telling MS-DOS that you omitted <databits>.)

MS-DOS confirms the settings:

```
COM1: 2400,n,7,2,-
```

## CONNECTING A SERIAL PRINTER

If you want to use a serial printer attached to a communications port, you must use the Mode command to tell MS-DOS to send printer output to the communications port instead of to the regular (parallel) printer port. This is called *redirecting* or *rerouting* the printer output. (You might recall from the earlier examples of controlling a dot-matrix printer that the MS-DOS responses to the Mode command included the line *LPT1: not rerouted*. Here, you can see the meaning of that message: MS-DOS was reporting that output to the regular printer port was not redirected to a serial port.)

Before you redirect the printer output, you must first set the parameters of the serial communications port to the values required by the printer, as described in the preceding section.

When used to redirect printer output to a serial communications port, the Mode command has one form:

**mode <printer>=<port>**

<printer> is the name of the printer port (*lpt1:*, *lpt2:*, or *lpt3:*) whose output is to be redirected.

<port> is the name of the serial communications port (*com1:* or *com2:* in all versions of MS-DOS, *com1:* through *com4:* in 3.3 and later versions). You must enter both parameters.

### Example of Connecting a Serial Printer

To redirect printer output from LPT1 to serial port COM1, you would first set the serial port to match the communications parameters of your printer and then type:

```
C:\>mode lpt1:=com1:
```

MS-DOS would acknowledge:

```
LPT1: rerouted to COM1:
```

Now all output that would normally go to LPT1: would be sent to COM1: instead. To cancel the redirection and restore the printer output to LPT1:, you would type:

```
C:\>mode lpt1:
```

# FINDING OUT ABOUT YOUR SYSTEM

You have, up to this point, seen a number of ways to use the Mode command to control the devices on your system. But just as it's useful to know how to control your devices, it's also helpful to know what devices MS-DOS is prepared to use and how it "sees" them. Beginning with version 4, you can use the Mode command not only to describe devices to MS-DOS but to find out about them.

To check on the status of any or all devices on your system, you use the command:

**mode <device> /status**

<device> is the name of a particular device you want to check on. If you omit <device>, MS-DOS reports on all the devices it recognizes.

*/status*, which you can abbreviate as */sta*, is needed only when you want to check the status of a parallel printer you've redirected. (The */sta* is needed because simply typing *mode lpt1:* would cancel the redirection.)

To check on the status of a single device, you type *mode* and the name of the device. For example, if the display were set to show 80 characters per line and 43 lines per screen, the command:

```
C:\>mode con
```

would produce a report like this:

```
Status for device CON:
----------------------
Columns=80
Lines=43

Code page operation not supported on this device
```

(The message *Code page operation not supported on this device* simply means that MS-DOS, on this computer, has not been told to recognize international language, date, decimal, and currency conventions. If you need this capability, refer to the online help for the Mode command.

To check on all the devices on your system, you would type:

```
C:\>mode
```

and MS-DOS would respond with a report like this:

```
Status for device LPT1:
-----  ----------------
LPT1: not rerouted
Retry=NONE

Code page operation not supported on this device

Status for device LPT2:
----------------------
LPT2: not rerouted

Status for device LPT3:
----------------------
LPT3: not rerouted

Status for device CON:
----------------------
Columns=80
Lines=25

Code page operation not supported on this device

Status for device COM1:
----------------------
Retry=NONE
```

Although parts of the report might look unfamiliar, here's what it means:

- The report covers five devices: three parallel ports (LPT1, LPT2, and LPT3), the display (CON), and a serial port (COM1).

- The message *LPT*x*: not rerouted* simply means that information sent to any of these output channels has not been diverted to another port.

- The message *Retry=NONE* means that, if the device connected to a port is busy, MS-DOS will not keep trying to send information to the device (a printer or modem, for example).

- The *Code page...* message means that MS-DOS has not been told to recognize international language, date, decimal, and currency conventions.

# COPYING FROM A DEVICE TO A FILE OR ANOTHER DEVICE

As you saw in earlier examples, you can use the Copy command to copy from a device to a file. You have used this technique several times to create sample files by copying from the keyboard to a file, and you will find it handy for creating short text files.

You can also copy from one device to another. Copying from the keyboard to the printer, for example, is a convenient way to print short notes or lists.

When you copy from one device to a file or another device, MS-DOS continues to copy until it encounters the character (Ctrl-Z) that marks the end of a file. Whenever you copy from the keyboard, you can send this end-of-file character by pressing the key labeled F6 and then pressing the Enter key (or, as you've done before, by pressing Ctrl-Z and Enter).

When used to copy from a device to a file or another device, the Copy command has two parameters:

**copy <source> <target>**

<source> is the name of the source device.
<target> is the name of the target file or device.

## Examples of Copying from a Device to a File or Another Device

To copy from the keyboard (CON) to the printer (PRN), make certain the printer is turned on and type:

```
C:\>copy con prn
```

Now everything you type will be both displayed and sent to the printer. Type a few lines, and then end the copy by pressing F6 or Ctrl-Z (shown as ^Z in the example because that's how MS-DOS displays it):

```
These lines are being
copied from the
keyboard to the printer.
^Z
        1 file(s) copied

C:\>_
```

NOTE: *If this command doesn't produce a printed copy, you might need to tell the printer to eject the printed page and move to a new page. Try taking your printer off line and pressing the formfeed button.*

## PRINTING GRAPHICS IMAGES

Pressing Shift-PrtSc prints the text displayed on either a monochrome or a color display, but it does not print graphics images from a display that is attached to a graphics adapter. The Graphics command enables MS-DOS to print these graphics images on any of several different printers.

You need enter the Graphics command only once. After you enter it, pressing Shift-PrtSc prints everything on the screen of the active display, including graphics images, accented characters, lines, and boxes. Color on noncolor printers is simulated with shading. Depending on the resolution of the display, the graphics image itself may be printed across the page (as you see it on screen), or it may be printed sideways (rotated 90 degrees) and enlarged.

The Graphics command loads a program that increases the amount of memory that MS-DOS uses. The command has four main parameters:

**graphics  <printer>  /R /B /lcd**

<printer> can be any of the IBM and non-IBM printers listed in Figure 7-4.

/R (Reverse) tells MS-DOS to print the screen as you see it—in other words, light characters on a dark background.

/B tells MS-DOS to print the background color if you have specified *color4* or *color8* for <printer>. If you don't specify /B, then MS-DOS doesn't print the background color.

*/lcd* tells MS-DOS to print the contents of the liquid crystal display of the IBM PC Convertible computer.

| *Specify as:* | *For printer model:* |
| --- | --- |
| color1 | IBM Personal Computer Color Printer with a black ribbon or the black band of a color ribbon |
| color4 | IBM Personal Computer Color Printer with a red-green-blue ribbon |
| color8 | IBM Personal Computer Color Printer with a cyan-magenta-yellow ribbon |
| compact | IBM Personal Computer Compact Printer (MS-DOS versions prior to 4) |
| graphics | IBM Graphics Printer, Proprinter, Pageprinter, or Quietwriter |

**Figure 7-4.**                                                                                     *(continued)*
*Printers supported by the Graphics command.*

**Figure 7-4.** *continued*

| Specify as: | For printer model: |
|---|---|
| graphicswide | IBM Quietwriter or Proprinter with an 11-inch carriage (MS-DOS versions 4 and later) |
| thermal | IBM PC Convertible Printers (MS-DOS versions 3.3 and later) |
| hpdefault | Any Hewlett-Packard PCL printer (MS-DOS versions 5 and later) |
| deskjet | Hewlett-Packard DeskJet (MS-DOS versions 5 and later) |
| laserjet | Hewlett-Packard LaserJet (MS-DOS versions 5 and later) |
| laserjetII | Hewlett-Packard LaserJet Series II (MS-DOS versions 5 and later) |
| paintjet | Hewlett-Packard PaintJet (MS-DOS versions 5 and later) |
| quietjet | Hewlett-Packard Quietjet (MS-DOS versions 5 and later) |
| quietjetplus | Hewlett-Packard Quietjet Plus (MS-DOS versions 5 and later) |
| ruggedwriter | Hewlett-Packard Rugged Writer (MS-DOS versions 5 and later) |
| ruggedwriterwide | Hewlett-Packard Rugged Writer with wide carriage (MS-DOS versions 5 and later) |
| thinkjet | Hewlett-Packard ThinkJet (MS-DOS versions 5 and later) |

When you enter the Graphics command, MS-DOS loads the program, adds it to the parts of the system kept in memory, and displays the system prompt. You needn't enter the command again until the next time you start MS-DOS.

If you're using a color display and you have a printer that can print graphics, you can test the Graphics command by entering the command and appropriate parameters, loading a graphics image on your display, and then pressing Shift-PrtSc.

## CHANGING THE KEYBOARD LAYOUT

Whenever you start MS-DOS, it assumes the language and keyboard layout of the country for which your computer was manufactured. Since the mid-1980s, however, successive releases of MS-DOS have offered increasing amounts of support for languages other than its original American English. As part of this international support, MS-DOS versions 3 and later include a Keyboard (Keyb) command that changes the keyboard layout to accommodate the special characters of different languages and to match the arrangement of keys used in different countries.

The first time the Keyboard command is carried out, it loads a small program that increases the size of MS-DOS in memory by about 5000 bytes. Subsequent Keyboard commands then tell MS-DOS to use different sets of characters that correspond to different country-specific keyboard layouts.

## Keyboard Layouts

When you use the Keyb command, you tell MS-DOS which keyboard layout you want by adding a two-letter country code to the command. If you're using any of IBM's PC-DOS releases 3.0 through 3.2 or MS-DOS version 3.2, you can choose from six layouts by typing the command as shown in the center column:

| Code | Command | Country |
|------|---------|---------|
| dv | keybdv | Dvorak (an alternative English-language layout) |
| fr | keybfr | France |
| gr | keybgr | Germany |
| it | keybit | Italy |
| sp | keybsp | Spain |
| uk | keybuk | United Kingdom |

If you're using version 3.3 or later, you have a significantly expanded group of keyboard codes to choose from because these versions of MS-DOS offer much more international support. The following table shows the keyboard codes readily available for IBM and compatible computers in most countries.

| Code | Command | Country |
|------|---------|---------|
| be | keyb be | Belgium |
| br | keyb br | Brazil (versions 5 and later) |
| cf | keyb cf | French-speaking Canada |
| cz | keyb cz | Czech Republic—Czech (versions 5 and later) |
| dk | keyb dk | Denmark |
| fr | keyb fr | France |
| gr | keyb gr | Germany |
| hu | keyb hu | Hungary (versions 5 and later) |
| it | keyb it | Italy |
| la | keyb la | Latin America |
| nl | keyb nl | Netherlands |
| no | keyb no | Norway |
| pl | keyb pl | Poland (versions 5 and later) |
| po | keyb po | Portugal |
| sf | keyb sf | French-speaking Switzerland |
| sg | keyb sg | German-speaking Switzerland |

*(continued)*

*continued*

| Code | Command | Country |
|------|---------|---------|
| sl | keyb sl | Slovakia—Slovak (versions 5 and later) |
| sp | keyb sp | Spain |
| su | keyb su | Finland |
| sv | keyb sv | Sweden |
| uk | keyb uk | United Kingdom |
| us | keyb us | United States, Australia, English-speaking Canada |
| yu | keyb yu | Yugoslavia (versions 5 and later) |

Because entering a Keyboard command changes the location of common keys (especially punctuation marks), the character that results from pressing a key doesn't always match the label on the key, as you'll see shortly.

## Typing Accented Characters with Dead Keys

Many languages use *accented characters* that combine an accent mark and a common character (such as Å or ñ). Some of these accented characters are assigned locations on the keyboard; on the French keyboard, for example, you type *è* by pressing the 7 key in the top row of the keyboard (to type the number 7, you press Shift-7).

Often there aren't enough available keys to provide all the accented characters, however, so MS-DOS also uses *dead keys* to combine accent marks and characters. Some typewriters use this same technique, so dead keys might be familiar.

A dead key is one that represents just an accent mark. Pressing a dead key doesn't produce any apparent result, but it tells MS-DOS to combine the accent mark with the next key you press. On the French keyboard, for example, you type *ô* by pressing the key labeled with a { and a [, which is the dead key for the circumflex (ˆ), and then pressing the key labeled O.

If you press a dead key and then press a character that cannot be combined with the accent mark represented by the dead key, MS-DOS beeps and displays the accent mark, followed by the key you pressed, to show you it can't combine them as an accented character. For example, ˆp indicates that MS-DOS cannot put a circumflex over the letter P. If the dead key represents the diaeresis (¨), MS-DOS displays a small dot (.) or a filled-in square (■) followed by the second key you pressed in an incorrect dead-key sequence.

To correct the error, backspace to erase the two characters and type the correct dead-key sequence.

## Example of Using the Keyboard Command

If you're using MS-DOS version 3.0 through 3.2, type:

```
C:\>keybfr
```

If you're using MS-DOS version 3.3 or later, type the following to change the keyboard arrangement to French:

```
C:\>keyb fr
```

If MS-DOS responds *Bad or missing Keyboard Definition File*, you need to expand the command to tell MS-DOS where to find the command file it needs. The file is named KEYBOARD.SYS, and it should be in your MS-DOS directory. Retype the command as follows, substituting the name of your MS-DOS directory if it is not C:\DOS:

```
C:\>keyb fr,,c:\dos\keyboard.sys
```

If you are accustomed to the United States layout, here are the most obvious changes with the French layout: You must hold down the Shift key to type a number; the locations of two pairs of letter keys are reversed (Q-A and W-Z); M is to the right of L (where the semicolon is located on the American English keyboard); and most symbols and punctuation marks are in different places.

Now that you have switched keyboards, you must follow the new layout. For example, the command to display a directory in wide format is *dir /w*. If you don't follow the French keyboard layout, you'll type something like *dir=z* because the equal sign or another character is where the forward slash used to be, and the W and Z have also changed places.

Suppose you wanted to type the sentence *L'hôtel célèbre est grand* (meaning *The famous hotel is big*). Both the é and the è are on the keyboard (2 and 7, respectively), but the ô is not, so you must use the dead key for the circumflex (to the right of P). And remember, the Q and the A keys have changed places. Here, step by step, is how you would type the phrase:

```
C:\>L
```

For the apostrophe, press the 4 key in the top row. After the apostrophe, type *h*:

```
C:\>L'h
```

Now you have to use the circumflex dead key, which is to the right of the P. Press the circumflex dead key ([). Nothing happens yet. Now type *o*; MS-DOS displays ô. Continue by typing *tel c*:

```
C:\>L'hôtel c
```

For é, press the 2 key in the top row; then type *l*:

```
C:\>L'hôtel cél
```

For è, press the 7 key in the top row; then type *bre est gr*:

```
C:\>L'hôtel célèbre est gr
```

And finally, press Q to get the a, and type *nd*:

```
C:\>L'hôtel célèbre est grand
```

Although that's a painfully long list of instructions just to type a simple sentence, in fact it goes quite quickly after a bit of practice. Press Esc to clear the line, and type *keyb us* to return to the United States layout.

If your computer was manufactured for use in the United States and you have an IBM keyboard or a strict compatible, you can switch from a foreign layout to the United States configuration by pressing Ctrl-Alt-F1 (hold down both the Ctrl and Alt keys and press the F1 function key). Notice that MS-DOS is still set to the foreign layout, even though functionally it uses the United States configuration. To switch back to the foreign configuration, press Ctrl-Alt-F2.

# A Tree of Files

As you have seen, when MS-DOS formats a disk it creates a directory that describes each of the files on the disk. The directory holds a fixed number of entries: 112 on a 360 KB or 720 KB floppy disk, 224 on a 1.2 MB or 1.44 MB floppy disk, and 512 or more on a hard disk (the number varies with the size of the disk).

To make your computer filing system more flexible, MS-DOS lets you create additional directories, called *subdirectories,* on a disk. The subdirectories divide the disk into different storage areas, each of which you can use as if it were a different disk.

To distinguish the main directory that MS-DOS creates from the subdirectories that you create, the main directory is known as the *root directory* (*root* because a multilevel directory structure can grow from it).

As you add levels to your file structure, a block diagram would show it spreading from the root directory and branching to other directories, like a tree branching from its root. This type of file structure is often called a *tree-structured* file system.

## DEFINING A SUBDIRECTORY

To MS-DOS, a subdirectory is simply a file that contains directory entries; these entries are identical in form to the entries in the main directory, but there is no limit to the number of entries you can put in a subdirectory.

You name a subdirectory as you name any other file, but because the subdirectory defines other files, you cannot use the normal file commands to copy or erase a subdirectory. This chapter shows you how to use several commands that enable you to do the following:

- Create a subdirectory with the Make Directory (md) command.

- Change or display the name of the current directory with the Change Directory (cd) command.

- Move files from one directory to another and rename directories with the Move command.

- Delete a subdirectory with the Remove Directory (rd) command.

- Delete a directory structure with the Deltree command.

- Display a list of files and the directories on a disk with the Directory (dir) and Tree commands.

- Tell MS-DOS where to look for a command file if it's not in the current directory by using the Path command.

■ Tell MS-DOS where to look for a data file if it's not in the current directory by using the Append command (3.3 and later versions).

Using these features of MS-DOS, you can create and manage a computer filing system that is tailored to the way you work.

## PREPARING FOR THE EXAMPLES

The examples in this chapter require one formatted floppy disk. Put the formatted floppy disk in drive A. If any files from earlier examples are stored on the floppy disk, delete them by typing the following; be sure to include the *a:* in the command:

```
C:\>del a:*.*
```

MS-DOS asks you to confirm that you want to erase all the files:

```
All files in directory will be deleted!
Are you sure (Y/N)?_
```

Before you respond, check the command you entered and be certain that you typed the drive letter (*a:*). If you didn't, press Ctrl-Break to cancel the Delete command, and retype the command correctly. If you did type the drive letter, respond *y*. Because a mistake in using the Delete command in this way could cause the loss of valuable files, you must also press the Enter key after typing *y* before MS-DOS will carry out the command.

After you have deleted the files, change the current drive to A by typing:

```
C:\>a:
```

This completes the preparation.

## CREATING A MULTILEVEL FILE STRUCTURE

Suppose you work at a small company and provide services to two departments, Marketing and Engineering. You keep all your papers in a file drawer. You keep miscellaneous items in the front of the drawer, and dividers labeled MKT and ENG separate the parts where you store papers that relate to each department.

Now that you're going to be using a computer, you can set up your computer file system to match your paper files by creating two subdirectories named MKT and ENG. You can store miscellaneous computer files in the main, or root, directory of the disk, and you can store the files relating to each department in separate subdirectories. Figure 8-1 on the following page shows the filing cabinet and a block diagram of this corresponding MS-DOS file structure.

**Figure 8-1.**
*Two-level file system.*

## Creating a Subdirectory

The Make Directory (md or mkdir) command creates a subdirectory. The only parameter that you must include is the name of the subdirectory you want to create. The command is described later in more detail; for now, type the following to create two subdirectories named MKT and ENG:

```
A:\>md mkt
```

```
A:\>md eng
```

You can see the subdirectories you just created by displaying the entries in the root directory. Type:

```
A:\>dir
```

MS-DOS shows two files named MKT and ENG:

```
Volume in drive A is EXAMPLES 2
Volume Serial Number is 1839-10EE
Directory of A:\

MKT            <DIR>       10-16-93  10:54a
ENG            <DIR>       10-16-93  10:54a
        2 file(s)              0 bytes
                        1212928 bytes free
```

Note that the directory identifies the files as subdirectories by displaying <DIR> after their names. The backslash (\) in the third line of the display is the character that MS-DOS uses to refer to the root directory of a disk. You've seen the backslash as part of the system prompt throughout this book; you'll see more of it and its uses in later examples.

Because MKT is a subdirectory, you can display its contents with the Directory command, just as you can display the contents of the root directory. Type the following command:

```
A:\>dir mkt
```

MS-DOS displays the contents of MKT:

```
Volume in drive A is EXAMPLES 2
Volume Serial Number is 1839-10EE
Directory of A:\MKT

.              <DIR>       10-16-93  10:54a
..             <DIR>       10-16-93  10:54a
        2 file(s)              0 bytes
                        1212928 bytes free
```

Even though you just created it, MKT seems to contain subdirectories named . (dot) and .. (double dot). These really aren't subdirectories; they're abbreviations you use to refer to other directories. You'll see how these abbreviations are used a bit later.

## The Path to a Directory

The third line of the preceding directory display tells you that you're looking at the directory of A:\MKT. The \ (backslash) refers to the root directory, and MKT is the name of the subdirectory whose contents you're displaying. Together, they are called the *path name* of the directory, or just the *path,* because they describe the path MS-DOS follows to find the directory. The path names of the two subdirectories you created, \MKT and \ENG, tell MS-DOS that the subdirectories are in the root directory.

You can also include a path name with a file name, to tell MS-DOS where to find a file. The path name goes just before the file name (after the drive letter, if one is included) and is separated from the file name by a backslash. For example, if the subdirectory \MKT contained a file named BUDGET.JAN, the full path and file name would be \MKT\BUDGET.JAN.

## The Current Directory

Just as MS-DOS keeps track of the current drive, it also keeps track of the current directory. If you start MS-DOS from a hard disk, the current directory after startup is usually either the root directory (C:\) or your MS-DOS directory (C:\DOS). If you start MS-DOS from a floppy disk, the current directory after startup is normally the root directory of the floppy disk drive (A:\).

Just as you can change the current drive, you can change the current directory so that you don't have to type the path name each time you want to work with a directory other than the current directory.

The Change Directory (cd or chdir) command changes or displays the name of the current directory. If you enter the command with no parameter, it displays the name of the current directory. To see what the current directory is, type:

```
A:\>cd
```

The current directory is the root directory, so the response is short:

```
A:\
```

It tells you that any command you enter will apply to the root directory of the floppy disk in drive A, unless you specify a different path name. Change the current directory to the subdirectory named MKT by typing:

```
A:\>cd mkt
```

If your system prompt normally shows the current directory, MS-DOS acknowledges:

```
A:\MKT>
```

as soon as it carries out the Change Directory command.

If your system prompt doesn't display the current directory, MS-DOS acknowledges the command merely by displaying the system prompt. But if you display the current directory again by typing:

```
A>cd
```

MS-DOS responds:

```
A:\MKT
```

**NOTE:** *Whenever you work with subdirectories, it's useful to have the current directory displayed as part of the system prompt. If your system prompt does not include the current directory, change it by typing* prompt $p$g. *Chapter 14, "Creating Your Own Commands," tells you how to make this command a normal part of your system's startup routine.*

You've changed the current directory to \MKT, so any command you enter applies to the subdirectory MKT in the root directory. Type the Directory command again:

```
A:\MKT>dir
```

MS-DOS displays the entries in the subdirectory \MKT:

```
Volume in drive A is EXAMPLES 2
Volume Serial Number is 1839-10EE
Directory of A:\MKT

.              <DIR>       10-16-93  10:54a
..             <DIR>       10-16-93  10:54a
        2 file(s)            0 bytes
                      1212928 bytes free
```

This display is the same as the one you saw earlier when you typed *dir mkt*, but this time you didn't have to name the subdirectory because you had changed the current directory to \MKT.

## Using Subdirectories

Your floppy disk now has the directory structure shown in Figure 8-1. You can use each of these directories as if it were a separate disk. The current directory is \MKT. Create a file named SAMPLE.TXT in the root directory by typing the following lines:

```
A:\MKT>copy con \sample.txt
This is a sample file.
^Z
        1 file(s) copied
```

Notice that you included the backslash to tell MS-DOS to put the file in the root directory. You also use the backslash to display the contents of the root directory when it's not the current directory. Type the following:

```
A:\MKT>dir \
```

Again MS-DOS displays the entries in the root directory:

```
Volume in drive A is EXAMPLES 2
Volume Serial Number is 1839-10EE
Directory of A:\
```

```
MKT            <DIR>       10-16-93  10:54a
ENG            <DIR>       10-16-93  10:54a
SAMPLE   TXT          24 10-16-93  11:13a
          3 file(s)           24 bytes
                        1212416 bytes free
```

The root directory contains two subdirectories and the file you just created.

### Copying from One Directory to Another

Because you can treat directories as if they were separate disks, you can copy a file from one directory to another. Copy SAMPLE.TXT from the root directory of drive A to a file named ACCOUNT in the current directory (\MKT) by typing:

```
A:\MKT>copy \sample.txt account
          1 file(s) copied
```

You included the path (the backslash, meaning the root directory) in front of SAMPLE.TXT to tell MS-DOS where to find the file; you didn't have to include a path for ACCOUNT because you were putting it in the current directory. Now display the current directory by typing the following:

```
A:\MKT>dir

 Volume in drive A is EXAMPLES 2
 Volume Serial Number is 1839-10EE
 Directory of A:\MKT

 .             <DIR>       10-16-93  10:54a
 ..            <DIR>       10-16-93  10:54a
ACCOUNT               24 10-16-93  11:13a
          3 file(s)           24 bytes
                        1211904 bytes free
```

The file is there. You can copy files from one directory to another as easily as you can copy them from one disk to another.

Just as MS-DOS doesn't confuse two files with the same name on different disks, it doesn't confuse two files with the same name in different directories. MS-DOS can tell the latter apart because their paths are different. You can demonstrate this by copying the file named ACCOUNT from \MKT to the subdirectory \ENG, giving it the same file name. Type the following:

```
A:\MKT>copy account \eng
          1 file(s) copied
```

You didn't include the file name after the path name of the target directory because you wanted to give the copy the same name as the original. Assure yourself that the file was copied correctly by displaying the directory of \ENG:

```
A:\MKT>dir \eng

 Volume in drive A is EXAMPLES 2
 Volume Serial Number is 1839-10EE
 Directory of A:\ENG

.               <DIR>      10-16-93  10:54a
..              <DIR>      10-16-93  10:54a
ACCOUNT                24 10-16-93  11:13a
        3 file(s)           24 bytes
                      1211392 bytes free
```

You now have two files named ACCOUNT on the same disk; but they are in different subdirectories, and their different path names make them as different to MS-DOS as if you had given them different file names.

## Time Out for a Quick Review

Before completing your multilevel file structure, take a few minutes to review the following definitions. They summarize the terms and concepts introduced in the preceding examples.

*Directory entry:* A description of a file that includes the name, extension, and size of the file, and the date and time it was created or last updated.

*Directory:* A list of directory entries. You'll also see it used with a sense of place: "Which directory am I in?"

*Root directory:* The list of directory entries that MS-DOS creates and maintains on each disk. It is called the root directory (or simply the root) because the entire directory structure on the disk grows from it. Because the root has no name to MS-DOS, it is represented by a backslash (\).

*Subdirectory:* A file that contains directory entries. Like the term *directory,* it is also sometimes used with a sense of place: "Which subdirectory is that file in?"

*Path name:* The list of directory names that defines the path to a subdirectory. The directory names are separated by backslashes (\). The root directory is represented by a backslash at the beginning of the path. If a file name is included at the end of the path, it is separated from the last directory name by a backslash.

*Current directory:* The directory that MS-DOS assumes you want to use unless you specify another in a command. The current directory is similar in concept and effect to the current drive.

# ADDING MORE LEVELS TO YOUR FILE STRUCTURE

The subdirectories you create can contain any type of file, including other sub-directories. Like putting dividers between other dividers in a file drawer, this further structuring narrows the subject of a storage area. Suppose you do the following type of work for the marketing and engineering departments:

| *Marketing* | *Engineering* |
|---|---|
| Word processing | Word processing |
| Budgets | Budgets |
| Customer lists | Project scheduling |
| Sales forecasts | |

You decide to set up your file structure to match your work.

The following list shows the subdirectories you could create to match your computer files to the work you do (MKT and ENG are the departmental subdirectories you created):

| *In MKT:* | *In ENG:* |
|---|---|
| WP | WP |
| BUDGET | BUDGET |
| CUSTOMER | SCHEDULE |
| SALES | |

You would then have created the file structure shown in Figure 8-2.

## Making a Subdirectory: The MD Command

As you saw earlier, the Make Directory (md or mkdir) command creates a subdirectory. The Make Directory command has three parameters:

**md <drive><path><directory>**

<drive> is the letter, followed by a colon, of the drive (such as *a:*) that contains the disk on which the subdirectory is to be created. If you omit <drive>, MS-DOS creates the subdirectory on the disk in the current drive.

<path> is the path name of the directory in which the subdirectory is to be created. If you omit <path>, the subdirectory is created in the current directory.

<directory> is the name of the new directory.

**Figure 8-2.**
*Three-level file systems.*

The current directory is \MKT. For the example in this chapter, you want four subdirectories in \MKT named WP, BUDGET, CUSTOMER, and SALES. Type the following Make Directory commands to create the subdirectories:

```
A:\MKT>md wp

A:\MKT>md budget

A:\MKT>md customer

A:\MKT>md sales
```

Display the directory of \MKT by typing:

```
A:\MKT>dir

Volume in drive A is EXAMPLES 2
Volume Serial Number is 1839-10EE
Directory of A:\MKT

.            <DIR>        10-16-93  10:54a
..           <DIR>        10-16-93  10:54a
ACCOUNT                24 10-16-93  11:13a
WP           <DIR>        10-16-93  11:22a
BUDGET       <DIR>        10-16-93  11:22a
CUSTOMER     <DIR>        10-16-93  11:23a
SALES        <DIR>        10-16-93  11:23a
        7 file(s)           24 bytes
                      1209344 bytes free
```

The directory shows the file you copied a few minutes ago (ACCOUNT) and the four subdirectories you just created.

Your file structure calls for subdirectories named WP and BUDGET in \ENG also. Remember, MS-DOS can distinguish between \MKT\WP and \ENG\WP, and \MKT\BUDGET and \ENG\BUDGET, because their paths are different.

To create the subdirectory \ENG\WP, type:

```
A:\MKT>md \eng\wp
```

You included the path (\ENG) because the current directory is \MKT. The Make Directory command doesn't change the current directory, so it's still \MKT, but you can verify that the subdirectory \ENG\WP was created by displaying the contents of \ENG. Include the path here, too, by typing:

```
A:\MKT>dir \eng

Volume in drive A is EXAMPLES 2
Volume Serial Number is 1839-10EE
Directory of A:\ENG

.            <DIR>        10-16-93  10:54a
..           <DIR>        10-16-93  10:54a
ACCOUNT                24 10-16-93  11:13a
WP           <DIR>        10-16-93  11:25a
        4 file(s)           24 bytes
                      1208832 bytes free
```

Now you're going to start moving around from subdirectory to subdirectory, so before creating the last two subdirectories in \ENG, here's a closer look at your navigator, the Change Directory command.

## Changing the Current Directory: The CD Command

You have already used the Change Directory (cd or chdir) command to change and display the current directory. The Change Directory command has two parameters:

**cd <drive><path>**

<drive> is the letter, followed by a colon, of the drive (such as *a:*) that contains the disk on which the current directory is to be changed. If you omit <drive>, MS-DOS changes the current directory of the disk in the current drive.

<path> is the path name of the directory that is to become the current directory. If you omit <path>, MS-DOS displays the current directory on <drive>.

If you omit both <drive> and <path> (enter the command with no parameters), MS-DOS displays the current directory of the disk in the current drive.

### Keeping Track of Where You Are

As a note earlier in this chapter showed, you can change the system prompt to display not only the current drive but other information, such as the current directory.

Up to this point, the system prompt has shown the current drive and directory in abbreviated form (for example, *A:\MKT>*). In the remainder of the chapter, you'll be changing directories fairly often, so change the prompt to one that helps you identify the current directory at a glance. Type the following, including a blank at the end of the line, just before you press the Enter key:

```
A:\MKT>prompt Current Directory is $p$_Command: <Enter>
```

Now the system prompt becomes:

```
Current Directory is A:\MKT
Command: _
```

You could restore the system prompt to its more familiar form by typing the Prompt command with no parameters (*prompt*) or by typing *prompt $p$g*, but leave it this way for the rest of the chapter. The prompt takes up a bit more space, but it helps you keep track of where you are—a useful feature, especially if you are still adjusting to the idea of moving from one directory to another.

### Using the Subdirectory Markers

Remember those markers (. and ..) listed in each subdirectory? They're designed to let you move quickly up and down a directory structure, particularly when several levels make the path names long.

147

The .. represents the directory that contains the current directory (sometimes called the *parent* of the current directory). The current directory is \MKT; to move the current directory up (toward the root directory) one level, type:

```
Current Directory is A:\MKT
Command: cd ..

Current Directory is A:\
Command: _
```

The system prompt still shows you the current directory, but, as you can see, the current directory has changed to the root directory, which is one level above \MKT.

To complete your file structure, you need two more subdirectories in \ENG. Change the current directory to \ENG, and then create \ENG\BUDGET and \ENG\SCHEDULE by typing the following:

```
Current Directory is A:\
Command: cd eng

Current Directory is A:\ENG
Command: md budget

Current Directory is A:\ENG
Command: md schedule
```

This completes the structure of your multilevel file system.

You have nine subdirectories, plus the root directory, any of which you can use as if it were a separate disk. To show you how easy this is, the next few examples have you put sample files in several of the subdirectories. Figure 8-3 shows how your final file system will look, including the path names of all directories (above the boxes) and the names of the files you'll add (inside the shaded boxes).

To create the sample files in \ENG\WP, first change the current directory to \ENG\WP and copy the file named ACCOUNT from \ENG, naming it LET1.DOC, by typing the following:

```
Current Directory is A:\ENG
Command: cd wp

Current Directory is A:\ENG\WP
Command: copy \eng\account let1.doc
        1 file(s) copied
```

**Figure 8-3.**
*Two-department file structure.*

Note that you must use \ENG in the command, even though \ENG\WP is a subdirectory of \ENG.

Now copy LET1.DOC twice, to create LET2.DOC and LET3.DOC, and display the directory by typing:

```
Current Directory is A:\ENG\WP
Command: copy let1.doc let2.doc
        1 file(s) copied

Current Directory is A:\ENG\WP
Command: copy let1.doc let3.doc
        1 file(s) copied
```

```
Current Directory is A:\ENG\WP
Command: dir

Volume in drive A is EXAMPLES 2
Volume Serial Number is 1839-10EE
Directory of A:\ENG\WP

.                <DIR>        10-16-93   11:25a
..               <DIR>        10-16-93   11:25a
LET1     DOC          24 10-16-93   11:13a
LET2     DOC          24 10-16-93   11:13a
LET3     DOC          24 10-16-93   11:13a
        5 file(s)              72 bytes
                          1206272 bytes free
```

From this subdirectory, you can copy all three of these files to \MKT\WP with one command. Type the following:

```
Current Directory is A:\ENG\WP
Command: copy *.* \mkt\wp
```

MS-DOS lists the source files as it copies them:

```
LET1.DOC
LET2.DOC
LET3.DOC
        3 file(s) copied
```

These files could be word processing files that contain letters. Now create three more files in \MKT\WP that could represent word processing files that contain reports. First, change the directory to \MKT\WP, then copy the three files whose names begin with LET, changing their names so they begin with RPT. Type:

```
Current Directory is A:\ENG\WP
Command: cd \mkt\wp

Current Directory is A:\MKT\WP
Command: copy let?.doc rpt?.doc
```

MS-DOS again lists the source files as it makes the copies:

```
LET1.DOC
LET2.DOC
LET3.DOC
        3 file(s) copied
```

To complete the files in this subdirectory, copy the same three files again, this time changing their extension to STY, which could identify word processing files that contain style sheets for formatting and printing documents. Type the following:

```
Current Directory is A:\MKT\WP
Command: copy let?.doc let?.sty
```

Now display the directory to verify that all nine files are there by typing:

```
Current Directory is A:\MKT\WP
Command: dir

 Volume in drive A is EXAMPLES 2
 Volume Serial Number is 1839-10EE
 Directory of A:\MKT\WP

 .              <DIR>      10-16-93   11:22a
 ..             <DIR>      10-16-93   11:22a
 LET1     DOC        24 10-16-93   11:13a
 LET2     DOC        24 10-16-93   11:13a
 LET3     DOC        24 10-16-93   11:13a
 RPT1     DOC        24 10-16-93   11:13a
 RPT2     DOC        24 10-16-93   11:13a
 RPT3     DOC        24 10-16-93   11:13a
 LET1     STY        24 10-16-93   11:13a
 LET2     STY        24 10-16-93   11:13a
 LET3     STY        24 10-16-93   11:13a
        11 file(s)        216 bytes
                      1201664 bytes free
```

To complete the file system, you'll need three files in \MKT\BUDGET named BGT1.XLS, BGT2.XLS, and BGT3.XLS, and you'll need three files in \ENG\BUDGET named BGT1.NEW, BGT2.NEW, and BGT3.NEW. First, use the Copy command to create the files in \MKT\BUDGET by typing:

```
Current Directory is A:\MKT\WP
Command: copy let?.doc \mkt\budget\bgt?.xls
```

MS-DOS lists three source files as it makes the copies and then displays the prompt.

To finish, you could create the files for \ENG\BUDGET from the current directory, but that would mean typing the full path and file name. To save some keystrokes, change to the \MKT\BUDGET directory by typing:

```
Current Directory is A:\MKT\WP
Command: cd ..\budget
```

The .. marker tells MS-DOS to move up to the parent (\MKT) of the current directory and, from there, move down to the \BUDGET directory. The prompt changes to the following:

```
Current Directory is A:\MKT\BUDGET
Command: _
```

Now you can finish creating the sample files by typing:

```
Current Directory is A:\MKT\BUDGET
Command: copy *.xls \eng\budget\*.new
```

MS-DOS lists three source files copied: BGT1.XLS, BGT2.XLS, and BGT3.XLS. Your file system now has the directories and files shown in Figure 8-3.

## Moving Files from One Directory to Another

Like the Copy command, the Move command (available in versions 6 and 6.2) makes a copy of one or more files on a different directory or disk; unlike Copy, Move doesn't leave the original in place. You can also use Move to change the name of a directory.

The Move command requires two parameters:

**move /Y <source> <target>**

/Y tells Move not to prompt you before creating the directory into which the specified files are moved.

<source> is the name of the file to be moved, and <target> is the name for the file in its new location. You can specify a drive letter and path name with both <source> and <target>. You can use wildcard characters to move a set of files, but if you do so you cannot change the files' names; if you want to give a file a different name in its new location, you can move only one file at a time.

If you are using version 6.2 and <target> is the name of an existing file, MS-DOS prompts you to confirm that you want to replace the existing file with <source>.

If you make <source> the name of a directory, you can rename the directory by specifying a different name in <target>. You cannot, however, move a directory to a different location in the directory structure.

### Examples of Moving Files

The next three examples not only show you how to use the Move command, they give you a chance to use the dot (.) and double-dot (..) markers listed in the subdirectories. First, you'll move the file BGT1.XLS from \MKT\BUDGET to \MKT\SALES. Type the following:

```
Current Directory is A:\MKT\BUDGET
Command: move bgt1.xls \mkt\sales
```

MS-DOS responds by displaying the source and target file names:

```
a:\mkt\budget\bgt1.xls => a:\mkt\sales\bgt1.xls [ok]
```

Use the Directory command to verify that BGT1.XLS has been moved to the new directory.

You can use wildcard characters to move more than one file with similar file names or extensions. Notice that in this example, instead of typing the full path name of the target, you'll use the double-dot representation for the directory that contains the current directory. Type the following Move command to move BGT2.XLS and BGT3.XLS to \MKT\SALES:

```
Current Directory is A:\MKT\BUDGET
Command: move bgt?.xls ..\sales
a:\mkt\budget\bgt2.xls => a:\mkt\sales\bgt2.xls [ok]
a:\mkt\budget\bgt3.xls => a:\mkt\sales\bgt3.xls [ok]
```

The Move command lists only BGT2.XLS and BGT3.XLS because you moved BGT1.XLS with the first Move command.

Now suppose you tell MS-DOS to move BGT1.XLS to BGT2.XLS. Type the following:

```
move ..\sales\bgt1.xls ..\sales\bgt2.xls
```

MS-DOS responds by prompting you to confirm that you want to replace (overwrite) BGT2.XLS with BGT1.XLS:

```
Overwrite a:\mkt\sales\bgt2.xls (Yes/No/All)?_
```

Yes means yes and No means no, but what does All mean? Well, if you had used a wildcard character to move a series of files with one command and knew that you wanted to overwrite an existing file in every instance, you could type *A* for All; if you type *Y*, MS-DOS prompts you for each instance where a file would be overwritten.

Type *N*; MS-DOS cancels the Move command and displays the system prompt.

The last Move command moves all three files back to the current directory. This time you'll use the single dot to represent the current directory instead of typing its complete path name:

```
Current Directory is A:\MKT\BUDGET
Command: move ..\sales\*.xls .
a:\mkt\sales\bgt1.xls => a:\mkt\budget\bgt1.xls [ok]
a:\mkt\sales\bgt2.xls => a:\mkt\budget\bgt2.xls [ok]
a:\mkt\sales\bgt3.xls => a:\mkt\budget\bgt3.xls [ok]
```

### Example of Renaming a Directory

Suppose you decide that a better name for the directory A:\ENG\WP is A:\ENG\EDIT. To change the name of the directory, type:

```
Current Directory is A:\MKT\BUDGET
Command: move a:\eng\wp a:\eng\edit
```

MS-DOS responds by displaying the old and new names of the directory:

```
a:\eng\wp => a:\eng\edit [ok]
```

Now when you use the Directory command to view the contents of the ENG directory, you'll see that the name has changed:

```
Current Directory is A:\MKT\BUDGET
Command: dir a:\eng

Volume in drive A is EXAMPLES 2
Volume Serial Number is 1839-10EE
Directory of A:\ENG
.              <DIR>      10-16-93   10:54a
..             <DIR>      10-16-93   10:54a
ACCOUNT           24      10-16-93   11:13a
EDIT           <DIR>      10-16-93   11:30a
BUDGET         <DIR>      10-16-93   11:30a
SCHEDULE       <DIR>      10-16-93   11:30a
```

## MANAGING YOUR SUBDIRECTORIES

Once subdirectories become part of your work with MS-DOS, they quickly become essential for organizing your programs and data files, especially on a hard disk. But the more subdirectories and files you create, the harder it is to keep track of where they are and what they contain. Giving descriptive names to your subdirectories and files is one way to maintain order. Another way is to group your files—especially data files—logically. At times, however, you'll still find yourself wondering what an old subdirectory contains and whether you still need it. And even if you're tremendously well organized, you'll also sometimes forget just where you saved *that* file (usually when you're in a desperate hurry to find it).

As you would expect, MS-DOS includes several commands that help you manage your subdirectories and the files they contain. You've already seen the Directory and Change Directory commands, which allow you to move around through your directory structure. The remainder of this chapter describes other commands that help you:

- Eliminate unneeded subdirectories (the Remove Directory command).

- Delete an entire directory structure, files and all (the Deltree command).

- Use command files from any subdirectory (the Path command).

- Search for particular files by name or attribute (the /S parameter of the Directory command).

- View the directory structure of a disk (the Tree and Check Disk commands).

- Help MS-DOS find data files in different subdirectories (the Append command).

## Removing a Subdirectory: The RD Command

As you work with a multilevel filing system, you might find that you no longer need a particular subdirectory, or that you want to combine the files from several subdirectories into one and then delete the unneeded subdirectories from your file structure. The Remove Directory (rd or rmdir) command removes a subdirectory. A subdirectory cannot be removed with this command if it contains any files or any other subdirectories.

The Remove Directory command has two parameters:

**rd <drive><path>**

<drive> is the letter, followed by a colon, of the drive that contains the disk with the subdirectory to be removed. You can omit <drive> if the subdirectory is on the disk in the current drive.

<path> is the path name of the subdirectory to be removed. You must specify <path> because MS-DOS will not remove the current directory.

Suppose you decide you don't need the subdirectory \ENG\EDIT. Tell MS-DOS to remove it by typing:

```
Current Directory is A:\MKT\BUDGET
Command: rd \eng\edit
```

MS-DOS responds *Invalid path, not directory, or directory not empty* because \ENG\EDIT isn't empty: You put three files—LET1.DOC, LET2.DOC, and LET3.DOC—in it.

This example points out the difference in the ways you handle files and subdirectories. As you saw in earlier chapters, you use the Delete command to delete a file from a disk. To remove a directory, however, you use the Remove Directory command. Versions 6 and 6.2 of MS-DOS offer a command for deleting directories and anything contained in them. See the next section for more information.

In the next example, you will delete three files with the Delete command and then remove a directory with the Remove Directory command. First, change the current directory to \ENG, and then delete the files with the Delete command by typing:

```
Current Directory is A:\MKT\WP
Command: cd \eng

Current Directory is A:\ENG
Command: del edit\*.doc
```

You changed the current directory to \ENG, rather than to \ENG\EDIT, because MS-DOS won't remove the current directory. Now that \ENG\EDIT is empty, type the Remove Directory command and verify the change by displaying the directory.

```
Current Directory is A:\ENG
Command: rd edit

Current Directory is A:\ENG
Command: dir

 Volume in drive A is EXAMPLES 2
 Volume Serial Number is 1839-10EE
 Directory of A:\ENG
            <DIR>      10-16-93   10:54a
 ..         <DIR>      10-16-93   10:54a
 ACCOUNT           24  10-16-93   11:13a
 BUDGET     <DIR>      10-16-93   11:30a
 SCHEDULE   <DIR>      10-16-93   11:30a
        5 file(s)          24 bytes
                      1200640 bytes free
```

The subdirectory \ENG\EDIT is gone.

If you want to remove a directory but need some of the files it contains, copy the files you need to another subdirectory, then erase all the files and remove the unneeded directory.

**NOTE:** *The next few topics cover features in version 5 and later of MS-DOS. If you don't have version 5 or later, skip to the heading "The Path to a Command: The Path Command."*

## Deleting a Subdirectory and Its Contents: Deltree

The Remove Directory command is perfectly adequate for getting rid of directories, but deleting several directories can get tedious, especially if some of the directories contain other subdirectories and all the directories and subdirectories contain files. Starting with version 6, MS-DOS gives you a way to cut through all the delays and rid yourself of all those directories in one fell swoop: the Deltree command. Deltree deletes a directory and *all* its contents, even if those contents include subdirectories with their own files and subdirectories. It deletes an entire branch, or subtree, from the directory tree structure. Because of Deltree's potential for damage, MS-DOS prompts you to confirm the action just as it does when you tell it to delete all the files in a directory. If you told MS-DOS to delete a directory named SALES, for example, Deltree would respond *Delete directory "sales" and all its subdirectories? [yn]*. If you reply by typing *N* (uppercase or lowercase), MS-DOS cancels the Deltree command.

Suppose you wanted to delete all the directories you created for the examples in this chapter. Using the Remove Directory command, you'd have to delete the directories one at a time, starting with the lowest in the directory structure, deleting the files with the Delete command before removing the directories with the Remove Directory (rd) command. Using Deltree, you could get rid of all the directories and files with just one command.

But there's a price to be paid for all this convenience: the danger that you'll inadvertently wipe out dozens, hundreds, even all of your files. Suppose that your root directory contained a directory named RUNBAS that contained several subdirectories and files—like the file structure you created for the examples in this chapter. You're ready to delete these directories and files, and you decide to save time by using the Deltree command instead of deleting the files and directories using several Delete and Remove Directory commands. You're tired, or rushed, or not paying attention, and you type *deltree* \ but forget to type *runbas*. If you were to respond affirmatively to the prompt, you'd erase every single file and directory on your hard disk.

So use Deltree with care. Make certain that you understand what you're telling MS-DOS to do before you use the command, and then go over it one more time before you press Y and Enter.

## Viewing Files in More than One Subdirectory

If you have version 5 or later, you can display the contents of the current subdirectory and all subdirectories below it by using the /S parameter of the Directory command. When used to display the contents of more than one subdirectory, the command is:

**dir <filename> /S**

If you include <filename>, MS-DOS searches for the file in the current directory and all subdirectories below it. You can use wildcards to specify a group of files. If you do not include <filename>, MS-DOS displays the names of all files in all the subdirectories.

You can also combine /S with other parameters of the Directory command. For example, you can include /P to halt the display after each screenful, and you can include the /W parameter to display the directories in wide format.

To see how the /S parameter works, begin by changing to the root directory of the disk in drive A to start at the highest level of your directory tree. Type the following Change Directory command (remember, \ means the root directory):

```
Current Directory is A:\ENG
Command: cd \
```

Now request a listing of all subdirectories and files stored in the root directory. The list is long, so use the /P parameter as well as /S so that MS-DOS will pause after each screenful. Type:

```
Current Directory is A:\
Command: dir /s /p
```

The first screenful looks like the following:

```
Volume in drive A is EXAMPLES 2
Volume Serial Number is 1839-10EE

Directory of A:\

MKT          <DIR>      10-16-93   10:54a
ENG          <DIR>      10-16-93   10:54a
SAMPLE   TXT         24 10-16-93   11:13a
        3 file(s)           24 bytes

Directory of A:\ENG

.            <DIR>      10-16-93   10:54a
..           <DIR>      10-16-93   10:54a
ACCOUNT             24 10-16-93   11:13a
BUDGET       <DIR>      10-16-93   11:30a
SCHEDULE     <DIR>      10-16-93   11:30a
        5 file(s)           24 bytes

Directory of A:\ENG\BUDGET

.            <DIR>      10-16-93   11:30a
..           <DIR>      10-16-93   11:30a
Press any key to continue . . .
```

Notice that MS-DOS displays the name of each subdirectory on a separate line above the list of subdirectory entries. If you want to display another screenful, press any key. If you want to cancel, press Ctrl-Break.

## Viewing Specified Files in More Than One Subdirectory

A listing of every file in every subdirectory on a disk can be very long. You can limit the display by telling MS-DOS to show only the names of files that you specify. For example, use the asterisk wildcard to tell MS-DOS to list any file in any subdirectory whose extension is DOC. Type:

```
Current Directory is A:\
Command: dir *.doc /s
```

MS-DOS responds:

```
Volume in drive A is EXAMPLES 2
Volume Serial Number is 1839-10EE

Directory of A:\MKT\WP

LET1        DOC        24 10-16-93   11:13a
LET2        DOC        24 10-16-93   11:13a
LET3        DOC        24 10-16-93   11:13a
RPT1        DOC        24 10-16-93   11:13a
RPT2        DOC        24 10-16-93   11:13a
RPT3        DOC        24 10-16-93   11:13a
        6 file(s)          144 bytes

Total files listed:
        6 file(s)          144 bytes
                       1200640 bytes free
```

Only the subdirectory \MKT\WP contains files with the extension DOC.

The /S parameter can be particularly useful if you remember the name of a file but you can't remember where you put it. Change to the root directory of the disk, and use the /S parameter to search every subdirectory. Use wildcards, if needed, to search for a group of files or for a file whose name you're not sure of.

## The Path to a Command: The Path Command

In a multilevel filing system, you'll probably change the current directory as you use data files in different subdirectories. But you'll use command files too, such as the external MS-DOS commands and application programs. When you type a command, MS-DOS looks for the command file in the current directory. If you have changed directories, chances are the current directory doesn't contain the command file you need.

The Path command lets you tell MS-DOS where to look for a command file if it's not in the current directory. You can name one or more directories—the root directory or any subdirectory on the disk in any disk drive. This command lets you work in any subdirectory you want and still be able to use any command file.

The Path command has three parameters:

**path <drive><path> ;**

<drive> is the letter, followed by a colon, of the drive (such as *a:*) with the disk that contains the command file. If you omit <drive>, MS-DOS looks on the disk in the current drive.

<path> is the path name of the directory that contains the command file.

You can specify several command paths in one command, separating them with semicolons. If you enter a Path command with no parameters (just type *path*), MS-DOS displays the command paths you have defined. If you type *path* followed only by a semicolon, MS-DOS cancels any command paths you have defined.

If you have a hard disk, the root directory probably contains a special file named AUTOEXEC.BAT that MS-DOS reads each time you start or restart your computer. AUTOEXEC.BAT contains instructions that help MS-DOS work well for you. One of those instructions is probably a Path command that enables you to use application programs, as well as external MS-DOS commands, no matter what the current directory is. For example, suppose you use Microsoft Word, Lotus 1-2-3, R:BASE, and MaxThink, and your MS-DOS files are in a directory named \DOS. Your Path command probably looks something like this:

```
path c:\dos;c:\word;c:\123;c:\rbfiles;c:\max
```

The order in which the directory names are specified determines the order in which MS-DOS searches for the command file. Because the drive letter and root-directory symbol (\) precede each subdirectory name, MS-DOS knows where to find each program, and you can use any program in any of these directories even if the current drive isn't C.

If MS-DOS has no trouble starting application programs or carrying out external commands when drive A is the current drive, you can be sure you have an AUTOEXEC.BAT file with a Path command in it. You can check on your own command path by typing *path* with no parameters. Type:

```
Current Directory is A:\
Command: path
```

If you do have any problems starting programs from another drive, consult Chapter 14, "Creating Your Own Commands," which describes how you can create or modify an AUTOEXEC.BAT file.

## Displaying the Directory Structure: Tree and Check Disk

As described in Chapter 11, "The MS-DOS Shell," the Shell lets you quickly display a diagram of the directory structure of any disk and use that diagram to move from one directory to another. Tree and Check Disk are commands that allow you to view your directory structure from the system prompt.

The Tree command has two main parameters:

**tree <drive> /F**

<drive> is the letter of the drive, followed by a colon, that contains the disk whose directory structure is to be displayed.

/F displays a list of the files in each directory.

## Checking the Directory Structure of a Disk

NOTE: *The following two examples use the Tree command. If your version of MS-DOS does not include this command, a later example shows you how to use the Check Disk command to see a list of directories and files on a disk.*

Suppose you're about to create a new file and you want to check on the most appropriate subdirectory for it. As its name implies, the Tree command shows you the structure of the directory tree on whichever disk you specify. For example, check the directories on your sample disk. To be sure you see the entire structure, first check that the current directory is the root directory. If it isn't, change directories by typing *cd\*. Now ask MS-DOS to show you the names and relative levels of the directories on the disk. Type:

```
Current Directory is A:\
Command: tree
```

If you're using version 4 or later of MS-DOS, you see a report like this:

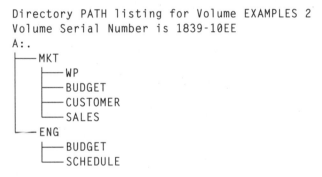

```
Directory PATH listing for Volume EXAMPLES 2
Volume Serial Number is 1839-10EE
A:.
├───MKT
│   ├───WP
│   ├───BUDGET
│   ├───CUSTOMER
│   └───SALES
└───ENG
    ├───BUDGET
    └───SCHEDULE
```

If you're using an earlier version of MS-DOS, you see a report like the following (some blank lines that appear on the screen have been removed to condense the display):

```
DIRECTORY PATH LISTING
Path: \MKT
Sub-directories:    WP
                    BUDGET
                    CUSTOMER
                    SALES
Path: \MKT\WP
Sub-directories:    None
Path: \MKT\BUDGET
Sub-directories:    None
Path: \MKT\CUSTOMER
Sub-directories:    None
Path: \MKT\SALES
```

```
Sub-directories:    None
Path: \ENG
Sub-directories:    BUDGET
                    SCHEDULE
Path: \ENG\BUDGET
Sub-directories:    None
Path: \ENG\SCHEDULE
Sub-directories:    None
```

But suppose a report on the directory structure isn't detailed enough. You want to know the name of each file in each subdirectory—perhaps because there is one file in particular you need. To do this, you use the /F parameter, which shows not only the directory structure of the disk but the names of the files in each directory. For example, versions 4 and later produce a report like this when you type *tree /f*:

```
Directory PATH listing for Volume EXAMPLES 2
Volume Serial Number is 1839-10EE
A:.
│       SAMPLE.TXT
│
├───MKT
│       ACCOUNT
│
│   ├───WP
│           LET1.DOC
│           LET2.DOC
│           LET3.DOC
│           RPT1.DOC
│           RPT2.DOC
│           RPT3.DOC
│           LET1.DOC
│           LET2.DOC
│           LET3.DOC
│
│   ├───BUDGET
│           BGT1.XLS
│           BGT2.XLS
│           BGT3.XLS
│
│   ├───CUSTOMER
│   └───SALES
└───ENG
        ACCOUNT
    │
    ├───BUDGET
            BGT1.NEW
            BGT2.NEW
            BGT3.NEW
    │
    └───SCHEDULE
```

Now the tree shows the names of your files beneath the names of the subdirectories that contain them.

If your version of the Tree command doesn't produce the graphic type of report shown above, or if your version of MS-DOS doesn't include a Tree command, you can use the /V parameter of the Check Disk command to see a list of files and directories. Type:

```
Current Directory is A:\
Command: chkdsk /v
```

MS-DOS responds with a report like this:

```
Volume Serial Number is 1839-10EE
Directory A:\
Directory A:\MKT
A:\MKT\ACCOUNT
Directory A:\MKT\WP
A:\MKT\WP\LET1.DOC
A:\MKT\WP\LET2.DOC
A:\MKT\WP\LET3.DOC
A:\MKT\WP\RPT1.DOC
A:\MKT\WP\RPT2.DOC
A:\MKT\WP\RPT3.DOC
A:\MKT\WP\LET1.STY
A:\MKT\WP\LET2.STY
A:\MKT\WP\LET3.STY
Directory A:\MKT\BUDGET
A:\MKT\BUDGET\BGT1.XLS
A:\MKT\BUDGET\BGT2.XLS
A:\MKT\BUDGET\BGT3.XLS
Directory A:\MKT\CUSTOMER
Directory A:\MKT\SALES
Directory A:\ENG
A:\ENG\ACCOUNT
Directory A:\ENG\BUDGET
A:\ENG\BUDGET\BGT1.NEW
A:\ENG\BUDGET\BGT2.NEW
A:\ENG\BUDGET\BGT3.NEW
Directory A:\ENG\SCHEDULE
A:\SAMPLE.TXT

   1213952 bytes total disk space
      4096 bytes in 8 directories
      9216 bytes in 18 user files
   1200640 bytes available on disk
```

```
 512 bytes in each allocation unit
2371 total allocation units on disk
2345 available allocation units on disk

655360 total bytes memory
528688 bytes free
```

Here, the directories are identified by *Directory* preceding the path and file name. The file in the root directory (SAMPLE.TXT) is listed at the end, above the usual Check Disk reports on disk space and memory.

A printed copy of either of these reports can be helpful, especially if your filing system has several levels. For a hard disk with several hundred files, however, bear in mind that either a Tree or a Check Disk report showing both directories and files could be several pages long. Here are some ways you can print the reports of either or both the Tree and Check Disk commands.

If you want to print a list of both directories and files, use the Tree command with the /F parameter or the Check Disk command with the /V parameter. If you have version 4 or later and your printer is not an IBM or IBM-compatible printer, either use the Check Disk command or use the /A parameter of the Tree command, which tells MS-DOS to use hyphens, backslashes, and other common characters to print the diagram. Without the /A parameter, your printout might include accented letters, small open circles, or other such characters in place of the horizontal and vertical lines showing the branches of your directory tree.

For example, to print a complete report for the disk in drive A, type:

```
Current Directory is A:\
Command: tree /f > prn
```

or:

```
Current Directory is A:\
Command: tree /f /a > prn
```

or:

```
Current Directory is A:\
Command: chkdsk /v > prn
```

To print only a list of directories on the disk in drive A, you can use either of the following commands.

With the Tree command, type:

```
Current Directory is A:\
Command: tree > prn
```

With the Check Disk command, you use techniques described in Chapter 13, "Taking Control of Your System," to filter out all the file names from the output of the Check Disk command, leaving just the subdirectory names, which are then sent to the printer. Try it. (Notice that a slash, not a backslash, precedes the *v*.) Type:

```
Current Directory is A:\
Command: chkdsk /v | find "Di" > prn
```

The printed output of this command shows only the names of the directories (the lines that contain *Di*).

Any of these guides to your file system can help you keep track of both files and subdirectories and can help you use your system more efficiently.

## Another Type of Path: The Append Command

If you're using 3.3 or a later version of MS-DOS, you can use the Append command as well as the Path command to tell MS-DOS where to look for a file if it's not in the current directory. Although it seems redundant to have two commands that can set a search path, there's a significant difference between Path and Append: Path sets the path to *command* files; Append sets the path to *data* files too. Just as with the Path command, you can name one or more directories on any disk drive.

The Append command has three main parameters related to helping MS-DOS find data files (and program files):

**append <drive><path> ;**

<drive> is the letter, followed by a colon, of the drive (such as *c:*) with the disk that contains the files. If you omit <drive>, MS-DOS looks on the current drive.

<path> is the path name of the directory that contains the files.

You can specify several appended paths in one command, separating them with semicolons. If you enter an Append command with no parameters (just type *append*), MS-DOS displays the paths you have defined. If you type *append* followed only by a semicolon, MS-DOS cancels any paths you have defined.

It's easy to try the Append command. The root directory is the current directory, and the file RPT1.DOC is in the directory \MKT\WP. First, try to display the file by using the Type command:

```
Current Directory is A:\
Command: type rpt1.doc
```

MS-DOS replies *File not found* because RPT1.DOC isn't in the current directory. Now type two Append commands to set the data path to \MKT\WP and display the data path:

```
Current Directory is A:\
Command: append \mkt\wp

Current Directory is A:\
Command: append
APPEND=\MKT\WP
```

Now try the Type command again:

```
Current Directory is A:\
Command: type rpt1.doc
This is a sample file.
```

This time MS-DOS finds the file because you told it where to look. Cancel the appended path by typing *append* with just a semicolon, then check again:

```
Current Directory is A:\
Command: append ;

Current Directory is A:\
Command: append
No Append
```

The Path and Append commands are valuable tools for improving the efficiency and convenience of using a hard disk. Appendix C, "MS-DOS Command Reference," includes a complete description of each.

If you're going to continue using your system, restart your computer or type the following to restore the system prompt:

```
Current Directory is A:\
Command: prompt $p$g

A:\>
```

## CHAPTER SUMMARY

Although this chapter introduced several new terms and concepts, it doesn't take many commands to set up a multilevel file system. The structure shown in Figure 8-3, for example, required only the 11 commands listed on the next page. (Don't enter them; this list is just to show you the commands you entered.)

```
md mkt
md eng
cd mkt
md wp
md budget
md customer
md sales
md\eng\wp
cd \eng
md budget
md schedule
```

You might not create a file structure with this many levels on a floppy disk, although it's certainly possible if you use high-density floppy disks. As you noticed, subdirectories require a great deal of work from the floppy disk drive. But you might find that two or three subdirectories reduce the number of floppy disks you use, or that they let you use your system more efficiently. The examples in this chapter showed you how to use all the commands you need to create and manage a multilevel filing system.

Save the floppy disk that contains the file system you created in this chapter. You'll use it again to copy sample files in the next chapter, "Managing Your Hard Disk."

# 9

# Managing Your Hard Disk

**A** hard disk holds far more data than a floppy disk, and MS-DOS can use it much more quickly. You don't remove a hard disk; it's permanently fixed in the drive. Like a floppy disk, a hard disk stores data in tracks and sectors; unlike a floppy disk, however, a hard disk stores data on magnetically coated, rigid metal—not plastic—disks that are enclosed in a nonremovable case.

A typical hard disk drive contains two or more separate disks that give it a total storage capacity of 40 to 120 megabytes, but hard disks with even higher capacities are becoming common. Several computers offer a hard disk that can hold 600 MB or more. This chapter focuses on how to use your hard disk efficiently.

Managing your hard disk requires more thought and planning than managing your floppy disks, simply because of the sheer number of files involved. But properly organized and managed, your hard disk is a fast and effective tool you use with a minimum of fuss. Two tasks are more important than any others in managing your hard disk efficiently. One is setting up a filing system that lets you take advantage of the disk's capacity without losing track of all your files; this chapter shows you how to plan a structure and use the commands to create that structure. The other task is backing up the files periodically, both to protect your data in the event your hard disk is inadvertently erased or damaged and to clear out old files you no longer use regularly; the topic of backing up is covered in the next chapter, "Protecting Your Disks and Files."

The previous chapter covered setting up and using a multilevel filing system. Everything you learned there applies to managing your hard disk properly. This chapter covers the additional tasks of organizing directories and files on your hard disk and managing large numbers of files.

In most ways, you treat a hard disk as if it were a large floppy disk, using the MS-DOS directory commands to create, change, and remove directories, and the MS-DOS file commands to copy, erase, rename, and otherwise work with your files. The Volume and Label commands described in Chapter 6, "Managing Your Floppy Disks," can also be used with a hard disk. But two commands— Diskcopy and Diskcomp—don't work with the hard disk because they are designed to work only with entire floppy disks.

This chapter suggests some guidelines to simplify the job of managing your hard disk; it shows you how to set up a filing system, control the archive attribute of a file with the Attribute command, copy files selectively with the Replace and Xcopy commands, increase the capacity and efficiency of your hard disk with the DoubleSpace and Defrag programs, and, if you have version 6.2, use a program called ScanDisk to check for and correct disk errors.

## PUTTING APPLICATION PROGRAMS ON YOUR HARD DISK

When you set up your directory structure, you'll have to copy the command and data files of your application programs onto the hard disk. Most application programs install themselves in their own subdirectories on a hard disk; others don't include an installation (or setup) program, leaving it to you to create the subdirectories and copy the files. You shouldn't put all your programs in the root directory or in a single large program directory. If you do, you'll have difficulty telling one program file from another, and you'll end up with as much disorganization as you would if you tossed all your program floppy disks into one big drawer.

Remember, too, that MS-DOS itself is a collection of command (program) files. Like application-program files, the MS-DOS files can be stored in a variety of places on your hard disk, including the root directory. Versions 4 and later, in fact, install themselves in a \DOS subdirectory. If, for some reason, your MS-DOS files are in the root directory, you should move them to a subdirectory named \DOS so they'll be easy to find and won't clutter up either your root directory or your directory displays. Instructions for doing this are in Appendix A, "Installing MS-DOS."

## PREPARING FOR THE EXAMPLES

The examples in this chapter rely on the information presented in the preceding chapter, "A Tree of Files," and use the directory structure and files you created there. If you haven't completed those examples, do so before continuing.

The examples in this chapter require the sample subdirectories and files in Figure 9-1 on the next page. You will create these on the hard disk in a subdirectory named \RUNDOS, which will keep all your examples in one place for easy removal.

If your system prompt doesn't show the current directory, change it to an abbreviated version of the *Current Directory is...* prompt you used in the last chapter. Type:

```
C>prompt $p$g<Enter>

C:\>
```

Now your system prompt shows both the current drive and the current directory and will help you keep track of where you are in your directory structure.

**Figure 9-1.**
*Subdirectories and files for hard disk examples.*

To create the \RUNDOS subdirectory, type:

```
C:\>md \rundos
```

Now change the current directory to \RUNDOS by typing:

```
C:\>cd \rundos
```

## Copying Files to Your Hard Disk

The remainder of your preparation depends on which version of MS-DOS you're using. If you have version 3.2 or later, follow the instructions under the heading "Copying Files with the Xcopy Command." If you have a version of MS-DOS prior to 3.2, follow the instructions under the heading "Copying Files with the Copy Command."

### Copying Files with the Xcopy Command

If you're using version 3.2 or later of MS-DOS, copying everything from your practice floppy disk to the \RUNDOS directory is simple. All you need is one Xcopy command, which copies subdirectories and files from the source disk to the target disk. The Xcopy parameter you use here, /S, copies all subdirectories as well as all files. Xcopy is described in more detail later. For now, put the floppy disk that contains your sample files in drive A and type:

```
C:\RUNDOS>xcopy a: /s
```

MS-DOS responds:

```
Reading source file(s)...
A:SAMPLE.TXT
A:MKT\ACCOUNT
A:MKT\WP\LET1.DOC
A:MKT\WP\LET2.DOC
A:MKT\WP\LET3.DOC
A:MKT\WP\RPT1.DOC
A:MKT\WP\RPT2.DOC
A:MKT\WP\RPT3.DOC
A:MKT\WP\LET1.STY
A:MKT\WP\LET2.STY
A:MKT\WP\LET3.STY
A:MKT\BUDGET\BGT1.XLS
A:MKT\BUDGET\BGT2.XLS
A:MKT\BUDGET\BGT3.XLS
A:ENG\ACCOUNT
A:ENG\BUDGET\BGT1.NEW
A:ENG\BUDGET\BGT2.NEW
A:ENG\BUDGET\BGT3.NEW
        18 File(s) copied
```

You don't need the file named SAMPLE.TXT, the directories named \ENG and
\ENG\BUDGET, or the files they contain. If you have version 6 or 6.2 of MS-DOS, remove them by typing:

```
C:\RUNDOS>del sample.txt

C:\RUNDOS>deltree eng
Delete directory "eng" and all its subdirectories? [yn] y
Deleting eng...
```

If you have an earlier version of MS-DOS, type:

```
C:\RUNDOS>del sample.txt
C:\RUNDOS>del eng\account
C:\RUNDOS>del eng\budget\*.new
C:\RUNDOS>rd eng\budget
C:\RUNDOS>rd eng
```

You're through.

### Copying Files with the Copy Command

If you're using a version of MS-DOS prior to 3.2, put the floppy disk that contains
your sample files in drive A and type the following commands to duplicate the
floppy disk's directory structure on your hard disk:

```
C:\RUNDOS>md mkt
C:\RUNDOS>md mkt\wp
C:\RUNDOS>md mkt\budget
```

Now type the following to copy the files from the floppy disk to the hard disk:

```
C:\RUNDOS>copy a:\mkt\account mkt
        1 File(s) copied

C:\RUNDOS>copy a:\mkt\wp\*.* mkt\wp
A:\MKT\WP\LET1.DOC
A:\MKT\WP\LET2.DOC
A:\MKT\WP\LET3.DOC
A:\MKT\WP\RPT1.DOC
A:\MKT\WP\RPT2.DOC
A:\MKT\WP\RPT3.DOC
A:\MKT\WP\LET1.STY
A:\MKT\WP\LET2.STY
A:\MKT\WP\LET3.STY
        9 File(s) copied

C\RUNDOS>copy a:\mkt\budget\*.* mkt\budget
A:\MKT\BUDGET\BGT1.XLS
A:\MKT\BUDGET\BGT2.XLS
A:\MKT\BUDGET\BGT3.XLS
        3 File(s) copied
```

This completes the preparation.

# CHANGING THE ATTRIBUTES OF A FILE OR A DIRECTORY

The Attribute command lets you control the following attributes of a file or directory: *read-only*, *hidden*, *archive*, and *system*. You can use the Attribute command to control access to a file or a group of files by using read-only and hidden attributes. In short, if a file has the read-only attribute, you can view the contents of a file but can't change it. If a file has the hidden attribute (which is available in version 5 or later of MS-DOS), the file is hidden from view; you won't see it listed when you use the Directory command.

The hidden attribute is particularly useful with directories, both because it can help reduce screen clutter by omitting hidden directories from directory listings and because it can also help you hide directories and the files they contain from casual view.

If you're using version 3.2 or a later version of MS-DOS, you can also use the Attribute command to control the archive attribute of a file, which tells MS-DOS (or any other program that checks it) whether the file has been changed since the last time it was backed up for archival storage. Another attribute is the system attribute that is used to tell MS-DOS to treat a file as a system (program) file. If you have version 5 or later, you can use the system attribute. This attribute is normally used only by programmers.

This chapter describes the Attribute command in more detail and shows other examples of its use. The command has the following parameters:

**attrib +R -R +A -A +H -H +S -S <filename> /S**

+R turns on the read-only attribute; -R turns it off.

+A turns on the archive attribute (sometimes called the *archive bit*); -A turns it off.

+H turns on the hidden attribute; -H turns it off. If you have version 5 or later, you can use the hidden attribute.

+S turns on the system attribute; -S turns it off. If you have version 5 or later, you can use the system attribute.

<filename> is the drive, path, and name of the file or directory whose attributes are to be changed or displayed. You can use wildcard characters to specify a group of files. In versions 5 or later, you can omit <filename> to view or change the attributes of all files in the current directory. In effect, omitting the <filename> parameter in versions 5 or later is the same as specifying <filename> as *.*.

/S, in versions 3.3 and later, applies the Attribute command to each subdirectory contained in <filename>. If you specify <filename> as the root directory of a disk and include /S, the Attribute command is applied to every subdirectory on the disk.

Through version 4 of MS-DOS, if you omit all parameters except <filename>, MS-DOS displays the name or names of the files preceded by an A if the file has the archive attribute, an R if the file has the read-only attribute, or both if the file has both attributes set.

In versions 5 and later, omitting all parameters, including <filename> if you choose, causes MS-DOS to display the name or names of all files in the current directory. It precedes the file names with A and R for archive and read-only as it does in earlier versions, and uses H and S to indicate the hidden and system attributes.

## Examples of Changing the Archive Attribute

The archive attribute is a part of the directory entry that isn't displayed by the Directory command but that can be examined or changed by MS-DOS or another program that checks it. This attribute can be used by the Xcopy command described later in this chapter under the heading "Using the Xcopy Command" and by some programs that back up files from a hard disk. The archive attribute is turned on by the MS-DOS Editor, by Microsoft Word, and by most other programs that change a file. Because the archive attribute tells MS-DOS or another program whether a file has been changed since the last time (if ever) it was backed up, it is used principally by Xcopy and other programs to determine which files must be backed up.

To complete the following examples, change the current directory to \RUNDOS\MKT\WP by typing:

```
C:\RUNDOS>cd mkt\wp
```

As a first step, check the attributes of the files in the current directory. Type the following command if you have version 5 or later:

```
C:\RUNDOS\MKT\WP>attrib
```

Type this command if you have an earlier version:

```
C:\RUNDOS\MKT\WP>attrib *.*
```

MS-DOS responds with a display like the following:

```
A              C:\RUNDOS\MKT\WP\LET1.DOC
A              C:\RUNDOS\MKT\WP\LET2.DOC
A              C:\RUNDOS\MKT\WP\LET3.DOC
A              C:\RUNDOS\MKT\WP\RPT1.DOC
A              C:\RUNDOS\MKT\WP\RPT2.DOC
A              C:\RUNDOS\MKT\WP\RPT3.DOC
A              C:\RUNDOS\MKT\WP\LET1.STY
A              C:\RUNDOS\MKT\WP\LET2.STY
A              C:\RUNDOS\MKT\WP\LET3.STY
```

MS-DOS displays the name of each file with an A in column 3 because the files have never been backed up.

To turn off the archive attribute of all files with the extension DOC and check the result, type the following (in this and the following examples, you can omit the *.* if you're using version 5 or later):

```
C:\RUNDOS\MKT\WP>attrib -a *.doc

C:\RUNDOS\MKT\WP>attrib *.*
               C:\RUNDOS\MKT\WP\LET1.DOC
               C:\RUNDOS\MKT\WP\LET2.DOC
               C:\RUNDOS\MKT\WP\LET3.DOC
               C:\RUNDOS\MKT\WP\RPT1.DOC
               C:\RUNDOS\MKT\WP\RPT2.DOC
               C:\RUNDOS\MKT\WP\RPT3.DOC
A              C:\RUNDOS\MKT\WP\LET1.STY
A              C:\RUNDOS\MKT\WP\LET2.STY
A              C:\RUNDOS\MKT\WP\LET3.STY
```

Now only those files whose extension is STY have the archive attribute.

If you're using 3.3 or a later version of MS-DOS, you can use the /S parameter to apply the Attribute command to all subdirectories. To turn off the archive attribute of all files in the directories \RUNDOS\MKT, \RUNDOS\MKT\WP, and

\RUNDOS\MKT\BUDGET and then check the results in all three, type the following commands to change the directory to \RUNDOS\MKT, turn off the archive attribute of all files in all subdirectories, and check the attributes of all files in all subdirectories:

```
C:\RUNDOS\MKT\WP>cd ..

C:\RUNDOS\MKT>attrib -a *.* /s

C:\RUNDOS\MKT>attrib *.* /s
              C:\RUNDOS\MKT\WP\LET1.DOC
              C:\RUNDOS\MKT\WP\LET2.DOC
              C:\RUNDOS\MKT\WP\LET3.DOC
              C:\RUNDOS\MKT\WP\RPT1.DOC
              C:\RUNDOS\MKT\WP\RPT2.DOC
              C:\RUNDOS\MKT\WP\RPT3.DOC
              C:\RUNDOS\MKT\WP\LET1.STY
              C:\RUNDOS\MKT\WP\LET2.STY
              C:\RUNDOS\MKT\WP\LET3.STY
              C:\RUNDOS\MKT\BUDGET\BGT1.XLS
              C:\RUNDOS\MKT\BUDGET\BGT2.XLS
              C:\RUNDOS\MKT\BUDGET\BGT3.XLS
              C:\RUNDOS\MKT\ACCOUNT
```

The response to the second Attribute command shows that you turned off the archive attribute of all the files in \RUNDOS\MKT\WP, \RUNDOS\MKT\BUDGET, and \RUNDOS\MKT.

If you don't have version 5 or later, type the following command to turn on the archive attributes of all files in all subdirectories in \RUNDOS\MKT. (Examples later in the chapter assume the attributes are turned on.)

```
C:\RUNDOS\MKT>attrib +a *.* /s
```

Now go on to the heading "Copying Selected Files."

If you do have version 5 or later, the following examples give you practice with other file attributes.

## Examples of Changing Other Attributes

As already mentioned, the hidden attribute can be useful in minimizing screen clutter and, to some extent, in hiding files and directories from casual view. Because an experienced user of MS-DOS would know how to search for hidden files and directories, however, consider this attribute more of a convenience than a security measure.

To apply and change the hidden attribute with both directories and files, begin by hiding the \RUNDOS\MKT\BUDGET directory. Type:

```
C:\RUNDOS\MKT>attrib +h budget
```

Now tell MS-DOS to show the directory for \RUNDOS and all its subdirectories, pausing after each screenful:

```
C:\RUNDOS\MKT>dir \rundos /s /p
```

MS-DOS lists \RUNDOS, \RUNDOS\MKT, and \RUNDOS\MKT\WP and the files they contain, but it does not list the BUDGET directory or any of its files. However, if you use the /A parameter of the Directory command to tell MS-DOS to list all hidden files and directories in \RUNDOS and its subdirectories:

```
C:\RUNDOS\MKT>dir \rundos /ah /s
```

MS-DOS displays:

```
    Volume in drive C is HARD DISK
    Volume Serial Number is 1608-5A30

Directory of C:\RUNDOS\MKT

BUDGET        <DIR>      10-16-93   8:21a
        1 file(s)             0 bytes

Total files listed:
        1 file(s)             0 bytes
                    15159296 bytes free
```

And if you check the attributes of \RUNDOS\MKT\BUDGET:

```
C:\RUNDOS\MKT>attrib budget
```

You see:

```
      H       C:\RUNDOS\MKT\BUDGET
```

Next, to see how hiding files differs from hiding a directory, first remove the hidden attribute from \RUNDOS\MKT\BUDGET:

```
C:\RUNDOS\MKT>attrib -h budget
```

To reduce your typing chores, change to the \RUNDOS\MKT\BUDGET directory:

```
C:\RUNDOS\MKT>cd budget
```

Now apply the hidden attribute to the three files in the directory:

```
C:\RUNDOS\MKT\BUDGET>attrib +h *.xls
```

Type the command *dir \rundos /s /p* to again display the directory for \RUNDOS and all its subdirectories. This time, MS-DOS shows that \RUNDOS\MKT\BUDGET exists, but notice that the directory doesn't seem to contain any files. You removed the hidden attribute from the directory, so MS-DOS has no trouble including it in the listing, but you added the hidden attribute to the files in the directory, so now MS-DOS refuses to report on the contents of the directory. Even when you display the directory itself, MS-DOS does not show the hidden files:

```
C:\RUNDOS\MKT\BUDGET>dir

 Volume in drive C is HARD DISK
 Volume Serial Number is 1608-5A30
 Directory of C:\RUNDOS\MKT\BUDGET

 .              <DIR>      10-16-93    8:21a
 ..             <DIR>      10-16-93    8:21a
        2 file(s)            0 bytes
                      15159296 bytes free
```

Check the attributes of the files in this directory, however, and MS-DOS responds:

```
C:\RUNDOS\MKT\BUDGET>attrib *.xls
      H        C:\RUNDOS\MKT\BUDGET\BGT1.XLS
      H        C:\RUNDOS\MKT\BUDGET\BGT2.XLS
      H        C:\RUNDOS\MKT\BUDGET\BGT3.XLS
```

When files are hidden, you can't change their other attributes. For example, suppose you decide to make the files read-only; try it by typing:

```
C:\RUNDOS\MKT\BUDGET>attrib +r *.xls
```

MS-DOS refuses:

```
Not resetting hidden file C:\RUNDOS\MKT\BUDGET\BGT1.XLS
Not resetting hidden file C:\RUNDOS\MKT\BUDGET\BGT2.XLS
Not resetting hidden file C:\RUNDOS\MKT\BUDGET\BGT3.XLS
```

You can, however, change other attributes if you also specify the hidden attribute. Make the files both read-only and hidden with one Attribute command:

```
C:\RUNDOS\MKT\BUDGET>attrib +r +h *.xls
```

Check the attributes again:

```
C:\RUNDOS\MKT\BUDGET>attrib *.xls
      HR       C:\RUNDOS\MKT\BUDGET\BGT1.XLS
      HR       C:\RUNDOS\MKT\BUDGET\BGT2.XLS
      HR       C:\RUNDOS\MKT\BUDGET\BGT3.XLS
```

MS-DOS reports the files are now both hidden (H) and read-only (R).

To return all the files in RUNDOS and its subdirectories to their original state, first remove the hidden and read-only attributes from the budget files:

```
C:\RUNDOS\MKT\BUDGET>attrib -r -h *.xls
```

Now change the current directory to C:\RUNDOS\MKT, and turn on the archive attribute of all files in C:\RUNDOS\MKT and all its subdirectories:

```
C:\RUNDOS\MKT\BUDGET>cd ..
C:\RUNDOS\MKT>attrib +a *.* /s
```

# COPYING SELECTED FILES

In earlier chapters, you saw that you can copy files with similar names or extensions by using the Copy command and wildcard characters. If you're using 3.2 or a later version of MS-DOS, you have even more flexibility in copying files:

- The Replace command lets you replace all files in every subdirectory of a target disk that have the same name as the files on a source disk. The Replace command also lets you copy only the files on a source disk that *don't* exist on the target disk or in a target directory. Beginning with version 4, the Replace command also lets you update files by replacing only those on the target disk that are *older* than those of the same name on the source disk.

- The Xcopy command, as you saw in preparing for this chapter's examples, lets you copy whole subdirectories and the files in them. It also lets you copy only files that have changed since they were last backed up or those that have changed since a particular date.

## Replacing Files on a Disk

The Replace command, like the Copy command, copies files from one disk or directory to another. The Replace command, however, is more selective:

- If used without the /A or /U parameter, the Replace command copies only source files that also exist on the target; it *replaces* files, hence its name.

- If used with the /A parameter, it lets you reverse the operation of the Replace command and tell it to copy only source files that *don't* exist on the target; with this option, it only *adds* files.

- If used with the /U parameter, the Replace command lets you copy only source files that are newer than files of the same name on the target; with this option, it *updates* files.

As a further refinement, the Replace command also lets you copy files not only from the source directory but also from all the subdirectories the source contains.

The Replace command has eight parameters:

**replace <source> <target> /A /S /R /P /U /W**

<source> is the name of the file to be copied. You can use wildcard characters to replace a set of files that have similar file names or extensions.

<target> specifies where <source> is to be copied. You can include a drive letter and a path name.

/A (for *add*) copies only the files specified in <source> that don't exist in <target>. This lets you add files to <target> without replacing files that already exist. If you don't specify /A, only files specified in <source> that also exist in <target> are copied. If you specify /A, you cannot specify /S or /U.

/S applies the Replace command to all subdirectories contained in <target>. If you specify <target> as the root directory of a disk, the command is applied to every subdirectory on the disk. If you specify /S, you cannot specify /A.

/R replaces those files in <target> that are read-only in addition to those that are normally replaced.

/P prompts you for confirmation before it replaces or adds each file.

/U (for *update*) replaces only those files on the target disk that are older than the corresponding files on the source disk. If you specify /U, you cannot specify /A.

/W prompts you to press a key before the Replace command begins. This lets you put in the correct floppy disk before starting to replace or add files.

To see how the Replace command works, copy the file named LET1.DOC from \RUNDOS\MKT\WP to \RUNDOS\MKT\BUDGET and then check the directory by typing:

```
C:\RUNDOS\MKT>copy wp\let1.doc budget
        1 file(s) copied

C:\RUNDOS\MKT>dir budget

 Volume in drive C is HARD DISK
 Volume Serial Number is 1608-5A30
 Directory of C:\RUNDOS\MKT\BUDGET

 .              <DIR>       10-16-93     8:21a
 ..             <DIR>       10-16-93     8:21a
 BGT1    XLS          24 10-16-93     8:17a
 BGT2    XLS          24 10-16-93     8:17a
 BGT3    XLS          24 10-16-93     8:17a
 LET1    DOC          24 10-16-93     8:17a
        6 file(s)           96 bytes
                     15157248 bytes free
```

Now use the Replace command with no parameters to replace every file in the directory \RUNDOS\MKT\BUDGET whose name begins with LET and whose extension is DOC that also exists in \RUNDOS\MKT\WP. Type:

```
C:\RUNDOS\MKT>replace wp\let*.doc budget
```

MS-DOS responds:

```
Replacing C:\RUNDOS\MKT\BUDGET\LET1.DOC

1 file(s) replaced
```

The Replace command copied only the file—the one you copied at the beginning of this example—that already existed in \RUNDOS\MKT\BUDGET. The message tells you that MS-DOS *replaced* one existing file.

Now type the Replace command again, but this time include the /A parameter, which tells MS-DOS to copy only those files that do *not* exist in the target; you're doing the opposite of what you did with the previous Replace command:

```
C:\RUNDOS\MKT>replace wp\let*.doc budget /a
```

MS-DOS responds:

```
Adding C:\RUNDOS\MKT\BUDGET\LET2.DOC

Adding C:\RUNDOS\MKT\BUDGET\LET3.DOC

2 file(s) added
```

This time the Replace command copied the files that it didn't copy in the previous example. The message tells you that MS-DOS *added* files to the target directory.

Finally, if you have version 4 or later of MS-DOS, see how you can update files. Begin by creating a newer version of LET1.DOC in the directory \RUNDOS\MKT\WP:

```
C:\RUNDOS\MKT>copy con wp\let1.doc
This is a newer file.
^Z
        1 file(s) copied
```

Now you have one version of the file in \RUNDOS\MKT\BUDGET and a newer version with the same file name in \RUNDOS\MKT\WP. Update all files in the BUDGET subdirectory by typing:

```
C:\RUNDOS\MKT>replace wp\let*.doc budget /u
```

MS-DOS responds:

```
Replacing C:\RUNDOS\MKT\BUDGET\LET1.DOC

1 file(s) replaced
```

This time, MS-DOS compared matching file names and updated only the one, LET1.DOC, that had a more recent version in the source directory than in the target directory.

## Using the Xcopy Command

In preparing for this chapter, you used the Xcopy command to move an entire directory structure from one disk to another. If the corresponding subdirectories don't exist on the target disk or directory, the Xcopy command creates them.

Unlike Copy and Replace, Xcopy can be used to copy only files whose archive attribute is on or files that have been changed since a date you specify.

The Xcopy command has 10 parameters:

**xcopy <source> <target> /A /M /D:<date> /E /P /S /V /W**

<source> is the name of the file to be copied. You can include a path name, and you can use wildcard characters to copy a set of files with similar file names or extensions.

<target> specifies where <source> is to be copied. You can include any combination of drive letter, path name, and file name. If you specify different drives, the target directory does not have to have the same name as the source directory.

/A copies only those files whose archive attribute is on and leaves the archive attribute of the source unchanged.

/M copies only those files whose archive attribute is on and turns off the archive attribute of the source. This tells MS-DOS (or any other program) that the file hasn't been changed since it was last backed up and therefore doesn't need to be backed up again.

/D:<date> copies only files created or changed on or after <date>. (The date of creation or last change is the date shown in the directory entry for any file. Enter <date> just as you would for the Date command.)

/E creates subdirectories in <target> even if they're empty in <source>. This parameter can be used only when /S is used.

/P prompts for confirmation before each file specified in <source> is copied.

/S applies the Xcopy command to all subdirectories contained in <source> that are not empty. If you specify <source> as the root directory of a disk, the Xcopy command is applied to every non-empty subdirectory on the disk.

/V verifies that the copy of the file on <target> was stored correctly. This can slow the operation of the Xcopy command somewhat, but it's good insurance if you're copying critical data and must be certain that it was copied correctly.

/W prompts you to press a key before the Xcopy command begins. This wait gives you a chance to put in the correct floppy disk before starting to copy files.

For this example, you create a temporary subdirectory named FRED in the root directory and dispose of it at the end of the example. First, change the current directory to \RUNDOS:

```
C:\RUNDOS\MKT>cd ..
```

Now type the following Make Directory command:

```
C:\RUNDOS>md \fred
```

and add the following sample file to \RUNDOS:

```
C:\RUNDOS>copy con test.doc
This is a test file.
^Z
        1 file(s) copied
```

All the files in \RUNDOS and its subdirectories have the archive attribute turned on. For the first Xcopy command, use the /A parameter to copy all the files in \RUNDOS whose extension is DOC and whose archive attribute is turned on:

```
C:\RUNDOS>xcopy *.doc \fred /a
```

MS-DOS responds by displaying the name of each source file as it is copied:

```
Reading source file(s)...
TEST.DOC
        1 File(s) copied
```

MS-DOS copied TEST.DOC, the only file in \RUNDOS whose extension is DOC. Verify this by displaying the directory of \FRED:

```
C:\RUNDOS>dir \fred

 Volume in drive C is HARD DISK
 Volume Serial Number is 1608-5A30
 Directory of C:\FRED

.            <DIR>      10-16-93  12:28p
..           <DIR>      10-16-93  12:28p
TEST     DOC        22 10-16-93  12:35p
        3 file(s)           22 bytes
                     14096384 bytes free
```

Now type the same Xcopy command, but add the /S parameter to copy all files whose extension is DOC and whose archive attribute is turned on, not only in \RUNDOS but also in all its subdirectories:

```
C:\RUNDOS>xcopy *.doc \fred /a /s
Reading source file(s)...
TEST.DOC
MKT\WP\LET1.DOC
MKT\WP\LET2.DOC
MKT\WP\LET3.DOC
MKT\WP\RPT1.DOC
MKT\WP\RPT2.DOC
MKT\WP\RPT3.DOC
MKT\BUDGET\LET1.DOC
MKT\BUDGET\LET2.DOC
MKT\BUDGET\LET3.DOC
        10 File(s) copied
```

This time MS-DOS copied 10 files; it also copied the subdirectories named MKT\WP and MKT\BUDGET. Verify this by displaying the directory of \FRED\MKT:

```
C:\RUNDOS>dir \fred\mkt

 Volume in drive C is HARD DISK
 Volume Serial Number is 1608-5A30
 Directory of C:\FRED\MKT

 .              <DIR>      10-16-93   12:28p
 ..             <DIR>      10-16-93   12:28p
 WP             <DIR>      10-16-93   12:39p
 BUDGET         <DIR>      10-16-93   12:39p
        4 file(s)              0 bytes
                       14071808 bytes free
```

The Xcopy command created the subdirectories named WP and BUDGET in \FRED, then copied the files whose extension is DOC and whose archive attribute is on from the \RUNDOS\MKT\WP directory to \FRED\MKT\WP and from the \RUNDOS\MKT\BUDGET directory to \FRED\MKT\BUDGET.

The value of the archive attribute, however, is that it can tell you which files have changed since they were last backed up—if the archive attribute is turned off when a file is backed up and it is turned on when a file is changed. The /M parameter, like the /A parameter, tells Xcopy to copy only those files whose archive attribute is on; but it also turns the archive attribute off on the source file so that you can mark the files as backed up. Type another Xcopy command to copy the files whose extension is DOC, but this time use /M instead of /A:

```
C:\RUNDOS>xcopy *.doc \fred /m /s
```

MS-DOS responds just as it did to the previous Xcopy command because it copied the same 10 files, but this time it turned their archive attributes off. It's easy to check this; retype the last Xcopy command:

```
C:\RUNDOS>xcopy *.doc \fred /m /s
        0 File(s) copied
```

This time no files were copied because the previous command turned off the archive attributes of the files.

Now suppose you change one of the files. A new file's archive attribute is on, just as if it were an existing file you changed with the MS-DOS Editor or with a word processor, so type the following to create a different version of \RUNDOS\TEST.DOC:

```
C:\RUNDOS>copy con test.doc
A new version of TEST.DOC.
^Z
        1 file(s) copied
```

Type the same Xcopy command you typed twice before; the first time Xcopy copied 10 files, the second time it copied no files, and this time it should copy one file:

```
C:\RUNDOS>xcopy *.doc \fred /m /s
Reading source file(s)...
TEST.DOC
        1 file(s) copied
```

Xcopy copied only the file whose archive attribute was on.

You'll be using only the RUNDOS directory structure in later chapters, so if you have version 6 or 6.2 of MS-DOS, type the following command to dispose of the directory you added for this example:

```
C:\RUNDOS>deltree \fred
Delete directory "\fred" and all its subdirectories? [yn] y
Deleting \fred...
```

If you have an earlier version, type the following commands:

```
C:\RUNDOS>del \fred\mkt\wp\*.doc
C:\RUNDOS>rd \fred\mkt\wp
C:\RUNDOS>del \fred\mkt\budget\*.doc
C:\RUNDOS>rd \fred\mkt\budget
C:\RUNDOS>rd \fred\mkt
C:\RUNDOS>del \fred\test.doc
C:\RUNDOS>rd \fred
```

Next change the current directory back to \RUNDOS\MKT:

```
C:\RUNDOS>cd mkt
```

and, finally, clean up your \RUNDOS\MKT\BUDGET directory:

```
C:\RUNDOS\MKT>del budget\let*.doc
```

# STRETCHING YOUR HARD DISK

A hard disk is fast, durable, holds a lot more than a floppy disk, and generally does its job with little attention from you. It has one drawback, though: Hard disks, like garages and kitchen drawers, tend to fill up much more quickly than we expect (or would like).

When your hard disk fills up, the quickest way to alleviate the problem is to delete files you no longer need and archive files you might need at some point in the future. This housekeeping is time consuming, but you should do it periodically to make sure that you don't lose track of important files in the welter of other files that inevitably accumulate.

For a longer term solution, you can attack the problem from either the hardware side or the software side. On the hardware side, you can buy a larger hard disk and transfer your files to it or buy another hard disk and add it to your system. Both of these are fairly expensive propositions, and transferring your files to a new hard disk can take quite a while.

The software solution is simpler and more appealing: Using mathematical techniques, a program can reduce the number of bytes in a file—*compress* the file—without losing any of the information in the file. Starting with version 6, MS-DOS includes the compression program DoubleSpace, which compresses your hard disk. That is, it compresses all the files on your hard disk. If you have version 5 or earlier, however, go on to the heading "MS-DOS and Your Hard Disk."

Although the files on your disk will be compressed, the only difference you'll see on your disk will be a lot more available space. MS-DOS does the compressing behind the scenes. When you write a file to the disk, MS-DOS automatically compresses it. When you read the file, MS-DOS expands it, returning the file to its original state. For example, when you use the MS-DOS Editor to read a file, MS-DOS expands that file so that Edit can read its contents. You'll also notice that when you use the Directory command to see a list of the files in a directory on your compressed disk, MS-DOS displays the files' expanded sizes. And, if you copy a file from your compressed disk to an uncompressed floppy disk, MS-DOS will expand the file before copying it.

## Compression Isn't Free

DoubleSpace will, indeed, make your disk seem about twice as large as it was before. Although the physical capacity of the disk doesn't change, compressing the files lets the disk hold about twice as much.

Nothing is free, of course. The price you pay for doubling the capacity of your hard disk is about 35 KB of memory that the DoubleSpace program requires. DoubleSpace will always be running after you compress your disk so that MS-DOS can compress and expand files as they're read from and written to the disk. Thanks to the memory management capabilities of MS-DOS, however, you can run DoubleSpace in upper memory so that you can minimize the effect of using up a lot of memory.

## Compressing Your Hard Disk with DoubleSpace

To compress your hard disk, run the DoubleSpace setup program by typing *dblspace* at the system prompt. DoubleSpace displays its opening setup screen, which lets you choose to continue, learn more about DoubleSpace setup, or quit. Press Enter to continue. The next screen tells you that you can either let DoubleSpace make most of the decisions about the setup for you (*Express Setup*) or make the decisions yourself (*Custom Setup*):

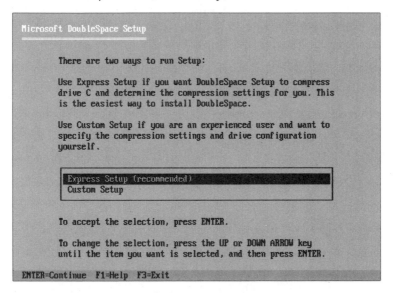

Press Enter to accept *Express Setup.*

The next screen gives you a chance to turn back before installing DoubleSpace and compressing your disk. Press C to start the process.

If you have MS-DOS version 6.2, the DoubleSpace setup program first runs the ScanDisk program to make sure that your hard disk is free of errors. (You'll read more about ScanDisk later in this chapter under the heading "Checking a Disk for Errors.") If you have version 6, the setup program runs ChkDsk at this point. The setup program then examines your system and restarts your computer. Next DoubleSpace compresses the files on your hard drive, which it assumes is drive C. This might take a long time; the larger your hard disk, the longer it will take. DoubleSpace lets you know how much time it estimates the process will take and displays the name of the file it is currently compressing. When it finishes with the compression, DoubleSpace runs the Defrag program (which we'll discuss later in this chapter under the heading "Storing Files Efficiently on Disk") to organize your hard disk. This, too, can take a while. DoubleSpace then restarts your system to complete the process.

After your system restarts, everything should work just as it did before. In normal use, the only difference you'll notice is a lot more room on your hard disk. A little checking, though, will reveal an extra disk drive that wasn't there before. If your hard disk is drive C, for example, now you have a drive H too.

But you haven't added a hard disk drive, of course, so how can there be another disk drive? DoubleSpace is responsible. To perform its magic, DoubleSpace creates a file called a *compressed volume file*, which acts as drive C (the compressed drive). Drive H is the uncompressed drive that contains the compressed volume file. Drive H also stores hidden system files that MS-DOS uses when you start your machine and any other files that you don't want compressed. By default, DoubleSpace leaves 2 MB of disk space free on drive H. Copy files to drive H only if you don't want them compressed.

## Compressing a Floppy Disk

You can use DoubleSpace to compress a floppy disk just as you compressed your hard disk. Insert the floppy disk in drive A, and type *dblspace*. This time, you see DoubleSpace's main screen (Figure 9-2), which shows you that drive C is a compressed drive.

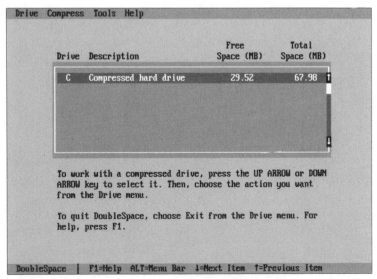

**Figure 9-2.**
*DoubleSpace's main screen.*

The bar at the top of the main screen contains four menus: Drive, Compress, Tools, and Help. These menus contain commands that cause DoubleSpace to perform actions. To access a menu, press the Alt key and then the first letter of the menu's name. (If you have a mouse, you can access a menu by positioning the mouse pointer over the menu name and pressing the left mouse button.) To compress a floppy disk, first open the Compress menu by pressing Alt and then C, and then choose the *Existing drive* command in the menu by pressing Enter. (You can access the other commands in a menu by pressing the Down arrow key until the command you want is highlighted.) DoubleSpace checks to see whether any drives can be compressed and then tells you which ones it found. Chances are your list includes only drive A, but if you have another hard disk that you didn't compress or if you've defined a RAM disk, the list might include more than one drive letter. Using the arrow keys if necessary, highlight the line for the A drive and press Enter.

Now DoubleSpace gives you a chance to change your mind; press C to start compressing the floppy disk in drive A. DoubleSpace tells you approximately how long the process will take and then starts compressing. When it finishes, it displays the list of compressed drives again, this time adding drive A and identifying it as a *Compressed floppy disk.*

Now your floppy disk has nearly twice as much space available as it did before. If it had files on it before you compressed the drive, you'll see that the files are still available. As when you compressed your hard disk, your system has another disk drive: drive G. DoubleSpace uses this uncompressed drive for maintaining the files on the disk. Because it doesn't contain much free space, drive G isn't much use for storing uncompressed files. If you need to put uncompressed files on a disk, simply use an uncompressed disk.

Note that you can use compressed floppy disks only on machines that are running DoubleSpace. If you want to transfer files to a computer that isn't using DoubleSpace, be sure to copy the files to an uncompressed floppy disk. Also, MS-DOS doesn't allow you to use the Format command to format a compressed disk. Instead, use the /format parameter with the DoubleSpace command. For example, when you type

```
C:\>dblspace /format a:
```

DoubleSpace reformats the compressed disk in drive A. It deletes all the files but keeps the information that makes it compressed.

## Mounting or Unmounting a Drive

> **NOTE:** *If you're using version 6.2 of MS-DOS, DoubleSpace automatically recognizes, or* mounts, *a compressed floppy disk; the following topic doesn't apply to your system unless you choose to turn off automatic mounting. Skip to the heading "Removing DoubleSpace."*

When you first compress a floppy disk, DoubleSpace makes it available to MS-DOS for you, a process DoubleSpace calls *mounting* the disk. The process of making the disk unavailable to MS-DOS is called *unmounting*. If you change floppy disks or restart your computer, you need to mount the floppy disk in order to use it.

The terms mount and unmount may seem odd. They are names that have survived from the earliest days of computing, long before personal computers were even imagined. Think about how computers are usually pictured in movies or cartoons: a refrigerator-like appliance with two large round devices at about eye level. This machine is a tape drive, used on early mainframe computers for most data storage because disk drives were enormously expensive. The round devices are the supply and take-up reels for the magnetic tape, and the act of loading a reel of tape into a tape drive was (and still is) called *mounting* the tape. DoubleSpace uses the term a bit differently.

Your hard disk should remain mounted at all times. In fact, DoubleSpace won't let you unmount the drive from which you start MS-DOS. But you have to mount a floppy disk drive each time you insert a different compressed floppy disk in it. Otherwise MS-DOS won't treat the disk as a compressed disk. In fact, if you use the Directory command to see what is on an unmounted compressed floppy disk, all you'll see is a file called READTHIS.TXT. To read it, type:

```
A:\>type readthis.txt
```

Here is the contents of the file:

```
This disk has been compressed by MS-DOS 6 DoubleSpace.

To make this disk's contents accessible, change to this drive and then type
   DBLSPACE /MOUNT
at the command prompt.
```

To mount a compressed floppy disk from the main DoubleSpace screen (Figure 9-2), insert the floppy disk in a drive. Use drive A for this example. Choose the Mount command from the Drive menu. (Press Alt then D to open the menu, then press the Down arrow key three times and press Enter.) DoubleSpace searches for unmounted compressed drives and displays the ones it finds, as shown at the top of the next page.

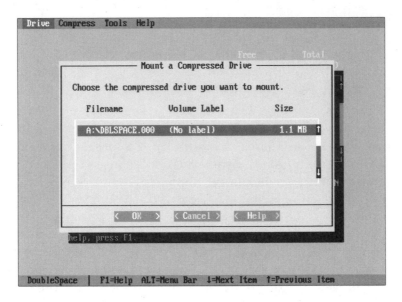

In addition to the name of the uncompressed drive, DoubleSpace lists the name of the compressed volume file, which is the file on your disk that contains the compressed drive. Next use the Up or Down arrow keys to select the compressed disk you want to mount. In this example, you would select A:\DBLSPACE.000. DoubleSpace mounts the floppy disk and then updates the list of compressed drives on the main DoubleSpace screen. Quit DoubleSpace by choosing Exit from the Drive menu. The compressed floppy disk remains mounted until you change floppy disks or restart your computer.

To mount a compressed floppy disk at the system prompt, insert the floppy disk in a drive. Type *dblspace /mount* and the letter of the drive the floppy disk is in. For example, if you're using drive A, type:

```
C:\>dblspace /mount a:
```

DoubleSpace displays messages telling you it is mounting the drive and then that it has mounted the drive successfully. The compressed floppy disk remains mounted until you change floppy disks or restart your computer.

Although it means a bit more effort when you use compressed floppy disks, DoubleSpace is nonetheless a virtually cost-free way to double the storage capacity of all the disks you use.

> **NOTE:** *You can use DoubleSpace to further manage your compressed drives. You can change their sizes, create new drives from free disk space, view information about all your drives, and more. See Appendix C, "MS-DOS Command Reference," and your* MS-DOS User's Guide *for more information.*

## Removing DoubleSpace

If you're using version 6.2 of MS-DOS and decide that you want to stop using file compression and return to the normal capacity of your hard disk, you can use the /U (Uncompress) parameter of the DoubleSpace command. The process takes about the same amount of time that it took to compress the disk.

If you're using version 6 or 6.2 of MS-DOS, you must copy all the compressed files that you want to keep to an uncompressed disk, then delete the hidden files that DoubleSpace uses. The additional hard disk volume that DoubleSpace created (probably drive H if you have one hard disk) is uncompressed, but it almost certainly doesn't have nearly enough space to hold all the files on your compressed disk (probably drive C).

> **NOTE:** *If you're not yet familiar with MS-DOS, you should probably get some assistance from a more experienced user before you delete DoubleSpace using version 6 or 6.2. Certain types of mistakes could cause the loss of some files or even the loss of the use of your hard disk. The following instructions are not meant to be a step-by-step example; follow these instructions* only *if you want to delete DoubleSpace from your system.*

If your hard disk was less than half full when you installed DoubleSpace and you haven't stored a lot of new files on the compressed disk since then, you can probably use DoubleSpace to increase the amount of uncompressed space and reduce the amount of available space on the compressed disk. Then you can simply use the Xcopy command to save the files you need.

To increase the amount of uncompressed space, start DoubleSpace by typing *dblspace*, then choose *Change Size* from the Drive menu. DoubleSpace displays a dialog box showing the current, minimum, and maximum sizes of the volume file (DBLSPACE.000) on both the uncompressed drive and the compressed drive (probably drive C). The cursor is in the field labeled *New size*, which should contain the same value as the *Current Size* field for DBLSPACE.000. Enter a value a bit larger than the *Minimum Size* field for DBLSPACE.000, and press Enter. DoubleSpace tells you that it's changing the size of drive C, then tells you that it's remounting drive C.

When control returns, leave DoubleSpace, and use the Xcopy command to copy all the files on drive C you want to keep to the uncompressed drive. For example, if you've got room for all the compressed files and the uncompressed drive is drive H, you would type *xcopy \*.\* h:\ /s*. At a minimum, you'll want to save the MS-DOS files and the root directory. When you've finished copying the files you want to save, you're ready to delete DoubleSpace.

If you don't have enough space on your hard disk to hold uncompressed versions of the files you want to save, you'll have to back them up to floppy disks using MSbackup or the Xcopy command. When you have backed them up, you're ready to delete DoubleSpace.

Now you must delete the Device command that DoubleSpace puts in CON-FIG.SYS and the files it creates in the root directory. You can use Edit to delete the line in CONFIG.SYS that reads *device=c:\dos\dblspace.sys*. The line might read *device-high=* instead of *device=*, and the command might include some parameters, such as */L:2,52272*.

Before you can delete the DoubleSpace files in the root directory, you'll have to make the files accessible with the Attribute command (*attrib -s -h -r h:\dblspace.\**), then delete them with the Delete command (*del h:\dblspace.\**). Press Ctrl-Alt-Del to restart the system, then type a Directory command and see how many bytes are available on the disk; your disk should be back to its non-compressed size.

## Checking a Disk for Errors

Starting with version 6.2, MS-DOS includes a program called ScanDisk that does a more thorough job of checking for and correcting disk errors than the Check Disk (chkdsk) command of earlier versions. The DoubleSpace program uses ScanDisk to make sure that the files on a disk can safely be compressed. (The Check Disk command remains in MS-DOS, but you should use ScanDisk whenever you want to check your disks.)

ScanDisk checks both the directory structure information of the files on a disk and the surface of the disk itself for errors. In many cases, ScanDisk can correct structure errors—thereby recovering lost data—or move files from areas where the disk surface is damaged to undamaged locations. You can also use ScanDisk to check the compressed volume file that contains the files stored on a disk compressed with DoubleSpace.

Like other MS-DOS programs, such as MSbackup and DoubleSpace, Scan-Disk displays its own menus and dialog boxes, letting you choose your options with either the keyboard or a mouse.

> **NOTE:** *You can specify all the ScanDisk options with command parameters, but this form of using ScanDisk is much less convenient and is included primarily to let you run the program from a batch file. If you would like to do this, the MS-DOS online help contains a complete description of all the parameters. Type* help scan-disk *for this information.*

The command to start ScanDisk has one parameter:

```
scandisk <drive>
```

<drive> is the letter, followed by a colon, of the drive to be checked. If you don't specify <drive>, MS-DOS checks the current drive.

```
Microsoft ScanDisk

ScanDisk is now checking the following areas of drive C:

     √    Media descriptor
     »    File allocation tables
          Directory structure
          File system
          Surface scan




     ◄ Pause ►    ‹ More Info ›    ‹ Exit ›


     78% complete    ▓▓▓▓▓▓▓▓▓▓▓▓▓▓▓▓▓▓▓▓▓
```

Start ScanDisk by typing *scandisk*. ScanDisk displays its opening screen and begins checking the disk. This screen tells you which area of the disk ScanDisk is checking. The process takes just a few moments.

If ScanDisk detects errors in the file structure, it displays a dialog box titled *Problem Found* and gives you the options of saving the questionable data in a file in the root directory (just as the Check Disk command does), deleting the data, or simply ignoring it (leaving the disk unchanged). Unless you're missing some data, choose Delete.

If you choose to delete the data, ScanDisk displays another dialog box, titled Create Undo Disk, that gives you the option of having ScanDisk create a file on a floppy disk—one that you can later use to reverse the steps that ScanDisk takes to delete the unwanted data and restore the disk to its previous condition. This only works if you use the undo disk before making any other changes to the disk, however. If you try to undo the deletion after changing the disk, ScanDisk won't be able to reconstruct the data and may damage the data structure, causing the loss of important files. Because the least bit of activity can cause one or two files to change on the disk, you probably shouldn't create an undo disk.

When ScanDisk finishes checking the file structure on the disk, it asks you whether you want to check the surface of the disk for defects. Although the estimates it displays are overly pessimistic, the process can still take several minutes. For now, choose No and return to the system prompt. You should, however, use ScanDisk to check the surface of your disk every couple of months to correct any problems that might develop before they cause the loss of valuable data.

## STORING FILES EFFICIENTLY ON DISK

As described in Chapter 6, "Managing Your Floppy Disks," files on a disk can become *fragmented* (stored in two or more chunks in different parts of the disk) as you work with them, leaving unused spaces scattered around the disk. This can slow down your system, especially if many files are fragmented, because it takes MS-DOS longer to read and write files that aren't stored neatly in one place. You could experience a significant slowdown if all the available space on a disk were broken up into many small unused areas, requiring MS-DOS to break up every file you work with.

If you have version 6 or 6.2, you can use the MS-DOS Defrag program to pack all the files on a disk into one compact area, with each file stored in one location. Defrag lets you choose your options from menus; to start it, type *defrag*. After displaying a copyright notice, the Defrag program tells you it's testing system memory and then displays its opening screen:

Most likely, Defrag will highlight the line containing *C:*, suggesting that you optimize (or reorganize the files on) drive C. If it did, press Enter; if not, use the arrow keys to highlight *C:* and then press Enter. (If you prefer using the mouse, you can double-click on *C:* to choose it.) Defrag reads the files on the disk and then displays a box titled *Recommendation* that suggests whether you should optimize only the files, do a full optimization (moving directories, too, if necessary), or possibly not optimize at all.

## Map of a Fragmented Disk

Regardless of the recommendation displayed in the dialog box, the main part of the screen shows a map of how the space on your disk is used. Each rectangle represents a portion of your disk. The map legend is in the lower right corner. Used areas appear white and unused areas appear gray, so if you see any large white areas that contain smaller gray areas, you're looking at a fragmented disk:

If your disk isn't badly fragmented, Defrag might recommend that you optimize only the files. Doing so will leave a few unused areas on the disk. To gain the maximum benefit from packing the files (and to see how full optimization works), you can request a full optimization. This isn't necessary, though; in most cases, if Defrag recommends that you optimize only the files, doing so will be sufficient.

If Defrag recommends full optimization, press Enter, and then go on to the next paragraph here. If Defrag does not recommend full optimization, press Esc to clear the Recommendation box. Defrag immediately displays the Optimize menu. Press the Down arrow key twice and then press Enter to choose *Optimization Method.* Now Defrag displays a box titled *Select Optimization Method* with *Full Optimization* selected. Press Enter, and then, when Defrag displays the Optimize menu again, highlight *Begin Optimization* by pressing the Up arrow key twice, and press Enter.

Now the optimization process begins. Defrag reorganizes all the files on the disk in order to pack them together. It displays a lowercase *r* in place of a white rectangle when it's reading a portion of a file to be moved, and an uppercase *W* when it writes the file in its new location. As you watch, any gray areas surrounded by white on the map should be disappearing, starting at the beginning of the disk (the upper left of the map).

Defrag displays *Finished condensing* when it finishes the defragmentation process. Press Enter to acknowledge the message. Next Defrag displays a dialog box that offers you the choice of condensing another drive, configuring the program, or exiting. Press the Right arrow key twice and press Enter to choose <Exit>, or press Esc to leave Defrag and return to MS-DOS.

You can also run Defrag by typing a command at the MS-DOS prompt and using parameters to specify the options. (The form of the command is shown in Appendix C, "MS-DOS Command Reference.") If you use a program that routinely modifies many files every day—for example, a word processor or data base program—and you want your system to run as quickly as possible, you could put the command *defrag c: /f* in your AUTOEXEC.BAT file. The /F parameter specifies a full optimization, so Defrag would fully optimize your hard disk every time you started or restarted your system.

## MS-DOS AND YOUR HARD DISK

Now that you're familiar with directories and with the commands you use to manage them, you can look at your own system and put some of your knowledge to work.

Because a hard disk can hold so many files, it's important to create a directory structure that lets you keep track of your files and programs. You can set up your subdirectories to match the way you use your computer, organizing them by department, application program, people's names, or any other way that's comfortable.

Until you get a directory structure established, however, files have a tendency to collect in the root directory, making it difficult to find a file you need. If you reserve the root directory for nothing but subdirectories and files that must be there, finding your way around your hard disk becomes much easier.

If you've been using your hard disk for some time and haven't known about or paid much attention to the idea of creating a directory structure on it, it's possible that the root directory of your hard disk contains many files that don't need to be there: MS-DOS files, for example, if MS-DOS is not in a subdirectory of its own; program files; data files; and perhaps files inherited from a former user of the computer. Some of these files, such as the MS-DOS command files, are essential but need not all be in the root directory; others, such as files you've inherited, might be unnecessary to your work; still others, such as application program files and data files, might be much easier to find and keep track of in directories of their own.

Few people, and certainly no book, can tell you the best way to organize your directories and files. If your root directory contains many files that should be in subdirectories of their own, the Make Directory, Copy, Xcopy, and (when you've moved files to new subdirectories) Delete commands can help you with your housekeeping. Ultimately, you are the best judge of your own work and work habits, but there are some general guidelines you can follow, either in setting up a new hard disk or in organizing one you've been using:

- Keep your MS-DOS command files in a subdirectory of their own. The only files that MS-DOS requires to be in the root directory are named COMMAND.COM, CONFIG.SYS, and AUTOEXEC.BAT. Versions 4 and later of MS-DOS install themselves so that these files are in the root directory, but all other MS-DOS files are in a separate subdirectory named \DOS. If you have an earlier version of MS-DOS and all of the MS-DOS files are in your root directory, read Appendix A, "Installing MS-DOS," to find out how to set up and move files to a \DOS subdirectory.

- Some application programs also require files in the root directory; the documentation that came with the program should tell you about this, and the program itself might create the necessary files when you install it. When in doubt, follow the advice given in the documentation.

- If your hard disk has been used by someone else, print a listing of the root directory before you try reorganizing or deleting the files in it. Be particularly careful about removing any files with the extensions COM, SYS, or EXE; remember, they are program files. If you don't know what a particular command file is supposed to do, ask someone who does know.

- When you install a new program, put it in its own subdirectory if you can. Some programs propose this during the installation procedure. If yours doesn't, you might still be able to put it in a subdirectory, provided it can be installed on a hard disk and has the ability to work with different drives and subdirectories. Check the program's documentation for instructions. After a program is installed in a subdirectory, all you need do is add the subdirectory name to the command path in order to make the program's command files available at any time.

- Think about the data files you create. These are generally the files that take up the most room on a hard disk. They are also the ones that can become the most confusing as file names begin to proliferate and come close to duplicating one another. Although this book uses files with the names LET1.DOC, LET2.DOC, and so on, real data files with such names would mean little in a root directory cluttered with a hundred other letters. On the other hand, such names might mean a great deal in subdirectories named for clients, projects, proposals, and the like. In short, pay as much attention to organizing your hard disk as you would to organizing a large set of files in a file cabinet.

### Taking Care of Your Hard Disk

Although MS-DOS can't help you physically protect your hard disk, there are some common-sense approaches you can use. Dire warnings aside, a hard disk is neither fragile nor temperamental. Many people use the same hard disk for years without encountering any problems. In fact, considering the close tolerances involved—the read/write heads literally float on air a tiny fraction of an inch above the disk itself—a hard disk is remarkably sturdy and reliable. All it normally needs is a little help from you. For example:

- Don't turn your system off and on repeatedly during the day. Leaving the system on minimizes wear on the mechanical parts of your hard disk.

- Don't turn the system off while the hard disk is active. By the same token, avoid bumping or jostling the system at those times too. You'll help preserve both disk and data.

- Keep the system and its surroundings reasonably clean. You don't have to sterilize anything; just clean and relatively dust-free will do.

- Save your work and turn off your system during windstorms and at other times when the power is likely to surge or be interrupted. A sudden loss of electricity or a sudden surge of excess power can cause problems, especially if the computer is reading from or writing to the hard disk at the time.

- If you have extra memory on your system, consider using some of it for a RAM disk. Not only will you reduce stress on your hard disk, you'll find that file access becomes noticeably quicker.

- Shut the system down before moving it. Don't worry about sliding it across your desk, but do be careful not to drop it or bang it into walls or furniture.

Barring equipment failure, about all it takes to keep your hard disk running smoothly are a little common sense and the same type of care you'd give your VCR or stereo system.

## CHAPTER SUMMARY

This chapter showed you how to set up a filing system, control the archive attribute, and copy files selectively with the Replace and Xcopy commands. It also showed how using the DoubleSpace and Defrag programs lets you increase the capacity and efficiency of your hard disk and how using ScanDisk can help you check for and correct disk errors.

Because you can't see it, it's easy to take your hard disk for granted. But the hard disk is an essential part of your computer system. If you organize your file structure to match the way you work, the hard disk lets you move from job to job or program to program with a minimum of effort. Setting up a filing system and doing some periodic housekeeping takes a bit of time but pays off by letting you work more efficiently. More than any other part of the system, the hard disk determines how well your computer works for you.

# 10

# Protecting Your Disks and Files

ou've seen that a hard disk is much faster and more convenient to use than floppy disks, even the latest high-capacity floppy disks that hold nearly three megabytes. But the same features that make a hard disk so valuable can also make loss of the disk or the files stored on it more distressing. It's bad enough to discover that MS-DOS either can't find or can't use files you stored on a floppy disk. It's almost always worse when the same thing happens to your hard disk.

MS-DOS tries to help protect your files by requesting confirmation before it carries out a Delete command that would remove all files in a directory. Recent versions of MS-DOS protect you from accidentally formatting a disk by requiring you to type a drive letter and, if you specify a hard disk, by prompting you to verify the command. In addition to these attempts to make you think twice before carrying out a potentially destructive command, MS-DOS also provides some commands that help you protect your valuable files.

The MSbackup command in versions 6 and 6.2 (and the Backup and Restore commands in earlier versions) lets you copy files from your hard disk to floppy disks for safekeeping and then copy them back to the hard disk if you need them.

If, despite these safeguards, you still lose files accidentally, MS-DOS, starting with version 5, includes the Undelete and Unformat commands that recover a file after you delete it or restore the contents of a disk you inadvertently format. Versions 6 and 6.2 continue this emphasis on guarding against or recovering from file damage by adding two extra levels of file protection to the Undelete command and by adding Undelete for Windows, a program that provides the same protection in Windows as the MS-DOS version of Undelete. Versions 6 and 6.2 also offer anti-virus programs that run under both MS-DOS and Windows.

This chapter shows you how to use these protective features, including the MS-DOS versions of Undelete and anti-virus protection. See the documentation that comes with MS-DOS for a description of how to use the Windows versions of these programs.

The examples in this chapter require some preparation. If you still have the floppy disk you used for the examples in Chapter 5, "Managing Your Files," put it in drive A and go on to the heading "Recovering Deleted Files." If you don't have the example floppy disk, put a formatted floppy disk in drive A and type the following commands:

```
C:\>copy con a:report.txt
This is a dummy file.
^Z
    1 file(s) copied
C:\>a:
A:\>copy report.txt bank.txt
    1 file(s) copied
A:\>copy report.txt forecast.txt
    1 file(s) copied
A:\>copy report.txt budget.jan
    1 file(s) copied
A:\>copy report.txt budget.feb
    1 file(s) copied
```

Use the Directory command to check that all five files are on the floppy disk:

```
A:\>dir
 Volume in drive A is EXAMPLES 1
 Volume Serial Number is 1A2C-13F5
 Directory of A:\

REPORT   TXT        23 10-16-93    9:16a
BANK     TXT        23 10-16-93    9:16a
FORECAST TXT        23 10-16-93    9:16a
BUDGET   JAN        23 10-16-93    9:16a
BUDGET   FEB        23 10-16-93    9:16a
       5 file(s)       115 bytes
                   1210903 bytes free
```

Depending on which floppy disk you put in drive A, your report may show more files than this, but the five file names shown here should appear there. The times and dates will be different, too, but the file names and sizes (23 bytes) should be the same.

This completes preparation for the examples in this chapter.

## RECOVERING DELETED FILES

Beginning with version 5, MS-DOS includes an Undelete command that can help you recover a file you've deleted. In most cases, when you delete a file, MS-DOS marks its storage space on the disk as unavailable for reuse, but it doesn't physically remove the information contained in that space. When MS-DOS manages storage space in this way, it's possible to use the Undelete command to recover a deleted file until (and only until) MS-DOS reuses part or all of the file's disk space for another file. MS-DOS versions 6 and 6.2 substantially change the

Undelete command by introducing two levels of file protection in addition to the one available in version 5. If you have version 5, skip to the heading "Undelete and Delete Tracking." The following section covers versions 6 and 6.2.

## Undelete's Levels of Protection

MS-DOS versions 6 and 6.2 offer an enhanced Undelete command that helps you recover a file you've deleted. It includes three levels of protection: standard, Delete Tracker, and Delete Sentry. Standard uses information recorded by MS-DOS to recover a deleted file. It works by reinstating the information about the disk location where the deleted file was stored. Of the three levels of guarding against file deletion, standard provides the lowest level of protection. You can use it to recover a deleted file as long as MS-DOS has not placed another file in any portion of the deleted file's location. The standard level of protection is available when you switch on your computer.

Delete Tracker offers the next higher level of Undelete's file protection. It uses a hidden file named PCTRACKR.DEL to hold disk-storage information about the files you delete. Once you start Delete Tracker for a disk drive, Undelete records storage information for all subsequent deleted files. Undelete can then use this information to try to recover one or more deleted files. If MS-DOS has placed another file over part of the deleted file's location, Undelete attempts to restore part of the file. Note that Delete Tracker in versions 6 and 6.2 works in the same way as the delete tracking feature in version 5, which is discussed in the next section, "Undelete and Undelete Tracking."

To choose the Delete Tracker level of protection, type the Undelete command and specify the /T switch and the drive you want to protect. For example, to activate Delete Tracker on drive A, you would type the following at the command prompt (do not type this command now):

```
A:\>undelete /ta
```

Delete Sentry offers the highest level of protection against accidental file deletion. It creates a hidden directory named SENTRY to which a deleted file is moved without changing the record of the file's location. When you undelete the file, MS-DOS moves the file back to its original location. With Delete Sentry protection, you don't have to worry about MS-DOS placing another file in the deleted file's place. The deleted file remains tucked away on your disk, safe and sound. Undelete truly removes the file from your hard disk either after seven days or when Undelete needs more room in the SENTRY directory.

To activate the Delete Sentry level of protection, specify the /S switch and the drive you want to protect. If you're selecting the current drive, you don't need to include the drive letter designation. For example, if the current drive is A, type the following at the command prompt (type this command now):

```
A:\>undelete /s
```

Now delete the test files you created earlier:

```
A:\>del report.txt
A:\>del bank.txt
A:\>del forecast.txt
A:\>del budget.jan
A:\>del budget.feb
```

Now check the directory again:

```
A:\>dir
Volume in drive A is EXAMPLES 1
Volume Serial Number is 1A2C-13F5
Directory of A:\

File not found
```

If there were other files on the floppy disk you put in drive A, they'll still appear in the report, but the five files you deleted should be gone.

If you have version 6 or 6.2, try using the Undelete command to retrieve the files you deleted. The following list describes most of the parameters for the versions 6 and 6.2 Undelete command. To find out about Undelete's advanced parameters, see Appendix C, "MS-DOS Command Reference."

**undelete <filename> /ds /dt /dos /all /list /status /U /S<drive>
/T<drive>**

<filename> is the name of the file or files you want to restore. You can specify a drive and path, and you can use wildcards to specify a set of files. If you don't include <filename>, Undelete assumes you want to recover all deleted files in the current directory of the current drive.

*/ds* recovers only those files protected by the Delete Sentry level, prompting for confirmation on each file. Undelete assumes */ds* if the SENTRY directory exists, even if you don't include this parameter.

*/dt* recovers only those files protected by the Delete Tracking level, prompting for confirmation on each file.

*/dos* recovers only those files that are internally listed as being deleted by MS-DOS, prompting for confirmation on each file. If a deletion-tracking file exists, this switch causes Undelete to ignore it.

*/all* recovers all deleted files without prompting for confirmation on each.

*/list* lists the deleted files that are available to be recovered but does not recover any files. You can restrict the resulting list by using the <filename> parameter and the */ds /dt,* and */dos* switches.

/U disables the Delete Tracker or Delete Sentry protection.

*/status* displays the type of delete protection in effect for each drive. You cannot specify any other parameters when you use /STATUS.

/S<drive> enables the Delete Sentry level of protection and loads the memory-resident portion of the Undelete program. If you omit <drive>, Undelete will protect the files on the current drive. You cannot specify any other parameters when you use /S<drive>.

/T<drive> enables the Delete Tracker level of protection and loads the memory-resident portion of the Undelete program. If you omit <drive>, Undelete will protect the files on the current drive. You cannot specify any other parameters when you use /T<drive>.

You just deleted several files from the disk in drive A. To request a list of these files, type

```
A:\>undelete /list
```

The Undelete command responds with a display like this:

```
UNDELETE - A delete protection facility
Copyright (C) 1987-1993 Central Point Software, Inc.
All rights reserved.

Directory: A:\
File Specifications: *.*

    Delete Sentry control file contains    5 deleted files.

    Deletion-tracking file not found.

    MS-DOS directory contains    5 deleted files.
    Of those,    0 files may be recovered.

Using the Delete Sentry method.

        REPORT   TXT      23  10-16-93  9:16a  ...A  Deleted:  10-17-93 3:24p
        BANK     TXT      23  10-16-93  9:16a  ...A  Deleted:  10-17-93 3:24p
        FORECAST TXT      23  10-16-93  9:16a  ...A  Deleted:  10-17-93 3:25p
        BUDGET   JAN      70  10-16-93  9:16a  ...A  Deleted:  10-17-93 3:25p
        BUDGET   FEB      23  10-16-93  9:16a  ...A  Deleted:  10-17-93 3:25p
```

Let's examine this report. Although it's long, it's not difficult to interpret. After three lines of introductory text, Undelete lets you know where it is searching for the deleted files and what type of files it is searching for. In this case, it's looking in the root directory of the disk in drive A, and it's looking for all deleted files.

The next section of the report gives information about each level of protection. You can see that Undelete found five files protected by the Delete Sentry level, no files protected by the Delete Tracking level, and five files protected by the standard level (MS-DOS directory). Notice that in this case Undelete says that it can't recover the five files by using the standard method. You need to use the Delete Sentry method.

Finally, the report lists the five deleted files, giving their names, sizes, and dates and times of creation. The *...A* tells you that the files have not been backed up (archived), and the remainder of each line tells you the date and time the file was deleted.

Suppose you want to use the Undelete command to recover the file REPORT.TXT. By default, Undelete recovers only those files protected by the Delete Sentry level. Because you have been using the Delete Sentry level of protection, all you have to do is type the following:

```
A:>undelete report.txt
```

(If you had been using Delete Tracking, you would have had to add the */dt* parameter, and if you had been using the standard level, you would have had to add */dos*.) You see the same introductory text as before, and then Undelete displays:

```
Directory: A:>
File Specifications: REPORT.TXT

    Delete Sentry control file contains    1 deleted files.

    Deletion-tracking file not found.

    MS-DOS directory contains    1 deleted files.
    Of those,    0 files may be recovered.

Using the Delete Sentry method.

    REPORT    TXT      23  10-26-93  9:16a ...A Deleted: 10-17-93 3:24p
This file can be 100% undeleted. Undelete (Y/N)?
```

Type *y*, and in a moment the recovery process ends:

```
    File successfully undeleted.
```

To recover all deleted files on this disk, or to search through the deleted files and recover only those you want, you would type *undelete*. For each file that Undelete could recover, it would display a message and prompt similar to those you just saw. In each case, you would type *y* or *n* to tell Undelete whether to recover or to ignore the file.

Before continuing, delete REPORT.TXT once again to return your sample disk to its earlier state.

## Undelete and Delete Tracking

In version 5 Undelete works by reinstating the information about the disk locations where the deleted file was stored. Bear in mind, however, that MS-DOS does not necessarily store an entire file in a single location on disk. Sometimes, especially on much-used disks, it tucks sections of a file into widely separated storage areas in order to make the best possible use of available space. As you save files, even small ones, MS-DOS assigns and reassigns these storage areas. Because disk storage is so changeable, Undelete is successful only if it can follow a file's chain of storage locations from beginning to end. If, as often happens, MS-DOS uses a link in this chain for storing part of another file, Undelete reaches a dead end and cannot recover the entire file.

> **NOTE:** *If you need Undelete, use it as soon as possible after realizing that you need to recover a deleted file. Each time MS-DOS saves another file on the disk, your chances of recovering the file are reduced.*

You can use the MS-DOS 5 version of Undelete either on its own or with a feature called *delete tracking*. Delete tracking is activated by the Mirror command, which creates a special file named PCTRACKR.DEL for holding disk-storage information about the files you delete. (MS-DOS versions 6 and 6.2 do not include the Mirror command because its functionality was added to Undelete.) Once you start delete tracking for a disk drive, the Mirror command records storage information for all subsequent deleted files. Undelete can then use this information to try to recover one or more deleted files. Because delete tracking uses a file for holding disk-storage information, it tends to be more effective than using MS-DOS–based information in recovering files. The following examples show you how to start delete tracking and use it to restore deleted files.

When used for tracking deleted files, the Mirror command has the form:

**mirror /T<drive>-<files>**

<drive> is the letter (without a colon) of the drive for which you want to start delete tracking. You must include this parameter.

<files> is the number of deleted files you want to track. If you include <files>, you can specify from 1 through 999, separating it from <drive> with a hyphen. If you omit <files>, the delete tracker assumes a generous number based on the size of the disk: 25 for a 360 KB floppy disk, 50 for a 720 KB floppy disk, 75 for a 1.2 MB or a 1.44 MB floppy disk, and 100 to 300 for a hard disk, depending on its capacity.

To start delete tracking for the sample floppy disk in drive A, type:

```
A:\>mirror /ta
```

Mirror responds with a set of messages, among them *Drive A being processed* and, when all goes well, *The MIRROR process was successful* and *Installation complete.*

Now delete the test files you created earlier:

```
A:\>del report.txt
A:\>del bank.txt
A:\>del forecast.txt
A:\>del budget.jan
A:\>del budget.feb
```

Now check the directory again:

```
A:\>dir
 Volume in drive A is EXAMPLES 1
 Volume Serial Number is 1A2C-13F5
 Directory of A:\

 File not found
```

If there were other files on the floppy disk you put in drive A, they'll still appear in the report, but the five files you deleted should be gone.

If you have version 5, try out the Undelete command to retrieve the files you deleted. (If you don't have version 5, skip to the heading "Reformatting and Unformatting Disks.")

The version 5 Undelete command has the following parameters:

**undelete <filename> /dt /dos /all /list**

<filename> is the name of the file or files you want to restore. You can specify a drive and path, and you can use wildcards to specify a set of files. If you don't include <filename>, Undelete assumes you want to recover all deleted files in the current directory of the current drive.

*/dt* tells Undelete to use the delete-tracking file recorded by the Mirror command. The */dt* parameter causes Undelete to prompt for confirmation before undeleting each file. Undelete assumes */dt* if a delete-tracking file exists, even if you don't include this parameter.

*/dos* tells Undelete to use information recorded by MS-DOS. Like the */dt* parameter, */dos* causes Undelete to prompt for confirmation. Because of the way MS-DOS deletes files, the */dos* parameter also causes Undelete to ask you to provide the first character in the name of the file. Undelete assumes the */dos* parameter if a delete-tracking file does not exist, even if you omit this parameter.

*/all* causes Undelete to recover all possible deleted files without stopping to prompt for confirmation.

*/list* causes Undelete to display a list of files it can recover, without actually undeleting them.

You just deleted several files from the disk in drive A. To request a list of these files, type:

```
A:\>undelete /list
```

The Undelete command responds with a display like this:

```
Directory: A:\
File Specifications: *.*
    Searching deletion-tracking file...
    Deletion-tracking file contains    5 deleted files.
    Of those,    5 files have all clusters available,
         0 files have some clusters available,
         0 files have no clusters available.

    MS-DOS directory contains    3 deleted files.
    Of those,    3 files may be recovered.

Using the deletion-tracking file.

        REPORT   TXT      23 10/16/93  9:16a  ...A  Deleted: 10/17/93  3:24p
        BANK     TXT      23 10/16/93  9:16a  ...A  Deleted: 10/17/93  3:24p
        FORECAST TXT      23 10/16/93  9:16a  ...A  Deleted: 10/17/93  3:25p
        BUDGET   JAN      23 10/16/93  9:16a  ...A  Deleted: 10/17/93  3:25p
        BUDGET   FEB      23 10/16/93  9:16a  ...A  Deleted: 10/17/93  3:25p
```

Although longer and more detailed than most MS-DOS reports, this display is not difficult to interpret. First, Undelete tells you that it is checking the disk in drive A for all deleted files (*File Specifications: *.**).

The middle section of the report tells you what Undelete has found. If you use the delete-tracking file, Undelete can completely restore the five deleted files. (The message *all clusters available* means that Undelete can find all storage units allotted to each file.) On the other hand, if you use the information recorded by MS-DOS (by specifying the */dos* parameter), Undelete can find and recover three of the deleted files.

Because you started delete tracking, Undelete gives precedence to the delete-tracking file, so the bottom section of the report lists the five deleted files, giving their names, sizes, and dates and times of creation. The ...*A* tells you that the files have not been backed up (archived), and the remainder of each line tells you the date and time the file was deleted.

> NOTE: *The delete-tracking file can help you recover files deleted after you have started delete tracking with the Mirror command. If you delete a file when this feature is not turned on, the delete-tracking file cannot help you recover it. However, because MS-DOS also records deletions, you might still be able to use the /dos parameter of the Undelete command instead.*

Suppose you want to recover one of the deleted files, REPORT.TXT, on the disk in drive A. Type:

```
A:\>undelete report.txt
```

You see some preliminary messages telling you the recovery process has been started, and then Undelete displays:

```
Using the deletion-tracking file.

    REPORT   TXT      23 10/16/93  9:16a  ...A  Deleted: 10/17/93  3:24p
All of the clusters for this file are available. Undelete (Y/N)?
```

Type *y*, and in a moment the recovery process ends:

```
    File successfully undeleted.
```

To recover all deleted files on this disk, or to search through the deleted files and recover those you wanted, you would type *undelete*. For each file that Undelete could recover, it would display a message and prompt similar to those you just saw. In each case, you would type *y* or *n* to tell Undelete whether to recover or to ignore the file.

Before continuing, delete REPORT.TXT once again to return your sample disk to its earlier state. Change the current directory to C:\ by typing the commands shown at the top of the next page.

```
A:\>c:
C:\>cd \
```

Inadvertently deleting a file or files isn't the only way to lose valuable data. Until version 5, formatting a disk meant irretrievably erasing any files on the disk. Now, however, you can recover from that error too.

# REFORMATTING AND UNFORMATTING DISKS

If you have version 5 or later of MS-DOS, insert a new floppy disk in drive A to experiment with the Unformat command. If you don't have version 5 or later, skip to the heading "Developing a Backup Procedure."

You should always be careful about formatting disks that already contain program or data files. Starting with version 5, however, MS-DOS can help you recover from an inadvertent format. As you have seen, the Undelete command can often restore the deleted files. In much the same way, the Unformat command can help you restore the disk to its earlier state after you've mistakenly formatted it. The following examples show you how to reformat a disk with the /Q (quick) parameter of the Format command and then reverse the format with the Unformat command.

> **NOTE:** *Version 5 of MS-DOS includes the Mirror command, which can be used to record the current status of a disk. This information can be used later when you unformat the disk. For more information about Mirror, see Appendix C, "MS-DOS Command Reference."*

If you have version 5 or later, type the following to create a small file on the floppy disk in drive A so that you can see a change when you reformat it:

```
C:\>copy con a:myfile.doc
This is my sample file.
^Z
```

Use the Directory command to verify that MYFILE.DOC is on the floppy disk in drive A. While you're looking at the display, also make a note of the volume serial number.

## Reformatting the Floppy Disk

Now reformat the floppy disk, this time using the /Q parameter of the Format command. Type:

```
C:\>format a: /q
```

MS-DOS responds much as it does when you don't use /Q. First, it asks you to insert a floppy disk in drive A. The floppy disk is in the drive, so press Enter. Next, MS-DOS checks the existing disk format and, because the floppy disk has already been formatted, it tells you it's *Saving UNFORMAT information*. This message appears whenever you reformat a disk because MS-DOS itself saves disk-storage information.

When the quick format starts, your floppy disk drive becomes active for a short time, and MS-DOS tells you the size of the disk it's quick-formatting. This message is followed almost immediately by:

```
Format complete
```

MS-DOS should now be asking you for a volume label:

```
Volume label (11 characters, ENTER for none)? _
```

Name the disk DOSDISK, and type *n* when MS-DOS asks:

```
QuickFormat another (Y/N)?
```

If you try the Directory command again, you'll notice two changes: MYFILE.DOC no longer appears in the directory, and the volume serial number is now different. The changes show that the floppy disk has, indeed, been reformatted.

## Unformatting the Floppy Disk

> **NOTE:** *The following example shows how you can try to rebuild a floppy disk after mistakenly formatting it. Don't assume that you can reformat and rebuild floppy disks whenever you want. As you'll see shortly from some of the messages MS-DOS displays, rebuilding a disk can cause loss of stored data. Examples are included here to help you in emergencies. Copying and careful handling are still your best methods of protecting the information on your floppy disks.*

Suppose now that you've just realized you formatted the wrong floppy disk. The one in drive A contained some valuable files that you want to recover. The Format command saves information that can be used to restore the disk to its former condition.

You can use the Unformat command to rebuild a disk, as long as you didn't use the /U parameter of the Format command in formatting the disk. This example uses only one parameter, the letter of the drive containing the disk to be unformatted. Other parameters for Unformat are described in Appendix C, "MS-DOS Command Reference."

To unformat the sample floppy disk in drive A, type:

```
C:\>unformat a:
```

MS-DOS responds with the message asking you to insert the floppy disk to rebuild. The floppy disk is in the drive, so press Enter to begin unformatting.

Now you see a rather wordy response from MS-DOS, but read through it all. The message tells you that the information needed to rebuild the disk has been found in a file named MIRROR.FIL and that MS-DOS will use the file in attempting to unformat the disk. You also see a message telling you that rebuilding the disk could cause loss of information. Keep this message in mind; rely on this command to rebuild a disk, but don't make it part of your everyday work with MS-DOS. That's not how it's meant to be used.

If you're using version 5, MS-DOS tells you the last time the Mirror file was updated and asks you to press *l* (lowercase L) if you want to rebuild the disk using the file it found, *p* if you want to use the prior file (you rarely will), or Esc to end the command. You want to continue, so press *l*.

Versions 5 and later give you one more chance to change your mind (the following message appears on one line on your screen):

```
Are you sure you want to update the system area
of your drive A (Y/N)? _
```

This time you're sure, so press *y*. The drive becomes busy for a few moments, and MS-DOS finishes up with the message:

```
The system area of drive A has been rebuilt.

You may need to restart the system.
```

(You don't have to restart the system with this disk.)

It's done. If you check the directory of drive A, you'll find that Unformat has not only recovered MYFILE.DOC, it has even restored the original volume serial number of the disk.

## Rebuilding a Hard Disk

Because of the extent of potential loss in terms of programs and data, recent versions of MS-DOS require deliberate effort on your part to format a hard disk. It's not a step to be taken lightly, and the most experienced computer user feels at least a small twinge after pressing Enter to start the process. Beginning with version 5, the Unformat command provides a means for you to undo the format of either a floppy disk or a hard disk.

Earlier in this chapter you used the Unformat command with floppy disks. You unformat a hard disk in the same way. Be aware, however, that files stored on a hard disk become unavailable after the disk has been formatted. In order for Unformat to work on a system with, for example, one hard disk and one floppy disk drive, you need a startup floppy disk with which you can start MS-DOS from drive A. You can create such a floppy disk with the Format /S command. Copy to this floppy disk the MS-DOS file UNFORMAT.COM and accurate copies of the files named AUTOEXEC.BAT and CONFIG.SYS, which are in the root directory of your startup disk.

You can use Unformat for one other task with your hard disk: rebuilding a damaged partition table. A damaged partition table means that MS-DOS can't find (and therefore start from) your hard disk. If you are unable to access your hard drive and you're using version 6 or 6.2 of MS-DOS, start your machine with a startup floppy disk and run the Unformat command. Unformat checks for a damaged partition table and fixes it if possible. If you are using version 5, you can use the Mirror command to save a copy of the partition table on a floppy disk. Then, if your hard disk's partition table becomes damaged, you can specify the */partn* parameter with the Undelete command to rebuild the partition table from the copy. See Appendix C, "MS-DOS Command Reference," for more information about Mirror and the version 5 parameters of Undelete.

## GUARDING AGAINST VIRUS PROGRAMS

*Computer virus* is a term used to describe a program that hides itself on a disk—usually inside a program file—and can spread itself from system to system; a virus eventually does something to irritate you or even destroy your files.

There are now thousands of such programs, but the danger from them has been exaggerated in recent years. A virus can be introduced to your computer only if you use an "infected" floppy disk or if your computer is connected to another machine that has a virus. Most software manufacturers check their disks for virus programs before boxing them, so if your machine isn't connected to any others and if you use only your disks and disks from programs you've bought, you shouldn't have to worry about viruses. However, it always makes sense to be cautious. We know that virus programs do exist and sometimes cause inconvenience or damage to your programs and data.

To let you protect your system against a virus, versions 6 and 6.2 of MS-DOS include programs that run under both MS-DOS and Windows to detect and remove virus programs from your disks. MS-DOS even includes a program you can install that runs all the time, guarding your system against a virus program that might wreak havoc on your files. We'll discuss the MS-DOS versions of these programs. See the *MS-DOS User's Guide*, which comes with MS-DOS, for a description of how to use the versions that were written for Microsoft Windows.

## Checking Your Hard Disk

It's easy to check your hard disk for a virus; to start Microsoft Anti-Virus, the anti-virus program, type *msav*. You'll notice that the program first gets information about your disk. As it does so, a box on the screen titled "Reading disk information" displays which disk the program is reading and how many directories it has read so far. When it's done, Anti-Virus displays its opening screen:

The window titled Main Menu offers five options, which are listed in the left half of the window: Detect, Detect & Clean, Select new drive, Options, and Exit. At this point the pane in the right half of the window describes the Detect option, which is the currently selected option. It lets you know that if you choose Detect, Anti-Virus will scan the disk for viruses and give you the choice of correcting the problem (cleaning), continuing without cleaning, or quitting the scan.

For this example, you're going to scan the disk and get rid of any virus that Anti-Virus finds. Press the Tab key once to select the second option, Detect & Clean. As the pane to the right explains, if you choose Detect & Clean, Anti-Virus scans your disk for viruses and, if it finds any, cleans them without giving you a choice. Press Enter to begin the process now.

Anti-Virus first checks that there isn't a virus already running on your machine in memory. It then checks every file on the hard disk, showing you its progress in the pane on the right and displaying the name of the file it's currently checking in the upper left corner of the screen:

When Anti-Virus completes, it displays a summary report showing how many disks and files it scanned and how many files it cleaned. Chances are your report shows that Anti-Virus found no infected files. If Anti-Virus does find an infected file, it cleans the file, adjusting for any changes the virus made to the file, and may prompt you to take additional action.

After checking the summary report (and taking any action recommended by Anti-Virus), close the report by pressing Enter to choose OK. Now quit the program by pressing the Tab key three times to select the Exit option. Then press Enter. Anti-Virus will display a box letting you know that you are closing Anti-Virus. If you're certain you want to quit, press Enter. If not, press Tab to select Cancel and then press Enter.

## Checking a Floppy Disk

As mentioned earlier, floppy disks can be the transportation method of viruses from one computer to another. If you're using a disk whose origins you don't know, you would be wise to check the disk for viruses before copying anything from it to your hard disk.

Insert the disk you want to check in the disk drive. For this example, we'll use the A drive. Start Anti-Virus by typing *msav*. Choose the Select New Drive option by pressing the Tab key until the option is highlighted and then pressing Enter. A list of your disk drives appears in the upper left corner of your screen:

Press the Left arrow key twice to select the A drive, and then press Enter. Anti-Virus gets information about your floppy disk the same way it gets information about your hard disk. After it finishes getting information, Anti-Virus is ready to check the disk. Choose the Detect option or the Detect & Clean option to start the scan.

## Checking for Unknown Viruses

Anti-Virus checks for every virus that it knows. Of course, there are some new viruses that Anti-Virus doesn't recognize. Anti-Virus has a way to combat those as well. As mentioned earlier, most viruses infect program files. The first time Anti-Virus runs, it notes the size, attributes, date, and time of all the program files on your disk. The next time you check the disk with Anti-Virus, it checks that none of those program files have changed. A change might indicate the presence of a virus. If it finds a modified program file as it scans, Anti-Virus displays a box like the following one:

Anti-Virus lets you know that a program file has changed and gives you some choices of action. If you know why the file has changed—for example, if you've updated your program—press Enter to select Update and let Anti-Virus know that the file was legitimately changed. Be sure to check the name of the directory that contains the program file. It might give you a clue to a reason the file was changed. Suppose you have recently updated your version of MS-DOS. You can see in the example above that the file HIMEM.SYS is in the MS-DOS directory. Even if you don't know what HIMEM.SYS does, the fact that it's in the MS-DOS directory gives you ample reason not to worry that it has been changed since the last time you checked for viruses. You should leave that file alone and simply select the Update choice. If you are absolutely positive that a file shouldn't have changed, then it might very well have a virus. Press Tab to select Delete, and then press Enter. This deletes the file from your disk.

## Using Anti-Virus When Updating Software

If you update any software, such as your word processor or spreadsheet program, or even MS-DOS, many files will be changed legitimately. When you run Anti-Virus after updating the software, you will be prompted to accept the changes for every one of those files. You can avoid this time-consuming task by deleting the information Anti-Virus has saved about your program files before you update your software.

First, type *msav* to start Anti-Virus. Next choose the Detect & Clean option to scan your disk for viruses. When Anti-Virus completes its scan, press the F7 function key. A message box appears asking whether you're sure that you want to delete the checklist files. Press Enter to begin the process. (Press Tab and then Enter to cancel the operation.) Anti-Virus runs through the directories on your disk and deletes the information it saved about the program files. A box on the right side of the window keeps you informed of the progress. When the procedure is complete, exit Anti-Virus by pressing Tab until the Exit option is highlighted and then pressing Enter. Now you're ready to update your software. Follow the installation instructions that came with the software.

When your software update is complete, run Anti-Virus one more time to reinstate the information about your program files. Simply choose the Detect & Clean option again. Because you deleted the information about the older versions of your program files, Anti-Virus won't prompt you to accept the new versions.

## Running Anti-Virus with a Command

You can also run Anti-Virus by typing a single command at the command prompt and using parameters to specify the options. The complete form of the command is shown in Appendix C, "MS-DOS Command Reference." For example, if you type the following:

```
C:\>msav c: /c
```

the /C parameter tells Anti-Virus to scan your memory and hard disk for viruses and clean any infected files it finds. If you want to be vigilant against viruses, you could run this command every time you start your computer. You can do this automatically by adding the command to your file named AUTOEXEC.BAT. See Chapter 14, "Creating Your Own Commands," for details about this special file. You probably don't need to run Anti-Virus that often, however, unless you routinely use a lot of disks or programs from other computer systems.

## Constant Protection with Vsafe

If you want your system continuously monitored against the unwanted effects of a virus program, you can run the Vsafe program, available in versions 6 and 6.2. This program monitors everything that happens in your system and makes sure that no unwanted programs are run. If Vsafe discovers something suspect, it will immediately display a message box containing a warning on your screen.

To load Vsafe, type *vsafe*. After Vsafe displays a message telling you it has successfully loaded, press Alt-V to display the Vsafe control menu, which contains a list of the actions Vsafe will protect against. The actions that are followed by an X are currently protected. An explanation of these actions and of the parameters that you can use with Vsafe is included in Appendix C, "MS-DOS Command Reference." To change whether a particular action is protected, type the number corresponding to the action. If the action is protected when you type the number, it will become unprotected; if the action is not protected, it will become protected. When you have finished making your selections, press Esc to return to the command line.

Vsafe uses quite a bit of memory (about 23 KB) and slows down your system because it checks all disk and memory activity. Note that you probably don't need the level of protection offered by Vsafe unless you routinely use a lot of disks or programs from other computer systems. You can unload Vsafe by typing *vsafe /u* or by pressing Alt-U when the control menu is displayed on the screen.

## DEVELOPING A BACKUP PROCEDURE

It could take a drawerful of floppy disks to back up all the files on a hard disk. If your average file were 10,000 bytes long (about 6½ double-spaced typed pages), a full 40 MB hard disk would have more than 4000 files, and you'd need almost 35 high-density (1.2 MB) floppy disks to back them all up. A full 120 MB hard disk could require more than one hundred 1.2 MB floppy disks.

But you don't have to back up all your files. You needn't back up program files, for example, because you already have the original MS-DOS and application-program floppy disks. Some data files, such as a spelling dictionary, don't usually change, so it isn't necessary to back them up either.

How often you back up your other data files, such as word processing documents or spreadsheets, depends on how often they change. For example, spreadsheets might change often while the budget is being prepared but remain unchanged the rest of the year. The backup procedures you use depend on how you use your computer. But no matter how you decide to back up your files, be certain to do so regularly. A system failure can happen, but if you back up your files regularly, such a failure will be merely an inconvenience instead of a disaster.

## BACKING UP AND RESTORING FILES WITH MSBACKUP

If you're using version 6 or 6.2, you can use the MS-DOS program MSbackup (Microsoft Backup) to make backup copies of your files on floppy disks and restore files from the backup floppy disks to your hard disk. MSbackup does not require you to type commands. Instead it presents you with menus from which you choose the tasks you want the program to carry out.

To see how MSbackup works, make sure you have two formatted floppy disks. Both floppy disks must be the same type, even if you have different type drives. Type *msbackup* at the system prompt. If this is the first time MSbackup has been run on your system, it tells you that *Microsoft Backup requires configuration for this computer* and starts a series of steps that let it determine what sort of hardware you're using (especially what sort of floppy disk drives you have). Press Enter to proceed with configuration.

The configuration process is an automated run-through of many of the MSbackup commands, flashing through the screens almost faster than you can read them. Occasionally it will pause, display a message, and wait for you to press Enter. The fourth such instance occurs when MSbackup displays a box titled Floppy Disk Compatibility Test. The message explains that to ensure that MSbackup will create reliable backups, it is necessary to perform a test backup. Press Enter to start the test. This is the portion of the configuration in which you'll need the two disks. MSbackup automatically backs up some files from the MS-DOS directory. In the middle of the test, MSbackup displays a box titled Backup To in which you should specify which floppy disk drive you will use:

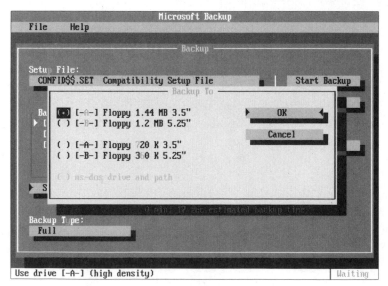

If you see a dot between the parentheses at the beginning of the line describing your floppy disk drive, your drive is selected. Simply press Enter. To select a different disk drive, type the character that is highlighted (if you have color, the letter is red) in the line you want to choose. You'll see that the dot between the parentheses moves to the correct line. Now press Enter to continue the process. MSbackup asks you to insert first one and then the other floppy disk in the drive you selected. The whole configuration process should take five minutes or so.

When configuration finishes, MSbackup displays a dialog box titled *Configure* with the option *Save* highlighted. Press Enter to save the configuration so that MSbackup will know how your system is configured from now on. This ends the configuration process.

Now, whether or not MSbackup checked the configuration of your system, it displays its main menu in a box titled *Backup* followed by a version number. The menu displays five choices: Backup, Restore, Compare, Configure, and Quit. Because *Backup* is highlighted, you can choose it now by pressing Enter. MSbackup displays the Backup screen:

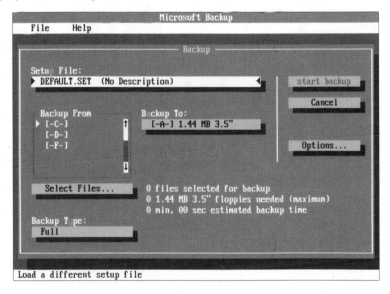

This is the window from which you'll do most of your work.

## Online Help

Like Anti-Virus and other menu-based MS-DOS programs, MSbackup includes online help that describes every function of the program. To see how it works, press F1. MSbackup displays a window titled *Backup Help*, which explains how to get help.

After reading this screen, press PgDn to move to the next screen, which shows a list of help topics (the choices on the Backup screen). Choose *Select Files button* by pressing the Tab key until it's highlighted and then pressing Enter; now MSbackup displays a description of the Select Backup Files screen and states how to select the files you want to back up. You'll see the Select Backup Files screen in a moment.

Scroll through the description; when you finish reading it, press Esc to return to the Backup screen. Remember, you can use online help to view a description of everything that MSbackup does.

## Types of Backup

MSbackup offers three types of backup:

- Full, which backs up every file you select.

- Incremental, which backs up every file you select that has changed since the last full or incremental backup.

- Differential, which backs up every file you select that has changed since the last full backup.

If you start by doing a full backup and then do an *incremental* backup each night, you'd need the floppy disks for the full backup and all incremental backups to recover all the files. If you start by doing a full backup and then do a *differential* backup each night, you'd need only the floppy disks for the full backup and the latest incremental backup to recover all the files. The method you choose depends on how many files you want to back up and how many of those files you change in a typical work day.

If you don't change many files—and especially if the files you change tend to be the same files—then a differential backup is probably the most effective for you. You'll have the most current copies of your files saved. But if you change quite a few files every day, you're probably better off doing incremental backups and keeping all the incremental backup floppy disks until you do your next full backup.

## Accessing the Parts of the Backup Screen

The Backup screen contains eight elements. The highlighted element is the one that is currently *selected*. To select a different element, press the Tab key until that element is highlighted. In most cases, once the highlight is on the element, you can press Enter to choose the element and perform an action. For example, press Tab until the highlight is on the element labeled Backup Type, and then press Enter. MSbackup displays a box that lets you choose the type of backup you want to perform:

This box contains a list of choices preceded by parentheses, one of which contains a dot. The dot represents a selected item, and you can select only one item in this kind of list. There are two ways to select the item you want: You can press the key of the highlighted character in the line you want to select, or you can use the Up and Down arrow keys to move the highlight to the line you want to select and then press the Spacebar to move the dot to the highlighted line. If you want to cancel your selection and return to the Backup screen, either press Tab until the word Cancel is selected and press Enter or press the Esc key. To accept your selection, simply press Enter.

Now that you have an idea of how to move around in MSbackup, press Esc to return to the Backup screen.

**NOTE:** *This tutorial gives instructions for using the keyboard. If you have a mouse, feel free to use it. For example, with a mouse, choosing elements in the Backup screen is easy. All you have to do is position the mouse pointer over the element you would like to choose and then click (press and release) the left mouse button once. You can just as easily choose items from a list.*

## Selecting Files to Back Up

The examples that follow require the directory structure and files you created in the previous chapter. If you haven't completed those examples, do so before continuing.

You're going to back up some files now, so first choose *Select Files...* from the Backup screen. MSbackup reads all the file names from the hard disk, then displays the Select Backup Files screen (you read the online help description of this screen a moment ago):

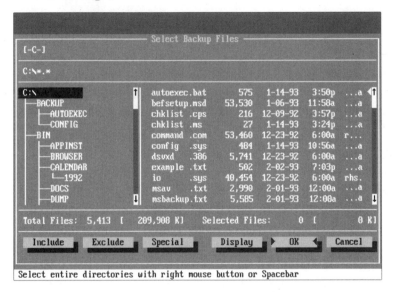

As you can see, this screen contains a list of the directories on your disk and a list of the files in the currently selected directory. When MSbackup first displays this screen, the highlight is in the list of directories. Press the Down arrow key until you highlight the WP subdirectory in the C:\RUNDOS\MKT directory. The following figure shows the resulting display. The directories shown in your screen will most certainly be different from the ones shown here. However, your list of files in the WP directory should be the same.

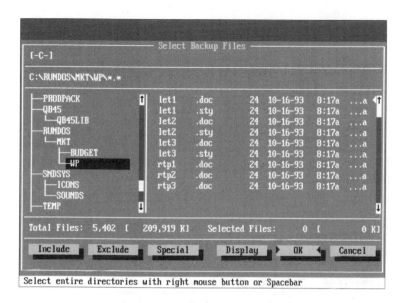

Now press the Tab key to move the highlight to the section of the screen that contains the file names. To select a file for backup, use the Up and Down arrow keys to select the file name and then press the Spacebar. (If you're using a mouse, position the mouse pointer on the file name and press the right mouse button.) Try it: Press the Down arrow key twice to select the file name *let2.doc*, and then press the Spacebar; a check mark should appear to the left of the file name. In the same way, select the files RPT1.DOC, RPT2.DOC, and RPT3.DOC.

> **NOTE:** *If you have a mouse, MSbackup makes it easy to select a series of files. All you have to do is position the mouse pointer over the first file name, press and hold the right mouse button, move the mouse pointer down to the last file in the series, and release the right mouse button.*

Once you select it, a file stays selected. You can reverse the selection of a file by highlighting the file name and pressing the Spacebar again.

You can also select all the files in a directory. Press Tab until the highlight is back on the list of directories. Now press the Up arrow key once to select the directory named *BUDGET*, and then press the Spacebar. Now look at the list of file names on the right side; each one is preceded by a check mark. Press the Spacebar again. All the check marks disappear. Move back to the WP directory.

## Backing Up the Files

You've marked four files to back up: LET2.DOC, RPT1.DOC, RPT2.DOC, and RPT3.DOC. The screen should look like this:

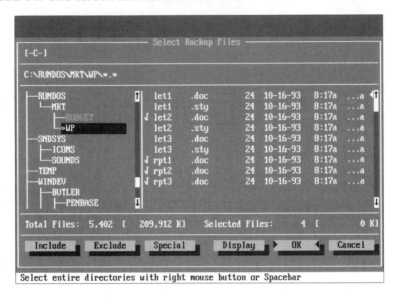

Press the Tab key until OK is selected, and then press Enter. MSbackup returns to the Backup screen. In the lower middle, the screen tells you that five files are to be backed up (the four you marked plus a catalog file that MSbackup creates), that you'll need one floppy disk, and that it will take about 15 seconds to back up the files. Insert one of the floppy disks that MSbackup used when it checked the configuration of your system, and then choose *Start Backup* at the upper right corner of the screen by highlighting it and pressing Enter.

Because you already have a disk in the drive, simply press Enter when MSbackup tells you to insert a disk in drive A. Because you're using a floppy disk that MSbackup wrote on while checking your system configuration, you will see a message telling you that you have inserted a disk that already contains backup files and asking whether to retry or to overwrite the disk. Because you won't need the files currently on the disk, select *Overwrite* and press Enter to continue.

It doesn't take long to back up the four files (probably less than the estimated 15 seconds). When MSbackup finishes, it displays a summary report and waits for you to press Enter. Now it returns once again to MSbackup's main menu.

MSbackup includes more options, but these are the basic functions you need to set up a backup procedure. The names of the files you chose to back up for this example are stored in a file named DEFAULT.SET. To make sure that these files won't be included in your backup procedure from now on, choose Backup to return to the Backup screen, choose *Select Files...*, and then remove the check marks from the four files (choose the directory \RUNDOS\MKT\WP, and then use the Spacebar to remove the check marks from the file names). Now choose *OK*, and check the description in the lower middle of the Backup screen; it should say you have zero (0) files selected.

Quit MSbackup by pressing Esc, pressing Enter when MSbackup asks if you want to save the changes to the DEFAULT.SET, and then choosing *Quit* from MSbackup's main menu.

## Restoring Files Using MSbackup

Restoring files works just about the same as backing them up. Now type the following to delete three files whose file names start with RPT:

```
C:\>cd rundos\mkt\wp
C:\RUNDOS\MKT\WP>del rpt?.doc
```

Start MSbackup again by typing *msbackup*. This time, choose *Restore* from the main menu by selecting it and pressing Enter. The Restore screen looks very much like the Backup screen. Choose *Select Files...* at the lower left.

Again, the display of directories and files looks much as it does when you're backing up files. Highlight the directory \RUNDOS\MKT\WP. The names of the four files you backed up should appear:

As you did in the Select Backup Files screen, put check marks next to *rpt1.doc*, *rpt2.doc*, and *rpt3.doc*. Then choose *OK*. The Restore screen tells you *3 files selected for restore*. Choose *Start Restore* at the upper right of the screen. When MSbackup prompts you to put the disk in drive A, press Enter to choose OK because the floppy disk you used for the backup is still there.

Again, the restore process itself takes just a few seconds, and then MSbackup displays a summary report. Press Enter, and MSbackup returns to the main menu.

You have used the main features of both the Backup and Restore parts of MSbackup. You can experiment with the other features just as you did here. Whenever the meaning of a term or the purpose of a choice isn't clear, use the online help to get an explanation.

### MSbackup for Windows

MSbackup for Windows works in much the same way as the version described here, although the appearance of the screens match Windows. It, too, offers online help; you should be able to use the Windows version, if you prefer, with no difficulty.

## BACKING UP FILES WITH THE BACKUP COMMAND

If you're using version 5 or earlier, you must use the Backup command to back up files. Although it lacks the convenient menus and mouse features of the MSbackup program included with versions 6 and 6.2, the Backup command (and its companion, the Restore command) nonetheless offers all the capability you need to back up your files.

The Backup command lets you select files on the basis of their path name, their file name, whether they have been changed since the last backup, or whether they have been changed since a particular date. The parameters can be combined, so you can back up files in just about any way you like.

The Backup command can have as many as nine parameters:

**backup <source> <drive> /A /S /M /F /D:<date> /T:<time> /L:<logfile>**

<source> is the file or set of files you want to back up. You can specify a drive (such as *a:*), a path (such as *a:\myfiles*), a file name with or without wildcards (such as *a:*.doc*), or a combination of these elements (such as *a:\myfiles\report.doc*).

<drive> is the letter, followed by a colon, of the drive (such as *a:*) that contains the disk that receives the backup files. You must specify <drive>.

/A adds the backup files to the backup disk, rather than erasing all files on the backup disk as the command usually does before making the backup copies.

/S backs up files from all subdirectories.

/M backs up only the files that have been modified since the last backup.

/F, in versions prior to 4, formats the target disk if it isn't already formatted. The /F parameter uses the Format command file (FORMAT.COM) to format the target disk, so FORMAT.COM must be in either the current directory or a directory that is in the command path. The /F parameter isn't required in versions 4 and later. If you haven't already formatted the disk, note that MS-DOS automatically formats the floppy disk for the normal capacity of the drive, again assuming that it can find FORMAT.COM. You can, however, use the /F parameter either to format a set of floppy disks or to format one or more floppy disks with a capacity other than the one MS-DOS assumes for the floppy disk drive (for example, specify */f:360* to format 360 KB floppy disks in a 1.2 MB drive). When MS-DOS finishes whatever formatting you choose, it moves on to the backup procedure you've requested in your Backup command.

/D:<date> backs up all files that have changed since <date>. Enter <date> just as you would for the Date command.

/T:<time> backs up all files that have changed since <time> on <date>. Enter <time> just as you would for the Time command.

/L:<logfile> creates a log file on the disk in the source drive. The log file contains the date and time of the backup procedure and, for each file that is backed up, the path name, the file name, and the number (assigned by MS-DOS) of the floppy disk that contains the file. If a log file already exists, the backup information is added at the end, creating a history of backups for the source drive. If you include /L but omit the colon and <logfile>, MS-DOS names the log file BACKUP.LOG and stores it in the root directory of the source drive.

> **NOTE:** *Although the Backup command exists in versions 2 and later of MS-DOS, not all the versions include all the parameters described here, nor are all the versions and releases of MS-DOS compatible with one another. For a list of the parameters available to you, check the documentation that came with your version of MS-DOS. You should use the same version of MS-DOS both to back up and to restore files.*

## Backing Up All the Files in a Directory

The simplest way to back up files is by directory. You back up all files in a directory by specifying just the path of the directory and the letter of the floppy disk drive that contains the backup floppy disk. To ensure that the examples proceed smoothly, have ready either a formatted blank floppy disk or a new floppy disk that matches the capacity of your floppy disk drive. (Remember, if you have version 3 or earlier, the floppy disk must be formatted before you back up any files.)

To back up all the files in the directory named \RUNDOS\MKT\BUDGET, type the following:

```
C:\RUNDOS\MKT>backup budget a:
```

MS-DOS displays a warning:

```
Insert backup floppy disk 01 in drive A:

WARNING! Files in the target drive
A:\ root directory will be erased
Press any key to continue . . .
```

If you don't use the /A parameter, MS-DOS erases any files on the backup floppy disk before it makes the backup copies. This warning gives you a chance to make certain the correct floppy disk is in the drive. Put your blank floppy disk in drive A, and press any key.

If you have version 4 or later and are using an unformatted floppy disk, MS-DOS begins the backup procedure by formatting the floppy disk. When the backup procedure begins, MS-DOS displays the name of each file as it makes the copies:

```
*** Backing up files to drive A: ***
Floppy disk Number: 01

\RUNDOS\MKT\BUDGET\BGT1.XLS
\RUNDOS\MKT\BUDGET\BGT2.XLS
\RUNDOS\MKT\BUDGET\BGT3.XLS
```

The directory of the backup floppy disk shows one or two files you might not expect. Type the following:

```
C:\RUNDOS\MKT>dir a:
```

If you're using version 3.3 or later, the MS-DOS response to your directory command looks something like this:

```
Volume in drive A is BACKUP  001
Volume Serial Number is 2543-14F7
Directory of A:\

BACKUP   001        72 10-16-93    1:48p
CONTROL  001       311 10-16-93    1:48p
    2 file(s)       383 bytes
                1212928 bytes free
```

MS-DOS has stored all the backed-up files in the file named BACKUP.001 and all the path names in the file named CONTROL.001. (On a second backup floppy disk, the extensions would be 002; on a third backup floppy disk, they would be 003.) Note that the size of BACKUP.001 corresponds to the total number of bytes in the three files it contains; CONTROL.001 contains all the extra information MS-DOS needs to restore those files.

If you're using version 3.2 or earlier, MS-DOS responds:

```
Volume in drive A has no label
Directory of  A:\

BACKUPID @@@       128  10-16-93  1:48p
BGT1     XLS       152  10-16-93  8:17a
BGT2     XLS       152  10-16-93  8:17a
BGT3     XLS       152  10-16-93  8:17a
         4 File(s)   358400 bytes free
```

BACKUPID.@@@ is a small file that MS-DOS stores on a backup floppy disk to identify it. Also, note that MS-DOS has added 128 bytes to each of the files you backed up; this addition contains the path and file name of the file that was backed up and is used by the Restore command. The Restore command deletes the path and file name information, so the restored version of the file is identical to the one you backed up. You'll work with the Restore command later in the chapter.

If a Backup command fills the floppy disk before backing up all the files you specified, MS-DOS prompts you to put in another floppy disk. It displays the same warning but refers to the second floppy disk as Floppy Disk Number 02.

If another floppy disk is required, MS-DOS prompts again, increasing the floppy disk number each time. If you were actually backing up files, you would label the floppy disk you just used with the contents and date and store it in a safe place.

## Backing Up All Subdirectories

You can back up the files in the current directory and all its subdirectories with the /S parameter. For example, the current directory is \RUNDOS\MKT. To back up all the files in it and all its subdirectories, you would type *backup \*.\* a: /s*. MS-DOS would display the names of all 13 files it backed up from the directories \RUNDOS\MKT, \RUNDOS\MKT\WP, and \RUNDOS\MKT\BUDGET. This backup floppy disk would contain all your marketing files, not just the files from one of the subdirectories.

## Backing Up a Specific File

You can back up a specific file by including a file name with the Backup command. For example, if the current directory were \RUNDOS\MKT\WP, you would type *backup let1.doc* to back up just the file LET1.DOC. You can use wildcard characters to back up a set of files with the same name or extension. For example, typing *backup \*.doc* would back up all files whose extension is DOC.

## Backing Up Only Files That Have Changed

As the number of your files increase, you might want to be even more selective about the ones you back up. For example, a word processing directory might contain hundreds of documents, but only a few you're working with now. The /M (Modify) parameter of the Backup command backs up only those files that have changed since the directory was last backed up. To see this parameter, you need a file that has changed since you backed up \RUNDOS\MKT in the last example. Create a short file by copying from the console:

```
C:\RUNDOS\MKT>copy con new.doc
This file has changed
since the last backup.
^Z
        1 file(s) copied
```

Now tell MS-DOS to back up any file that has changed since the directory was last backed up:

```
C:\RUNDOS\MKT>backup *.* a: /m
```

MS-DOS displays its warning and, when you press a key, displays the backed up files:

```
*** Backing up files to drive A: ***
Floppy disk Number: 01

\RUNDOS\MKT\NEW.DOC
```

Only the new file is backed up.

You can also back up only those files that have changed since a particular date with the /D:<date> parameter. For example, if you typed the command *backup \*.\* /d:10-16-93*, MS-DOS would back up all files that were created or changed after October 16, 1993, whether or not they had been backed up before.

### Adding Files to a Backup Floppy Disk

Each form of the Backup command you have used so far starts by erasing any files on the backup floppy disk. There might be times, however, when you want to back up files from several different directories on one floppy disk or add a file or two to an existing backup floppy disk. The /A parameter adds a file to a backup floppy disk without erasing any backup files it contains.

If you periodically back up a few files from several different directories, you can use the /A parameter to put all the backup files on one floppy disk. A word of caution about this technique: With versions of MS-DOS through 3.2, if a file you add to a backup floppy disk has the same name and extension as a file already on the floppy disk, MS-DOS changes the extension of the added file to @01, regardless of what it was before.

## RESTORING FILES TO THE HARD DISK WITH THE RESTORE COMMAND

It's easy to restore a file from a backup floppy disk to the hard disk using the Restore command. Simply insert the backup floppy disk in the floppy disk drive and type *Restore*, specifying the name of the file or files to be restored. The Restore command needs the path and file name information added to files by the Backup command, so you can restore only files that were backed up with the Backup command. The Restore command in versions 5 and later can restore files backed up with the Backup command in any prior version of MS-DOS. If you don't have version 5 or later, however, you should use the same version of MS-DOS for both the Backup and Restore commands.

The Restore command can have as many as 12 parameters:

**restore <drive> <path><filename> /S /P /M /N /D /A:<date> /A:<date> /E:<time> /L:<time>**

<drive> is the letter, followed by a colon, of the drive (such as *a:*) that contains the backup floppy disk. You must include <drive>.

<path> is the path name, preceded by a drive letter and a colon, if appropriate, of the directory to which the file is to be restored. If you omit <path>, the file is restored to the current directory.

<filename> is the name of the file to be restored. You can use wildcard characters to restore a set of files. You must specify either <path> or <filename>.

/S restores files to all subdirectories.

/P tells MS-DOS to prompt you for confirmation before restoring read-only files or files that have changed since they were last backed up.

/M restores files that were *modified* since they were backed up.

/N restores files that have been deleted from the original source disk since they were backed up.

/D doesn't restore any files; it displays a list of the files stored on the backup floppy disk that match the path and file names you specified as part of the Restore command (version 5 only).

/B:<date> restores only those files that were changed on or *before* <date>. Enter <date> just as you would for the Date command.

/A:<date> restores only those files that were changed on or *after* <date>. Enter <date> just as you would for the Date command.

/E:<time> restores only those files that were changed at or *earlier than* <time> on <date>. Enter <time> just as you would for the Time command.

/L:<time> restores only those files that were changed at or *later than* <time> on <date>. Enter <time> just as you would for the Time command.

> **NOTE:** *Although the Restore command exists in versions of MS-DOS numbered 2 and later, not all the versions include all the parameters described here. For a list of the parameters available to you, check the documentation that came with your version of MS-DOS.*

> **WARNING:** *Don't use the Backup or Restore command if you have entered an Assign, Join, or Substitute command to alter the way MS-DOS interprets drive letters. Because these commands can mask the type of drive, MS-DOS could damage or delete the files you specify in the commands or other files on the disk.*

To prepare for the Restore command examples that follow, type the following command to back up all the files in \RUNDOS\MKT\WP:

```
C:\RUNDOS\MKT\WP>backup *.* a: /l
```

MS-DOS issues the usual warnings; press a key to back up the files. After MS-DOS displays the names of the files it backed up, delete all the files from the hard disk by typing:

```
C:\RUNDOS\MKT\WP>del *.*
```

This completes preparation for the Restore examples.

## Restoring a Specific File

Inadvertently erasing or changing a file is probably the most common reason for restoring a file. You can restore a specific file by specifying the source drive and the target drive, path name, and file name with the Restore command. (You must include the path if you are restoring a file to a directory other than the current directory, and the path you specify must be the same as the path from which the file was originally backed up.)

For example, if the current directory were \RUNDOS\MKT\WP, you would type *restore let1.sty* to restore only the file LET1.STY. (You can omit the drive and path because you're restoring the file to the current directory.)

You can use wildcard characters to restore a set of files with the same name or extension. For example, to restore all the files whose extension is DOC that you backed up from the current directory (\RUNDOS\MKT\WP), you would type *restore a: *.doc*.

If you enter the Restore command with a path name and the wildcard specification *.*, MS-DOS restores all files that belong in that directory.

## Restoring All Subdirectories

Just as the /S parameter of the Backup command backs up the files in a directory and all its subdirectories, the /S parameter of the Restore command restores the files in a directory and all its subdirectories. To restore the files in \RUNDOS and all its subdirectories, you would type *restore a: \rundos\*.* /s*.

## Selecting Files to Be Restored

A file you restore replaces a file with the same name on the hard disk. You might not want this replacement, especially if you have changed the file on the hard disk since the backup floppy disk was made. You can protect yourself from unwanted changes by using the /P (Prompt) parameter of the Restore command, which tells MS-DOS to prompt for confirmation if the file on the hard disk has changed since the backup was made.

> **WARNING:** *If you're using version 3.2 or earlier and are restoring files that were backed up with a previous version of MS-DOS, be sure to use the /P parameter. If MS-DOS asks whether to restore files named MSDOS.SYS, IO.SYS, IBMBIO.COM, or IBMDOS.COM, reply* n *(no). Otherwise, you would replace parts of your MS-DOS program with portions of an earlier version, and MS-DOS wouldn't start from your hard disk.*

Remember, backing up your files is your best and cheapest insurance against hard disk problems and those occasional lapses that lead us to make mistakes. It doesn't matter how well you know how to use the backup capabilities if you don't use them.

# The MS-DOS Shell

**V**ersions 4 through 6 of MS-DOS include a program called the MS-DOS Shell that lets you use menus and small on-screen images to manage your files and disks without typing MS-DOS commands or file names at the system prompt. With the Shell, you can see your directory structure outlined on-screen, and you can navigate from one directory to another with the keyboard or a mouse. You can also set up your application programs so you can run them by selecting from a list. If you have version 5 or later of MS-DOS, you can even switch among multiple programs without having to quit one before you start another.

This program is called a *shell* because it surrounds MS-DOS. When you use it, you see the Shell and its menus rather than MS-DOS or its system prompt. The Shell even adds some capabilities that MS-DOS commands don't offer. For example, you can rename a directory, move one or more files without having to copy and erase them, and view the contents of two disks or directories at the same time.

This chapter gives you a quick tour of the Shell for versions 5 and later. It shows you how to use the Shell's major capabilities with either the keyboard or the mouse. If you have version 4 of MS-DOS, your Shell is visually similar but differs in some significant respects. You can use this chapter as a general guide to the Shell, but refer to your documentation and to online Help in your Shell for specifics. If you have version 6.2 of MS-DOS and would like to use the Shell, you can order the Supplemental Diskette (see the manual that came with MS-DOS).

## STARTING THE SHELL

MS-DOS can be installed so that it runs the Shell whenever you start or restart your computer, or so that it waits until you give the command to run the Shell. If MS-DOS runs the Shell automatically, the Shell appears as soon as MS-DOS finishes its startup routine. If MS-DOS does not run the Shell automatically, you see the normal MS-DOS startup, ending with the system prompt. In this case, you start the Shell by typing its name:

```
C:\>dosshell
```

When you start the Shell, the program begins by reading the name of each directory and file from the disk in the current drive. If the disk contains many directories and files, the Shell reports on its progress in a box headed *Reading Disk Information*. The Shell then displays its opening screen, which looks like the illustration at the top of the next page. For simplicity, the illustration shows only the files most likely to be in the root directory of a hard disk. You might see others.

**NOTE:** *If your opening Shell screen doesn't show areas headed* Directory Tree *and* Main, *you can change the display by choosing Program/File Lists from the View menu at the top of the screen. If you don't know how to do this, refer to the illustrations and disregard your display for a few minutes.*

The Shell operates either in *text mode*, as shown in the preceding illustration, or in *graphics mode*. Text mode uses text characters only—no pictures—to create the display you see. Graphics mode, which you can use on EGA, VGA, and similar displays, combines text characters and some graphic images. Figure 11-1 on the next page shows how the screen in the preceding illustration looks in graphics mode. Notice that the mouse pointer is arrow-shaped instead of rectangular and that small images of disk drives and file folders replace the square brackets used in text mode.

The rest of this chapter shows screens in graphics mode. If you would like to switch to graphics mode, press the Alt key, then press the letter O, and then press the letter D. When a box labeled *Screen Display Mode* appears, press the Down arrow key until the dark highlight rests on the choice that begins with the word *Graphics*. Press Enter, and your screen will change to graphics mode.

## Parts of the Shell Window

The opening Shell screen shows a large *window* containing a number of different elements. This window also shows two major parts of the Shell, the *File List* at the top and the *Program List* below it. From top to bottom, the principal elements in the Shell's opening window are listed at the top of the next page and labeled in Figure 11-1.

- The top line of the screen (title bar) identifies the MS-DOS Shell.

- The second line (menu bar) displays the names of the available menus: File, Options, View, Tree, and Help. You choose commands from these menus.

- The next two lines identify the current drive and directory (probably C:\, as shown earlier) and show the disk drives attached to your system.

- The next one-third to one-half of the window comprises the File List area, which is divided vertically into two smaller sections.

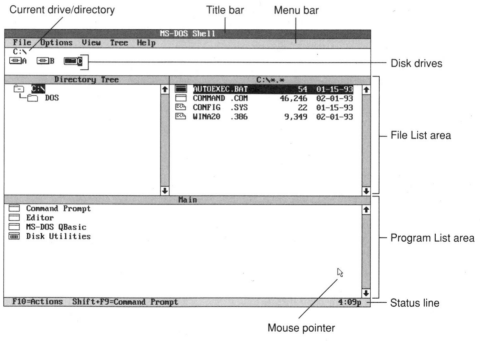

**Figure 11-1.**
*Parts of the MS-DOS Shell window in versions 5 and later.*

The left-hand portion, titled *Directory Tree*, shows all the directories on the current disk, arranged with subdirectories indented to the right and connected by lines that show the directory structure. This display is like the output of the Tree command. A minus sign inside the symbol that represents a directory (for example, the symbol to the left of C:\) means the directory contains one or more subdirectories that are currently displayed in the directory tree. A plus sign inside the symbol that represents a directory means that the directory contains one or more subdirectories that are not currently displayed.

The right-hand portion lists the files in the current drive and the directory (C:\*.* in the preceding illustration). Like a directory listing, these entries list the name, size, and date of creation or last change of each file in the selected directory.

■ The lower section of the Shell window, titled *Main*, is the Program List area. It displays a list of programs you can run. Until you add your own programs to this window, it contains at least two basic choices, Command Prompt and Disk Utilities.

■ Finally, the bottom line of the screen (status line) shows you the time of day and the effect of using two shortcut keystrokes, F10 and Shift-F9 (produced by holding down either Shift key and pressing F9). The F10 key activates the menus in the menu bar; Shift-F9 lets you temporarily leave the Shell and work at the MS-DOS system prompt. (To return to the MS-DOS Shell from the system prompt, type *exit* and press Enter.)

## Using the Keyboard and Mouse

Before you begin to explore the Shell, it's useful to know how to get around in it with a mouse or with the keyboard.

If you have a mouse, you already know that using one is easy and relatively standard among different application programs. In the Shell, maneuvering is as simple as you'd expect: Just roll the mouse on your desktop until the pointer is wherever you want it to be on the screen. Once you've pointed to the item or to the part of the window you want, you can select it by clicking the left mouse button. (The right button is inactive in the Shell.) For certain tasks, you double-click on an item by pressing the left button twice in rapid succession. In addition, you sometimes drag an item, as when you move a file from one directory to another, by pressing and holding the left button and moving the mouse pointer to a new location before releasing the button.

With the keyboard, you use the Tab key to move from one area of the Shell to another—for example, to move from the list of drives to the Directory Tree and then to the list of files in the current directory. To reverse direction, press Shift-Tab.

Figure 11-2 on the next page describes basic techniques you can use to perform the most common Shell operations with the keyboard or a mouse.

If you're a keyboard user who is unfamiliar with menu-based programs, don't be concerned if the techniques don't have much meaning as yet; they soon will. For both mouse and keyboard, the hands-on examples in this chapter also help you along when necessary.

| *Keyboard* | *Mouse* |
|---|---|
| **To select a menu:** | |
| Press either Alt or F10 to activate the menu bar; press the key letter of the menu name (underlined in graphics mode, highlighted in text mode). | Click on the menu name. |
| **To select a menu command:** | |
| Press the key letter of the command you want (underlined in the command name). | Click on the command. |
| **To select a file:** | |
| Highlight the file name by using the arrow keys. | Click on the file name. |
| **To choose (carry out) a command:** | |
| Highlight the command name by using the arrow keys, then press the Enter key. | Double-click on the command name. |

**Figure 11-2.**
*Basic keyboard and mouse techniques.*

**NOTE:** *For the sake of standardization, this chapter assumes a computer with a hard disk (drive C) and at least one subdirectory (C:\DOS). If your system differs, the examples are still appropriate but might not work exactly as described.*

## HELP IS A KEYSTROKE AWAY

The Shell includes on-screen help information that can guide you through most of its features. You can request either general information or direct help with a specific situation. General help is a good way of finding out about the Shell and how it works—which keys you use, what procedures are available, and so on. Direct help provides details about whatever task you're working on at the time you request help. To request general help, you use the Help menu at the top of the screen. To request direct help, you choose the item or command you want and then press F1. You'll try both types of help in the following examples.

Start with general help by choosing the Help menu using one of the methods described below:

- With the keyboard, press Alt or F10 to activate the menus, and then press H.

- With the mouse, click on Help.

The Help menu opens, showing a list of choices with Index highlighted. Press Enter, and the Shell displays a window headed *MS-DOS Shell Help*:

The top line of the Help window contains the title of the screen. The main part of the Help window, titled *MS-DOS Shell Help Index*, describes what you can do next. The bottom line of the Help window—no matter what Help information is displayed—offers you five choices:

- *Close* ends Help, removes the Help window, and returns you to whatever you were doing.

- *Back* returns to the previous Help display if you've moved from one topic to another within Help.

- *Keys* displays a list of topics related to using the keyboard with the Shell.

- *Index* displays the Help index you're looking at now.

- *Help* displays help on Help.

Right now, notice that the box labeled *MS-DOS Shell Help Index* starts with a few lines that tell you how to choose an index topic. Just below this is the heading *Keyboard Help*, which is followed by a group of topics beginning with *General MS-DOS Shell Keys*. The index breaks Help information into broad categories with related topics grouped under them. To see what help is available, press the PgDn key a few times, stopping when you see the heading *MS-DOS SHELL BASICS HELP* and the topic *Welcome to MS-DOS Shell*. Now try requesting some help using one of the two methods listed at the top of the next page:

- With the keyboard, press the Tab key as many times as necessary to move the highlight or the small arrow at the left edge of the window to *Welcome to MS-DOS Shell*; press Enter.

- With the mouse, double-click on *Welcome to MS-DOS Shell*.

The title at the top of the window changes to *Welcome to MS-DOS Shell*, and the old display is quickly replaced by a description of the Shell. Press the PgDn key several times. At the end of the description, you see the the words *Next topic* followed by *Scroll Bars*. Press the Tab key to select this new topic and press Enter, or double-click on it with the mouse. The window changes again, this time to one that tells you how to use the scroll bar the Shell displays along the right edge of certain windows.

Instead of moving deeper into Help, now try moving back the way you came. Choose the button marked *Back* at the bottom of the window. Either press the Tab key until the mouse pointer is on *Back* and press Enter, or click on *Back* with the mouse. The Help display changes to the previous screenful of information, *Welcome to MS-DOS Shell*. Choose *Back* again, and you see the original index screen.

If you want, experiment with other Help topics or with the other buttons at the bottom of the window. When you're ready to stop, either press Esc or use the Close button by tabbing to it and pressing Enter or by clicking on the button with the mouse.

Before leaving the subject of Help entirely, try requesting some direct help. First, choose the File menu (press Alt-F or click on File). Notice that the Open command is highlighted. Ask Help what this command does. Press the F1 key, and a Help window appears, this one telling you not only about the File Open command, but also referring you to additional information if you need it. Press Esc to close the Help window.

If you plan to use the Shell frequently, consider browsing through Help as you just did. It's a good way to learn to use the Shell. And remember the F1 key; it's all you need to request help on a particular task.

## THE FILE LIST

If you're using the keyboard to operate the Shell, you use the Tab key to activate the screen area you want to work in. If you're using a mouse, clicking in an area is enough to activate that portion of the window.

The current drive—probably drive C—should be highlighted. To prepare for the next examples, select the Directory Tree by pressing the Tab key or by clicking the mouse anywhere in that area. If the highlight is on the root directory (for example, C:\), use the Down arrow key or the mouse to highlight a different directory.

**NOTE:** *If you're using the Shell with a monochrome display and you see only two colors, one dark and one light, you can make your screen more closely match the shading in the illustrations in this chapter by changing to four-color monochrome. To do this, press the Alt key and then press the letter O twice. When a box labeled* Color Scheme *appears, press the Down arrow key until the dark highlight is on* Monochrome-4 Colors. *Press Enter, and your screen will change to shades of light and dark.*

## The File Menu

The Shell menus are lists of choices. Although they are menus like those in a restaurant, they show you both what items you can choose and whether the Shell will ask for more information when you make a choice. To see this, select the File menu again. The screen should look like this:

Notice that the menu items are displayed in both light (dimmed) and dark characters. The Shell uses dimmed characters to let you know which menu options you can't choose because they're not appropriate for what you're doing at the time.

Right now, the File menu tells you that you can open a file (to work with), run a program file, search for a file, delete (careful!) or rename the current directory, create a directory, or exit the Shell. Until you select one or more files, these are the only actions you can perform from the File menu. You can't print, for example, because you haven't selected a file to print.

The ellipsis (...) following certain choices, such as Run, means that the Shell needs a little more information before it can carry out the command. When you see an ellipsis following a command name, you can expect the Shell to prompt you for more information before it carries out the command. You'll see how this works a bit later. Keys and key combinations, such as *F8* and *Alt-F4* along the right edge of the menu, represent shortcut keys you can press instead of using the menu to choose the commands they carry out.

Press Esc to close the File menu.

## Selecting a Directory

The Directory Tree outlines the directory structure of the disk in the current drive. If it's not already highlighted, select your \DOS directory. There are faster ways to move through a list, but for now, press an arrow key until DOS or the name of your MS-DOS directory is highlighted, or click on DOS (press the PgDn key, if necessary, to bring the directory into view). The area to the right should show the MS-DOS files.

(If you don't have a hard disk, substitute the root directory of your startup disk for the \DOS directory unless the instructions here tell you otherwise.)

Select the files area to the right of the Directory Tree by pressing the Tab key or by clicking anywhere in that portion of the screen.

## Scrolling Through the Directories

The list of files in \DOS is probably too long to fit on the screen, so to see it all you need to *scroll* through the directory. Using the keyboard, you can scroll through this or any other long list of files or directories in any of several ways:

- By pressing the Down (or Up) arrow key to move a line at a time.

- By pressing the PgDn (or PgUp) key to move a screen at a time.

- By pressing a letter key to move directly to the first entry that begins with that letter.

- By pressing the Home key to move to the first entry in the list or by pressing the End key to move to the last entry.

If you're using a mouse, the Shell includes a mechanism that makes scrolling even easier: the *scroll bar*, for which you saw Help earlier. The scroll bar is the vertical bar at the right margin of each window. It has an arrow at the top and at the bottom and contains a shaded box. Clicking on one of the arrows moves a list one line in the direction of the arrow. Clicking in the blank part of the scroll bar moves a screenful, and dragging the shaded box to any position between the top and bottom moves you the same relative distance in the list.

To try scrolling through a list, use one of the techniques described on the previous page to view different parts of the \DOS directory.

## Selecting Files

In order to work with your files, both MS-DOS and the Shell require you to indicate which files you want to affect with any particular command. From the MS-DOS command prompt, you type a file name, with or without wildcards, to specify files. Within the Shell, you mark the names of the files you want to affect.

With the mouse, a file is selected as soon as you point to it and click the left button. With the keyboard, you tab to the list of file names and use the arrow keys to highlight the file name you want. In graphics mode, the symbol to the left of the file name is highlighted as soon as you select the file. In text mode, an arrow and a triangle appear before the file name. Your next file-oriented action will affect that particular file.

With a file selected, open the File menu again. Notice that all of the choices except Create Directory are now available. That's because all the other commands on the menu can be applied to a selected file. Press Esc to close the menu.

You can select more than one file at a time—for copying, perhaps, or moving to another directory:

- To select a series of files with the keyboard, move the highlight to the name of the first file, press and hold the Shift key, and extend the selection with the arrow keys.

- To select a series of files with the mouse, click on the first file name, press and hold the Shift key, and click on the last file in the group you want to select.

- To use the keyboard to select files scattered throughout a list, press and release Shift and the F8 key. When you do this, the word *ADD* appears near the right edge of the status line at the bottom of the screen. Using the arrow keys to highlight file names, press the Spacebar to select each file you want. To switch back to normal selection, press Shift-F8 again.

- To use the mouse to select files scattered throughout a list, hold down the Ctrl key instead of the Shift key as you click on each file name you want.

If you've practiced selecting groups of files, reduce the selection to one file by choosing Deselect All from the File menu. (Press Alt, then F, then L, or click on File and then on Deselect All.)

The next few topics show you some of the File menu items; you can explore the rest. Most of the items are self-explanatory, but a few might not seem obvious. *Associate*, for example, lets you tell the Shell to run an application program when you choose a file with a particular file extension. You might associate your word processing program, for example, with files whose extension is DOC. If you need explanations you don't find here, remember that Help is always available.

## Copying a File

To see how the Shell prompts you for additional information, move to the files area and highlight APPNOTES.TXT from your \DOS directory. Now press F8 or select Copy from the File menu.

The screen should look like this:

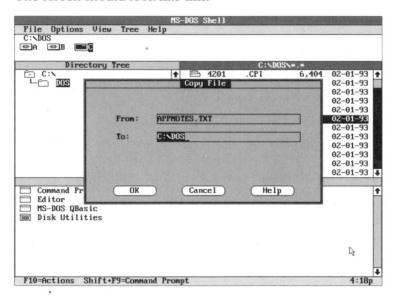

The Shell displays a box titled *Copy File* in the middle of the screen. The box, called a *dialog box*, is what the Shell uses to ask for any additional information it needs in order to carry out a menu command. As you can see, the Shell makes some assumptions. Here, for example, the From field is already filled in with APPNOTES.TXT, the file you selected to copy.

Because you can include a drive letter and path name when you copy files, the Shell tries to help here too by suggesting the current directory, placing the cursor at the end, and highlighting its guess. To add to this drive and path, you would press the Right arrow or the End key and start typing. To replace the suggested drive and path, you would simply start typing; the characters you typed would replace what the Shell displayed.

You're going to copy APPNOTES.TXT to a file named APPNOTES.NEW in the current directory, so type *appnotes.new* and press Enter. The dialog box disappears, and APPNOTES.NEW is added to the list of files. It's as if you had typed the command *copy appnotes.txt appnotes.new* at the system prompt.

Moving a file with the Move command works just like copying a file, but the Shell deletes the original file after making the new copy. If you used the Shell to move APPNOTES.NEW from the current directory (\DOS) to the root directory, for example, the result would be the same as if you had typed in MS-DOS version 6 or 6.2 *move appnotes.new* \ or, in earlier versions of MS-DOS, *copy appnotes.new* \ and *del appnotes.new*.

**NOTE:** *If you're using a mouse, you can move a file easily by selecting it and, holding down the left mouse button, dragging the file to the name of a different directory. When you do this, the Shell asks if you're sure you want to move the file. If you are, click on Yes or press Enter. The file is moved. No need to copy and delete; no need even to choose the Move command from the File menu.*

### Viewing a File

Viewing a file is a quick way to see what's in it; you can't change the file—you can only look at it. DOSSHELL.INI is a text file created when you install MS-DOS. Among other things, this file tells the Shell about your system and the way it should look when it starts. Select DOSSHELL.INI from the list of files, then select View File Contents from the File menu. The screen should look like this:

```
═══════════════════ MS-DOS Shell ─ DOSSHELL.INI ═══════════════════
  Display  View  Help
 ┌──────────────────────────────────────────────────────────────────┐
 [   To view file's content use PgUp or PgDn or ↑ or ↓.              ]

 *************** WARNING ***********************
 This file may contain lines with more than 256
 characters. Some editors will truncate or split
 these lines. If you are not sure whether your
 editor can handle long lines, exit now without
 saving the file.

 Note: The editor which is invoked by the
         MS-DOS 5.0 EDIT command can be used
         to edit this file.
 *************** NOTE ***********************
 Everything up to the first left square bracket
 character is considered a comment.
 **********************************************
 [savestate]
 screenmode = text
 resolution = low
 startup = filemanager
 filemanagermode = shared
 sortkey = name
 pause = disabled
 explicitselection = disabled
 swapmouse = disabled
 tasklist = disabled
 switching = disabled
 ──────────────────────────────────────────────────────────────────
  ←┘=PageDown  Esc=Cancel  F9=Hex/ASCII                      4:25p
```

The top line identifies the file (DOSSHELL.INI), the next line lists the menus available (Display, View, Help), and the third line tells you which keys you can press to scroll through the file. (If you're using a mouse, you can also scroll by clicking on the PgUp, PgDn, and arrow symbols on this third line of the screen.) The main part of the screen shows part of DOSSHELL.INI.

The Shell can display files in either of two modes, ASCII or hexadecimal. As you see it now, the file is displayed as an *ASCII file*, so called because it is translated into readable text characters according to the American Standard Code for Information Interchange, or ASCII. In hexadecimal format, the characters in a file are translated into the mathematical language of computers—specifically, the base-16 numbering system often used by programmers. To see the hexadecimal view, press F9.

It's certainly different. Each line of the hexadecimal view shows 16 characters. The first column of numbers at the left margin is the address—in hexadecimal, of course—of the beginning of each line, starting at 0 at the beginning of the file. Each of the middle four columns of numbers is the hexadecimal representation of four characters, two digits per character. The 16 columns at the right show the ASCII characters that correspond to the hexadecimal digits in the line.

Press F9 again, and the display returns to the ASCII view. Press Esc to return to the File List display.

### Deleting a File

Using the Shell, you can delete one file, several files, all files in a directory, or any directory except the root (\) simply by selecting the file, files, or empty directory you want to delete, and then pressing Del or selecting Delete from the File menu. Because it's so easy to change directories and select files in the Shell, using the Shell to delete files you no longer need is a snap compared to typing comparable commands at the MS-DOS system prompt.

Simply because the Shell makes it so quick and easy to delete files, however, it's a good idea to give yourself some protection by making sure that the Shell asks you to confirm each deletion. With the Shell, in fact, you can protect yourself not only from inadvertently deleting a file with the Delete command, but also against inadvertently replacing a file by copying another in its place.

### Protecting Yourself

To protect yourself against inadvertently deleting a file, select the Options menu, then choose Confirmation. The Shell displays the dialog box shown on the facing page.

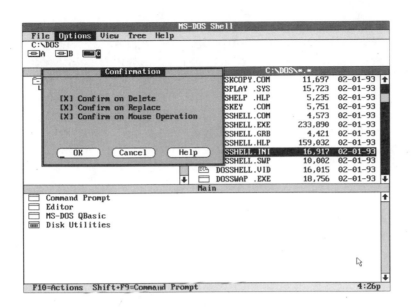

The brackets to the left of each option contain an X if the option is active. Selecting an active option turns it off; selecting an inactive option turns it on.

Confirm On Delete determines whether the Shell prompts you for confirmation before deleting a file. Confirm On Replace protects you against a less obvious way of losing a file: It determines whether the Shell prompts you for confirmation before copying over an existing file. Confirm On Mouse Operation determines whether the Shell warns you before carrying out a mouse operation that moves or copies a file.

All three options should be on (contain an X between the brackets). If one is off, tab to it and press the Spacebar to turn it on. When you're finished, press Enter to close the dialog box.

Now to delete a file. A while ago you created APPNOTES.NEW by copying APPNOTES.TXT. You don't need APPNOTES.NEW, so select it (don't select APPNOTES.TXT by mistake), then press Del or choose Delete from the File menu. The Shell displays a dialog box headed *Delete File Confirmation*.

This is how the Shell gives you a second chance. The dialog box shows the name of the file to be deleted, and the buttons at the bottom ask you to choose Yes, No, or Cancel. Press Enter to choose Yes. The Shell deletes APPNOTES.NEW and returns you to the File List display.

You can delete an entire directory and its contents in two quick steps with the Shell. Because the Shell refuses to delete a directory that contains files, you first select the directory in the Directory Tree, and then select and delete all files in it with the Select All and Delete commands on the File menu. Once the files are gone, you can use Delete again, this time to remove the directory itself. Because it's so easy, make sure you do, indeed, want to erase both the directory and everything in it—a few valuable files might be hidden in a welter of unnecessary ones.

Whether or not you have set Confirm On Delete, you must delete all files in a directory before you can delete the directory, just as when you use the MS-DOS Remove Directory command. Likewise, you cannot delete any directory that contains subdirectories, nor can you delete (or rename) the root directory, because each disk must contain this directory.

## Using the Options and View Menus

You just used the Confirmation command from the Options menu to protect against inadvertently deleting or copying over a file. Other choices on the Options and View menus let you display file names in a particular order; display information about the selected file, directory, and disk; display the files in two directories at once; display all the files on the selected disk; display only the File List; or display the Program List and File List at the same time, as the Shell is doing now.

### Controlling the Order in Which File Names Are Displayed

When you first start the Shell, the File List displays the file names in alphabetic order. You can change this order to display the files arranged (sorted) by extension, date, size, or even the order in which they are stored on the disk. To display the files arranged by extension, choose File Display Options from the Options menu. The Shell displays the Display Options dialog box, which looks like this:

In addition to specifying the order in which files are to be displayed, this dialog box lets you tell the Shell whether to display hidden and system files and whether to display files in ascending (A to Z) or descending (Z to A) order.

To change Display Hidden/System Files or Descending Order with the keyboard, you would tab to the option and press the Spacebar. With the mouse, you would simply click anywhere on the option. Either way, if the option is turned on, an X appears in the brackets; if the option is off, as it should be now, the brackets are empty.

The different ways you can sort files are in the list at the right side of the dialog box. These options are mutually exclusive, so only one can be active at any time. The active choice is indicated by a dark dot inside the circle (a dot between parentheses in text mode).

To try changing one of the settings, press Tab to move to the list and press the Down arrow key once to select *Extension*. Then press Enter or click on OK to close the dialog box. When the full window reappears, the files are listed alphabetically by extension—BAS files before COM files, and so on—rather than by name as they were before. Finding files arranged alphabetically by name is generally easier than if they're arranged by extension, so use the File Display Options command again and return to sorting by name.

### Displaying File, Directory, and Disk Information

The Show Information command on the Options menu displays information about the currently selected file, directory, and disk. Highlight APPNOTES.TXT, then choose the Show Information command. The screen should look like this:

There's nothing in this window for you to type or select; it simply shows you the following information:

- *File* shows the name and attributes of the selected file.

- *Selected* shows the letter of the selected disk drive and the number and total size of all selected files. If you're displaying directories from two disks, it shows both disk letters and the number and total size of all selected files on both disks.

- *Directory* shows the name of the directory that contains the file named under *File*, the number of bytes taken up by all the files in the directory, and the number of files in the directory. Knowing the size of a directory can be quite useful in certain operations, such as copying a directory from a hard disk to a floppy disk.

- *Disk* shows the name (volume label), capacity, available space, number of files, and number of directories on the disk that contains *File*.

Press Esc or click on Close to remove the Show Information window from the screen.

## Changing the View

The Shell lets you display the File List, the Program List, or both (as you're doing now). You choose what you want to see with the View menu. To change the view, open the View menu. The screen should look like this:

The first choice (Single File List) is highlighted; the item Program/File Lists is dimmer than the other choices because that's what the Shell is displaying now, so you can't choose it. Press Enter to select the highlighted choice. Now the File List takes up the entire window:

```
                          MS-DOS Shell
 File  Options  View  Tree  Help
 C:\DOS
 ⊟A   ⊟B   ▬C

         Directory Tree                      C:\DOS\*.*
 ┌─ C:\                          ↑   4201     .CPI      6,404  02-01-93  ↑
    └─ DOS                           4208     .CPI        720  02-01-93
                                     5202     .CPI        395  02-01-93
                                     ANSI     .SYS      9,029  02-01-93
                                     APPEND   .EXE     10,774  02-01-93
                                     APPNOTES .TXT      9,058  02-01-93
                                     ASSIGN   .COM      6,399  02-01-93
                                     ATTRIB   .EXE     15,796  02-01-93
                                     CHKDSK   .EXE     16,216  02-01-93
                                     CHKSTATE .SYS     38,752  02-01-93
                                     CHOICE   .COM      1,754  02-01-93
                                     COMP     .EXE     14,282  02-01-93
                                     COMMAND  .COM     53,022  02-01-93
                                     CMP      .EXE     14,282  02-01-93
                                     CONFIG   .SYS        215  02-01-93
                                     COUNTRY  .SYS     17,069  02-01-93
                                     CPSHELP  .OVL     29,828  02-01-93
                                     DBLSPACE .BIN     63,868  02-01-93
                                     DBLSPACE .EXE    286,338  02-01-93
                                     DBLSPACE .HLP     35,342  02-01-93
                                     DBLSPACE .INF      1,113  02-01-93
                                     DBLSPACE .SYS        217  02-01-93
                                ↓    DEBUG    .EXE     20,522  02-01-93  ↓
 F10=Actions   Shift+F9=Command Prompt                            4:35p
```

## Displaying Two Directories at Once

The Shell lets you display the files in two directories, on the same or on different drives. To see this, choose Dual File Lists from the View menu. The Shell divides the middle portion of the screen horizontally into two areas, one above the other. The areas are identical: Each includes the disk-drive icons, the Directory Tree, and the names of the files in the selected directory.

In the example shown at the top of the next page, the upper file area lists the names of the files in the \DOS directory on the system disk (usually drive C), and the lower file area lists the names of the files in the root directory.

When you're viewing a dual file list, you can select files in either list for copying, deleting, moving, and so on. You can select files in more than one directory by displaying two directories and activating Select Across Directories on the Options menu, and you can even view directories on two disks by selecting different drives for the two areas.

Choose the Single File List command again to return the display to one directory.

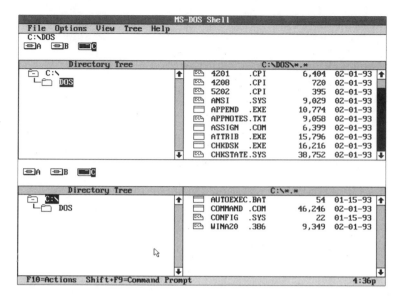

### Finding That File

The bigger the disk, the more you can store on it. That's the good part. The more you store, the harder it can be to find a particular file. That's the bad part. Eventually, everyone who uses a computer for a while confronts the same frustrating question: Where did I save that file?

If you use MS-DOS version 5 or later, that question becomes, if not negligible, at least less irritating. Rather than search through each directory, you can tell the Shell to do the work with the Search command on the File menu. Suppose, for example, that you wrote a bid proposal last year, and you think you saved it as PROPOSAL.DOC. You're pretty sure the proposal is still on your hard disk somewhere, and now you'd like to resurrect the document, change it a bit, and submit it as a different bid. With one command, you can tell the Shell to go look for what you want. When you choose Search from the File menu, you see a dialog box like the one on the next page.

Notice that the Shell initially proposes to search the entire disk for all files (*.*). That approach can be useful in some situations, particularly because the Shell's report on what it finds includes the path to each file. In this example, however, you're interested in a particular file name and extension, so you'd type *proposal.doc* in the field labeled *Search For*. (To find a set of files, you could use wildcard characters—for example, *.doc* to see a list of all files on the disk with the extension DOC.) To search the entire disk, leave the X next to the *Search entire disk* option. To limit the search to the current directory and its subdirectories, you turn off this option.

260

To try this command, tell the Shell to search the entire disk for the file UNDELETE.EXE. When you press Enter or click on OK to start the search, the Shell might become still for a short time. Don't be concerned; it's working, just as MS-DOS is working when you use Check Disk or a similar command. When the search is complete, a new window appears, displaying a list of all files that match the path (if any), file name, and extension you specified. Press Esc to clear the window.

## Displaying All the File Names on a Disk

Whereas the Search command gives you a way to find one or more needles in a haystack, the All Files command on the View menu lets you see the whole pile of hay—every file in every subdirectory on a disk. Choose the All Files command from the View menu.

When you choose the All Files command, the Shell combines two types of displays in one. At the right side of the screen, it lists the names of all files on the disk, showing the same directory information it normally shows in the File List area. Along the left side of the screen, it provides the same information you see when you choose the Show Information command from the Options menu. This combined display not only lets you see the directory information for each file on the disk, it also provides you with the directory name, attributes, directory size, and other details displayed by the Show Information command. As you select different file names, the Shell updates the information on the left side of the screen to tell you about the currently selected file.

Return to displaying the directory tree by choosing Program/File Lists from the View menu.

## Viewing the Directory Tree

When you use directories and subdirectories to organize your files, you can create a directory tree with many levels. The Tree menu lets you control how many directory levels are displayed in the Directory Tree area of the File List. If you want, you can choose to see only the root directory of a disk. On the other hand, you can tell the Shell to outline the entire tree, including every subdirectory of every directory on the disk. Between these extremes, you can selectively collapse and expand single directories or subdirectories according to the level of detail that interests you at the time.

You can use the various commands on the Tree menu to expand and collapse directories, but the Shell also recognizes certain keys that make your work much easier. Here are the commands on the Tree menu and what they do, as well as the keys you use:

- *Expand One Level* expands the selected directory to display the next directory level. Speed key: + (plus).

- *Expand Branch* expands the selected directory to show all directory levels under it. Speed key: ∗ (asterisk).

- *Expand All* expands the entire directory tree to show all subdirectories under all directories. Speed key: Ctrl-∗ (hold down Ctrl and press asterisk).

- *Collapse Branch* collapses the selected directory. Speed key: − (minus).

The Tree menu does not include a command or a key combination that collapses the entire directory tree once you've expanded all levels. You don't have to collapse the branches one by one, however. To return to the Shell's normal display of the directory tree, select the root directory and press the minus key to collapse the entire tree. Once that's done, press the plus key to expand the root directory one level.

Beyond this description, all you need is a little bit of experimentation with your own directory tree in order to become comfortable with the Shell's ability to show you different levels of your directory structure from the root directory to the entire tree. Notice, as you select different directories, that the file list at the right side of the File List area changes to show the files in the selected directory.

Although the Shell isn't suited for everything you'll do with MS-DOS, you can see that it makes many routine file-management tasks much simpler and quicker.

The next part of this chapter deals with a different side of the Shell—the Program List. If you want to stop temporarily, you can leave the Shell and return to MS-DOS by pressing F3 or choosing Exit from the File menu.

# THE PROGRAM LIST

If you think of the File List area as the part of the Shell window that provides information, you can think of the Program List area as the part that provides functionality. The Program List area can contain two different types of items: programs and program groups. Although both represent applications and other programs you can run directly from the Shell, programs are stand-alone items that run as soon as you activate them. Program groups are umbrella items that include several programs. (In graphics mode, a program group has a different icon from a program. In text mode, a program group is enclosed in square brackets [ ].)

When you start the Shell, the Program List area displays a list of programs and the name of one program group. Typically, the programs and the program group are:

- *Command Prompt*, which temporarily stops the Shell and displays the MS-DOS system prompt so that you can type MS-DOS commands. You return to the Shell by typing *exit*.

- *Editor*, which starts the versions 5 and later MS-DOS Editor program that you meet briefly here and learn about in more detail in the next chapter.

- *MS-DOS QBasic*, which starts the QBasic program, a version of the Microsoft QuickBasic programming language.

- *Disk Utilities*, which is a program group that displays another list of choices when you select it. In this case, Disk Utilities groups a set of commonly used MS-DOS disk and file operations.

You'll experiment with these and add programs and a group of your own. Before you start, however, prepare for one of the later examples by copying one file to a floppy disk in drive A. Put a formatted floppy disk in drive A, then highlight the file named DOSSHELL.INI, which you viewed earlier, in your \DOS directory. Now press F8 or choose Copy from the File menu to copy DOSSHELL.INI to A:\. You won't need the File List area for now, so clear the window a bit by choosing Program List from the View menu.

## Starting a Program

To start a program or display the items in a program group, you simply choose from the Program List. For example, Command Prompt should be highlighted now. Although you wouldn't necessarily consider this the name of a program, it does in fact start a program that causes MS-DOS to temporarily leave the Shell and display the system prompt. Press Enter or double-click on Command Prompt, and in a few moments the screen clears, MS-DOS displays an opening message, and you see the MS-DOS prompt.

To return to the Shell, type:

```
C:\DOS>exit
```

Unless you're running a program that has its own quit command, this is the command you use to return to the Shell.

## Switching Among Programs

Have you ever, while using one program (a word processor, for example), needed to use another program (a spreadsheet, say, or a graphics program)? If so, you had to leave the first program, start the second, finish with the second program, leave it, and start the first program again. Sometimes this can happen fairly often, making you spend too much time just starting and stopping programs.

The Shell includes a feature called the Task Swapper, which lets you start one or more programs and then switch from the Shell to each program with just a few keystrokes. You'll test this with the MS-DOS Editor and QBasic, both of which come with MS-DOS.

> **NOTE:** *If you're interested in trying the Task Swapper with your own application programs, you can follow the instructions given here by substituting the names of your application programs when you're told to activate the Editor and QBasic. A word processing program, such as Microsoft Word, will do. But try not to use a memory-resident ("pop-up") program, such as Doskey; you might see a message telling you to quit the program before returning to the Shell.*

To start the Task Swapper, display the Options menu. The fifth item is Enable Task Swapper, and this choice is turned either on or off. If it's on, it's preceded by a dot. If it's off, select it and press Enter to turn it on. When you're finished, press Esc to clear the Options menu.

Now the Program List area should be divided into two parts: The left half should be titled *Main*; the right half should be titled *Active Task List*. The right side displays the names of all programs that you have started and left running; you haven't left any running, so the list should be blank.

Start the Editor by choosing Editor from the Main window. When the Editor dialog box asks you which file to edit, type *edfile* and press Enter or click on OK. When the Editor starts, it displays a blank window. So that your applications will be easy to recognize, type the following line:

```
This is my Editor file.
```

Now return to the Shell without stopping the Editor. To do this, press Ctrl-Esc. In a few moments the Shell displays the Program List screen again. This time, Editor appears in the Active Task List to tell you that you can rejoin the Editor any time you like. To do so, you simply select it from the Active Task List.

Start a second program by choosing MS-DOS QBasic from the Main window. When the program asks you the name of the file to edit, type *basfile* and press Enter or click on OK. When QBasic starts, type:

```
This is my QBasic file.
```

Again, press Ctrl-Esc to return to the Shell. Now the Active Task List shows two entries, MS-DOS QBasic and Editor.

To switch to the Editor, select it from the Active Task List. There's the Editor again, just as when you left it. Now suppose you were using the Editor and remembered that you wanted to check something with QBasic. Hold down the Alt key and press Tab until the title bar at the top of the screen displays *MS-DOS QBasic*. Release the Alt key, and you're back to your other program. Press Ctrl-Esc to return to the Shell.

You can switch among your programs and the Shell at will by pressing Alt-Tab. When you press Alt-Tab, the Shell cycles through the name of each active program (including itself) in round-robin fashion. Unless you have started several programs, Alt-Tab is the only key combination you need to switch back and forth. If you'd like to see what other key combinations you can use, choose Keyboard from the Help menu, then choose Active Task List Keys.

If you want to start a program but won't use it right away, you can add it to the Active Task List without ever leaving the Shell. Highlight Command Prompt, but press Shift-Enter instead of just Enter. Now the Active Task List should contain Command Prompt, MS-DOS QBasic, and MS-DOS Editor.

When you're through using a program, just end it as you normally would; the Shell displays the Program List screen again, but now the name of the program you left doesn't appear in the Active Task List.

To stop the three tasks you've started, do the following: Choose Command Prompt from the Active Task List, and type *exit* when MS-DOS displays the system prompt. When the Shell reappears, Command Prompt is gone from the list of tasks. Next, switch to QBasic, and choose Exit from the File menu. Choose No when QBasic asks if you want to save the sample file. When you return to the Shell, switch to the Editor, choose Exit from the File menu, and again choose No when asked if you want to save the file. This time when you return to the Shell, there are no entries in the Active Task List.

You'll find that switching among programs like this lets you make much better use of your time at the computer.

## Selecting a Program Group

The symbol or brackets associated with Disk Utilities in the Main area tells you that selecting this item displays a different list of choices. To see the list, choose Disk Utilities.

The area of the screen is now titled *Disk Utilities*—the name of the program group you selected—rather than *Main*, and you see a different list of choices: Main (which returns you to the Main Program List screen), Disk Copy, Backup Fixed Disk, Restore Fixed Disk, Quick Format, Format, and Undelete. As you'll see shortly, you can customize this list of choices by adding your own program items and program groups. Choose Main to return to the Main screen.

When the Program List area is active, the menus aren't the same as when the File List is active. The Tree menu disappears because it isn't needed here. The Options and Help menus remain the same, and the View menu remains almost the same. (Refresh is not available from the Program List area.) The File menu, however, contains a number of different choices.

## The Program List File Menu

Rather than offering choices that deal with files, the Program List's File menu lets you manage its list of program items and program groups. Display the File menu; the choices include:

- *New*, which adds a new program item or program group to the Program List.

- *Open*, which starts the highlighted program item or displays the items in a selected program group. (It has the same effect as highlighting an item and pressing Enter.)

- *Copy*, which copies a program item to a program group you specify.

- *Delete*, which deletes a program item or a program group (from which you've already deleted all program items).

- *Properties*, which lets you specify the title, startup command, and other definitions of a program item or program group.

- *Reorder*, which lets you change the order in which the program items and program groups are displayed.

- *Run*, which lets you start any program, whether or not it is displayed in the list of program items and program groups.

- *Exit*, which leaves the Shell.

## Adding a Program Item

Adding a program item to the Shell can be fairly simple. You can even add a program that requires more than one command simply by separating the commands with semicolons.

Suppose you wanted to add an entry called Memory Check that would carry out the MS-DOS Mem command. Choose New from the File menu. The Shell displays a dialog box that gives you the choice of adding a Program Group or a Program Item. The Shell assumes you want to add a Program Item, which you do, so press Enter or click on OK.

Now the Shell displays the Add Program dialog box:

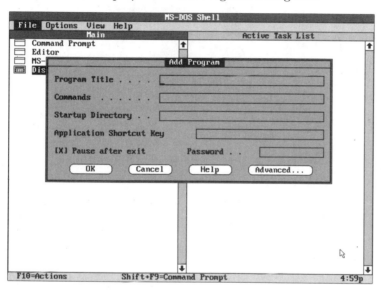

The Shell requires that you fill out only the Program Title and Commands fields to define a new entry. The Program Title field specifies how the Program List item will be displayed; type *Memory Check*. Press Tab to move to the Commands field, which specifies the command (or commands) to be carried out; type *mem* and press Enter. The Add Program dialog box disappears, and the item Memory Check is added to the list of programs.

Choose the new item by highlighting it and pressing Enter or by double-clicking on it; the screen clears, and in a few moments MS-DOS displays the report of the Mem command, followed by the message *Press any key to return to MS-DOS Shell.* Press any key to return to the Shell.

### Changing a Program Item

You can change any of the characteristics of a program item—the title, commands to be carried out, and so forth. The Shell refers to these characteristics as *properties*; to change them, you highlight the program item to be changed and select Properties from the File menu. Highlight Memory Check, and then select Properties from the File menu. The Shell displays the Program Item Properties dialog box:

This dialog box contains the same fields as the Add Program dialog box. Because it lets you change an existing definition, however, fields to which values have been assigned—in this case, Program Title and Commands—are filled in.

To change one of the properties or add a new one, you simply enter the new value in the appropriate field. Suppose, for example, you decide that you want the program item to be named Mem Command instead of Memory Check. You also want to assign it the password IQ.

Type *Mem Command* in the Program Title field, type *IQ* (notice the capitals) in the Password field, and press Enter to carry out the change. Try the command again. This time, a dialog box appears, asking for the password. Type *IQ*—be sure to type in capital letters, because the Shell can tell the difference—then press Enter. Once you've entered the password, the dialog box disappears, the screen clears, and the memory report is displayed. Your program item is the same command, but you've now given it a new definition.

### Deleting a Program Item

This Mem Command example has served its purpose, so you'll delete it. Make sure that Mem Command is highlighted, and select Delete from the File menu. The Shell displays the Delete Item dialog box shown below.

Like the Delete File dialog box, the Delete Item dialog box lets you confirm the name of the item to be deleted. Because you've assigned a password to Mem Command, the dialog box reminds you of the fact. The dialog box offers two choices, Delete and Do Not Delete. The Delete option is highlighted, and you are asked to choose OK, Cancel, or Help. You want to delete the item, so press Enter. The dialog box disappears, and the Shell continues to display the Main Program List screen, but Mem Command is gone.

## Customizing the Program List

You can customize the list of program items and program groups that the Shell displays, tailoring the Shell to reflect the programs you use. You might add a program group named Word Processing, for example, to include your word processor and associated programs, or you might add a program group named Financial for your spreadsheet or accounting programs. Once you create the groups, you will add program items to them. The program items run the programs.

### Adding a Program Group

Suppose you wanted to create a separate program group named Text Files that would let you edit, display, and print files from the Shell. You'll add the program group and then add the MS-DOS Editor to it.

269

**NOTE:** *If you want, you can try adding your word processor as the program item. Assuming that your word processor accepts a file name as part of the startup command, the following instructions should work for you. Just remember to use the command that starts your program instead of the Edit command that starts the MS-DOS Editor.*

To create the program group, choose New from the File menu just as when you added the Memory Check program item. As before, the Shell displays the New Program Object dialog box. This time, however, you don't want to accept the Shell's choice of the Program Item option, so select Program Group instead and then press Enter (or click on OK). The Shell displays the Add Group dialog box:

As the dialog box shows, the only field you must complete is Title, which specifies the group name you want in the Program List area. If you wish, you can also specify the Help text that the Shell displays if F1 is pressed when the group name is highlighted, and (as before) you can designate a password that must be entered in order to use the group. For this program group, you'll enter a title and some help text.

First type *Text Files* in the Title field, then tab to the Help Text field. Type *This group lets you edit text files*, and press Enter to save these entries; the Shell displays the Program List area again, with the added group Text Files.

Now activate the Text Files group by highlighting it and pressing Enter or by double-clicking on it. The title line at the top of the display changes from *Main* to *Text Files*, and even though you haven't added any program items yet, the list contains one choice: Main. The Shell adds this program item for you so you can return to the Main Program List screen. (You can also return by pressing Esc.)

## Specifying a Command Parameter

The first program item you'll add to the Text Files program group will run the MS-DOS Editor or the alternative you've chosen. (Yes, you can already run the Editor from the Main list, but it's used as an example here because most computer users have a text-handling program of some type.)

Choose the New command from the File menu. The Shell displays the New Program Object dialog box, just as it did when you added Memory Check and Text Files. Press Enter or click on OK to create a program item. The Shell displays the Add Program dialog box. Type *Text Editor* and tab to the Commands field.

When you specified the Memory command in the earlier example, you entered just the command name in the Commands field. A text editor, however, normally lets you specify the name of a file you want to work on. For example, if you include a file name with the command that starts the MS-DOS Editor, MS-DOS opens the file if it exists or creates the file if it doesn't exist; if you don't include a file name, MS-DOS starts the Editor without opening or creating a file.

To tell the Shell that you want a program item to accept one parameter, such as a file name, you include a percent sign followed by the numeral 1 (%1) in the Commands field. For the MS-DOS Editor, type *edit %1*. (For a different editor or a word processor, type the appropriate startup command. For example, type *word %1* if you're using Microsoft Word.) This process of creating a parameter is explained later, in the section "Designing Your Own Dialog Box." Now tab to the Startup Directory field.

## Specifying a Path

If you routinely use directories in your work, you probably organize your data files in different directories, depending on what they contain or what type of application you use them with. Your word processing files, for example, might be categorized by type (letters, memos, reports), client, department, or in any of a number of other ways.

In setting up a program to run from the Shell, you can use the Startup Directory field in the Add Program dialog box to change to a particular drive or directory whenever you start the associated program. If you write a lot of letters, for example, you might change to your LETTERS directory when you start your word processor.

To see how the startup directory works, tell the Shell to use the root directory of drive A whenever it starts by typing *a:\* in the Startup Directory field. Now tab to the Application Shortcut Key field.

### Specifying a Shortcut Key

Just as some Shell menu selections have keyboard shortcuts—F8 for Copy in the File Menu of the File List, for example—you can specify a shortcut key combination for a program item or program group. The shortcut key must be Shift, Alt, or Ctrl, combined with another key on the keyboard. To make Alt-E the shortcut key for the Editor, press Alt plus the E key. *Alt-E* appears in the Application Shortcut Key field. Finally, tab to the Pause After Exit field.

### Controlling the Pause Message

When you tried the Memory Check examples, you saw that the Shell displayed *Press any key to return to MS-DOS Shell* and waited to let you read the message and press a key. This pause isn't required, however, and you can control it with the Pause After Exit field. There's an X between the brackets now, to show that the option is turned on. Press the Spacebar (or click on the X) to turn the option off.

Chances are you won't want to keep anyone from using the Editor, so there's no need for a password. Besides, you've already seen how the password option works, so press Enter to tell the Shell you've finished with the dialog box. Instead of returning to the Program List, however, the Shell displays another dialog box titled Add Program.

### Designing Your Own Dialog Box

The command you entered for the Editor was *edit %1*, telling the Shell that you wanted the command to accept one parameter (a file name) of your choice. The Shell will have to prompt for this parameter, and the dialog box you're looking at now lets you specify the contents of the dialog box that displays the prompt.

The cursor is at the beginning of the Window Title field; this field specifies the title displayed in the bar at the top of the dialog box (*Add Program* in the dialog box you're working with now). Type *File To Edit* and tab to the Program Information field.

The Program Information field specifies the explanatory text that appears below the title but still at the top of the dialog box. (In the box you're working in now, the text reads *Fill in information for %1 prompt dialog.*) Type *Enter the name of the file to be edited (or press Enter to start the Editor with no file)*. Tab to the Prompt Message field.

The Prompt Message field specifies the text that appears to the left of the field to be filled in (here it's *Prompt Message* for the field you're working in now). The Edit command parameter must be a file name, so type *File name:* and tab to the Default Parameters field.

The Default Parameters field lets you specify a value that the Shell fills in for the command parameter. (You'll see how this works shortly.) Type *fred*, then press Enter to complete the definition of the Text Editor program item. The Shell displays the Text Files program list again, this time with two items: Main and Text Editor.

## Testing the New Program Item

To try out your new program item, check that the floppy disk with DOSSHELL.INI is in drive A. Highlight *Text Editor* and press Enter to start the program. First, the Shell displays the File To Edit dialog box that you just designed:

Check the title of the dialog box, the instruction line at the top, and the prompt to the left of the entry field. They should match the text you entered in the Window Title, Program Information, and Prompt Message fields a moment ago.

The entry field contains *fred*, the default parameter you specified in the Default Parameters field. If you pressed Enter now, the Shell would tell MS-DOS to run the Edit command, using FRED as the name of the file to edit. Because there is no such file, first MS-DOS would create it, and then the Editor would show you a blank screen.

Instead, request the DOSSHELL.INI file that you copied to the floppy disk in drive A earlier in the chapter. The Shell erases the default file name as soon as you start typing, so just type *dosshell.ini.*

Now press Enter. Drive A becomes active, and soon the screen fills with the lines of DOSSHELL.INI.

Right now you're just verifying that the Text Editor program item works, so select Exit from the Editor's File menu (or use the appropriate Quit command if you're using a different program). The Editor quits, and the Shell screen returns, showing your Text Files group and its two choices.

## The Disk Utilities Program Group

You can learn still more about defining program items and groups by selecting a program item from the Disk Utilities group and seeing how the fields are filled out. Just don't change anything. For example, return to the Main screen, and select Format in the Disk Utilities group. The screen looks like this:

Notice that the Parameters field is filled in with *a:*, suggesting that the floppy disk in drive A should be formatted. Now press Esc (not Enter) to return to the Program List and, with Format still highlighted, choose Properties from the File menu to see how the Format program item is defined. The screen should look like this:

One parameter, %1, is specified in this dialog box. To see how this parameter is defined, press Enter or click on OK. The Shell displays the Program Item Properties dialog box for %1:

Compare the fields of this dialog box with the dialog box itself, as illustrated earlier; the text in the fields matches the text that defines the title, instructions, and prompt of the Format dialog box. Press Enter or click on OK to clear the screen.

The Editor example showed the degree to which you can tailor the Shell to your own use. Although the example prepared only one command for MS-DOS to carry out (the Edit command with a file name as a parameter), remember that you can specify more than one command, if necessary, by separating the commands with a semicolon (surround each with blank spaces).

You've also seen how to specify and define a parameter for the Edit command. In your own work, you can specify more than one parameter, each of which has its own dialog box with separate instructions, prompts, and default values. Together, multiple commands and multiple parameters should let you add any program you like to the Shell Program List, providing all the startup information the program might need.

You added only one program item to the Text Files group, but you could add several more, using the same method you used to add the Editor. If you want, you can experiment with programs that are part of MS-DOS. You could, for example, add an item named Display File that runs a Type command.

Using the same techniques, you could add program groups such as Desktop Publishing or Financial Management to run all the application programs you use. With the Task Swapper, you could then start several of your application programs and switch among them without having to exit from one to start another. With the help of the Associate command on the File List's File menu, you can even set up your system so that the Shell starts a particular program and opens the specified file whenever you choose a file name with a specified extension.

Just as you can structure your file system to match your work, you can structure the program choices of the Shell to run the programs that you use.

## Deleting a Program Group

When you're through experimenting with the MS-DOS Editor program item, you can delete the program item from the Text Files group, and you can delete the Text Files group itself. A short while ago, you deleted the Mem Command program item. Deleting a program group is just as easy; the only catch is that you cannot delete a group that contains any program items. In this respect, deleting a program group is like using the Remove Directory command to delete a directory: It works only if the group or directory is empty.

To return the Program List to its original state, return to the Main Program List screen if necessary. Next, activate your Text Files group and highlight the Text Editor program item. Choose Delete from the File menu, and press Enter or click on OK when the Shell displays the Delete Item dialog box. (If you've added other program items to this group, delete them, too.)

Once you've deleted all of the program items in a group, you can delete the group itself. It's the same procedure you just followed. First, return to the Main Program List screen. Next, highlight Text Files, choose Delete from the File menu, and press Enter or click on OK to delete the group. When you're finished, the Shell displays the Main Program List screen again, this time without the Text Files group.

This chapter hasn't covered all the features of the Shell, but it has shown you the most common ones. Because the operating techniques are fairly consistent throughout the Shell and because the Help information is quite thorough, you should be able to learn what isn't covered by selecting the menu items and using the Help feature to guide you.

# 12

# Creating and Editing Files of Text

lthough computers were once thought of primarily as machines for mathematics—you still occasionally hear them referred to as "number crunchers"—word processing is the most common use of personal computers today. Word processing programs offer a stunning array of features, accommodating not only the usual memos and reports, but even book-length documents that include multiple columns, a table of contents, an index, and many graphics.

But this array of capabilities is a mixed blessing because a high-end word processor is a large program requiring a significant commitment from both the computer (memory and disk space) and the person using it (learning time).

Beginning with version 5, MS-DOS includes a simple menu-based text editor that offers a good alternative to a word processor for smaller jobs. The official name for this program is the *MS-DOS Editor,* but this chapter will use the name *Edit* instead, both because it's simpler and because that's the name of the command that starts the MS-DOS Editor.

Edit lacks many of the capabilities of a word processor: You must press Enter at the end of each line, for example, and you can't control the capabilities of your printer much beyond the simple printing of text. These very limitations, however, make Edit small, fast, and easy to learn. It's admirably suited for writing short memos and lists and for creating sets of MS-DOS commands known as *batch files.* If you have used a word processor, especially one with drop-down menus, Edit's basic operation should feel familiar.

This chapter shows you around Edit by using an example situation that could occur in any office: You're in charge of a project, and your team has completed several spreadsheets, a 10-page proposal, and a cover letter. You've copied these files to a floppy disk and want the team to review the results one last time before the presentation. You're going to send copies of the floppy disk to the team members, and you need a short memo to tell them what's on it.

NOTE: *If you don't have version 5 or later, you have a different editor, named Edlin, which is not described in this book. For a description of how to use this program, see the manual that came with your computer.*

## USING THE KEYBOARD AND THE MOUSE

Like many application programs, Edit responds to either the keyboard or a mouse for most operations. On-screen, the keyboard cursor is represented, as usual, by a flashing underline; the mouse is represented by a rectangular block (the mouse pointer). You use the keyboard and the mouse much as you do in the

Shell, so if you haven't yet tried out the Shell, turn to the heading "Using the Keyboard and Mouse" near the beginning of Chapter 11 for a description of how to display a menu and select a menu item or a file name. The text you find there, plus Figure 11-2, summarizes the techniques and defines possibly unfamiliar mouse terms, such as *click, double-click, drag,* and *select*. The first few examples in this chapter give instructions for both keyboard and mouse, but the remaining examples simply ask you to open a menu or choose a menu command.

In addition to choosing from menus, however, you'll frequently use two techniques with Edit that you don't need in the Shell: positioning the cursor where you want to edit text and selecting a block of text. The following descriptions provide some needed background information. Examples later in the chapter provide specifics.

## Positioning the Cursor

You can use either the keyboard or the mouse to position the cursor. You'll probably find yourself using both at different times, depending upon where your hands are positioned when you have to move the cursor. Figure 12-1 shows the main cursor-movement keys and their effect.

| Key | Moves the Cursor To |
| --- | --- |
| Right arrow | Next character |
| Left arrow | Previous character |
| Up arrow | Previous line |
| Down arrow | Next line |
| End | Last character in the line |
| Home | First nonblank character in the line |
| Ctrl-Right arrow | Beginning of the next word |
| Ctrl-Left arrow | Beginning of the previous word |
| Ctrl-Enter | Beginning of the next line |
| Ctrl-End | End of the document |
| Ctrl-Home | Beginning of the document |

**Figure 12-1.**
*Edit's cursor-movement keys.*

To position the cursor with the mouse, move the mouse pointer to the text location you want, and then click the left mouse button.

## Selecting a Block of Text

Some edit operations, such as moving and copying text, require you to select the block of text to be affected. Other operations, such as printing, let you select a portion of the document if you wish; otherwise, the action applies to the entire document.

To select a block of text with the keyboard, position the cursor at the first character to be selected, hold down the Shift key, and then use any of the cursor-movement keys described in Figure 12-1 to select the text you want. Edit highlights the selected text as you move the cursor. When you release the Shift key, the block remains selected until you move the cursor.

To select a block of text with the mouse, position the mouse pointer on the first character to be selected, press and hold the left mouse button, and move the mouse pointer to the last character of the block. The selected text is highlighted as you move the mouse. Just as when you select text with the keyboard, the text remains selected until you move the cursor again or position the mouse pointer elsewhere and click the left mouse button.

# STARTING EDIT

To start Edit from the MS-DOS system prompt, type its name:

```
C:\>edit
```

MS-DOS copies the Edit program into memory, and after a moment Edit displays its opening screen.

The screen looks substantially different from a normal MS-DOS display and is noticeably different from the opening Shell screen too. If you take a closer look, however, you can see that the Edit screen has the same essential features as the Shell: A large window in which you work, a menu bar across the top, scroll bars along the edges, and a bar across the bottom telling you how to carry out basic operations. For the most part, you can think of the differences between Edit and the Shell as comparable to the differences between a sedan and a station wagon: They don't look the same, but if you can drive one, you can drive the other. And, as you'll soon see, Edit is easy to work with.

# HELP

Right now, you should be looking at a large dialog box in the middle of the screen. As in the Shell, dialog boxes are Edit's means of displaying and requesting information. The flashing cursor suggests that you *<Press Enter to see the Survival Guide>*, so press Enter. The screen changes to this:

```
 File  Edit  Search  Options                              Help
                    HELP: Survival Guide
╔══════════════════════════════════════════════════════════════╗
Using the MS-DOS Editor:

  ▪ To activate the MS-DOS Editor menu bar, press Alt.
  ▪ To activate menus and commands, press the highlighted letter.
  ▪ To move between menus and commands, use the direction keys.
  ▪ To get help on a selected menu, command, or dialog box, press F1.
  ▪ To exit Help, press Esc.

Browsing the MS-DOS Editor Help system:

  ▪ To select one of the following topics, press the Tab key or the first
    letter of the topic. Then press the Enter key to see information on:

    ◀Getting Started▶   Loading and using the MS-DOS Editor and the
                        MS-DOS Editor Help system
    ◀Keyboard▶          Editing and navigating text and MS-DOS Editor Help

Tip: These topics are also available from the Help menu.

─────────────────────── Untitled ───────────────────────
 <F1=Help> <F6=Window> <Esc=Cancel> <Ctrl+F1=Next> <Alt+F1=Back>
```

The Survival Guide is the introductory screen to Edit's online help. (*Online* is a venerable computer term meaning that a program or a device is available; hence, online help.) Most of the information you need to operate Edit is available from online help whenever Edit is running.

As in the Shell, Edit's help feature explains what you can do at any point in using the program. And, as in the Shell, you can request two types of help: general information and specific instructions (known as *context-sensitive* help) for using a particular command or dialog box. The examples in this chapter direct you to display both types of help, but you can also request assistance any time you want by pressing F1 or by choosing a command from the Help menu. Because Edit's Help differs substantially from the Shell's, the next few pages describe Edit's Help in some detail.

Some help screens include several topics you can choose among. These topics are enclosed in left-pointing and right-pointing arrowheads. The cursor right now, for example, is under the *G* in the topic *Getting Started*. To see Edit's own description of how to use it and its help feature, select this topic by pressing Enter or by moving the mouse pointer anywhere between the arrowheads and clicking the right mouse button. Edit responds by displaying a set of topics on *Getting Started*.

At the top of the Help window, Edit displays *HELP: Getting Started* to remind you of the topic you chose. Below this are three choices: *Getting Started*, *Keyboard*, and *Back*. *Getting Started* is highlighted to show that it is the current topic; its choices are displayed in the lower part of the Help window. *Keyboard* displays additional help, and *Back* returns you to the previous help screen.

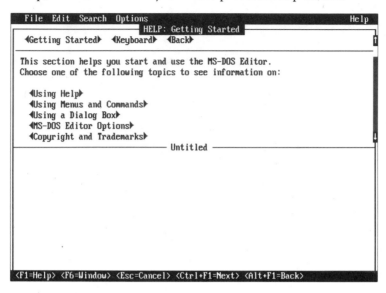

To see a little more help, select *Using Help*. Either press the Tab key until the cursor is under the *U* and then press Enter, or move the mouse pointer anywhere between the arrowheads and press the right mouse button. Edit now displays the *Using Help* screen:

This screen describes the help capabilities and how you use them. After you have read the description, press Enter or select *Back* to return to the *Getting Started* screen.

The bottom line of the screen displays some additional help information—in this case, the effect of pressing function and other special keys. No matter what you're doing with Edit, the bottom line displays information specific to what you're doing. Right now, the bottom line tells you what happens if you press the following keys:

| Key | Description | Effect of Pressing |
|-----|-------------|--------------------|
| F1 | Help | Displays the help screen of the selected item. |
| F6 | Window | Switches windows. In this case, moves the cursor to the Edit window (now labeled *Untitled*); if the cursor were in the Edit window, F6 would move it to the Help window. |
| Esc | Cancel | Closes the Help window, and return to the Edit window. |
| Ctrl-F1 | Next | Displays the next help topic. (Steps through all the help topics, whether or not they apply to what you're doing right now.) |
| Alt-F1 | Back | Displays the previous help topic. |

## Customizing Help

Right now, the Edit window where you create documents is between the Help window and the bottom line. If you're using a color display, the background color of the Edit window probably isn't the same as that of the Help window. The Edit window is labeled *Untitled* because you didn't name a file when you started Edit.

When you're using Help, you can leave all or part of its current display visible and move between the Edit window and the Help window by pressing F6 or by placing the mouse pointer in the window you want and clicking the left button. That way, you can work on a file and yet refer to help whenever you need it. As you may already have noticed, however, the help screens vary in size. Some, like the one you're looking at now, take about half the screen. Others take only a line or two, and some, like the *Using Help* screen, take almost all the available space.

To help you control your workspace, Edit lets you increase or decrease the size of the active window—the one that contains the cursor. Using the keyboard, press Alt-Plus (hold down Alt and press the plus sign) to make the active window larger; press Alt-Minus to make the active window smaller. With the mouse, simply place the pointer at the top of the Edit window, hold down either mouse button, and move the window border up or down until the Help and Edit windows are the size you want.

If you resize windows and find that either window is too small to display an entire help topic or the file you're working on, you can either change the size again or use the PgUp, PgDown, and arrow keys to scroll through the text with the keyboard. You can also scroll with the mouse by using the scroll bar at the right edge of the active window.

Viewing both windows can be helpful when you're exploring Edit on your own, but for now press Esc to clear the Help window.

## ENTERING LINES

It's time to enter the first few lines of the sample memo. If you make a typing error, you can backspace and correct it before pressing Enter. But don't worry if you press Enter before you realize a line contains errors; as you'll learn, it's easy to correct mistakes. Type the following lines, pressing Enter at the end of each line (press Enter without typing anything where there's a blank line):

```
This floppy disk has 5 files on it.
Please check the spreadsheets and print the
documents to make sure they agree with our
assumptions.

You can review the documents on the
screen. To check the proposal, type:

TYPE A:PROPOSAL.DOC | MORE

This displays one screen at a time.
Press the Spacebar to display the
next screen, or press Ctrl-Break to stop.

Let's do this quickly; it's due Thursday.

Tom
```

The screen shows the lines you have entered.

## ADDING TEXT TO A FILE

You insert text in a file by positioning the cursor where the text is to be inserted and typing the new text. For example, to insert the phrase *and recommendations* after the word *assumptions*, use the arrow keys or the mouse to position the cursor under the period that follows *assumptions*, and type *and recommendations* (but don't press Enter).

Now suppose you also decide to add a title to your memo. Use the mouse or press Ctrl-Home to move the cursor to the beginning of the file, the *T* in the word *This*. Type the following lines (press Enter twice after *team* to add a blank line):

```
Final Project Review -- 10/16/93
To: Project team
```

Oops. You also wanted a blank line between the title lines. Move the cursor to the *T* in *To* and press Enter.

Now you decide you want to include a list of file names after the first sentence. Position the cursor at the beginning of the line that starts *Please check*. Press Enter to insert a blank line, press Tab to indent the line, then type the following (don't forget to press Enter at the end of the line):

```
FORECAST.WKS
```

Look at the cursor. It moved down to the next line, but it isn't at the left margin. It's indented so that it's directly below the beginning of the line you just inserted. What's going on?

## WHERE'S THE MARGIN?

If you indent a line with spaces or tabs (which Edit converts to spaces), Edit assumes that you want the next line to start with the same indent. This assumption can be quite a convenience when you're writing an outline or other type of document that has many indented lines, and that's why pressing the Home key moves the cursor to the first nonblank character in a line, not to the left margin.

Type the following lines to enter four more file names in the indented list, pressing Enter at the end of each:

```
OPTION1.WKS
OPTION2.WKS
LETTER.DOC
PROPOSAL.DOC
```

The assumption that you want to continue an indent isn't always true, of course, so sometimes you'll have to erase the spaces Edit inserts at the beginning of a line. To reduce the inconvenience, Edit lets you erase all the spaces at the beginning of a line by pressing Backspace once when the cursor is under the first nonblank character in an indented line.

Try it. Press Enter once to put a blank line between the last file name in the list and the first line of the following paragraph. Check that the cursor is under the *P* in *Please*, which should be indented eight spaces. Press Backspace; Edit erases the indent and moves the cursor and the line beginning with *Please* to the left margin.

This completes the first draft of the memo. The following illustration shows how your screen should look.

## PRINTING A FILE

A file stored on disk is perfect for distribution but is otherwise of limited value. In most cases, you want a printed copy of the documents you create. To print this version of the memo, make sure your printer is turned on, and then choose Print from the File menu using one of the two methods described below:

- Using the keyboard, press Alt, F, and then P.

- Using the mouse, click on File in the menu bar at the top of the screen, then click on Print.

**NOTE:** *From now on, use keystroke or mouse sequences like this whenever you're asked to choose a command from a particular menu.*

Edit responds with a dialog box asking whether you want to print the entire document or just the part that is selected. The small dot in parentheses tells you that Edit proposes to print the complete document. This is what you want, so press Enter or click on OK; Edit should print the file. If your printer isn't ready, Edit displays the message *Device fault*. Check the printer, and try again by pressing the Enter key.

## SAVING A FILE

Your memo so far is stored just in the computer's memory, not on disk. If you turned the computer off, the document would be lost. To save the file on disk, choose Save As from the File menu. Edit displays a dialog box that asks you to name the file:

The cursor is in the text box titled *File Name* because Edit is waiting for you to type a file name. Below File Name is the name of the current directory (it should read C:\). The box that follows, titled *Dirs/Drives*, lets you save the file in a different directory or even on a disk in a different drive.

Edit can save a file to any directory or drive on your system. For this example, you'll simply type a drive letter and a file name in the File Name text box. Make sure that a formatted floppy disk is in drive A and type:

```
a:memo.txt
```

Now press Enter, or choose OK at the bottom of the dialog box. The file is saved, as you can see from the title block at the top of the screen, which has changed from *Untitled* to *MEMO.TXT*.

## More About Directories and Drives

As you saw in Chapters 8 and 9, directories are invaluable tools. Before you move on, choose the Save As and Open commands from the File menu, and take a few moments to examine the dialog boxes they display a little more closely. (Press Esc or choose Cancel to clear the screen when you're through.)

To help you find or save a file in any directory on any drive, the Dirs/Drives text box in these dialog boxes lists the names of all subdirectories of the current directory and ends with the names of all the drives on your system. The drives are easy to recognize because they are enclosed in square brackets like this: [-A-].

To use the Dirs/Drives text box, you move the cursor to the text box with the Tab key, use the arrow keys to highlight the directory or drive you want, and press Enter (or double-click with the mouse) to change the current drive/directory. To move farther down the directory tree, you repeat the same steps.

Once you've chosen a new drive or directory in the Save As dialog box, the highlight returns to the File Name text box so that you can type the name you want to give the file. If you're using the Open dialog box, you can either type a file name or choose a drive or directory to display a list of files in the Files box. The list will contain all of the files from that drive or directory that match the pattern in the File Name box, such as *.txt. You can then choose a file from this list. The Dirs/Drives text box is particularly useful when you want to scan your drives and directories, either to store a file or to load one whose location you're not sure of.

# DELETING TEXT

To delete the character at the location of the cursor, press Del. To delete more than one character, select them all and either press Del or use the Clear command from the Edit menu. Using either the keyboard or the mouse, you can select any amount of text, from a single character to the entire document, as described early in this chapter.

To practice deleting text, you'll return to the file MEMO.TXT. Begin by deleting the words *on it* at the end of the line that precedes the list of file names. Position the cursor under the period at the end of the line. Although it seems as if you're starting at the wrong end, remember that you can extend the selection either to the left or to the right. Hold down the Shift key, and press the Left arrow key until *on it* and the preceding blank are highlighted. Now simply press Del or choose Clear from the Edit menu. The words are gone.

To delete an entire line and not leave any odd line spacing in your document, you delete everything: text, blank spaces, even the invisible carriage return that Edit uses to mark the end of a line. Suppose, for example, you decide not to include the file named LETTER.DOC and want to delete the entire line from the memo. Simply highlighting the file name won't do the job because the carriage return will still be there, creating a blank line. Instead, start by positioning the cursor. If you're using the keyboard, hold down Ctrl and press Enter several times to move the cursor to the *L* in *LETTER*. Press Backspace to delete the indent. Now hold down the Shift key and press the Down arrow key once. The entire line is selected.

With the mouse it's even easier: Position the cursor at the left edge of the line, press and hold the left mouse button, and move the mouse slightly to drag the mouse pointer one row down.

When the line is selected, press Del or choose the Clear command to delete the line.

# ENDING AN EDITING SESSION

To leave Edit and return to MS-DOS, choose Exit from the File menu. You have changed the file since the last time you saved it, so Edit asks you whether it should save the file first; select Yes. Edit saves the file, then ends and returns to MS-DOS, which displays the system prompt.

If you make some changes to a file, then decide you don't want to change the file after all, you can cancel the editing session without saving the changes by selecting No when Edit asks whether it should save the file.

# EDITING AN EXISTING TEXT FILE

When you type *edit* followed by the name of a file, Edit checks to see whether the file you named exists. If the file exists, Edit copies the file into memory; if the file doesn't exist, Edit shows you an empty window but uses the file name as a title and remembers the file name when you save the file.

To work with the file you just created, type the following:

```
C:\>edit a:memo.txt
```

Edit starts and displays the memo.

## Copying and Moving Text

You can copy or move text from one place in a document to another by using a special area of Edit's memory called the *Clipboard*. Copying, of course, leaves the text in the original location unchanged, while moving deletes the text from its original location.

To copy text, you first copy it to the Clipboard, then copy it from the Clipboard to the cursor location. (When you insert your text in the new location, you *paste* it, from the phrase *cut and paste*.) Suppose you wanted to copy the list of file names in MEMO.TXT to the end of the memo, following the signature line. First, select the file names. To use the keyboard, position the cursor under the *F* in *FORECAST.WKS*, hold down either Shift key, and press the Down arrow key four times; to use the mouse, move the mouse pointer to the *F*, hold down the left mouse button, and move the mouse down until all four lines are highlighted.

Next, open the Edit menu. All the choices show a highlighted letter; the second choice is Copy, with a highlighted C (notice that the shortcut key for copying to the Clipboard is Ctrl-Ins); click on Copy or press C. The Edit menu disappears. There's no indication that anything has happened, but Edit has copied the four lines to the Clipboard.

Now move the cursor down to the line that follows *Tom*, and select the Edit menu again. This time, only Paste shows a highlighted letter, meaning that it's the only valid choice from the menu (its shortcut key is Shift-Ins). Paste is an option only when something is on the Clipboard, so the dark characters and the highlighted P tell you that the lines were indeed copied to the Clipboard. Press P, and the four file names appear in the new location.

Moving text is almost the same as copying; the only difference is that you select Cut instead of Copy from the Edit menu. To move the new set of file names back immediately following the original list, select the lines you just pasted and select Cut from the Edit menu (the shortcut key for Cut is Shift-Del). The lines disappear from the screen, just as if you had deleted them. But move the cursor up to the blank line that follows the last file name in the original location and press Shift-Ins (the shortcut key for Paste). The second list of file names appears immediately below the first.

Pasting from the Clipboard doesn't erase its contents. Press Shift-Ins again, and the four lines of file names are inserted again. You should now see 12 file names.

Copying, cutting, and pasting make it easy to rearrange a document. You don't want to keep this version of the memo, so select Open from the File menu, type *a:memo.txt* in the File Name text box, and select *No* when Edit asks if you want to save the loaded file. The changed version of the file is replaced by the original.

## SEARCHING FOR A GROUP OF CHARACTERS

As a file gets longer, it takes you longer to find a particular word or line, and there's more chance that you'll miss it. Edit eliminates this problem by searching for any character or group of characters you specify.

This memo isn't long enough to require that sort of help, but you can still see how it works. Suppose you wanted to check the names of all the files whose extension is DOC. Choose Find from the Search menu. Edit asks you what you want to find and proposes whatever word the cursor is currently beneath. Type *doc* in the Find What text box and press Enter.

Almost immediately, Edit highlights *DOC* in *PROPOSAL.DOC*. Notice that although you typed *doc*, Edit found *DOC* too. As you'll see in a moment, you can tell Edit whether to distinguish between uppercase and lowercase letters.

If you want to find the same characters again, you don't have to repeat the whole process: Just press F3, which tells Edit to repeat the last search. This time it highlights *doc* in the word *documents*. That's not quite what you had in mind, but it's perfectly normal behavior for Edit: It searches for the characters you specify in either uppercase or lowercase, anywhere within a word, unless you specify otherwise.

Select Find from the Search menu again (it should show *doc* in the Find What text box). First, type *DOC* to replace *doc*. Next, notice the option labeled Match Upper/Lowercase. Select the option by pressing Tab and then pressing the Spacebar or by clicking the mouse anywhere in the option. An X appears inside the brackets.

Now press Enter or choose OK to search again. Edit jumps down and highlights *DOC* in the line beginning *TYPE A:PROPOSAL.DOC*. Press F3 to repeat the search, and the highlight moves up to the preceding PROPOSAL.DOC. Now press F3 again; instead of highlighting *doc* in *documents*, Edit again highlights DOC in the line beginning *TYPE*. You told Edit you didn't want to find *doc*, just *DOC*.

## REPLACING ONE GROUP OF CHARACTERS WITH ANOTHER

One of the most common reasons you'll want to find a particular word or group of characters in a document is so that you can change it. Edit will not only find the characters for you, as you just saw, it will also make the change for you. Suppose you want to change the file extension WKS to XLS wherever it occurs in the memo.

Select Change from the Search menu. Edit displays the Change dialog box, as shown at the top of the next page.

```
 File  Edit  Search  Options                                    Help
                           MEMO.TXT
Final Project Review -- 10/16/93                                     ↑

To: Project team
                         ┌─────────── Change ───────────┐
This flopp             │                              │
              │  Find What: ▓DOC▓                    │
        FO    │                              │
        OP    │                              │
        OP    │  Change To: [                        ]│
        PR    │                              │
              │                              │
Please che    │                              │
documents     │    [X] Match Upper/Lowercase      [ ] Whole Word │
assumption    │                              │
              │                              │
You can re    │ < Find and Verify > < Change All > < Cancel > < Help >│
screen. To    └──────────────────────────────┘

TYPE A:PROPOSAL.▓DOC▓ | MORE                                         ↓

This displays one screen at a time.                                 ↓
←                                                                →
 F1=Help   Enter=Execute   Esc=Cancel   Tab=Next Field   Arrow=Next Item
```

In addition to the Find What text box you saw in the Find dialog box, there's a Change To text box. The Find What text box should contain *DOC*; you want to change every occurrence of WKS to XLS, so type *WKS*. Move to the Change To text box and type *XLS*. Leave the Match Upper/Lowercase option turned on so that Edit will search only for *WKS* and not *wks*. Find and Verify is highlighted at the bottom of the dialog box as the action to take, so press Enter to start the search.

Edit highlights the first occurrence of *WKS* (in *FORECAST.WKS*) and asks you whether to change or skip this occurrence. Press Enter (or click on Change) to change it; Edit displays the next occurrence of *WKS* and repeats the question. Change this occurrence too. When Edit displays the last occurrence of *WKS* (in *OPTION2.WKS*), change it as well. Press Enter or click OK when Edit tells you *Change complete*. The screen shows that all three file extensions have changed from WKS to XLS.

To tell Edit to change all occurrences without prompting for verification, you would select Change All instead of Find and Verify in the Change dialog box.

## INSERTING AND OVERSTRIKING TEXT

You probably used the Backspace key to correct typing errors while you were entering the memo. After writing a memo or a report, however, you'll usually want to make some changes after you read through the first draft. To change text after you have entered it, you start by positioning the cursor where you want to make the change. At that point you can delete incorrect characters, insert new ones, or type correct characters in place of the incorrect ones (the latter is called *overstriking*). The next few examples show you how to make typical changes in a document.

To change the word *Project* to *Product* in the first line of the memo, move the cursor to the *j* and press the Insert key. The cursor changes from an underline to a flashing block. Each time you press Insert, you alternate back and forth between inserting characters (signified by the flashing underline) and replacing characters (signified by the flashing block). Now, with the flashing block showing, whatever you type won't be inserted; it will replace what is on the screen. Type *du*; the new characters replace the old, changing *Project* to *Product*.

Press Insert again to change the cursor back to an underline so that characters you type are inserted.

Insert the word *New* before *Project* in the second title line by moving the cursor to the *P* and typing *New* followed by a space (but don't press Enter, because you don't want to enter a carriage return character). The remainder of the line moves over to make room for the new characters.

Next, change the 5 to a 4 in the third line, and change the period at the end of the third line to a colon. Position the cursor under the 5, press Insert to change to overstrike, and type *4*. Then move the flashing block to the period, and type a colon. Press Insert to return to inserting rather than overstriking characters.

Finally, add a file description to the second file name (OPTION1.XLS). Move the cursor to the space after *XLS*, press the Spacebar three times, and type *Higher sales*. Do the same to add the file description *No staff increase* three spaces after the third file name (OPTION2.XLS).

## COPYING FROM ANOTHER FILE

Suppose you had another file that contained the mailing address of the project team members, and you wanted to include that list at the beginning of the memo. You wouldn't have to type the list; you could simply copy it from the other file. You can try this feature by creating another file of addresses and copying it into MEMO.TXT.

You'll create a file named ADDRESS.TXT that contains six dummy address lines. First, save MEMO.TXT by choosing Save from the File menu, and then remove the file from memory by choosing New from the File menu. Edit clears the screen to show you that you're starting a new file.

Next, type the following line:

```
XXX ADDRESS LIST XXX
```

Now make five more copies of the line. To do this, select the line (make sure that the entire line, from the left margin to the right edge of the screen, is highlighted), press Ctrl-Ins to copy it to the Clipboard, press Home to remove the highlight, and press Shift-Ins five times to copy the lines. You should see six identical lines. Copy all six of the lines to the Clipboard, and then save the file by choosing Save As from the File menu, typing *a:address.txt*, and pressing Enter.

Now copy the lines from the Clipboard into a different file. Load the MEMO.TXT file by choosing *Open* from the File menu, typing *a:memo.txt* in the File Name box, and pressing Enter. You want to paste the address list just after *To: New Project team*, so position the cursor at the beginning of the blank line below *To*. Press Enter to add an extra blank line for spacing. Now press Shift-Ins to insert the six lines from the Clipboard. This is the final version of the memo; the screen should look like this:

Save this final version of the memo. Now for something a bit less tedious before you leave Edit.

## CHANGING THE SCREEN DISPLAY

If you have a color monitor, Edit probably displayed white text against a blue background when you first started it. You can change this color scheme to any combination of foreground (text) and background (screen) color your display is capable of showing. Select Display from the Options menu. The screen should look like this:

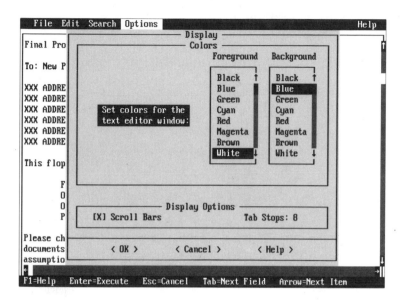

Before you start customizing your display, turn to Edit's Help again, this time to see how Edit can advise you on the Display dialog box. Press F1, and Edit displays the Help box that tells you how to use the Display dialog box. Read the explanation, and then press Esc to remove the Help box.

The cursor is now in the text box that lists possible foreground colors. Using the arrow keys or the mouse, select different colors (you can move the cursor between the foreground and background color boxes by pressing Tab and Shift-Tab). The text block to the left of the color boxes changes to show the effect of each color selection.

When you find a combination you like, press Enter to return to Edit. It will use these colors the next time you start it. (If you prefer the standard combination, press Esc to cancel the dialog box; Edit leaves the colors unchanged.) Leave Edit by choosing Exit from the File menu.

## CHAPTER SUMMARY

This chapter showed you the basics of using Edit. You're ready to use it for many of the short text-editing jobs that don't require a word processor.

There's more to Edit, such as different methods of cutting and pasting text and shortcut keys based on the WordStar word processor. You can explore further on your own, using Help as your guide: Display a help screen—the Keyboard help screens are a good place to start—and use the F6 key to switch back and forth between the Help and Edit windows as you try out new features. You'll find that Help is the most patient instructor you've ever had.

# 13

# Taking Control of Your System

**U** p until now in this book, you have used the MS-DOS commands in their standard form. MS-DOS, however, gives you a great deal of flexibility in controlling the way some commands do their work for you. This chapter describes two ways in which you can take control of your system.

The first part of the chapter introduces the concept of input and output *redirection*. Essentially, redirection is a form of traffic control that allows you to route input and output between devices and files you specify. You'll also see how to use redirection with MS-DOS commands that let you control both the form and content of command input and output.

If you have version 5 or later of MS-DOS, the second part of this chapter takes you further into the Doskey program introduced in Chapter 3, "Getting Your Bearings." Using Doskey, you'll see not only how to edit commands you've already used, but also how to enter and carry out more than one command at a time.

## REDIRECTING COMMAND OUTPUT

It is easy to visualize what happens with command output, so even though it might seem odd to discuss results before discussing causes, this section on command output gives you a foundation for understanding command input as well.

The result, or output, of most commands is some action, such as copying a file (with the Copy command) or controlling the operation of a device (with the Mode command). The output of some commands, however, such as Directory, Check Disk, and Tree, is a report. Up to now, you have used these reports primarily as displays—MS-DOS has sent them to the *standard output device*, the console. (Recall from Chapter 7, "Managing Your Devices," that MS-DOS uses the name CON, or console, for both the keyboard, which is input only, and the display, which is output only.)

As you'll see in this chapter, MS-DOS lets you send reports and other output to a different device, such as a printer, or to a file. This is called *redirecting* the output of the command; you did it a few times in previous chapters with such commands as *dir > prn*. The technique is simple: To redirect the output of a command that normally sends its results to standard output (the display), you type the command name followed by > and the name of the device or file to which the output is to be sent. The > looks something like an arrowhead pointing toward the alternate output device or file. If you redirect output to a file that doesn't exist, MS-DOS will create the file.

Using redirection it's easy to print a copy of the directory as you did in Chapter 4, "A Look at Files and Floppy Disks," for example. To repeat that example, but this time with an understanding of what happens, be sure the printer is turned on and type the following:

```
C:\>dir > prn
```

The > tells MS-DOS to redirect the output of the Directory command, and PRN tells MS-DOS where to send it: to the printer. The directory should be printing now. If it's long and you want to cancel the printing, press Ctrl-Break.

## REDIRECTING COMMAND INPUT

You've seen how quickly and easily you can redirect output to a device or a file. You can just as easily redirect input, in effect telling certain MS-DOS commands to get their data from a source other than the one (often called *standard input device*) they would normally use. To redirect input, follow the command name with the < character and the name or device from which the input is coming.

Together, redirected input and output are known as redirection. Although redirection might sound complicated, it is easy to understand, as the examples in this chapter show.

Three MS-DOS commands, known collectively as *filter commands*, make particularly effective use of redirection.

## FILTER COMMANDS

Filter commands take input from a device or a file, change the input in some way, and send the result to an output device or file. They are called filter commands because they work much like a filter in a water system, which takes incoming water, changes it in some way, and sends it along the system.

MS-DOS includes three filter commands:

- *Sort* arranges lines in ascending or descending order.

- *Find* searches for a string of characters.

- *More* temporarily halts the display after one screenful (to give you a chance to read the lines).

You can redirect both the input and the output of a filter command. The filter commands aren't really intended to be used with keyboard input. Rather, they are designed to get their input from a file or even from the output of another command. This chapter shows you how to use and combine the filter commands to create your own powerful, specialized commands.

## PREPARING FOR THE EXAMPLES

Redirection and filter commands give you the elements of a simple file-management program. While they won't replace a file manager, they let you use MS-DOS to search and sort simple lists without spending extra money or time on another program.

The examples in this chapter use a sample file that almost everyone needs: a list of names and telephone numbers. Too often, files of telephone numbers and business cards are out of date, incomplete, or in the other office. Questions arise: "Was that number in the telephone index or the business-card file?" Or "Did I file the number under Jones or under Accountants?" This example shows you how to let MS-DOS keep track of your phone list and eliminate these questions.

Change the current directory to \RUNDOS by typing the following:

```
C:\>cd \rundos
```

### Entering the Sample File

The sample file is named PH.TXT. You can use Edit to create it from MS-DOS, or you can use your own word processor if it can save documents as unformatted text files—that is, files that don't contain any of the program's own formatting codes.

Each line of the file contains six items of data: last name, first name, area code, telephone number, a key word that identifies a category, and a short description. The key words are: *cust* for customer, *cons* for consultant, and *vend* for vendor. You'll enter the items in specific columns so you can sort the list by any item.

To use Edit to create the file, start Edit and name the file in a single command by typing the following:

```
C:\RUNDOS>edit ph.txt
```

Now you can begin to enter the items in the file. To help you get the items in the correct columns, the following entry shows the first line, with a period marking each space. Type the line as shown, pressing the Spacebar once for each period shown:

```
Jones.....Michele...(747).429-6360..cons.chemist
```

End the line by pressing Enter.

Enter the remaining lines in the sample file, shown in Figure 13-1, using the spacing of the first line as a guide. When you've typed all the lines, save the file and quit the editor.

```
Jones     Michele    (747) 429-6360    cons chemist
Smith     John       (747) 926-2945    vend furniture
White     Alice      (747) 425-7692    cust Accountant
Green     Fred       (541) 926-4921    cust math teach
Black     John       (747) 426-3385    cons mech eng pkg
Smith     Ed         (541) 835-8747    vend caterer
Jones     Alison     (747) 429-5584    cons Chem engineer
IBM       sales      (747) 463-2000    vend Dave Hill
Jones     James      (747) 636-3541    cust architect
Black     Alice      (747) 426-7145    cust Elec eng
```

**Figure 13-1.**
*Telephone and business-card list.*

Now you're ready to use the file. To see the entry for Alice White, type the following (notice the capital W):

```
C:\RUNDOS>find "Wh" ph.txt
```

```
---------- PH.TXT
White     Alice      (747) 425-7692   cust Accountant
```

That's fast, but it's just the beginning.

# THE SORT FILTER COMMAND

The Sort filter command arranges, or sorts, lines of input and sends them to standard output (the display) unless you redirect the output—for example, to the printer. If you enter the command with no options, it sorts the lines of input in ascending order (alphabetically from A to Z, or numerically from lowest to highest number), starting the sort on the character in the first column.

The Sort command has two parameters:

**sort /R /+<column>**

/R (*Reverse*) sorts the lines in reverse order (Z to A, or highest to lowest number).

/+<column> sorts the lines starting at the specified column, rather than starting in the first column.

To sort a particular file, you can redirect the input of the Sort command by following the command name with < and the name of the file to be sorted. If you don't have version 4 or later of MS-DOS, be sure to use a space both before and after the <. If you don't redirect the input, the Sort command sorts lines that you type at the keyboard (standard input).

## Sort Command Examples

Figure 13-2 shows the column number of each of the six items in the telephone list: last name, first name, area code, telephone number, key word, and description. You'll use these column numbers to sort the file in different ways.

```
1          11         21   27        37   42
Jones      Michele    (747) 429-6360 cons chemist
```

**Figure 13-2.**
*Column numbers of items in the telephone list.*

The simplest way to sort the file is in ascending order, starting in the first column. (In the sample file, this sorts the entries by last name.) Type:

```
C:\RUNDOS>sort < ph.txt
```

MS-DOS quickly displays the sorted result:

```
Black      Alice      (747) 426-7145  cust Elec eng
Black      John       (747) 426-3385  cons mech eng pkg
Green      Fred       (541) 926-4921  cust math teach
IBM        sales      (747) 463-2000  vend Dave Hill
Jones      Alison     (747) 429-5584  cons Chem engineer
Jones      James      (747) 636-3541  cust architect
Jones      Michele    (747) 429-6360  cons chemist
Smith      Ed         (541) 835-8747  vend caterer
Smith      John       (747) 926-2945  vend furniture
White      Alice      (747) 425-7692  cust Accountant
```

The file itself isn't changed; what you see is simply the result of MS-DOS reading, sorting, and displaying the lines of the file.

To sort the file in reverse order, use the /R option:

```
C:\RUNDOS>sort /r < ph.txt
```

It doesn't take MS-DOS any longer to sort backward:

```
White      Alice      (747) 425-7692  cust Accountant
Smith      John       (747) 926-2945  vend furniture
Smith      Ed         (541) 835-8747  vend caterer
Jones      Michele    (747) 429-6360  cons chemist
Jones      James      (747) 636-3541  cust architect
Jones      Alison     (747) 429-5584  cons Chem engineer
IBM        sales      (747) 463-2000  vend Dave Hill
Green      Fred       (541) 926-4921  cust math teach
Black      John       (747) 426-3385  cons mech eng pkg
Black      Alice      (747) 426-7145  cust Elec eng
```

Suppose you wanted to arrange the list by the key word—first the consultants, then the customers, then the vendors. The first letter of the key word is in column 37, so use the column option:

```
C:\RUNDOS>sort /+37 < ph.txt
```

Now it's easy to pick out the different categories:

```
Jones    Alison    (747) 429-5584   cons Chem engineer
Jones    Michele   (747) 429-6360   cons chemist
Black    John      (747) 426-3385   cons mech eng pkg
White    Alice     (747) 425-7692   cust Accountant
Jones    James     (747) 636-3541   cust architect
Black    Alice     (747) 426-7145   cust Elec eng
Green    Fred      (541) 926-4921   cust math teach
Smith    Ed        (541) 835-8747   vend caterer
IBM      sales     (747) 463-2000   vend Dave Hill
Smith    John      (747) 926-2945   vend furniture
```

Sorting is fast, easy, and useful.

## THE FIND FILTER COMMAND

The Find filter command searches lines of input for a string of characters you specify. If you enter the command with no parameters other than the string and the file name, the Find command displays all lines that contain the string.

The Find command has six parameters:

**find /V /C /N /I "<string>" <filename>**

/V displays all lines that do not contain the string.

/C (*Count*) displays just the number of lines found, not the lines themselves.

/N (*Number*) displays the input line number with each line found.

/I (*Ignore*), in versions 5 and later, causes the Find command to ignore differences between uppercase and lowercase—for example, to treat *a* and *A* as the same letter.

"<string>" is the string of characters you want to find; it must be enclosed in quotation marks. Keep in mind that unless you specify the /I parameter, the Find command distinguishes between uppercase and lowercase letters, so "cons" and "CONS", for example, are different strings.

<filename> is the name of the file to be searched. If you omit <filename>, the Find command searches standard input. You can include several different file names in a single Find command simply by separating the file names with blanks. If some of the files are in a different directory or on a disk in a different drive, precede the file name with the appropriate path name or drive letter.

## Find Command Examples

To display the entries for all consultants in the file named PH.TXT, type the following:

```
C:\RUNDOS>find "cons" ph.txt
```

The first line of output identifies the input file, PH.TXT. Each line that contains the string *cons* is displayed immediately after:

```
---------- PH.TXT
Jones      Michele    (747) 429-6360   cons chemist
Black      John       (747) 426-3385   cons mech eng pkg
Jones      Alison     (747) 429-5584   cons Chem engineer
```

To see how the Find command works with more than one file, type the following to make a duplicate copy of the phone list:

```
C:\RUNDOS>copy ph.txt ph1.txt
```

Now type the Find command you used in the preceding example, but this time include both files:

```
C:\RUNDOS>find "cons" ph.txt ph1.txt
```

MS-DOS displays the name of each file as it finds *cons* in PH.TXT and PH1.TXT:

```
---------- PH.TXT
Jones      Michele    (747) 429-6360   cons chemist
Black      John       (747) 426-3385   cons mech eng pkg
Jones      Alison     (747) 429-5584   cons Chem engineer

---------- PH1.TXT
Jones      Michele    (747) 429-6360   cons chemist
Black      John       (747) 426-3385   cons mech eng pkg
Jones      Alison     (747) 429-5584   cons Chem engineer
```

Obviously, using the Find command to search for a character string in several files is more productive when the contents of the files differ, but this example shows the method, if not the full capability, of the command. You don't need PH1.TXT anymore, so type *del ph1.txt* to keep your disk uncluttered.

Return now to the original phone list, PH.TXT. If you just want to know how many consultants are in the list, use the /C option:

```
C:\RUNDOS>find /c "cons" ph.txt
```

This time, the line that identifies the input file also shows the number of lines that contain the string:

```
---------- PH.TXT: 3
```

Three lines in the file contain *cons*.

As often happens in a real telephone index, the sample file uses different words or abbreviations to mean the same thing. Both *engineer* and *eng* are used, for example, to describe an engineer. Both words contain *eng*, however, so you can find all the engineers by typing the following:

```
C:\RUNDOS>find "eng" ph.txt

---------- PH.TXT
Black     John       (747) 426-3385   cons mech eng pkg
Jones     Alison     (747) 429-5584   cons Chem engineer
Black     Alice      (747) 426-7145   cust Elec eng
```

As also happens in real life, capitalization in the sample file is not consistent. One entry, for example, contains the notation *Chem engineer*, and another contains the all-lowercase *chemist*. You could avoid the inconsistency by specifying the string as *hem* rather than as *chem* or *Chem*. But if you have version 5 or later, you can use the /I parameter instead to tell the Find command to ignore uppercase/lowercase differences. If you have version 5 or later, type:

```
C:\RUNDOS>find /i "chem" ph.txt
```

MS-DOS quickly responds:

```
---------- PH.TXT
Jones     Michele    (747) 429-6360   cons chemist
Jones     Alison     (747) 429-5584   cons Chem engineer
```

## Finding Lines That Don't Contain the String

With any version of MS-DOS, you can also use the /V parameter to display lines that *don't* contain a string. For example, to display the entries *not* in the 747 area code, type:

```
C:\RUNDOS>find /v "(747" ph.txt

---------- PH.TXT
Green     Fred       (541) 926-4921   cust math teach
Smith     Ed         (541) 835-8747   vend caterer
```

Including the left parenthesis with 747 distinguishes between entries with an area code of 747 and entries that might contain 747 in the phone number. Try the example without the left parenthesis:

```
C:\RUNDOS>find /v "747" ph.txt

---------- PH.TXT
Green     Fred       (541) 926-4921   cust math teach
```

Ed Smith's telephone number is 835-8747, so his entry wasn't displayed even though his area code is 541. When you enter the characters to find, be sure to include enough information to specify what you're looking for. In the sample file, for example, typing "(7" would be enough to specify the 747 area code; it wouldn't be enough, however, if the file contained another area code beginning with 7. And, as you saw, you must include the left parenthesis to distinguish an area code from some other set of numbers.

### Including Line Numbers with the Output

To display the entries for people named Smith and to include the line numbers of the entries, use the /N option:

```
C:\RUNDOS>find /n "Smith" ph.txt

---------- PH.TXT
[2]Smith     John       (747) 926-2945  vend furniture
[6]Smith     Ed         (541) 835-8747  vend caterer
```

The two entries displayed are the second and sixth lines of the sample file.

### Combining Find Command Options

You can combine Find command options. For example, to display the entries not in the 747 area code and to include their line numbers, use both the /V and /N options:

```
C:\RUNDOS>find /v /n "(7" ph.txt

---------- PH.TXT
[4]Green     Fred       (541) 926-4921  cust math teach
[6]Smith     Ed         (541) 835-8747  vend caterer
```

(If you used Edit to create the sample file, you might also see *[11]* appear at the end of this report. That's probably because you pressed Enter when you finished typing the last entry and, in doing so, created a blank line that Find has included in its search. The blank line is listed because you told Find to show the *numbers* of all lines that *don't* contain the 747 area code.)

## MORE ON REDIRECTING

Earlier in this chapter, you redirected input to the Sort command by specifying the file PH.TXT. You can also redirect the output of a filter command. To print the entries for all vendors (that is, to redirect output from the display to the printer), type the following:

```
C:\RUNDOS>find "vend" ph.txt > prn
```

The entries are printed. If your phone list has two or three hundred entries, this technique of using options and redirecting output is a quick way to print a copy showing a selected group of entries.

## Redirecting Both Input and Output

You can redirect both input and output by following the command name with < and the name of the input file or device and then > and the name of the output file or device. (Be sure to include blanks before and after both < and > if you don't have version 4 or later of MS-DOS.)

For example, to print the alphabetized version of PH.TXT, check that your printer is on and then type:

```
C:\RUNDOS>sort < ph.txt > prn
```

The input for the Sort command comes from PH.TXT, and the output is redirected to the printer.

MS-DOS allows you to redirect both the input and output of a single command from and to the same file. That is, MS-DOS does not report any error if, for example, you type the command *sort < ph.txt > ph.txt*. Doing this, however, can make a large file unusable. If you want to sort a file and keep the same file name, do the following:

- Redirect the output to a temporary file, such as PH-TMP.TXT. To sort PH in reverse order, you would type *sort /r < ph.txt > ph-tmp.txt*.

- If you're certain you don't need it, delete the original file (*del ph.txt*). If you want to keep the original, give it a different name, such as OLDPH.TXT, using the Rename command (*ren ph.txt oldph.txt*).

- Then use the Rename command to give the temporary file the original file name (*ren ph-tmp.txt ph.txt*).

- The new version of PH.TXT would contain the telephone list sorted in reverse order. You could verify the contents by displaying PH.TXT with the Type command.

## Adding Redirected Output to a File

When you redirect output to an existing file, the redirected output replaces the original file. But you can also *add* redirected output to the end of an existing file by using >> instead of >. If the file doesn't already exist, it is created, just as when you use >.

## CONNECTING COMMANDS WITH A PIPE

A powerful way of using a filter command is to redirect the output of some other command to the input of the filter command. In effect, the two commands are connected, with the output of the first command feeding directly into the filter command. Continuing the analogy to a water system, this connection is called a *pipe*.

You tell MS-DOS to pipe the output of one command to the input of another by typing ¦ between the names of the two commands; the ¦ provides the connection between the two commands. The More filter command provides a simple example.

### The More Filter Command

The More filter command displays one screenful (24 lines unless you've specified otherwise with the Mode command) followed by the line -- *More* --, and then it pauses. When you press any key, More displays the next screenful and pauses again if necessary, continuing in the same way until all the input has been displayed.

For the following example, you need a disk or directory that contains more than one screenful of files. Your \DOS directory will do; type the following:

```
C:\RUNDOS>dir \dos ¦ more
```

This command tells MS-DOS to redirect the output of the Directory command to the input of the More command. The More command displays the first screenful of the directory and -- *More* -- at the bottom of the screen. Press any key to see the rest of the directory, or press Ctrl-Break to cancel the More command and return to the system prompt. The More command lets you review a long output sequence or file without having to press Pause or Ctrl-Num Lock to start and stop the display.

### Combining Filter Commands

You can pipe the output of one Find command to the input of another Find command to make a more specific search. A real-life list like the sample phone list, for example, might include several dozen customers. Suppose you want to display the names of customers in the 747 area code only. To do this, pipe the output of a Find command that searches for *cust* to another Find command that searches for *(7*. Type:

```
C:\RUNDOS>find "cust" ph.txt ¦ find "(7"
White      Alice      (747) 425-7692   cust Accountant
Jones      James      (747) 636-3541   cust architect
Black      Alice      (747) 426-7145   cust Elec eng
```

If you check an earlier list of the file, you'll see that Fred Green is a customer, but his area code is 541, so the second Find command eliminated the entry for his name. Notice that the line that identifies the file (----------PH.TXT) isn't displayed. The first Find command pipes ----------PH.TXT as part of its output to the second Find command, but because the line does not contain the string *(7,* it is not included as part of the output of the second Find command.

You can also pipe the output of the Find command to the Sort command. To see all the consultants sorted by last name, type the following:

```
C:\RUNDOS>find "cons" ph.txt ¦ sort

        ---------- PH.TXT
Black    John      (747) 426-3385  cons mech eng pkg
Jones    Alison    (747) 429-5584  cons Chem engineer
Jones    Michele   (747) 429-6360  cons chemist
```

You can combine as many commands as you like. Suppose you want to print a list of all customers in the 747 area code, sorted by telephone number. You can search PH.TXT for *cust*, pipe that output to a Find command that searches for *(7,* pipe that output to a Sort command that sorts at column 27 (the telephone number), and redirect the output to the printer. Try this by typing the following:

```
C:\RUNDOS>find "cust" ph.txt ¦ find "(7" ¦ sort /+27 > prn
```

The printed output includes:

```
White    Alice     (747) 425-7692  cust Accountant
Black    Alice     (747) 426-7145  cust Elec eng
Jones    James     (747) 636-3541  cust architect
```

If your list included several dozen customers, this could be a handy way to organize a calling campaign.

## The Difference Between > and ¦

Sometimes the distinction between > and ¦ isn't readily apparent. > redirects output to a file or device; ¦ redirects output to another command. This difference is easy to demonstrate. Sort is a filter command. To make the output of the Directory command the input to the Sort command, type the following:

```
C:\RUNDOS>dir c:\ ¦ sort
```

As you would expect, MS-DOS displays the directory sorted in alphabetic order. (If the directory includes two files whose names look like 072F2321 or %PIPE1.$$$, don't be alarmed. These are temporary files MS-DOS creates in order to pipe the output of one command to the input of another; MS-DOS deletes the files automatically.)

Now type:

```
C:\RUNDOS>dir c:\ > sort
```

This time you don't see anything on the screen because you told MS-DOS to redirect the output of the Directory command to a file named SORT. Confirm this by displaying the file with the Type command:

```
C:\RUNDOS>type sort
```

The file contains the directory, which is not sorted. You created the file when you redirected the output of the Directory command. You don't need this file, so delete it by typing *del sort*.

# EDITING AN MS-DOS COMMAND WITH DOSKEY

As you've seen, commands that redirect and filter input, output, or both can become long and complex, especially if you also include subdirectory names, file names, and extensions. By now you've also used many MS-DOS commands over and over again—to the point where you probably have no idea, other than "a lot," of the number of times you've typed *dir* followed by a drive letter, path, or file name.

If you have version 5 or later, you can repeat (or edit) any recent command by using the small program named Doskey that you first encountered in Chapter 3, "Getting Your Bearings." (If you don't have version 5 or later, you don't have Doskey, so you can go on to Chapter 14, "Creating Your Own Commands.")

Typing *doskey* for the first time during a session with your computer causes MS-DOS to load the Doskey program into memory. Once in memory, Doskey keeps track of the commands you type and allows you to go back and review or repeat them by pressing the arrow and function keys.

But even though Doskey lets you reuse a command you typed earlier, you might want to change it slightly, to specify a different drive or file name. When you've recalled a previous command, Doskey lets you use the keys described in Figure 13-3 to edit the command.

To see how to edit commands with Doskey, start by loading the program into memory. Type:

```
C:\RUNDOS>doskey
DOSKey installed.
```

Now type a command and press Enter to carry it out:

```
C:\RUNDOS>find "Smith" ph.txt | sort /+11
```

| Key | Action |
| --- | --- |
| Home | Moves the cursor to the beginning of the command |
| Ctrl-Home | Deletes from the cursor location to the beginning of the command |
| End | Moves the cursor to the end of the command |
| Ctrl-End | Deletes from the cursor location to the end of the command |
| Left arrow | Moves the cursor one character left |
| Ctrl-Left arrow | Moves the cursor one "word" (group of characters without blanks) left |
| Right arrow | Moves the cursor one character right |
| Ctrl-Right arrow | Moves the cursor one "word" (group of characters without blanks) right |
| Ins | Adds typed characters at the location of the cursor the first time you press it; overstrikes existing characters the next time you press it; toggles between these two actions |
| Del | Deletes the character at the location of the cursor; does not move the cursor |
| Esc | Erases the displayed command |

**Figure 13-3.**
*The Doskey editing keys.*

What if you wanted to type another command almost like that one? Instead of having to retype the whole thing, Doskey lets you recall the command to the screen, make any changes you like, then press Enter to carry out the command again. You start by using the Up arrow key to display the command you want to reuse, so press the Up arrow key. MS-DOS dutifully redisplays the Find command you just typed.

Your first edit will change *Smith* to *Black*. Press Home to move the cursor to the beginning of the command. Press Ctrl-Right arrow once to move the cursor to the quotation mark preceding *Smith*, and then press the Right arrow key to move the cursor under the *S* in *Smith*:

```
C:\RUNDOS>find "Smith" ph.txt | sort /+11
```

Now type *Black*. Notice that the characters you type replace the characters that were there. To insert characters rather than replace them, you would press Ins before beginning to type. To delete characters, you would press Del once for each character you wanted to remove.

Your command should look like this:

```
C:\RUNDOS>find "Black" ph.txt | sort /+11
```

Press Enter, and this time MS-DOS lists all people named Black, alphabetizing them by their first names. Press the Up arrow key again to display the last command. Now try moving the cursor around.

Press Home to move the cursor to the beginning of the command. Next, press Ctrl-Right arrow three times to move the cursor right three words:

```
C:\RUNDOS>find "Black" ph.txt | sort /+11
```

As a final exercise, try deleting parts of the command. Press Ctrl-End, and all characters from the cursor to the end of the line vanish:

```
C:\RUNDOS>find "Black" ph.txt _
```

Press Ctrl-Left arrow to move the cursor to the *p* in *ph.txt*:

```
C:\RUNDOS>find "Black" ph.txt
```

Press Ctrl-Home. This time, you delete all characters between the cursor and the beginning of the command:

```
C:\RUNDOS>ph.txt
```

What's left isn't very meaningful, so clean up by pressing Esc to erase the entire line:

```
C:\RUNDOS>_
```

## ENTERING MULTIPLE COMMANDS WITH DOSKEY

In this chapter, you've seen many ways to use the redirection (< and >) and pipe (|) symbols to carry out more than one command at the same time. But what about other commands? While using MS-DOS you might sometimes have thought it would be nice to type two or more related (or unrelated) commands and have MS-DOS carry them out one after the other. With Doskey, you can type as many commands as you want, up to a maximum of 128 characters. To tell Doskey where one command ends and the next begins, you press Ctrl-T, which is displayed as a paragraph mark (¶).

To see how this feature works, try the following example, which clears the screen, creates a new directory named TEST, makes TEST the current directory, and displays the directory listing. You'll enter all four commands on the same line, separating them by pressing Ctrl-T:

```
C:\RUNDOS>cls <Ctrl-T> md test <Ctrl-T> cd test <Ctrl-T> dir
```

When you press Enter, the screen clears and the commands are carried out one at a time. It happens quickly, but each command is displayed as it is carried out, so you can see the results:

```
C:\RUNDOS> md test

C:\RUNDOS> cd test

C:\RUNDOS\TEST> dir

 Volume in drive C is HARD DISK
 Volume Serial Number is 1608-5A30
 Directory of C:\RUNDOS\TEST

 .              <DIR>     10-16-93  11:27a
 ..             <DIR>     10-16-93  11:27a
         2 file(s)            0 bytes
                      14069807 bytes free
```

The next example uses the Copy command to create a sample file by copying from the console (CON). Type:

```
C:\RUNDOS\TEST>copy con example <Ctrl-T> type example
```

When you press Enter this time, the system pauses after the first command is displayed. MS-DOS is waiting for you to create the sample file, so type the following:

```
This is a sample file named EXAMPLE.
<Ctrl-Z>
```

When you press Enter, you see the familiar *1 file(s) copied* message followed by your
second command:

```
C:\RUNDOS\TEST> type example
This is a sample file named EXAMPLE.
```

This time, you created a file and displayed it.

Finally, clean up your directory by typing the following set of commands:

```
C:\RUNDOS\TEST>del example <Ctrl-T> cd .. <Ctrl-T> rd test
```

## CHAPTER SUMMARY

As you've seen, redirection, filter commands, and pipes let you create powerful,
specific commands. When you consider these—and all the other MS-DOS commands you've encountered—you can begin to see ways in which you can adapt
MS-DOS to your own needs and circumstances.

This chapter ends the part of the book that deals with MS-DOS as it is provided on disk. The next three chapters show you how to combine MS-DOS commands in sets known as *batch files* to put more of the power of MS-DOS to work. You
have the building blocks. Now it's time to use them to customize MS-DOS.

# 14

# Creating Your Own Commands

s the preceding chapters show, MS-DOS gives you a great deal of control over your computer system. But MS-DOS is necessarily general purpose, because many people use it for many different tasks. So that you can adapt the computer to your work, MS-DOS lets you combine existing MS-DOS commands to create your own special-purpose commands.

The technique is simple: To make your own command, you create a text file that contains MS-DOS commands. And you can give such a file—called a *batch file*—any valid name except the name of an existing command; the extension of the file must be BAT. To use your command, simply type the name of the batch file; MS-DOS carries out the commands contained in the file as if you had typed each of them separately. Commands that you create in this way are called *batch commands*.

This chapter describes how to create batch files and batch commands. It also describes the Remark command, which is intended for batch files, and it shows you how to modify the MS-DOS startup procedure if there are certain commands you always want MS-DOS to carry out when you start your system.

## A BATCH OF WHAT?

The term *batch* has its origins in the early days of large computers, when most work was done by submitting a deck of punched cards to the data-processing department. The punched cards had to contain all the instructions required for the program to run correctly. There was no chance to interact with the system. The data-processing personnel ran these jobs in batches and delivered the output.

In effect, you do the same thing when you use a batch command because a batch file contains all the instructions needed to carry out a job. *Batch,* then, is used to describe a set of commands that are run one after the other. You can use batch files to automate frequently used command sequences and to make the system more accessible to colleagues who use application programs but might not know MS-DOS as well as you do.

## HOW MS-DOS SEARCHES FOR A COMMAND

If you type something when MS-DOS is displaying the system prompt, MS-DOS assumes you have typed a command name. It then follows a particular sequence in trying to carry out the command:

1. It checks to see whether you typed the name of a built-in command, such as *dir* or *copy*. If you did, MS-DOS carries out that command.

2. If what you typed isn't the name of a built-in command, MS-DOS checks to see if you typed the name of a file with the extension COM or EXE (a command file). If you did, MS-DOS searches the current directory for the file and, if it finds the file, loads the program contained in the file and runs it.

3. If what you typed isn't the name of a command file, MS-DOS checks to see if you typed the name of a file with the extension BAT (a batch file). If you did, MS-DOS searches the current directory for the file and, if it finds the file, carries out the commands in the batch file.

4. If MS-DOS doesn't find the file in the current directory, it performs steps 2 and 3 of this sequence in each of the directories specified in the Path command.

The sequence is important because it explains why MS-DOS won't carry out a command file with the same name as a built-in command and why it won't carry out a batch file that has the same name as either a built-in command or a command file.

## CREATING THE SAMPLE FILES

Change to the \RUNDOS directory:

```
C:\>cd \rundos
```

Because you'll be creating your own commands in this chapter, the system prompt will be shown as a simple C> to keep it unobtrusive. If your system prompt normally shows the current directory, you can simplify it temporarily by typing:

```
C:\RUNDOS>prompt
```

When you next start or restart your computer, the system prompt will revert to showing both the current drive and the current directory.

You'll use three sample files in this chapter: LETR1.DOC, LETR2.DOC, and LETR3.DOC. Type the text shown at the top of the next page to create the sample files. (Remember, press either F6 or Ctrl-Z, and then press Enter where you see ^Z.)

```
C>copy con letr1.doc
This is the sample file.
^Z
        1 file(s) copied

C>copy letr1.doc letr2.*
        1 file(s) copied

C>copy letr1.doc letr3.*
        1 file(s) copied


C>_
```

## CREATING A BATCH FILE

A batch file is simply a text file, whose extension is BAT, that contains MS-DOS commands. There are several ways to create a batch file. If the batch file is short and you're confident that it will work correctly, you can simply copy from the console to a file. If you think you might want to tinker with the file before saving it, you can use Edit or a word processor that can store files without inserting its own formatting codes. If want to see how the commands work together, you can use Doskey for a test-as-you-go approach as described later in this chapter under the heading "Using Doskey to Create a Batch File."

Because the examples in this chapter are short and have already been checked for usability, you'll copy from the console to create your first batch files. You can't go back to correct an error after you press Enter at the end of a line, but if you make a typing error you can recover easily by pressing Ctrl-Break and reentering the batch file.

Suppose one of the application programs you use is a word processor, and you name the files that contain letters LETR1.DOC, LETR2.DOC, LETR3.DOC, and so forth. You use the Directory command fairly often to display the names of those particular files. Instead of typing *dir letr*.doc* each time, you could put the Directory command in a batch file named DIRLET.BAT.

Type the following to create the batch file:

```
C>copy con dirlet.bat
dir letr*.doc
^Z
        1 file(s) copied


C>_
```

The first line you typed names the batch file; the second line contains the command MS-DOS carries out. Test your batch command by typing its name:

```
C>dirlet

C>dir letr*.doc

 Volume in drive C is HARD DISK
 Volume Serial Number is 1608-5A30
 Directory of C:\RUNDOS

LETR1     DOC       26 10-16-93    3:13p
LETR2     DOC       26 10-16-93    3:13p
LETR3     DOC       26 10-16-93    3:13p
         3 file(s)           78 bytes
                      13277184 bytes free
```

It's possible that you'll see a double prompt like the following when your batch file finishes running:

```
C>
C>_
```

Don't worry about this prompt.

The first line displayed after you type your batch command is the Directory command that you entered into your batch file. MS-DOS displays the commands in a batch file as they are carried out, as if you had typed the command itself.

You could make the batch command even easier to type by naming the batch file simply LDIR.BAT. In the long run, however, it's usually better to make the name long enough to give a good hint of what the command does, especially if you create a large number of batch files.

## Displaying Messages from a Batch File

The Remark (rem) command doesn't cause MS-DOS to do anything, but it is a valid command. You can include a message with the Remark command. The command form is:

**rem <message>**

Although this command isn't especially useful at the MS-DOS command level, it lets you display a message from a batch file. To see how the Remark command works, create another version of DIRLET.BAT that displays a descriptive message; type the following:

```
C>copy con dirlet.bat
rem DIRECTORY OF LETTERS
dir letr*.doc
^Z
        1 file(s) copied
```

The new version of DIRLET.BAT replaces the first version you created a few minutes ago. Test this new version by typing:

```
C>dirlet
```

The Remark command you included causes MS-DOS to display the message before it displays the directory:

```
C>rem DIRECTORY OF LETTERS

C>dir letr*.doc

 Volume in drive C is HARD DISK
 Volume Serial Number is 1608-5A30
 Directory of C:\RUNDOS
LETR1    DOC       26 10-16-93   3:13p
LETR2    DOC       26 10-16-93   3:13p
LETR3    DOC       26 10-16-93   3:13p
        3 file(s)           78 bytes
                    13277184 bytes free

C>_
```

## Carrying Out the Same Batch Command with Different Data

You have seen that most MS-DOS commands include one or more parameters that you can use to make your instructions more specific. When you enter a Directory command, for example, you can specify a file name to display some portion of the files on a disk and the /W option to display the wide form of the directory. The Copy command is another example. It requires two parameters: the name of the file to be copied and the name to be given to the new copy.

Parameters let you use the same MS-DOS command with different data. You can give a batch file the same capability with a feature called a *replaceable parameter*. A replaceable parameter is a special symbol you put in a batch file. When you use the batch file, MS-DOS replaces the symbol with a parameter you include when you type the batch command. The symbol consists of a percent sign followed by a one-digit number, such as %1. You can use the numbers 1 through 9 in replaceable parameters, and you can include more than one replaceable parameter in a batch file. (MS-DOS also recognizes %0 as a replaceable parameter but reserves this parameter to mean the drive, path, and file name of the batch file itself.)

The number of the symbol identifies which parameter replaces the symbol. If a batch command takes two parameters, for example, MS-DOS replaces %1 wherever it occurs in the batch file with the first parameter you type with the batch command, and it replaces %2 with the second parameter you type. Replaceable parameters can be used anywhere in a batch command.

For example, suppose you wanted a batch command that would print a file by copying it to the printer. (You already have a MS-DOS Print command, but go through the example anyway; it illustrates the use of replaceable parameters.) All the batch file needs is a Copy command and one replaceable parameter that identifies the file to be printed. The batch command is called *Prnt* to avoid confusion with the Print command. Type the following:

```
C>copy con prnt.bat
copy %1 prn
^Z
        1 file(s) copied
```

To test your Prnt batch command, make certain the printer is turned on and type the following:

```
C>prnt letr1.doc
```

MS-DOS displays the command after replacing %1 with the batch-command parameter, LETR1.DOC, and prints the file:

```
C>copy letr1.doc prn
        1 file(s) copied
```

Figure 14-1 shows several versions of PRNT.BAT that you might create for printing other documents. Each version contains at least one replaceable parameter; the last version contains two. To the left of each version is an example of how the batch command would be typed, and to the right are the corresponding commands that would be carried out after MS-DOS replaced the replaceable parameters. The batch-command parameters, the replaceable parameters in each version of the batch file, and the result after MS-DOS replaces them with the batch-command parameters are shown in *italics*.

| Batch Command You Would Type | Contents of PRNT.BAT | Commands That Would Be Carried Out |
|---|---|---|
| C>prnt *memo.doc* | copy *%1* prn | copy *memo.doc* prn |
| C>prnt *memo* | copy *%1*.doc prn | copy *memo*.doc prn |
| C>prnt *memo rept* | copy *%1*.doc prn<br>copy *%2*.doc prn | copy *memo*.doc prn<br>copy *rept*.doc prn |

**Figure 14-1.**
*Replaceable parameters in a batch file.*

Replaceable parameters make batch files much more flexible. Your batch commands needn't be limited to handling the same files or devices all the time—they can be used just like MS-DOS commands to operate with any file or device.

## Canceling a Batch Command

As with other MS-DOS commands, you press Ctrl-Break to cancel a batch command. But when you cancel a batch command, MS-DOS prompts you to confirm. To see this, create a short new batch file named DIRS.BAT that first displays the entries in your \DOS directory and then displays the entries in the current directory (\RUNDOS).

Create the DIRS.BAT file by typing the following:

```
C>copy con dirs.bat
dir \dos
dir
^Z
        1 file(s) copied
```

The directory displays should be long enough to give you time to press Ctrl-Break. Type the name of the Dirs batch command, then press Ctrl-Break as soon as MS-DOS starts displaying the file names:

```
C>dirs

C>dir \dos

 Volume in drive C is HARD DISK
 Volume Serial Number is 1608-5A30
 Directory of C:\DOS

 .            <DIR>      01-15-93    6:05p
 ..           <DIR>      01-15-93    6:05p
EGA      SYS     4885      02-01-93  12:00a
DISPLAY  SYS    15682      02-01-93  12:00a
FORMAT   COM    32285      02-01-93  12:00a
PACKING  LST     3492      02-01-93^C

Terminate batch job (Y/N)?_
```

If you respond *n*, the command being carried out is canceled, but MS-DOS continues with the next command in the batch file. Type *n*; MS-DOS carries out the next command, which displays the current directory:

```
C>dir

 Volume in drive C is HARD DISK
 Volume Serial Number is 1608-5A30
 Directory of C:\RUNDOS

 .            <DIR>      10-16-93    8:21a
 ..           <DIR>      10-16-93    8:21a
```

```
PH        TXT        526      10-16-93    1:43p
LETR1     DOC         26      10-16-93    3:13p
LETR2     DOC         26      10-16-93    3:13p
LETR3     DOC         26      10-16-93    3:13p
DIRLET    BAT         41      10-16-93    3:17p
PRNT      BAT         13      10-16-93    3:24p
DIRS      BAT         15      10-16-93    3:30p
        9 file(s)              673 bytes
                      13265422 bytes free
```

If you respond *y* to the "Terminate?" question, MS-DOS cancels the entire batch command and displays the system prompt. Type the Dirs batch command, and cancel it again, but this time respond *y*:

```
C>dirs

C>dir \dos

 Volume in drive C is HARD DISK
 Volume Serial Number is 1608-5A30
 Directory of C:\DOS

.                <DIR>     01-15-93    6:05p
..               <DIR>     01-15-93    6:05p
EGA       SYS      4885     02-01-93   12:00a
DISPLAY   SYS     15682     02-01-93   12:00a
FORMAT    COM     32285     02-01-93   12:00a
PACKING   LST      3492     02-01-93   12:00a
ANSI      SYS      8868     02-01-93^C

Terminate batch job (Y/N)?y
```

MS-DOS returns to command level without completing the batch command.

## DEVELOPING YOUR OWN STARTUP PROCEDURE

Each time you start or restart the system, MS-DOS goes through a startup procedure that includes searching the root directory of the startup disk for a special batch file named AUTOEXEC.BAT. If it finds the file, MS-DOS carries out whatever commands the file contains. Typically, AUTOEXEC.BAT is used to hold the commands you don't want to have to type each time you start or restart the system—a Path command, for example, that tells MS-DOS where to find command files on a hard disk and a Prompt command that sets the system prompt to show the current directory.

Versions 4 and later of MS-DOS create AUTOEXEC.BAT (or modify the existing version) as part of the installation procedure. Earlier versions of MS-DOS don't create the file automatically, but because AUTOEXEC.BAT is so useful, most systems include one.

Although MS-DOS gives special treatment to AUTOEXEC.BAT, that doesn't mean the file is untouchable. You can add commands to it at any time, but you should always be careful not to change or delete any existing commands, especially those you don't clearly understand. (You *can* encounter such commands in AUTOEXEC.BAT, particularly on systems that connect to a network and those that have been set up by someone else.)

The following examples show you some commands you might want to include in AUTOEXEC.BAT to tailor MS-DOS and your computer more closely to your needs or preferences. If you follow these examples, however, you'll replace the AUTOEXEC.BAT file you have now, so before you start, you'll check for, and protect, your existing file.

## A Safety Check

It's easy to check for AUTOEXEC.BAT. Remember, it must always be in the root directory of the system disk, so a simple Directory command does the job. The current directory should still be C:\RUNDOS, so type the following command to check the root directory:

```
C>dir \autoexec.bat
```

If MS-DOS responds *File not found*, you don't have an AUTOEXEC.BAT file, and you won't hurt a thing by trying the following examples. If, however, MS-DOS responds by showing an entry for AUTOEXEC.BAT, type the following to rename your existing file so that you won't lose it:

```
C>ren \autoexec.bat autoexec.sav
```

Type the Directory command again to search for AUTOEXEC.BAT in the root directory. This time, MS-DOS should respond *File not found*.

You'll restore your original AUTOEXEC.BAT later.

## Creating an AUTOEXEC.BAT File

Depending on how your system is set up and what you want to do with it, an AUTOEXEC.BAT file can contain anywhere from a few to many commands. As mentioned earlier, however, two that are usually included are a Path command that tells MS-DOS where to find command files and a Prompt command that sets the system prompt to display the current directory.

Although your normal AUTOEXEC.BAT file might well include more than these two commands, the following example shows you how to create just such a simple AUTOEXEC.BAT file. The file is short, so copy from the console to create it.

Type the following:

```
C>copy con \autoexec.bat
rem SAMPLE STARTUP PROCEDURE
path c:\;c:\dos;c:\rundos
prompt $p$g
^Z
```

You created the file in the root directory of the system disk because that's where MS-DOS always looks for AUTOEXEC.BAT. To test your startup procedure, you must restart the system.

NOTE: *Be sure to open the latch or remove any floppy disk in the floppy disk drive so that MS-DOS restarts from the hard disk.*

Now restart the system by pressing Ctrl-Alt-Del. MS-DOS might display some messages before carrying out the commands in your new AUTOEXEC.BAT file, but regardless of your version of MS-DOS, the end of the startup screen looks like this:

```
C>rem SAMPLE STARTUP PROCEDURE

C>path c:\;c:\dos;c:\rundos

C>prompt $p$g

C:\>_
```

So far so good, but, as you've probably realized, a simple batch file like this just begins to tap the power of AUTOEXEC.BAT. Suppose, now, that you want MS-DOS to clear the screen and display its version number each time you start your computer. You also want MS-DOS to change to a particular directory and display a directory listing. Here's a new AUTOEXEC.BAT file that does what you want. You can use Edit or a word processor if you want to try your editing skills. Otherwise, simply copy from the console again (as shown in the example) to replace the sample AUTOEXEC.BAT file with a new version.

Type the following:

```
C:\>copy con autoexec.bat
rem SAMPLE STARTUP PROCEDURE
path c:\;c:\dos;c:\rundos
prompt $p$g
cls
ver
cd \rundos
dir
^Z
```

Again, restart the system to test your new AUTOEXEC.BAT file. This time, you see (though briefly):

```
C>rem SAMPLE STARTUP PROCEDURE

C>path c:\;c:\dos;c:\rundos

C>prompt $p$g
```

The screen clears, and then MS-DOS displays:

```
C:\>ver

MS-DOS Version 6.0

C:\>cd \rundos

C:\RUNDOS>dir

 Volume in drive C is HARD DISK
 Volume Serial Number is 1608-5A30
 Directory of C:\RUNDOS

 .            <DIR>      10-16-93   8:21a
 ..           <DIR>      10-16-93   8:21a
 PH      TXT       526    10-16-93   1:43p
 LETR1   DOC        26    10-16-93   3:13p
 LETR2   DOC        26    10-16-93   3:13p
 LETR3   DOC        26    10-16-93   3:13p
 DIRLET  BAT        41    10-16-93   3:17p
 PRNT    BAT        13    10-16-93   3:24p
 DIRS    BAT        15    10-16-93   3:30p
         9 file(s)            673 bytes
                        13265422 bytes free
```

Your new startup procedure not only tells MS-DOS where to find the files it needs, it also clears the screen, displays the version number, changes the current directory, and then displays the entries in the current directory.

You can also use AUTOEXEC.BAT to handle special startup requirements. For example, if your system has equipment options that require special setup instructions with the Mode command, put the commands in AUTOEXEC.BAT so that you needn't type them each time you start or restart the system. Or, if you have a device attached to your system that requires a special program to operate it (such as a CD-ROM drive or a scanner), you can put the command in your AUTOEXEC.BAT file so that you don't have to enter the command each time you start the system. And by all means, put the command to load Doskey in AUTOEXEC.BAT if it isn't there already.

If you renamed your existing AUTOEXEC.BAT file at the beginning of this example, type the following to save the example as AUTOEXEC.TST and restore the original:

```
C:\RUNDOS>ren \autoexec.bat autoexec.tst
```

```
C:\RUNDOS>ren \autoexec.sav autoexec.bat
```

Now your real AUTOEXEC.BAT will be executed the next time you start up your system. The version you created in the example is still in the root directory as AUTOEXEC.TST, in case you want to experiment with it further.

If you didn't have an AUTOEXEC.BAT file to begin with, type the following so that MS-DOS won't carry out your example file the next time you start your system:

```
C:\RUNDOS>ren autoexec.bat autoexec.tst
```

The version you created in the example is still present in the root directory as AUTOEXEC.TST, in case you want to experiment with it further.

Finally, to rid your system of a possibly invalid Path command, restart your computer by pressing Ctrl-Alt-Del.

## SOME USEFUL COMMANDS

The following examples describe a few batch commands you might find useful; they might also give you some ideas for other commands you could create. Each topic includes a description of what the command does, the contents of the batch file, and one or two examples of its use.

These examples are illustrative; they are not hands-on exercises because you might not have the necessary files or devices to use them. But remember that they're here; you'll probably find a situation in which they can be helpful.

### Printing a File

Earlier in the chapter you created the Prnt batch command, which prints a file by copying it to the printer. PRNT.BAT contains *copy %1 prn*. To use it, you type the name of the batch file followed by the name of the file to be printed. (For example, to print a file named REPORT.DOC, you would type *prnt report.doc*.)

As the examples in Figure 14-1 showed, you can make batch commands more specific by including common parts of a file name or extension in the batch file. For example, if you frequently print files that have the extension DOC, you could enter the command in the batch file as *copy %1.doc*; to print the file named REPORT.DOC, you would only have to type *prnt report*.

## Printing a File in Small Type

If your printer is compatible with Epson or IBM dot-matrix printers, you can use the Mode command to print 132 characters on a line. This type size is handy for wide reports or spreadsheets, and putting the Mode and Copy commands in a batch file named SMALL.BAT makes them easy to use. SMALL.BAT contains:

```
mode lpt1: 132
copy %1 lpt1:
mode lpt1: 80
```

If your printer is attached to a different port, change *lpt1* to *lpt2* or *lpt3*, as necessary. The Small command takes one parameter, the name of the file to be printed in small type. To use the Small command to print the file REPORT.DOC, you would type:

```
C:\>small report.doc
```

MS-DOS would display the Mode and Copy commands and print the file in small type:

```
C:\>mode lpt1: 132

LPT1: not rerouted

LPT1: set for 132

No retry on parallel printer time-out

C:\>copy report.doc lpt1:
        1 file(s) copied

C:\>mode lpt1: 80

LPT1: not rerouted

LPT1: set for 80

No retry on parallel printer time-out
```

The second Mode command resets the printer to normal type.

## Eliminating Old BAK Files

Because many word processors create a backup file with an extension of BAK each time you edit a file, your disks can get crowded with files you might not need. The two batch files here work together to let you find all the BAK files on your disk and erase the ones you don't need.

First, FINDBAK.BAT consists of one Directory command that uses the /S parameter to look in all subdirectories of the root directory and the /B parameter to display only the path and file name of each file it finds:

```
dir \*.bak /s /b
```

The backslash before *.bak* starts the search in the root directory and, because all other subdirectories are contained in the root, the /S parameter makes the command find every BAK file on the disk. Use the Findbak command to locate the files you want to delete.

Next, CLEAN.BAT consists of one Delete command that erases all files in the specified directory that have the extension BAK:

```
del %1*.bak
```

The Clean command takes one parameter, the directory name followed by a backslash. If you omit the parameter, the command cleans up the current directory. You can clean up the disk in a different drive by preceding the path name with the drive letter and a colon. For example, after using FINDBAK.BAT to find your BAK files, you would erase all files whose extension is BAK in the current directory, simply by typing *clean*. To erase all the BAK files in the directory \MKT\WP, you would type *clean \mkt\wp\*. To erase all BAK files in the directory \LASTYEAR\RPT on the disk in drive A, you would type *clean a:\lastyear\rpt\*.

# CREATING COMMANDS WITH DOSKEY

> **NOTE:** *Doskey is included with versions 5 and later of MS-DOS. If you have an earlier version, go on to Chapter 15, "Creating Smart Commands."*

You've seen how batch files can help you customize MS-DOS by combining commands to perform special tasks. To create a batch file, you can copy from the console, as in the preceding examples, or use a text editor or a word processor. If you have version 5 or later, you can also use Doskey.

Chapters 3 and 13 showed how Doskey can help you edit and repeat MS-DOS commands you've already used. This section introduces several Doskey parameters that help you not only view but save commands in either of two forms: as batch files or as keyboard shortcuts called *macros*.

## Batch Files and Macros

You know that batch files are sets of MS-DOS commands that you save in a text file and carry out by typing the name of the batch file. A macro is a similar type of work saver. You create a macro by assigning a descriptive name to one or more commands. Once you've defined a macro in this way, you simply type the name to carry out the commands. You benefit by saving time and keystrokes, especially with often-used, long, or complicated sets of commands.

In some respects, macros are very much like batch files. Both are your creations; both cause MS-DOS to carry out one or more commands to do a specific job; and both let you start the command sequence by typing a short, descriptive name.

### Doskey Command Parameters

In earlier chapters, you've typed *doskey* to start the Doskey program, and you've used function and editing keys to retrieve, display, and edit commands. Doskey also includes several parameters you can use to create and view commands and macros. Three important ones are:

**doskey /history <macro>=<command> /macros**

Doskey is the name of the program. When you type *doskey* by itself, MS-DOS loads the program into memory, where it remains until you turn the system off or restart MS-DOS.

*/history*, which you can abbreviate as */H*, tells Doskey to show you a list of all commands currently in memory. You can use the */history* parameter to create a batch file, by redirecting the commands from memory to a file.

<macro>=<command> tells Doskey to create a macro. As already mentioned, you assign a name (shown here as *macro*) to one or more commands (*command*). An equal sign must follow the macro name.

*/macros*, which you can abbreviate as */M*, tells Doskey to display the macros currently in memory. You can use the */macros* parameter to save macros by redirecting them from the computer's memory, where they will be lost when you shut down the system, to a file.

Doskey includes a few other parameters you can use to control its behavior. You don't need these parameters here; the details are in Appendix C, "MS-DOS Command Reference."

## Using Doskey to Create a Batch File

When you use Doskey, you can retrieve and edit commands you typed earlier because the commands remain in a special portion of your computer's memory until you turn off the computer or restart Doskey, or until you've typed so many commands that the oldest ones are discarded to make room for newer ones.

Because commands remain in memory, you can use Doskey as an alternative to a text editor for creating some batch files. The following example shows how to redirect Doskey's list of commands to a batch file. Begin by starting Doskey. Type:

```
C:\>doskey
```

(If Doskey is already running, press Alt-F7. This clears the list of commands Doskey has recorded and assures you of a fresh start.)

Now type some commands:

```
C:\>cd \rundos

C:\RUNDOS>dir /oe > prn

C:\RUNDOS>cd \
```

These three commands change the current directory, print a directory listing sorted by extension, and return to the root directory of drive C. These commands could form a small but useful batch file for keeping track of the files you create with your applications, especially if you can specify the directory you want to list and print. You can create the file in a two-step process.

First, use the Doskey /H parameter to redirect the commands to a file. This example uses the extension BAT, but you could just as easily save the commands as a standard text file with an extension such as TXT or DOC. Type:

```
C:\>doskey /h > list.bat
```

That's really all there is to using Doskey to save a sequence of commands you've typed. If you want to save the commands as a usable batch file, however, your work isn't quite done, so use Edit to add a few finishing touches. Type:

```
C:\>edit list.bat
```

When Edit displays the file, change \RUNDOS to a replaceable parameter so you can specify any directory you choose. Change:

```
cd \rundos
```

to:

```
cd %1
```

Notice, too, that Doskey has included the command you typed to create the batch file. You have to omit this command to avoid accidentally redirecting some future list of unrelated Doskey commands to your batch file, so delete the line that contains *doskey /h > list.bat*. Save the file, and you're done. From now on, whenever you want to print the directory entries of the files in a particular directory, sorted by extension, just type *list* followed by the name of the directory.

Using Doskey in this way can be especially useful when you're developing a batch file and aren't certain the commands you're putting together will do the job you have in mind. Start Doskey, and type each command you intend to use.

Because each command is carried out immediately, you can see exactly what it does, and you can see how all the commands work together before you save them as a batch file.

## Using Doskey to Create a Macro

Creating a macro with Doskey is just as easy as creating a batch file, perhaps even easier. To define a macro to Doskey, you type a macro name, an equal sign, and the command or commands you want the macro to carry out. You can use replaceable parameters as you do in batch files, but instead of %1, %2, %3, and so on, you use $1, $2, $3, and so on through $9.

The following examples use the Directory and Mode commands to create some macros you might want to use.

In versions 5 and later, the /O parameter of the Directory command allows you to sort a directory in a number of ways: by name, extension, size, or date and time, or with subdirectories grouped at the beginning of the listing. Depending on what you're doing, you might choose to look at a directory in any of these ways. To keep typing to a minimum, you can create a macro for each type of listing and add the /P parameter so that MS-DOS will pause after each screenful.

If you haven't turned off or restarted your computer, clear Doskey's memory by pressing Alt-F7. If you have turned off your computer, turn it back on, and type *doskey* to load the program. Now create the macros by typing the following:

```
C:\>doskey dname=dir $1 /on /p

C:\>doskey dext=dir $1 /oe /p

C:\>doskey dsize=dir $1 /os /p

C:\>doskey ddate=dir $1 /od /p

C:\>doskey dsubs=dir $1 /og /p
```

Now try them out. Using your \DOS directory as an example, type *dname \dos* to list the entries alphabetically by file name, *dext \dos* to list them by extension, *dsize \dos* to list them by size, and *ddate \dos* to list them by date and time. If you want, type *dsubs c:* to list the directories on drive C before the files.

If you have a monitor that can change between a normal display (25 lines) and a condensed display (43 or 50 lines) with the Mode command, you can create macros that switch you quickly back and forth. You might, for example, prefer a condensed display for directory listings but a regular 25-line display for most other work. Type the following:

```
C:\>doskey big=mode con lines=25

C:\>doskey little=mode con lines=43
```

Now, when you want a condensed display, simply type *little*. To switch back to 25 lines, type *big*. (If you try these examples and MS-DOS responds *ANSI.SYS must be installed to perform requested function*, you need to identify a file named ANSI.SYS to MS-DOS as part of your startup procedure. Chapter 17, "Tailoring Your System," tells you how.)

You can also combine the screen macros with the directory-display macros by taking advantage of Doskey's ability to accept more than one command on a line. At the system prompt, you separate commands by pressing Ctrl-T. In a macro, you do the same thing by typing *$T* (or *$t*). For example, the following macro changes the screen to a condensed display, lists by size the entries in the directory you specify, waits for you to press a key, and then returns to a 25-line display. Note the *$t* separating the Mode, Pause, and Directory commands. Although the macro is shown on two lines here, don't press Enter until you reach the end:

```
doskey dir43=mode con lines=43 $t dir $1 /os /p
$t pause $t mode con lines=25<enter>
```

To see a condensed listing of your \DOS directory, you would type *dir43 \dos*.

## Saving Macros for Later Use

Although macros act much like batch files, they are stored in your computer's memory, not on disk, so they are not automatically saved when you turn off or restart the computer. You can save the macros you create, however, by using either the /H or the /M parameter to redirect the macros into a file. The difference between the two parameters is an important one:

- If the macro-definition commands are in the list of commands Doskey can retrieve, /H saves the *commands* that create the macros.

- If the macros are currently in your computer's memory, /M saves the macros themselves.

To see how these parameters work, first use the /H parameter to save the macro definitions currently in your computer's memory. Type:

```
C:\>doskey /h > macros1.txt
```

Now, save the macros themselves by typing:

```
C:\>doskey /m > macros2.txt
```

Use the Type command to view the two files you just saved. The commands saved with /H look something like this (you probably won't see them all if you've been trying out the macros because other commands will take up space in the list):

```
doskey dname=dir $1 /on /p
doskey dext=dir $1 /on /p
doskey dsize=dir $1 /on /p
doskey ddate=dir $1 /on /p
doskey big=mode con lines=25
doskey little=mode con lines=43
doskey dir43=mode con lines=43 $t dir $1 /os /p
   $t pause $t mode con lines=25
doskey /h > macros1.txt
```

The file saved with /M looks like this:

```
DNAME=dir $1 /on /p
DEXT=dir $1 /on /p
DSIZE=dir $1 /on /p
DDATE=dir $1 /on /p
DSUBS=dir $1 /og /p
BIG=mode con lines=25
LITTLE=mode con lines=43
DIR43=mode con lines=43 $t dir $1 /os /p
   $t pause $t mode con lines=25
```

The first file contains the *commands* that created the macros. You can easily turn such a file into a batch file by entering the macro-definition commands, giving the file a BAT extension, and deleting the last line (which will be something like *doskey /h > macros1.txt*).

The second file contains the *macros* you created. It forms a useful record of your macros, but in order to run the macros again in your next session with MS-DOS, you must edit the file, adding *doskey* in front of each one to turn the macro into the command that creates it. You can then turn the file of macro-definition commands into a batch file by giving the file a BAT extension.

Thus, although the /M parameter might appear to be more useful because it saves the actual macros, the reverse is true. Each time you start MS-DOS, you must also define any macros you want to use. If you're going to save a macro, you'll want to save the macro definition because you must run the command that creates the macro before you can use the macro itself. You can, if you want, put a macro-definition command in a batch file and run it without any problems. You cannot, however, run the macro itself from a batch file, even if you first define it in the same batch file. Macro names can be typed only at the MS-DOS system prompt.

# 15

# Creating Smart Commands

he previous two chapters showed how redirection, filter commands, pipes, batch files, and macros let you build your own commands or change the way that MS-DOS commands work. This chapter shows how MS-DOS gives you more control over the way it carries out the commands you build into a batch file. The techniques in this chapter help you create powerful commands tailored to your needs.

You can make your commands display their own instructions or warning messages. Or you can specify the circumstances under which MS-DOS carries out one command—or a different sequence of commands altogether. You can even make the system pause until you tell it to proceed.

This chapter shows you how to develop a batch file that uses most of these capabilities. The next chapter extends the example, describes two additional batch commands, and shows several useful commands you can create. When you complete these two chapters, you'll be ready to apply the full power of MS-DOS to your needs.

## PREPARING FOR THE EXAMPLES

For these examples, you'll need a formatted floppy disk and some sample files. If you completed the examples in Chapter 13, "Taking Control of Your System," use the \RUNDOS directory, which contains the phone-list file. Put the formatted floppy disk in drive A, and change the current directory to \RUNDOS by typing:

```
C:\>cd \rundos
```

If you want, change the prompt to C>, as shown in the following examples, by typing *prompt*. You'll use six sample files in this and the next chapter:

| | |
|---|---|
| P.DOC | Q.DOC |
| P.BAK | Q.BAK |
| P.OLD | Q.OLD |

Type the following to create the files (as usual, press F6 or Ctrl-Z and Enter where you see ^Z):

```
C>copy con p.doc
This is a sample file.
^Z
        1 file(s) copied

C>copy p.doc p.bak
        1 file(s) copied

C>copy p.doc p.old
        1 file(s) copied
```

```
C>copy p.* q.*
P.DOC
P.BAK
P.OLD
          3 file(s) copied
```

This completes the preparation for the examples.

# CREATING AN ARCHIVE COMMAND

Disk files proliferate as you use your computer. You'll probably archive files from time to time, copying them to long-term-storage floppy disks and then erasing them from your working disks, just as you occasionally remove documents from your paper files and put them in long-term storage.

Although MS-DOS versions 6 and later include the MSbackup command and earlier versions include the Backup and Restore commands to help you archive old files, this chapter shows you how to use the MS-DOS batch commands to develop an Archive command that all users can use, whether or not they're comfortable with MS-DOS commands.

You start with just a Copy command, and then you expand the batch file to display instructions, provide a safeguard against inadvertently erasing a previously archived file, and erase the file after it is archived.

The floppy disk in drive A is the archive floppy disk, the one you store in a safe place. Your hard disk is the working disk that contains files you want to archive.

Your Archive command will be a file named ARCHIVE.BAT. The initial version contains only a Copy command. To create the file, type the following:

```
C>copy con archive.bat
copy %1 a:%1
^Z
          1 file(s) copied
```

This file is the starting point for your Archive command. It requires only one parameter, the name of the file to be archived. The Copy command copies this file (*%1* in the Copy command) to the floppy disk in drive A, giving it the same name (*a:%1*) as the original. To see how the batch file works, make certain the archive floppy disk is in drive A; archive P.DOC by typing:

```
C>archive p.doc
```

MS-DOS responds by displaying and carrying out the Copy command in the batch file:

```
C>copy p.doc a:p.doc
          1 file(s) copied
```

This isn't much, but then it's only a starting point. You'll add significantly to this simple command as you go through the examples in this chapter.

## MODIFYING THE SAMPLE BATCH FILE

This chapter describes four batch commands: Echo, Pause, If, and Goto. Each command description explains the purpose of the batch command, then adds it to ARCHIVE.BAT. The modified version of the batch file is shown with the changed or added lines shaded. Either use the MS-DOS text editor (Edit) to make the indicated changes or enter each updated version by copying from the console.

## CONTROLLING SYSTEM MESSAGES

The Echo command controls whether commands in a batch file are displayed, and it lets you display your own messages. It has three parameters:

**echo on off <message>**

*on* causes commands to be displayed as they are carried out. (This is called "turning echo on.") Echo is on unless you turn it off.

*off* causes commands not to be displayed as they are carried out. (This is called "turning echo off.") Eliminating the commands from the display can make a batch file easier to use by reducing clutter on the screen.

<message> is a string of characters, such as a reminder or a warning, that you want to display. <message> is displayed whether echo is turned on or off.

You can include only one parameter with an Echo command. If you omit all parameters (just type *echo*), MS-DOS displays the status of echo (either *ECHO is on* or *ECHO is off*).

The first changes to your Archive command add an Echo command at the beginning to turn echo off and another Echo command after it to display a title message.

Here is the modified version of ARCHIVE.BAT:

```
echo off
echo Archive Procedure
copy %1 a:%1
```

To archive P.DOC with your new Archive command, type the name of the batch file and the name of the file to be archived:

```
C>archive p.doc
```

Because echo is always on when MS-DOS starts carrying out the commands in a batch file, MS-DOS displays the first Echo command, which turns echo off. Then it carries out the second Echo command, which displays the title *Archive Procedure*. Finally, it carries out the Copy command from the original ARCHIVE.BAT and copies the file:

```
C>echo off
Archive Procedure
         1 file(s) copied
```

Messages produced by a command itself (such as *1 file(s) copied* in the preceding example) are displayed whether echo is on or off.

Starting with version 3.3, you can prevent any individual command from being echoed by preceding it with the @ symbol. This means that you can eliminate even that first *echo off* message by changing the first line of ARCHIVE.BAT to *@echo off*. If you're using 3.3 or a later version, edit the file again to add the @ symbol at the beginning of line 1. From now on, all examples will show the @ symbol; if you're not using 3.3 or a later version, simply ignore it.

Your Archive command is starting to take shape. It's time to add some instructions for the person who uses it.

## MAKING THE SYSTEM PAUSE

Some MS-DOS commands, such as Format and Diskcopy, display a message and wait for you to respond, giving you a chance to confirm your intention or to complete preparation by inserting a floppy disk or by turning on the printer. You can have your batch files do the same by using the Pause command, which displays the message *Press any key to continue...* and makes the system wait until you press any key. (The message is *Strike a key when ready...* in versions prior to 4.)

The Pause command has one parameter:

**pause <message>**

<message> is a string of characters, such as a reminder or a warning, that you want the Pause command to display. <message> is displayed only if echo is on.

You'll add a Pause command to ARCHIVE.BAT now. You'll also add a message—a reminder to make certain that the archive floppy disk is in drive A before the file is copied.

But wait: Any message you include as a parameter with the Pause command is displayed only if echo is on, and you have turned echo off in line 1 of ARCHIVE.BAT.

You can still use the Pause command, however. Instead of using the message capability of the Pause command, just use an Echo command to display the reminder, then add a Pause command without a message. This approach is a bit more work than simply adding a message after the Pause command, but the result is a command that's easier to use because you avoid cluttering the display with all the commands that MS-DOS would display if you were to turn echo on.

The modified version of ARCHIVE.BAT is:

```
@echo off
echo Archive Procedure
echo Make sure archive floppy disk is in drive A
pause
copy %1 a:%1
```

Remember, if you're not using version 3.3 or later, ignore the @ in line 1. Test this version by typing:

```
C>archive p.doc
Archive Procedure
Make sure archive floppy disk is in drive A
Press any key to continue . . .
_
```

The Echo command displays the reminder, the Pause command displays its message telling you to press a key, and the system waits. Complete the command by pressing any key. MS-DOS copies the file and acknowledges:

```
1 file(s) copied
```

## CONTROLLING WHICH COMMANDS ARE CARRIED OUT

Besides carrying out MS-DOS commands as though you had typed them individually, batch files let you specify that a command should be carried out only if some condition is true—for example, only if a specific file exists. This capability makes your batch files more flexible, letting you adapt them to a variety of situations.

The If command specifies the condition to be checked and the MS-DOS command to be carried out. It has three parameters:

**if not <condition> <command>**

*not* reverses the meaning of the If command so that <command> is carried out only if <condition> is not true.

<condition> is the condition to check. It has two commonly used forms:

- *exist* <filename> checks whether the named file exists. You can include a path name, if necessary. If <filename> exists, the condition is true.

- <string1>==<string2> compares the two character strings you specify. If they are identical, the condition is true. Note that there are two equal signs.

<command> is any MS-DOS command.

You'll add an If command to ARCHIVE.BAT to control when it displays a warning message.

## Adding Protection to Your Archive Command

When you copy a file with the Copy command, you tell MS-DOS the name of the original and the name to be given to the new copy. MS-DOS checks to see whether there is already a file with the same name as the copy on the target disk; if there is, MS-DOS replaces the existing file with the copy. What if you didn't realize that a file with the same name existed on the disk? You might inadvertently lose a valuable file.

To protect yourself against such an oversight, you'll include two more commands in ARCHIVE.BAT. First, you'll add an If command that checks to see whether the file to be archived already exists on the archive floppy disk in drive A. If it does, an Echo command in the second part of the If command displays a warning message telling you that you can cancel the command by pressing Ctrl-Break. You'll also add a Pause command to give you time to read the warning message and, if necessary, cancel the Archive command by pressing Ctrl-Break.

Here is the modified version of ARCHIVE.BAT. Type the fifth line on one line, even though it is shown on two lines in the text:

```
@echo off
echo Archive Procedure
echo Make sure archive floppy disk is in drive A
pause
if exist a:%1 echo a:%1 exists. Press
CTRL-BREAK to cancel, or
pause
copy %1 a:%1
```

Test this version of your Archive command by typing:

```
C>archive p.doc
Archive Procedure
Make sure archive floppy disk is in drive A
Press any key to continue . . .
_
```

343

Press any key to continue the command:

```
a:p.doc exists. Press CTRL-BREAK to cancel, or
Press any key to continue . . .
_
```

Don't press any key yet.

You might not want to replace the copy of the file in drive A. Press Ctrl-Break to cancel the command. MS-DOS asks whether you really mean it:

```
Terminate batch job (Y/N)?_
```

Type *y* to confirm. MS-DOS cancels the rest of your Archive command and displays the system prompt without copying the file. If you had not pressed Ctrl-Break, the file would have been copied as before, erasing the previously archived version of P.DOC.

## Smoothing a Rough Edge

Your Archive command is getting more useful; you've protected yourself from inadvertently erasing an existing file. But there's a problem now. See what happens if the name of the file to be archived isn't the name of a file already on the floppy disk in drive A. Delete P.DOC from drive A, and archive it again:

```
C>del a:p.doc

C>archive p.doc
Archive Procedure
Make sure archive floppy disk is in drive A
Press any key to continue . . .
_
```

Fine so far. Press the Spacebar to continue:

```
Press any key to continue . . .
_
```

That's not too good. The system comes right back and pauses again, even though everything is OK, because the Pause command that follows the If command is always carried out. Press the Spacebar again:

```
1 file(s) copied
```

MS-DOS copies the file as it should. Your Archive command is working properly, but the two pauses could be confusing, especially if someone else uses your batch command. How can you fix this?

You could delete the first Pause command, but if you did, you wouldn't have a chance to make certain that the correct floppy disk had been placed in drive A. That's not a very good solution.

Or you could delete the second Pause command and change the If command, making the "file exists" warning a Pause message instead of an Echo message, as it is now. But then, recall that you would have to delete the command *echo off* at the beginning of the batch file so that the message following the new Pause command would be displayed. And that would mean all your commands in the file would be displayed. This solution would make the response to your Archive command cluttered and confusing, so it isn't very good either.

There is, however, a way to change your Archive command so that the second Pause command is carried out only if the file to be archived is already on the floppy disk in drive A. This solution requires using another command for batch files—the Goto command.

## CHANGING THE SEQUENCE OF COMMANDS

The batch files you have created up to now carry out the MS-DOS commands they contain in the order in which the commands appear. Your batch commands would be more flexible if you could control the order in which the commands are carried out. The Goto command gives you this control by telling MS-DOS to go to a specific line in the command file, rather than to the next command in the sequence.

You tell MS-DOS where to go in the batch file by specifying a *label*. A label, which is located on a line in a batch file, consists of a colon (:) immediately followed by a string of characters (for example, *:start*). A label is not a command. It merely identifies a location in a batch file. When MS-DOS goes to a label, it carries out whatever commands follow the line on which the label appears.

The Goto command has one parameter:

**goto <label>**

<label> is the label that identifies the line in the batch file where MS-DOS is to go.

The Goto command is often used as part of an If command. For example, the If command checks some condition. If the condition is not true, MS-DOS carries out the next command; if the condition is true, MS-DOS carries out the Goto command and moves to some other part of the batch file.

Remember the problem with your Archive command? If the file to be archived is already on the floppy disk in drive A, you want MS-DOS to display a warning message and pause; otherwise, you just want to copy the file. This situation is tailor-made for an If command that includes a Goto command.

The modified version of ARCHIVE.BAT is:

```
@echo off
echo Archive Procedure
```

```
echo Make sure archive floppy disk is in drive A
pause
if not exist a:%1 goto safe
echo a:%1 exists. Press CTRL-BREAK to cancel, or
pause
:safe
copy %1 a:%1
```

These changes warrant a bit more explanation:

- The If command still checks whether the file to be archived exists on the floppy disk in drive A. Now, however, the command includes the parameter *not*, which means that the command in the second part of the If command is carried out only if the reverse of the condition is true (that is, if the file does *not* exist on the floppy disk in drive A).

- The second part of the If command—the command to be carried out if the condition is true—is changed to a Goto command that tells MS-DOS to skip to a label called *:safe*.

- If the file to be archived doesn't exist on the floppy disk in drive A, the Goto command is carried out and MS-DOS jumps to the label *:safe*, skipping the Echo and Pause commands. The Copy command following *:safe* copies the file.

- If the file to be archived does exist on the floppy disk in drive A, the Goto command is not carried out and MS-DOS continues with the Echo and Pause commands. If you don't cancel by pressing Ctrl-Break, MS-DOS carries out the Copy command. In this instance, MS-DOS ignores the line that contains the label *:safe* because the only purpose of the label is to identify a location in a batch file.

P.DOC is on the floppy disk in drive A (you archived it again a bit earlier), so first see if this version of your Archive command warns you that the file exists. Type the following:

```
C>archive p.doc
Archive Procedure
Make sure archive floppy disk is in drive A
Press any key to continue . . .
_
```

Press any key to continue the command:

```
a:p.doc exists. Press CTRL-BREAK to cancel, or
Press any key to continue . . .
_
```

There's the warning. Press any key to complete the command:

```
1 file(s) copied
```

But the problem came up when the file wasn't on the archive floppy disk: You got the second pause anyway. Test your revised Archive command in this situation by archiving P.BAK, which hasn't yet been archived:

```
C>archive p.bak
Archive Procedure
Make sure archive floppy disk is in drive A
Press any key to continue . . .

_
```

Press a key:

```
1 file(s) copied
```

Problem solved. Because P.BAK wasn't on the archive floppy disk in drive A, the Goto command was carried out; the Goto command caused MS-DOS to skip over the intervening Echo and Pause commands and to copy the file.

Your Archive command works properly. You had to do a little more work to avoid the double pause, but now the command is less confusing and easier to use. You'll probably encounter this kind of circumstance fairly often as you create batch commands. Just remember: It takes a little more time to make a command easy to use, but the investment is usually worthwhile, especially if other people will be using the command.

## Using Wildcard Characters with a Batch File

You can use wildcard characters to archive a series of files with your Archive command. Type the following command to archive all the files named P:

```
C>archive p.*
Archive Procedure
Make sure archive floppy disk is in drive A
Press any key to continue . . .

_
```

Press any key:

```
a:p.* exists. Press CTRL-BREAK to cancel, or
Press any key to continue . . .

_
```

You archived P.DOC and P.BAK in earlier examples, so they're on the archive floppy disk. The Archive command doesn't identify the specific file that exists, but it does give you a chance to cancel if you don't want to overwrite a file.

Press Ctrl-Break to cancel the rest of the command, and respond to the MS-DOS prompt for confirmation with *y*:

```
Terminate batch job (Y/N)?y
```

If you had pressed any key other than Ctrl-Break, all the files named P would have been copied to the floppy disk in drive A, replacing any that were already there.

## Erasing the Original of an Archived File

Archiving involves not only copying a file to an archive floppy disk, but also means deleting the original. Your Archive command only copies; now it's time to make it delete too. But just as it's prudent to check whether the file exists on the archive floppy disk before you make the copy, it's also prudent to check again before deleting the original, just to be sure the file was copied to the archive floppy disk.

You need only one additional If command to check whether the file to be archived is on the archive floppy disk and, if it is, to delete the original from the working disk. Here is this modified version of ARCHIVE.BAT:

```
@echo off
echo Archive Procedure
echo Make sure archive floppy disk is in drive A
pause
if not exist a:%1 goto safe
echo a:%1 exists. Press CTRL-BREAK to cancel, or
pause
:safe
copy %1 a:%1
if exist a:%1 del %1
```

The screen responses of this version of your Archive command are the same as in the previous version, but the new command deletes the original file after copying it. Test it by archiving P.DOC again:

```
C>archive p.doc
Archive Procedure
Make sure archive floppy disk is in drive A
Press any key to continue . . .
_
```

Press any key:

```
a:p.doc exists. Press CTRL-BREAK to cancel, or
Press any key to continue . . .
_
```

You want to copy the file to the archive floppy disk, so press any key:

```
1 file(s) copied
```

See if the original version of P.DOC still exists by typing:

```
C>dir p.doc

    Volume in drive C is HARD DISK
    Volume Serial Number is 1608-5A30
    Directory of C:\RUNDOS

    File not found
```

The original is gone. Your Archive command does copy the specified file to the archive floppy disk and then deletes the original.

Functionally, the command is complete.

# DRESSING UP YOUR ARCHIVE COMMAND

The value of your batch files depends not only on what they do but also on how easy it is to use them correctly. This ease of use is particularly important if you use a batch file only occasionally or if someone else uses it; it's vital if the batch file deletes other files, as your Archive command does.

That's why, for example, your Archive command starts by turning echo off: An uncluttered screen helps to make the responses less confusing. You can also do some other things to make a batch file easy to use:

- Clear the screen.

- Use the Echo command to display messages that report on progress or results.

- Use spaces or insert tabs so you can position messages displayed by the Echo command where they are prominent on the screen.

- Use the Echo command to include blank lines that further improve the readability of the screen.

You can also use the Remark command to put notes to yourself in the batch file. As long as echo is off, these remarks aren't displayed. Remarks can help you remember how a batch file works, in case you have to change it or you want to create a similar command using the same technique. Remarks are especially useful if the batch file is long or if it's one you may not look at very often.

## Echoing a Blank Line

Up to now, you have used the Echo command either to turn echo off or to display a message. You can also use the Echo command to display a blank line—something you'll probably want to do fairly often to improve the appearance of the display.

You've seen that you turn echo on or off by following *echo* with either *on* or *off*. If you follow *echo* with some other words, they are displayed as a message, and if you simply type *echo*, MS-DOS tells you whether echo is on or off. How do you tell MS-DOS to echo a blank line? Beginning with version 3.1, typing *echo.* (*echo* and a period, with no space between) causes MS-DOS to display a blank line. If this does not work with your version of MS-DOS, you can also type *echo*, press the Spacebar once, hold down the Alt key, and use the numeric keypad (not the numbers in the top row of the keyboard) to type *255*. When you release the Alt key, the cursor moves over one column. You don't see any characters displayed, but when MS-DOS carries out your Echo command, it will echo a blank line on the screen.

The following example modifies ARCHIVE.BAT. If your version of MS-DOS doesn't respond to *echo.*, substitute Alt-255 in the appropriate lines. The changes in this batch file don't add any capability to your Archive command, but they do make it easier for someone to understand what's happening. The changes are described in more detail in a moment. Here is the modified version of ARCHIVE.BAT:

```
@echo off
cls
Rem Three tabs in following echo command
echo<tab><tab><tab>***ARCHIV PROCEDURE***
echo.
echo Make sure archive floppy disk is in drive A
pause
Rem Branch around warning if file not archived
if not exist a:%1 goto safe
echo.
echo a:%1 exists. Press CTRL-BREAK to cancel, or
pause
:safe
copy %1 a:%1
if exist a:%1 del %1
echo.
echo %1 archived
```

The purpose of each change is as follows:

- In line 2, the Clear Screen command starts your Archive command off with a blank screen, giving you complete control over what is displayed.

- In line 3, the Remark command reminds you that the space at the beginning of the Echo command in line 4 is created by pressing the Tab key three times.

- In line 4, the title (***ARCHIVE PROCEDURE***) is made more prominent and is displayed in the center of the screen by the insertion of three tabs.

- In line 5, an Echo command displays a blank line below the title.

- In line 8, the Remark command explains the purpose of the Goto command included in line 9.

- In line 10, another Echo command displays a blank line to make the warning message in line 11 more visible.

- In line 16, the Echo command displays another blank line to make the message in line 17 more visible.

- In line 17, the Echo command's message tells which file has been archived.

Make the necessary changes, and compare your batch file with the modified form of ARCHIVE.BAT shown earlier. If there are any differences, correct them before saving the revised version.

Although you haven't changed anything your Archive command does, its screen responses are quite different now. Test the new version by archiving P.OLD (which isn't on the archive floppy disk):

```
C>archive p.old
```

Because ARCHIVE.BAT now starts by clearing the screen, everything you see from this point on is displayed by your Archive command. When the command prompts you to check the floppy disk in drive A, press any key. The screen now looks like this:

```
                ***ARCHIVE PROCEDURE***

Make sure archive floppy disk is in drive A
Press any key to continue . . .

            1 file(s) copied

p.old archived
```

Test ARCHIVE.BAT again to see how it responds when the file already exists on the archive floppy disk. P.DOC and P.OLD are no longer on the disk in drive C (you archived them after making the change that erases the file), so archive P.BAK. Type the following, pressing any key to continue the command after each pause:

```
C>archive p.bak
```

The screen looks like this:

```
                    ***ARCHIVE PROCEDURE***

Make sure archive floppy disk is in drive A
Press any key to continue . . .

a:p.bak exists. Press CTRL-BREAK to cancel, or
Press any key to continue . . .

        1 file(s) copied

p.bak archived
```

ARCHIVE.BAT is quite a bit longer than when you began, but your Archive command doesn't look much like a homemade command any more. Although you needn't always go to such lengths when you create a command, it's nice to know that a little extra effort can make your work look professional. If others will use the batch files you create, the investment of your effort can quickly pay off in shorter training time, more efficient use of the system, and fewer mistakes.

## CHAPTER SUMMARY

This chapter covered a lot of ground. Experimenting is the best way to put what you learned here into practice. Just be certain to use floppy disks that don't contain files you need until you're sure your batch commands are working properly.

The next chapter describes two additional batch commands that let you create even more flexible batch files, and it shows you several useful batch files you can use to start your personal collection. You need the archive floppy disk in drive A. Remove this floppy disk, and label it ARCHIVED FILES.

# 16

# Creating More Smart Commands

he previous chapter showed you how to use the advanced capability of batch files. Knowing how to create batch files is only half the job, however; the other half is finding uses for them. This chapter shows you how to create some commands to search through the phone-list file you created in Chapter 13, "Taking Control of Your System"; it also describes four advanced batch commands and shows several useful batch files to give you some ideas for your own use.

## PREPARING FOR THE EXAMPLES

For the first examples in this chapter, you need the phone-list file (PH.TXT) that you created in Chapter 13. If you haven't gone through the examples in Chapters 13, 14, and 15, you should do so before proceeding. PH.TXT should already be in the directory named \RUNDOS. Change the current directory to \RUNDOS by typing:

```
C>cd \rundos
```

If your prompt doesn't appear as C>, you can change it to match the following examples by typing *prompt*. This completes the preparation for the examples.

## COMMANDS FOR SEARCHING THROUGH A FILE

In Chapter 13, you created a file of names, addresses, and telephone numbers, and you used the Find and Sort commands to display entries. You can also put the Find and Sort commands in batch files to create your own search commands and achieve some of the capabilities of a simple record-management program.

For example, the simplest search uses the Find command to display all records that contain a particular string. Create a batch file named SHOW.BAT by typing the following:

```
C>copy con show.bat
@echo off
find "%1" ph.txt
^Z
         1 file(s) copied
```

This batch file gives you a Show command that displays all records from PH.TXT that contain the string you specify as the parameter to your Show command. To search the phone list, type *show* followed by the string. For example, to display the entries for all consultants (entries that contain the string *cons*), type:

```
C>show cons
```

MS-DOS displays all entries for consultants:

```
---------- PH.TXT
Jones     Michele    (747) 429-6360  cons chemist
Black     John       (747) 426-3385  cons mech eng pkg
Jones     Alison     (747) 429-5584  cons Chem engineer
```

**NOTE:** *As it stands, your Show command requires that you specify the string in the same combination of uppercase and lowercase letters that appears in the file. If you have version 5 or later of MS-DOS, remember that you can include the /I parameter to tell the Find command to ignore differences in case. For example, if you entered the Find command as* find /i "%1" ph.txt, *you could type the Show command in the preceding example as* show cons, show Cons, *or* show CONS *and still be assured of finding the entries you wanted. For simplicity, the following examples omit the /I parameter of the Find command. If you want, however, you can include it to make your batch files even more flexible.*

As you've seen, typing *show cons* is easier than typing *find "cons" ph.txt*. Read on, and you'll find that you can use similar batch files to conduct even more powerful searches just as easily.

## Compound Searches

As the examples in Chapter 13, "Taking Control of Your System," showed, you can also combine Find commands to search for records that contain various combinations of character strings—for example, all consultants named Jones or all entries that are outside the 747 area code. Putting these Find commands in a batch file saves even more typing than the Show command you just created.

For example, suppose you want to create a command to show all entries that contain both one string and another. This requires two Find commands, with the output of the first piped to the second. You could call such a command Showand. Create a file named SHOWAND.BAT by typing:

```
C>copy con showand.bat
@echo off
find "%1" ph.txt | find "%2"
^Z
        1 file(s) copied
```

This batch command takes two parameters—the two strings the Find command searches for. Now you can search the phone list for entries that contain two strings as easily as you can search it for entries containing one string; just type *showand* followed by the two strings. For example, to display all consultants named Jones, type:

```
C>showand cons Jones
```

MS-DOS displays the records that contain both strings:

```
Jones      Michele    (747) 429-6360   cons chemist
Jones      Alison     (747) 429-5584   cons Chem engineer
```

This is definitely easier than typing *find "cons" ph.txt ¦ find "Jones"*.

What if you want to create a command that shows all entries except those that contain a particular string? Use a Find command with the /V parameter. You could call this command Showxcpt; create SHOWXCPT.BAT by typing the following:

```
C>copy con showxcpt.bat
@echo off
find /v "%1" ph.txt
^Z
        1 file(s) copied
```

This batch command requires one parameter, the string you don't want to see. For example, to display all entries not in the 747 area code, type the following:

```
C>showxcpt (7
```

MS-DOS displays all lines from PH.TXT that don't contain *(7*.

```
---------- PH.TXT
Green      Fred       (541) 926-4921   cust math teach
Smith      Ed         (541) 835-8747   vend caterer
```

These three batch files—SHOW, SHOWAND, and SHOWXCPT—let you search a file quickly in several ways. You can combine all three searches into a single command just by changing SHOW.BAT.

## Chaining Batch Files to Create Powerful Commands

As your skill in creating batch files grows, you'll sometimes find that you want to use one batch file to carry out the commands in another batch file. One way to do this is to *chain* the batch files. Another, described later in this chapter, is to use the Call command.

When you chain batch files, you use the name of one batch file as a command in another. MS-DOS then carries out the commands in the second batch file as if you had typed its name; if the second batch file contains the name of a third batch file, MS-DOS carries out its commands, and so on. When the commands in the last chained batch file have been carried out, MS-DOS returns to the system prompt.

To see how this works, modify SHOW.BAT to cover all three types of searches you just performed by chaining it to either SHOWAND.BAT or SHOWXCPT.BAT. When you do this, the parameters you type with the revised Show command must specify the type of search as well as the string or strings to search for.

You're creating your own Show command with the following parameters:

**show xcpt and <string1> <string2>**

*xcpt* searches for entries that don't contain the specified string.

*and* searches for entries that contain two specified strings.

<string1> and <string2> are the strings to search for. If you include *and*, you must include both <string1> and <string2>; otherwise just include <string1>.

If you don't specify either *xcpt* or *and*, your Show command searches for all entries that contain <string1>.

This more powerful version of SHOW.BAT is still fairly short; type the following:

```
C>copy con show.bat
@echo off
if %1==xcpt showxcpt %2
if %1==and showand %2 %3
find "%1" ph.txt
^Z
        1 file(s) copied
```

The first If command checks whether the first parameter (%1) typed with the Show command is *xcpt* (recall that the == compares two strings to see if they are identical). If %1 is the same as *xcpt*, SHOWXCPT.BAT is carried out. The second parameter (%2) you type with the Show command is the string to search for; it is the single parameter that SHOWXCPT.BAT requires.

The second If command checks whether the first parameter typed with the Show command is *and*. If it is, SHOWAND.BAT is carried out. The second and third parameters (%2 and %3) typed with the Show command are the two strings to search for; they are the two parameters that SHOWAND.BAT requires.

If the first parameter (%1) typed with the Show command is neither *xcpt* nor *and*, the Find command is carried out to perform a simple search.

Except for the Echo command, only one of the commands in SHOW.BAT is carried out in any particular search. Figure 16-1 shows the contents of SHOW.BAT and an example of each type of search you can make. For each example, the figure lists the Show command as you would type it and substitutes values for the replaceable parameters in SHOW.BAT. The command in SHOW.BAT that is carried

357

out is not shaded. An arrow to the right represents chaining to SHOWXCPT or
SHOWAND; the contents of each chained batch file, with values substituted for its
replaceable parameters, are shown below the chained batch file.

```
C>type show.bat
@echo off
if %1==xcpt showxcpt %2
if %1==and showand %2 %3
find "%1" ph.txt

C>show cust

@echo off
if cust==xcpt showxcpt
if cust==and showand
find "cust" ph.txt
C>show xcpt cust

@echo off
if xcpt==xcpt showxcpt cust  - - - > showxcpt cust
if xcpt==and showand cust
find "xcpt" ph.txt                        @echo off
                                          find /v "cust" ph.txt
C>show and cust Jones

@echo off
if and==xcpt showxcpt cust
if and==and showand cust Jones  - -> showand cust Jones
find "and" ph.txt
                                          @echo off
                                          find "cust" ph.txt!find "Jones"
```

**Figure 16-1.**
*Chaining batch files.*

Now you can perform any of the three types of searches with the Show command. The simple search works as it did in the earlier Show command. For example, to display all entries that contain *Jones*, type:

```
C>show Jones

---------- PH.TXT
Jones     Michele   (747) 429-6360  cons chemist
Jones     Alison    (747) 429-5584  cons Chem engineer
Jones     James     (747) 636-3541  cust architect
```

To display all entries that don't contain a particular string, type *xcpt* as the first parameter. For example, to display all entries outside the 747 area code, type:

```
C>show xcpt (7

---------- PH.TXT
Green     Fred      (541) 926-4921   cust math teach
Smith     Ed        (541) 835-8747   vend caterer
```

Or, to search for two strings, type *and* as the first parameter. For example, to see all engineers named Jones, type:

```
C>show and Jones eng
Jones     Alison    (747) 429-5584   cons Chem engineer
```

If you put your telephone numbers and business cards in a text file like this, these three batch files put the contents of the file at your fingertips. Not only can you search for an entry quickly, you can easily display groups of related entries.

This application, like Edit, is another example of how MS-DOS can make your computer more useful without additional software.

## SOME USEFUL BATCH FILES

To give you some ideas about the sort of batch commands that might help you from day to day, several useful batch files are shown here. These are not step-by-step examples; each description gives the purpose of the batch file, shows its contents, explains how it works, and describes how you would use it.

An effective way to become familiar with batch commands is to experiment. You could enter the following batch files, for example, then experiment with them, making changes and seeing the effects of the changes. If your batch files include commands that can modify or delete files, be sure to test the batch files on disks that contain files you don't need.

You can create the batch files by copying from the console to a file or by using a text editor. Most of the batch files include one or more Echo commands to add a blank line to the display (for readability); they are shown as *echo* followed by a period (*echo.*). If you don't have version 3.1 or later, echo a blank line by typing *echo*, holding down the Alt key, and typing *255* using the numeric keypad.

## Viewing a Long Directory Listing

Even though you back up old files and clear out unneeded ones regularly, a directory can soon contain more files than MS-DOS can list on one screen. And some often-used directories—word processing directories, for example, or collections of spreadsheets and charts—can become quite large.

If you have version 4 or later of MS-DOS and an EGA or VGA display, you can use the LONGDIR.BAT file described here to change the display to 43 lines per screen, display a long directory one screenful at a time, and then change the display back to 25 lines.

LONGDIR.BAT contains:

```
@echo off
cls
mode con lines=43
dir %1 /p
pause
mode con lines=25
```

The first Mode command switches the display to 43 lines. The Directory command then finds the listings for the directory (%1) you specify as a parameter with the Longdir command, displays the entries 43 lines at a time, and waits for you to press a key. The Pause command displays *Press any key to continue* when the directory listing is complete, and the second Mode command returns the screen display to 25 lines.

To use the command, you type *longdir* followed by the directory listing you want to see. You can include a drive letter, followed by a colon, a path name, and a file name including wildcard characters. For example, you can type the command as *longdir a:*, *longdir \clients\wp* or *longdir \clients\wp\*.doc*. If you don't include a drive, path, or file name (type just *longdir*), the command displays the current directory.

(Depending on how your system is set up, LONGDIR.BAT might list the directory you specify but refuse to change to 43 lines per screen after telling you that *ANSI.SYS must be installed to perform requested function*. If this happens, you need to identify a file named ANSI.SYS to MS-DOS. Chapter 17, "Tailoring Your System," tells you how to do this.)

## Cleaning Up Disk Storage

Because many word processors and other application programs create a backup file with the extension BAK each time you change a file, your disks can get crowded with backup files you don't need. The CLEANUP.BAT batch file described here replaces one you created earlier; it displays the directory entries of all files with an extension of BAK and then pauses. At that point, you can cancel the command by pressing Ctrl-Break; if you press any key to proceed, the command erases the files.

CLEANUP.BAT contains:

```
@echo off
cls
echo *** Will erase the following files: ***
dir %1*.bak
echo.
echo Press CTRL-BREAK to cancel, or
pause
del %1*.bak
```

Notice that there is no blank between *%1* and *\*.bak* in the Directory and Delete commands; this lets you specify a drive letter or a path name as a parameter with the file name, but be sure to end a path name with a backslash (\).

To erase all BAK files from the current directory on the disk in the current drive, type *cleanup* and press any key when the Pause command prompts you.

To erase all BAK files from another directory, type the path name followed by \ as a parameter; you can also precede the path name with a drive letter and colon (for example, *cleanup a:\* or *cleanup \mkt\wp\*).

## Directory of Subdirectories

If a directory contains many subdirectories and files, sometimes you'd like to see just the subdirectories. The DIRSUB batch file described here lets you do just that; it uses different techniques depending on the version of MS-DOS you're using.

If you're using version 5 or later, DIRSUB.BAT contains:

```
@echo off
echo *** Subdirectories in %1 ***
echo.
dir %1 /ad
```

The /AD (Attribute Directory) parameter tells MS-DOS to display just the subdirectories.

You can type one parameter (%1) with the Dirsub command to specify the directory whose entries are to be displayed. The parameter can include a drive letter and colon, a path name, or both. If you don't include a parameter, this Dirsub command displays the subdirectories in the current directory (but doesn't display the directory name because you didn't type any characters to replace %1 in the message line).

If you're using an earlier version of MS-DOS, you can take advantage of the fact that the Directory command displays *<DIR>* to identify a subdirectory. This version of DIRSUB.BAT contains:

```
@echo off
echo *** Subdirectories in %1 ***
echo.
dir %1 | find "<"
```

In this file, the output of the Directory command is piped to a Find command that displays all directory lines that contain a less-than sign (<).

With either version of DIRSUB.BAT, to see the subdirectories in the current directory you would type *dirsub*. To see those in the current directory of drive A, you would type *dirsub a:*, and to see the subdirectories in \MKT\WP, you would type *dirsub \mkt\wp*.

The special entries . and .., which the Directory command identifies as subdirectories, are in all directories except the root. You can modify DIRSUB.BAT so that it doesn't display these entries by piping the output of the Directory command to a Find command that uses the /V parameter to eliminate all lines that contain a period. For version 5 or later, the command would be:

```
dir %1 /ad | find /v "."
```

For an earlier version of MS-DOS, the command would be:

```
dir %1 | find "<" | find /v "."
```

The added Find command uses the /V parameter to eliminate all lines that contain a period. You would use this version of the Dirsub command just as you would use the earlier version.

If you created DIRSUB.BAT, it's a snap to reverse the action so that it displays only files instead of subdirectories. The DIRFIL batch file requires only a simple change to the last line of DIRSUB.BAT.

If you're using version 5 or later, simply put a hyphen before the D in the /AD parameter to reverse its meaning:

```
dir %1 /a-d
```

If you're using an earlier version, add the /V parameter to the Find command to reverse its meaning:

```
dir %1 | find /v "<"
```

You would use this command just as you used Dirsub.

## Moving Files from One Directory to Another

In a tree-structured file system, you'll sometimes want to move files from one directory to another. Versions 6 and 6.2 of MS-DOS include the Move command, which makes it simple to move files. If you have an earlier version, you can move files only by copying the file to the new directory with the Copy command and then erasing the original with the Delete command. MOVE.BAT combines these in one command.

MOVE.BAT contains:

```
@echo off
copy %1 %2
cls
echo Files in target directory:
echo.
dir %2 /p
echo.
echo If files to be moved are not in directory,
echo press CTRL-BREAK to cancel. Otherwise
pause
del %1
```

Here is how the batch file works, line by line:

- In line 1, the Echo command turns echo off.

- In line 2, the Copy command copies the files to the target directory.

- In line 3, the Clear Screen command clears the screen.

- In lines 4 and 5, Echo commands display a message and a blank line.

- In line 6, the Directory command displays the contents of the target directory. The /P parameter is included to ensure time enough to view even a very long directory.

- In lines 7 through 9, Echo commands display a blank line and a warning message.

- In line 10, the Pause command makes the system pause to let you cancel the Delete command in line 11 if the files you moved are not displayed in the listing of the target directory.

You have created a command with two parameters:

**move <source> <target>**

<source> is the name of the file to be moved (copied and then deleted). You can include a drive letter and path name. If you use wildcard characters in the file name, MS-DOS displays the name of each file it copies.

<target> is the name of the directory to which the <source> files are to be copied. If you omit <target>, the files are copied to the current directory.

For example, assume that the current directory is \MKT\WP. To move the file REPORT.DOC to the directory \ENG\WP, you would type *move report.doc \eng\wp*. To move the file BUDGET.JAN from \ENG\WP to \MKT\WP, you type the command as *move \eng\wp\budget.jan*. To move all files from \MKT\WP to \WORD\MKT, you would type *move *.* \word\mkt*.

# FOUR ADVANCED BATCH COMMANDS

> **NOTE:** *The batch commands you have worked with up to this point are sufficient for you to create useful batch files like the search commands for the phone-list file. Rather than continue with the rest of this chapter right now, you might want to put the book aside for awhile and experiment, and then return to learn the last four batch commands this book discusses.*

The four remaining batch commands—Shift, For, Call, and Choice—give you even more control over how your batch files work. They're somewhat more complicated than the other batch commands, but the examples should make their use clear.

## Preparing for the Advanced Examples

The remaining examples in the chapter require the P.* and Q.* files that should still be in your RUNDOS directory from the exercises you did in Chapter 15, "Creating Smart Commands." You also need to put the floppy disk you labeled ARCHIVED FILES in drive A.

## The Shift Command: Shifting the List of Parameters

The Shift command moves the list of parameters you type with a batch command one position to the left. For example, suppose you type a Shift command with three parameters. After the Shift command is carried out once, what was %3 becomes %2 and what was %2 becomes %1; what was %1 is gone. After a second Shift command, what started out as %3 is %1; what started as %2 and %1 are both gone.

This command lets a short batch file handle any number of parameters; the following sample batch file illustrates the technique. ARCH1.BAT archives any number of files. Here are its contents:

```
@echo off
:start
if "%1"=="" goto done
echo *** Archiving %1 ***
if not exist a:%1 copy %1 a:
shift
goto start
:done
```

Here's a description of how it works:

- As usual, the first line is an Echo command to turn echo off.

- The label *:start* marks the beginning of the commands that will be repeated for each parameter.

- The If command checks to see whether a parameter was entered for %1. It does this by comparing "%1" with two quotation marks enclosing nothing at all (""). You're telling MS-DOS to compare the first parameter (if one was typed) with nothing, or no parameter. When the comparison is true, meaning that there are no more parameters, the Goto command sends MS-DOS to the label *:done* in line 8.

- The Echo command displays the name of the file that is being archived.

- The If command checks whether the file to be archived exists on drive A; if it doesn't, the Copy command copies the file from the current drive to drive A.

- The Shift command moves the list of parameters one position left.

- The Goto command sends MS-DOS back to the label *:start*.

- The label *:done* marks the end of the command file.

To use this batch file you type *arch1* followed by the names of the files to be archived. The command stops when "%1" equals ""—in other words, when there are no more file names to be substituted for %1.

To test the command, copy the file named P.OLD, which you archived in Chapter 15, "Creating Smart Commands," from the floppy disk in drive A to the current drive by typing:

```
C>copy a:p.old
```

Now archive P.OLD, Q.DOC, and Q.OLD by typing the command shown at the top of the next page.

```
C>arch1 p.old q.doc q.old
*** Archiving p.old ***
*** Archiving q.doc ***
        1 file(s) copied
*** Archiving q.old ***
        1 file(s) copied
```

The confirming messages show that MS-DOS did not copy the file that was already on the floppy disk in drive A (P.OLD) but that it did copy the files that weren't on the floppy disk (both Q.DOC and Q.OLD).

This short archive command doesn't display instructions or warnings like the batch file you created in Chapter 15, "Creating Smart Commands," but it does show how you can use the Shift command to write a batch file that handles any number of parameters. The technique is simple: Do something with %1, shift the parameters, then use a Goto command to send MS-DOS back to the beginning to do it all over again. Just make sure you define a way to stop the process, or MS-DOS will carry out the command forever.

## The For Command: Carrying Out a Command More than Once

Sometimes you might want MS-DOS to carry out a command more than once in a batch file—for instance, to carry out a command for each file that matches a file name with wildcard characters. The For command does just that. Like the If command, the For command has two parts: The first part defines how often a command is to be carried out, and the second part is the command to be carried out.

The For command is somewhat more complex than the other batch commands. If you don't fully understand the description of its parameters, read on and try the examples. As with many other aspects of using a computer, it's easier to use the For command than it is to read about it.

The For command has three parameters:

**for %%p in (<set>) do <command>**

The words *in* and *do* are required in the command; they are not parameters.

%%p is a replaceable parameter used inside the For command. MS-DOS assigns to it, in turn, each value included in (<set>).

(<set>) is the list of possible values that can be given to %%p. You separate the values with blanks, and you must enclose the entire list in parentheses—for example, *(1 2 3)*. You can also specify a set of values with a file name that includes wildcard characters—for example, *(a:*.doc)*.

<command> is any MS-DOS command other than another For command. You can use both batch-command parameters (such as %1) and the For command replaceable parameter (%%p) in <command>.

It's all less complicated than it sounds. When MS-DOS carries out a For command, it assigns to %%p, in turn, each value that you specify in (<set>), then it carries out <command>. Each time it carries out <command>, MS-DOS first substitutes for %%p the current value taken from (<set>).

A brief example shows how the For command works. The following batch command carries out an Echo command three times, displaying each of the three words enclosed in parentheses. Create FOR1.BAT by typing:

```
C>copy con for1.bat
for %%p in (able baker charlie) do echo %%p
^Z
        1 file(s) copied
```

In this For command, *(able baker charlie)* is (<set>) and *echo %%p* is <command>. The For command tells MS-DOS to carry out the Echo command once for each word in parentheses, substituting, in turn, *able*, *baker*, and *charlie* for %%p. Test it by typing:

```
C>for1
```

For a change, this batch file doesn't begin by turning echo off, so MS-DOS displays each command it carries out, starting with the For command:

```
C>for %p in (able baker charlie) do echo %p
```

MS-DOS then displays and carries out the Echo command once for each value in the set, each time substituting the next value from the set for the replaceable parameter in the Echo command:

```
C>echo able
able

C>echo baker
baker

C>echo charlie
charlie
```

Instead of specifying actual values in the set, you can use replaceable parameters, such as %1. This technique works as it does in any other batch command but can be confusing in this case because now you can have %1 and %%p in the same command. Here's how it works: %1 refers to the first parameter typed with the batch command, %2 refers to the second parameter typed with the batch command, and so forth; %%p refers to the value selected from the set enclosed in parentheses within the For command.

The next example shows you the difference. Here, the words to be displayed are typed as parameters of the batch command, instead of being included as part of the For command. Create FOR2.BAT by typing:

```
C>copy con for2.bat
for %%p in (%1 %2 %3) do echo %%p
^Z
         1 file(s) copied
```

This For command tells MS-DOS to carry out the Echo command (*echo %%p*) once for each value in parentheses, substituting for %%p the first, then the second, and finally the third parameter you type with the For2 command. Test it by typing:

```
C>for2 dog easy fox
```

MS-DOS displays each command it carries out. First it displays the For command:

```
C>for %p in (dog easy fox) do echo %p
```

Note that MS-DOS has substituted values for all replaceable parameters. The set in parentheses is now *(dog easy fox)* because those are the three parameters you typed; they have replaced *(%1 %2 %3)*. As you may have noticed in the preceding example, MS-DOS has also dropped one of the percent signs from %%p. MS-DOS removes the first percent sign when it substitutes the parameters you type with the command for %1, %2, and so forth. It does, however, leave one percent sign to show that a value must still be substituted for %p.

MS-DOS then displays and carries out three Echo commands, each time substituting one value from the set in parentheses for %p:

```
C>echo dog
dog

C>echo easy
easy

C>echo fox
fox
```

If you wish, you can specify the set in a For command with a file name and wildcard characters. MS-DOS then assigns to %%p, in turn, each file name that matches the wildcard characters. You can use this technique to create a simple Archive batch file using only a For command. The following command doesn't display instructions and warnings, but it does show you how much can be done with a single batch command.

Create a batch file named ARCH2.BAT by typing the following:

```
C>copy con arch2.bat
for %%p in (%1) do if not exist a:%%p copy %%p a:
^Z
        1 file(s) copied
```

Q.DOC and Q.OLD are on the floppy disk in drive A (you copied them in the example of the Shift command). Use them to test ARCH2.BAT by archiving all Q files:

```
C>arch2 q.*
```

MS-DOS displays each command it carries out, starting with the For command (remember, you have not turned echo off):

```
C>for %p in (q.*) do if not exist a:%p copy %p a:
```

MS-DOS then displays and carries out three If commands, each time substituting a file name that matches the set enclosed in parentheses for the replaceable parameter in the If command:

```
C>if not exist a:Q.DOC copy Q.DOC a:
```

```
C>if not exist a:Q.BAK copy Q.BAK a:
        1 file(s) copied
```

```
C>if not exist a:Q.OLD copy Q.OLD a:
```

The messages displayed by the Copy command confirm that MS-DOS did not copy either Q.DOC or Q.OLD because they were already on the archive floppy disk, but did copy Q.BAK, which hadn't been archived.

The For command gives you a quick way to carry out an MS-DOS command several times. As shown in some of the sample batch files that conclude this chapter, the For command makes it possible to create powerful batch commands.

## The Call Command: Using a Batch Command in a Batch File

Earlier in this chapter, in the final version of SHOW.BAT, you used batch commands (Showand and Showxcpt) in a batch file. MS-DOS didn't return to SHOW.BAT after carrying out these batch commands even though neither command was actually the last command in SHOW.BAT; the last command was Find. You can use this capability, called *chaining*, with any version of MS-DOS. Once you chain to another batch command, you can't go back to the first.

If you're using version 3.3 or later, however, you can also use the Call command in a batch file to tell MS-DOS to carry out the commands in another batch file. Unlike chaining, the Call command causes MS-DOS to come back and continue with the next command in the original batch file. This lets you use a batch command of your own making in a batch file, just as you would use an MS-DOS command.

The Call command has two parameters:

**call <batchfile> <parameters>**

<batchfile> is the name of a batch command that you want MS-DOS to carry out from within the calling batch file.

<parameters> represents any parameters that <batchfile> requires.

Two short batch files demonstrate the usefulness of the Call command. First, create a batch file named ECHOIT.BAT by typing the following:

```
C>copy con echoit.bat
@echo off
echo %1
^Z
        1 file(s) copied
```

ECHOIT.BAT simply echoes the parameter you enter with it. For example, to echo *fred*, type the following:

```
C>echoit fred
fred
C>_
```

Now create another batch file named ECHOALL.BAT that uses a For command to carry out ECHOIT.BAT for each of up to three parameters, pauses until you press a key, and displays an ending message:

```
C>copy con echoall.bat
@echo off
for %%p in (%1 %2 %3) do call echoit %%p
pause
echo End of ECHOALL.BAT
^Z
        1 file(s) copied
```

The For command carries out the Call command for each of up to three parameters that can be entered with the Echoall batch command. The Call command carries out the batch command ECHOIT.BAT, specifying, in turn, each parameter entered with the Echoall batch command.

Now type the following to echo the words *xray*, *yankee*, and *zulu*:

```
C>echoall xray yankee zulu
xray
yankee
zulu
Press any key to continue . . .
```

Press a key, and MS-DOS displays the final message in ECHOALL.BAT:

```
End of ECHOALL.BAT
```

If you hadn't included the Call command, MS-DOS would have carried out ECHOIT.BAT once to display the first parameter (*xray*) and then would have returned to the system prompt. Because you did use the Call command, MS-DOS carried out ECHOIT.BAT three times, once for each parameter, and then returned to the final lines of ECHOALL.BAT before displaying the system prompt.

## The Choice Command: Writing an Interactive Batch Command

Most of the programs you use are interactive. They occasionally ask you for some information (such as the name of a file or whether you want to exit the program), wait for you to respond, then take some action based on your answer. Starting with version 6 of MS-DOS, you can give your batch commands the same capability with the Choice command.

The Choice command lets you list the one-character responses that are acceptable and, if you like, the text of a message to be displayed. When it's carried out, the Choice command displays the message (if you specify one) and a prompt that lists the characters that can be chosen, then waits for a keyboard response.

So that you can determine which response was entered, Choice sets a value called *errorlevel* to 1 if the first response you listed was chosen, 2 if the second response was chosen, and so forth. You use the *errorlevel* option of the If command to check what the response was and take the appropriate action in the batch file.

The Choice command has three commonly used parameters. (See Appendix C, "MS-DOS Command Reference," for an explanation of all the parameters.)

**choice /C:<keys> /N <text>**

/C:<keys> specifies which characters (letters, numbers, or punctuation marks) are permitted as responses. Don't separate the characters with spaces or commas.

/N tells Choice not to display the prompt.

<text> specifies a message to be displayed before the prompt.

You can use the Choice command to make a simple menu system. Suppose that you use Procomm Plus, Microsoft Money, and Microsoft Works and want to display a menu that lets you start any of these three programs just by pressing a letter. The single batch file MENU.BAT would let you do just that:

```
@echo off
cls
echo CHOOSE A PROGRAM
echo.
echo Procomm Plus
echo Money
echo Works
echo.

choice /c:pmwq /n Press P, M, W, or Q to quit:

if errorlevel 4 goto end
if errorlevel 3 goto works
if errorlevel 2 goto money
if errorlevel 1 goto pcplus

:works
\msworks\msworks
menu

:money
\msmoney\msmoney
menu

:pcplus
\pcplus\pcplus
menu

:end
```

The first section of the batch file clears the screen and displays the menu of your three programs. The Choice command then waits for a reply and sets *errorlevel* to the proper value. Here's a closer look at the three parameters of this Choice command:

- */c:pmwq* specifies the four permitted responses: P (for Procomm Plus), M (for Money), W (for Works), and Q (for Quit).

- */n* tells the Choice command not to display the prompt (which, in this case, would be *[P,M,W,Q]?*).

- *Press P, M, W, or Q to quit* is the message that the Choice command displays before waiting for a reply.

Next the batch file checks the value of *errorlevel* set by the Choice command and runs the appropriate program. Because the If command actually checks whether *errorlevel* is equal to or greater than the specified value, you check for the largest possible value first, then the next largest, and so forth. The first reply listed in the Choice command's /C parameter is P, so Choice assigns *errorlevel* the value of 1 if P is pressed; the fourth reply listed is Q, so Choice assigns *errorlevel* the value of 4 if Q is pressed.

After you're done running the program you chose, the batch file runs Menu, a batch command that carries out this batch file. How can a batch file carry out itself? When MS-DOS finds a batch command in a batch file, it stops carrying out the current batch file and starts the one named. In this case, MS-DOS stops MENU.BAT and starts it again at the beginning; it doesn't matter that the same batch file is being started again. Because this batch command appears before the end of the batch file, it causes the menu to be displayed again after you exit one of the program choices. The only way to leave the menu is to press Q (or Ctrl-Break, which stops any batch file).

When you type *menu*, MS-DOS clears the screen and displays your menu:

```
CHOOSE A PROGRAM

Procomm Plus
Money
Works

Press P, M, W, or Q to quit:_
```

If you press any key other than one of the four listed, MS-DOS beeps and waits for you to press another key. If you press W, MS-DOS carries out the command that starts Microsoft Works because the Choice command set *errorlevel* to 3. When you exit Microsoft Works, MS-DOS displays your menu again. To leave the menu, press the Q key.

You can adapt this batch file to your own programs by replacing the program names in the first part of the file (using more lines if necessary) and changing the commands that start the programs (again, add more commands if you add items to the menu).

## SOME MORE USEFUL BATCH FILES

The following batch files use the advanced batch commands. Again, they aren't step-by-step examples; they're working samples to give you an idea of what can be done with the full set of batch commands. You can enter the batch files by copying from the console or by using a text editor.

### Displaying a Series of Small Text Files

If you work with many small text files, such as batch files or boilerplate paragraphs for word processor documents, it's handy to be able to review several files with one command, rather than having to print or display them one at a time. The batch file shown here, REVIEW.BAT, uses the Shift, Type, and Pause commands to display any number of files one at a time. Remember, *echo.* (or *echo* Alt-255) echoes a blank line. REVIEW.BAT contains:

```
@echo off
:start
if "%1"=="" goto done
cls
echo<space><tab><tab>*** FILENAME: %1 ***
echo.
type %1
echo.
echo.
pause
shift
goto start
:done
```

This batch file uses the same technique as the earlier examples of the Shift command. The first Echo command displays the file name (moved toward the center of the screen with two tabs) so that you'll know what file is displayed. The last two Echo commands display two blank lines to separate the file from the Pause command message.

With this Review command, you type the names of the files as parameters. To display the P.* files, for example, you type *review p.doc p.old p.bak*. MS-DOS clears the screen and displays the first file, then displays the Pause command message and waits for you to press any key before clearing the screen and displaying the next file. When the If command finds a null parameter (""), MS-DOS returns to command level.

374

## Searching Files for a String of Characters

Have you ever searched through your paper files to find a specific letter or reference? To help you find all lines that contain a particular string, SCAN.BAT lets you specify a file to be searched and a string to search for. It displays each line in the file that contains the string. You can also use wildcard characters to search a set of files. Here are the contents of SCAN.BAT:

```
@echo off
cls
echo<space><tab><tab>***LINES IN %1 THAT CONTAIN %2***
echo.
for %%p in (%1) do find "%2" %%p
```

All the work here is done in the last line of the batch file. The earlier lines clear the screen and display a title. The For command actually carries out the Find command for each file name that matches the first parameter you type with the Scan command; the Find command is the one that searches for the string that you type as the second parameter.

As mentioned earlier in the chapter, remember that if you have version 5 or later of MS-DOS, you can use the /I parameter to tell the Find command to ignore differences between uppercase and lowercase characters (*for % %p in (%1) do find /i "%2" % %p*).

To display each line that contained the word *sales* in all files with an extension of DOC, you would type *scan *.doc sales*. MS-DOS would clear the screen and display each line that contained the word *sales*.

## Displaying a Sorted Directory

Beginning with version 5, you can use the /O parameter of the Directory command to sort a directory by name, extension, size, or date and time. If you don't have version 5, however, you can sort a directory by name, extension, or size by creating the four small batch files described here.

Because the items in a directory entry always begin in the same column, you can sort the directory entries by extension or size by using the column parameter (/+<number>) of the Sort command. (Sorting by name doesn't require the column parameter because the file name starts in column 1.) These are the columns where the information begins:

- Name—column 1 (doesn't need to be specified).

- Extension—column 10.

- Size—column 16.

Although directory entries include the date and time, sorting them by date (column 24) or time (column 34) doesn't work properly. Sorting by date, for example, would cause January of one year to appear in the list before December of the preceding year (that is, 1-1-94 would *precede* 12-31-93). If you sorted by time, a file created at 9 in the morning on October 16, 1993, would appear in the list *before* a file created at 11 in the morning a month earlier. Then, too, if you're using version 4 of MS-DOS, which displays time based on a 12-hour clock rather than a 24-hour clock, a file created at 5 in the evening would be listed before a file created at 9 that morning.

Sorting by date or time, therefore, is not particularly useful. On the other hand, the benefits of sorting a directory alphabetically by file name or by extension are obvious. Furthermore, if you need to delete some files to make space on a disk, or if you're just interested in the relative sizes of files, sorting by size is useful.

To create a command that displays a directory sorted by name, extension, or size, you create three batch files that sort and display the directory, and you create a fourth batch file that chains to the correct one of the other three.

First, copy from the console, as you have done before, to create the following one-line batch files; their names tell how they sort the directory:

DIRNAME.BAT:

```
dir %1 | sort | find "-" | more
```

DIREXT.BAT:

```
dir %1 | sort /+10 | find "-" | more
```

DIRSIZE.BAT:

```
dir %1 | sort /+16 | find "-" | more
```

Each of these batch files sorts and displays the contents of the directory specified in the parameter %1 and pipes the output of the Sort command to a Find command that selects only the lines that contain a hyphen, limiting the output to just those lines that contain an entry. (The hyphens separate the parts of the date.) The output of the Find command is then piped to the More command to handle directories more than one screen long. If no parameter is specified, the batch command sorts and displays the current directory. The only difference among the batch files is the column in which sorting begins.

You now need the batch file that chains to the correct one of the previous three. Name the file DIRSORT.BAT; it contains:

```
@echo off
for %%p in (name ext size) do if "%1"=="%%p" dir%%p %2
echo First parameter must be name, ext, or size
```

Be sure *not* to put a blank between dir and %%p in the second line, or the result won't be a valid file name for any of the chained batch files. The quotation marks around %1 and %%p prevent MS-DOS from displaying an error message if no parameter is typed with the command.

In the DIRSORT batch file, the For command sets %%p, in turn, to each of the words in the set in parentheses, then carries out the If command, which compares %%p to the first parameter typed with the Dirsort command. If there is a match, the If command adds the value of %%p to *dir* to produce the name of one of the three sort batch files and chains to that file (for example, *dir + name* would become *dirname*). The second parameter (%2), if any, typed with the Dirsort command is the %1 parameter (the directory name) needed by the chained batch file.

If the first parameter you type with the Dirsort command isn't one of the three words in the set in parentheses, the condition in the If command is not true. Then the Echo command in the next line is carried out, displaying a message that lists the correct parameters, and the Dirsort batch command ends without chaining to one of the files that display a sorted directory.

To display a sorted directory, you would type the Dirsort command with one or two parameters: The first, which is required, would specify how to sort and would have to be *name*, *ext*, or *size*; the second parameter, which is optional, would be the drive letter, path name, or name of the directory to be displayed. If you didn't include the second parameter, the command would display the current directory of the disk in the current drive.

For example, to display the current directory of the disk in the current drive, sorted by size, you would type *dirsort size*. To display the root directory, sorted by name, of the disk in drive A, you would type *dirsort name a:\*.

## CHAPTER SUMMARY

These batch files should give you a good start on a collection of special-purpose commands, and they might give you some ideas for creating more of your own. This is where the flexibility of MS-DOS really becomes apparent: The wide range of MS-DOS commands and capabilities is only the starting point for putting MS-DOS to work. With redirection, filter commands, batch files, and macros, you can combine all the other MS-DOS commands into a set of custom-tailored commands to make your personal computer truly personal.

# 17

# Tailoring Your System

**I**f you have followed the examples in the book, you have used all the major features of MS-DOS. Although it might sometimes seem that MS-DOS offers more options than you need, those options give you flexibility in tailoring MS-DOS; they let you adapt the computer to yourself rather than adapt yourself to the computer.

This chapter shows several ways you can tailor MS-DOS to your needs or preferences. Not only does this tailoring make MS-DOS fit your work needs better, but some of the techniques described here can also make your system immediately useful without your having to buy an application program. Some of these techniques can also make the system more accessible to people who may need to use the computer but who don't have your experience with MS-DOS. And tailoring can also make it easier to achieve consistency in procedures such as backing up a hard disk when several people use the computer.

This chapter describes:

- How to define configuration commands, which you put in the file named CONFIG.SYS to tell MS-DOS how to use the hardware devices that make up your system.

- How to use the MemMaker program, which helps you maximize the amount of available conventional memory.

- How to run MS-DOS, device drivers, and other programs in upper memory, leaving conventional memory for application programs.

- How to manage your portable computer with two programs: Power, which can conserve battery life, and Interlink, which transfers files quickly over a serial cable between two computers.

- How to start your system *without* carrying out the commands in CONFIG.SYS or AUTOEXEC.BAT.

- How to step through the commands in CONFIG.SYS and AUTOEXEC.BAT one at a time, choosing whether or not to carry out each one.

- How to set up multiple configurations and choose the one you want when you start or restart the system.

- Some less frequently used MS-DOS commands.

Examples are included, but they're not step-by-step exercises. This chapter gives you some ideas about how to tailor MS-DOS by applying what you have learned in previous chapters.

# DEFINING YOUR SYSTEM CONFIGURATION

Unlike the other MS-DOS commands, which tell MS-DOS what to do, the configuration commands tell MS-DOS *how* to do something, such as using a device or communicating with a disk drive. These commands help define the computer setup, or *configuration*, so that MS-DOS can work well with your equipment. You don't type the configuration commands at the keyboard as you do other MS-DOS commands. You put them in a special file called CONFIG.SYS, which must be in the root directory of your MS-DOS disk. MS-DOS carries out the commands in CONFIG.SYS only when you start or restart the system, so if you change a command in this file, you must restart MS-DOS for the command to take effect.

If you purchase an application program or an accessory device that requires certain commands in CONFIG.SYS, either the installation program adds or modifies the needed commands or the documentation provides step-by-step instructions. Most other times, however, the system configuration remains stable, so you don't change the configuration commands very often. But as you become more familiar with MS-DOS and your computer, you might want to experiment with commands in CONFIG.SYS as a means of speeding up or refining the way your system works.

In version 5 or later, MS-DOS itself either creates a basic CONFIG.SYS file (and an AUTOEXEC.BAT file) for you or it modifies the existing version of each file as part of its installation procedure. In version 4, MS-DOS creates CONFIG.SYS and AUTOEXEC.BAT if they don't already exist; if they do exist, MS-DOS creates versions named CONFIG.400 and AUTOEXEC.400, which you can later combine with your existing CONFIG.SYS and AUTOEXEC.BAT files. Earlier versions of MS-DOS do not automatically create either CONFIG.SYS or AUTOEXEC.BAT.

You create or edit CONFIG.SYS with a text editor just as you create or edit a batch file. The following topics describe some of the configuration commands you might use on your system.

## The Device Command and Device Drivers

The Device configuration command specifies a program (a special type of file whose extension is usually SYS) that tells MS-DOS how to use a particular device. Such a program is called a *device driver*. The form of the Device command is:

**device=<filename>**

<filename> is the name of the file that contains the device driver. You can include a path name if the file is not in the root directory. If you have a mouse, for example, and the program that tells MS-DOS how to use it is named MOUSE.SYS in the C:\MOUSE directory, the device command you put in your CONFIG.SYS file would be *device=c:\mouse\mouse.sys*.

Although the word *device* brings hardware to mind, a Device command needn't always refer to a piece of equipment you can touch or carry. In certain instances, a "device" is actually a program that simulates hardware. For example, MS-DOS includes a special program file that enables it to use a portion of memory on your system as if that memory were disk-based storage. The file, RAMDRIVE.SYS, enables MS-DOS to use memory as if it were an extremely fast disk drive instead. RAMDRIVE.SYS is described shortly. First, though, a little information about your computer's memory will help you understand how and when to use these device drivers.

## Types of Memory and How They Differ

Your computer uses memory for temporary storage of calculations, data, active programs, and other work in progress. Computer memory comes in three flavors: *conventional, extended,* and *expanded.*

### Conventional Memory

Conventional memory is the type sometimes referred to as RAM (for *random access memory*). Computers that run MS-DOS usually come with 1 MB of conventional memory. This memory can be used to hold MS-DOS, application programs, and data. All computer programs can use conventional memory, but IBM and compatible computers running MS-DOS are limited to a maximum of 1 MB (1024 KB) of this type of memory.

Even if your computer has 1 MB of conventional memory, however, not all of it is freely available for applications, data, or even MS-DOS. In actuality, MS-DOS normally uses only the first 640 KB of conventional memory for applications and data. The remaining 384 KB of conventional memory is known as the *upper memory area* or *reserved* memory and is set aside for special purposes such as hardware control and video memory. This reserved portion of memory is used by memory-management software in units called *upper memory blocks,* or UMBs. Beginning with version 5, MS-DOS can load device drivers and programs such as Doskey into unused UMBs, thus helping you conserve as much as possible of your computer's first 640 KB of memory for applications and data.

### Extended Memory

Extended memory is additional memory that begins at the 1 MB boundary where conventional memory ends, so it literally extends beyond the limits of conventional memory. You can add many megabytes' worth of extended memory to a computer, but that does not necessarily mean you can use it. Extended memory can be used for storage only by programs specifically designed to find and take advantage of it. If your programs cannot use extended memory, you might as well not have any. Extended memory is often managed by a program called an *extended memory manager,* which keeps two applications from trying to use the same portion of extended memory at the same time.

## Expanded Memory

If you think of extended memory as "high" memory that a program can reach with the right tools, you can think of expanded memory as a separate reservoir from which a program can draw through a pipeline. Expanded memory must be handled by a program called an *expanded memory manager.* An expanded memory manager should come with any expanded memory you install in your system.

Once your computer is set up with extended memory, expanded memory, or both, you really needn't worry about what type you have or how it's used. It's the job of the managing software to do all that for you. But you can use MS-DOS, especially version 5 or later, to take advantage of extended, expanded, and reserved memory to make your system run faster and more efficiently.

> **NOTE:** *If you don't have version 5 or later of MS-DOS, the following few topics don't apply to your system. Skip to the heading "Creating a Disk Cache with SMARTDRV.EXE" if you have the Microsoft release of version 4. Skip to the heading "Simulating a Disk Drive in Memory with RAMDRIVE.SYS" if you have version 3 or IBM's version 4 of MS-DOS.*

## Managing Memory

Your computer needs nothing more than MS-DOS to manage conventional memory, but when you add extended or expanded memory to a system, MS-DOS needs some extra help. In version 5, help appears in the form of two device drivers named HIMEM.SYS and EMM386.EXE.

HIMEM.SYS is an extended memory manager. If extended memory is installed in your system when MS-DOS version 5 is installed, MS-DOS finds the memory and adds to CONFIG.SYS an appropriate Device command that names this device driver. If you install extended memory after installing MS-DOS, you can add your own Device command to CONFIG.SYS. For example, if HIMEM.SYS is in the C:\DOS directory, the command would be:

```
device=c:\dos\himem.sys
```

Once you've identified HIMEM.SYS (or another extended memory manager) in CONFIG.SYS, you can turn some of the extended memory into a fast-access storage area, a simulated disk drive, or a home for MS-DOS itself.

On a computer with an 80386 or 80486 microprocessor, you can perform additional memory management with EMM386.EXE. This memory manager performs two tasks listed at the top of the next page.

- If your system has extended memory but your applications require expanded memory, EMM386.EXE can help MS-DOS treat a specified amount of that extended memory as if it were expanded memory.

- If your system has unused portions of the upper memory area available after all necessary amounts have been parceled out for hardware control, video, and other special purposes, EMM386.EXE can make those unused portions of memory available to MS-DOS for loading device drivers and programs.

EMM386.EXE includes a number of parameters, most of which are needed only by programmers. Three that you might use, however, are described here. Assuming that EMM386.EXE is in the C:\DOS directory, the Device command and the three parameters look like this:

**device=c:\dos\emm386.exe <memory> ram noems**

<memory> tells MS-DOS how much extended memory, in kilobytes, to treat as expanded memory. You can specify 16 to 32768. If you don't include <memory>, MS-DOS assumes all available memory, rounding down to the nearest multiple of 16 if necessary. When you use this parameter, MS-DOS sets aside the required amount of extended memory for use as expanded memory. It also sets up your system's upper memory area so that part can be used to make the expanded memory available to programs, and the remainder can, if requested, be used for loading device drivers and programs.

*ram* tells MS-DOS to provide access to both expanded memory and upper memory (UMBs).

*noems* tells MS-DOS to set aside all available upper memory for loading device drivers and programs. If you use this parameter, you cannot use any expanded memory.

Include either *ram* or *noems* in the Device command that names EMM386.EXE. For example, a basic Device command in CONFIG.SYS would be:

```
device=c:\dos\emm386.exe
```

To treat 640 KB of extended memory as expanded memory and make UMBs available, the command would be:

```
device=c:\dos\emm386.exe 640 ram
```

To set aside all available reserved memory for loading programs and device drivers, the command would be:

```
device=c:\dos\emm386.exe noems
```

Once you give MS-DOS access to upper memory, you can use this memory with either the Loadhigh command or the Devicehigh configuration command described in the section headed "Using the Upper Memory Area."

## Running MS-DOS in High Memory

Through version 4, MS-DOS loaded itself into conventional memory, reducing the amount of memory available for applications and data by the amount of space it needed. Beginning with version 5, MS-DOS includes a simple configuration command named Dos that can help you conserve conventional memory on a system with extended memory, upper memory, or both.

If your system has at least 64 KB of extended memory, you can use the Dos command to tell MS-DOS to position itself in a portion of extended memory called the *high memory area* (HMA). If your system has at least 350 KB of extended memory (typical of 80386 systems with 1 MB of RAM), you can use the Dos command to make part or all of the upper memory area available for use by device drivers and programs. By moving MS-DOS, device drivers, and utility programs such as Doskey and other memory-resident software out of conventional memory, you leave as much of that valuable storage space as possible for your applications and data to use.

The Dos configuration command is:

**dos=high/low,umb/noumb**

*high* tells MS-DOS to load itself into the high memory area if it can. *low* tells MS-DOS to load itself into conventional memory. If you don't specify *high*, or if MS-DOS can't load itself into high memory, MS-DOS automatically moves into conventional memory.

*umb* (short for upper memory blocks) tells MS-DOS to use the upper memory area for device drivers and programs. *noumb* tells MS-DOS not to use the upper memory area. If you don't specify *umb*, MS-DOS does not use the upper memory area.

You can put this command anywhere in CONFIG.SYS, and you can specify both parameters in one command by separating them with a comma. If you use the *high* parameter, however, also include a Device command that names HIMEM.SYS so that you can be sure MS-DOS can find and use extended memory. If you use the *umb* parameter, also include a Device command that names EMM386.EXE or another manager that makes the upper memory area available for use. The following two examples show different ways to use these commands in CONFIG.SYS.

To load MS-DOS into high memory on a system with at least 64 KB of extended memory, you would include these commands in CONFIG.SYS:

```
device=c:\dos\himem.sys
dos=high
```

To load MS-DOS into high memory and provide access to all of the available upper memory area on an 80386 or 80486 system with at least 350 KB of extended memory, you would include the following commands in CONFIG.SYS:

```
device=c:\dos\himem.sys
dos=high,umb
device=c:\dos\emm386.exe noems
```

**NOTE:** *The Device command naming HIMEM.SYS must precede the Dos command and the Device command naming EMM386.EXE.*

If you tell MS-DOS to load itself into extended memory, you can check its position with the Mem command. MS-DOS should respond *MS-DOS resident in High Memory Area.* If MS-DOS cannot find the High Memory Area and load itself in extended memory, you don't have to worry. It will load into conventional memory just as it always has.

## Letting MS-DOS Help You Manage Memory

To take full advantage of the MS-DOS memory-management features in version 5 and later, the proper configuration commands must be placed in CONFIG.SYS, specific device drivers should be loaded into high memory with the Doshigh command, and memory-resident programs should be loaded into high memory with Loadhigh commands in AUTOEXEC.BAT. You can add these commands yourself, or an experienced MS-DOS user can do it for you.

Starting with version 6, MS-DOS itself offers the same sort of help that the experienced user would. The MemMaker program analyzes your computer's memory and other programs that you use, and then adds the appropriate commands to CONFIG.SYS and AUTOEXEC.BAT to make best use of the memory installed in your system.

You should run MemMaker early in your quest to develop the perfect configuration. As you'll see later in this chapter, versions 6 and 6.2 of MS-DOS allow you to specify multiple configurations in your CONFIG.SYS file. MemMaker doesn't take the multiple configurations into account when it performs its memory optimization, so if you run it after breaking your CONFIG.SYS file into multiple configurations, your work might be lost.

To start MemMaker, just type *memmaker* at the system prompt. In a moment, MemMaker displays its opening screen, which describes the process it follows:

```
Microsoft MemMaker
_____

Welcome to MemMaker.

MemMaker optimizes your system's memory by moving memory-resident
programs and device drivers into the upper memory area. This
frees conventional memory for use by applications.

After you run MemMaker, your computer's memory will remain
optimized until you add or remove memory-resident programs or
device drivers. For an optimum memory configuration, run MemMaker
again after making any such changes.

MemMaker displays options as highlighted text. (For example, you
can change the "Continue" option below.) To cycle through the
available options, press SPACEBAR. When MemMaker displays the
option you want, press ENTER.

For help while you are running MemMaker, press F1.

            Continue or Exit? Continue

ENTER=Accept Selection  SPACEBAR=Change Selection  F1=Help  F3=Exit
```

After you press Enter to continue, MemMaker displays a screen that allows you to choose between letting MemMaker use its default settings (Express Setup) or specifying the settings yourself (Custom Setup). Press Enter to choose Express Setup. The default settings will do a good job of optimizing your memory.

There isn't much for you to do from here on. As the instructions say, you'll be given a few choices, but these are mostly limited to decisions such as choosing between continuing with MemMaker or returning to MS-DOS. In the course of deciding how best to manage your system's memory and putting the required commands in CONFIG.SYS and AUTOEXEC.BAT, MemMaker restarts your system twice.

After the second restart, MemMaker displays a summary of its actions, letting you know how much memory it freed for you. If your system wasn't set up for memory management before, you should see significantly more conventional memory available (it isn't unusual for 610 KB or even more to be free). You might be able to free a bit more conventional memory by fine-tuning the commands in CONFIG.SYS and AUTOEXEC.BAT, but, by and large, MemMaker should do the job well enough by itself.

## Creating a Disk Cache with SMARTDRV.EXE

If your computer has a hard disk, either extended or expanded memory, and version 6 or 6.2 of MS-DOS, you can load the device driver SMARTDRV.EXE in AUTOEXEC.BAT to turn part of this additional memory into a rapid-access storage area known as a *disk cache*. (If you have version 4 or 5, you use the Device command and the device driver SMARTDRV.SYS in CONFIG.SYS to do the same thing.) A disk cache speeds up your system because information that your computer reads from disk into memory remains in the cache. It's much faster for your computer to read information that's already in memory, so a disk cache can substantially reduce the amount of time your computer spends going out to disk, finding the information you need, and reading it into memory.

> **NOTE:** *If you're using the DoubleSpace program to compress your hard disk, don't use SmartDrive to create a disk cache on the compressed disk. It will actually slow down access to that disk. You should, however, use SmartDrive on your uncompressed hard disk drive.*

To create a disk cache with SMARTDRV.EXE, add a command in the following form to AUTOEXEC.BAT:

**smartdrv.exe <size> <minsize>**

SMARTDRV.EXE is the name of the file that contains the device-driver program. If the program is not in the root directory of the current disk, precede the name with a drive and path—for example, *c:\dos\smartdrv.exe*.

<size> is the size you want the cache to be, in kilobytes. It can be any value from 128 to 8192 (8 MB). If you don't specify <size>, SMARTDRV.EXE sets the cache size to 256 KB. When the cache is created, MS-DOS rounds <size> to the nearest multiple of 16. If there is too little memory to create the size cache you specify, SMARTDRV.EXE creates a smaller one, using the memory that is available.

<minsize> is the smallest size you want the cache to be, again in kilobytes. You don't have to specify <minsize>, but if you don't, and you use a program such as Microsoft Windows version 3 or later, the program might be able to reduce the size of your cache to suit its own purposes. In some cases, the program might reduce the cache size to 0.

In MS-DOS versions 6 and 6.2, the disk cache is always created in extended memory. In versions 4 and 5, you can specify the /A parameter to create the cache in expanded memory. Because the disk cache is created in extended or expanded memory, you must include a command in your CONFIG.SYS file that identifies your extended or expanded memory manager. If you have version 4 or 5 of MS-DOS, the Device command specifying SMARTDRV.SYS must appear after the memory manager command in CONFIG.SYS.

Also, when you specify the size, leave enough memory for other programs that also run in extended or expanded memory. If you're not certain how much of this memory you have (or have available), use the Mem command to ask MS-DOS to report on memory usage.

> **NOTE:** *SMARTDRV.EXE has other parameters that further specify how the disk cache is created and managed. See Appendix C, "MS-DOS Command Reference," for details.*

The following example creates a 1 MB (1024 KB) disk cache with a minimum size of 256 KB. The example assumes that SMARTDRV.EXE is in the C:\DOS directory:

```
c:\dos\smartdrv.exe 1024 256
```

## Simulating a Disk Drive in Memory with RAMDRIVE.SYS

Disk drives are mechanical and quite slow compared to the computer's memory. Starting with version 3.2, MS-DOS lets you set aside a portion of the computer's memory for use as a simulated disk, making it possible for disk operations to be performed at memory speeds.

This simulated disk is called a *RAM disk* or *RAM drive* because it exists in your computer's memory (RAM) rather than as a solid piece of hardware. It's also known as a *virtual disk* because having a RAM disk is virtually the same as having another disk drive. A RAM disk is particularly useful on a system with extended or expanded memory because MS-DOS can create the RAM disk in either of these types of memory, leaving the computer's conventional memory for other uses.

On the surface, a RAM disk might not seem much different from a disk cache, described in the preceding section. However, it is different. You can think of a disk cache—one created either by SMARTDRV.EXE or by a separate disk-caching program—as a warehousing area for information you've already used. In contrast, creating a RAM disk is like adding an extremely fast disk drive to your system.

A RAM disk behaves like any other disk: It has a drive letter and a directory, and you can specify it in any command that refers to a disk. It is much faster than a real disk drive, however, and the difference is especially noticeable when you use commands, such as Copy, that work with disk drives or when you use application programs that access the disk frequently, as many word processors and database programs do. To use a RAM disk, you copy the files you need from a physical disk to the RAM disk after MS-DOS has started, then copy them back to the disk after you have completed the work. Copying them back is particularly important because any changes you make to the files are recorded only in memory when you are using a RAM disk, and the contents of memory disappear whenever you turn off your computer.

MS-DOS assigns the next available drive letter to the RAM disk. On a system with one or two floppy disk drives and a hard disk, the next available letter is usually D. (If you're using the DoubleSpace disk compression program, the next available letter is usually I.)

Although a real disk drive has a fixed capacity, such as 360 KB or 1.44 MB, a RAM disk can have whatever capacity you want, within the limits described below for the command parameters. If your computer has enough memory, you can define more than one RAM disk by including more than one RAM-disk Device command in CONFIG.SYS.

If your computer is equipped with expanded or extended memory, you should tell MS-DOS to use this additional memory for your RAM disk, leaving your computer's conventional memory space for programs to use. If you have version 5 or later of MS-DOS and an 80386 or 80486 computer, you can also use the Devicehigh configuration command described later to load the program that creates the RAM disk into the upper memory area. (You can check on available upper memory blocks with the /C parameter of the Mem command.)

As efficient as it is, the remarkable increase in speed offered by RAM disks can have some drawbacks. If your computer doesn't have expanded or extended memory (or if you don't tell MS-DOS to use it), the memory used for a RAM disk reduces the amount of memory available to programs. Furthermore, the contents of a RAM disk are lost each time you turn the computer off.

If the RAM disk is large enough, you can speed operations by copying both programs and data files to it. Otherwise, make certain that your RAM disk leaves enough memory for the programs you use. In either case, be sure to copy the files you want to keep onto a real disk before you turn the computer off. You can automate this process by using a batch file to copy your working files to the RAM disk, to start the application program, and then to copy the revised working files back to the real disk after you leave the application program.

Depending on your version of MS-DOS, the file that creates a RAM disk is called either RAMDRIVE.SYS or VDISK.SYS. To avoid excessive detail, the following description applies to RAMDRIVE.SYS as it can be used with versions 6 and 6.2 of MS-DOS. Differences in earlier versions and in VDISK.SYS are not major, but they do exist. If you need exact values, refer to Appendix C, "MS-DOS Command Reference."

To define a RAM disk, the Device command is:

**device=ramdrive.sys \<size\> \<sector\> \<directory\> /E /A**

RAMDRIVE.SYS (or VDISK.SYS) is the name of the device-driver program. If it isn't in the root directory of the MS-DOS disk, you must include the drive letter and path name of its directory—for example, *c:\dos\ramdrive.sys*.

<size> is the size, in kilobytes, of the RAM disk. The minimum is 4 KB, and the maximum is 32,767 KB (4 MB). If you omit <size> or specify an incorrect value, RAMDRIVE.SYS sets <size> to 64.

<sector> is the size, in bytes, of each sector on the RAM disk. You can specify 128, 256, or 512. If you omit <sector> or specify an incorrect value, RAMDRIVE.SYS sets <sector> to 512.

<directory> is the number of directory entries allowed in the root directory of the RAM disk. You can specify any value from 2 to 1024. Each directory entry takes up 32 bytes of the RAM disk. If you omit <directory> or specify an incorrect value, RAMDRIVE.SYS sets <directory> to 64.

/E puts the RAM disk in extended memory. It is valid only if the computer contains extended memory. Using extended memory for a RAM disk leaves the maximum amount of conventional memory for programs. If you use /E, you cannot use /A.

/A puts the RAM disk in expanded memory. Like the /E option, it leaves the maximum amount of conventional memory available for programs. If you use /A, you cannot use /E.

If there isn't enough memory to create the RAM disk as you specify it, and you're creating the disk in conventional memory, RAMDRIVE.SYS doesn't create the disk. If you're creating the disk in extended or expanded memory, RAMDRIVE.SYS creates a disk using all available memory.

The following examples show the commands that would create RAM disks in conventional, extended, and expanded memory. All three examples assume that RAMDRIVE.SYS is in the C:\DOS directory.

To create a small (64 KB) RAM disk in conventional memory, accepting the values MS-DOS assumes for <sector> and <directory>, you would place either of the following commands in CONFIG.SYS:

```
device=c:\dos\ramdrive.sys 64
```

or:

```
device=c:\dos\ramdrive.sys
```

To create a much larger (720 KB) RAM disk in extended memory, again accepting the values MS-DOS assumes for <sector> and <directory>, you would need two commands: first, a Device command to identify the extended memory manager to MS-DOS and second, a Device command to create the RAM disk in extended memory. The commands would look like this:

```
device=c:\dos\himem.sys
device=c:\dos\ramdrive.sys 720 /e
```

Finally, to create the RAM disk described in the preceding example, but in expanded rather than extended memory, the commands would be:

```
device=<manager>
device=c:\dos\ramdrive.sys 720 /a
```

When you create this RAM disk on your own system, you would replace *manager* with the drive, path, and file name of your expanded memory manager.

## Using the Upper Memory Area

If you have an 80386 or 80486 computer, chances are your system has 1 MB of memory. If you have version 5 or later of MS-DOS, you can use the Loadhigh and Devicehigh commands to load programs and certain device drivers into upper memory blocks (UMBs). Both commands can help you conserve regular memory for applications and data.

Loadhigh is an MS-DOS command that you type or use in a batch file. Devicehigh is a configuration command that you put in CONFIG.SYS. Because MS-DOS doesn't normally treat the upper memory area as part of your computer's available memory, you can use the Loadhigh and Devicehigh commands only after you have loaded:

- The HIMEM.SYS device driver, which enables MS-DOS to use high memory.

- The Dos configuration command, which tells MS-DOS whether to use available upper memory blocks (UMBs).

- The EMM386.EXE device driver or a similar device driver that makes unused blocks of the upper memory area available.

Once you've used the Dos command and have identified the appropriate memory managers to MS-DOS with Device configuration commands, you can use the Loadhigh and Devicehigh commands to tell MS-DOS what to load into the upper memory area. To see if you have enough memory for a particular program or device driver, compare the file's size with the available memory reported by the Mem /C command.

The following sample CONFIG.SYS file shows the Dos and Device commands you need to use Loadhigh and Devicehigh. Files are assumed to be in the C:\DOS directory. In this example, the Dos command also tells MS-DOS to run in high memory; the *noems* parameter of the Device command naming EMM386.EXE indicates that the system has no need for expanded memory:

```
device=c:\dos\himem.sys
dos=high,umb
device=c:\dos\emm386.exe noems
```

## Loading Programs with Loadhigh

The Loadhigh command can be used either from the system prompt or, for programs you want to load regularly into the upper memory area, from your AUTOEXEC.BAT file. Loadhigh, which can be abbreviated lh, is particularly well suited for use with the type of program known as a TSR (*Terminate and Stay Resident*). Such programs sit in memory but usually reside quietly in the background, as opposed to word processors and other application programs that remain in control of the system as long as they are active. MS-DOS includes a number of TSRs, among them Doskey, Graphics, Mode, and Append.

To load a program into upper memory, the form of the Loadhigh command is:

**loadhigh <filename> <parameters>**

<filename> is the name of the program you want to load, including a drive and path if necessary.

<parameters> represents any parameters you type when starting the program.

For example, after starting with the CONFIG.SYS file described earlier, you would load Doskey into upper memory with the command:

```
loadhigh doskey
```

MS-DOS would then attempt to load the program into the upper memory area. If there weren't enough room, MS-DOS would load Doskey into conventional memory instead.

## Loading Device Drivers with Devicehigh

The Devicehigh command lets you load device drivers, such as RAMDRIVE.SYS, into the upper memory area and thus conserve as much of your computer's conventional memory as possible. Device drivers that are included with MS-DOS and that can be loaded into the upper memory area are EGA.SYS, DISPLAY.SYS, DBLSPACE.SYS, INTERLNK.SYS, ANSI.SYS, RAMDRIVE.SYS, and DRIVER.SYS. (MS-DOS versions prior to 6 also included PRINTER.SYS.)

You can also load device drivers that aren't part of MS-DOS into reserved memory. Some, however, need more memory than expected when they're loaded and might cause your system to halt. If this happens, you might be able to fix the problem by using the *minsize* parameter of the Devicehigh command to specify the amount of memory the driver needs.

> **NOTE:** *Before experimenting, create a startup floppy disk (use the /S parameter of the Format command), and copy your CONFIG.SYS and AUTOEXEC.BAT files to it. Then if you experience difficulties with a device driver, you have an alternative means of starting your computer so that you can correct the situation. Versions 6 and 6.2 of MS-DOS makes it possible to skip the loading of CONFIG.SYS and AUTOEXEC.BAT, so there's no need to create the startup disk. See the section "Starting Without CONFIG.SYS or AUTOEXEC.BAT" later in this chapter.*

The form of the Devicehigh command in versions 6 and 6.2 is:

**devicehigh=/L:<region>,<minsize> /S <filename>**

/L:<region>,<minsize> lets you specify where in upper memory you want to place the driver and the minimum amount of memory needed by the device driver. <region> specifies the region in upper memory into which you want to put the device driver. To list the regions available in upper memory, use the Mem command with the /F parameter. <minsize> tells MS-DOS the smallest amount of memory into which the device driver will fit. If a device driver needs two or more regions of memory, separate the region numbers with semicolons. Use <minsize> if you experience problems loading a device driver into the upper memory area.

/S shrinks the UMB to its smallest size as MS-DOS loads the device driver. This switch is normally used only by the MemMaker program.

<filename> is the name, including extension, of the device driver you want to load. Include a path if the driver is not in the root directory of the disk from which you start MS-DOS. You can also include parameters required by the device driver.

Version 5 of MS-DOS has a slightly different form:

**devicehigh size=<memsize> <filename>**

*size*=<memsize> is the amount of memory, given as a hexadecimal value, required by the device driver. Use *size* if you experience problems loading a device driver into the upper memory area. Although the value must be a hexadecimal (base 16) number, you don't have to calculate it yourself; you can use the Mem command with the /C parameter to list the size of the driver. The second column of the Mem command report gives the size of the device driver in decimal; the third column gives the size in hexadecimal. If hexadecimal is new to you, don't be disconcerted if you see a combination of letters and numerals; both 0004A0 and 0038E0, for example, are valid hexadecimal numbers.

<filename> is the name, including extension, of the device driver you want to load. Include a path if the driver is not in the root directory of the disk from which you start MS-DOS. You can also include parameters that are required by the device driver.

When you use Devicehigh, MS-DOS attempts to load the specified device driver in the upper memory area. If there isn't enough room, MS-DOS loads the driver into conventional memory instead.

The following sample CONFIG.SYS file for version 6 or 6.2 of MS-DOS includes the commands shown earlier plus a Devicehigh command that loads RAMDRIVE.SYS into the upper memory area and creates a 640 KB RAM disk in extended memory:

```
device=c:\dos\himem.sys
dos=high,umb
device=c:\dos\emm386.exe noems
devicehigh=/L:1,640 c:\dos\ramdrive.sys
```

## Controlling the Display with ANSI.SYS

MS-DOS includes a device driver called ANSI.SYS that defines a standard set of methods for managing a display, including how to display and erase characters, move the cursor, and select colors. Some programs, including parts of the MS-DOS Mode command, require your system disk to have a CONFIG.SYS file that contains the command *device=c:\dos\ansi.sys* (assuming the file is in your C:\DOS directory). ANSI is an acronym for American National Standards Institute.

## Configuration Commands for Your Portable Computer

Portable computers have special needs, some of which are met by two device drivers introduced in version 6 of MS-DOS:

- POWER.EXE extends battery life by shutting down portions of the computer's circuitry when no activity is taking place. If the computer conforms to the Advanced Power Management (APM) specification, POWER.EXE can extend battery life as much as 25 percent.

- INTERLNK.EXE lets you connect a portable computer to a desktop computer with a cable and quickly copy files back and forth.

Both programs are fairly simple to use. To take advantage of POWER.EXE, for example, add the configuration command *devicehigh=c:\dos\power.exe* to your CONFIG.SYS file. After you start the system, type the command *power*. If you plan to use the power-saving features permanently, add the Power command to AUTOEXEC.BAT.

To use INTERLNK.EXE, you must have a cable to connect the computers; the most common is a 3-wire serial cable, but you can also use a 7-wire null modem cable or a bidirectional parallel cable. If version 6 or 6.2 is installed on both computers, add the configuration command *devicehigh=c:\dos\interlnk.exe* to CONFIG.SYS on the portable computer. On the larger computer, simply type the command *intersvr* (you don't have to add a command to CONFIG.SYS). Disk drives attached to the larger computer appear as drives to the portable; copying from one machine to the other is simply a matter of using the Copy or Xcopy commands to copy files from one drive to another.

For more information about using these two device drivers, use the MS-DOS Help facility (for example, type *help power.exe* or *help intersvr*) or consult the manual that came with MS-DOS versions 6 and 6.2.

# OTHER CONFIGURATION COMMANDS

Several configuration commands control internal operating characteristics of your system and usually deal with how MS-DOS handles files or reads disks. Some application programs or devices include detailed instructions for adding or changing these configuration commands. The configuration commands discussed in this section are described in more detail in Appendix C, "MS-DOS Command Reference."

## Defining Temporary Work Areas

The Buffers configuration command defines the number of work areas in memory (*buffers*) that MS-DOS uses to read from and write to a disk. The effect of this configuration command on system performance depends on the type of disk drive you use and the types of programs you use. The form of the Buffers command is:

**buffers=<number>**

Unless otherwise noted, versions of MS-DOS through 3.2 use two or three buffers, depending on your system and the amount of memory it has. If you're using version 3.3, MS-DOS sets the number of buffers primarily according to the amount of memory your system has. You can, of course, override these values by including or changing the Buffers configuration command in CONFIG.SYS. For optimum performance, some programs require you to set buffers to a higher number than MS-DOS assumes. Fastback, for example, needs 40. For a list of values that MS-DOS uses, see the description of the Buffers command in Appendix C.

## Specifying the Number of Open Files

The Files configuration command tells MS-DOS how many files it can use at one time. Unless otherwise instructed, MS-DOS can use a maximum of eight files at a time. The form of the Files command is:

**files=<number>**

<number> can be any number from 8 through 255.

## Setting the Highest Drive Letter

The Lastdrive configuration command specifies the highest drive letter that MS-DOS recognizes as valid. If CONFIG.SYS doesn't contain a Lastdrive command, the highest drive letter MS-DOS recognizes is E. This command is usually used to specify a higher letter (up to Z) if MS-DOS needs more than five drive letters. MS-DOS might need more drive letters because the computer is part of a network, because it uses many RAM disks, or because a large hard disk is divided into sections, each of which is referred to by a different drive letter. The form of the Lastdrive command is:

**lastdrive=<letter>**

<letter> is any letter from A to Z.

## Troubleshooting and Tailoring System Startup

When your system behaves erratically—one or more programs won't run or run incorrectly, or perhaps a device doesn't work properly—one of the most valuable troubleshooting techniques is to remove commands from CONFIG.SYS and AUTOEXEC.BAT until the problem goes away. Starting with version 6, MS-DOS takes much of the tedium out of this procedure by letting you start the system without carrying out any of the commands in CONFIG.SYS or AUTOEXEC.BAT or by letting you choose, command by command, whether to carry out the commands in CONFIG.SYS and AUTOEXEC.BAT.

You can also structure the commands in CONFIG.SYS so that MS-DOS displays a menu of alternate configurations and lets you choose which combination of configuration commands to carry out.

### Starting Without CONFIG.SYS or AUTOEXEC.BAT

If you install a new program or device and your system stops working properly—or if someone else uses your system and now it won't do what it's supposed to—there's a chance that a configuration command in CONFIG.SYS or a command in AUTOEXEC.BAT is causing the problem.

To confirm the diagnosis, press Ctrl-Alt-Del to restart the system and when MS-DOS displays *Starting MS-DOS*, press F5; MS-DOS skips both CONFIG.SYS and AUTOEXEC.BAT. If the system starts properly (although it may behave differently from the way it usually does because you aren't carrying out your normal configuration or startup commands), edit your CONFIG.SYS and AUTOEXEC.BAT files to double-check any commands you might have added. If you didn't add any commands recently, you'll need to do further investigating. The next topic tells you how to use another feature to pinpoint the problem.

### Choosing Individual Startup Commands

If there's a problem in CONFIG.SYS or AUTOEXEC.BAT, you can test their commands one at a time by pressing F8 when MS-DOS displays *Starting MS-DOS* at startup. In response, MS-DOS displays each configuration command in CONFIG.SYS, starting with the first, and prompts you *[Y,N]?* Step through the file this way until you locate the offending configuration command; then either correct it or remove it.

When MS-DOS has completed processing CONFIG.SYS, it prompts you *Process AUTOEXEC.BAT [Y,N]?* To step through each command in AUTOEXEC.BAT just as you did in CONFIG.SYS, press *Y*.

**NOTE:** *If you call or chain to other batch files in AUTOEXEC.BAT, MS-DOS steps through those files one command at a time, too, giving you complete control of your diagnostic process.*

### Defining a Menu of Configurations

Suppose you have a device that you use rarely—for example, a color scanner—whose device driver is very large and cannot run in high memory. You have also found that it runs much better if you create a RAM drive to hold some temporary files created during the scan, which uses more memory. But because the driver and the created RAM drive take up memory that otherwise would be available for other programs, you'd like to load the device driver and set up the RAM drive only when you're going to use the scanner. Versions 6 and 6.2 let you do just that by adding some commands to your CONFIG.SYS file.

Let's look at an example. When you start your machine using the following CONFIG.SYS file, MS-DOS displays a screen titled "MS-DOS 6.2 Startup Menu" that lists two menu items—*NoScanner* and *Scanner*. MS-DOS reads different parts of your CONFIG.SYS file depending on the item you choose.

```
device = c:\dos\himem.sys
device = c:\dos\emm386.exe noems
dos = high,umb
lastdrive = f

[Menu]
menuitem = NoScanner
menuitem = Scanner

[NoScanner]

[Scanner]
device = c:\scan\colrscan.sys
devicehigh = c:\dos\ramdrive.sys 1024 512 64 /e

[Common]
devicehigh = c:\dos\dblspace.sys /move
devicehigh = c:\dos\ansi.sys
buffers = 20
files = 40
```

The first four commands set up upper memory management and specify the highest drive letter that MS-DOS will recognize; these configuration commands are always carried out.

The line that contains *[Menu]* marks the beginning of the list of menu choices. There are two choices in this configuration menu—*NoScanner* and *Scanner*. You'll need a separate section in CONFIG.SYS for each of these choices to specify what configuration commands, if any, are to be carried out when each choice is made.

The first menu item section starts with the line *[NoScanner]*. This section contains no configuration commands because you don't want to take any special action if you're not going to use the scanner.

The second menu item section starts with the line *[Scanner]*. This section contains two configuration commands that are carried out if you choose *Scanner* from the startup menu. They load the device driver named COLRSCAN.SYS and create a 1-megabyte RAM drive.

The four configuration commands following *[Common]* are carried out regardless of what you choose from the startup menu. These commands complete the job of specifying to MS-DOS how your system is set up and how to manage its resources.

By setting up your CONFIG.SYS file this way, you don't have to give up the use of the memory required to run your scanner when you don't use it. Each time you start your system, you'll have the chance to tell MS-DOS how to configure the system. You can use this technique to handle any special configurations, such as running a network or installing drivers for seldom-used hardware.

## COMMANDS FOR OCCASIONAL USE

This book has described all the commands you routinely use to operate MS-DOS. There are a few remaining commands you might occasionally need, and there are several commands that you won't need unless you plan to program or use some of the advanced capabilities of MS-DOS. The less commonly used commands are described briefly here and in more detail in Appendix C, "MS-DOS Command Reference."

### Displaying the MS-DOS Version Number

The Version command displays the number of the version of MS-DOS you're using. If you use more than one version, or if you are using someone else's machine, this gives you a quick way to check the version.

The Version command has no parameters:

**ver**

If you're using version 6, for example, MS-DOS replies *MS-DOS Version 6.00* in response to the command.

## Changing the System Prompt

As shown in examples in earlier chapters, you can change the system prompt with the Prompt command to display much more than just the current drive letter. The change takes effect as soon as you enter the command.

The Prompt command has one parameter:

**prompt <string>**

<string> is a string of characters that defines the new system prompt. You can use any characters you want. You can also instruct the new prompt to include one or more items of useful information by including a dollar sign and one of the following characters to specify what you want the prompt to contain:

| *Character* | *Produces* |
|---|---|
| d | The current date |
| p | The current drive and directory |
| n | The current drive |
| t | The current time |
| v | The MS-DOS version number |
| g | A greater-than sign (>) |
| l | A less-than sign (<) |
| b | A vertical bar ( ¦ ) |
| q | An equal sign (=) |
| e | An escape character |
| h | A backspace |
| $ | A dollar sign ($) |
| _ | A signal to end the current line and start a new one (The character is an underscore, not a hyphen.) |

You can include as many combinations of $, followed by a character, as you wish. MS-DOS ignores any combination of $ followed by a character that is not in the preceding list.

If you enter the Prompt command with no parameter (just type *prompt*), MS-DOS restores the prompt to the standard MS-DOS version: the letter of the current drive followed by a greater-than sign (for example, C>).

The Prompt command takes effect immediately, so it's easy to experiment. You saw how to change the system prompt to a courteous request (*May I help you?*) in Chapter 3, "Getting Your Bearings," and you've changed it to suit your needs in other chapters. To restore the system prompt to its most common form, type *prompt $p$g.*

Several examples follow. Notice how the system prompt changes each time to show the effect of the previous Prompt command. Press the Spacebar before pressing the Enter key to end each command in order to leave a blank space between the end of the system prompt and the beginning of the command that you type next.

To define the system prompt as the current drive and directory, type:

```
C:\MKT\WP>prompt $p

C:\MKT\WP _
```

The example assumes that the current drive is C and that the directory is \MKT\WP. To define the system prompt as two lines that show the date and time, type:

```
C:\MKT\WP prompt $d$_$t

Sat 10-16-1993
14:57:10.11 _
```

The time and date will vary, depending on how you have set them in your system. Press the Enter key several times to see that MS-DOS keeps the time current.

Finally, combining several of the options shows just how much you can include in a prompt:

```
Wed 10-16-1991
15:02:10.11 prompt $v$_$d $t$_Current directory $q $p$_Command:

MS-DOS Version 6.00
Sat 10-16-1993 15:02:57.68
Current directory = C:\MKT\WP
Command: _
```

The Prompt command lets you easily tailor the system prompt to the balance of information that you prefer. When you design a system prompt that you like, put it in AUTOEXEC.BAT, and you'll never have to type it again; MS-DOS will carry out the command every time you start the system.

## Speeding Up File Access

Each time you (or an application program) need a file, MS-DOS might first need to search for the subdirectory that contains the file and then search the directory entries for the file itself. On a hard disk with hundreds or thousands of files, all this searching can take some time.

The Fastopen command tells MS-DOS to keep track (in memory) of the locations of subdirectories and files as it uses them. The next time it's asked for a file or subdirectory, MS-DOS checks in memory before it searches the disk. If it finds the location of the file or subdirectory in memory, MS-DOS can go directly to it on the disk instead of searching for it.

If you or your application programs tend to use the same files or directories over and over, the Fastopen command can make MS-DOS visibly faster. The Fastopen command works only with hard disks. (Note that you shouldn't use Fastopen if you're running Microsoft Windows.) Fastopen has three parameters:

**fastopen <drive>=<files> /X**

<drive> is the drive letter, followed by a colon, of the hard disk whose files and subdirectories you want MS-DOS to track (for example, *c:*).

<files> is the number of files and subdirectories whose location MS-DOS will keep in memory; it must be preceded by an equal sign. You can specify a value for <files> from 10 through 999. For example, if you had one hard disk, drive C, and wanted MS-DOS to keep track of the last 75 files and subdirectories used, you would type *fastopen c:=75*.

/X tells MS-DOS to keep track of the locations in expanded memory. If you use /X, check to be sure your expanded memory conforms to the current standard, which is LIM EMS 4.0.

If you're using MS-DOS from a hard disk, the installation program might have set up a Fastopen command telling MS-DOS to keep track of the last *x* files and subdirectories you used. This command would have been placed in your configuration file in a form like this: *install=c:\dos\fastopen.exe c:=(50,25)*. Although the command looks a bit more complicated than *fastopen c:=50*, its purpose is the same. The *install* part of the command (described in Appendix C, "MS-DOS Command Reference") simply tells MS-DOS to use your computer's memory as efficiently as it can. If you want to change the number of files, you can change the command in CONFIG.SYS. For example, to keep track of the last 75 files and subdirectories, change the command to *install=c:\dos\fastopen.exe c:=(75, 25)*.

## Treating a Directory As If It Were a Disk Drive

The Substitute (subst) command lets you treat a directory as if it were a separate disk. If your directory structure includes long path names, or if you use application programs that accept a drive letter but not a path name, you can use the Substitute command to tell MS-DOS to treat all future references to a particular drive as references to a directory on the disk in a different drive.

After naming a drive letter in a Substitute command, you cannot refer to that drive letter in any other command, so you will probably want to use a drive letter that doesn't refer to an existing drive. In order to do this, you must tell MS-DOS to accept more drive letters than there are disk drives. You can put a Lastdrive command in the CONFIG.SYS file in the root directory of your MS-DOS system disk. The Substitute command has two parameters:

**subst <drive> <pathname> /D**

<drive> is the letter, followed by a colon, to be used to refer to <pathname>.

<pathname> is the path name of the directory to be referred to by <drive>.

D deletes any substitutions that involve <drive>. If you include /D, you cannot include <pathname>.

If you omit all parameters and type only *subst*, MS-DOS displays a list of any substitutions in effect. For example, suppose you find yourself frequently referring to a directory whose path name is C:\SPREAD\SALES\FORECAST and you would like to use a shorter synonym. To substitute *x:* for the path name, you would make certain that your CONFIG.SYS file contained a Lastdrive command that specified the letter *x*, and then you would type *subst x: c:\spread\sales\forecast*. The substitution would remain in effect until you restarted MS-DOS or canceled the substitution by typing *subst x: /d*.

# PART III

# APPENDIXES

Part III includes three appendixes. Appendixes A and B contain reference material for occasional use or for background information. Appendix A, ``Installing MS-DOS,'' is a guide to installing and upgrading to versions 3 through 6.2 of MS-DOS. It supplements the step-by-step instructions you receive with a new version of MS-DOS. Appendix B, ``Glossary,'' contributes to your background knowledge by defining commonly used terms and those presented in the main portion of this book. Appendix C, ``MS-DOS Command Reference,'' is a comprehensive reference to MS-DOS commands and their parameters. It provides easy-to-find answers to questions about the form and use of commands.

A

# Installing MS-DOS

his appendix shows you how to install versions 3 through 6.2 of MS-DOS. Although MS-DOS was probably preinstalled on your system, someday you might need to reinstall MS-DOS or upgrade to a newer version. If you need more background information or specific instructions, refer to the documentation that comes with your version of MS-DOS.

## INSTALLING OR UPGRADING TO VERSION 5 OR LATER

Although MS-DOS has grown in capability over the years, it has also become easier to install. Versions 5 and later are the easiest to set up, whether you're intalling MS-DOS on a brand-new system or upgrading from an earlier version. The first of the floppy disks on which versions 5 and later are supplied contains a setup program (SETUP.EXE) that does almost all the work for you.

Whether you're upgrading or installing MS-DOS on a brand-new machine, *use the Setup program*. Even if you've installed earlier versions of MS-DOS by copying files from the MS-DOS floppy disks, you can't install version 5 or later in this way. Many of the MS-DOS files are shipped in a special condensed format that Setup expands during the installation procedure. In addition, Setup checks the memory and devices on your system (so you don't have to), offers help at each stage, prompts whenever it needs a response from you, displays an indicator showing how much of the installation is complete, and even tells you what it's doing as it prepares MS-DOS to work on your computer.

### Installing Version 5 or Later for the First Time

If your system is new, chances are that MS-DOS has already been installed for you, especially if your computer has a hard disk. If MS-DOS is not installed, start by inserting the floppy disk labeled *Disk 1* in drive A. Then start or restart your computer.

Setup guides you through the entire installation process, asking you to provide some responses and to make a few choices (for example, whether you want to install the MS-DOS or Microsoft Windows versions of some features, or both). Setup proposes a response whenever it asks you to make a choice, usually either the one most people choose or the one that Setup has determined suits your system best. If you need further information before deciding to accept or change a proposed response, press the F1 key. Accepting all the choices Setup proposes will set up a basic working system for you. Once you're comfortable with this system, you can make any necessary modifications by tailoring the files AUTOEXEC.BAT and CONFIG.SYS to suit your own preferences. These files are described in Chapter 14, "Creating Your Own Commands"; Chapter 17, "Tailoring Your System"; and Appendix C, "MS-DOS Command Reference." After it's done installing MS-DOS, Setup restarts your machine.

## Upgrading to Version 5 or Later

If you have a hard disk and are upgrading from an earlier version of MS-DOS, you can upgrade without a worry. Setup provides the Uninstall program, which is a built-in program that lets you restore your earlier version of MS-DOS if the installation fails or if you find that some of your programs cannot work with the new version.

Label a blank floppy disk *Uninstall*. Then place the floppy disk labeled *Disk 1* in drive A, and type the following:

```
C>a:
A>setup
```

After generating a preinstallation report of your machine's configuration and checking your system, Setup displays a welcoming message and tells you which keys to press to request help, continue with the installation, or quit. From this point on, follow the on-screen instructions. If you are uncertain about any responses, press the F1 key for help and further information. After it's done installing MS-DOS, Setup restarts your machine.

After the new version is installed, place the *Uninstall* floppy disk in a safe place. It's unlikely that you'll need to return to your old version of MS-DOS, but if you do, place the *Uninstall* floppy disk in drive A, restart the system, and follow the instructions that appear on the screen.

# INSTALLING OR UPGRADING TO VERSION 4

Version 4 of MS-DOS comes with an installation program that prompts you through the installation process. The installation program includes online help that explains most of the choices.

Essentially, all you do is place the floppy disk labeled *Install* in drive A, start or restart your computer, and then press the Enter key to begin. From that point onward, the installation program, named Select, asks you questions about your computer system and tells you which of the original MS-DOS floppy disks it needs and when you need them. Before you start, however, there are a few things you should know or prepare for to make the procedure as easy as possible.

## Your Computer

Find out (roughly) how much memory your system has. The Select program doesn't ask you for the exact amount, but during installation it asks you to choose how you want to balance the memory used by MS-DOS and by your programs.

If your system contains less than 512 KB of memory, choose the first option (*Minimum MS-DOS function; maximum program workspace*) to give your programs as much working room as possible. If your system has 512 KB of memory, choose the option Select proposes (*Balance MS-DOS function with program workspace*). If your system has more than 512 KB of memory, choose the third option (*Maximum MS-DOS function; minimum program workspace*) so that both MS-DOS and your programs have plenty of room to work in.

Check the make and model of printer you use. Also, find out whether it is a serial or a parallel printer, and find out the number of the port it is connected to (for example, LPT1: for a parallel printer or COM1: for a serial printer). The Select program will ask you to choose your printer from a list. It will also propose a printer port, so it is up to you to know whether Select is correct.

## The Installation/Upgrade Process

NOTE: *If you're using a hard disk and are upgrading to version 4 from an earlier version of DOS, don't try to install IBM's release of DOS if your computer is currently running a version of DOS released by another manufacturer. There is a small but significant difference between IBM's release and others that prevents successful installation. You can install the IBM release, but to do so you must back up your hard disk, reformat it, and then install DOS. If you're not sure whose release of DOS you have, start your computer to display the information; if DOS doesn't display the manufacturer's name and the version number, type* ver *(the Version command).*

Whether you install MS-DOS on a hard disk or on floppy disks, Select needs one or more blank floppy disks for the installation. One of the first things Select does is display a list showing the number and capacity of floppy disks it needs for installing MS-DOS on various types of disk drives.

## AUTOEXEC.BAT and CONFIG.SYS

When Select finishes putting MS-DOS on a hard disk that contains an earlier version of MS-DOS, its final message might tell you that Select has saved information about your computer, printer, display, screen, and the MS-DOS Shell in two files that it named AUTOEXEC.400 and CONFIG.400. You'll want MS-DOS to be able to find this information whenever you start or restart your computer, and for that to happen, you'll have to rename the files AUTOEXEC.BAT and CONFIG.SYS. Only then will MS-DOS automatically search for the information saved by the Select program.

# INSTALLING VERSION 3

Versions 3 and earlier of MS-DOS do not include an installation program, so it's up to you to determine how you want to set up MS-DOS to work on your system. If your computer doesn't have a hard disk, all you really need to do is make copies of your MS-DOS floppy disks with the Diskcopy command described in Chapter 6, "Managing Your Floppy Disks." Diskcopy makes an exact duplicate of a floppy disk, so once you've copied your original MS-DOS floppy disks, you can store them safely away and use the copies in your everyday work with MS-DOS.

If you have a hard disk, you use a two-step procedure to copy MS-DOS from your MS-DOS floppy disk(s) to the hard disk. The first step uses the System (sys) command to copy two hidden files that MS-DOS needs in order to start from your hard disk. The second step uses the Copy command to copy the remaining MS-DOS files to your hard disk.

> NOTE: *The following instructions assume that your hard disk has already been formatted (prepared for use). If it has not, or if you want to wipe it clean and start anew, you can use the command* format c: /s *to prepare the disk and copy the system files. If you try this command, however, and MS-DOS displays a* WARNING *message followed by a request for you to confirm the format, be very sure you want to continue. Once MS-DOS begins formatting the hard disk, you'll lose whatever files it contains—forever.*

## Copying the System Files

Place your MS-DOS startup floppy disk in drive A. Depending on the version you're installing, this floppy disk is labeled either *Startup* or *MS-DOS*. Turn on the computer or restart it by simultaneously pressing the keys marked Ctrl, Alt, and Del.

If you're upgrading to a newer release of version 3, or if your hard disk is already formatted, use the System command to move the hidden MS-DOS files to your hard disk. Type the following:

```
A>sys c:
```

MS-DOS responds *System transferred.*

**NOTE:** *If you're installing version 3.3 on a system using version 3.1 or earlier, MS-DOS might display the message* Insufficient memory for system transfer. *If you see this, it means that MS-DOS cannot transfer the files properly. You must back up all the files on your hard disk, format it, and later restore all the files you've backed up.*

Whether you use Format or System, your next step is to copy the MS-DOS files from the MS-DOS floppy disks to a directory named \DOS on your hard disk. The question now is, Where do they go? If you're working with a new or newly formatted hard disk, follow the instructions in the next section, "Copying MS-DOS to a DOS Directory." If you're upgrading an existing MS-DOS version from one release to another (for example, from 3.1 to 3.3), skip to the heading "Upgrading with Version 3."

## Copying MS-DOS to a DOS Directory

If you've just formatted your hard disk, it's an empty storage area you can use as you like, so make your future work easier by copying MS-DOS to a special section—a directory—of its own. Doing this keeps your MS-DOS files separate from application and data files, and it generally helps keep your hard disk neat and organized.

If you're new to MS-DOS, the following commands probaby won't mean much to you, but if you type them exactly as shown, you should be able to install any release of version 3 without problems.

First, check that your startup disk is still in drive A, and copy the MS-DOS file named COMMAND.COM to the base (root) directory or your hard disk, where it normally goes. Type:

```
A>copy command.com c:\
```

Now create the MS-DOS directory by typing:

```
A>md c:\dos
```

Copy the files from your MS-DOS disk to the new DOS directory:

```
A>copy *.* c:\dos
```

If you have more than one MS-DOS disk, repeat the Copy command to copy the rest of your MS-DOS files.

When you typed *.* (meaning "all files") in your Copy command, you recopied COMMAND.COM. You don't need two copies of this file, so delete the one in your DOS directory by typing:

```
A>del c:\dos\command.com
```

Finally, create a special file, again in the root directory of your hard disk, that tells MS-DOS where to find its own command files. Type the following. Press Enter at the end of each line, and press—at the same time—the two keys marked Ctrl and Z where you see <Ctrl-Z>.

```
A>copy con c:\autoexec.bat
path=c:\dos
<Ctrl-Z>
```

If all goes well, MS-DOS should respond *1 File(s) copied.* If it does not, retype the preceding lines.

Your new version of MS-DOS should now be ready for use. Remove any disk from drive A, and restart the computer by pressing Ctrl, Alt, and Del. When MS-DOS starts up, the system prompt should be *C>*. You can verify that MS-DOS can find its own command files by typing:

```
C>chkdsk
```

If MS-DOS produces a report on your hard disk, you're all set. If it does not start from drive C, repeat the setup procedure. If MS-DOS responds *File not found* to your Check Disk command, retype the preceding commands that start with *copy con c:\autoexec.bat.*

## Upgrading with Version 3

If you're upgrading from one version of MS-DOS to another, your earlier version might be in a DOS directory, or it might be in the main (root) directory of your hard disk. It all depends on how your hard disk was organized.

Checking on, and possibly reorganizing, your hard disk assumes some knowledge of disks, directories, and directory commands. If this is familiar territory, the following instructions should help you out. If you and MS-DOS are relative strangers and you have a currently functional system, you might prefer to work through the examples in this book or ask someone for advice before trying to organize your hard disk.

### If You Have a DOS Directory

If you already have a DOS directory, use the Replace command to replace all the old MS-DOS files with those in the new version. Change the current drive to C by typing:

```
A>c:
```

Now, for each new MS-DOS disk you place in drive A, type the following two commands. If necessary, change *dos* to the name of your DOS directory:

```
C>replace a:\*.* c:\ /s
C>replace a:\*.* c:\dos /a
```

The first command replaces existing files; the second adds any files from the MS-DOS disk that don't exist on drive C. That's it. You're done.

### If You Don't Have a DOS Directory

If you don't have a DOS directory and all your MS-DOS files are in the root directory of the hard disk, you have two tasks to perform: first, to upgrade your current version of MS-DOS; second, to clear old MS-DOS files out of the root directory.

You've already moved the new system files to your hard disk. Now, to upgrade your current version and place your MS-DOS files in a DOS directory, start by creating the new DOS directory:

```
A>md c:\dos
```

Next, copy the file named COMMAND.COM to the root directory of your hard disk:

```
A>copy command.com c:
```

Now copy the other MS-DOS files from the MS-DOS disk to the DOS directory:

```
A>copy *.* c:\dos
```

If you have another MS-DOS disk, repeat the preceding Copy command. Next, check for an AUTOEXEC.BAT file by typing:

```
A>type c:\autoexec.bat
```

If MS-DOS displays a file and one of the lines is a Path command like this:

```
PATH=C\;C:\WP;C:\SPREAD;C:\DB
```

use Edit or your word processor (if it can save unformatted files) to add your new DOS directory to the Path command:

```
PATH=C:\;C:\DOS;C:\WP;C:\SPREAD;C:\DB
```

If MS-DOS responds *File not found* to your Type command, you need to create a basic AUTOEXEC.BAT file with a Path command as follows (press Ctrl and Z together where you see <Ctrl-Z>):

```
A>copy con c:\autoexec.bat
path=c:\dos
<Ctrl-Z>
```

Use the Type command again, this time to check for a file named CONFIG.SYS. If MS-DOS displays a file, use Edit or your word processor to edit it, adding the name of the DOS directory to all references to MS-DOS files. For example:

```
DEVICE=C:\DOS\ANSI.SYS
DEVICE=C:\DOS\VDISK.SYS
```

(If MS-DOS responds *File not found* to this command, you don't have to create a *CONFIG.SYS* file for it to use. You might want to at some point, but for now your system will work without such a file.)

Finally, for the second stage in reorganizing your hard disk, turn on your printer, and print a listing of the root directory with the command:

```
A>dir c:\ > prn
```

Using the files in your MS-DOS directory or the files on the disks for your old version of MS-DOS as a guide, carefully mark the printout, noting all MS-DOS files in the root directory other than COMMAND.COM, AUTOEXEC.BAT, and CONFIG.SYS. That is, mark files such as FORMAT.COM, PRINT.COM, DISKCOPY.COM, and so on.

Once you've marked these files names (and double-checked them to be sure you didn't include any non-DOS files), type a Delete command for each to remove it from the *root* directory. For example, type:

```
A>del c:\format.com
```

```
A>del c:\print.com
```

```
A>del c:\diskcopy.com
```

When you're finished, the root directory should contain only COMMAND.COM, AUTOEXEC.BAT, and CONFIG.SYS, as well as the non-DOS files and directories it held before. The remainder of your MS-DOS files should all be in C:\DOS.

# Glossary

# A

**Adapter** A term sometimes used to refer to printed-circuit cards that plug into a computer and control a device, such as a display or a printer.

**Anti-Virus** A program in versions 6 and 6.2 that checks your system for the presence of virus programs. If it finds a virus, it alerts you and, if possible, eliminates the offending file or files that contain the program. *See also* Virus.

**Application program** A program, such as a word processor or spreadsheet, that performs a specific task; an application of the computer to a particular type of work.

**Archive** To transfer files to a separate disk or a backup tape for safekeeping. In versions 6 and 6.2 of MS-DOS, the MSbackup command helps archive files, and if necessary, it can be used to return archived files to the disk from which they were backed up. (In earlier versions, you use the Backup and Restore commands.)

**ASCII** A standardized coding scheme that uses numeric values to represent letters, digits, symbols, and so on. ASCII is an acronym for *American Standard Code for Information Interchange* and is widely used in coding information for computers.

**AUTOEXEC.BAT** A name reserved for a batch file that contains commands that are carried out by MS-DOS each time the system is started. An AUTOEXEC.BAT file can be used to perform a desired set of startup procedures without your having to type the commands each time.

**AUX** Short for *auxiliary*. The communications port MS-DOS uses unless instructed otherwise. AUX can be either COM1 or COM2 in versions of MS-DOS through 3.2; it can be COM1, COM2, COM3, or COM4 in versions 3.3 and later.

# B

**Backspace key** The key labeled with a single, left-pointing arrow and, often, the word *Backspace*; erases characters you have typed, one at a time.

**Back up** To copy one or more files to disks or tapes for safekeeping.

**BAK** An extension assigned by Edlin and by many word processors to the next-most-recent (penultimate) version of a text file. If the working copy of a file is damaged, the BAK file can be used to salvage a near-current version of the document.

**Basic** A programming language included with MS-DOS. When originally developed, Basic was an acronym for *Beginner's All-purpose Symbolic Instruction Code*. Through version 4, MS-DOS includes either Basic and BASICA (Advanced Basic) or GW-BASIC. Versions 5 and later include a more sophisticated, visually oriented form called QBasic.

**Batch file** A text file whose extension is BAT; contains MS-DOS commands. When you type the name of a batch file while MS-DOS is at the command level, MS-DOS carries out the commands in the file.

**Baud** Broadly, the rate at which data is transmitted over a communications link; more specifically, *baud* refers to the number of changes per second (representing coded data) carried by the signal. For commonly used modem rates, approximately one character per second is transmitted for each 10 baud.

**Binary** The base-2 numbering system whose only digits are 0 and 1. The binary system is particularly well suited to use with computers because the two digits can be represented by the presence or absence of a voltage.

**Bit** The smallest unit of information used with computers; corresponds to a binary digit (either 0 or 1). Eight bits make up one byte.

**Boot** To start up a computer; derived from the saying "pull yourself up by your own bootstraps."

**Byte** The unit of measure used for computer memory and data storage. One byte contains eight bits and can store one character (a letter, number, punctuation mark, or other symbol).

C

**Character string** A group of characters that you tell MS-DOS to treat as a set of letters or numbers rather than as a command. The Find filter command searches for character strings enclosed in quotation marks (""). In other commands, such as Search and Replace, the quotation marks are not needed.

**Chip** *See* Integrated circuit.

**Color Graphics Adapter (CGA)** A printed-circuit card in the system unit of a computer that controls the display; shows both text and graphics at low resolution in up to 16 colors.

**COM1, COM2, COM3, COM4** Short for *communications*. The names of the serial communications ports. All versions of MS-DOS recognize COM1 and COM2; versions 3.3 and later also recognize COM3 and COM4.

**Command** An instruction you give to control a computer program such as MS-DOS or an application program.

**Command file** A file that contains the program or instructions required to carry out a command. If the file's extension is COM or EXE, the command file contains machine instructions; if its extension is BAT, the command file is a batch file and contains MS-DOS commands.

**Communications** The transmission of data between computers; also called telecommunications.

**Communications port** *See* Port.

**Compression** *See* File compression.

**CON** Short for *console*. The name by which MS-DOS refers to the keyboard (input) and the display (output).

**Control key** The key labeled Ctrl; use it as you do the Shift key by holding it down while pressing another key. The Ctrl key in combination with another key can prompt an action or create a character with special significance. For example, when the Ctrl key is pressed with Break, any command that was being executed is interrupted. The Ctrl key pressed with Z creates a special character called the end-of-file marker. If displayed on the screen, Ctrl is shown as ^, as in the end-of-file marker ^Z (Ctrl-Z).

**Conventional memory** The name used for the first megabyte of random access memory in an IBM or compatible computer. MS-DOS and application programs can freely use the first 640 KB of conventional memory. Memory between 640 KB and 1 MB can be used by versions 5 and later of MS-DOS.

**CPU** Short for *central processing unit*. The part of a computer that performs calculations and processes information. In microcomputers that use MS-DOS, the CPU is an 8086/8088, 80286, 80386, or 80486 microprocessor.

**Ctrl** *See* Control key.

**Ctrl-Break** The key combination that cancels a command; entered by holding down the Ctrl key and pressing the Break key.

**Ctrl-C** Same as Ctrl-Break.

**Ctrl-Num Lock** The key combination that stops MS-DOS until you press any other key. On keyboards without a Pause key, Ctrl-Num Lock is used to freeze the display so you can view long displays. Entered by holding down the Ctrl key and pressing the Num Lock key.

**Ctrl-P** Same as Ctrl-PrtSc.

**Ctrl-PrtSc** The key combination that controls simultaneous printing and displaying. Pressing Ctrl-PrtSc once causes MS-DOS to print everything that is displayed; pressing Ctrl-PrtSc again causes MS-DOS to stop printing everything that is displayed. Entered by holding down the Ctrl key and pressing the PrtSc key.

**Ctrl-S** Same as Ctrl-Num Lock.

**Ctrl-Z** The key combination that creates the special character (displayed as ^Z) that MS-DOS uses to mark the end of a file. Created by holding down the Ctrl key and pressing Z or by pressing the function key labeled F6.

**Current directory** The directory in which MS-DOS looks for and writes files unless otherwise instructed.

**Current drive** The drive containing the disk on which MS-DOS looks for and saves files unless otherwise instructed.

# D

**Data** The information processed by a computer in doing its work.

**Data bit** A signal used in serial communications to represent part of a character. Seven or eight data bits can be used to represent one transmitted character.

**Data file** A file that contains the data needed by a program; the data can be numbers, text, graphics images, or a combination.

**Defragment** The process of rearranging the files on a disk so that all available space is combined into a single area. *See also* Fragment.

**Device** A piece of computer equipment, such as a display or a printer, that performs a specific task. The program that controls a device is called a device driver.

**Device name** The name by which MS-DOS refers to a device (for example, PRN, LPT1, LPT2, or LPT3 for a printer). Device names are treated like file names by MS-DOS.

**Directory** The index of files that MS-DOS maintains on a disk. The directory entry for each file includes the file's name, extension, size, date and time it was created or last changed, and the location of the beginning of the file. All but the last item can be displayed by the Directory command.

**Disk** A magnetically coated disk used to store information. The term is used when no distinction need be made between a floppy disk and a hard disk.

**Disk cache** A portion of memory set aside for use as a temporary, rapid-access storage area for information read from disk. A disk cache speeds operations by cutting down on the number of times the computer must perform relatively slow disk reads.

**Disk drive** The device that rotates a disk in order to read (retrieve) and write (store) information.

**Diskette** *See* Floppy disk.

**Display** The screen on which the computer shows both what you type at the keyboard and the result of its work; assumed by MS-DOS to be the standard output device unless a different device is specified.

**Doskey** A program in versions 5 and later of MS-DOS that records commands and enables you to repeat, edit, or store them as batch files or keyboard macros.

**DoubleSpace** A program in versions 6 and 6.2 that compresses the files on your hard disk, increasing the effective capacity of your hard disk by up to 100 percent.

**Drive letter** The letter that identifies a disk drive; can be any letter from A to Z.

**E**

**Edit** As a verb, to change the contents of a file, usually with a word processor or an editing program. As a noun, Edit is the name of the command that starts the MS-DOS Editor, the menu-based text editor included with versions 5 and later of MS-DOS.

**Editor** A program used to create or change text files; also called a *text editor*.

**Edlin** One of the two MS-DOS text editors. (The other, new with version 5, is the MS-DOS Editor. *See* Edit.) Edlin numbers the lines in a file and uses those numbers as references in finding, changing, or deleting lines.

**Enhanced Graphics Adapter (EGA)** A printed-circuit card in the system unit of a computer that controls the display. Shows both text and graphics at medium resolution in up to 64 colors.

**Enter key** The key you press to tell MS-DOS that you have finished typing a line. Labeled *Return* on some keyboards.

**Escape key** The key labeled Esc; cancels a line you have typed but have not yet entered by pressing the Enter key.

**Expanded memory** Additional memory that can be installed on any early PC-compatible computer. Use of this memory requires a special program called an expanded memory manager, and programs must be written specifically for such memory. Standardized use of expanded memory is governed by the Lotus-Intel-Microsoft (LIM) specification.

**Extended memory** Memory above 1 MB that can be installed on an IBM PC/AT, IBM PS/2 Models 50 or above, or any computer compatible with those models that has an 80286, 80386, or 80486 microprocessor. Extended memory is often handled by a program called an extended memory manager.

**Extension** A suffix of up to three characters that can be added to a file name to identify the contents of the file more precisely.

**F**

**File** A named collection of information stored on a disk; usually contains data, graphics, or a program.

**File compression** The technique of reducing the amount of space a file requires on a disk by replacing common character combinations with shorter codes. If you compress all files on a disk, the effect is to increase the apparent capacity of a disk, often by a factor of two or more.

**File name** A name of up to eight characters that you assign and that MS-DOS uses to find a file on a disk; can be followed by a period and three additional characters called the file-name extension.

**Filespec** The complete specification of a file; can include a drive letter, path name, file name, and extension.

**Filter command** An MS-DOS command that reads standard input, processes it in some way (for example, sorts it in alphabetic order), and writes the result to standard output.

**Fixed disk** *See* Hard disk.

**Floppy disk** A disk for storing files, made of thin plastic and enclosed in a protective jacket.

**Floppy disk drive** A disk drive used for floppy disks.

**Format** To prepare a disk for use.

**Fragment** The division of the available storage space on a disk into smaller and smaller pieces as MS-DOS erases and stores files. Such a condition slows down MS-DOS file operations. A fragmented disk can be corrected by moving files into the unused areas until all available storage space is combined into a single, contiguous area. *See also* Defragment.

**Function key** One of 10 or more keys—usually labeled F1, F2, and so on—that cause MS-DOS (or an application program) to perform a certain function, such as copying characters in a line of text.

**H**

**Hard disk** A disk of large capacity (10 MB or more) that cannot be removed from its drive. Also called a *fixed disk*.

**Hardware** The equipment that makes up a computer system, as opposed to the programs, or software.

**Hexadecimal** The base-16 numbering system whose digits are 0 through 9 and A through F (the letters A through F correspond to the decimal numbers 10 through 15); often used in computer programming because it is easily converted to and from binary, the base-2 numbering system the computer uses.

**Hidden file** A file that is not normally listed when you display the directory. MS-DOS uses two special, hidden files on any startup disk. They are hidden so that they cannot be altered or deleted under normal circumstances. Beginning with version 5, directories and data files can also be hidden for a certain amount of privacy.

**Hierarchical filing system** *See* Multilevel filing system.

**High Memory Area (HMA)** The name given to the first 64 KB of extended memory (additional memory starting at 1 MB). On a computer with extended memory, versions 5 and later of MS-DOS can run in the HMA, leaving more conventional memory available for applications and data.

## I

**Initialize** *See* Format.

**Input** The data that a program reads.

**Input/output** A term that refers to the devices and processes involved in the computer's reading (input) and writing (output) of data.

**Integrated circuit** An electronic device that combines thousands of transistors on a small wafer of silicon. Such devices are the building blocks of computers. Also referred to as a *chip*.

**Interface** The boundary between two systems or entities, such as a disk drive and the computer, or the user and a program.

**I/O** Abbreviation for *input/output*.

**I/O redirection** *See* Redirection.

## K

**Keyboard** The device consisting of alphabetic keys and other keys on which instructions and data are typed into the computer; assumed by MS-DOS to be the standard input device unless a different device is specified.

## L

**LPT1, LPT2, LPT3** Short for *line printer*. The names that MS-DOS uses to refer to the three ports to which parallel printers can be attached.

## M

**Macro** A set of keystrokes or commands that you assign a name and store either temporarily in memory or permanently on disk. A macro is a means of saving time by assigning a short name to a long or involved set of commands you use frequently. You can create macros with the Doskey program in versions 5 and later of MS-DOS.

**Memory** A type of electronic circuitry that the computer uses to store programs and data. Unlike disk storage, which is permanent, a computer's working memory is temporary—its contents are lost when power is removed. Memory is usually measured in units of 1024 bytes, called kilobytes and abbreviated K or KB; a megabyte (M or MB) is equal to 1024 kilobytes, or 1,048,576 bytes.

**Microcomputer** A small computer system whose central processing unit is a microprocessor; usually used by only one person.

**Microprocessor** An integrated circuit, or chip, that contains the circuits needed to carry out program instructions. The microprocessor performs calculations, briefly stores instructions and data, and transfers information to and from a computer's memory.

**Modem** Contraction of *modulator-demodulator*. A device that enables transmission of computer data over telephone lines.

**Monitor** A television-like device that displays computer input and output; often used synonymously with *display*.

**Monochrome** A term used to describe a computer display capable of displaying one color (usually white, green, or amber).

**Monochrome Display Adapter (MDA)** A printed-circuit card, in the system unit of a computer, that controls the display. Shows text only, not graphics, at medium resolution in one color.

**Multicolor Graphics Array (MCGA)** A printed-circuit card, in the system unit of a computer, that controls the display. Shows both text and graphics at low to medium resolution in up to 256 colors; used in IBM PS/2 model computers.

**Multilevel filing system** A computer filing system that lets you define directories within other directories, creating a structure with many levels. Also called a *tree-structured* or *hierarchical filing system*.

## N

**Network** A group of computers that are linked by printed-circuit cards, cables, and network software and can share resources, such as programs, data, disk drives, and printers.

## O

**Operating system** A program that coordinates the operation of all parts of a computer system.

**Output** The result of a program's processing input data.

## P

**Parallel communications** A communications technique that uses multiple wires to send all eight bits of a byte at once (in parallel).

**Parallel port** A port for parallel communications; the port to which the printer is usually attached.

**Parameter** A qualifier that you include with a command to define more specifically what you want MS-DOS to do; also called an *argument* or an *option*.

**Parity** An error-detection technique that is used to ensure accuracy during data communication.

**Path** The list of directory names that defines the location of a directory or file.

**Path name** The portion of a file specification that defines the path to the file; can include a drive letter followed by a colon.

**Pipe** To direct the output of one command for use as the input of another command. The pipe symbol MS-DOS uses is the broken vertical bar ( ¦ ).

**Port** The electrical connection through which the computer sends and receives data to and from devices or other computers.

**Printed-circuit card** A thin, rectangular card or board, usually made of fiberglass or epoxy and coated with copper. Electrical circuits and connections are etched into the copper, and electronic devices, such as integrated circuits, are soldered to the circuits. These cards are at the heart of a computer system, giving the machine its ability to perform calculations, store and transfer data, and use the display, disk drives, mouse, printer, modem, and other devices.

**Printer** A device that produces images of text and graphics on paper.

**Print queue** The list of files to be printed; you can create, examine, and modify the print queue with the Print command.

**PRN** Short for *printer*. The printer MS-DOS uses unless instructed otherwise. Can refer to LPT1, LPT2, or LPT3.

**Program** A set of instructions for a computer.

**Prompt** A request displayed by the computer for you to provide some information or perform an action.

**Q**

**Queue** *See* Print queue.

**R**

**RAM** Short for *random access memory*. The memory that MS-DOS uses for programs and data; RAM content changes often while you use the computer and is lost when the computer is turned off.

**RAM disk** A portion of the computer's random access memory reserved for use as a simulated disk drive. Also called an *electronic* or *virtual* disk. Unless saved on a physical disk, the contents of a RAM disk are lost when the computer is turned off.

**Read-only file** A file whose read-only attribute is set so that its contents can be displayed and read but not changed.

**Redirection** The process of causing a command or program to take its input from a file or device other than the keyboard (standard input), or of causing the output of a command or program to be sent to a file or device other than the display (standard output). The MS-DOS redirection symbols are the greater-than ($>$) and less-than ($<$) signs.

**Replaceable parameter** A symbolic reference, consisting of a percent sign followed by a one-digit number (such as %1), that can be included with commands in a batch file to refer to the parameters entered with the batch command. In versions 5 and later of MS-DOS, replaceable parameters can also be used with Doskey; they are represented by a dollar sign followed by a one-digit number (such as $1).

**Return key** The Enter key.

**ROM** Short for *read-only memory*. A type of computer memory that is permanently recorded in hardware. ROM contains instructions that help a computer carry out routine tasks, such as starting itself. The contents of ROM cannot be changed and are not lost when the computer is turned off. On some computers, such as the IBM PS/1 series, MS-DOS is contained in ROM.

**Root directory** The main directory that MS-DOS creates on each disk; the top directory in a multilevel filing system.

## S

**ScanDisk** A program in version 6.2 that checks both the structure of the files on a disk and the surface of the disk itself for errors. In many cases, it can correct the structure errors (recovering lost data) or move files from areas where the disk surface is damaged to undamaged locations.

**Serial communications** A communications technique that transfers information one bit at a time (serially) rather than one byte at a time (in parallel); used in modem communications and with some printers and other devices, such as mice.

**Serial port** The communications port (COM1, COM2, COM3, or COM4) to which a device, such as a modem or a serial printer, can be attached.

**Shell** A program that shows itself to the person using the computer and then passes commands to a different program to be carried out. It's called a shell because it effectively surrounds the other program, hiding it from view. Versions 4 and later of MS-DOS include shell programs that let you use many MS-DOS commands without having to type commands or file names at the system prompt. Other MS-DOS shell programs are also available.

**Software** The programs that are used with a computer system, as opposed to the equipment, or hardware.

**Standard input** The device from which a program reads its input unless the input is redirected; in normal MS-DOS operation, standard input is the keyboard.

**Standard output** The device to which a program sends its output unless the output is redirected; in normal MS-DOS operation, standard output is the display.

**Stop bit** A signal used in serial communications that marks the end of a character.

**Subdirectory** A file that contains directory entries; sometimes also used to refer to the group of files whose directory entries are in the same file.

**System program** A program whose purpose is to control the operation of all or part of the computer system, such as managing the printer or interpreting commands.

**System prompt** The characters MS-DOS displays when it is at the command level (ready to accept a command). Unless you specify otherwise, the system prompt usually shows the current drive and directory followed by a greater-than sign (for example, C:\MS-DOS>).

## T

**Telecommunications** *See* Communications.

**Temporary file** A file that MS-DOS or an application program creates for holding interim data. MS-DOS, for example, creates temporary files when redirecting input or output. Temporary files are deleted by the program when they are no longer needed.

**Text** Ordinary, readable characters, including the uppercase and lowercase letters of the alphabet, the numerals 0 through 9, and punctuation marks.

**Text editor** A program that you use to create or change text files. Also called simply an *editor*.

**Text file** A file that you can read (contains ordinary letters, numerals, and punctuation marks).

## U

**Update** To change a file, creating a new (or updated) version.

**Upper memory area** The area of memory between 640 KB and 1 MB that can be used by versions 5 and later of MS-DOS.

**Upper Memory Block (UMB)** A portion of the upper memory area that can be allocated for use by MS-DOS.

## V

**Video Graphics Array (VGA)** A printed-circuit card, in the system unit of a computer, that controls the display. Shows both text and graphics at medium to high resolution in up to 256 colors.

**Virtual disk** *See* RAM disk.

**Virus** A program that hides itself on a disk or inside a file and can spread itself from system to system. Virus programs eventually do something irritating or even destructive, such as destroying files or formatting a disk.

**Volume label** An identifying name of up to 11 characters that you can assign to a disk.

## W

**Wildcard character** A special character that, like the wild card in a poker game, can be used to represent any other character. MS-DOS recognizes two wildcard characters: the question mark (?), which can represent any single character, and the asterisk (*), which can represent any number of characters.

**Write-protect** To cover the small notch on a 5.25-inch floppy disk or to uncover the opening on a 3.5-inch floppy disk so that new or changed information cannot be written onto the floppy disk.

C

# MS-DOS Command Reference

## <COMMAND> /?
## Command Help

*See* Help (versions 5 and later).

## ANSI.SYS
## Control Program for Screen and Keyboard
### Versions 2 and later

*Page 393*

ANSI.SYS is a program that lets you control the console device. With it, you can manipulate the characters assigned to keys on the keyboard and the color, position, and other attributes of the display. A program that controls a device is called a *device driver;* ANSI.SYS is a device driver that follows the conventions adopted by the American National Standards Institute (ANSI) for screen and keyboard control.

ANSI.SYS is widely used and offers many ways to extend your control over the console. It is used by a few MS-DOS commands, such as Mode, but is not required in your everyday use of MS-DOS. A full description is beyond the scope of this book. Details, explanations, and examples are in *MS-DOS to the Max* by Dan Gookin (Microsoft Press, 1993) and might also be in your MS-DOS manual.

## ANTI-VIRUS
## Look for Viruses

*See* MS Anti-Virus (MSAV) *and* Vsafe.

## APPEND
## Define a Data Path
### Versions 3.2 and later

*Page 165*

The Append command specifies one or more directories that MS-DOS searches for a data file that isn't in the current directory. You can use the Append command on a network. The Append command is entered in either of the following two forms.

As the first use of Append after starting or restarting the system:

**append /E /X**

At any time during a session with MS-DOS:

**append <path> /X:on /X:off /path:on /path:off**

/E makes the data path part of the MS-DOS environment. You can specify /E only if you're using Append for the first time after starting the system. You cannot specify any search directories with this form of the command. Use Append a second time to define appended directories.

/X, beginning with version 3.3, enables MS-DOS to search appended directories for command files (files with the extension COM, EXE, or BAT) as well as data files. The /X parameter lets Append act like the Path command, letting you use program files as if they were in the current directory. In versions 4 and later of MS-DOS, this parameter can be typed as either /x or /x:on.

<path> is the name of the directory to be added to the search path. You can specify a directory on the same or a different drive, or you can specify only a drive letter (such as a:). If you specify more than one drive or directory, separate the path names with a semicolon (;).

/X:on and /X:off, in versions 4 and later, turn the search path on and off. Using /X:off tells MS-DOS not to search appended directories for command files. It has the reverse effect of /X:on (or /X). MS-DOS assumes /X:off unless you specify otherwise.

/path:on and /path:off in versions 4 and later tell MS-DOS whether to search the appended directories for data files in which the file name is preceded by a drive letter, a path, or both. The /path:on parameter tells MS-DOS to include the drive letter or path name; /path:off tells MS-DOS to ignore them. If you don't specify otherwise, MS-DOS assumes /path:on.

If you type append without any parameters, MS-DOS displays the current data path. If you type append ; (note the semicolon), MS-DOS removes all appended directories from the data path.

> **NOTE:** *If you define a data path consisting of several directories, MS-DOS doesn't tell you where it found a file you requested. Nor does MS-DOS necessarily save a revised file in its original directory if the directory is part of the data path. It might instead save the file in the current directory. If you're not using version 4 or later, use the Append command with care. If you are using one of these versions, the /path:off parameter helps to overcome this problem.*

### Examples

To tell MS-DOS to search the appended data path for command files as well as data files (versions 4 and later):

```
C:\>append /x:on
```

To tell MS-DOS to search for data files in \MKT\WP and \ENG\WP on drive C:

```
C:\>append \mkt\wp;\eng\wp
```

433

To display appended directories:

```
C:\>append
```

To remove all directories from the data path:

```
C:\>append ;
```

## ASSIGN
## Route Disk Operations to a Different Drive
### Versions 3 through 5, IBM releases 2 through 5

The Assign command routes requests for disk operations on one drive to a different drive. Its primary use is with application programs that look for files on a specific drive (such as B) and don't let you specify a different drive (such as C).

**assign <drive1>=<drive2> /sta**

<drive1> is the letter of the drive to be assigned.

<drive2> is the letter of the drive that is to be used instead of <drive1>.

*/sta* (short for *status*) exists in version 5 only; it tells MS-DOS to display a report on drives you've assigned.

Both <drive1> and <drive2> must refer to existing disk drives, including hard disks and RAM drives. Do not, however, assign your hard disk (such as C) to another drive. You can assign more than one drive in a single Assign command by separating the <drive1>=<drive2> pairs with blanks.

If you omit all parameters (just type *assign*), MS-DOS deletes all drive assignments so that all drive letters refer to their original drives.

> **NOTE:** *The Assign command masks the actual type of disk drive from MS-DOS, so use it only when necessary, and don't enter a Backup, Restore, Label, Join, Substitute, or Print command that uses an assigned drive. Two MS-DOS commands—Format and Diskcopy—ignore any drive assignments made with the Assign command. If you have version 3.1 or later, use the Substitute command instead of the Assign command; for example, type* subst b: c:<path> *instead of* assign b=c.

### Examples
To assign drive B to drive C:

```
C:\>assign b=c
```

To assign drives A and B to drive D:

```
C:\>assign a=d b=d
```

To display a report of assigned drives:

```
C:\>assign /sta
Original A: set to D:
Original B: set to D:
```

To reset all drive letters to their original drives:

```
C:\>assign
```

## ATTRIBUTE
## Display or Change File Attributes
### Versions 3 and later

*Page 174*

The Attribute command (attrib) displays or changes any of up to four attributes of a file: read-only, archive, hidden, and system.

If a file is read-only, you cannot change or delete the file. If a file's archive attribute is on, the Backup, Restore, and Xcopy commands can use the attribute's status to determine whether the file should be copied (archived) to another disk.

Beginning with version 5, you can also give a file the hidden and system attributes. Neither hidden nor system files appear in directory listings unless you specifically request them with the /A (Attributes) parameter of the Directory command. These files are also unaffected by Rename and certain other commands.

The hidden attribute can be applied to data files you want to keep personal or keep from cluttering the screen. The system attribute is traditionally reserved for a command file used only by MS-DOS. It's usually used only by programmers and is included here for completeness only.

**attrib +R -R +A -A +H -H +S -S <filename> /S**

+R assigns the read-only attribute; −R removes it.

+A (versions 3.2 and later) assigns the archive attribute; −A removes it.

+H (versions 5 and later) assigns the hidden attribute; −H removes it.

+S (versions 5 and later) assigns the system attribute; −S removes it.

You can set or change more than one attribute in a single command by separating the attributes with a blank.

<filename> is the name of the file whose attribute or attributes are to be displayed or changed. The file name can include a drive letter, followed by a colon, and a path name if appropriate.

/S applies the Attribute command to all subdirectories contained in <filename> (versions 3.3 and later).

If you type only *attrib <filename>*, MS-DOS displays the attribute status of the file(s) to the left of their file names.

### Examples

Assume that drive C includes a directory named C:\MKT. To make the file named REPORT.DOC in C:\MKT a read-only file:

```
C:\>attrib +r \mkt\report.doc
```

To make the file named BUDGET.XLS in C:\MKT both read-only and hidden:

```
C:\>attrib +r +h \mkt\budget.xls
```

To display the attributes of all files in C:\MKT:

```
C:\>attrib \mkt\*.*
```

MS-DOS responds:

```
A    R      C:\MKT\REPORT.DOC
A           C:\MKT\FORECAST.DOC
A           C:\MKT\SALESREP.DOC
A    HR     C:\MKT\BUDGET.XLS
            C:\MKT\FIRSTQTR.XLS
```

To remove the hidden attribute from BUDGET.XLS:

```
C:\>attrib -h \mkt\budget.xls
```

# BACKUP
## Make a Backup Copy of Files
### Versions 2 through 5

*Page 232*

The Backup command makes a backup copy of files so that you can safeguard data against damage or other loss. Files can be backed up from and to any type of source and target disk. Rather than making an exact copy of the file, as the Copy command does, the Backup command records the directory from which each file was backed up. The Restore command uses this data to reinstate files in the correct locations.

Although the Backup command is present in versions 2 through 5, not all the parameters described here are in every release of MS-DOS; refer to your MS-DOS manual to find out which parameters are available to you.

**backup <path><filename> <drive> /A /S /M /F:<size> /D:<date> /T:<time> /L:<logfile>**

<path> and <filename> specify the file or files to be backed up. You must specify at least a drive letter, followed by a colon. You can include a path name or a file name, or both, and you can use wildcard characters.

<drive> is the letter, followed by a colon, of the drive that contains the backup disk (such as *a:*). In versions earlier than 3.3, the backup disk must be formatted.

/A adds the backup files to the backup disk. If you don't use /A, MS-DOS displays a warning message and then erases any files on the target disk before copying the files. If you omit /A, be sure the backup disk doesn't contain any files you want to keep.

/S backs up all files in all subdirectories contained in the current directory or the specified directory.

/M backs up only files that have been modified since they were last backed up.

/F:<size>, available in versions 3.3 through 5, formats the target disk if it isn't already formatted. If you specify /F, the current command path must include the directory containing the file FORMAT.COM.

- In version 3.3, you cannot specify <size>. Backup formats the target disk to match the capacity of the drive, so if you use /F, do not put a low-density floppy disk in a high-density drive; put a 1.2 MB floppy disk in a 1.2 MB drive, a 1.44 MB floppy disk in a 1.44 MB drive, and so on. Lower-capacity floppy disks (such as 360 KB floppy disks) formatted for high capacity (such as 1.2 MB) cannot always be read reliably.

- In versions 4 and 5, Backup automatically formats an unformatted floppy disk to match the normal capacity of the floppy disk drive. Specify /F:<size> only if the capacity of the target disk does not match that of the drive in which you put it—for example, a 360 KB floppy disk in a 1.2 MB drive. <size> can be 160, 180, 320, 360, 720, 1.2, 1.44, or (in version 5) 2.88.

/D:<date> backs up only files that have been modified since the date specified in <date>. Specify <date> as you would for the Date command.

/T:<time> backs up all files that have changed since <time> on <date>. Specify <time> as you would for the Time command.

/L:<logfile> creates a log file on the source drive that contains the date and time of the backup, the path name and file name of each file that is backed up, and the backup number that MS-DOS assigned to the floppy disk on which the file is backed up. If a log file already exists, the backup information is added at the end, creating a history of backups for the source drive. If you don't specify a name for the log file, MS-DOS names it BACKUP.LOG and stores it in the root directory of the source drive.

MS-DOS displays the name of each file as it is backed up. If the target disk is a floppy disk, the backup files are stored in its root directory. If the target disk is a hard disk, the backup files are stored in a directory named \BACKUP.

If the files to be backed up require more than one floppy disk, MS-DOS prompts you to insert another floppy disk; be sure to label these disks because the Restore command asks for them by number. Files can't be backed up from a write-protected floppy disk.

When it finishes, the Backup command reports to MS-DOS on the backup procedure by setting an internal value named *errorlevel* to one of the following:

- 0: Backup was completed successfully.

- 1: No files were found to back up.

- 2: Some files were not backed up because of conflicting file-sharing needs (networks only).

- 3: Ctrl-C was pressed to end the backup process before all files were backed up.

- 4: System problems stopped the backup process.

If you use batch files to help with your backup procedure, you can check this value with the *errorlevel* option of the If batch command and use the result to control which other commands are carried out in a batch file.

NOTE: *Because the Backup command varies among different versions of MS-DOS, it's advisable to use the same version both to back up and to restore files. In particular, do not try to use version 3.3 or later to restore files backed up with version 3.2 or earlier.*

*Do not back up files from a drive that is affected by an Assign, Substitute, or Join command; restoring the files with the Restore command can damage the directory structure of the disk to which the files are restored.*

### Examples

To back up all files with the extension DOC from the current drive and directory to the disk in drive A and create the log file named BACKUP.LOG:

```
C:\>backup c:*.doc a: /l
```

To back up to drive A all files in all subdirectories on drive C that have been modified since they were last backed up:

```
C:\>backup c:\ a: /s /m
```

(If the disk in drive A is filled before all the files are backed up, you are prompted to insert a new disk. If you're using a version earlier than 3.3 and you regularly back up large files from a hard disk to floppy disks, prepare an adequate supply of formatted floppy disks before beginning a backup procedure. If you're using version 3.3 with unformatted floppy disks, use the /F parameter.)

To back up all files whose extension is DOC from the current directory and all its subdirectories in drive D to the disk in drive A and add them to the backup disk:

```
C:\>backup d:*.doc a: /s /a
```

To back up all files whose extension is DOC that were changed on or after October 16, 1993, backing them up from the directory \WORD\MKT on the disk in drive C to the disk in drive A:

```
C:\>backup c:\word\mkt\*.doc a: /d:10-16-93
```

## BACKUP (MSBACKUP)
## Make a Backup Copy of Files or Restore Files

*See* MSbackup (MSBACKUP).

## BATCH COMMANDS AND BATCH FILES
## Executing a File of MS-DOS Commands

*Chapters 14 through 17*

In addition to typing MS-DOS commands at command level, you can put one or more commands in a batch file—a file with the extension BAT. When you create a batch file, you group commands in the order and combination in which you want them carried out. MS-DOS carries out all the commands, in order, when you type the name of the batch file. Batch files can save typing time, tailor MS-DOS to work with your equipment, and make MS-DOS commands easy to use, even for people who know little about computers.

One widely used batch file is the special file named AUTOEXEC.BAT, which must be in the root directory of the startup disk. MS-DOS carries out the commands in AUTOEXEC.BAT whenever you start or restart the system, so this file lets you set up MS-DOS to match your system and preferences.

### Batch Commands

Several MS-DOS commands are intended primarily for use in batch files:

- Call carries out the commands in another batch file, then returns to complete the original batch file (versions 3.3 and later). *See* Call.

- Choice displays a prompt and allows the user to make a choice. You can then use If commands to take action based on the user's response. *See* Choice.

- Echo controls whether MS-DOS displays (echoes) each command it carries out. You can also use the Echo command to display a message or to tell you whether the echo option is on or off. *See* Echo.

- For repeatedly carries out an MS-DOS command according to limits that you set. *See* For.

- Goto tells MS-DOS to skip to a different location in a batch file, rather than carry out the next sequential command. *See* Goto.

- If tests a condition and, if the condition is true, carries out an MS-DOS command you specify. *See* If.

- Pause stops carrying out commands and waits for a key to be pressed before continuing with the next command in a batch file. *See* Pause.

- Rem lets you include comments (remarks) in a batch file. *See* Rem.

- Shift moves a series of command-line parameters entered with a batch command one position to the left. The first parameter is lost, the second parameter becomes the first, and so on. *See* Shift.

## BREAK
## Controlling When MS-DOS Checks for Ctrl-C
**Versions 2 and later**

The Break command lets you control how often MS-DOS checks to find out whether you typed Ctrl-C (or Ctrl-Break on some machines) to end a program. Normally, MS-DOS checks for Ctrl-C only when it reads or writes characters from or to a standard character device, such as the display, a printer, or a communications port.

**break on off**

*on* tells MS-DOS to extend its Ctrl-C checking—for example, to include each time it reads from or writes to a disk drive.

*off* tells MS-DOS to check for Ctrl-C only when it reads from or writes to a standard character device.

If you enter *break* with no parameters, MS-DOS displays the current break status: either *BREAK is on* or *BREAK is off.*

If break is off, your system runs somewhat faster than when break is on, but you have fewer opportunities to stop a program that spends a lot of time doing computations without using an input or output character device.

MS-DOS starts with break off unless you specify otherwise. You can use the Break command described here to set break on any time after starting MS-DOS, or you can tell MS-DOS to start with break on by including the similar Break configuration command in CONFIG.SYS. For information on the Break configuration command, see the next entry.

### Examples

To turn break on:

```
C:\>break on
```

To turn break off:

```
C:\>break off
```

To display the break status:

```
C:\>break
```

## BREAK (CONFIGURATION COMMAND)
## Controlling When MS-DOS Checks for Ctrl-C

### Versions 2 and later

Like the MS-DOS Break command, the Break configuration command controls how often MS-DOS checks for Ctrl-C. MS-DOS normally starts with break off, meaning that it checks for Ctrl-C whenever it reads from or writes to a character device, such as the keyboard or display. You can set the break status with the MS-DOS Break command any time while you're using MS-DOS. You can also start MS-DOS with break on by placing a *break=on* configuration command in CONFIG.SYS. If you need more information on this command, refer to the documentation that came with your version of MS-DOS.

## BUFFERS (CONFIGURATION COMMAND)
## Controlling the Number of Disk Buffers

### Versions 1 and later

*Page 396*

The Buffers configuration command specifies how many disk buffers MS-DOS sets aside each time it starts. A disk buffer is an area of memory that MS-DOS uses to hold data being read from or written to disk. MS-DOS creates the buffers in a portion of the computer's memory. Each buffer holds one sector (about 530 bytes, or 0.5 KB) of information, so the more buffers you use, the less memory is available for programs. If you have version 5 and are running MS-DOS in the HMA portion of extended memory, the buffers are also placed in the HMA and thus leave more conventional memory for programs and data.

Unless you specify otherwise with a Buffers command in CONFIG.SYS, MS-DOS uses the following number of buffers:

2   If the system has 360 KB floppy disk drives and less than 128 KB of memory.

3   If the system has a floppy disk drive with a capacity greater than 360 KB.

5   If the system has more than 128 KB of conventional memory (versions 3.3 and later).

10  If the system has more than 256 KB of conventional memory (versions 3.3 and later).

15  If the system has 512 KB to 640 KB of conventional memory (versions 3.3 and later).

The optimum number of buffers depends on several factors, among them:

- The type and size of disk drives you use. If you have a hard disk, you can increase speed by setting the number of buffers to 20 for a hard disk up to 40 MB, 30 for a disk of 40 to 79 MB, 40 for a disk of 80 to 119 MB, or 50 for a disk of 120 MB or more.

- The type of programs you use. If you use applications that normally access files sequentially rather than by jumping from one place to another, 10 to 20 buffers can increase speed by keeping information in memory and reducing the number of times MS-DOS must go out to disk.

- The type of file structure you use. If you have a large, multilevel subdirectory structure, using 10 to 25 buffers can significantly speed disk operations.

Beginning with version 4, the Buffers command also includes a secondary-cache feature. This feature tells MS-DOS that, whenever it reads one sector, it should also "look ahead" at following sectors and read them into memory as well. Using this look-ahead feature, especially with programs that access information sequentially, increases the store of information that MS-DOS keeps in memory and can find quickly without resorting to relatively slow disk-read operations.

The Buffers command can have three parameters:

**buffers=<number>,<look-ahead> /X**

<number> is the number of buffers to set aside, from 1 through 99. If you have version 4 and a system with expanded memory, you can place buffers in

expanded memory with the /X parameter. In this case, <number> can be from 1 through 10000.

<look-ahead>, in versions 4 and later, is the number of buffers for holding sectors you want MS-DOS to read beyond the sector currently being used. <look-ahead> can be from 1 through 8. Each look-ahead buffer takes about 530 bytes of additional memory. If you already use a disk-caching program, such as Smart-Drive in versions 4 and later, you can ignore this look-ahead feature because your program should work as well as, or better than, a secondary cache created with the Buffers command.

/X, in version 4 only, tells MS-DOS to put the buffers in expanded memory.

### Examples

To allocate 30 buffers, put the following Buffers command in CONFIG.SYS:

```
buffers=30
```

To allocate 30 regular buffers and allow 4 look-ahead buffers:

```
buffers=30,4
```

## CALL (BATCH COMMAND)
## Carry Out Another Batch File
### Versions 3.3 and later

*Page 369*

You can use the Call batch command in a batch file to tell MS-DOS to carry out the commands in a second batch file, then return to the original batch file and continue with the next command in it instead of returning to the system prompt. This lets you use a batch command of your own making in a batch file just as you would use any other MS-DOS command.

### call <batchfile> <parameters>

<batchfile> is the name of the file of commands you want MS-DOS to carry out. Include a drive letter, path, or both if the batch file you call is not in the current directory.

<parameters> represents any parameters that <batchfile> requires. You can enter the parameters themselves, or you can use replaceable parameters so that parameters typed on the command line with the name of the first batch file are passed along to the batch file being called.

### Example

Suppose you have two batch files. One, named SORTFILE.BAT, first uses the Sort command to sort the file whose name you type as a parameter with *sortfile*, then

443

redirects the sorted output to the printer; the other, WEEKRPT.BAT, carries out several commands to print a series of sorted lists that make up a weekly report.

To use the SORTFILE batch command in WEEKRPT.BAT to print the sorted version of the file named REPORT.LST, include the following Call command in WEEKRPT.BAT:

```
call sortfile report.lst
```

MS-DOS carries out the commands in SORTFILE.BAT—printing the sorted version of REPORT.LST—and continues with the command that follows the Call command in WEEKRPT.BAT.

## CHANGE CODE PAGE (CHCP)
## Display or Change System-Wide Code Page
### Version 3.3

The Change Code Page command (chcp) tells MS-DOS which code page to use for all devices that have been prepared for code-page switching. You use it to display the current code page or to change code pages when you want to change the language or character set that MS-DOS uses. The *codepage select* option of the Mode command changes the code page for individual devices.

**chcp <codepage>**

<codepage> is the three-digit number from the list below that specifies a particular code page (852, Slavic, is in versions 5 and later only).

| Code-Page Number | Code Page |
|---|---|
| 437 | United States |
| 850 | Multilingual (Latin I) |
| 852 | Slavic (Latin II) |
| 860 | Portuguese |
| 863 | French Canadian |
| 865 | Nordic |

If you omit <codepage>, MS-DOS displays the number of the current code page. If you specify a code page but it cannot be activated for all devices that support code-page switching, MS-DOS responds *Code page nnn not prepared for all devices.*

You must execute the National Language Support Function (nlsfunc) command before you can use the Change Code Page command to change a code page.

### Examples

To change the system code page to multilingual (850):

```
C:\>chcp 850
```

To display the current code page (assume that it's 850):

```
C:\>chcp
```

MS-DOS responds *Active code page: 850.*

## CHANGE DIRECTORY (CD)
## Change Current Directory

### Versions 2 and later

*Page 147*

The Change Directory command (cd or chdir) changes or displays the current directory.

> **cd <drive><path>**

<drive> is the letter, followed by a colon, of the drive whose current directory is to be displayed or changed.

<path> is the path name of the directory that is to become the current directory.

If you omit <path>, MS-DOS displays the current directory of the disk in <drive>. If you omit both <drive> and <path>, MS-DOS displays the current directory of the disk in the current drive.

### Examples

To change the current directory on the disk in the current drive to \MKT\WP:

```
C:\>cd \mkt\wp
```

To change the current directory on the disk in drive A to \MKT\WP:

```
C:\>cd a:\mkt\wp
```

To display the current directory of the disk in the current drive:

```
C:\>cd
```

To display the current directory of the disk in drive D:

```
C:\>cd d:
```

## CHECK DISK (CHKDSK)
## Check Disk Status

### Versions 1 and later

*Pages 107, 160*

> **NOTE:** *If you're using version 6.2, the ScanDisk program is a better tool for detecting and correcting disk errors. See the topic "Checking a Disk for Errors" in Chapter 9, "Managing Your Hard Disk," and the ScanDisk entry in this appendix.*

The Check Disk command (chkdsk) checks the allocation of storage on a disk and displays a report that shows the total amount of disk space, how much is used by directories and files, including hidden files, and how much is not available because of disk imperfections. Chkdsk also tells you how much memory is in the system and how much is free for use. Beginning with version 4, chkdsk also reports on disk usage in terms of allocation units (storage units consisting of groups of bytes).

> **chkdsk <drive><filename> /V /F**

<drive> is the letter, followed by a colon, of the drive that contains the disk to be checked (such as *a:*). If you omit <drive>, MS-DOS checks the disk in the current drive.

<filename> specifies one or more files to be checked for fragmentation (stored in two or more nonadjacent locations on the disk). If you don't specify a drive, chkdsk checks the disk in the current drive. If you don't specify a path, chkdsk checks the current directory. If you omit <filename>, chkdsk checks storage on the entire disk.

/V displays the full path name and file name of each file and directory on the disk being checked (versions 2 and later).

/F tells chkdsk to correct allocation errors, if it finds any and if you respond *y* when it notifies you of the errors and asks whether to correct them. Correcting allocation errors requires changing the information on the disk and may cause loss of some data, so this parameter safeguards against disk changes unless you approve them (versions 2 and later).

If chkdsk finds errors in the allocation of disk space, it refers to this space as *allocation units* (or *clusters*) and *chains* and asks whether you want to recover the space into a file. If you reply *y*, chkdsk corrects the errors only if you included the /F parameter. The space is then recovered into a file named FILE*nnnn*.CHK in the root directory of the drive being checked (*nnnn* is a sequence number that starts with 0000).

If you specify a file name or a set of file names (by using wildcards) when you enter the chkdsk command, the chkdsk report tells you whether any of the files are fragmented by displaying the name of each file, followed by the message

*Contains* n *non-contiguous blocks.* A badly fragmented disk can slow performance. If too many files on a floppy disk are fragmented and you have version 6 or 6.2 of MS-DOS, use the Defrag program to restore the files to contiguous sectors. If you have an earlier version, copy all the fragmented files to another floppy disk with the Copy command (*copy* *.*). If too many files on a hard disk are fragmented, restore them to contiguous sectors with Defrag (or another disk-reorganizing program if you don't have version 6 or 6.2) or by using MS-DOS to back up all the files, reformat the hard disk, and restore the files to the hard disk.

> NOTE: *Chkdsk cannot be used with a drive created or affected by the Assign, Join, or Substitute command, nor can it be used with a network drive. Chkdsk can be used on a disk compressed by the DoubleSpace program, but it only checks the drive's file allocation tables. Use the DoubleSpace command with the /chkdsk parameter to verify the integrity of the compressed drive.*

### Examples

To check the disk in the current drive:

```
C:\>chkdsk
```

If there are no errors, chkdsk displays a report like this:

```
Volume HARD DISK  created 10-16-1993 3:31p
Volume Serial Number is 1608-5A30

 33462272 bytes total disk space
   112640 bytes in 5 hidden files
    86016 bytes in 34 directories
 25919488 bytes in 967 user files
    10240 bytes in bad sectors
  7333888 bytes available on disk

     2048 bytes in each allocation unit
    16339 total allocation units on disk
     3581 available allocation units on disk

   655360 total bytes memory
   513072 bytes free
```

To check the disk in drive A, checking all files in the directory \MKT\WP to see if they are fragmented:

```
C:\>chkdsk a:\mkt\wp\*.*
```

Chkdsk displays its usual report, followed by a list of any fragmented files:

```
A:\MKT\WP\REPORT.DOC Contains 2 non-contiguous blocks
A:\MKT\WP\FORECAST.DOC Contains 5 non-contiguous blocks
A:\MKT\WP\SALESREP.DOC Contains 4 non-contiguous blocks
```

To check the disk in the current drive and tell chkdsk you want to be able to recover any lost clusters:

```
C:\>chkdsk /f
```

Chkdsk displays its usual report. If there are allocation errors, it displays a message similar to this:

```
x lost allocation units found in y chains.
Convert lost chains to files (Y/N)?
```

If you want to recover the lost units, reply *y*. When the command has completed, display the files named FILE*nnnn*.CHK. Rename them if they contain data you want to keep, or delete them to make the disk space available to other files.

## CHOICE (BATCH COMMAND)
## Prompt the User to Make a Choice
### Versions 6 and 6.2

*Page 371*

The Choice batch command displays a prompt and then waits for the user to press one of the specified keys. This allows you to write batch files that can take various actions based on the user's response.

**choice /C:<keys> /N /S /T:<character>,<seconds> <prompt>**

/C:<keys> specifies the characters that are allowable responses. If you don't specify /C:<keys>, Choice uses YN. If the user presses the first key, Choice sets the MS-DOS *errorlevel* value to 1, and if the user presses the second key, Choice sets *errorlevel* to 2, and so forth. You can then use the If command to take action based on the value of *errorlevel*.

/N tells Choice not to display the allowable keys at the end of the prompt. By default, Choice displays in brackets the characters you specified in /C:<keys>, followed by a question mark. (Even if you use /N, the specified keys still work.)

/S causes Choice to distinguish between uppercase and lowercase letters. If you don't specify /S, Choice considers the uppercase and lowercase form of a given letter to be the same.

/T:<character>,<seconds> tells Choice to act as though the user pressed a particular key if the user makes no choice within the specified length of time. <character> must be one of the characters you specified in /C:<keys> (or Y or N if you didn't use /C:<keys>), and <seconds> is the number of seconds (from 0 through 99) Choice will wait for the user to make a choice. If you specify 0 for <seconds>, Choice will continue only after the user makes a choice.

<prompt> is text you want Choice to display. Unless you use /N, Choice will display the allowable keys in brackets and a question mark after <prompt>.

448

If the user presses a key that is not allowed, Choice beeps. If Choice encounters an error, it sets the *errorlevel* value to 255. If the user presses Ctrl-C or Ctrl-Break, Choice sets *errorlevel* to 0.

## Examples

To ask the user to simply choose between Yes and No, type:

```
C:\>choice Continue
```

Choice will display the following prompt and wait for the user to respond:

```
Continue [Y,N]?
```

To ask the user whether to delete a file (with the option to cancel the operation) and have Choice assume No if the user presses no key within 15 seconds:

```
C:\>choice /C:YNC /T:N,15 Do you want to delete this file
```

Choice displays the following prompt:

```
Do you want to delete this file [Y,N,C]?
```

If the user does not respond after 15 seconds have elapsed, Choice will display *N* after the question mark and set the *errorlevel* value to 2. (For a sample batch file using this command, see the Goto batch command.)

# CLS
# Clear the Screen

### Versions 2 and later

*Page 118*

The Clear Screen command clears the screen and displays the system prompt in the upper left hand corner. Clear Screen has no parameters.

**cls**

## Example

To clear the screen:

```
C:\>cls
```

# COMMAND
# Start a New Command Processor

### Versions 1 and later

The Command command loads another copy of the MS-DOS command processor (COMMAND.COM), the program that displays the system prompt and responds to the commands you type.

**command /P /C <command>**

/P makes the new copy of COMMAND.COM permanent. It displays the sign-on message and system prompt and waits for a command. There is no way to return to the previous command processor (versions 2 and later).

/C <command> loads the new copy of COMMAND.COM, carries out the command specified by <command>, and returns control to the previous command processor (versions 2 and later).

If you enter a Command command with no parameters, the new copy of COMMAND.COM displays the sign-on message and system prompt and waits for a command. The new copy of COMMAND.COM remains in memory until you type *exit*. Control then returns to the previous command processor.

If you put a Command command with the /C parameter in a batch file and use it to carry out another batch file, MS-DOS continues with the next statement in the first batch file when the second batch file completes. This allows a batch file to call another batch file, as well as to chain to another batch file. This technique is unnecessary in versions 3.3 and later because they include the Call command.

### Examples

To load a new copy of COMMAND.COM that remains in control until you type *exit*:

```
C:\>command
```

To load a permanent new copy of COMMAND.COM:

```
C:\>command /p
```

To cause a batch file (BATCH1.BAT) to load a new copy of COMMAND.COM, carry out the commands in a second batch file (BATCH2.BAT), finish carrying out the commands in the first batch file, and return to the previous command processor, put the following command in BATCH1.BAT:

```
command /c batch2.bat
```

## COMPARE (COMP)
## Compare Two Files

### Version 3.3, IBM releases 1 through 5

*Page 83*

The Compare command (comp) compares two files or sets of files byte by byte and reports up to 10 differences for each comparison. If it finds any differences, Compare displays the location of each. In all versions of MS-DOS in which it appears, Compare displays the hexadecimal (base-16) value of the differing bytes. In version 5, you can specify decimal values or ASCII characters instead, and you can also tell Compare to display line numbers, compare a specified number of lines, and ignore differences between uppercase and lowercase.

If the files are the same, Compare displays *Files compare OK.* If the files are different lengths, Compare displays *Files are different sizes* and quits comparing the files. If the files are the same length but their content differs, Compare displays the locations and values of up to 10 bytes that differ; if more than 10 bytes differ, it displays the message *10 Mismatches - ending compare.* After completing any comparison, Compare asks whether you want to compare more files. If you type *y,* Compare prompts for the names of the next files to compare and, if you have version 5, any options, such as decimal, ASCII, or line numbers, that you want to specify.

### comp <file1> <file2> <option>

<file1> is the name of the first file to be compared. You can include a drive and path, and you can use wildcard characters to specify a group of files with similar names or extensions.

<file2> is the name of the second file to be compared. You can include a drive and path, and you can use wildcard characters. If you specify only a drive letter or path name, Compare compares <file1> to the file with the same name on the drive or in the directory you specified in <file2>. If you use wildcard characters in <file1>, Compare finds and compares all files in the second set that match the file specification.

If you omit <file2>, Compare prompts for it. If you omit both <file1> and <file2> by typing *comp* with no parameters, Compare prompts for both file names (and options in version 5).

<option> is the version 5 parameter that lets you specify the type of comparison you want. If you don't specify an option, Compare displays any differences it finds in hexadecimal, which, though invaluable to programmers, is generally indecipherable to other people. To help you make the report more understandable and to let you refine the comparison, version 5 offers these alternatives:

- /D to display decimal rather than hexadecimal numbers.

- /A to translate numbers into recognizable characters according to the widely used code called ASCII.

- /L to display the line number where a difference occurs.

- /N=*xxx* to compare only a specified (*xxx*) number of lines.

- /C to ignore the difference between uppercase and lowercase letters.

### Examples

Suppose that the current directory (C:\) contains FILE1 and FILE2. FILE1 contains the words *This is a sample file.* FILE2 contains the words *This one is different.* The directory \DOCS on the same drive contains identical files—same names, same contents.

To compare the two files in the current directory:

```
C:\>comp file1 file2
```

Because the files are the same lengths but more than 10 bytes differ, Compare would display the locations and values of the differences followed by *10 Mismatches - ending compare.*

To compare FILE1 in the current directory with \DOCS\FILE1:

```
C:\>comp file1 \docs\file1
```

Because the files are the same, Compare would display *Files compare OK.*

To compare FILE1 in the current directory with \DOCS\FILE2 and display the characters that differ:

```
C:\>comp file1 \docs\file2 /a
```

Compare would display 10 characters that differ in each file and end the comparison.

Finally, suppose each file were 100 lines long. To compare the first 20 lines of FILE1 and FILE2 and display the line numbers where differences occur:

```
C:\>comp file1 file2 /n=20 /l
```

# CONFIG.SYS
## File of System Configuration Commands

*Page 381*

CONFIG.SYS is a file that contains configuration commands that define the hardware and software that make up your system. It must be in the root directory of the system disk. Each time MS-DOS starts, it carries out the commands in the CONFIG.SYS file. If there is no file named CONFIG.SYS in the root directory of the system disk, MS-DOS assumes certain configuration values.

The configuration commands include:

- Break, which controls how often MS-DOS checks for Ctrl-C. *See* Break.

- Buffers, which specifies how many disk buffers MS-DOS sets aside. *See* Buffers.

- Country, which specifies the country whose date and time format is to be used. *See* Country.

- Device, which identifies a file that contains a program to control a device (such a program is called a *device driver*). *See* Device.

- Devicehigh, which enables MS-DOS to load device drivers into the upper memory area (the portion of memory between 640 KB and 1 MB) on computers with an 80386 or 80486 microprocessor and extended memory. *See* Devicehigh.

- Dos, which serves two functions: telling MS-DOS whether to load itself into conventional or extended memory and maintaining access to the upper memory area so that programs can be loaded into it. *See* Dos.

- Drivparm, which defines the operating characteristics of a disk or a tape drive. *See* Drive Parameters—Drivparm.

- FCBS, which specifies the number of files controlled by File Control Blocks (FCBs) that can be open at the same time. *See* FCBS.

- Files, which specifies how many files controlled by handles can be open at the same time. *See* Files.

- Include, which includes all of one configuration block inside another configuration block. *See* Include.

- Install, which loads a command file from CONFIG.SYS. *See* Install.

- Lastdrive, which sets the highest drive letter that MS-DOS recognizes. *See* Lastdrive.

- Menucolor, which sets the colors for the startup menu. *See* Menucolor.

- Menudefault, which specifies the default choice for the startup menu. *See* Menudefault.

- Menuitem, which defines an item on the startup menu. *See* Menuitem.

- Numlock, which tells MS-DOS whether to set the Num Lock key on or off. *See* Numlock.

- Rem, which lets you add a comment within CONFIG.SYS or temporarily disable a line. *See* Rem.

- Set, which creates an environment variable and assigns a value to it. *See* Set.

- Shell, which specifies the name of a command processor to be used instead of COMMAND.COM. *See* Shell.

- Stacks, which tells MS-DOS how much memory to reserve for its temporary use. *See* Stacks.

- Submenu, which defines an item on the startup menu that, when chosen, takes you to another set of choices. *See* Submenu.

- Switches, which blocks enhanced keyboard functions. *See* Switches.

CONFIG.SYS is a text file; you can create it or modify an existing version with a text editor, such as Edit or Edlin, or with a word processor that lets you store a file without formatting codes.

## COPY

### Copy a File or Device

**Versions 1 and later**

Copy is one of the most flexible and often-used MS-DOS commands. It lets you duplicate, store, move, display, and even print files. Because Copy can be used in different ways, the command is described in four entries that cover:

- Copying one or more files from one location (drive or directory) to another.

- Copying one or more files to a device, such as a printer.

- Copying from a device, such as the keyboard, to a file or another device.

- Combining files.

## COPY

### Copy a File to Another File (Location)

*Page 74*

This form of the Copy command duplicates a file on the same or a different disk. You can give the copy the same file name if you're copying to another drive or directory. If you want to duplicate a file in the same directory (for example, to create a second copy for editing), you must give it a different name or extension because MS-DOS doesn't allow two files with the same name in the same directory.

**copy <file1> <file2> /A /B /V**

<file1> is the file to be copied. You can include a drive letter, a path name, or both, and you can use wildcard characters to copy a set of files with similar names or extensions.

<file2> is the file to which <file1> is copied. If <file1> is not on the current drive or in the current directory and you omit <file2>, MS-DOS copies <file1> to a file with the same name in the current directory of the current drive. If you specify <file2> as a drive letter, a path name, a file name (and extension), or all three, MS-DOS copies <file1> as follows:

| Target | Source File Is Copied To |
|--------|--------------------------|
| Drive letter | A file with the same name in the current directory of the specified drive |
| Path name | A file with the same name in the specified directory |
| File name | A file with the specified name in the current directory |
| All three | A file with the specified file name, in the specified drive and directory |

**NOTE:** *Be very careful when you specify <file2> if you're using version 6 or earlier. If a file with the same name already exists in the drive and directory you specify, those versions of MS-DOS replace the existing file with the copy, deleting the original version without warning you.*

/A (for *ASCII*) treats the file as a text file. You can include /A either before or after <file2>. If /A precedes <file2>, MS-DOS copies up to the first Ctrl-Z character in each file specified by <file1>. The Ctrl-Z and any data that follows are not copied. If /A follows <file2>, MS-DOS adds a Ctrl-Z character to the end of each file specified by <file2>. When MS-DOS combines files or copies to or from a device, it uses the /A option.

/B (for *binary*) treats the file as a non-text file. If /B precedes <file2>, MS-DOS copies everything, including the end-of-file mark, in each file specified by <file1>. If /B follows <file2>, MS-DOS does not add a Ctrl-Z character at the end of each file it copies.

Both /A and /B affect the preceding file and all subsequent file names in the command up to, but not including, a file name followed by /A or /B.

/V verifies that the file was copied correctly. MS-DOS turns verification on, copies the file, then turns verification off. You don't need this parameter if you've turned on the MS-DOS verify option with the Verify command. Verification slows the copy process.

### Examples

To copy the file named LETTER.DOC from the disk in drive A to the current directory (MKT\WP) of the current drive (C):

```
C:\MKT\WP>copy a:letter.doc
```

To copy the file named FORECAST.DOC from the directory \MKT\BUDGET on the disk in drive A to the directory \MKT\WP on the disk in the current drive (C):

```
C:\>copy a:\mkt\budget\forecast.doc \mkt\wp
```

To copy the file named REPORT.TXT from the root directory of drive A to a file named FINAL.RPT in the directory named \MKT\WP on the disk in the current drive:

```
C:\>copy a:\report.txt \mkt\wp\final.rpt
```

To copy all files with the extension TXT from the current directory of the disk in drive D to the current drive and directory (C:\MKT\WP), giving the copies the extension DOC:

```
C:\MKT\WP>copy d:*.txt *.doc
```

# COPY
## Copy a File to a Device
### Versions 1 and later

*Page 76*

This form of the Copy command copies one or more files from a disk to a device such as the printer.

#### copy <filename> <device> /A /B

<filename> is the name of the file or files to copy. You can use wildcards to specify more than one file, and you can precede the file name with a drive letter (followed by a colon), a path name, or both.

<device> is the name of the device, usually CON or PRN, to which <file> is to be copied.

/A and /B specify ASCII and binary files, as described in the preceding entry.

### Examples

To copy the file named REPORT.TXT to the screen (CON) from the current drive and directory:

```
C:\WP>copy report.txt con
```

The file is displayed, just as if you had entered *type report.txt.*

To copy the file named LETTER.DOC to the printer (PRN) from the directory \DOCS on the disk in drive A:

```
C:\>copy a:\docs\letter.doc prn
```

# COPY
## Copy from a Device to a File or Another Device
### Versions 1 and later

*Page 128*

This form of the Copy command copies from a device to a file or to a different device.

> **copy <source> <target>**

<source> is the device to copy from.

<target> is the file or device to copy to. If you specify a file, you can include a drive and path, but you cannot use wildcards.

### Examples

To copy from the keyboard (CON) to the printer (PRN), effectively treating your computer as if it were a typewriter:

```
C:\>copy con prn
```

To copy from the keyboard to a file named SAMPLE.TXT in the directory named \EXAMPLES on the disk in drive A:

```
C:\>copy con a:\examples\sample.txt
```

MS-DOS copies all characters you type until you end the file by pressing Ctrl-Z or F6 and the Enter key.

# COPY
## Combine Files
### Versions 1 and later

*Page 77*

This form of the Copy command combines two or more source files into a destination file you specify.

> **copy <source>+<source>+... <target> /A /B /V**

<source> is the name of each file to be combined. You can include a drive letter, a path name, or both, and you can use wildcards to specify a set of files. Use a plus sign (+) when you specify two or more file names. If a source file does not exist, MS-DOS doesn't notify you. It simply goes on to the next file in the list.

<target> is the name of the file into which the source files are combined. If you don't specify <target>, the files are combined into the first source file in the series.

457

> **NOTE:** *When you use wildcards to combine one or more source files into a target file that already exists in the same directory, the original contents of the target file are replaced by the contents of the combined source files. MS-DOS doesn't warn you that data will be lost but does display the message* Content of destination lost before copy *when the copy procedure is completed. If you want to add files to an existing file but keep the original information intact, use the plus sign between the names of the source files, and specify the target file name first.*

/A and /B specify ASCII and binary files, as described in an earlier entry on the Copy command. /V tells MS-DOS to verify the copy.

### Examples

To combine the files named APR.DOC, MAY.DOC, and JUN.DOC in the current directory into a file named 2Q.DOC in the current directory:

```
C:\MKT\WP>copy apr.doc+may.doc+jun.doc 2q.doc
```

To add the files named MAY.DOC and JUN.DOC to the file in the current directory named APR.DOC:

```
C:\MKT\WP>copy apr.doc+may.doc+jun.doc
```

To combine all the files in the current directory whose extension is DOC, in the order in which their directory entries appear, into another file, named TOTAL.DOC, which is also in the current directory:

```
C:\MKT\WP>copy *.doc total.doc
```

# COUNTRY (CONFIGURATION COMMAND)
## Set the International Date and Currency Format
### Versions 2.1 and later, IBM releases 3 and later

The Country command specifies a country code that tells MS-DOS to follow date, time, and other conventions for a particular country. If there is no Country command in CONFIG.SYS, MS-DOS follows the conventions of the country for which it was manufactured.

MS-DOS also uses the country code to choose the currency symbol and the character that separates the thousands and decimal fraction parts of a number. Although these characters aren't used in normal MS-DOS operation, the country code is available to application programs so that they can use the proper conventions.

**country=<code>,<codepage>,<countryfile>**

<code> is the three-digit country code that specifies the country whose date format is to be followed; it is the same as the international telephone dialing prefix. MS-DOS can recognize the country codes listed in Figure C-1. You must include all three digits, including any zeros at the beginning.

| Country or Language | Country Code | Valid Code Pages | MS-DOS Versions/Notes |
|---|---|---|---|
| Arabic | | 864, 850 | Special version of MS-DOS version 4 or later with country-specific supplement |
| Belgium | 032 | 850, 437 | Versions 2.1 and later |
| Brazil | 055 | 850, 437 | Versions 5 and later |
| Canada (French) | 002 | 863, 850 | Versions 3.3 and later |
| Croatia | 038 | 852, 850 | Versions 5 and later |
| Czech Republic | 042 | 852, 850 | Versions 5 and later |
| Denmark | 045 | 850, 865 | Versions 2.1 and later |
| Finland | 358 | 850, 437 | Versions 2.1 and later |
| France | 033 | 437, 850 | Versions 2.1 and later |
| Germany | 049 | 437, 850 | Versions 2.1 and later |
| Hebrew | | 862, 850 | Special version of MS-DOS version 4 or later with country-specific supplement |
| Hungary | 036 | 852, 850 | Versions 5 and later |
| International English | 061 | 437, 850 | Versions 2.1 and later |
| Italy | 039 | 437, 850 | Versions 2.1 and later |
| Japan | | 932, 437 | Special version of MS-DOS Asian edition of version 4 or later on a computer manufactured for use in Asia |
| Korea | | 934, 437 | Special version of MS-DOS Asian edition of version 4 or later on a computer manufactured for use in Asia |
| Latin America | 003 | 850, 437 | Versions 3.3 and later |
| Netherlands | 031 | 437, 850 | Versions 2.1 and later |

**Figure C-1.** *(continued)*
*Valid country codes and code pages for different versions of MS-DOS.*

**Figure C-1.** *continued*

| Country or Language | Country Code | Valid Code Pages | MS-DOS Versions/Notes |
|---|---|---|---|
| Norway | 047 | 850, 865 | Versions 2.1 and later |
| People's Republic of China | | 936, 437 | Special version of MS-DOS Asian edition of version 4 or later on a computer manufactured for use in Asia |
| Poland | 048 | 852, 850 | Versions 5 and later |
| Portugal | 351 | 850, 860 | Versions 3.3 and later |
| Serbia/Yugoslavia | 038 | 852, 850 | Versions 5 and later |
| Slovakia | 042 | 852, 850 | Versions 6 and 6.2 |
| Slovenia | 038 | 852, 850 | Versions 5 and later |
| Spain | 034 | 850, 437 | Versions 2.1 and later |
| Sweden | 046 | 437, 850 | Versions 2.1 and later |
| Switzerland | 041 | 850, 437 | Versions 2.1 and later |
| Taiwan | | 938, 437 | Special version of MS-DOS Asian edition of version 4 or later on a computer manufactured for use in Asia |
| United Kingdom | 044 | 437, 850 | Versions 2.1 and later |
| United States | 001 | 437, 850 | Versions 2.1 and later |

<codepage> is a three-digit number, also listed in Figure C-1, that specifies the code page that MS-DOS is to use (versions 3.3 and later).

<countryfile> is the name of the MS-DOS file that contains the country-specific information. If you omit the <countryfile> parameter, MS-DOS assumes the file is COUNTRY.SYS, which is stored in the root directory of the current drive (versions 3.3 and later).

## Example

In Belgium, the date is formatted as dd/mm/yyyy; for example, 16/10/1993 for October 16, 1993. To specify the Belgian format, put the following Country command in CONFIG.SYS:

```
country=032
```

## CTTY
## Change the Console Device
### Versions 2 and later

The CTTY command specifies the device that is to be used for standard input and standard output. You can assign standard input and output to a communications port, for example, to permit remote operation of the computer, or you can assign them to special devices supported by custom control programs.

Not all programs recognize the assignment of standard input and standard output. The Microsoft Basic interpreter, for example, does not, and so it is unaffected by the Change Console command.

**ctty <device>**

<device> is the name of the device that is to be used for standard input and standard output; the device must be capable of both input and output. If <device> specifies a device other than CON, AUX, PRN, LPT*n*, or COM*n*, CONFIG.SYS must include a Device command that names the file that contains the control program (device driver), and MS-DOS must have access to that file.

### Examples

To assign standard input and standard output to communications port COM1:

```
C:\>ctty com1
```

To reassign standard input and standard output to the keyboard and display:

```
C:\>ctty con
```

## DATE
## Change or Display the System Date
### Versions 1 and later

*Page 17*

The Date command displays the date kept by MS-DOS and prompts you to enter a new date. The sequence of the day, month, and year depends on the country code set with the Country or Select command. The sequence here is for the United States.

**date <mm-dd-yy>**

<mm-dd-yy> is the new date to be set. <mm> is the month (1 through 12), <dd> is the day (1 through 31), and <yy> is the year (1980 through 1999—or through 2099 if you type all four digits). You can separate the day, month, and year with hyphens, slashes, or periods: 10-16-93 or 10/16/93 or 10.16.93.

If you type only *date*, MS-DOS displays the current date and prompts you to enter the new date. Type a new date or press the Enter key to leave the date unchanged.

### Examples

To set the date to October 16, 1993:

```
C:\>date 10-16-93
```

To display the current system date and respond to the prompt for a new date:

```
C:\>date
```

MS-DOS responds:

```
Current date is Sat 10-16-1993
Enter new date (mm-dd-yy): _
```

Type the new date, or press the Enter key to leave the current date unchanged.

# DEFRAG
# Defragment a Disk

### Versions 6 and 6.2

*Page 196*

The Defrag command reorganizes the way files are stored on a disk so that each file is located in one contiguous portion of the disk, and, optionally, all the free space is consolidated in one area. This can shorten the time MS-DOS takes to find and load files.

> **WARNING:** *Do not use the Defrag command if you are running Microsoft Windows. Exit Windows first; then you can safely run Defrag.*

**defrag <drive> /U /F /S:<sortorder> /B /skiphigh /lcd /bw /g0 /H**

<drive> is the letter, followed by a colon, of the drive you want to defragment. If you omit <drive>, Defrag defragments the current drive.

/U tells Defrag to defragment the files but not to consolidate any free space between files. If you use /U, you can't use /F or /S.

/F tells Defrag to both defragment the files and consolidate all free space. If you use /F, you can't use /U.

/S:<sortorder> causes Defrag to sort the directory order of the files. If you use /S, you can't use /U. If you omit /S, MS-DOS doesn't change the existing order. <sortorder> can be any combination of the following settings:

| Setting | Sorted |
|---------|--------|
| N | By file name (A through Z) |
| N- | By file name (Z through A) |
| E | By extension (A through Z) |
| E- | By extension (Z through A) |
| S | By size (smallest to largest) |
| S- | By size (largest to smallest) |
| D | By date (earliest to latest) |
| D- | By date (latest to earliest) |

/B (for *boot*) restarts your computer after Defrag is finished.

*/skiphigh* loads Defrag into conventional memory. If you omit */skiphigh*, Defrag loads into upper memory if any is available.

*/lcd* causes Defrag to use colors that are easily viewed on an LCD screen. If you use */lcd*, you can't use */bw* or /g0.

*/bw* displays Defrag in monochrome ("black and white"). If you use */bw*, you can't use */lcd* or /g0.

/g0 forces Defrag to run without using graphics characters. If you use /g0, you can't use */lcd* or */bw*.

/H allows Defrag to move hidden files. If you omit /H, Defrag will not move hidden files.

## Examples

To fully defragment drive C:

```
C:\>defrag /f
```

To defragment the files on drive D, leaving the free space as is and placing the files in alphabetic order, first by extension and then by file name:

```
C:\>defrag d: /u /s:en
```

# DELETE (DEL)
# Delete (Erase) a File

**Versions 1 and later**

*Page 79*

The Delete command (del or erase) deletes a file or set of files.

**del <filename> /P**

<filename> is the name of the file to be deleted. You can use wildcard characters to delete a set of files with similar file names or extensions.

/P tells MS-DOS to prompt for verification before deleting a file (versions 4 and later).

If you don't use the /P parameter, MS-DOS deletes the file or files you specified as soon as you press the Enter key. The only exception occurs when you use the wildcard specification *.* to indicate all files or when you specify only a directory name (which implies *.*). Because *.* deletes the contents of an entire disk or directory, MS-DOS prompts for confirmation with a message like this: *All files in directory will be deleted! Are you sure (Y/N)?* You must press Y to carry out the command.

Beginning with version 5, MS-DOS offers you some protection if you inadvertently delete one or more files you meant to keep. The Undelete command can help you recover lost files, but in most cases it can work effectively *only* if you use Undelete as soon as possible—preferably immediately after deleting needed files. Because MS-DOS might save new information in the space formerly occupied by your deleted files, any delay in using the Undelete command can mean loss of some portion(s) of the files you want to recover. For more details, see the entry on the Undelete command.

### Examples

To delete the file named REPORT.DOC in the current directory on the disk in the current drive:

```
C:\MKT\WP>del report.doc
```

To delete all files with the extension BAK in the directory named \MKT\WP on the disk in drive A, telling MS-DOS to prompt for verification:

```
C:\>del a:\mkt\wp\*.bak /p
```

## DELTREE
## Delete an Entire Directory
### Versions 6 and 6.2

*Page 156*

The DelTree command allows you to delete an entire directory, including any files and subdirectories it contains. Be warned: This is a dangerous command. Double-check the drive and directory names before you press Enter!

**deltree /Y <drive><path>**

/Y causes DelTree to skip the prompt that normally confirms the deletion. Do not use this switch unless you are certain you have typed the correct location.

<drive> is the letter, followed by a colon, of the drive containing the disk with the directory to be removed (such as *c:*).

<path> is the path name of the directory you want to remove. You can use wildcard characters (? and *), but be very careful if you do so. You can accidentally delete files and directories that you meant to keep.

### Example

To remove the subdirectory C:\MKT and all its files and subdirectories:

```
C:\>deltree c:\mkt
```

## DEVICE (CONFIGURATION COMMAND)
## Define a Device-Control Program

### Versions 2 and later

*Page 381*

The Device configuration command identifies a file that contains a program to control a device. MS-DOS automatically recognizes and works with certain devices, such as the keyboard and the display. But other devices, such as a mouse, can be added to a computer system. If you add a device that MS-DOS doesn't already know about, you must tell MS-DOS the name of the device's controlling program. Such a control program, called a *device driver,* usually has the extension SYS and comes with the device. You can put more than one Device command in CONFIG.SYS.

**device=<filename>**

<filename> is the name of the file that contains the device driver. You can include a drive and path if necessary.

The device drivers listed in Figure C-2 are included with MS-DOS.

| Driver Name | MS-DOS Version(s) | Controls |
| --- | --- | --- |
| ANSI.SYS | 2 and later | Display and keyboard. This is an advanced use of MS-DOS; details may be in your MS-DOS manual and can also be found in the book *MS-DOS to the Max.* |
| DBLSPACE.SYS | 6 and 6.2 | Position in memory of the DoubleSpace disk compression program. This enables MS-DOS to load the program in upper memory; *see* the entry DoubleSpace in this appendix. |
| DISPLAY.SYS | 3.3 and later | Code-page switching for the display. |
| DRIVER.SYS* | 3.2 and later | Floppy disk drives. This device driver enables you to assign a drive letter to an internal or external floppy disk drive. |

**Figure C-2.**                                                                    *(continued)*
*Device drivers shipped with MS-DOS.*

**Figure C-2.** *continued*

| Driver Name | MS-DOS Version(s) | Controls |
|---|---|---|
| EGA.SYS | 5 and later | Screen restoration on an EGA display when the MS-DOS Shell's Task Swapper is used. |
| EMM386.EXE | 5 and later | Extended memory. This device driver, for use on 80386 and 80486 systems only, allows you to treat extended memory as expanded memory and to gain access to the reserved portion of conventional memory known as upper memory blocks (the memory between 640 KB and 1 MB); *see* Chapter 17, "Tailoring Your System," and the entries EMM386 and EMM386.EXE in this appendix. |
| HIMEM.SYS | 5 and later | Extended memory and the High Memory Area (HMA). Among other features, this device driver enables MS-DOS to load itself into extended memory and thus leave more conventional memory available for programs to use; *see* Chapter 17 and the entry HIMEM.SYS in this appendix. |
| INTERLNK.EXE | 6 and 6.2 | Interlink utility; *see* the entries for Interlink and Interlink Server in this appendix. |
| POWER.EXE | 6 and 6.2 | Power management; *see* the entry for Power in this appendix. |
| PRINTER.SYS | 3.3 through 5 | Code-page switching for the printer. |
| RAMDRIVE.SYS | 3.2 and later | RAM drive; *see* Chapter 17 and the entry RAMDRIVE.SYS in this appendix. |
| SETVER.EXE | 5 | Table of MS-DOS version numbers needed by applications and other programs; *see* the entry Set Version in this appendix. |
| SMARTDRV.EXE | 4 and later | Disk cache in extended or expanded memory. Called SMARTDRV.SYS in versions 4 and 5; *see* Chapter 17 and the entry SMARTDRV.EXE in this appendix. |
| VDISK.SYS | IBM releases 3 and later | RAM drive; *see* Chapter 17 and the entry RAMDRIVE.SYS in this appendix. |
| XMAEM.SYS* | IBM release 4 | Extended/expanded memory. |
| XMA2EMS.SYS* | IBM release 4 | Expanded memory. |

*Describing these device drivers is beyond the scope of this book; for details, refer to your computer's manual(s) and to your MS-DOS manual.

### Example

To load (from the root directory) a mouse driver named MOUSE.SYS, put the following Device command in CONFIG.SYS:

```
device=mouse.sys
```

To manage extended memory and the High Memory Area (HMA), assuming a \DOS directory:

```
device=c:\dos\himem.sys
```

If used to load MS-DOS into the HMA, this command must be accompanied by the *dos=high* command in CONFIG.SYS.

## DEVICEHIGH (CONFIGURATION COMMAND)
## Load Device Drivers into the Upper Memory Area

### Versions 5 and later

*Page 393*

The Devicehigh command tells MS-DOS to load a device driver into available upper memory blocks (UMBs) in the upper memory area (memory between 640 KB and 1 MB). The Devicehigh command requires a computer with at least 350 KB of extended memory. It also requires HIMEM.SYS and either EMM386.EXE or a comparable memory manager that provides access to UMBs. If you use EMM386.EXE, your computer must have either an 80386 or an 80486 microprocessor. Loading one or more device drivers into UMBs helps make more of your system's conventional memory available to programs.

You can load any of the following MS-DOS device drivers into UMBs: ANSI.SYS, DISPLAY.SYS, DBLSPACE.SYS, DRIVER.SYS, EGA.SYS, INTERLNK.EXE, PRINTER.SYS, RAMDRIVE.SYS, and SMARTDRV.SYS. If you normally load any of these drivers into conventional memory, you can place them in UMBs instead by adding the Dos and Device commands shown in the example for this entry and by changing the Device command for each driver to Devicehigh.

> **NOTE:** *Device drivers other than those listed here might cause problems with your system. Before using Devicehigh, consult your MS-DOS documentation, and refer to the section on Devicehigh in Chapter 17, "Tailoring Your System."*

The following applies to versions 6 and 6.2 only:

**devicehigh /L:<region>,<minsize> /S =<driver> <dparameters>**

/L:<region>,<minsize> lets you specify where you want to place the driver and the minimum amount of memory needed by the device driver. <region> specifies the region number into which MS-DOS should load the device driver;

<minsize> tells MS-DOS the smallest amount of memory into which the device driver will fit. If a device driver needs two or more regions of memory, separate the region numbers with semicolons.

/S shrinks the UMB to its smallest size as MS-DOS loads the device driver. This switch is normally used only by the MemMaker program; see the MemMaker entry in this appendix.

<driver> is the name of the device driver. You can include a path name.

<dparameters> represents any parameters required by the device driver.

The following applies to version 5 only:

**devicehigh size=<memsize> <driver> <dparameters>**

*size*=<memsize> lets you specify the minimum amount of the upper memory area, given as a hexadecimal (base-16) value, needed by the device driver. If you don't include this parameter and the driver attempts to use more memory than is available, the system might halt. You can find <memsize> by using a Device configuration command to load the driver in conventional memory and then using the */classify* parameter of the Mem command, which displays the names and sizes (in decimal and hexadecimal) of programs in memory.

<driver> is the name of the device driver. You can include a path name.

<dparameters> represents any parameters required by the device driver.

### Example

To tell MS-DOS to use the upper memory area, make it available to device drivers, and load RAMDRIVE.SYS in UMBs with instructions to create a 1024 KB RAM disk in extended memory, put commands like the following in CONFIG.SYS:

```
dos=high,umb
device=c:\dos\himem.sys
device=c:\dos\emm386.exe noems
devicehigh=c:\dos\ramdrive.sys 1024 /e
```

## DIRECTORY (DIR)
## Display Directory Entries

### Versions 1 and later

*Pages 69, 157*

The Directory command (dir) displays the directory entry of one or more files. A Directory command display looks like the following:

```
Volume in drive C is HARD DISK
Volume Serial Number is 1608-5A30
Directory of C:\MKT\WP
```

```
.               <DIR>     07-02-93   5:24p
..              <DIR>     07-02-93   5:24p
REPORT   DOC    60780  08-15-93   1:09a
FORECAST DOC    18256  10-10-93   7:46p
SALESREP DOC    25728  10-13-93   8:42a
LETTERS         <DIR>
FCST-APR DOC     4328  10-12-93   9:07a
FCST-MAY DOC    20982  09-24-93  10:09p
STYLE           <DIR>
FCST-MAR DOC      996  10-12-93   5:36p
WKRPT    STY     2688  10-12-93   5:50p
BUDGET   DOC     5888  10-11-93   9:28a
       12 file(s)       139646 bytes
                      23633152 bytes free
```

The first three lines show the volume label of the disk (HARD DISK), the volume serial number (beginning with version 4), and the drive and path name of the directory whose entries are displayed (C:\MKT\WP). The last lines show the number of directory entries displayed (12), the number of bytes (139,646) used by the files (versions 5 and later), and the available space on the disk (23,633,152 bytes).

The directory entry for a file includes the file name and extension, size in bytes, and the date and time it was created or last changed. The directory entry for a subdirectory (LETTERS and STYLE in the preceding example) includes the file name and extension, followed by <DIR>.

The first two subdirectory entries in the preceding example are symbolic; the first (one period) represents the directory whose entries are displayed, and the second (two periods) represents the directory that contains the directory whose entries are displayed (sometimes referred to as the *parent* directory). The entries . and .. do not appear in the listing of the root directory of a disk.

### dir <filename> /W /P /A<attribute> /O<sortorder> /S /B /L /CH

<filename> is the name of the file whose directory entry is to be displayed. You can use wildcard characters to display the entries of a set of files with similar names or extensions. If you omit <filename>, MS-DOS displays the directory entry of each file in the specified or current directory. If you specify only a drive letter, MS-DOS displays the directory entry of each file in the current directory of the specified drive. If you specify a filename but no extension, MS-DOS displays the directory entry for each file with that file name, regardless of extension.

/W (for *wide*) displays only the file name and extension of each directory entry in five columns across the screen. Beginning with version 5, the names of subdirectories are enclosed in square brackets for readability—for example, *[DOS]* instead of *DOS*.

469

/P (for *pause*) displays the directory one screenful at a time, displaying *Press any key to continue...* (*Strike a key when ready...* in versions prior to 4) at the bottom of the screen. Pressing any key displays the next screenful of entries; pressing Ctrl-Break or Ctrl-C cancels the command. Beginning with version 5, MS-DOS heads each new screenful of entries with the message *(continuing <pathname>)* to help you keep your bearings.

The following parameters are available in versions 5 and later of MS-DOS.

/A<attribute> displays the entries for files with the attribute you specify. (The colon is optional; omit it if you want.) <attribute> can be any of the following:

- H displays hidden files—that is, files whose hidden attribute is on.

- S displays system files—that is, files normally used by MS-DOS. These files are typically hidden as well to avoid inadvertent change or deletion. MS-DOS requires two system files named MSDOS.SYS and IO.SYS (IBMDOS.COM and IBMBIO.COM in IBM releases) on any disk you use to start your system. Don't tamper with these.

- D displays only the names of directories.

- A displays files whose archive attribute is on—that is, files that have not been archived since they were created or last changed.

- R displays read-only files—that is, files that can be read but not changed.

You can precede any of these attributes with a hyphen (minus sign) to omit files or directories with the specified attribute.

/O<sortorder> specifies the order in which directory entries are displayed. <sortorder> can be any of the following. As with attributes, you can use a hyphen to reverse the order.

- N sorts entries alphabetically by file name from A to Z.

- E sorts alphabetically by extension from A to Z.

- D sorts by date, oldest to newest.

- S sorts by size, smallest to largest.

- G groups directories ahead of files. (-G groups directories after files.)

/S displays every file in every subdirectory on the disk that matches <filename>. So that you know where the files are stored, MS-DOS identifies each subdirectory with the words *Directory of* <path> before displaying the directory entries.

/B displays only the name and extension of each file in the specified directory that matches <filename>.

/L displays the directory entries in lowercase letters.

/CH, available only in versions 6 and 6.2, displays the compression ratio of files in a compressed drive, based on the cluster size of the physical disk drive. If you omit the H, the compression ratio is based on a cluster size of 8 KB. If you use /W or /B, /CH and /C are ignored.

NOTE: *Beginning with version 5, you can use the Set command with a variable named* dircmd *to tailor directory listings to your preferences. For an example, see the entry on the Set command.*

### Examples

To display the directory entry of each file with the extension DOC in the current directory on the disk in drive A:

```
C:\>dir a:*.doc
```

To display the directory entry of each file in the directory \MKT\WP on the disk in the current drive, in wide format:

```
C:\>dir \mkt\wp /w
```

To display the directory entry of each file in the parent directory (MKT) of the current directory on the disk in the current drive, pausing after each screenful:

```
C:\MKT>dir .. /p
```

To display the directory entry of each file without an extension in the current directory on the disk in the current drive:

```
C:\>dir *.
```

To display only subdirectories (not files) in the current directory:

```
C:\>dir /ad
```

To display files (but not subdirectories) in the current directory:

```
C:\>dir /a-d
```

To display the files in the current directory alphabetically by extension:

```
C:\>dir /oe
```

To display the files in the current directory in order from newest to oldest, placing directories at the end of the listing:

```
C:\>dir /o-d /o-g
```

## DISK COMPARE (DISKCOMP)
## Compare Two Floppy Disks

**Versions 3.2 and later, IBM releases 1 and later**

*Page 105*

The Diskcomp command compares two floppy disks of the same size and capacity track by track and reports the side and track of any sectors that differ. If the disks are identical, Diskcomp reports *Compare OK.* Because it compares the tracks of the floppy disks without regard to the names of the files, Diskcomp does not report that two disks containing the same files are identical if the files are stored in different locations.

The Diskcomp command automatically determines the number of sides and sectors per track from the disk in the first drive specified (which it calls the source). You cannot compare a floppy disk in a double-sided drive to a floppy disk in a single-sided drive, nor can you compare two floppy disks with different numbers of sectors per track. You can, however, use the Diskcomp parameters to compare just one side of disks in double-sided drives or just the first 8 sectors of each track on disks written with 9 sectors per track.

> **NOTE:** *The Diskcomp command cannot be used with a hard disk, with a drive created or affected by an Assign, Join, or Substitute command, or with a network drive.*

**diskcomp <drive1> <drive2> /1 /8**

<drive1> is the letter of the floppy disk drive, followed by a colon, that contains the first floppy disk to be compared (such as *a:*).

<drive2> is the letter of the floppy disk drive, followed by a colon, that contains the second floppy disk to be compared.

If you have two floppy disk drives of matching types and one is the current drive, specifying only the second drive in the Diskcomp command causes MS-DOS to compare the disk in the second drive to the disk in the current drive.

If you have one floppy disk drive and it is the current drive, Diskcomp prompts you through a one-drive comparison if you type the command in any of the following forms: *diskcomp, diskcomp a:, diskcomp a: a:, diskcomp b:,* or *diskcomp a: b:.*

If you have a hard disk and it is the current drive, you must specify both <drive1> and <drive2> because Diskcomp is for floppy disks only.

/1 compares only the first side of the floppy disks, even if they are in double-sided disk drives.

/8 compares only the first 8 sectors of each track, even if the floppy disks have more sectors per track.

After it has compared the floppy disks, the Diskcomp command prompts *Compare another diskette (Y/N)?* If you reply *y*, it again prompts you to insert the source and target disks in the specified drives.

### Examples

To compare the floppy disk in drive A to the floppy disk in drive B:

```
C:\>diskcomp a: b:
```

If you have only one floppy disk drive, Diskcomp tells you when to swap disks.

To compare the first side of the disk in drive A to the first side of the disk in the current drive (B):

```
B:\>diskcomp a: /1
```

To compare two floppy disks using only the current drive (A):

```
A:\>diskcomp
```

## DISKCOPY
## Copy a Complete Floppy Disk
### Versions 2 and later

*Page 103*

The Diskcopy command makes a sector-by-sector copy of a floppy disk. If the target floppy disk isn't formatted to match the source floppy disk, Diskcopy formats the floppy disk for you in versions 4 and 5 and in all earlier IBM releases of DOS.

Because the Diskcopy command makes an identical copy, it does not consolidate fragmented files; to consolidate fragmented files, use the Copy command and specify *.* to copy all files from the source disk to the target disk. (Use the Defrag program if you have version 6 or 6.2.)

> **NOTE:** *The Diskcopy command cannot be used with a hard disk, with a drive created or affected by an Assign, Join, or Substitute command, or with a network drive. You cannot use Diskcopy with dissimilar floppy disk types—for example, a 720 KB and a 1.2 MB disk.*

> **diskcopy <source> <target> /1 /V**

<source> is the letter, followed by a colon, of the floppy disk drive that contains the disk to be copied (such as *a:*). If you enter only one drive letter, MS-DOS assumes it contains the source disk.

<target> is the letter of the floppy disk drive, followed by a colon, that contains the disk to which <source> is copied.

If you have two floppy disk drives of matching capacity and one is the current drive, specifying only the second drive in the Diskcopy command causes MS-DOS to copy from the disk in the second drive to the disk in the current drive.

If you have one floppy disk drive and it is the current drive, Diskcopy prompts you through a one-drive copy if you type the command in any of the following forms: *diskcopy, diskcopy a:, diskcopy a: a:, diskcopy b:*, or *diskcopy a: b:*.

If you have a hard disk and it is the current drive, you must specify both <source> and <target> because Diskcopy is for floppy disks only.

/1 copies only the first side of <source>, even if <source> is a double-sided disk.

/V verifies that the copy is indeed an exact copy of the source disk. Using this switch causes Diskcopy to take longer to complete the process (versions 5 and later).

After it has copied the disk, MS-DOS prompts *Copy another (Y/N)?* If you reply *y*, MS-DOS prompts you to insert the source and target disks. After ending the Diskcopy command by replying *n* to the concluding prompt, you can verify the copy with the Diskcomp command.

The Diskcopy command reports the side, track, and sector of any disk errors it encounters. If these reported sectors contain valid data, the copy may not be usable.

## Examples

To copy the floppy disk in drive A to the floppy disk in drive B:

```
C:\>diskcopy a: b:
```

If you have only one floppy disk drive, MS-DOS prompts you through a one-drive copy.

On a system with two floppy disk drives, to copy the first side of the disk in drive B to the first side of the disk in the current drive (A):

```
A:\>diskcopy b: /1
```

To copy a floppy disk using only the current drive (A):

```
A:\>diskcopy
```

## DOS (CONFIGURATION COMMAND)
## Load MS-DOS into High Memory

**Versions 5 and later**

*Page 385*

The Dos configuration command tailors MS-DOS to use memory above 640 KB, the upper limit of conventional memory, and thus leave more room for programs and data. In order to function correctly, the Dos command requires a computer with extended memory (above 1 MB), reserved memory (the upper memory area between 640 KB and 1 MB), or both. Depending on the parameters you use, your computer must also be based on an 80286, 80386, or 80486 (or better) microprocessor.

On an 80286, 80386, or 80486 machine with extended memory, the Dos command can be used with the *high* parameter to tell MS-DOS to load part of itself into the first 64 KB of extended memory—the region known as the high memory area, or HMA. On a computer with at least 350 KB of extended memory, the Dos command can be used with the *umb* parameter to enable loading of device drivers and other programs into available portions of the upper memory area known as upper memory blocks (UMBs).

Because the Dos command deals with memory that is not normally accessible to MS-DOS, it is used with the Device configuration command and two device drivers: HIMEM.SYS, which manages extended memory, and EMM386.EXE (or a comparable program), which manages extended/expanded memory and provides access to UMBs. The examples at the end of this entry show such commands. Like other configuration commands, the Dos command belongs in the file CONFIG.SYS.

### dos=high/low,umb/noumb

*high* tells MS-DOS to load part of itself into the HMA whenever you start or restart the computer. In order to succeed, this command must be accompanied in CONFIG.SYS by a Device command that tells MS-DOS where to find HIMEM.SYS, the program that manages extended memory.

*low* tells MS-DOS to load itself into conventional memory. If you don't use the Dos command, MS-DOS assumes *low*. If you specify *high* but MS-DOS can't find or use the HMA at startup, it loads itself into conventional memory instead.

*umb* (for *upper memory blocks*) tells MS-DOS to allow device drivers and other programs to be loaded into the upper memory area. The actual loading of programs is done by the Devicehigh and Loadhigh commands described in Chapter 17, "Tailoring Your System," and elsewhere in this appendix.

*noumb* (for *no upper memory blocks*) tells MS-DOS not to allow device drivers and other programs to be loaded into the upper memory area. If you don't use the Dos command, MS-DOS assumes *noumb*.

You can use both the *high/low* and *umb/noumb* parameters in the same command.

### Examples

To load MS-DOS into the HMA on an 80286-based computer (such as an enhanced PC-compatible computer) with at least 64 KB of extended memory, put the following commands in CONFIG.SYS:

```
device=c:\dos\himem.sys
dos=high
```

(The example assumes that HIMEM.SYS is in the C:\DOS directory.)

To load MS-DOS into the HMA and allow device drivers and other programs to be loaded into the upper memory area on an 80386-based computer with 350 KB or more of extended memory, put the following commands in CONFIG.SYS:

```
device=c:\dos\himem.sys
device=c:\dos\emm386.exe noems
dos=high,umb
```

The example assumes that HIMEM.SYS, the extended memory manager, and EMM386.EXE, the program that manages upper memory blocks, are both in C:\DOS. The *noems* option used with EMM386.EXE tells MS-DOS you don't need access to both the upper memory area and expanded memory. If you do need both, use the *ram* parameter described in the entry EMM386.EXE.

## DOSKEY
## Command History and Macro Recorder
### Versions 5 and later

*Pages 16, 34, 312*

Doskey performs two main tasks: It maintains a log of the commands that you type, and it records sequences of keystrokes for later playback as macros. Doskey is something like an editor but one that works on commands rather than on documents or other files. Typing *doskey* causes MS-DOS to load the program into

476

memory, where it remains until you restart your system. As you work, you can then retrieve, edit, and carry out earlier commands without retyping them. In addition, you can create macros by assigning short, easy-to-remember names to long, complex, or often-used sequences of MS-DOS commands.

**doskey /insert /overstrike /reinstall /bufsize=<size> /macros /history <macro>=<commands>**

*doskey*, typed with no parameters, tells MS-DOS to install the Doskey program.

*/insert* causes Doskey to insert text rather than replace characters as you edit commands and macros.

*/overstrike* causes Doskey to type over (replace) existing characters with those you type. If you don't specify */insert* or */overstrike*, Doskey assumes */overstrike*.

*/reinstall* causes Doskey to load a new copy of the program into memory. When you reinstall Doskey, previously recorded commands and macros are no longer available for use. The old copy remains in memory, but the new copy takes over the tasks of recording commands and macros.

*/bufsize=<size>* is the size (in bytes) of the storage area (called the buffer) in which Doskey saves commands as you enter them. You can specify */bufsize* only when you start or reinstall Doskey. If you don't specify */bufsize*, Doskey assumes 512 bytes—enough for about 25 commands, each about 20 characters long. The smallest value you can use for <size> is 256.

*/macros* (or */m*) tells Doskey to display all macros currently in memory.

*/history* (or */h*) tells Doskey to display all commands currently in memory. If you've used Doskey to create macros, you can use the */history* parameter with the redirection symbol (>) to send the commands to a file—a batch file, for example, so that you can save and reuse the macros in a later session.

<macro>=<commands> tells Doskey to create the macro named <macro> and save it in memory. <macro> is the name you want to assign to a set of commands; <commands> are the MS-DOS commands to be carried out whenever you type the macro name. To delete a macro, omit the <commands> part of the parameter; that is, type the macro name followed by an equal sign, and then press Enter.

You can include multiple commands in a macro by separating them with a dollar sign followed by the letter *t* ($t). You can also use replaceable parameters, which function just as they do in batch files but are typed with a dollar sign rather than a percent sign ($1 through $9 instead of %1 through %9).

Just as the Prompt command lets you include character combinations that begin with $ to represent characters you can't type, Doskey lets you include the combinations shown in Figure C-3. Doskey also uses special editing keys, described in Chapter 13, "Taking Control of Your System," Figure 13-3.

| Character | Use |
|-----------|-----|
| $g | Redirect output; same function as >. |
| $g$g | Append output; same function as >>. |
| $l | Redirect input; same function as <. |
| $b | Pipe output to another command; same function as ¦. |
| $t | Separate commands. |
| $$ | Dollar sign (for use in file names). |
| $1–$9 | Replaceable parameters; same function as %1–%9 in batch files. |
| $* | Special-purpose replaceable parameter used to include everything typed after the macro name as part of the parameter. |

**Figure C-3.**
*Doskey special character combinations.*

## Examples

To load the Doskey program:

```
C:\>doskey
```

To reinstall Doskey and specify a 256-byte buffer:

```
C:\>doskey /reinstall /bufsize=256
```

To save the commands currently in memory by redirecting them to a file named MINE.TXT:

```
C:\>doskey /h > mine.txt
```

To create a macro that formats a 360 KB floppy disk in whatever disk drive you specify on the command line:

```
C:\>doskey 360=format $1 /f:360
```

To format the floppy disk in drive A, you would type *360 a:*. To display the macros currently in memory:

```
C:\>doskey /m
```

## DOSSHELL
## Start the MS-DOS Shell

### Versions 4 through 6

*Page 242*

Dosshell is the command that starts the MS-DOS Shell, the program that provides a visual environment in which you use menus and graphics, rather than typed commands, to work with MS-DOS, your applications, and your data files.

The Shell was modified both functionally and in appearance between versions 4 and 5 of MS-DOS. Both versions are easier to use than MS-DOS commands; the version 5 or 6 Shell is faster and makes more use of graphics than its version 4 predecessor. Use of the Shell in its version 5 or 6 form is described in Chapter 11, "The MS-DOS Shell."

The following command format and examples apply to the version 5 or 6 Shell:

**dosshell /T:<res> /G:<res> /B**

/T starts the Shell in text (character mode). <res> is an optional letter, such as L for low or H for high, that specifies screen resolution. The values you can use depend on your display hardware. If you don't know what resolutions are available, start the Shell without any parameters, and choose the Display command on the Options menu to see a list of display modes that can run on your system.

/G starts the Shell in graphics mode; as with /T, you can specify a particular resolution if you want.

/B starts the Shell in black and white rather than in color.

### Examples

To start the version 5 or 6 Shell in text mode on a system capable of graphics:

```
C:\>dosshell /t
```

To start the Shell in black and white on a color monitor:

```
C:\>dosshell /b
```

## DOUBLESPACE (DBLSPACE)
## Disk-Compression Program

### Versions 6 and 6.2

*Page 187*

The DoubleSpace command (dblspace) allows you to install automatic disk compression, effectively as much as doubling the size of your disks.

**dblspace /chkdsk /compress /convstac /create /defragment /delete /format /info /list /mount /unmount /ratio /size**

If you run DoubleSpace (dblspace) without adding any parameters, the full-screen version of the program will start. The first time you run DoubleSpace, the program takes you through a series of steps to set up disk compression on your system. To bypass the full-screen version, you can type any of the following variations.

**NOTE:** *The following form of the DoubleSpace command works only with version 6 of MS-DOS. To check a disk using version 6.2 or later, use the ScanDisk command.*

**dblspace /chkdsk /F <drive>**

*/chkdsk* tells DoubleSpace to verify the integrity of a compressed drive. It is similar to the Check Disk (chkdsk) command in that it can identify (and attempt to fix, if you include the /F parameter) allocation errors. However, it cannot check the drive's file allocation table; use the Check Disk command to do that.

/F tells DoubleSpace to correct errors on the disk, if it finds any.

<drive> is the letter, followed by a colon, of the drive to be checked (such as *a:*). If you omit <drive>, DoubleSpace checks the current drive.

**dblspace /compress <drive1> /newdrive=<drive2> /reserve=<size>**

*/compress* (or */com*) tells DoubleSpace to compress the files in an existing drive, making more room available on that drive. (You can't compress a drive that's completely full. A hard disk needs at least 1 MB of free space; a floppy disk, at least 200 KB.)

<drive1> is the letter, followed by a colon, of the drive you want to compress.

*/newdrive=*<drive2> (or */new=*<drive2>) specifies the drive letter for the new uncompressed drive that DoubleSpace creates. (The compressed drive will be named <drive1>.) If you omit */newdrive*, DoubleSpace uses the next available drive letter.

*/reserve=*<size> (or */res=*<size>) specifies, in megabytes, how much free space the new uncompressed drive will have. Some files (such as the Microsoft Windows swap file) can't be stored in a compressed drive, so you should leave enough room to allow for these files (and any future growth).

**dblspace /create <drive1> /newdrive=<drive2> /size=<size>
/reserve=<size>**

*/create* tells DoubleSpace to create a new compressed drive from free space on the specified drive.

<drive1> is the letter, followed by a colon, of the drive in which you want to create the new compressed drive.

*/newdrive*=<drive2> (or */n*=<drive2>) specifies the drive letter for the new compressed drive. If you omit */newdrive,* DoubleSpace uses the next available drive letter.

*/size*=<size> (or */si*=<size>) specifies, in megabytes, how much of the free space on the uncompressed drive DoubleSpace will use to create the new compressed drive. If you type */size,* you can't use */reserve.*

*/reserve*=<size> (or */re*=<size>) specifies, in megabytes, how much space DoubleSpace will leave uncompressed. To make the new compressed drive as large as possible, set <size> to 0. If you type */reserve,* you can't use */size.* If you omit both */size* and */reserve,* DoubleSpace will reserve 1 MB of uncompressed space.

**dblspace /defragment <drive>**

*/defragment* (or */def*) tells DoubleSpace to defragment a compressed drive. When you defragment a drive, you consolidate all the free space. Then if you decrease the size of your compressed disk, you can free as much space as possible.

<drive> is the letter, followed by a colon, of the compressed drive you want to defragment. If you omit <drive>, DoubleSpace defragments the current drive.

**dblspace /delete <drive>**

*/delete* (or */del*) causes DoubleSpace to delete a compressed drive. Note that when you delete a compressed drive, you also delete all the files contained in that drive.

<drive> is the letter, followed by a colon, of the compressed drive you want to delete. You can't delete drive C.

If you accidentally delete a compressed drive, you can try to restore it by using the Undelete command. Look for a file named DBLSPACE.### (such as DBLSPACE.000). After you undelete the volume file, you can begin using it as a compressed drive by using the DoubleSpace */mount* parameter.

**dblspace /format <drive>**

*/format* (or */f*) tells DoubleSpace to format a compressed drive. This effectively erases all the files stored in the drive. The disk keeps the information that makes it compressed. (Because you can't unformat a formatted compressed drive, be careful when using this command.)

<drive> is the letter, followed by a colon, of the compressed drive you want to format. You can't format drive C.

**dblspace /info <drive>**

*/info* causes DoubleSpace to display information about a compressed drive. Using the */info* switch is not required; you can simply specify *dblspace <drive>* if you want.

<drive> is the letter, followed by a colon, of the compressed drive you want to examine.

**dblspace /list**

*/list* (or */l*) tells DoubleSpace to list all of your computer's drives, both compressed and uncompressed (but not including any network drives).

**dblspace /mount=<extension> <drive1> /newdrive=<drive2>**

*/mount*=<extension> (or */mo*=<extension>) tells DoubleSpace to *mount,* or make available for use, an unmounted compressed drive. DoubleSpace mounts a drive by assigning a drive letter to the file that contains the compressed drive's contents. This file is called the DoubleSpace volume file. (You need to mount a compressed drive only if you have previously unmounted a drive or you want to mount a drive that's located on a floppy disk.) <extension> specifies the file name extension of the volume file. If you omit <extension>, DoubleSpace tries to mount the file named DBLSPACE.000.

<drive1> is the letter, followed by a colon, of the drive that contains the volume file.

*/newdrive*=<drive2> (or */new*=<drive2>) specifies the drive letter for the new compressed drive. If you omit */newdrive*, DoubleSpace uses the next available drive letter.

**dblspace /unmount <drive>**

*/unmount* (or */u*) tells DoubleSpace to *unmount,* or make unavailable, a compressed drive. When you unmount a compressed drive, you can no longer access

the files stored in that drive, although the files still exist. To restore access to the files, use the */mount* form of this command.

<drive> is the letter, followed by a colon, of the compressed drive that you want to unmount. If you omit <drive>, DoubleSpace unmounts the current drive.

### dblspace /ratio=<value> <drive> /all

*/ratio=*<value> (or */ra=*<value>) changes the compression ratio of a compressed drive. DoubleSpace adjusts the compression ratio every time you start your computer, so you normally do not need to use this form of the command. <value> is a ratio from 1.0 through 16.0; if you omit <value>, DoubleSpace sets the compression ratio to the average of the compression ratios for the files currently stored in the drive.

<drive> is the letter, followed by a colon, of the compressed drive for which you want to set the compression ratio. If you specify <drive>, you can't use the */all* switch. If you don't specify either <drive> or */all*, DoubleSpace sets the compression ratio of the current drive.

*/all* tells DoubleSpace to change the compression ratio of all mounted compressed drives. If you use */all*, you can't specify <drive>.

### dblspace /size=<drivesize> /reserve=<size> <drive>

*/size=*<drivesize> (or */si=*<drivesize>) causes DoubleSpace to change the size of a compressed drive. If you specify <drivesize> (in megabytes), DoubleSpace changes the uncompressed space occupied by the compressed drive to <size>. You can't use */reserve* if you specify <drivesize>.

*/reserve=*<size> (or */res=*<size>) specifies, in megabytes, how much space to leave uncompressed. If you specify */reserve=*<size>, you can't specify <drivesize>. If you omit both <drivesize> and */reserve=*<size>, DoubleSpace will make the compressed drive as small as possible.

<drive> is the letter, followed by a colon, of the compressed drive you want to resize.

NOTE: *The following form of the DoubleSpace command works only with version 6.2 of MS-DOS. To remove DoubleSpace from a system running version 6 of MS-DOS, see the topic "Removing DoubleSpace" in Chapter 9, "Managing Your Hard Disk."*

### dblspace /uncompress<drive>

*/uncompress* tells DoubleSpace that you want to remove DoubleSpace from the specified drive. If <drive> is the only (or last remaining) compressed drive on your system, this form of the command also removes the DoubleSpace program.

<drive> is the drive letter, followed by a colon, of the compressed drive you want to uncompress.

### Examples

To start the DoubleSpace program:

```
C:\>dblspace
```

To compress drive H, leaving 6 MB uncompressed as drive I:

```
C:\>dblspace /com h: /new=i: /res=6
```

To display information about the compressed drive H:

```
C:\>dblspace /info h:
```

To uncompress drive H (removing DoubleSpace if this is the only compressed drive):

```
C:\>dblspace /uncompress h:
```

## DRIVE PARAMETERS—DRIVPARM (CONFIGURATION COMMAND)
## Define a Disk or Tape Drive
### Versions 3.2 and later, non-IBM releases only

The Drive Parameters configuration command (drivparm) defines the operating characteristics of a disk drive or tape drive. If you don't specify device characteristics with Drivparm, MS-DOS assumes standard characteristics for that type of device. In general, you need to use the Drivparm command only when you need to change the way MS-DOS defines a disk or tape drive on your system. If you need more information, refer to the documentation that came with the drive and with your version of MS-DOS.

## ECHO (BATCH COMMAND)
## Display a Message
### Versions 2 and later

*Page 340*

The Echo command sends a message to the standard output device (usually the display), controls whether MS-DOS displays batch commands as it carries them out (echo on), or displays the status of echo (on or off). MS-DOS turns echo on when it starts carrying out the commands in a batch file, unless the file is started by another batch file that has turned echo off.

**echo on off <message>**

*on* tells MS-DOS to display each command as it is carried out.
*off* tells MS-DOS not to display each command as it is carried out.
<message> is a message to be sent to standard output.

If you enter an Echo command with no parameters (just type *echo*), MS-DOS displays the status of echo (either *ECHO is on* or *ECHO is off*).

To avoid displaying a line in a batch file, start the line with the @ symbol (versions 3.3 and later). To echo blank lines to the screen and improve the appearance of a batch file, either type *echo* followed immediately by a period (*echo.*) or type *echo*, hold down the Alt key, and type *255* on the numeric keypad.

### Examples

To turn echo on:

    echo on

To turn echo off:

    echo off

To display a blank line, the message *Put the backup disk in drive A*, and another blank line:

    @echo.
    @echo Put the backup disk in drive A
    @echo.

To display the echo status:

    C:\>echo

## EDIT
## Create or Change Text Files
### Versions 5 and later

*Page 279*

The Edit command starts the MS-DOS Editor, a text editor that allows you to choose from menus to create, change, and save files.

The MS-DOS Editor, called Edit for short in this book, is described in 'Chapter 12, "Creating and Editing Files of Text." The program's on-screen help can also be used both for learning and as a reference tool. Edit offers two types of help: general information and context-sensitive help that can be requested after a command is chosen.

**NOTE:** *In order to run Edit, MS-DOS must be able to find the file QBASIC.EXE. Be sure this file is in the command path.*

### edit <filename> /B /G /H /nohi

<filename> is the name of an existing file you want to view or edit. Omit <filename> to start Edit without loading a file into memory.

/B starts Edit in monochrome if you have a color monitor.

485

/G used with a CGA display and adapter causes Edit to update the screen contents as rapidly as possible. If this parameter produces white streaks or dots on the screen, restart the editor without /G.

/H causes Edit to display as many lines per screen as your monitor can manage.

*/nohi* tells Edit that your display does not support high-intensity characters (bright white, for example).

The following lists briefly describe each of the menus used with Edit.

**File menu:** Used for creating, loading, saving, and printing files. It also quits the editor. The File commands are:

- New—creates a new file. If another document is on the screen, Edit prompts you to save or close the open file or to cancel the File New command.

- Open—opens an existing file. This command causes the editor to display a dialog box. The dialog box asks for the name of the file to open and also includes a list of other drives and directories you can choose from if the file is not on the current drive or in the current directory.

- Save—saves the current file under the name already assigned to it. If the file has not been named, the editor asks you to name it.

- Save As—both names and saves a file. This command produces a dialog box in which you enter the name you want to give the file and, optionally, choose a different drive, directory, or both in which to save the file.

- Print—prints the current file. This command produces a dialog box in which you can choose to print the entire document or a selected portion of it.

- Exit—quits the editor. If you choose File Exit before saving the latest changes to a file, the editor prompts you to save or close the file or to cancel the command.

**Edit menu:** Lets you rearrange a file by cutting, copying, and inserting text in different locations. When you cut text, you delete it from the document; when you copy text, you duplicate it. Edit temporarily stores cut or copied text in a special area of memory called the Clipboard. The Edit commands are:

- Cut—deletes selected text to the Clipboard, where it remains until replaced by other text you cut or copy.

- Copy—copies selected text to the Clipboard, where it remains until replaced by other text you cut or copy.

- Paste—inserts the text most recently cut or copied to the Clipboard in the document at the cursor location.

- Clear—deletes selected text without placing it on the Clipboard. Text deleted with this command cannot be retrieved.

**Search menu:** Searches the current document for a string of characters you specify. Searches begin at the current cursor position and cycle back to the beginning of the document if necessary. The commands on the Search menu are:

- Find—searches for a particular string. This command produces a dialog box that asks you to specify the string, choose to match or ignore uppercase and lowercase letters, and either limit the search to complete words (occurrences of the string surrounded by blanks) or include occurrences found as part of other words (for example, *whole* in *wholesome*).

- Repeat Last Find—repeats the last search. If no earlier search has been performed, this command searches for the next occurrence of the word the cursor is on (or the word to the left of the cursor if it is between words).

- Change—replaces one string with another. This command produces a dialog box that allows you to specify the string to change and the string to change it to, whether to match or ignore uppercase and lowercase, whether to limit the search to whole words, and whether the editor is to confirm before making each change.

**Options menu:** Controls the screen and lets you set the path to Edit's online help (stored in a file named EDIT.HLP). The Options commands are:

- Display—controls three screen features: color, the display of scroll bars at the side and bottom of the screen, and the number of spaces in each tab.

- Help Path—sets the path to EDIT.HLP.

**Help menu:** At the top right corner of the screen, provides access to online help. The Help commands are:

- Getting Started—includes help on using Edit, help on getting help, and help on starting the editor with various options.

- Keyboard—tells you about the keystrokes used with Edit.

- About—displays version and copyright information about Edit.

## EDLIN
## Create or Modify a Text File
### Versions 1 through 5

Edlin is a line-oriented text editor. It includes a variety of commands for insert-ing, deleting, changing, copying, and moving lines. Each line can be up to 253 characters long. In addition to the Edlin commands, you can use the MS-DOS edit-ing keys to edit individual lines.

Edlin is called a line-oriented editor because it displays a line number at the beginning of each line; these numbers are for reference only and are not part of the file. Edlin renumbers lines after any command that changes the sequence or number of lines in the file, to maintain an unbroken sequence.

When you enter the Edlin command (type *edlin* followed by a file name) at the system prompt, Edlin loads the file to be edited (or creates it, if it's a new file), displays an asterisk (its prompt), and waits for a command.

Most Edlin commands consist of a single character preceded by one or more parameters (usually line numbers). The command characters can be entered in either uppercase or lowercase, and you can enter more than one command on a line by separating them with semicolons.

Just as MS-DOS keeps track of a current drive and current directory, Edlin keeps track of the *current line,* which is the target for many commands if you don't specify a line number. Many of the Edlin commands operate on a range of lines, which you define by specifying the beginning and ending line numbers.

All Edlin commands that accept a line number or range of line numbers recognize the following symbolic references:

| | |
|---|---|
| # | means the line after the last line in the file |
| . | (a period) means the current line |
| + or − | specifies line numbers relative to the current line; for example, +3 means three lines past the current line |

When you end an editing session and write a revised file back to disk, Edlin renames the original version to give it the extension BAK, thus saving a backup copy of the original. If a file with the same name and the extension BAK exists on the same disk, Edlin deletes the existing file before renaming the original.

To start Edlin, you enter the Edlin command at the MS-DOS system prompt.

**edlin <filename> /B**

<filename> is the name of the text file to be created or changed. If the file exists, Edlin copies it into memory. If the file doesn't exist, Edlin creates it. Except in version 3.3, Edlin won't edit a file whose extension is BAK. To edit a file whose extension is BAK, first change the extension with the MS-DOS Rename command.

/B causes Edlin to ignore any Control-Z (end-of-file) characters in the file.

Brief descriptions of Edlin commands follow, with examples showing representative uses of each.

**Append:** Reads additional lines of a file into memory. Use Append when a file is larger than 75 percent of available memory.

**<lines>a**

<lines> specifies the number of lines to append.

For example, to append 200 lines to the file in memory:

```
*200a
```

**Copy:** Copies one or more lines from one place in a file to another.

**<from>,<to>,<target>,<count>c**

<from> is the number of the first line to be copied; <to> is the number of the last. <target> is the number of the line *above* which the lines are to be copied. <count> specifies how many times the lines are to be copied. If you omit <from>, <to>, or both, be sure to type their trailing comma(s) in your command.

The following examples assume that line 20 is the current line. To copy lines 20 through 25 above line 5:

```
*20,25,5c
```

To copy line 20 above line 30:

```
*20,20,30c
```

or, using symbolic references:

```
*,,+10c
```

**Delete:** Deletes specified lines from a file.

**<from>,<to>d**

<from> is the number of the first line to be deleted; <to> is the number of the last. If you omit the <from> parameter, be sure to type its trailing comma in your command. If you omit both <from> and <to> and simply type *d*, Edlin deletes the current line.

The following examples assume that line 20 is the current line. To delete lines 20 through 25:

```
*20,25d
```

or, using symbolic references:

```
*,+5d
```

To delete the current line:

```
*d
```

**Edit:** Not strictly a command. To edit a line, type the line number and press Enter. You can edit the current line by typing a period and pressing Enter. You can edit the line that follows the current line by just pressing Enter.

> **<line> or .**

<line> is the number of the line to be edited.

The following examples assume that line 20 is the current line. Pressing the Enter key is represented by <Enter>. To edit line 25:

```
*25<Enter>
```

or, using symbolic references:

```
*+5<Enter>
```

To edit the current line (line 20):

```
*.<Enter>
```

To edit line 21:

```
*<Enter>
```

**End Edit:** Ends the editing session and writes the current file to disk. (To end the session without saving the file, you use the Quit command, described later.)

> **e**

The End Edit command has no parameters. To end the editing session and save the current file:

```
*e
```

**Insert:** Enters new lines into the file being edited. Edlin prompts with the number of the new line and continues to prompt until you press Ctrl-C to stop inserting lines.

> **<target>i**

<target> is the line before which the new line(s) are to be inserted. If you don't specify <target>, the lines are inserted above the current line. To add lines to the end of the file, you can specify <target> as # or as a number larger than the highest line number in the file.

The following examples assume that line 20 is the current line. To insert lines after line 20:

```
*21i
```

To insert lines at the beginning of the file:

```
*1i
```

To insert lines at the end of the file:

```
*#i
```

**List:** Displays one or more lines of the file.

**<from>,<to>l**

<from> is the number of the first line to be displayed; <to> is the number of the last. If you don't specify <from>, Edlin starts 11 lines before the current line. If you don't specify <to>, Edlin displays one screenful starting with <from>. If you omit <from>, be sure to type the trailing comma in your command. If you omit both <from> and <to> and simply type *l*, Edlin displays one screenful centered around the current line.

The following examples assume that the current line is 30. To list lines 30 through 40:

```
*30,40l
```

To list one screenful centered around the current line:

```
*l
```

**Move:** Moves one or more specified lines from one location in a file to another, deleting them from the original location.

**<from>,<to>,<target>m**

<from> is the number of the first line to be moved; <to> is the number of the last; <target> is the line above which the line or lines are to be moved. If you omit <from>, Edlin starts with the current line. If you omit <to>, Edlin stops with the current line. If you omit <from>, <to>, or both, be sure to type the trailing comma(s) in your command.

The following examples assume that line 20 is the current line. To move lines 20 through 25 above line 5:

```
*20,25,5m
```

To move line 20 above line 30:

```
*20,20,30m
```

or, using symbolic references:

```
*,,30m
```

**Page:** Displays up to one screenful of a file at a time.

**<from>,<to>p**

<from> is the number of the first line to be displayed; <to> is the number of the last. If you omit <from>, Edlin starts with the line after the current line. If you omit <to>, Edlin displays one screenful starting with <from>. If you omit <from>, be sure to type the trailing comma. If you omit both <from> and <to> and simply type *p*, Edlin displays one screenful, starting with the line after the current line.

The following examples assume that the current line is 30. To display lines 30 through 40:

```
*30,40p
```

To display one screenful, starting with the line after the current line:

```
*p
```

**Quit:** Ends an editing session without saving the current file. The Quit command has no parameters. To avoid inadvertent loss of a file, however, Edlin prompts for confirmation before quitting.

**q**

To quit the editing session without saving the current file:

```
*q
```

Edlin responds:

```
Abort edit (Y/N)?
```

Press Y to quit; press N to remain in Edlin.

**Replace:** Replaces one character string with another in one or more lines of a file. You can tell Edlin to prompt for confirmation before each replacement by including a question mark (?) in the command.

**\<from>,\<to>?r\<string1>\<Ctrl-Z or F6>\<string2>**

\<from> is the number of the first line in which the string is to be replaced; \<to> is the number of the last. The ? tells Edlin to prompt before replacement. \<string1> is the string to be replaced; \<string2> is the replacement string. You must separate the two strings by pressing Ctrl-Z or the F6 key. If you omit \<from>, be sure to type the trailing comma in your command.

The following examples assume that line 20 is the current line. To replace all occurrences of *company* with *corporation* in lines 21 through 30:

```
*21,30rcompany<Ctrl-Z>corporation
```

To replace all occurrences of *March* with *April* from line 21 through the end of the file, requesting a prompt before each replacement:

```
*21,#?rMarch<Ctrl-Z>April
```

**Search:** Searches a file for a specified string of characters. Because the file might contain more than one occurrence of the string, you can tell Edlin to prompt for confirmation before stopping the search.

**\<from>,\<to>?s\<string>**

\<from> is the number of the first line to be searched; \<to> is the number of the last. The ? tells Edlin to prompt for confirmation before ending the search. \<string> is the string to search for. If you omit \<from>, be sure to type the trailing comma in your command.

The following examples assume that line 20 is the current line. To find the first occurrence of *value* in lines 21 through 30:

```
*21,30svalue
```

To find a particular occurrence of *value*, searching the entire file and instructing Edlin to prompt for confirmation:

```
*1,#?svalue
```

**Transfer:** Merges the contents of another file into the current file.

**\<target>t\<filename>**

\<target> is the number of the line above which the incoming file will be transferred. If you don't specify \<target>, Edlin assumes the current line. \<filename> is the name of the file whose contents are to be transferred. In versions 3 and later, you can include a directory path with \<filename>.

The following example assumes that line 20 is the current line. To merge the contents of REPORT.DOC above line 20:

```
*20treport.doc
```

or

```
*treport.doc
```

**Write:** Starting at the beginning of the current file, writes a specified number of lines from memory to disk. Write makes room for more lines to be read into memory with the Append command.

### &lt;lines&gt;w

&lt;lines&gt; specifies the number of lines to write. If you omit &lt;lines&gt;, Edlin writes lines until available memory is 25 percent full.

For example, to write 200 lines to disk:

```
*200w
```

## EMM386
## Enable and Disable Expanded Memory
### Versions 5 and later

The EMM386 command works with the EMM386.EXE device driver described in the following entry. You can use the EMM386 command to control access to expanded memory on a computer with an 80386 or 80486 microprocessor.

### EMM386 on off auto

*on* enables access to expanded memory controlled by the EMM386.EXE device driver.

*off* suspends access to expanded memory, making this type of memory temporarily unavailable to programs requesting it.

*auto* provides access to expanded memory only if a program requests it.

This command includes two additional parameters, *w=on*, and *w=off*, that apply to a computer with a Weitek coprocessor. If you need this additional support, refer to the documentation that came with your version of MS-DOS.

## EMM386.EXE
## Simulate Expanded Memory and
## Provide Access to Upper Memory Blocks
### Versions 5 and later

*Pages 383, 392*

EMM386.EXE is the name of a device driver included with versions 5 and later of MS-DOS. This program has two functions: to treat extended memory as if it were expanded memory and to provide access to the upper memory area located between 640 KB and 1 MB. As its name implies, EMM386.EXE requires a computer based on the 80386 (or 80486 or better) microprocessor.

To use EMM386.EXE (or the related EMM386 command), you must tell MS-DOS this device driver exists by including a Device command in your CONFIG.SYS file. EMM386.EXE includes a number of parameters, most of which are useful primarily to programmers and are beyond the scope of this book. The basic form for identifying the device driver is:

**device=<path>emm386.exe <size> ram noems**

<path> specifies the path to the file EMM386.EXE. Most likely, it is C:\DOS. If you don't specify <path>, MS-DOS looks in the root directory of the system disk.

<size> specifies the amount of extended memory, in kilobytes, that you want to use as if it were expanded memory. You do this for programs that can use expanded memory but not extended memory. The amount you need depends on the memory requirements of your programs. <size> can be any value from 16 through 32768. If you don't include <size>, MS-DOS assumes 256; if you specify a value that can't be divided evenly by 16, MS-DOS rounds the value down to the nearest multiple of 16.

*ram* allows you to use both expanded memory and blocks of memory (UMBs) in the upper memory area.

*noems* provides access to the upper memory area but not to any expanded memory. Use either *ram* or *noems* if you plan to load device drivers or programs into reserved memory with the Devicehigh configuration command or the Loadhigh command.

### Example

Because memory management is a complex task for MS-DOS, you include several related commands in CONFIG.SYS along with the Device command you use to identify EMM386.EXE. The following example shows a sample CONFIG.SYS file that includes the commands you need. In this example, the Dos command is used both to load MS-DOS into high memory and to enable MS-DOS to use UMBs. The Device command identifying EMM386.EXE requests access to the upper memory area but not to expanded memory, and the sample Devicehigh command loads the ANSI.SYS device driver into upper memory.

```
dos=high,umb
device=c:\dos\himem.sys
device=c:\dos\emm386.exe noems
devicehigh=c:\dos\ansi.sys
```

## ERASE
## Erase a File

*See* Delete.

## EXE2BIN
## Convert an Executable (EXE) File to COM Format

**Versions 1 through 5**

The Exe2bin command converts a program command file from EXE format to COM format. Exe2bin is an advanced MS-DOS command, usually used by programmers, and a description of its use is beyond the scope of this book; if you need details, refer to the MS-DOS *Technical Reference* or the *Programmer's Reference* manual.

## EXIT
## Leave COMMAND.COM

**Versions 2 and later**

*Page 264*

The Exit command leaves the currently active version of COMMAND.COM and returns control of the system to the program from which that version was started. Essentially, the Exit command returns you to a prior task.

COMMAND.COM is the part of MS-DOS that interacts with you by waiting for and responding to commands. When you or a program activates the COMMAND.COM program, you start a new version of it, adding a new layer to the processes that MS-DOS keeps track of in the system. For example, if you're using the MS-DOS Shell and leave it by choosing Command Prompt from the Main window, you start a new version of COMMAND.COM. That's why you must type *exit* to return to the Shell. You're exiting one copy of COMMAND.COM and returning to the program from which you started it.

The Exit command has no parameters:

**exit**

The command has no effect if COMMAND.COM was activated by a Command command with the /P (for *permanent*) parameter.

## EXPAND
## Expand Compressed MS-DOS Files

**Versions 5 and later**

Expand is the name of a utility program that can be used to transfer individual MS-DOS files from the original MS-DOS floppy disks to a working MS-DOS disk, such as a hard disk. This program is included with MS-DOS because most command files in versions 5 and later are stored on the MS-DOS floppy disks in a special compressed format. Compressed files have extensions ending in an underscore (for example, COMMAND.CO_). They are not usable in compressed form, and they cannot be transferred to a working MS-DOS disk with Copy, Replace, or a similar command. Expand decompresses such a file, at the same time placing the file in a target disk or directory you specify.

**expand <source> <target>**

<source> is the drive, path, and file name of the compressed file you want to expand. You cannot use wildcards to expand more than one file at a time.

If you omit <target>, MS-DOS prompts you for the target. If you omit both <source> and <target>, MS-DOS prompts you for both.

<target> is the destination drive, path, and file name of the expanded file. When you expand a file, use the same file name, but replace the underscore with the letter needed to form a recognizable MS-DOS extension; for example, change CO_ to COM, SY_ to SYS, or EX_ to EXE.

### Example

Suppose you deleted the RAMDRIVE.SYS file from your \DOS directory because you wanted to reduce the amount of storage space needed by MS-DOS on the hard disk. You recently added an extra-memory board and now want to reinstate the file you deleted. To expand the file and place it in C:\DOS, first place your MS-DOS floppy disk labeled *Disk 1* in drive A, and type *type a:packing.lst | more* to see which MS-DOS floppy disk contains the files. Then place the MS-DOS floppy disk with RAMDRIVE.SY_ in drive A and type:

```
C:\>expand a:ramdrive.sy_ c:\dos\ramdrive.sys
```

# FASTHELP
## Command Help

*See* Help.

# FASTOPEN
## Speed Up File Access
### Versions 3.3 and later

*Page 401*

The Fastopen command tells MS-DOS to keep in memory the storage locations of subdirectories and files on one or more hard disks that have been used during the current session. When the Fastopen command is used, MS-DOS checks in memory before searching the disk whenever it is told to find a file or a subdirectory. If the file or subdirectory has already been used, its disk location is in memory, and MS-DOS can go directly to the storage location, instead of searching through each directory in the path. Fastopen cannot be used to keep track of files stored on floppy disks or on a network drive.

If you and your applications tend to use the same files or directories over and over, the Fastopen command can make your system noticeably faster. You can enter the Fastopen command only once during a session with MS-DOS, so if you want to increase or decrease the number of files and directories Fastopen tracks, you must restart your system.

**fastopen <drive>=<files> /X**

<drive> is the drive letter, followed by a colon, of the hard disk whose files and subdirectories you want MS-DOS to track. The drive letter must refer to a hard disk.

<files> is the number of file and subdirectory locations MS-DOS is to keep in memory. The number of files must be separated from <drive> by an equal sign. You can specify up to 999 files; each file requires about 50 bytes of memory. If you don't specify <files>, MS-DOS keeps track of the last 48 files and subdirectories (this number varies in different releases of MS-DOS).

/X keeps Fastopen information in expanded memory (versions 4 and later).

Because your CONFIG.SYS or AUTOEXEC.BAT file might already include a Fastopen command, check their contents before entering the command at the system prompt. If you do use Fastopen and find that it does speed your system, you can put the command in either CONFIG.SYS or AUTOEXEC.BAT in the forms shown in the following examples.

### Examples

To keep track of the last 30 files and subdirectories used on the hard disk in drive C, you can type the following command or put it in AUTOEXEC.BAT:

```
fastopen c:=30
```

Assuming that the file FASTOPEN.EXE is in C:\DOS, the following command in CONFIG.SYS is equivalent to the command in the preceding example:

```
install=c:\dos\fastopen.exe c:=30
```

## FC (FILE COMPARISON)
## Compare Two Files

### Versions 2 and later, primarily non-IBM releases

*Page 83*

The File Comparison command (FC) compares two files and sends the differences to standard output—normally the display. By redirecting output, you can also send the results of a comparison to a file or to another device, such as a printer.

**NOTE:** *Another way to compare files is with the Compare command, available in IBM versions of MS-DOS and in Microsoft's versions 3.3 through 5. See the entry on Compare.*

You can use FC to compare either text files or command files (program files with such extensions as EXE, COM, and SYS). Depending on the parameters you specify, you can compare files either line by line or byte by byte.

In a line-by-line comparison, FC starts by reading as many lines from each file as will fit in the portion of memory it uses (enough to hold 100 lines, unless you specify otherwise). It then compares the lines of the first file with the lines of the second. If it finds any differences, it displays the last line in each file that matched, the lines that don't match, and the first lines in each file that once again match.

When it finds differences, FC assumes that the lines of the two files are no longer synchronized—they don't correspond on a one-to-one basis. Unless you specify otherwise, FC looks for two sequential matching lines before it once again assumes the files are synchronized. If none of the succeeding lines in memory match up, FC displays the message *Resync failed. Files are too different* ( *\*\*\*Files are different \*\*\** in some versions of MS-DOS).

In a byte-by-byte, or binary, comparison, FC compares the two files from beginning to end. It does not display mismatched lines, but it does tell you which bytes, counting from the beginning of the file, are different, and it tells you what their coded values are in the hexadecimal (base-16) numbering system. If one file is shorter than the other, FC displays the message *FC: FILEx longer than FILEy* at the end of the comparison. Binary comparisons are primarily useful for checking nontext files, such as programs.

The FC command includes the following parameters:

**fc /A /B /C /L /LB*n* /N /*nnnn* /T /W <filename1> <filename2>**

/A tells FC to abbreviate its report, displaying only the first and last lines of each group of matched/mismatched lines (versions 3.2 and later).

/B specifies that the files are to be compared byte by byte. If you use /B, you cannot use any parameters other than <filename1> and <filename2>.

/C tells FC to ignore differences between uppercase and lowercase.

/L tells FC to compare the files as ASCII text. The command assumes this parameter for all text files (those without program-file extensions, such as COM, SYS, and EXE).

/LB*n*, where *n* is a number you supply, specifies how many lines FC reads into memory. If you omit *n* (specify just /LB), FC assumes 100.

/N tells FC to display line numbers in its report of an ASCII comparison.

/*nnnn*, where *nnnn* is a number you supply, tells FC how many matching lines it must find after a mismatch to assume the files again correspond on a line-by-line basis. If you don't specify /*nnnn*, FC assumes 2 lines (3 in MS-DOS versions through 3.2).

/T tells FC to treat tabs as tabs rather than as strings of spaces.

/W tells FC to convert tabs and consecutive spaces within a line to a single space.

<filename1> and <filename2> are the names of the files to be compared. Each can include a drive letter and a path, and you can include wildcard characters.

### Examples

To compare two text files (C:\CLIENTS\MEMO.DOC and A:MEMO.DOC) line by line, using the values FC assumes:

```
C:\>fc c:\clients\memo.doc a:memo.doc
```

To compare the same files, displaying line numbers as part of the output:

```
C:\>fc /n c:\clients\memo.doc a:memo.doc
```

To compare the files, ignoring case and redirecting the output to the printer:

```
C:\>fc /c c:\clients\memo.doc a:memo.doc > prn
```

To perform a byte-by-byte comparison of two nontext files (Q1.DAT and JAN-MAR.DAT):

```
C:\>fc /b q1.dat jan-mar.dat
```

## FCBS (CONFIGURATION COMMAND)
## Set Maximum Open File Control Blocks (FCBs)
### Versions 3 and later, IBM releases 3.1 and later

One of the two ways MS-DOS keeps track of file usage is by means of small blocks of information called file control blocks, or FCBs. The FCBS configuration command lets you specify the largest number of files controlled by file control blocks that can be open at the same time when file sharing is in effect. The FCBS command also lets you protect some or all of the open files from being automatically closed. Unless you specify otherwise, MS-DOS assumes four FCB-controlled files, none of them protected from closure.

You're unlikely to need the FCBS configuration command in everyday use of your computer. If you need more information on this command, refer to the documentation that came with your version of MS-DOS.

# FDISK
## Configure a Hard Disk
### Versions 3.2 and later, IBM releases 2 and later

The Fdisk command prepares a hard disk for use by MS-DOS and, if you choose, by another operating system as well. In preparing the disk, Fdisk creates one or more independent areas—subsections—called *partitions.*

Computers are usually delivered with the hard disk already prepared and, often, with MS-DOS already installed and ready to start from the hard disk. You use Fdisk if your hard disk is not prepared or if you decide to change or delete one or more partitions.

> **WARNING:** *If you use Fdisk to modify a hard disk that already contains information, be sure to back up any of the information you want to save before using Fdisk. Otherwise, you'll lose it all.*

The Fdisk command in versions through 5 has no parameters; the versions 6 and 6.2 Fdisk command has one parameter:

**fdisk /status**

*/status* causes Fdisk simply to display partition information without starting the program.

When you type *fdisk*, you start a program that steps you through available choices and procedures via a series of question-and-answer menus. Fdisk uses a few terms you don't encounter in your everyday use of MS-DOS, so the following definitions might help if you're planning to use Fdisk.

**Partition:** As mentioned earlier, a partition is a portion of the hard disk. You can have two types of MS-DOS partitions on a hard disk: the *primary MS-DOS partition* and an *extended MS-DOS partition.*

The primary MS-DOS partition is the one you dedicate to MS-DOS. Beginning with version 4, the primary MS-DOS partition can be any size, up to the full capacity of a hard disk. In earlier versions, this partition can be no larger than 32 MB.

The extended MS-DOS partition, available in versions 3.3 and later, lets you create a second partition and thus divide the storage space on a large hard disk into two smaller units, both of them usable by MS-DOS.

**Active partition:** This is the partition from which you start MS-DOS. If you want MS-DOS to start from your hard disk, the primary MS-DOS partition must also be the active partition. Fdisk lets you choose the active partition.

**Logical drive:** In relation to Fdisk, this is a portion of the extended MS-DOS partition that you use as if it were a separate disk drive. A logical drive is not physically separate from your hard disk, but MS-DOS treats it as if it were. When you create a logical drive with Fdisk, you (or MS-DOS) assign it a drive letter (such as D:) and a size (such as 20 MB). Each logical drive you create behaves—and can be treated—as if it were a real (physical) disk drive.

**Cylinder:** This is a way of referring to storage space on a hard disk. You see this term if you're using Fdisk with version 3.3. The program tells you how large your hard disk is (in cylinders) and, if you're creating an extended MS-DOS partition, asks you how large the partition should be—again, in cylinders. You can estimate roughly how many cylinders equal a given percentage of your hard disk by deciding on a percentage and then multiplying the total number of cylinders by that amount.

The actual process of using Fdisk is documented thoroughly in the manual that comes with MS-DOS. Read these details carefully before you prepare or try to change a hard disk, especially one that already contains programs or data.

## FILES (CONFIGURATION COMMAND)
## Set Maximum Open File Handles

### Versions 2 and later

*Page 396*

One of the two ways MS-DOS keeps track of file usage is by assigning a number called a *handle* to each open file. The Files configuration command sets the maximum number of files controlled by file handles that can be open at one time.

**files=<number>**

<number> specifies how many files can be open at the same time. It can be from 8 through 255; if you don't specify <number>, MS-DOS assumes 8. Each additional open file above 8 increases the memory used by MS-DOS.

When you install MS-DOS, it might create or modify CONFIG.SYS to include a Files command. If a program you're using requires more open files, edit your CONFIG.SYS file. Often the program's documentation will specify an appropriate Files command. If you need more information on this command, refer to the documentation that came with your version of MS-DOS.

# FIND
## Search Files for a Character String
### Versions 2 and later

*Page 305*

The Find filter command searches one or more files for a character string and sends each line that contains the string to standard output (usually the display).

> **find /V /C /N /I "&lt;string&gt;" &lt;filename&gt;**

/V finds lines that *don't* contain &lt;string&gt;.

/C sends the total number of lines (the *count*), rather than the lines themselves, to standard output. If you specify both /C and /N, the Find command ignores /N.

/N includes the line number with each line of output.

/I, beginning with version 5, tells Find to ignore uppercase and lowercase differences in the search.

"&lt;string&gt;" is the character string to search for. You must enclose the string in quotation marks. To include a quotation mark in &lt;string&gt;, type two quotation marks.

&lt;filename&gt; is the name of the file or files to be searched. You can specify more than one file name, separating them with spaces. If you omit &lt;filename&gt;, the Find command searches its standard input; you can either redirect standard input or pipe the output of another command to the Find command. You can include a path, but you cannot use wildcards in &lt;filename&gt;.

### Examples

To find all lines that contain the string *Sales* (note the capital *S*) in the file REPORT.DOC in the current directory:

```
C:\MKT\WP>find "Sales" report.doc
```

To find all lines that contain the string *April* in the file LETTERS.DOC in the current directory, include the line numbers, and redirect the output to the printer:

```
C:\MKT\WP>find /n "April" letters.doc > prn
```

With version 5 or later of MS-DOS, to find all lines in REPORT.DOC that contain the word *company* in any combination of uppercase and lowercase letters:

```
C:\MKT\WP>find /i "company" report.doc
```

In any version of MS-DOS, to find all lines that don't contain the string &lt;DIR&gt; in the output of a Directory command:

```
C:\>dir | find /v "<DIR>"
```

Or, in version 5 or later only:

```
C:\>dir | find /i /v "<dir>"
```

(Note that the versions 5 and later command *dir /a:-d* would be easier to use here.)

# FOR (BATCH COMMAND)
## Carry Out a Batch Command Several Times

### Versions 2 and later

*Page 366*

The For batch command carries out an MS-DOS command once for each member specified by a set of character strings, such as a set of file names.

**for %%p in (<set>) do <command> <parameters>**

%%p is a replaceable parameter that is given the value of each member of <set> by MS-DOS before <command> is carried out. It is represented by two percent signs (%%) followed by any character except one of the redirection symbols: <, >, or |.

<set> is a series of strings separated by blanks. <command> is carried out once for each member of <set>. If <set> is empty, <command> isn't carried out. <set> can contain character strings, path names, or file names. If one of the strings is a file name that includes wildcard characters, MS-DOS sets %%p, in turn, to each file name that matches the wildcard character, then carries out <command>.

<command> is any MS-DOS command except another For command. Through version 3.2, you can carry out another batch command without returning to the system prompt by making <command> a Command command with the /C parameter and specifying the batch file as the string that follows the /C parameter (see the second example that follows). If you're using version 3.3 or later, you can accomplish the same thing by using the Call command.

<parameters> specifies any parameters needed by <command>.

NOTE: *You can type a For command at the system prompt, rather than enter it in a batch file. If you do, use %p instead of %%p. Everything else is the same.*

## Examples

To copy up to nine files named in the batch command line to the current directory of the disk in drive A:

```
for %%p in (%1 %2 %3 %4 %5 %6 %7 %8 %9) do copy %%p a:
```

To carry out the batch files named BAT1.BAT, BAT2.BAT, and BAT3.BAT in versions 3.3 and later:

```
for %%p in (1 2 3) do call bat%%p
```

In versions prior to 3.3, the For command would be:

```
for %%p in (1 2 3) do command /c bat%%p
```

If you specified the command to be carried out as *bat%%p* (omitting *command /c*), MS-DOS would return to the system prompt after carrying out BAT1.BAT.

## FORMAT
## Prepare a Disk

### Versions 1 and later

*Pages 16, 101, 214*

The Format command prepares a disk for use by MS-DOS. Beginning with version 5, MS-DOS normally carries out a safe format that can be undone with the Unformat command. Through version 4, however, formatting a disk destroys the directory information MS-DOS uses to locate files. That means information previously stored on the disk can no longer be retrieved. Because inadvertent formatting can be inconvenient or can mean the loss of valuable programs and data, MS-DOS does not begin to format a disk until you press Enter to verify that the disk you want to format is in the drive you specified.

> **NOTE:** *With MS-DOS 3.1 and earlier, be careful to specify a drive letter and verify that the disk to be formatted is actually in that drive. If you don't specify the drive, these versions of MS-DOS format the disk in the current drive, even if it's a system disk or a hard disk.*

Don't use Format with a drive affected by a Join or Substitute command. Format cannot be used with a network drive. You also shouldn't use Format with a drive compressed by DoubleSpace. Use *dblspace /format* instead. The following description includes some parameters not mentioned in earlier chapters. Not all parameters are available with all versions of MS-DOS.

**format <drive> /1 /4 /8 /F:<size> /N:<sectors> /T:<tracks> /S /B /V:<label> /Q /U**

<drive> is the letter of the drive, followed by a colon, that contains the disk to be formatted. Early versions of MS-DOS don't require <drive>, but including the drive letter with every Format command is a good habit to form.

/1, a parameter that maintains compatibility with older computers and early versions of MS-DOS, formats only the first side of a 5.25-inch floppy disk, even if the disk is in a double-sided drive.

/4 formats a 5.25-inch, 360 KB floppy disk in a 1.2 MB drive. If used with the /1 parameter, /4 formats a 180 KB floppy disk. Disks formatted with this parameter in a high-capacity drive do not always work reliably in a 180 KB or a 360 KB drive.

/8, another parameter that maintains compatibility with older systems, formats a 5.25-inch floppy disk for 8 sectors per track (320 KB floppy disk capacity).

/F:<size> specifies the capacity (in kilobytes) for which the floppy disk should be formatted. Valid entries for <size> are 160, 180, 320, 360, 720, 1200, 1440, and (in versions 5 and later), 2880. The following examples, using 1200 KB as a model, show the various ways you can specify <size>: 1200, 1200K, 1200KB, 1.2, 1.2M, or 1.2MB. /F:<size> is in versions 4 and later.

/N:<sectors> and /T:<tracks> specify the number of sectors and tracks to format if you want to format less than the maximum capacity of the disk drive. These parameters are available in versions 3.2 and later. If you specify the parameter /N:<sectors>, you must also specify /T:<tracks>. Valid combinations of sectors and tracks for standard disk sizes are as follows:

| Size | Sectors | Tracks |
| --- | --- | --- |
| 360 KB | 9 | 40 |
| 720 KB | 9 | 80 |
| 1.2 MB | 15 | 80 |
| 1.44 MB | 18 | 80 |
| 2.88 MB | 36 | 80 |

/S creates a system disk by copying MS-DOS system files to the formatted disk.

/B formats a floppy disk and reserves space for the MS-DOS hidden files. You can later copy these files to the disk with the System (sys) command. If you specify /B, you cannot specify /S.

/V:<label> in versions 4 and later assigns <label> as a volume label to the formatted disk. In earlier versions, /V (without the colon and <label>) tells MS-DOS to prompt for a volume label when formatting is complete.

The remaining two parameters are in versions 5 and later.

/Q (for *quick*) performs a fast reformat of an already formatted disk. In a quick format, MS-DOS clears away the directory records of previously stored files, but it does not check the disk for unusable areas. The reformatted disk retains the same storage capacity for which it was originally formatted.

/U (for *unconditional*) performs an irreversible format that destroys all previously stored information and cannot be undone with the Unformat command. An unconditional format is the type normally performed by earlier versions of MS-DOS.

### Examples

To format the floppy disk in drive A for its maximum capacity:

```
C:\>format a:
```

To format the floppy disk in drive A for its maximum capacity and assign it the volume label LETTERS (versions 4 and later):

```
C:\>format a: /v:letters
```

To format a system disk in drive A and assign it a volume label when formatting is complete (versions prior to 4.0):

```
C:\>format a: /v /s
```

After formatting the disk, MS-DOS prompts you to type a volume label of 11 characters or less. You can change or delete this label later with the Label command.

To format a 360 KB floppy disk in a 1.2 MB drive (versions 3.2 and later):

```
C:\>format a: /4
C:\>format a: /n:9 /t:40
```

Another way to format a 360 KB disk in a 1.2 MB drive in versions 4 and later:

```
C:\>format a: /f:360
```

To perform a quick format on a previously formatted disk in drive A (versions 5 and later):

```
C:\>format a: /q
```

To perform an unconditional format on the disk in drive A, making any existing files unrecoverable (versions 5 and later):

```
C:\>format a: /u
```

## GOTO (BATCH COMMAND)
## Jump to a Label
### Versions 2 and later

*Page 345*

The Goto batch command tells MS-DOS to jump to a specified label in a batch file and carry out the commands that follow. A label is a line that consists of a colon (:) followed by a string up to eight characters long.

**goto <label>**

<label> is the label in the batch file you want MS-DOS to jump to.

### Example

The batch file includes four labels (lines 2, 11, 13, and 16). These labels specify locations to which the Goto commands can refer.

The If command in the sixth line includes a *goto end* command that sends MS-DOS to the label *:end* and ends the batch file if the user presses *C*. The *errorlevel* option of the If command checks a special *errorlevel* value that the Choice command sets to report the user's choice. (See the entry for Choice in this appendix.) Thus, *goto end* is carried out and the batch file ends if the Choice command in line 5 reports an *errorlevel* of 3 or greater. Otherwise, MS-DOS continues on to the If command in the seventh line.

```
@echo off
:start
echo.
echo %1
choice /C:YNC /T:N,15 Do you want to delete this file
if errorlevel 3 goto end
if errorlevel 2 goto skip
del %1
echo %1 deleted
goto next
:skip
echo %1 NOT deleted
:next
shift
if not "%1"=="" goto start
:end
```

# GRAFTABL
## Enable Graphics Character Set
### Versions 3 through 5

The Load Graphics Table command (graftabl) enables MS-DOS to display special characters, such as accented letters, symbols, and line-drawing characters (character codes 128–255). When you use the Graftabl command, MS-DOS can display the characters when the Color Graphics Adapter is in graphics mode. The command is unnecessary with an Enhanced Graphics Adapter and has no effect when the Monochrome Display Adapter is used. You can use Graftabl only once during a session with MS-DOS.

**graftabl <codepage> /status ?**

<codepage> is the three-digit number that specifies the code page that MS-DOS is to use. You cannot specify <codepage> in versions prior to 3.3. Valid code pages are:

| | |
|---|---|
| 437 | United States |
| 850 | Multilingual (Latin I) |
| 852 | Slavic (Latin II) — MS-DOS 5 only |
| 860 | Portuguese |
| 863 | Canadian French |
| 865 | Nordic |

/status displays the current code page (versions 3.3 through 5). You can abbreviate this parameter as /sta.

? (typed as *graftabl ?*) displays the current code page, a description of the parameters you can use, and a list of the numbers and names of available code pages (version 4). In version 5, typing *graftabl /?* (note the slash) causes MS-DOS to display online help for this command.

### Examples

To enable MS-DOS to display the graphics characters in graphics mode:

```
C:\>graftabl
```

MS-DOS reads the table of character definitions into memory and tells you it has done so.

To enable MS-DOS to display the Canadian French character set (code page 863) in graphics mode (versions 3.3 through 5):

```
C:\>graftabl 863
```

To display the current graphics code page (versions 3.3 through 5):

```
C:\>graftabl /sta
```

## GRAPHICS
## Enable Printing of a Graphics Display
**Versions 3.2 and later, IBM releases 2 and later**

*Page 129*

The Graphics command loads a program that MS-DOS keeps in memory to print the display produced by the Color Graphics Adapter (CGA), Enhanced Graphics Adapter (EGA), or Video Graphics Array (VGA) used in a graphics mode. After you enter the Graphics command, pressing Shift-PrtSc enables MS-DOS to print either a color graphics screen or the text-based display produced by a mono-chrome adapter.

NOTE: *Not all printers can reproduce graphics images. The Graphics command itself is not compatible with Hercules monochrome graphics adapters or with Enhanced Graphics Adapters in enhanced display modes.*

The Graphics command can include several parameters or none at all; to see which, if any, are available to you, check the documentation that came with your version of MS-DOS.

**graphics <printer> <profile> /R /B /LCD /PB:<id> /C /F /P<port>**

<printer> is one of the following printers supported by the Graphics command. If you don't specify <printer>, MS-DOS assumes *graphics.*

| Specify As | For Printer Model |
|---|---|
| color1 | IBM Personal Computer Color Printer with a black ribbon or the black band of a color ribbon |
| color4 | IBM Personal Computer Color Printer with a red-green-blue-black ribbon |
| color8 | IBM Personal Computer Color Printer with a cyan-magenta-yellow-black ribbon |
| compact | IBM Personal Computer Compact Printer (versions prior to 4) |
| graphics | IBM Graphics Printer, Proprinter, Pageprinter, or Quietwriter |
| graphicswide | IBM Quietwriter or Proprinter with an 11-inch carriage (versions 4 and 5 only) |
| thermal | IBM PC Convertible Printer (versions 3.3 and later) |
| hpdefault | Any Hewlett-Packard PCL printer (versions 5 and later) |
| deskjet | Hewlett-Packard DeskJet (versions 5 and later) |
| laserjet | Hewlett-Packard LaserJet (versions 5 and later) |
| laserjetII | Hewlett-Packard LaserJet Series II (versions 5 and later) |
| paintjet | Hewlett-Packard PaintJet (versions 5 and later) |
| quietjet | Hewlett-Packard Quietjet (versions 5 and later) |
| quietjetplus | Hewlett-Packard Quietjet Plus (versions 5 and later) |
| ruggedwriter | Hewlett-Packard Rugged Writer (versions 5 and later) |
| ruggedwriterwide | Hewlett-Packard Rugged Writer with wide carriage (versions 5 and later) |
| thinkjet | Hewlett-Packard ThinkJet (versions 5 and later) |

<profile> specifies the name of the file that provides detailed information about the printer you're using. The file GRAPHICS.PRO, supplied with MS-DOS, describes all the printers listed for <printer> (versions 4 and later).

/R prints the screen as you see it on the display: light images on a dark background.

/B prints the background in color. It is valid only if <printer> is *color4* or *color8*.

/LCD prints the image from the liquid crystal display (LCD) screen of the IBM PC Convertible (versions 3.3 and later).

/C centers the printed image on the paper. It works with an image resolution of 640 by 200 or with a 320-by-200 image printed with the /F parameter (versions 3.2 and 3.3 of MS-DOS only; not in IBM releases).

/F (for *flip*) prints a 320-by-200 image sideways by rotating it 90 degrees (versions 3.2 and 3.3 of MS-DOS only; not in IBM releases).

/P <port> specifies the printer port. It can be *1* (LPT1), *2* (LPT2), or *3* (LPT3) (versions prior to 4).

/PB:<id> tells MS-DOS what aspect ratio (ratio of display width to display height) to use when printing a graphics image. Valid entries for <id> are STD, which specifies the aspect ratio of a standard display, and LCD, which specifies that the aspect ratio of an LCD display should be used (versions 4 and later).

On a noncolor printer, the Graphics command prints the screen with up to four shades of gray. On a color printer, screen colors are reproduced with or without the background color, depending on the Graphics parameter you specify. If the display is in a 640-by-200 or a higher-resolution graphics mode, the printed image is rotated 90 degrees (printed sideways).

### Examples

To enable printing a graphics display on an IBM Personal Graphics Printer:

```
C:\>graphics
```

To enable printing a graphics display with a colored background on an IBM Personal Computer Color Printer with an RGB ribbon:

```
C:\>graphics color4 /b
```

To enable printing a graphics display on a Hewlett-Packard LaserJet Series II, reversing the image so that a reverse-video image (white on black) is printed:

```
C:\>graphics laserjetII /r
```

## HELP
## Command Help

**Versions 5 and later**

*Page 66*

Beginning with version 5, MS-DOS provides online help with command formats. Requesting help for a particular command causes MS-DOS to display a description of the command, the form in which it is typed, and a list of parameters (if any) with descriptions of what they do. Parameter descriptions do not include the values MS-DOS accepts for variables (those shown in angle brackets in this book, as in Format /F:<size>).

Help can be requested either by typing:

**help <command>**  (in version 5)
**doshelp <command>**  (in version 6)
**fasthelp <command>**  (in versions 6 and 6.2)

or by typing:

**<command> /?**

<command>, in either request, is any MS-DOS command other than a configuration command or an Edlin, MS-DOS Editor, or MS-DOS Shell command.

### Example

To request online help for the Diskcopy command:

```
C:\>help diskcopy
```

or

```
C:\>diskcopy /?
```

MS-DOS displays:

```
Copies the contents of one floppy disk to another.

DISKCOPY [drive1: [drive2:]] [/1] [/V]

    /1   Copies only the first side of the disk.
    /V   Verifies that the information is copied correctly.

The two floppy disks must be the same type.
You may specify the same drive for drive1 and drive2.
```

## HELP
## Full-Screen Command Help
### Versions 6 and 6.2

*Page 66*

In versions 6 and 6.2, the Help command became a full-screen help system that provides help with all MS-DOS commands, including configuration and batch commands.

**help /B /G /H /nohi <command>**

/B starts Help in monochrome if you have a color monitor.

/G used with a CGA display and adapter causes Help to update the screen contents as rapidly as possible. If this parameter produces white streaks or dots on the screen, restart Help without /G.

/H causes Help to display as many lines per screen as your monitor can manage.

*/nohi* tells Help that your display does not support high-intensity characters (bright white, for example).

<command> is the name of the MS-DOS command for which you want help. If you omit <command>, Help displays an index of all the available commands.

### Examples

To start Help and display the index of commands:

```
C:\>help
```

To go directly to the help for the Choice command:

```
C:\>help choice
```

## HIMEM.SYS
## Manage Extended Memory
### Versions 5 and later

*Pages 383, 392*

HIMEM.SYS is a device driver that manages extended memory (memory above 1 MB). As a memory manager, HIMEM.SYS ensures that applications don't attempt to use the same portions of extended memory. Equally important, HIMEM.SYS enables MS-DOS to load a large part of itself into the portion of extended memory known as the High Memory Area (HMA). The ability to run MS-DOS "high" helps conserve conventional memory (0 KB to 640 KB) for other programs and for data.

513

**device=<path>himem.sys**

<path> is the path to the directory containing HIMEM.SYS. If you don't include <path>, MS-DOS assumes the device driver is in the root directory of the startup drive.

NOTE: *HIMEM.SYS accepts a number of parameters that refine its behavior. You can, for example, specify the amount of memory an application must require if it is to use the HMA. These parameters are beyond the scope of this book; if you need them, refer to the documentation that came with your version of MS-DOS.*

### Example

The following example shows the two commands needed in CONFIG.SYS to identify HIMEM.SYS to MS-DOS and to enable MS-DOS to run in high memory. The example assumes that HIMEM.SYS is in the \DOS directory.

```
device=c:\dos\himem.sys
dos=high
```

HIMEM.SYS and the Dos command shown here are also needed if you want to use the upper memory area (640 KB to 1 MB) for loading device drivers and programs. Additional examples are in the entries on EMM386.EXE and the Devicehigh, Dos, and Loadhigh commands.

## IF (BATCH COMMAND)
## Deciding Whether to Carry Out a Batch Command

**Versions 2 and later**

*Page 342*

The If batch command tests a condition and carries out another command if the condition is met.

**if not <condition> <command>**

*not* reverses the meaning of <condition>. That is, <command> is carried out only if <condition> is *not* true.

<condition> is the condition to be tested. Using <condition>, a batch file can be used to check the outcome of a command such as Backup or Restore (with the *errorlevel* option), check whether a file exists, or check whether two strings are identical. <condition> takes one of the following forms:

| | |
|---|---|
| errorlevel <number> | True if *errorlevel* is equal to or greater than <number>. *errorlevel* represents a special value that is set by some MS-DOS commands (and other programs) primarily to indicate whether or not they were completed successfully. |
| exist <filename> | True if <filename> exists in the specified directory. |
| <string1>==<string2> | True if <string1> and <string2> are identical; remember, uppercase and lowercase are different. Notice that two equal signs separate the strings. This form of the If command can be used to compare file names, replaceable parameters entered on the command line with the batch command, or character strings. |

<command> is the command to be carried out. It can be any MS-DOS command, including another If command.

### Examples

To jump to the label *:end* if *errorlevel* is equal to or greater than 3:

```
if errorlevel 3 goto end
```

(For a sample batch file using this command, see the Goto batch command.)

To copy the file named in the first replaceable parameter from the disk in the current drive to the disk in drive A if the file doesn't exist on the disk in drive A:

```
if not exist a:%1 copy %1 a:%1
```

## INCLUDE (CONFIGURATION COMMAND)
## Include the Contents of Another Configuration Block

### Versions 6 and 6.2

The Include configuration command allows you to include the contents of one configuration block within another block in your CONFIG.SYS file. This can save you from having to enter the same set of configuration commands in two or more blocks, which makes your CONFIG.SYS file smaller and simplifies later changes.

**include=<block>**

<block> is the name of the configuration block you want to include.

## INPUT/OUTPUT REDIRECTION
### Redirecting Standard Input and Standard Output
**Versions 2 and later**

*Page 300*

Unless instructed otherwise, MS-DOS takes its input from standard input (usually the keyboard) and sends its output to standard output (usually the screen). You can redirect standard input and output, however, to a file or a device by using the symbols <, >, and >>. The < and > symbols redirect the input or output of a command or program.

The < symbol redirects input. For example, to tell the Sort filter command to read its input from the file named LIST.DOC, you would type *sort < list.doc.*

Similarly, you redirect output with the > symbol. For example, to send the output of a Directory command to a file named DIRFILE.DOC in the current directory, you would type *dir > dirfile.doc.* If there were no file named DIRFILE.DOC, MS-DOS would create it. If a file named DIRFILE.DOC already existed, MS-DOS would replace its contents with the output of the Directory command.

You can, however, tell MS-DOS to *add* output to the end of an existing file by using the symbols >>. For example, to add the output of the Directory command to an existing file named DIRFILE.DOC, you would type *dir >> dirfile.doc.* If the file didn't exist, MS-DOS would create it, as in the previous example, which used the > symbol.

You can redirect input and output from and to devices as well as files, and you can redirect both the input and output of a program. For example, to tell the Sort command to read its input from the file LIST.DOC and write its output to the printer (PRN), you would type *sort < list.doc > prn.*

Rather than redirecting output to a file or device, you can send the output of a command or program to the input of another command or program by separating the program or command names with a broken vertical bar ( ¦ ). Because the programs or commands are logically connected, this connection is called a *pipe.*

Pipes are used primarily with the filter commands: Find, More, and Sort. These commands read standard input and write to standard output, so they can be combined through redirection and pipes in a variety of useful ways. For example, *dir ¦ sort* sends the output of the Directory command to the input of the Sort command.

You can combine redirection and piping: For example, you could pipe the output of the Directory command to the Sort command, pipe the output of the Sort command to the Find command, and, finally, redirect the output of the Find command to the printer by typing *dir ¦ sort ¦ find ".DOC" > prn.*

## INSTALL (CONFIGURATION COMMAND)
## Load a Command from CONFIG.SYS

### Versions 4 and later

The Install command loads into memory the command file for any memory-resident programs. Examples of such programs are the following five MS-DOS commands: Doskey, Fastopen, Keyboard (keyb), National Language Support Function (nlsfunc), and Share. Once loaded, these command files remain in memory until you restart your computer. Install helps MS-DOS manage your computer's use of memory.

> **install=<filename> <cmdparms>**

> <filename> is the name of the command file to be installed. You must include the extension (COM or EXE) and can include a drive letter and path.

> <cmdparms> represents the parameters, if any, of the command to be installed.

### Examples

Assuming that all MS-DOS files are in the C:\DOS directory, the following command in CONFIG.SYS would tell MS-DOS to keep track of the last 50 files opened on the hard disk (drive C):

```
install=c:\dos\fastopen.exe c:=50
```

Assuming that all MS-DOS files are in the C:\DOS directory, the following commands in CONFIG.SYS would tell MS-DOS to provide national language support and start the system with the French keyboard layout:

```
install=c:\dos\nlsfunc.exe
install=c:\dos\keyb.com fr,,c:\dos\keyboard.sys
```

## INTERLINK (INTERLNK)
## Connect Interlink Client to Server

### Versions 6 and 6.2

The Interlnk command connects your computer to a computer that is running the Intersvr command. This gives you access to all the drives and printer ports located in the second computer.

> **interlnk <local>=<remote>**

> <local> is the drive letter you want to assign to a server drive.

<remote> is the letter of the drive in the server that you want to access. If you specify <local> but omit <remote>, Interlnk removes access to the server drive that had been associated with <local>.

Before you can use the Interlnk command, you need to install the INTERLNK.EXE device driver in the CONFIG.SYS file of the client computer and restart the computer.

### Examples

To associate the drive letter G with the server's drive C:

```
C:\>interlnk g=c
```

To remove the association of drive G:

```
C:\>interlnk g=
```

# INTERLINK SERVER (INTERSVR)
## Start Interlink Server
### Versions 6 and 6.2

*Page 395*

The Intersvr command establishes your computer as a server, which a second computer can then access as an Interlnk client. Intersvr includes several parameters, some of which are beyond the scope of this book. The basic form of the command is:

**intersvr <drives1> /X=<drives2> /baud:<rate> /B**

<drives1> are the letters, each followed by a colon, of the drives you want to make available to the client computer.

*/X*=<drives2> specifies the letters, each followed by a colon, of the drives you *don't* want to make available to the client computer. If you omit both <drives1> and */X*=<drives2>, Intersvr makes all drives available.

*/baud*:<rate> specifies the fastest baud rate that Intersvr will use. <rate> can be 9600, 19200, 38400, 57600, or 115200. If you omit */baud*, the baud rate defaults to 115200.

*/B* starts Intersvr in monochrome.

### Example

To start Intersvr and specify that floppy disk drives A and B should not be redirected:

```
C:\>intersvr /x=a: b:
```

## INTERLNK.EXE
## Redirect Drive and Printer Requests to Server
### Versions 6 and 6.2

*Page 395*

INTERLNK.EXE is the name of a device driver included with versions 6 and 6.2 of MS-DOS. This program *redirects* requests for drives or printer ports to an Interlnk *server,* a second computer that is connected to your computer via a serial or parallel cable.

To use INTERLNK.EXE (or the related Interlnk command), you must tell MS-DOS this device driver exists by including a Device or Devicehigh command in your CONFIG.SYS file. INTERLNK.EXE includes several parameters, some of which are beyond the scope of this book. The basic form for identifying the device driver is:

**device=<path>interlnk.exe /drives:<numdrives> /noprinter /auto /noscan /baud:<rate>**

<path> specifies the path to the file INTERLNK.EXE. Most likely, it is C:\DOS. If you don't specify <path>, MS-DOS looks in the root directory of the system disk.

*/drives:*<numdrives> specifies the number of drives that Interlnk will redirect. If you specify 0 for <numdrives>, Interlnk will redirect only the printer ports. If you omit */drives,* Interlnk will redirect three drives.

*/noprinter* tells Interlnk not to redirect the printer ports.

*/auto* first attempts to establish a connection with the server. If the connection doesn't exist, MS-DOS will not load INTERLNK.EXE into memory. If you omit */auto,* MS-DOS installs INTERLNK.EXE whether or not a connection exists when you restart the client computer.

*/noscan* prevents Interlnk from establishing a connection with the server. To establish the connection later, use the Interlnk command.

*/baud:*<rate> specifies the fastest baud rate that Interlnk will use. <rate> can be 9600, 19200, 38400, 57600, or 115200. If you omit */baud,* the baud rate defaults to 115200.

### Example

To load INTERLNK.EXE only if the client computer is already connected to the server, and to redirect only the disk drives (not the printers):

```
device=c:\dos\interlnk.exe /auto /noprinter
```

## JOIN
## Join a Disk Drive to a Directory
### Versions 3 through 5

The Join command connects one disk drive to an empty directory on a second drive. MS-DOS then treats the disk in the joined drive as if it were a directory on the disk in the drive to which it is joined.

> **join <drive> <pathname> /D**

<drive> is the drive that is to be joined to a directory on the second drive. The complete directory structure of <drive> is joined, starting at the root. Once you join <drive> to a directory on another drive, you cannot use the letter of <drive> in any MS-DOS command. If you do, MS-DOS responds *Invalid drive specification.*

<pathname> is the drive letter and path name of the drive and directory to which <drive> is to be joined. The directory must be a subdirectory of the root directory. If the directory doesn't exist, the Join command creates it; if the directory does exist, it must be empty. You cannot join <drive> to the root directory of another drive.

/D disconnects any join involving <drive>. The specified directory remains on the disk until it is removed with a Remove Directory command (rd).

If you omit all parameters (type just *join*), MS-DOS displays any joins in effect.

**NOTE:** *You should avoid using the Assign, Backup, Diskcopy, Format, Restore, and Substitute commands on a drive to which another drive is joined. If you want to use one of these commands, or if you need to use the drive that is joined, delete the join with the /D parameter. Join cannot be used with a network drive.*

### Examples

To join drive B to C:\DRIVEB:

```
C:\>join b: driveb
```

To delete the join from the preceding example:

```
C:\>join b: /d
```

Assume that you joined drive A to C:\DRIVEA and drive B to C:\DRIVEB. To display the joins in effect:

```
C:\>join
```

MS-DOS displays:

```
A: => C:\DRIVEA
B: => C:\DRIVEB
```

## KEYB
## Select a Keyboard Layout
### Versions 3.3 and later

*Page 131*

The Keyboard command (keyb) selects a keyboard layout that matches the layout used in the country you specify. Keyb replaces the Keyb*xx* command used in releases through 3.2. If you have one of those versions of MS-DOS, refer to the entry KEYB*xx*, following this one.

**keyb <code>,<codepage>,<keybfile> /ID:<kbdid> /E**

<code> is one of the following two-letter keyboard codes:

| Country | Keyboard Code | Code Page(s) | Keyboard ID |
|---|---|---|---|
| Belgium | be | 437,850 | |
| Brazil | br | 437,850 | |
| Canada (French) | cf | 863,850 | |
| Czech Republic (Czech) | cz | 852,850 | |
| Denmark | dk | 865,850 | |
| Finland | su | 437,850 | |
| France | fr | 437,850 | 120,189 |
| Germany | gr | 437,850 | |
| Hungary | hu | 852,850 | |
| Italy | it | 437,850 | 141,142 |
| Latin America | la | 437,850 | |
| Netherlands | nl | 437,850 | |
| Norway | no | 865,850 | |
| Poland | pl | 852,850 | |
| Portugal | po | 860,850 | |
| Slovakia (Slovak) | sl | 852,850 | |
| Spain | sp | 437,850 | |
| Sweden | sv | 437,850 | |

*(continued)*

| Country | Keyboard Code | Code Page(s) | Keyboard ID |
|---------|---------------|--------------|-------------|
| Switzerland (French) | sf | 437,850 | |
| Switzerland (German) | sg | 437,850 | |
| United Kingdom | uk | 437,850 | 166,168 |
| United States | us | 437,850 | |
| Yugoslavia (Croatia, Serbia, Slovenia) | yu | 852,850 | |

<codepage> is a three-digit number that specifies the code page that MS-DOS is to use. Valid code pages for each keyboard are listed in the preceding table.

<keybfile> is the name of the system file that contains the keyboard layouts. If you don't specify <keybfile>, MS-DOS assumes that the file is named KEYBOARD.SYS and that it is stored in the root directory of the system disk. If, as is likely, this file is in your MS-DOS directory, you must include the path to the file.

/ID:<kbdid> is a three-digit code that specifies a keyboard layout to be used when a country has more than one keyboard ID, as listed in the preceding table. If you don't specify /ID:<kbdid>, and more than one keyboard ID is listed for the country specified, MS-DOS assumes the first keyboard ID listed (versions 4 and later).

If your computer was manufactured for use in the United States, you can return to the U.S. keyboard layout after entering a Keyboard command by pressing Ctrl-Alt-F1. To return to the keyboard you defined with the Keyboard command, press Ctrl-Alt-F2.

/E lets you inform MS-DOS that you are using an enhanced keyboard with an 8086 computer. (If you're using an 80286 or higher computer, you don't need this switch.)

## Examples

To select the French keyboard layout, let MS-DOS assume the value for the code page, and tell MS-DOS that the keyboard definition file is KEYBOARD.SYS in the C:\DOS directory:

```
C:\>keyb fr,,c:\dos\keyboard.sys
```

Notice the two commas following *fr*; if you omit <codepage>, you must still type the comma that would follow, to show MS-DOS that you omitted it.

To display the currently active keyboard code and its code page, as well as the code page currently being used by CON:

```
C:\>keyb
```

If you had selected the U.S. keyboard and code page 850 for the keyboard and console, MS-DOS would respond:

```
Current keyboard code: US  code page: 850
Current CON code page: 850
```

## KEYB*xx*
## Select a Keyboard Layout
### Version 3.2, IBM releases 3 through 3.2

*Page 131*

The Keyboard command (keyb*xx*) in versions of MS-DOS prior to 3.3 loads a program that MS-DOS keeps in memory to change the keyboard layout to match the keyboard used in a particular country.

If you specify a keyboard layout other than the one you normally use, you can return to the layout MS-DOS assumes by pressing Ctrl-Alt-F1. You can also switch back to the other keyboard layout by pressing Ctrl-Alt-F2.

This Keyboard command has six forms, one for each keyboard that MS-DOS supports. Each begins with *keyb*; you replace the *xx* with one of the following two-letter codes:

| Description | Code | Typed As |
|---|---|---|
| Dvorak keyboard (non-IBM versions of MS-DOS) | dv | keybdv |
| France | fr | keybfr |
| Germany | gr | keybgr |
| Italy | it | keybit |
| Spain | sp | keybsp |
| United Kingdom | uk | keybuk |

### Example
To select the French keyboard layout:

```
C:\>keybfr
```

## LABEL

## Change or Delete the Volume Label of a Disk

**Versions 3.1 and later, IBM releases 3 and later**

*Page 110*

The Label command displays, adds, changes, or deletes the volume label of a disk. MS-DOS provides two ways to assign a volume label: the /V parameter of the Format command, which you use when preparing a disk for use, and the Label command, which you can use at any time on any formatted disk. To change or delete an assigned volume label, however, you must use the Label command.

The Label command has two parameters:

**label <drive><newlabel>**

<drive> is the letter, followed by a colon, of the drive containing the disk whose volume label is to be affected.

<newlabel> is the volume label you want to assign to the disk in <drive>. The label can be up to 11 characters long; it can include spaces as well as any characters that are valid for a file name. If you specify <newlabel>, MS-DOS assigns the label to the disk in <drive>, whether or not the disk already has a volume label. If you omit <newlabel> (type just *label* or *label* plus a drive letter), MS-DOS displays the volume label (if there is one) of the disk in the current or specified drive, then prompts you to type a new volume label or to press Enter. If you press Enter and the disk already has a volume label, MS-DOS asks if you want to delete the current label.

> **NOTE:** *You cannot use the Label command on a network drive. You should also avoid using it on a drive affected by the Assign, Join, or Substitute command. If you just want to display the volume label of a disk, use the Volume (vol) command.*

### Examples

To assign the volume label CLIENT LIST to the disk in drive A:

```
C:\>label a:client list
```

To display the volume label of the disk in drive A:

```
C:\>label a:
```

MS-DOS responds:

```
Volume in drive A is CLIENT LIST
Volume Serial Number is 3F68-1AFF
Volume label (11 characters, ENTER for none)?
```

If you type a label, MS-DOS renames the disk. If you press Enter, MS-DOS displays:

```
Delete current volume label (Y/N)?
```

To delete the volume label, press Y; to leave the label unchanged, press N.

## LASTDRIVE (CONFIGURATION COMMAND)
## Define the Highest Drive Letter

### Versions 3 and later

*Page 396*

The Lastdrive configuration command specifies the highest drive letter that MS-DOS recognizes as valid. If you don't use the Lastdrive command, MS-DOS assumes five drive letters, A through E. Using Lastdrive, you can specify letters up to Z—for example, on a system with two floppy disk drives, one or more hard disks, and several RAM disks or on a system with a large hard disk divided into a number of sections (called logical drives), each referred to by a different drive letter. You can also use Lastdrive if you need one or more unique drive letters (such as X) to refer to disk drives on a network.

**lastdrive=<letter>**

<letter> specifies the highest drive letter that MS-DOS recognizes. It can be any letter from A through Z. If <letter> specifies fewer disk drives than the actual number attached to the computer, MS-DOS ignores the Lastdrive command.

### Example

To allow eight drive letters, include the following, in CONFIG.SYS:

```
lastdrive=h
```

## LOADFIX
## Loads a Program Above 64 KB

### Versions 5 and later

A few programs cause the error message *Packed file corrupt* to appear if they are loaded in the first 64 KB of conventional memory. To tell MS-DOS to load a program above the first 64 KB of memory, use the Loadfix command.

**loadfix <filename> <parameters>**

<filename> is the name of the program you want to run. You can include a drive and path if necessary.

<parameters> represents any parameters required by the program.

## LOADHIGH (LH)
## Load Programs into the Upper Memory Area

### Versions 5 and later

*Page 392*

The Loadhigh command, abbreviated *lh*, tells MS-DOS to load a program into the portion of memory known as the upper memory area, which is used in units called upper memory blocks (UMBs). When you use Loadhigh, you can increase the amount of conventional memory available.

Loadhigh is useful for loading the types of programs known as TSRs (for "terminate and stay resident"). Such programs stay in memory even when they are not actively working. You probably want to reserve the maximum possible amount of conventional memory for applications, so TSRs are natural candidates for loading into the upper memory area. You can use Loadhigh with the following MS-DOS programs: Doskey, the MS-DOS Shell, Keyboard, Graphics, Nlsfunc, Mode, Share, Print, and Append.

The Loadhigh command requires a computer with at least 350 KB of extended memory, and it requires a memory-management program that can make UMBs available. If your computer has an 80386 or 80486 microprocessor, you can use the EMM386.EXE device driver described in this appendix.

In addition, because the Loadhigh command makes use of memory that is normally unavailable to MS-DOS, your CONFIG.SYS file must include a Dos command and two Device commands, all of which tell MS-DOS at startup that memory beyond 640 KB is accessible. These commands are shown in the example for this entry:

**loadhigh /L: <region>,<minsize> /S <filename> <parameters>**

/L:<region>,<minsize> lets you specify where you want to place the program and the minimum amount of memory needed by the program. <region> specifies the region number into which MS-DOS should load the program; <minsize> tells MS-DOS the smallest amount of memory into which the program will fit. If a program needs two or more regions of memory, separate the region numbers with semicolons.

/S shrinks the UMB to its smallest size as MS-DOS loads the program. This switch is normally used only by the MemMaker program; see the MemMaker entry in this appendix.

<filename> is the name of the program you want to load into the upper memory area. Include a drive letter and path (if necessary) if the program file is not in the current search path.

<parameters> represents any parameters that <filename> requires.

You use a separate Loadhigh command for each program to be loaded into the upper memory area. If there isn't enough upper memory to load a program, MS-DOS loads the program into conventional memory instead. If you load the same program or programs into upper memory whenever you start up, you can put the appropriate Loadhigh command(s) in your AUTOEXEC.BAT file.

## Example

Assuming that all MS-DOS files are in the C:\DOS directory and you want access to all available upper memory, these commands must be in CONFIG.SYS if you intend to load programs into the upper memory area:

```
device=c:\dos\himem.sys
device=c:\dos\emm386.exe noems
dos=umb
```

The Device commands identify two device drivers, HIMEM.SYS and EMM386.EXE, that MS-DOS needs in order to manage nonconventional memory. The Dos command enables MS-DOS to maintain access to reserved memory after startup.

To load Doskey into upper memory:

```
C:\>loadhigh doskey
```

To load Doskey into the upper memory area each time you start your system, put this Loadhigh command in AUTOEXEC.BAT.

## MD (MAKE DIRECTORY)
## Make a New Directory

**Versions 2 and later**

*Page 144*

The Make Directory command (md or mkdir) creates a new subdirectory.

**md <drive><path>**

<drive> is the letter, followed by a colon, of the drive containing the disk on which the directory is to be created. If you omit <drive>, MS-DOS creates the directory on the disk in the current drive.

<path> is the path name of the subdirectory to be created. If <path> begins with a backslash (\), MS-DOS makes the new directory a subdirectory of the root directory of the disk in the current or specified drive; if <path> doesn't begin with a backslash, MS-DOS makes the new directory a subdirectory of the current directory. There is no absolute limit to the number of levels of subdirectories you can create, but a good practical limit is about four or five; beyond this, a multilevel directory structure can become more confusing and unwieldy than helpful. The maximum length of a path name from the root directory is 63 characters, including backslashes.

**NOTE:** *Because the Assign, Join, and Substitute commands mask the real identities of directories, you shouldn't create directories when those commands are in effect.*

### Examples

To create a subdirectory named WP in the *current* directory of the current drive:

```
C:\ENG>md wp
```

To create a subdirectory named WP in the *root* directory of the current drive:

```
C:\DOS>md \wp
```

To create a subdirectory named WP in the directory \MKT of the disk in drive A:

```
C:\DOS>md a:\mkt\wp
```

## MEM (MEMORY)
## Display Memory Use

**Versions 4 and later**

*Page 116*

The Memory command displays the amount of memory installed and available for use, including extended and expanded memory and memory in the upper memory area. It can also display the name, location, size, and type of each program in memory.

**mem /program /debug /classify /free /module <name> /page**

*/program,* available in versions 4 and 5 only, specifies that the name, location, size, and type of each program in memory be displayed. If you have version 5, you can type this parameter as */p.*

*/debug* specifies that additional detail beyond that provided by the */program* parameter be included in the report. If you have version 5 or later, you can type this parameter as */d.*

*/classify* reports on use of conventional memory and the upper memory area used by the Loadhigh and Devicehigh commands. Unlike the */program* and */debug* parameters, */classify* gives the size of programs in decimal as well as hexadecimal. It also summarizes memory use and reports the largest available block in the upper memory area. If you have version 5 or later, you can type this parameter as */c.*

The following parameters are available only in versions 6 and 6.2:

*/free* (or */f*) displays the free areas in both conventional and upper memory.

*/module* <name> (or */M* <name>) displays exactly how a given program is using memory. <name> is the name of a program that is currently in memory. If you use */module,* you can't use any other parameters except */page.*

*/page* displays the memory information one screenful at a time, displaying *Press any key to continue...* at the bottom of the screen. Pressing any key displays the next screenful of information; pressing Ctrl-Break or Ctrl-C cancels the command.

### Examples

To display the types and amount of memory installed and available:

```
C:\>mem

Memory Type       Total = Used  +  Free
----------------  ------   ------   ------
Conventional      640K     40K      600K
Upper              91K     42K       49K
Adapter RAM/ROM   293K    293K        0K
Extended (XMS)*  3072K   2112K      960K
----------------  ------   ------   ------
Total memory     4096K   2487K     1610K

Total under 1 MB  731K     82K      650K

Total Expanded (EMS)              1408K (1441792 bytes)
Free Expanded (EMS)*              1024K (1048576 bytes)

  * EMM386 is using XMS memory to simulate EMS memory as needed.
    Free EMS memory may change as free XMS memory changes.

Largest executable program size   600K  (614368 bytes)
Largest free upper memory block    49K   (50256 bytes)
MS-DOS is resident in the high memory area.
```

This is the display produced by version 6 of MS-DOS on a system with 4 MB of extended memory, 1 MB of which is being emulated as expanded memory by the EMM386.EXE device driver. The system has a 1024 KB SmartDrive disk cache and a 512 KB RAM drive in extended memory, MS-DOS loaded in the high memory area, and Doskey loaded in upper memory. Your report will differ to reflect the way your system is set up. If you have version 4 or 5, the report is less detailed.

To see a more detailed report showing the name and size of each program loaded into memory, you could use the */classify* option:

```
C:\>mem /c
```

To see a very detailed report that not only shows the names and sizes of programs but gives their locations and tells you what types of programs they are, you would type *mem /d*.

## MEMMAKER
## Optimize Use of Memory

**Versions 6 and 6.2**

*Page 386*

The MemMaker program helps you make the best use of your memory by moving to upper memory as many device drivers and programs as possible. Doing this manually can be a frustrating and time-consuming task; MemMaker makes it simple. The basic form of the MemMaker command is:

**memmaker /B /batch /undo**

/B starts MemMaker in monochrome mode.

*/batch* tells MemMaker to run in "batch" mode. MemMaker makes the default choice for all prompts and automatically restores your computer to its original configuration if an error occurs. To see what actions MemMaker took, view the file MEMMAKER.STS after MemMaker is finished.

*/undo* reverses all the changes MemMaker made during its most recent run. If you experience problems with your computer after MemMaker makes changes, or you simply don't like what MemMaker has done, type *memmaker /undo*.

## MENUCOLOR (CONFIGURATION COMMAND)
## Set Startup Menu Colors

**Versions 6 and 6.2**

The Menucolor command lets you specify the colors that MS-DOS will use to display the CONFIG.SYS startup menu. Use this command only following the header *[menu]* in CONFIG.SYS.

**menucolor=<foreground>,<background>**

<foreground> specifies the color of the menu text.

<background> specifies the color of the screen background. If you omit <background>, MS-DOS uses 0 (black).

| Value | Color | Value | Color |
|-------|-------|-------|-------|
| 0 | Black | 8 | Gray |
| 1 | Blue | 9 | Bright blue |
| 2 | Green | 10 | Bright green |
| 3 | Cyan | 11 | Bright cyan |
| 4 | Red | 12 | Bright red |
| 5 | Magenta | 13 | Bright magenta |
| 6 | Brown | 14 | Yellow |
| 7 | White | 15 | Bright white |

Don't choose the same number for <foreground> and <background>—the menu will be invisible!

### Example

To set the colors of the startup menu to cyan on black:

```
menucolor=1
```

## MENUDEFAULT (CONFIGURATION COMMAND)
## Set Startup Menu Default

### Versions 6 and 6.2

The Menudefault command lets you specify your default choice for the CONFIG.SYS startup menu. You can also tell MS-DOS to select the default choice after waiting for the specified length of time. Use this command only following the header *[menu]* in CONFIG.SYS.

**menudefault=<block>,<seconds>**

<block> is the name of the configuration block that you want to make the default block.

<seconds> is the number of seconds (from 0 to 90) MS-DOS will wait for the user to make a choice. If <seconds> is 0, MS-DOS won't even wait for the user. If you omit <seconds>, MS-DOS waits until the user presses the Enter key.

**Example**

To tell MS-DOS that it should default to the configuration block named Nor-malBoot after 15 seconds:

```
menudefault=NormalBoot,15
```

## MENUITEM (CONFIGURATION COMMAND)
## Add Item to Startup Menu

### Versions 6 and 6.2

The Menuitem command lets you add up to nine items to the CONFIG.SYS startup menu. Each item corresponds to a configuration block within the CONFIG.SYS file. Use this command only following the header *[menu]* in CONFIG.SYS.

**menuitem=<block>,<text>**

<block> is the name of the configuration block that MS-DOS will execute if the menu item is chosen by the user.

<text> is any text (up to 70 characters) that you want displayed on the startup menu. If you omit <text>, MS-DOS displays the name of the configuration block.

**Example**

To create a CONFIG.SYS startup menu with three menu items:

```
menuitem=standard,Standard setup
menuitem=network,Standard setup with network
menuitem=barebones,Debugging setup
```

When MS-DOS starts, it displays the following startup menu:

```
MS-DOS 6.2 Startup Menu
=======================

    1. Standard setup
    2. Standard setup with network
    3. Debugging setup

Enter a choice: 1
```

## MIRROR
## Save Disk Information for File Recovery
### Version 5

*Page 210*

The Mirror command, available in version 5 only, is a disk- and file-recovery program. Mirror saves disk-storage information that you can use to unformat an inadvertently formatted floppy disk or hard disk, rebuild a damaged hard disk, or recover deleted files. The command is named Mirror because it creates special files that duplicate the directory and disk-storage information MS-DOS uses internally to keep track of files and their storage locations on disk. Depending on the parameters you specify, the Mirror command can help you record the latest file and directory structure on the disk you specify, track the storage locations of files you delete, or store information about the way a hard disk is set up for use by MS-DOS.

**mirror <drive> /1 /T<drive>-<files> /partn /U**

    <drive> is the letter, followed by a colon, of the drive whose file and directory information you want to record. You can specify more than one drive letter, separating them with spaces. If you don't specify <drive>, the Mirror command records information about the disk in the current drive. For each drive you specify, Mirror creates a read-only file named MIRROR.FIL in the root directory. This file, which can be surprisingly large for a hard disk, contains the information needed to rebuild the disk or to recover files and directories in the root directory.

    /1 (the numeral 1) tells Mirror to keep only the latest information about the disk in the drive you specify. If you don't use /1 and Mirror finds an earlier version of MIRROR.FIL, it renames the old file MIRROR.BAK and creates a new file named MIRROR.FIL for the latest disk information. MIRROR.BAK then becomes a backup in case the new MIRROR.FIL is unusable.

    /T<drive>-<files> tells Mirror to load a program that records the storage locations of files you delete. When you use this feature, known as *delete tracking*, Mirror saves information about all the files you delete while delete tracking is in effect. This information is stored in a system file named PCTRACKR.DEL. If you in-advertently delete a needed file, you can use PCTRACKR.DEL and the Undelete command to try to recover the file.

<drive> is the letter (without a colon) of the drive for which you want to track deleted files; you must include this parameter. <files> is the number of de-leted files you want to track. If you choose to include <files>, you can specify any number from 1 through 999, separating it from <drive> with a hyphen. If you don't specify <files>, Mirror assumes a certain number depending on the size of the disk, as shown in the following table:

| Disk Size | Number of Files | Size of PCTRACKR.DEL |
| --- | --- | --- |
| 360 KB | 25 | 5 KB |
| 720 KB | 50 | 9 KB |
| 1.2 MB | 75 | 14 KB |
| 1.44 MB | 75 | 14 KB |
| 20 MB hard disk | 101 | 18 KB |
| 32 MB hard disk | 202 | 36 KB |
| Hard disk larger than 32 MB | 303 | 55 KB |

Notice that PCTRACKR.DEL can require a fair amount of storage in its own right.

/partn (for partition) tells Mirror to save information about the way a hard disk is set up. MS-DOS uses this information, called a partition table, to find and use a hard disk. Because you need this information only if the partition table is dam-aged, but MS-DOS can not recognize the hard disk without the partition table, Mirror saves partition information on a floppy disk rather than on the hard disk itself. The information is stored in a file named PARTNSAV.FIL.

/U (for unload) removes the delete-tracking program from memory so that Mirror no longer records the storage locations of files you delete from disk.

NOTE: *Do not attempt to use the Mirror command with a drive affected by the Join or Substitute command. If you plan to use delete tracking with an assigned drive (Assign command), assign the drive first.*

### Examples

To record disk-storage information for drives C and D:

```
C:\>mirror c: d:
```

Mirror responds with a message like this (the copyright line is incomplete):

```
Creates an image of the system area.

Drive C being processed.

Drive D being processed.

The MIRROR process was successful.
```

A Directory command shows the file MIRROR.FIL in the root directory of each drive.

To start delete tracking for the current drive:

```
C:\>mirror /tc
```

As in the preceding example, Mirror displays a message describing its response. As soon as a file on this drive is deleted, Mirror will create PCTRACKR.DEL to hold information about it and other deleted files.

To stop delete tracking for the current drive:

```
C:\>mirror /u
```

Mirror responds *Deletion-tracking software removed from memory.*

To record partition information about the hard disk (drive C):

```
C:\>mirror /partn
```

Mirror responds with the message *Disk Partition Table saver* and a message asking you to insert a formatted floppy disk in the drive in which you want to save the table. (Unless you specify otherwise, Mirror assumes drive A.) When you press Enter to carry out the command, Mirror saves the partition table on the disk and, if all goes well, responds:

```
Successful
```

## MODE
## Control Device Mode

**Versions 3.2 and later, IBM releases 1 and later**

The Mode command is used in several different ways to enable MS-DOS to work with the display and with printer and communications ports. In versions 3.3 and later, the Mode command is also used to set code-page information that enables MS-DOS to display and print accented and foreign-language characters. Mode has eight basic uses:

- Set display characteristics, such as monochrome instead of color, or 40 columns instead of 80 columns.

- Set number of display lines and columns (versions 4 and later).

- Set keyboard repeat rate (versions 4 and later).

- Set communications parameters for a serial communications port.

- Set line width and spacing for a parallel printer attached to a parallel port or tell MS-DOS to use a printer attached to a parallel port other than LPT1.

- Connect a serial printer by redirecting output from a parallel port (such as LPT1) to a serial port (such as COM1).

- Check the status of system devices.

- Prepare and select code pages for national language support (versions 3.3 and later).

Each of these uses is described separately in the following entries.

## MODE
## Set Display Characteristics

**Versions 3.2 and later, IBM releases 2 and later**

*Page 119*

This form of the Mode command selects a display adapter, either Monochrome or Color Graphics. If you select a Color Graphics Adapter, you can also set the width of the display and enable or disable color. If the image on a display isn't centered, you can use Mode to shift the image left or right and display a test pattern.

**mode <method>,<shift>,T**

<method> selects the Monochrome or Color Graphics Adapter and specifies the width and color characteristics of the display attached to the Color Graphics Adapter. <method> can be specified as one of the following values listed.

| Value | Characteristics |
|-------|-----------------|
| mono | Monochrome Display Adapter |
| 40 | Color Graphics Adapter, 40-column display |
| 80 | Color Graphics Adapter, 80-column display |
| co40 | Color Graphics Adapter, color enabled, 40-column display |
| co80 | Color Graphics Adapter, color enabled, 80-column display |
| bw40 | Color Graphics Adapter, color disabled, 40-column display |
| bw80 | Color Graphics Adapter, color disabled, 80-column display |

<shift> can be specified as either *l* or *r* to shift left or right an off-center image on a display attached to the Color Graphics Adapter. The image is shifted two columns if the display width is 80 characters, one column if the display width is 40 characters. <shift> has no effect on an EGA or VGA display or on a display attached to a Monochrome Display Adapter.

T displays a test pattern after shifting the image so that you can see whether the display is centered. It also displays a prompt asking whether you can see the leftmost (or rightmost) character in the pattern. If you reply *n*, the Mode command shifts the image and displays the prompt again, continuing until you reply *y*. MS-DOS then returns to the system prompt.

## Examples

To select the display attached to the Color Graphics Adapter, enable color, and set the display to 80 columns:

```
C:\>mode co80
```

To select the display attached to the Color Graphics Adapter, disable color, set the display to 80 columns, shift the display two columns to the right, and display a test pattern:

```
C:\>mode bw80,r,t
```

Note the commas.

To select the display attached to the Monochrome Display Adapter:

```
C:\>mode mono
```

# MODE
## Set Display Lines

**Versions 4 and later**

*Page 119*

This form of the Mode command lets you specify whether 40 or 80 columns and 25, 43, or 50 lines should be displayed on the screen. The command is effective only if the line DEVICE=ANSI.SYS (preceded by a path if necessary) is included in your CONFIG.SYS file and if the display attached to your system can display the number of lines you specify. You can set either columns or lines, or both, with the command.

**mode con cols=<columns> lines=<lines>**

CON is the name of the console device; the display is the output portion of CON (the keyboard is the input portion of CON).

*cols*=<columns> specifies the number of columns in a line. <columns> can be either 40 or 80.

*lines*=<lines> specifies the number of lines displayed on the screen. <lines> can be 25, 43, or 50.

**NOTE:** *If you specify 43 or 50 lines and an application program, such as a word processor, resets the display to 25 lines whenever it returns to MS-DOS, you can avoid the need to enter the Mode command each time by starting the application program with a batch file that ends with a Mode command that sets the number of display lines to the number you prefer.*

### Example

To set the number of display lines to 43 and leave the number of columns unchanged:

```
C:\>mode con lines=43
```

# MODE
## Set Keyboard Repeat Rate

**Versions 4 and later**

*Page 118*

This form of the Mode command lets you control how long the keyboard waits before starting to repeat when you hold down a key and how quickly the character is repeated.

**mode con rate=<speed> delay=<pause>**

CON is the name of the console device; the keyboard is the input portion of CON (the display is the output portion of CON).

*rate*=<speed> specifies the speed of the repeat action. <speed> can be from 1 through 32. A value of 1 specifies the slowest rate, about 2 repetitions per second; 32 specifies the fastest rate, about 30 repetitions per second. If you specify *rate*, you must also specify *delay*.

*delay*=<pause> specifies how long the keyboard should wait, after you press a key, before starting to repeat. <pause> represents units of one quarter of one second and can range from 1 through 4; a value of 1 causes a delay of 0.25 second, and a value of 4 causes a delay of one second. If you specify *delay*, you must also specify *rate*.

### Example

To set the keyboard repetition rate to 10 and the delay to 0.5 second, type:

```
C:\>mode con rate=10 delay=2
```

## MODE
## Set Serial Communications Parameters
### Versions 3.2 and later, IBM releases 1.1 and later

*Page 123*

This form of the Mode command sets the communications parameters for a serial port. You use these parameters in situations such as setting up the port for a modem or a serial printer.

In versions 4 and later, the command and its parameters are entered as shown below. An alternative command format that can be used with all versions of MS-DOS is described later in this entry.

**mode <port> baud=<rate> parity=<type> data=<databits>
stop=<stopbits> retry=<action>**

<port> is the name of the serial port whose communications parameters are to be set. <port> can be COM1, COM2, COM3, or COM4. You must specify <port>.

*baud*=<rate> specifies the baud rate (speed of transmission). <rate> can be 110, 150, 300, 600, 1200, 2400, 4800, 9600, or 19200 (if the system is capable of supporting that speed). You must specify <baud>, but only the first two digits are required.

*parity*=<type> specifies the type of error checking to be performed. <type> can be *n* for none, *o* for odd, *e* for even, *m* for mark, or *s* for space. If you don't specify parity, MS-DOS assumes *e*.

*data*=<databits> specifies the number of electrical signals used to represent one character (such as *a*). <databits> can be 5, 6, 7, or 8. If you don't specify <databits>, MS-DOS assumes 7.

*stop*=<stopbits> specifies the number of electrical signals that mark the end of each character. <stopbits> can be 1, 1.5, or 2. If you don't specify <stopbits>, MS-DOS assumes 2 if the baud rate is 110; otherwise, it assumes 1.

*retry*=<action> specifies how the Mode command should respond when the serial port is busy. Possible values are *e* for error, *b* for busy, *p* for keep trying, *r* for ready, and *n* for no action. If you don't specify <action>, the Mode command assumes *n* (*e* in MS-DOS versions prior to 5). Unless the instructions for a program suggest otherwise, don't specify this parameter. You should also avoid it if you use the Mode command over a network.

With any version of MS-DOS, including versions prior to 4, you can also use the following form of the Mode command to set serial communications parameters. If you omit any parameter when you use this form of the command, be sure to include the following comma.

**mode <port> <baud>,<parity>,<databits>,<stopbits>,P**

<port> is the name of the serial port whose parameters are to be set. As with the preceding form of the command, <port> can be COM1, COM2, or (with versions 3.3 and later) COM3 or COM4. You must specify <port>.

<baud> is the baud rate. It can be any of the values listed for <baud> in the preceding form of the command, but 19200 is available only in versions 3.3 and later.

<parity> is the type of error checking performed. It can be *n*, *o*, or *e* in any version of MS-DOS and can also be *m* or *s* in versions 4 and later.

<databits> is the number of signals per character. It can be 7 or 8 in any version of MS-DOS and can be 5, 6, 7, or 8 in versions 4 and later.

<stopbits> is the number of signals marking the end of each character. It can be 1 or 2 in any version of MS-DOS and can be 1, 1.5, or 2 in versions 4 and later.

P, in versions through 3.3, tells MS-DOS to try continuously to send output to the serial port if the device attached to the port is not ready to receive data (for example, if the device is busy or is not turned on). Specify P when a printer is attached to the serial port. If MS-DOS is waiting for the printer and you want to return to the system prompt, press Ctrl-C or Ctrl-Break to cancel continuous retries. The P parameter is equivalent to the retry=b parameter in versions 4 and later.

### Examples

To set COM1 to 1200 baud, 8 data bits, and no parity, letting MS-DOS assume a value for stop bits and retries, use the following command in versions 4 and later:

```
C:\>mode com1 baud=1200 data=8 parity=n
```

For the same settings in any version of MS-DOS:

```
C:\>mode com1: 1200,n,8
```

To set COM2 to 2400 baud, no parity, and continuous retries, letting MS-DOS assume values for data bits and stop bits, use the following command in versions 4 and later:

```
C:\>mode com2 baud=2400 parity=n retry=b
```

Or, in earlier versions of MS-DOS:

```
C:\>mode com2: 2400,n,,,p
```

(Note the commas showing that values for data bits and stop bits are omitted.)

## MODE

## Set Parallel Printer Width and Spacing

**Versions 3.2 and later, IBM releases 1 and later**

*Page 120*

This form of the Mode command sets the number of characters per line and the number of lines per inch for a printer attached to a parallel port. In versions 4 and later, you can use the following form of the command. An alternative command format that can be used with all earlier versions of MS-DOS is described later in this entry.

**mode <printer> cols=<width> lines=<spacing> retry=<action>**

<printer> is the name of the parallel printer port: LPT1, LPT2, or LPT3. You must specify <printer>.

*cols*=<width> specifies the maximum number of characters that are to be printed on a line. <width> can be 80 or 132. If you don't specify <width>, MS-DOS assumes 80.

*lines*=<spacing> specifies the number of lines per vertical inch. <spacing> can be 6 or 8. If you don't specify <spacing>, MS-DOS assumes 6.

*retry*=<action> specifies how the Mode command should respond when the parallel port is busy. Possible values are *e* for error, *b* for busy, *p* for keep trying, *r* for ready, and *n* for no action. If you don't specify <action>, the Mode command assumes *n* (*e* in MS-DOS versions prior to 5). Unless the instructions for a program suggest otherwise, don't specify this parameter. You should also avoid it if you use the Mode command over a network.

With any version of MS-DOS, including versions prior to 4, you can also use the following form of the Mode command to set printer width and spacing:

**mode <printer> <width>,<spacing>,P**

<printer>, <width>, and <spacing> are the same parameters described earlier in this entry. If you use this form of the command, be sure to include the trailing comma if you omit <width> or <spacing>.

P, in versions prior to 4, tells MS-DOS to continuously try to send output to the printer, even if the printer is busy or not ready. If MS-DOS is waiting for the printer and you want to return to the system prompt, press Ctrl-C or Ctrl-Break to cancel continuous retries. The P parameter is equivalent to the retry=b parameter in versions 4 and later.

### Examples

To set LPT1 to 132 characters per line and 8 lines per inch, letting MS-DOS assume a value for retries, use the following form of the Mode command in versions 4 and later:

```
C:\>mode lpt1 cols=132 lines=8
```

Or, in any version of MS-DOS:

```
C:\>mode lpt1: 132,8
```

To set LPT2 to 8 lines per inch and specify continuous retries, use the following form of the Mode command in versions 4 and later:

```
C:\>mode lpt2 lines=8 retry=b
```

Or, in earlier versions of MS-DOS:

```
C:\>mode lpt2: ,8,p
```

## MODE
## Redirect Parallel Printer Output
**Versions 3.2 and later, IBM releases 1.1 and later**

*Page 125*

This form of the Mode command redirects output from a parallel port to a serial port. Before using a serial printer, you must set the communications parameters of the serial port as described previously under the heading "MODE: Set Serial

543

Communications Parameters" and then redirect output from a parallel port to the serial port with the following form of the Mode command:

**mode &lt;printer&gt;=&lt;port&gt;**

&lt;printer&gt; is the name of the parallel printer whose output is to be redirected. &lt;printer&gt; can be LPT1, LPT2, or LPT3.

&lt;port&gt; is the name of the serial communications port to which the parallel printer port is to be redirected. If you're using 3.2 or an earlier version of MS-DOS, &lt;port&gt; can be COM1 or COM2. If you're using version 3.3 or later, &lt;port&gt; can be COM1, COM2, COM3, or COM4.

To cancel redirection, omit the equal sign and &lt;port&gt; from the Mode command (that is, type just *mode &lt;printer&gt;*).

### Examples

To redirect output from LPT1 to COM2:

```
C:\>mode lpt1:=com2:
```

To cancel redirection of LPT1:

```
C:\>mode lpt1:
```

## MODE
## Check Device Status

**Versions 4 and later**

*Page 126*

Beginning with version 4, this form of the Mode command enables you to request a report on the status of any or all devices on your system.

**mode &lt;device&gt; /status**

&lt;device&gt; is the name of the device you want to check on, such as CON, LPT1, or COM1. If you omit &lt;device&gt;, MS-DOS reports on all the devices it recognizes.

*/status* tells MS-DOS you want to check on device status. You can abbreviate this parameter as */sta*, and you can omit it from the command altogether unless you are checking on a parallel printer whose output you've redirected.

### Example

To check the status of a parallel printer attached to LPT1 whose output has been redirected to COM2, with no retries if the port is busy:

```
C:\>mode lpt1 /sta

Status for device LPT1:
-----------------------
LPT1: rerouted to COM2:
Retry=NONE

Code page operation not supported on this device
```

(The last line means that the device has not been set up for international language support, as described in the following entries.)

## MODE
## Preparing a Code Page
### Versions 3.3 and later

This form of the Mode command defines the code page or code pages to be used with a hardware device. To use this form of the Mode command, you must already have installed code-page switching. See your MS-DOS manual for details.

**mode <device> cp prep=((<codepage>) <filename>)**

<device> is the name of the device for which the code page or code pages are to be prepared. It can be CON, PRN, LPT1, LPT2, or LPT3.

<codepage> is the code page to be used with <device>. If you specify more than one code page, separate the numbers with blanks. Note that the code-page numbers are enclosed in their own set of parentheses. You can use the following code-page numbers: 437 (United States), 850 (multilingual, or Latin I), 852 (Slavic, or Latin II—version 5 only), 860 (Portuguese), 863 (Canadian French), and 865 (Nordic).

<filename> is the name of the code-page information file MS-DOS needs to prepare the code page for <device>. A code-page information file has the extension CPI. The following files are standard in MS-DOS versions 3.3 and later:

| | |
|---|---|
| EGA.CPI | Enhanced Graphics Adapter (EGA) or Video Graphics Array (VGA) |
| 4201.CPI | IBM Proprinter and Proprinter XL or compatible (versions 3.3 through 5 only) |
| 4208.CPI | IBM Proprinter X24E Model 4207 and Proprinter XL24E Model 4208 or compatible (versions 4 and 5 only) |
| 5202.CPI | IBM Quietwriter III printer or compatible (versions 3.3 through 5 only) |
| LCD.CPI | IBM PC Convertible liquid crystal display (LCD) |

### Example

To prepare code pages 437 and 850 for an EGA or compatible display, assuming that EGA.CPI, the code-page information file, is in the C:\DOS directory:

```
C:\>mode con cp prep=((437 850)c:\dos\ega.cpi)
```

## MODE
# Selecting a Code Page

**Versions 3.3 and later**

This form of the Mode command selects a code page for a device. To use this form of the Mode command, you must already have installed code-page switching. See your MS-DOS manual for details.

**mode <device> cp select=<codepage>**

<device> is the name of the device for which the code page is to be selected. It can be CON, PRN, LPT1, LPT2, or LPT3.

<codepage> is the three-digit number of the code page to be used with <device>. You can use the following code-page numbers: 437 (United States), 850 (multilingual, or Latin I), 852 (Slavic, or Latin II—version 5 only), 860 (Portuguese), 863 (Canadian French), or 865 (Nordic). <codepage> must be one previously prepared with the *cp prepare* option of the Mode command.

### Example

To select code page 850 for the console:

```
C:\>mode con cp select=850
```

## MODE
# Displaying the Code-Page Status

**Versions 3.3 and later**

This form of the Mode command displays the status of the code pages. To use this form of the Mode command, you must already have installed code-page switching. See your MS-DOS manual for details.

**mode <device> cp /status**

<device> is the name of the device whose code-page status is to be displayed. It can be CON, PRN, LPT1, LPT2, or LPT3.

*/status* is optional.

### Example

To display the status of the console device:

```
C:\>mode con cp
```

## MODE
### Restoring a Code Page That Was Lost
#### Versions 3.3 and later

This form of the Mode command restores a code page that was selected for a device, then erased from memory. To use this form of the Mode command, you must already have installed code-page switching. See your MS-DOS manual for details.

**mode <device> cp refresh**

<device> is the name of the device whose most recently selected code page is to be restored. It can be CON, PRN, LPT1, LPT2, or LPT3.

### Example

To restore the most recently selected code page for the printer that is attached to the LPT2 port:

```
C:\>mode lpt2 cp refresh
```

## MORE
### Display a File One Screenful at a Time
#### Versions 2 and later

*Page 310*

The More filter command reads standard input (normally the keyboard) and sends lines to standard output (normally the display); after each screenful of lines it displays the line -- *More* -- and waits for you to press a key.

Because the input and output of the More command can be redirected, input can also come from a file, a device other than the keyboard, or the output of another command. Likewise, you can redirect the output of the More command to a file or a device other than the display. (*See* Input/Output Redirection.)

Thus, by redirecting or piping output to the More command, you can display a file one screenful at a time, pressing a key to see the next screenful. To stop displaying, you press Ctrl-Break. The More command has no parameters:

**more**

### Examples

To display the current directory one screenful at a time:

```
C:\>dir | more
```

To display the file REPORT.DOC one screenful at a time, the More command can be used in either of two ways. The first uses the redirection symbol < to get input from the file REPORT.DOC:

```
C:\MKT\WP>more < report.doc
```

The second pipes output from the Type command to the More command:

```
C:\MKT\WP>type report.doc | more
```

# MOVE
## Move a File or Rename a Directory

**Versions 6 and 6.2**

*Pages 79, 152*

The Move command moves one or more files to a new location. It differs from the well-known Copy command in that it doesn't leave a copy of the file in its original location. The Move command can also rename a directory.

### move /Y <filename> <target>

/Y tells Move not to prompt you before creating the directory into which the specified files are moved.

<filename> is the name of the file you want to move or the directory you want to rename. You can include a drive letter, a path name, or both, and you can use wildcard characters to move a set of files with similar names or extensions. You can specify more than one file by placing a comma between the file names.

<target> is the location to which <filename> is moved or the new name of the directory. If you are moving only one file, you can rename it at the same time by specifying the new file name as part of <target>.

> NOTE: *Be very careful when you specify <target> if you're using version 6 or earlier. If a file with the same name already exists in the location you specify, those versions of MS-DOS replace the existing file with the moved file, deleting the original version without warning you.*

### Examples

To move the file named FORECAST.TXT from the current directory (\MKT\WP) of the current drive (C:) to the root directory of drive A:

```
C:\MKT\WP>move forecast.txt a:\
```

To move the file named REPORT.TXT from the root directory of drive C to the current directory:

```
C:\MKT\WP>move c:\report.txt .
```

To rename the directory WP to WORDPROC:

```
C:\MKT>move wp wordproc
```

## MS ANTI-VIRUS (MSAV)
## Look for Viruses

### Versions 6 and 6.2

*Page 217*

*See also* Vsafe.

The Microsoft Anti-Virus program (MSAV) helps you locate and destroy any viruses that have found their way into your system. Anti-Virus has a number of parameters, most of which deal with the way the program appears. Its basic form is as follows:

**msav <drive> /S /C /A /L /video**

If you run Anti-Virus with none of these parameters, the full-screen version of the program starts.

<drive> specifies the drive that Anti-Virus checks for viruses. If you omit <drive>, Anti-Virus checks the current drive.

/S (for *scan*) tells Anti-Virus to inform you of any viruses it finds but not to remove them.

/C (for *clean*) causes Anti-Virus to remove any viruses it finds.

/A (for *all*) tells Anti-Virus to check all drives (except drives A and B).

/L (for *local*) tells Anti-Virus to check all drives except for network drives.

/video causes Anti-Virus to display a list of the parameters you can use to change how Anti-Virus appears when you run the full-screen version.

### Examples

To start the full-screen version of Anti-Virus:

```
C:\>msav
```

To tell Anti-Virus to check all drives and remove any viruses it finds:

```
C:\>msav /c /a
```

## MSBACKUP (MSBACKUP)
## Make a Backup Copy of Files or Restore Files

### Versions 6 and 6.2

*Page 223*

The MSbackup program, new in version 6, replaced the older Backup and Restore commands with a full-screen program that simplifies the important task of backing up your files on a regular basis.

**msbackup <setupfile> /bw /lcd /mda**

<setupfile> is the name of a setup file that tells MSbackup what type of backup you want to perform and what files to back up. If you omit <setupfile>, MSbackup assumes DEFAULT.SET.

*/bw* runs MSbackup in monochrome.

*/lcd* starts MSbackup using a color scheme that is easily visible on LCD screens (such as those in many laptop computers).

*/mda* tells MSbackup to use the monochrome display adapter.

## MS CD EXTENSION (MSCDEX)
### Identifies a CD-ROM Drive
**Versions 6 and 6.2**

The MScdex command identifies a CD-ROM drive to MS-DOS and assigns the drive a letter, such as E, F, or G. If you need more information about this command, type *help mscdex* at the system prompt.

## MS DIAGNOSTICS (MSD)
### List Information About Your Computer
**Versions 6 and 6.2**

The Microsoft Diagnostics program (MSD) displays a wealth of technical information about your computer.

**msd /B /I /F<filename> /P<filename> /S<filename>**

If you run the program without the /F, /P, or /S parameters, the full-screen version of MSD appears. This lets you quickly examine the areas in which you are interested.

/B runs MSD in monochrome.

/I tells MSD not to attempt to detect what hardware is part of the computer. Try using this switch if MSD refuses to run properly.

/F<filename> prompts you for information such as your name, address, and telephone number and then writes a complete report in the file specified by <filename>. This is useful if you need to send information about your system to the technical support department of a hardware or software company.

/P<filename> produces the same report that the /F parameter does, except that it doesn't prompt you for information.

/S<filename> creates a shorter summary report. If you omit <filename>, MSD prints the report on the screen.

### Example

To write a complete report to the file CURRENT.MSD in the root directory of drive C:

```
C:\>msd /p c:\current.msd
```

## NLSFUNC (NATIONAL LANGUAGE SUPPORT FUNCTION)
## Support National Language and Conventions

### Versions 3.3 and later

The National Language Support Function command (nlsfunc) enables MS-DOS to use code-page switching and loads the file that contains country-specific information, such as date format, time format, and currency symbol. You need to enter the Nlsfunc command before you can use the Change Code Page (chcp) command.

#### nlsfunc <countryfile>

<countryfile> is the name of the country information file (COUNTRY.SYS in most versions of MS-DOS). If you omit <countryfile>, MS-DOS assumes the file is the one specified in the Country configuration command in CONFIG.SYS; if there is no Country configuration command in CONFIG.SYS, MS-DOS assumes that the file is named COUNTRY.SYS and looks for it in the root directory of the current drive.

### Examples

The following command, typed at the system prompt (C:\>), starts the national language support program and tells MS-DOS to use the file COUNTRY.SYS in the C:\DOS directory:

```
C:\>nlsfunc c:\dos\country.sys
```

If you have version 4 or later of MS-DOS, you can place the following Install command in CONFIG.SYS to load the national language support program and specify the file COUNTRY.SYS (both stored in the C:\DOS directory) at startup:

```
install=c:\dos\nlsfunc.exe c:\dos\country.sys
```

NOTE: *If you have version 3.3 of MS-DOS, you can load national language support at startup by placing the command shown in the first example* (nlsfunc c:\dos\country.sys) *in AUTOEXEC.BAT.*

## NUMLOCK (CONFIGURATION COMMAND)
## Set Num Lock State

### Versions 6 and 6.2

The Numlock command lets you determine whether your Num Lock key is on or off when MS-DOS starts.

**numlock=<state>**

<state> is either *on* or *off.* MS-DOS sets the Num Lock to the specified state when it starts.

# PATH
## Define the Command Path
### Versions 2 and later

*Page 159*

The Path command tells MS-DOS where to search for a command file (a file whose extension is COM, EXE, or BAT) that isn't in the current directory. A command path becomes part of the MS-DOS environment, so it is available to every program.

**path <drive><path> ;**

<drive> is the letter, followed by a colon, of the drive containing the disk on which you want MS-DOS to look for command files (such as c:).

<path> is the path name of the directory that you want MS-DOS to search for command files. You can enter a series of path names, separated by semicolons. If you omit <drive> and <path> but include the semicolon, MS-DOS deletes any paths in effect.

If you enter the Path command with no parameters (type just *path*), MS-DOS displays the current command path. If no path has been specified, MS-DOS displays *No path.*

Include a Path command in AUTOEXEC.BAT if application programs or batch files on your hard disk are stored in separate subdirectories.

## Examples

To tell MS-DOS to search the root directory and the directories named \DOS, \WINDOWS, and \WORD of the current drive for command files:

```
C:\>path c:\;c:\dos;c:\windows;c:\word
```

To display the command path:

```
C:\>path
```

For the command path in the preceding example, MS-DOS responds:

```
PATH=C:\;C:\DOS;C:\WINDOWS;C:\WORD
```

To delete the command path:

```
C:\>path ;
```

## PAUSE (BATCH COMMAND)
## Temporarily Stop a Batch File

### Versions 1 and later

*Page 341*

The Pause batch command displays the message *Press any key to continue...* (*Strike a key when ready...* in versions before 4) and waits for you to press a key before carrying out any more commands. You can cancel a batch file while it is paused by pressing Ctrl-C.

The Pause command also lets you include a message to be displayed before *Press any key to continue....*

**pause <message>**

<message> is the message to be displayed before *Press any key to continue....*

### Examples

To temporarily stop a batch file:

```
pause
```

To temporarily stop a batch file and echo the message *Put the data disk in drive B and* before the *Press any key to continue...* message:

```
@echo off
echo Put the data disk in drive B and
pause
```

When MS-DOS carries out the commands in the batch file, it displays the following messages and waits for any key to be pressed:

```
Put the data disk in drive B and
Press any key to continue . . .
```

## POWER
## Control Power Management

### Versions 6 and 6.2

The Power command controls the power-management features found in many battery-powered computers. You must load the POWER.EXE device driver before you can use the Power command.

**power adv:<setting> std off**

If you type *power* with no parameters, Power displays the current power setting.

adv:<setting> changes the type of power management in effect. <setting> can be one of the following keywords:

| Keyword | Meaning |
| --- | --- |
| *max* | Maximum power conservation |
| *reg* | Regular power conservation (default) |
| *min* | Minimum power conservation |

*std* tells your computer to use only the power-conservation measures that are built into your computer's hardware. If your computer does not support the APM (Advanced Power Management) specification, *std* turns off power management.

*off* turns off power management.

## POWER.EXE
## Enable Power Management

### Versions 6 and 6.2

*Page 395*

POWER.EXE is the name of a device driver included with versions 6 and later of MS-DOS. This program allows you to control the power-management features found in many battery-powered computers.

**device=<path>power.exe adv:<setting> std off /low**

<path> specifies the path to the file POWER.EXE. If you don't specify <path>, MS-DOS looks in the root directory of the system disk.

adv:<setting> changes the type of power management in effect. <setting> can be one of the following keywords:

| Keyword | Meaning |
| --- | --- |
| *max* | Maximum power conservation |
| *reg* | Regular power conservation (default) |
| *min* | Minimum power conservation |

*std* tells your computer to use only the power-conservation measures that are built into your computer's hardware. If your computer does not support the APM (Advanced Power Management) specification, *std* turns off power management.

*off* turns off power management.

*/low* loads POWER.EXE into conventional memory. If you omit */low*, POWER.EXE loads into upper memory if any is available.

## PRINT
## Print a File

**Versions 2 and later**

*Page 87*

The Print command loads the MS-DOS Print program, which manages a queue of files waiting to be printed. The Print program, also known as a *print spooler,* can print the files in the queue while another program is running. It does this by using small portions of the computer's processing time.

The Print command is used in two forms. You use the first when you load the print program and set up its operating characteristics, and you use the second to manage the contents of the print queue. These forms are described separately in the following two entries.

## PRINT
## Set Operating Characteristics

**Versions 2 and later**

*Page 91*

The first time you enter the Print command after you start MS-DOS, you can define the operating characteristics of the print program with the command:

**print /D:<printer> /Q:<size> /B:<size> /S:<slice> /M:<max> /U:<wait>**

/D:<printer> specifies the name of the print device. If you do not specify <printer> in the first Print command you enter after starting the system, MS-DOS prompts you for the device name by displaying *Name of list device [PRN]:*. You can specify LPT1, LPT2, LPT3, COM1, COM2, AUX, or PRN. If you're using version 3.3 or later, you can also specify COM3 or COM4. If you press Enter without specifying a device, MS-DOS assumes PRN. If you use /D to name the print device, it must be the first parameter in the Print command (versions 3 and later).

/Q:<size> specifies how many files can be in the print queue. The range is 4 through 32; if you don't specify /Q:<size>, MS-DOS assumes 10.

/B:<size> specifies the number of bytes, up to 16384, in the print buffer (an area of memory used for data by the Print program). If you don't specify /B:<size>, MS-DOS assumes 512 bytes (versions 3 and later).

/S:<slice> specifies the length of time (time slice), measured in ticks of the computer's internal timer, that Print is allowed to control the computer. <slice> can be a value from 1 through 255; if you don't specify /S:<slice>, MS-DOS assumes 8 (versions 3 and later).

/M:<max> specifies how long, again in ticks of the computer's internal timer, that Print can take to print one character. <max> can be from 1 through 255; if you don't specify /M:<max>, MS-DOS assumes 2 (versions 3 and later).

/U:<wait> specifies how many timer ticks Print waits before giving up its time slice if the printer is busy or unavailable. <wait> can be from 1 through 255; if you don't specify /U:<wait>, MS-DOS assumes 1 (versions 3 and later).

Because MS-DOS assumes values for all these parameters, you needn't use any of them unless you want to change these assumed values. Depending on such factors as how often you use the Print command, how many files you typically put in the print queue, the average length of the files you print, and the size of your printer's buffer, you may be able to improve overall system performance by experimenting with some of the values that MS-DOS assumes.

### Example

To specify COM1 as <printer>, a queue that can hold up to 16 files, and a buffer size of 2048 bytes:

```
C:\>print /d:com1: /q:16 /b:2048
```

NOTE:  *Remember that you define these characteristics the first time you enter a Print command. To change the operation of the Print command if your AUTOEXEC.BAT file already contains a Print command, edit AUTOEXEC.BAT and restart your computer.*

## PRINT
## Manage the Print Queue
### Versions 2 and later

*Page 89*

Files are placed in the print queue in the order in which you specify them in the Print command, and they are printed in the same order. You can add files to and delete files from the print queue in the same command.

MS-DOS continues printing a file until it reaches an end-of-file marker (Ctrl-Z), then stops, even if it has not reached the actual end of the file, and goes on to the next file in the queue. After printing a file, MS-DOS advances the paper to the top of the next page.

### print <filename> /P /C /T

<filename> is the name of the file to be added to or deleted from the print queue. You can use wildcard characters to print a set of files with similar file names or extensions, and you can specify more than one file in a single Print

command, separating the file names with blanks. In versions 3 and later, you can also include a path name.

/P adds to the print queue the preceding and all subsequent files in the command line up to a /C parameter. If you enter a Print command with a file name but no other parameter, MS-DOS assumes /P.

/C deletes from the print queue the preceding and all subsequent files in the command line up to a /P parameter. If one of the deleted files is being printed, MS-DOS prints *File* <filename> *canceled by operator,* sounds the printer's bell (if there is one), and advances the paper to the top of the next page.

/T terminates printing. MS-DOS deletes all files from the print queue, cancels any file being printed, prints *All files canceled by operator,* sounds the printer's bell, and advances the paper to the top of the next page.

If you enter the Print command with no parameters, MS-DOS displays the names of the files in the print queue.

### Examples

To add all files in the current directory with the extension DOC (or as many as the queue will hold) to the print queue:

```
C:\MKT\WP>print *.doc
```

To remove the file named REPORT.DOC from the print queue and at the same time add the files named SLSRPT.DOC and SLSFCST.DOC to the print queue:

```
C:\MKT\WP>print report.doc /c slsrpt.doc /p slsfcst.doc
```

To cancel printing and remove all files from the print queue:

```
C:\MKT\WP>print /t
```

## PROMPT
## Set the System Prompt
**Versions 2 and later, IBM releases 2.1 and later**

*Page 400*

The Prompt command defines the system prompt, which recent versions of MS-DOS normally display as the current drive and directory, followed by a greater-than sign (such as *C:\>*). If you change the system prompt, you can include any character MS-DOS can display, and such items of system information as the time and date, in addition to the current drive and current directory.

**prompt <string>**

<string> is a string that defines the new prompt. It can contain any character MS-DOS can display, plus any number of the following two-character codes, which tell MS-DOS to include specific information in the prompt (each code must begin with a dollar sign):

| Code | Information Displayed |
|------|----------------------|
| $t | The time |
| $d | The date (preceded by the day of the week) |
| $p | Current directory of the current drive |
| $v | MS-DOS version number |
| $n | Current drive |
| $g | A greater-than sign (>) |
| $l | A less-than sign (<) |
| $b | A vertical bar (¦) |
| $q | An equal sign (=) |
| $h | A backspace (which erases the previous character) |
| $e | An escape character |
| $_ (underscore) | Start a new line |
| $$ | A dollar sign ($) |

If any other character follows the $, MS-DOS ignores both characters.

If you enter a Prompt command that includes no parameters, MS-DOS sets the system prompt to display the current drive followed by a greater-than sign (for example, *C>*).

## Examples

Each of the following examples shows a Prompt command followed by the prompt it produces (<space> represents pressing the Spacebar once).

To set the system prompt to display the word *Command* followed by a colon:

```
C:\>prompt Command:<space>
Command: _
```

To change the prompt from the preceding example to show the time—with six backspaces to erase seconds and hundredths of seconds—followed by a blank space, the date, and a colon:

```
Command: prompt $t$h$h$h$h$h$h<space>$d:<space>
16:07 Wed 10-16-1993: _
```

Finally, to reset the system prompt to the usual display (current drive and directory, followed by a greater-than sign):

```
16:07 Wed 10-16-93: prompt $p$g
C:\>_
```

# QBASIC
## Start the QBasic Interpreter
### Versions 5 and later

*Page 263*

The Qbasic command, in versions 5 and later of MS-DOS, starts the program that enables you to use MS-DOS QBasic, the successor to the GW-BASIC and BASICA programming languages shipped with earlier versions of MS-DOS. When you use the Qbasic command, you start the QBasic interpreter, a menu-based program. You use the interpreter to create QBasic programs, and the interpreter translates them into a form the computer can carry out. The QBasic interpreter includes online help; it does not teach you to program, but it does help you learn to use QBasic and the interpreter.

# RAMDRIVE.SYS
## Create a RAM Drive in Memory
### Versions 3.2 and later

*Page 389*

> NOTE: *In IBM releases of MS-DOS, the RAM-disk program is called VDISK.SYS. The following description applies to both RAMDRIVE.SYS and VDISK.SYS. Differences between the two are noted where appropriate.*

RAMDRIVE.SYS (and VDISK.SYS) are programs that create a RAM disk by setting aside a certain portion of the computer's memory and treating it as if it were a disk drive. To install a RAM disk, you add a Device command to CONFIG.SYS that identifies the RAM-disk program and specifies the size and characteristics of the RAM disk. You can create more than one RAM disk by including a Device command for each in CONFIG.SYS.

When you create a RAM disk, MS-DOS assigns the first available drive letter to it. MS-DOS normally assumes five available drive letters, A through E. If you need a drive letter higher than E, you should include or modify a Lastdrive command in CONFIG.SYS.

A RAM disk is faster than a physical disk drive because it is electronic—there are no moving parts. Because it is not a physical unit, however, a RAM disk has two characteristics that affect the way you use your system. First, you must be sure to save the contents of a RAM disk on a floppy disk or a hard disk. If you don't, any information it contains will be lost when you shut the system down. Second, the memory used for a RAM disk is unavailable for other use. If your system has extended or expanded memory, you can use either for a RAM disk without reducing conventional memory available to applications and data. If your system has 640 KB (or less) of conventional RAM, however, you should consider the memory needs of your programs and data and balance those needs against the extra speed provided by a RAM disk.

The Device command format and parameters for RAMDRIVE.SYS are described below. Differences for IBM's VDISK.SYS are noted.

### device=ramdrive.sys <size> <sector> <directory> /E /A

RAMDRIVE.SYS (or VDISK.SYS) is the name of the RAM-disk program. Include a drive letter and path name if the program is not in the current directory of the system disk. For example, specify *c:\dos\ramdrive.sys* if the program is in the C:\DOS directory.

<size> specifies the size, in kilobytes, of the RAM disk. If you don't specify <size>, MS-DOS assumes 64 KB. If you do specify <size>, acceptable minimum and maximum values for different versions of DOS are:

- Versions 6 and 6.2: minimum = 4 KB, maximum = 32767 KB (32 MB)

- Version 5: minimum = 16 KB, maximum = 4096 KB (4 MB)

- Earlier Microsoft releases: minimum = 16 KB, maximum = all of available memory.

- Earlier IBM releases: minimum = 1 KB, maximum = all of available memory.

<sector> specifies the size, in bytes, of each RAM-disk sector. Acceptable values for <sector> in different versions of DOS are listed below:

- Versions 5 and later: 128, 256, or 512. If you don't specify <sector>, MS-DOS assumes 512.

- Microsoft version 4: 128, 256, 512, or (in some releases) 1024. If you don't specify <sector>, MS-DOS assumes 512.

- Microsoft version 3: 128, 256, 512, or (in some releases) 1024. If you don't specify <sector>, MS-DOS assumes 128.

- IBM versions 3 and 4: 128, 256, or 512. If you don't specify <sector>, DOS assumes 128.

<directory> specifies the number of directory entries the root directory can hold. Acceptable values are 2 through 1024 in Microsoft releases of MS-DOS, 2

through 512 in IBM releases. If you don't specify <directory>, MS-DOS assumes 64. Each directory entry requires 32 bytes; if the entries you specify require a fraction of a sector, MS-DOS increases the number to fill the final sector.

/E tells MS-DOS to create the RAM disk in extended memory. If you use extended memory, any required Device command identifying this memory to MS-DOS must precede the RAM-disk command in CONFIG.SYS.

/A tells MS-DOS to create the RAM disk in expanded memory (additional memory conforming to the Lotus-Intel-Microsoft Expanded Memory Specification). If you use expanded memory, any required Device command identifying this memory to MS-DOS must precede the RAM disk command in CONFIG.SYS.

NOTE: *In IBM's release of version 4, this parameter is /X, not /A. If you want to use version 4 to install a RAM disk in expanded memory, check your documentation for details.*

### Examples

The following examples show equivalent Device commands for RAMDRIVE.SYS and VDISK.SYS. Such commands would be included in CONFIG.SYS. All examples assume RAMDRIVE.SYS or VDISK.SYS is in the C:\DOS directory.

To create a 64 KB RAM disk, using all the values that MS-DOS assumes:

```
device=c:\dos\ramdrive.sys
device=c:\dos\vdisk.sys
```

To create a 4 MB RAM disk in expanded memory, specifying 512-byte sectors and 224 directory entries:

```
device=c:\dos\ramdrive.sys 4096 512 224 /a
device=c:\dos\vdisk.sys 4096 512 224 /a
```

(Substitute /x for /a in the second command with IBM's version 4 of MS-DOS.)

To create a 1 MB RAM disk in extended memory, specifying 512-byte sectors and 112 directory entries:

```
device=c:\dos\ramdrive.sys 1024 512 112 /e
device=c:\dos\vdisk.sys 1024 512 112 /e
```

## RECOVER
### Recover Files from a Damaged Disk
**Versions 2 through 5**

The Recover command attempts to reconstruct files from a disk that has damaged sectors or a damaged directory. It names the recovered files FILE*nnnn*.REC, where *nnnn* is a sequence number that starts with 0001. Recovered files may include extraneous material at the end, which you'll need to edit out of the file.

The Recover command excludes data from all damaged sectors; recovered files may or may not be complete and may or may not be usable by an application program. Files can be recovered from subdirectories, but they are placed in the root directory of the disk, not in the subdirectory in which they were originally saved.

NOTE: *Recover cannot be used on a network, nor can it be used with a drive affected by a Join or Substitute command.*

### recover <filename>

<filename> is the name of the file to be recovered. If you specify a drive letter rather than a file name, MS-DOS assumes that the directory of the disk in the drive is damaged and recovers the directory as a single file containing the names of the files it originally contained. The original directory is erased, however, so don't use this form of the command unless you're sure the directory is unusable.

## Examples

To recover the file named REPORT.DOC in the current directory of the current drive:

```
C:\MKT\WP>recover report.doc
```

To recover as many files as MS-DOS can fit into the root directory of the disk in drive B:

```
C:\>recover b:
```

## REM (BATCH COMMAND)
## Include a Remark in a Batch File

### Versions 1 and later

*Page 321*

The Remark batch command (rem) lets you include remarks in a batch file. Remarks are displayed if echo is on and are not displayed if echo is off.

### rem <remark>

<remark> is the remark.

**NOTE:** *You can also insert* rem *at the beginning of a line in your AUTOEXEC.BAT or CONFIG.SYS file. When you do this, you tell MS-DOS to ignore the line during startup. Using the Rem command in this way allows you to disable a command in AUTOEXEC.BAT or CONFIG.SYS yet keep the command in case you decide to reinstate it later.*

### Example

The following batch command includes the remark *This batch file requires the data disk* in a batch file:

```
rem This batch file requires the data disk
```

## REMOVE DIRECTORY (RD)
## Remove a Directory

### Versions 2 and later

*Page 155*

The Remove Directory command (rd or rmdir) removes a subdirectory. You cannot remove the current directory or the root directory, nor can you remove a directory that contains files or other directories. (If you have version 6 or 6.2, you can use the Deltree command to remove directory structures. See the entry Deltree in this appendix.)

**rd <drive><path>**

<drive> is the letter, followed by a colon, of the drive containing the disk with the directory to be removed (such as c:).

<path> is the path name of the directory that is to be removed.

**NOTE:** *Because the Assign, Join, and Substitute commands can mask the actual subdirectory names, you shouldn't remove a directory with the RD command when any of these commands are in effect.*

### Examples

The following examples assume that the current directory is C:\.

To remove the subdirectory C:\MKT:

```
C:\>rd mkt
```

To remove the subdirectory C:\MKT\WP:

```
C:\>rd \mkt\wp
```

To remove the subdirectory \WORD\LETTERS from the disk in drive A:

```
C:\>rd a:\word\letters
```

## RENAME (REN)
## Change the Name of a File
### Versions 1 and later

*Pages 82, 153*

The Rename command (ren) changes the name of a file or a set of files. The re-named file must be in the same directory as the original and can't be given the name of an existing file in the same directory. You cannot rename a directory with Rename. (If you have version 6 or 6.2, you can use the Move command to re-name a directory.)

> **ren <oldname> <newname>**

<oldname> is the name of the file to be renamed. You can include a drive and path, and you can use wildcards (∗ or ?) to specify a set of files.

<newname> is the new name to be assigned to the file. If you include a drive letter or path name, MS-DOS responds *Invalid parameter* or *Invalid filename or file not found* and doesn't change the name. If <newname> is the same as the name of an existing file, MS-DOS responds *Duplicate file name or file not found* and leaves <oldname> unchanged.

### Examples

To change the name of the file REPORT.DOC to FINALRPT.DOC:

```
C:\MKT\WP>ren report.doc finalrpt.doc
```

To change the name of the file FINALRPT.SAV to FINALRPT.DOC:

```
C:\MKT\WP>ren finalrpt.sav *.doc
```

To change the names of all files named REPORT in the directory D:\MKT\WP to the name FINALRPT, keeping the same extension:

```
C:\>ren d:\mkt\wp\report.* finalrpt.*
```

## REPLACE
## Replace or Add Files on a Disk
### Versions 3.2 and later

*Page 180*

The Replace command lets you copy files selectively, either by replacing files that already exist on the target disk or by adding files to the target. The Replace com-mand can also search subdirectories on the target disk for files to be replaced. The Replace command does not affect files with the hidden or system attribute.

> **replace <source> <target> /A /S /R /P /W /U**

<source> is the name of the file to be copied. You can use wildcard characters to copy a set of files with similar file names or extensions.

<target> specifies where <source> is to be copied. You can include a drive letter and path name but not a file name.

/A (for *add*) copies only the files in <source> that don't exist in <target>. This lets you add files to <target> without replacing files that already exist. If you don't specify /A, only files specified in <source> that also exist in <target> are copied. If you specify /A, you cannot specify /S or /U.

/S applies the Replace command to all subdirectories contained in <target>. If you specify <target> as the root directory of a disk, the Replace command is applied to every subdirectory on the disk. If you specify /S, you can't specify /A.

/R extends replacement to include read-only files in <target>.

/P prompts for confirmation before replacing or adding each file.

/W waits and prompts you to press a key before the Replace command begins. This gives you a chance to put in the correct floppy disk before starting to replace or add files on it.

/U replaces only files in the target drive or directory that are older than their counterparts in the source drive or directory.

When it finishes, Replace sets *errorlevel* to one of the following values:

| | |
|---|---|
| 0 | Completed normally. |
| 1 | There was an error in the command line (versions 3.3 and earlier).<br>The version of MS-DOS can't run this version of Replace (versions 6 and 6.2). |
| 2 | No files were found to replace. |
| 3 | The source or destination path name was entered incorrectly or does not exist. |
| 5 | A read-only file was encountered in <target>, but the /R parameter was not included in the command. |
| 8 | Not enough memory. |
| 11 | Command-line error (versions 4 and later). |
| 15 | The command includes an invalid drive letter. |

You can check this value with the *errorlevel* option of the If batch command and use the outcome of the Replace procedure to control the behavior of a batch file.

### Examples

To replace all files whose extension is DOC in the directory C:\MKT\WP and all its subdirectories with the files whose extension is DOC on the disk in drive A and prompt for confirmation before each file is copied:

```
C:\>replace a:*.doc c:\mkt\wp /s /p
```

To add all files from the disk in drive A whose extension is DOC and that don't exist in the current directory on the disk in the current drive:

```
C:\MKT\WP>replace a:*.doc /a
```

# RESTORE
## Restore Backed-Up Files
### Versions 2 and later

*Page 237*

The Restore command copies files that were backed up with the Backup command in versions 2 through 5, restoring them from the backup disk to the original disk. (If you used the version 6 or 6.2 MSbackup command to back up the files, use the same command to restore them.) Files are restored to the directories from which they were backed up, so the same directory structure must exist on the disk to which the files are restored. If you have a series of backup floppy disks, MS-DOS prompts for them, as they are needed, in the same sequence in which they were backed up with the Backup command.

The Restore command includes a number of parameters that help you fine-tune the restoration procedure, but not all parameters are available in all versions of MS-DOS. Check the documentation that came with your version of MS-DOS to determine which parameters you can use.

**restore <drive> <filename> /S /P /B:<date> /A:<date> /M /N /E:<time> /L:<time> /D**

<drive> specifies the drive that contains the backup disk from which files are to be restored. If you don't specify a drive letter, the files are restored from the disk in the current drive.

<filename> specifies the file or files to be restored. You can include a drive letter and path and use wildcard characters to restore a set of files with similar names or extensions. If you don't specify a path, the files are restored to the current directory.

/S restores files from all subdirectories of the specified directory.

/P causes MS-DOS to prompt for confirmation before restoring a read-only file or a file that has changed since it was backed up. In versions 3.3 and later, the Restore command does not affect the system files (IO.SYS and MSDOS.SYS) that MS-DOS needs in order to function. In earlier versions, the /P parameter causes MS-DOS to prompt when it encounters hidden as well as read-only files, so you can use this parameter to avoid replacing the system files with copies from a different version of MS-DOS.

/B:<date> restores only files that were created or changed on or before <date>.

/A:<date> restores only files that were created or changed on or after <date>.

/M restores only files that have been changed since they were backed up.

/N restores only files that don't exist on the target.

/E:<time> restores only files that were created or changed earlier than <time>.

/L:<time> restores only files that were created or changed later than <time>.

/D, in versions 5 and later, displays the names of all files on the backup disk that match <filename>.

When it is finished, Restore sets one of the following *errorlevel* values:

| | |
|---|---|
| 0 | Completed normally. |
| 1 | No files were found to restore. |
| 3 | The restore process was canceled because the user pressed Ctrl-C or Ctrl-Break. |
| 4 | A system error occurred, and the restore process was stopped. |

You can check this value with the *errorlevel* option of the If batch command and thus use the outcome of the restore procedure to control the behavior of a batch file.

WARNING: *Trying to restore files that were backed up when an Assign, Substitute, or Join command was in effect can damage the directory structure of the disk.*

## Examples

To restore the file named REPORT.DOC from the disk in drive A to the directory \MKT\WP (from which it was backed up) on the disk in drive C:

```
C:\>restore a: c:\mkt\wp\report.doc
```

To restore all files in the root directory and all subdirectories on the disk in drive A to the same subdirectories on the disk in drive C:

```
C:\>restore a: c:\ /s
```

With versions 5 and later, to see a list of all files on the disk in drive A that were backed up from C:\MKT\WP and would be restored by specifying *.DOC:

```
C:\>restore a: c:\mkt\wp\*.doc /d
```

To restore the files in the preceding example, prompting for confirmation if the file has changed since it was backed up or if the file is read-only:

```
C:\>restore a: c:\mkt\wp\*.doc /p
```

## SCANDISK
## Scan a Disk for Errors

### Version 6.2

*Pages 107, 194*

ScanDisk checks both the directory structure information of the files on a disk and the surface of the disk itself for errors. In many cases, ScanDisk can correct structure errors—thereby recovering lost data—or move files from areas where the disk surface is damaged to undamaged locations. You can also use ScanDisk to check the compressed volume file that contains the files stored on a disk compressed with DoubleSpace.

**scandisk <drive>**

<drive> is the letter of the drive to be checked. If you don't specify <drive>, MS-DOS checks the current drive.

ScanDisk displays its opening screen, which tells you the area of the disk being checked. This process takes just a few moments. If ScanDisk detects errors, it gives you the option of correcting or ignoring the errors.

When ScanDisk finishes checking the file structure on the disk, it asks you whether you want to check the surface of the disk for defects.

### Examples

To start the full-screen version of ScanDisk and check the current drive:

```
C:\>scandisk
```

To check drive D instead:

```
c:\>scandisk d
```

If you prefer, you can specify all the program options with the command. This lets you run ScanDisk from a batch file. For a description of the parameters that you can enter with the command, type *help scandisk*.

## SELECT
## Start the Installation Program

### Version 4

*Page 409*

In version 4, the Select command starts the MS-DOS installation program, which prompts you for information about how to set up your operating system and then installs MS-DOS either on your hard disk or on floppy disks. The MS-DOS version 4 Install disk contains an AUTOEXEC.BAT file that automatically starts the Select program. To start the program, put the MS-DOS Install disk in drive A and turn the system on (or, if the system is running, press Ctrl-Alt-Del).

## SELECT
# Create a Country-Specific System Disk
### Version 3.3, IBM releases 3 through 3.3

The Select command creates a system disk tailored to the date format and keyboard layout of a particular country.

**select <source> <target> <country> <keyboard>**

<source> is the letter, followed by a colon, of the drive that contains the MS-DOS system disk; it must include the system files, COMMAND.COM, the Format command, and the Xcopy command. <source> must be either drive A or drive B; if you don't specify <source>, MS-DOS assumes drive A (versions 3.2 and 3.3).

<target> is the letter, followed by a colon, of the drive that contains the target disk. If you don't specify <target>, MS-DOS assumes drive B (versions 3.2 and 3.3).

<country> is the three-digit code, corresponding to the long-distance telephone prefix, of the country whose date and time format you want to use.

<keyboard> is the two-letter code for the keyboard layout you want to specify.

Valid country and keyboard codes through version 3.3 are listed in the following table (not all are available in all versions of MS-DOS).

| Country | Country Code | Keyboard Code |
|---------|--------------|---------------|
| Australia | 061 | US |
| Belgium | 032 | BE |
| Canada (English) | 001 | US |
| Canada (French) | 002 | CF |
| Denmark | 045 | DK |
| Finland | 358 | SU |
| France | 033 | FR |
| Germany | 049 | GR |
| International (English) | 061 | — |
| Israel | 972 | — |
| Italy | 039 | IT |
| Latin America | 003 | LA |
| Middle East (Arabic) | 785 | — |
| Netherlands | 031 | NL |
| Norway | 047 | NO |
| Portugal | 351 | PO |

*(continued)*

*continued*

| Country | Country Code | Keyboard Code |
|---------|--------------|---------------|
| Spain | 034 | SP |
| Sweden | 046 | SV |
| Switzerland (French) | 041 | SF |
| Switzerland (German) | 041 | SG |
| United Kingdom | 044 | UK |
| United States | 001 | US |

When you create a system disk with the Select command, MS-DOS also creates a CONFIG.SYS file and an AUTOEXEC.BAT file containing Date, Time, and Version commands. In version 3.2, if you specify a country whose keyboard file is not on the source disk, MS-DOS prompts you to insert the correct disk. Once a country-specific disk is created, you can use it to start MS-DOS with the date format and keyboard layout appropriate to that country.

### Example

To create a system disk for France and the French keyboard layout:

```
C:\>select 033 fr
```

## SET
## Change or Display an Environment Variable
### Versions 2 and later

The Set command changes or displays the value assigned to an environment variable. The environment is an area of memory in which MS-DOS keeps track of such information as the command path and definition of the system prompt. You can also use the Set command to define replaceable parameters for use with batch files. Set commands are usually included in AUTOEXEC.BAT. In versions 6 and 6.2, you can also include Set commands in CONFIG.SYS.

**set <variable>=<value>**

<variable> is the name of the variable you want to affect. One common variable is *temp*, which gives the path to a directory where applications can store temporary files. Another variable, useful in versions 5 and later of MS-DOS, is *dircmd*, which can be used to specify how MS-DOS should display the output of the Directory command. If you omit <value>, MS-DOS deletes the environment variable named <variable>.

If you type *set* with no parameters, MS-DOS displays the names and values of all current environment variables.

<value> is the string to be assigned to <variable>.

Although you don't need the Set command for everyday use, it can be helpful in refining your use of MS-DOS. If you need more information, refer to the documentation that came with your version of MS-DOS.

### Examples

To use C:\TEMP for temporary files, create the directory and include the following command in AUTOEXEC.BAT:

```
set temp=c:\temp
```

In versions 5 and later, to change the normal Directory command display to a wide format, with directories grouped before file names, you can include the following command in AUTOEXEC.BAT:

```
set dircmd=/w /og
```

To override the wide format, you would type a Directory command as *dir /-w.*

## SETUP
## Install MS-DOS

### Versions 5 and later

*Page 408*

The Setup command, in versions 5 and later, starts a program that installs MS-DOS on your system. To start Setup in version 5, place the first MS-DOS disk in drive A and start or restart the system. If you have version 6 or 6.2, start Setup by starting your system, placing the first disk in drive A (or B), and typing *a:setup* (or *b:setup*). The installation procedure itself is simple and almost entirely self-contained. If you need information on Setup, refer to the brief description in Appendix A, "Installing MS-DOS," or to the documentation that came with MS-DOS.

## SET VERSION (SETVER)
## Set MS-DOS Version Number

### Versions 5 and later

The Setver command lets you make versions 5 and later of MS-DOS appear to be a different (earlier) version to an application that requires a different version of MS-DOS. Version requirements for different programs are kept internally by MS-DOS in a format called a *version table.* You are unlikely to need this command in your everyday use of MS-DOS. If you do use it, first consult your documentation and the application's vendor to verify that you can use the Setver command without risk to your data.

**setver \<path\> \<application\> n.nn /delete /quiet**

\<path\> is the drive and path to the MS-DOS file named SETVER.EXE, which loads the version table into memory. The versions 5 and later Setup program ensures that MS-DOS will automatically load SETVER.EXE at startup by placing a Device command in CONFIG.SYS. To display the version table, type *setver* or *setver* <path>.

<application> is the file name and extension of the program for which you want to set the MS-DOS version number.

*n.nn* is the MS-DOS version number you want to specify (for example, 4.01).

*/delete* tells MS-DOS to remove a file from the version table. Use this parameter with caution.

*/quiet* keeps messages from being displayed. You can use this parameter only with */delete*.

### Example

To let PROGRAM.EXE use version 5 or later of MS-DOS as if it were version 3.3:

```
C:\>setver program.exe 3.3
```

## SETVER.EXE
## Load Version Table
### Versions 5 and later

SETVER.EXE is a device driver that loads the MS-DOS version table into memory. The version table is a list of program names and the versions of MS-DOS under which they were designed to run. SETVER.EXE and the related Setver command are used with programs that expect to work with a particular (earlier) version of MS-DOS, such as version 3.3.

SETVER.EXE is loaded into memory with a Device command, which should be placed in your CONFIG.SYS file by the MS-DOS Setup program.

#### device=setver.exe

SETVER.EXE is the name of the device driver. If you must add the command to CONFIG.SYS, precede the file name with a drive and path if the file is not in the current directory—for example, specify *c:\dos\setver.exe* if the file is in your /DOS directory.

## SHARE
## Allow Files to Be Shared
### Versions 3 and later

The Share command allows files to be shared by more than one program. If your computer is part of a network, you must enter a Share command before joining the network. Consult with the administrator of your network for information on how to use the Share command.

If your computer isn't part of a network, you probably don't need to use the Share command.

## SHELL (CONFIGURATION COMMAND)
### Specify the Command Processor
**Versions 2 and later**

The Shell configuration command specifies the command processor—the program that receives your instructions at the keyboard and relays them to the appropriate MS-DOS program—that MS-DOS is to use. Unless you specify otherwise with a Shell command, MS-DOS uses the program named COMMAND.COM. If you need to use a different command processor, the program requiring it should give you instructions on its use.

> NOTE: *The Shell command is not the same command that starts the MS-DOS Shell in versions 4 and later. To start the Shell, you type* dosshell *at the system prompt.*

## SHIFT (BATCH COMMAND)
### Move Batch Parameters One Position Left
**Versions 2 and later**

*Page 364*

The Shift batch command moves the command-line parameters entered with a batch command one position to the left; the leftmost parameter is lost, and all other parameters move one position left. You can use the Shift command to process more than 10 replaceable parameters in a batch file.

**shift**

### Example

The following batch file, named SHIFT_IT.BAT, uses the Shift command to process as many parameters as you can enter in the command line:

```
@echo off
echo %0
shift
:start
if "%0"=="" goto all_done
echo %0 %1 %2
shift
shift
shift
goto start
:all_done
echo ALL DONE
```

The Echo command in the second line displays the name of the batch file, and the Shift command in the third line shifts all command-line parameters one position to the left; the previous %0 (the name of the batch file) is lost, what was %1 becomes %0, what was %2 becomes %1, and so forth. The fifth line of the batch

573

file checks the left-most parameter to see if there is one. If there isn't, the command *goto all_done* ends the batch file. If there is a leftmost parameter, the sixth line displays the three leftmost parameters, lines 7 through 9 shift the parameters three positions to the left, and line 10 goes back to repeat the process.

Entering the SHIFT_IT batch command with the following parameters produces the display shown below:

```
C>shift_it 1 2 3 4 5 6 7 8 9 10 11 12 13 14 15
shift_it
1 2 3
4 5 6
7 8 9
10 11 12
13 14 15
ALL DONE
```

## SMARTDRV
## Manage a Disk Cache
### Versions 6 and 6.2

*See also* SMARTDRV.EXE.

The Smartdrv command lets you manage the contents of the disk cache created by SMARTDRV.EXE. You can use this command to clear the contents of the cache, change which drives are being cached, and change the type of caching being performed for each drive.

### smartdrv <disk><cachetype> /C /R

<disk> is the name of the drive whose caching is being modified.

<cachetype> specifies the type of caching that will be performed on the specified drive. There are two types of caching. Read-caching caches the information read from a disk. Write-caching caches the information written to a disk. <cachetype> can be a plus sign (+) or a minus sign (-). If you use a plus sign, <drive> is both read-cached and write-cached. If you use a minus sign, the disk is not cached at all. If you don't specify <cachetype> and <drive> is a floppy disk drive (or, in version 6.2, a CD-ROM drive), the disk is read-cached. If you don't specify <cachetype> and <drive> is a hard disk drive, the disk is both read-cached and write-cached in version 6 and read-cached only in version 6.2.

/C forces SmartDrive to write to disk everything waiting in its cache.

/R restarts SmartDrive, clearing the cache of all its previous contents.

### Example

To stop caching information from drive A and add read-caching only for floppy disk drive B, type the following:

```
C:\>smartdrv a- b
```

To restart SmartDrive and clear the cache of its contents, type

```
C:\> smartdrv /r
```

# SMARTDRV.EXE
## Create a Disk Cache
### Versions 6 and 6.2

*Page 385*

The SMARTDRV.EXE device driver creates a disk cache in extended memory and loads the SmartDrive program, which manages the cache. A disk cache is an area of memory that MS-DOS uses to store information recently read from or written to disk. Using a disk cache can speed operations significantly because MS-DOS can retrieve information directly from memory much faster than it can find the information on a disk. You create a disk cache in version 6 or 6.2 by adding the SMARTDRV.EXE command to AUTOEXEC.BAT. After the disk cache is created, you can use the Smartdrv command to manage the contents of the cache. Because the cache is created in extended memory, you must identify in CONFIG.SYS a program (such as EMM386.EXE) that manages your system's extended memory.

**smartdrv <drive> /E:<blocksize> <size> <minsize> /B:<buffersize> /C /F /N /R /L /Q /V**

*smartdrv* is the name of the device driver. Include a drive and path if SMARTDRV.EXE isn't in the root directory of your startup disk.

<drive> is the drive that will be cached. If you don't specify <drive>, all your drives are cached. See the Smartdrv entry in this appendix for details on how to modify the type of caching that SmartDrive performs.

/E:<blocksize> specifies, in bytes, the size of the blocks that SmartDrive moves. You can specify 1024, 2048, and 8192. If you don't specify /E:<blocksize>, the block size is set to 8192.

<size> is the size of the disk cache, in kilobytes. <size> can be any value from 128 to the amount of available extended memory. If you don't specify <size>, the size of the disk cache depends on the available amount of extended memory.

<minsize> is the smallest you want the cache to be, again in kilobytes. You don't have to specify <minsize> unless you're using Microsoft Windows version 3 or later. Windows might reduce the cache to suit its own needs, even if that means reducing <size> to 0.

/B:<buffersize> specifies the amount of additional information that SmartDrive reads and saves in memory when you read from the disk. If you don't specify /B:<buffersize>, SmartDrive reads 16 KB. <buffersize> can be any multiple of <blocksize>.

/C forces SmartDrive to write to disk everything waiting in its cache.

/F, in version 6.2 only, causes SmartDrive to write to disk before a program returns to the command prompt.

/N, in version 6.2 only, allows SmartDrive to wait until the system is idle before writing to disk. To force an immediate write, specify /C.

/R restarts SmartDrive, clearing the cache of all its previous contents.

/L loads SmartDrive into conventional memory. By default, the SmartDrive device driver is loaded into the upper memory area.

/Q prevents SmartDrive from displaying any output when it is loaded.

/V requires SmartDrive to display status messages when it is loaded. If you use /V, you can't use /Q.

### Example

To create a disk cache for all your drives, include the following command in AUTOEXEC.BAT:

```
c:\dos\smartdrv
```

To create a 1024 KB disk cache (minimum size 256 KB) for drive C, use this command:

```
c:\dos\smartdrv c 1024 256
```

## SMARTDRV.SYS
## Create a Disk Cache

### Versions 4 (Microsoft releases) and 5

*Page 387*

The SMARTDRV.SYS device driver creates a disk cache in either extended or expanded memory. A disk cache is an area of memory that MS-DOS uses to store information recently read from disk. Using a disk cache can speed operations significantly because MS-DOS can retrieve information directly from memory much faster than it can find the information on a disk. You create a disk cache in versions 4 and 5 by placing a Device configuration command in CONFIG.SYS. Whether you use extended or expanded memory, the Device command that creates a disk cache must follow a Device command that identifies for MS-DOS the program that manages your system's extended or expanded memory.

**device=smartdrv.sys <size> <minsize> /A**

SMARTDRV.SYS is the name of the device driver. Include a drive and path if SMARTDRV.SYS isn't in the root directory of your startup disk.

<size> is the size of the disk cache, in kilobytes. <size> can be any value from 128 to 8192 (8 MB). If you don't specify <size>, the cache is set to 256 KB. In creating the cache, SMARTDRV rounds <size> to the nearest multiple of 16. If there is not enough memory for the size you specify, it creates a smaller cache using the memory available.

<minsize>, in version 5 only, is the smallest you want the cache to be, again in kilobytes. You don't have to specify <minsize> unless you're using Microsoft Windows version 3 or later. Windows might reduce the cache to suit its own needs, even if that means reducing <size> to 0.

/A tells SMARDTRV to create the cache in expanded memory. If you don't specify /A, it creates the cache in extended memory.

### Example

The following example shows the two commands needed to create a 1024 KB disk cache (minimum size 256 KB) in extended memory with version 5 of MS-DOS:

```
device=c:\dos\himem.sys
device=c:\dos\smartdrv.sys 1024 256
```

The commands assume the device drivers named are in the C:\DOS directory. HIMEM.SYS is the version 5 extended memory manager; specify your own if you use a different one.

## SORT
## Arrange Lines of a File
**Versions 2 and later**

*Page 303*

The Sort filter command reads lines from standard input, arranges (sorts) them in alphabetic or numeric order, and writes the sorted lines to standard output.

In version 2, uppercase and lowercase letters are treated separately, so *Zurich* comes before *aardvark* in a sorted list. In versions 3 and later, however, uppercase and lowercase letters are treated identically, so *aardvark* comes before *Zurich.*

The input and output of the Sort command normally come from the keyboard and go to the display. Both, however, can be redirected from or to a file or device or piped from or to another command. For example, you can redirect input to a file to sort the lines of the file, then redirect the output to another file to store the sorted version on disk. The largest file that the Sort program can handle is 64 KB. If you redirect both the input to and the output from the Sort command to a file, use different file names; sorting a file to itself can destroy the contents of the file.

### sort /R /+<column>

/R sorts the file in reverse order (Z to A instead of A to Z, or highest number to lowest number).

/+<column> specifies the column on which the sorting is to be based; if you don't specify /+<column>, MS-DOS assumes 1.

### Examples

To sort the lines of a file named CLIENTS.LST and display the result:

```
C:\MKT>sort < clients.lst
```

To sort the file CLIENTS.LST in reverse order, placing the result in the file named CLIENTS.SRT:

```
C:\MKT>sort /r < clients.lst > clients.srt
```

## STACKS (CONFIGURATION COMMAND)
## Reserve Memory for Temporary Program Use

### Versions 3.2 and later

The Stacks configuration command tells MS-DOS how much memory to reserve for its own temporary use. Some application programs may require a Stacks command in CONFIG.SYS, and should tell you how to do it; otherwise, you shouldn't need to use this command.

## SUBMENU (CONFIGURATION COMMAND)
## Add Submenu to Startup Menu

### Versions 6 and 6.2

The Submenu command lets you add more than one level of menus to the MS-DOS startup menu. Use this command only following the header *[menu]* in CONFIG.SYS.

**submenu=<block>,<text>**

<block> is the name of the menu block to which MS-DOS will jump.

<text> is any text (up to 70 characters) that you want displayed on the startup menu. If you omit <text>, MS-DOS displays the name of the menu block.

### Example

To create a menu item that displays another set of menu items:

```
submenu=type_of_network, Install network
```

If the user chooses the menu item *Install network*, MS-DOS looks for a menu block named *type_of_network* and displays the menu items listed there.

## SUBSTITUTE (SUBST)
## Treat a Directory as a Disk Drive

### Versions 3.1 and later

*Page 402*

The Substitute command (subst) tells MS-DOS to treat a subdirectory as if it were an additional disk drive in your system. This lets you use subdirectories with an application program that doesn't recognize path names or use a drive letter in place of a long subdirectory name, because you can substitute a drive letter for a path to a subdirectory.

### subst <drive> <pathname> /D

<drive> is the letter, followed by a colon, of the drive to be substituted for <pathname> (such as c:). <drive> cannot be the current drive. If you specify <drive>, you must also specify <pathname>.

<pathname> is the path to the subdirectory for which <drive> is to be substituted; <pathname> must begin at the root directory (start with \). If you include a drive letter in <pathname>, it must be different from the letter you specified for <drive>. You must specify at least a backslash to name the root directory.

/D deletes a substitution, returning the drive letter to its original meaning. Do not use this parameter from within the substituted drive or directory.

If you enter the Substitute command with no parameters (type just *subst*), MS-DOS displays all substitutions in effect.

If you substitute a drive letter for one subdirectory, then want to substitute the same drive letter for a different subdirectory, you must first delete the original substitution.

If you want to use several subdirectories, enter a Substitute command for each subdirectory and use a different drive letter for each. If you need drive letters beyond E (the highest letter MS-DOS recognizes unless you specify otherwise), add or edit a Lastdrive configuration command in CONFIG.SYS to tell MS-DOS the highest drive letter.

> **NOTE:** *Because the Substitute command masks the actual type of disk drive from MS-DOS, you shouldn't use the Assign, Backup, Check Disk, Diskcomp, Diskcopy, Fdisk, Format, Join, Label, or Restore command when a substitution is in effect. Because the Substitute command can mask the true directory structure, you should also avoid using the Change Directory, Make Directory, Remove Directory, and Path commands when a substitution is in effect. If you want to use one of these commands, delete the substitution. The Substitute command cannot be used with a network drive.*

## SWITCHES (CONFIGURATION COMMAND)
## Set Various MS-DOS Options

### IBM release 4, MS-DOS versions 5 and later

The Switches configuration command lets you set several options in MS-DOS.

### switches=/K /F /N /W

/K tells MS-DOS not to use the enhanced keyboard functions. This prevents MS-DOS from using the additional keys on the enhanced keyboard. You would most likely need to use /K only if pressing one of the additional keys on the enhanced keyboard caused problems with one of your application programs.

The following parameters apply only to versions 6 and 6.2:

/F tells MS-DOS not to wait for 2 seconds after it displays the message *Starting MS-DOS.*

/N causes MS-DOS not to recognize the F5 and F8 function keys during startup. Normally, F5 and F8 allow you to skip configuration commands during startup.

/W informs MS-DOS that the file WINA20.286 is not in the root directory. You need to use /W only if you are using version 3 of Microsoft Windows and you have moved WINA20.286 to some other directory.

## SYSTEM (SYS)
## Transfer System Files

### Versions 1 and later

*Page 411*

The System command (sys) copies the MS-DOS system files—IO.SYS and MSDOS.SYS or IBMBIO.COM and IBMDOS.COM, depending on whose version of DOS you're using—from the disk in the current drive to a formatted disk. The system files are hidden and have special storage requirements. You don't see them in the output of the Directory command, but they must be present on any disk from which you want to start MS-DOS. Except in versions 5 and later of MS-DOS, the System command does not copy COMMAND.COM, which must also be on a startup disk. If you don't have version 5 or later, you must copy COMMAND.COM with the Copy command. If you have version 6 or 6.2, System also copies the file DBLSPACE.BIN, which is used with DoubleSpace disk compression.

You use the System command to transfer the MS-DOS system files to a hard disk, to a formatted blank floppy disk, or to a disk (such as an application disk) on which space has been reserved especially for these files. You can also use the

System command to replace existing system files with a newer version (3.3 and earlier versions, however, require the new system files to fit into the space occupied by the older files).

**sys <source> <drive>**

<source> specifies where the system files are to be copied from. You can specify a drive letter and a directory path name. If you don't specify <source>, MS-DOS copies the system files from the current drive (versions 4 and later).

<drive> is the letter of the drive, followed by a colon, that contains the disk to which the system files are to be copied (such as c:).

NOTE: *The System command cannot be used on a network drive.*

## Example
To copy the system files from the disk in drive C to a floppy disk in drive A:

```
C:\>sys a:
```

# TIME
# Change or Display the System Time
### Versions 1 and later

*Page 19*

The Time command displays the time maintained by MS-DOS, to the hundredth of a second, and prompts you to enter a new time. The time is displayed and entered according to a 12-hour or a 24-hour clock, depending on the custom of the country specified in the Country command in CONFIG.SYS. If you're using version 4 or later in a country, such as the United States, that normally uses a 12-hour clock, you can specify the time in 12-hour format, followed by an *a* or a *p* (for example, *10:15a* or *3:15p*), or in 24-hour format (for example, *15:15* for 3:15 P.M.).

The command form shown here uses the traditional United States format (hours:minutes:seconds).

**time <hh:mm><:ss><.xx>**

<hh:mm> is the new time to be set. <hh> is the hour (1 through 24 or 1 through 12 AM or PM), and <mm> is minutes (0 through 59). <hh> and <mm> are separated by a colon (:).

<:ss> specifies seconds (0 through 59), preceded by a colon (:). If you don't specify <:ss>, MS-DOS assumes 0.

<.xx> specifies hundredths of a second (0 through 99), preceded by a decimal point (.). If you don't specify <.xx>, MS-DOS assumes 0.

If you enter the Time command with no parameter (type just *time*), MS-DOS displays the current time and prompts you to enter the new time. You can either enter the new time or just press the Enter key to leave the time unchanged. If your system does not keep the time current when the computer is switched off, consider putting Date and Time commands in your AUTOEXEC.BAT file.

**NOTE:** *The Time command might not permanently change the system clock on computers with built-in or add-on clock/calendars. If you have a system with a built-in clock/calendar (such as an enhanced PC-compatible) and the Time command does not permanently change the time, use the SETUP program on your Diagnostics disk. If you have an add-on clock/calendar, use the software that came with the clock/calendar card.*

### Examples

To set the time to 6:00 A.M.:

```
C:\>time 6:00
```

Or, in version 4 or later:

```
C:\>time 6:00a
```

To set the time to 6:00 P.M.:

```
C:\>time 18:00
```

Or, in version 4 or later:

```
C:\>time 6:00p
```

To display the current time and respond to the prompt for a new time:

```
C:\>time
```

MS-DOS responds:

```
Current time is  6:02:01.60p
Enter new time: _
```

Or, if you're not using version 4 or later:

```
Current time is 18:02:01.60
Enter new time: _
```

Type the new time, or press the Enter key to leave the current time unchanged.

## TREE
## Display a Directory Structure
### Versions 3.2 and later, IBM releases 2 and later

*Page 160*

The Tree command shows the structure of a disk or directory by displaying the directory and subdirectory names and, optionally, the names of the files in each directory. In versions 4 and later, the Tree command diagrams the structure of a disk or a multilevel directory by using line-drawing and box-drawing characters. Earlier versions produce a list of directory names and, if requested, file names.

**tree <drive><path> /F /A**

<drive> is the letter of the drive, followed by a colon, that contains the disk whose directory structure is to be displayed.

<path> is the path to a specified directory. If you omit <path>, MS-DOS displays the current directory of the specified drive.

/F displays a list of the files in each directory.

/A specifies that alternative characters (plus signs, hyphens, and vertical bars) be used to draw the tree diagram so that it can be printed by printers that don't support the line-drawing and box-drawing characters (versions 4 and later).

NOTE: *You can also display a list of the directories and files on a disk with the /V option of the Check Disk command.*

### Examples

Assume that the root directory of the disk in drive C contains four directories: DOS, MKT, MFG, and ENG; \MKT and \ENG, in turn, contain subdirectories named WP and SPREAD. To display this directory structure, type:

```
C:\>tree
```

In versions 4 and later, MS-DOS displays the following diagram:

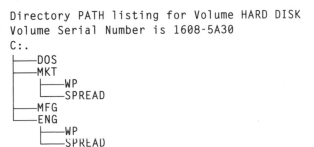
```
Directory PATH listing for Volume HARD DISK
Volume Serial Number is 1608-5A30
C:.
├───DOS
├───MKT
│   ├───WP
│   └───SPREAD
├───MFG
└───ENG
    ├───WP
    └───SPREAD
```

To print the diagram using the alternative characters, add the /A parameter and redirect the output to the printer:

```
C:\>tree /a > prn
```

MS-DOS prints the following diagram:

```
Directory PATH listing for Volume HARD DISK
Volume Serial Number is 1608-5A30
C:.
+---DOS
+---MKT
¦    +---WP
¦    \---SPREAD
+---MFG
\---ENG
     +---WP
     \---SPREAD
```

To display the directory structure of the disk in drive B, including all file names and pausing after each screenful:

```
C:\>tree b: /f ¦ more
```

## TYPE

## Display a File

### Versions 1 and later

*Page 73*

The Type command sends a file to standard output. If you don't redirect standard output, the file is displayed.

**type <filename>**

<filename> is the file to be sent to standard output. The Type command doesn't accept wildcard characters.

**NOTE:** *Some files include characters other than alphabetic and numeric characters and punctuation marks. Program files are one example; another is a word processor document that includes special formatting codes designed to be read by programs, rather than by people. If you use the Type command to display such a file, you'll probably see unintelligible characters and hear occasional beeps. Don't worry; your computer can handle the display, even though the results might be meaningless to you.*

### Examples

To display the file named REPORT.DOC in the current directory:

    `C:\MKT\WP>`type report.doc

To print the file REPORT.DOC from the directory \MKT\WP on the disk in drive A:

    `C:\DOS>`type a:\mkt\wp\report.doc > prn

# UNDELETE
# Recover Deleted Files

### Versions 5 and later

*Page 205*

The Undelete command restores files deleted with the Delete command, replacing them on the drive and in the directory from which they were removed.

Although Undelete can save you considerable time and aggravation when you've inadvertently deleted one or more needed files, files *cannot always* be completely recovered. When you delete a file, MS-DOS assumes that its storage space is available for saving other files. Undelete can succeed only if MS-DOS has not yet reassigned the file's disk space to another file. Once MS-DOS uses the space formerly occupied by a deleted file, the original information is lost and cannot be recovered by any means. For this reason, it is important to undelete files as soon as possible—preferably before any other files have been saved on the same disk.

**undelete <filename> /ds /dt /dos /all /list /load /S<drive>**
**/T<drive>=<files> /U /purge<drive>**

<filename> is the name of the file or files you want to restore. You can specify a drive and path, and you can use wildcards (* or ?) to specify a set of files. If you don't include <filename>, Undelete assumes you want to recover files in the current directory of the current drive.

*/ds* (available only in versions 6 and 6.2) tells Undelete to recover deleted files that were moved to the Delete Sentry directory by the Delete Sentry feature of the version 6 or 6.2 Undelete command. To use this parameter, you must already have started Delete Sentry. Undelete can then try to recover any files subsequently deleted. The */ds* parameter causes Undelete to display the name of each deleted file it finds and prompt you to confirm the recovery. If the only parameter you specify is <filename>, Undelete in versions 6 and 6.2 assumes */ds*.

*/dt* tells Undelete to recover deleted files recorded by the delete-tracking feature of the version 5 Mirror command or the version 6 or 6.2 Undelete command. To use this parameter, you must already have started delete tracking.

585

Undelete can then try to recover any files subsequently deleted. The /dt parameter causes Undelete to display the name of each deleted file it finds and to prompt you to confirm the recovery.

/dos tells Undelete to use the information recorded by MS-DOS to recover deleted files. When you use this parameter, Undelete prompts for confirmation before recovering each file it can restore. Because MS-DOS clears the first character in the name of a deleted file, you are also asked what the first character should be before the file is undeleted. If the only parameter you specify is <filename>, Undelete in version 5 assumes /dos if a delete-tracking file does not exist.

/all tells Undelete to recover all deleted files without stopping at each and prompting for confirmation. If the Delete Sentry feature is in place or if a delete-tracking file exists, /all causes all recoverable files to be restored under their original file names. Otherwise, /all causes all recoverable files to be restored with # or another unique character as the first character in the file name. You can then use the MS-DOS Rename command to replace the # symbol with an appropriate character.

/list tells Undelete to display a list of the files it can recover. Unrecoverable files are marked with a double asterisk (**).

The following parameters are available only in versions 6 and 6.2:

/load causes Undelete to load itself into memory, using the parameters stored in the file UNDELETE.INI.

/S<drive> tells Undelete to load itself into memory and move deleted files to a special directory. When you use this feature, known as *Delete Sentry*, Undelete moves the files you delete while Delete Sentry is in effect. If the delete-sentry directory becomes full, Undelete permanently deletes the oldest files until it has enough room to move the newly deleted file. This is the most certain method of undeleting files because the files aren't actually deleted. Just the same, you should undelete a file as soon as you know you need it because Undelete will permanently delete the file if it runs out of room or after seven days pass.

/T<drive>-<files> tells Undelete to load itself into memory and record the storage locations of files you delete. When you use this feature, known as *Delete Tracking*, Undelete saves information about all the files you delete while Delete Tracking is in effect. Although Delete Tracking isn't as certain a method of locating deleted files as is Delete Sentry, it doesn't require the extra disk space that the delete-sentry directory requires. This information is stored in a system file named PCTRACKR.DEL.

<drive> is the letter (without a colon) of the drive for which you want to track deleted files; you must include this parameter when you use /T. <files> is

the number of deleted files you want to track. If you choose to include <files>, you can specify any number from 1 through 999, separating it from <drive> with a hyphen. If you don't specify <files>, Undelete assumes a certain number depending on the size of the disk, as shown in the following table:

| Disk Size | Number of Files | Size of PCTRACKR.DEL |
|-----------|-----------------|----------------------|
| 360 KB | 25 | 5 KB |
| 720 KB | 50 | 9 KB |
| 1.2 MB | 75 | 14 KB |
| 1.44 MB | 75 | 14 KB |
| 20 MB hard disk | 101 | 18 KB |
| 32 MB hard disk | 202 | 36 KB |
| Hard disk larger than 32 MB | 303 | 55 KB |

/U (for *unload*) removes Undelete from memory so that it no longer tracks deleted files. If you want to change the method that Undelete uses to track deleted files, you need to first unload Undelete and then load it again using the appropriate parameters.

*/purge*<drive> permanently deletes all the files that are currently in the delete-sentry directory for the specified drive. If you omit <drive>, Undelete purges the current drive.

NOTE: *Do not attempt to load the Undelete command into memory to track a drive that's affected by the Join or Substitute command. If you plan to use Undelete with an assigned drive (Assign command), assign the drive first. If you need to restore a deleted subdirectory, you can try the Unformat command.*

## Examples

To undelete all recoverable files in the current directory of the current drive, using the delete-tracking file and prompting for confirmation each time:

```
C:\MKT>undelete /dt
```

To undelete all recoverable files with the file extension DOC in the directory C:\MEMOS, using the MS-DOS record of deleted files and prompting for confirmation each time:

```
C:\>undelete \memos\*.doc /dos
```

To undelete all recoverable files with the file extension DOC in the directory C:\MEMOS, not prompting for confirmation:

```
C:\>undelete \memos\*.doc /all
```

To list all deleted files in the directory C:\MEMOS and to note which can be recovered:

```
C:\>undelete \memos /list
```

## UNFORMAT
## Undo a Disk Format

### Versions 5 and later

*Page 214*

The Unformat command helps you undo the effects of formatting either a floppy disk or a hard disk. With Unformat, you can restore a disk, its files, and its directories to their status before the disk was formatted. Like the complementary Undelete command, Unformat provides a safeguard against accidental loss of programs and data.

Because no prior files, including the Unformat command file, can be read from a hard disk you've formatted by mistake, you should also keep on hand an MS-DOS startup disk containing UNFORMAT.COM and a current copy of the system's CONFIG.SYS file for use in gaining access to the disk after formatting.

**NOTE:** *Unformat cannot restore a disk formatted with the /U parameter of the Format command.*

### unformat <drive> /J /L /test /partn /P /U

<drive> is the letter, followed by a colon, of the drive containing the disk to unformat (such as c:). <drive> cannot refer to a network drive.

/J (available only in MS-DOS version 5) checks the disk in <drive> for disk-information files recorded by the Mirror command, but it does not unformat the disk at the same time. If you use /J, Unformat tries to verify that the contents of the Mirror files agree with the information it finds on the disk. Because of the way Unformat searches the disk, it can find a Mirror file even after the disk has been formatted. It cannot work, however, if you have used the Fdisk command to partition a hard disk.

*/test* checks the disk in <drive> but does not use files recorded by the version 5 Mirror command. Like the /J parameter, */test* examines the state of the disk but does not actually unformat it.

/L (versions 6 and 6.2) causes Unformat to search the disk directly, listing all the files and directories it finds in the root directory. This parameter causes Unformat to first search the disk and then ask if you're sure you want to restore it. Because Unformat cannot fully recover fragmented files (files stored in separate areas on the disk), it displays the name of each fragmented file and asks whether you want to truncate or delete it. You must choose one or the other, and in either case, you can expect to lose at least some information. If you don't use /L, Unformat normally displays only the names of files and subdirectories that are fragmented and are not fully recoverable.

/L (version 5) causes Unformat to react in one of two ways, depending on whether you also use the */partn* parameter. If you specify /L without the */partn* parameter, Unformat assumes there is no Mirror file and proceeds as described above for the versions 6 and 6.2 /L switch. If you specify /L with the */partn* parameter, Unformat displays the disk's partition table (information about the way the disk is set up for use by MS-DOS).

*/partn* without the /L parameter tells Unformat to restore the disk's partition table. To do this, Unformat must have access to a file named PARTNSAV.FIL, which you create with the Mirror command and keep on a disk, separate from the hard disk.

/P tells Unformat to send its messages to the printer attached to LPT1.

/U (available only in version 5) tells Unformat to rebuild the disk without using the Mirror file.

### Examples

To check on the inadvertently formatted hard disk in drive C without actually unformatting the disk:

```
A:\>unformat c: /test
```

To unformat the hard disk in drive C:

```
A:\>unformat c:
```

To unformat an inadvertently formatted floppy disk in drive A:

```
C:\>unformat a:
```

## VDISK.SYS
## Define a RAM Disk

*Page 390*

The device driver VDISK.SYS is used with the Device configuration command to create a virtual disk drive in your computer's memory. This file is in IBM's releases starting with version 3. The equivalent MS-DOS file is called RAMDRIVE.SYS. Refer to that entry if your system includes VDISK.SYS.

## VERSION (VER)
## Display the MS-DOS Version Number

**Versions 2 and later**

*Page 399*

The Version command (ver) displays the MS-DOS version number, which consists of the major version number, a period, and the minor version number (for example, 4.01).

The Version command has no parameters.

**ver**

### Example

To display the MS-DOS version number:

```
C:\>ver
```

For version 6.2, MS-DOS responds with a message like this:

```
MS-DOS Version 6.20
```

## VERIFY
## Verify Data Written to Disk

**Versions 2 and later**

The Verify command turns the verify feature of MS-DOS on or off. The verify feature confirms that data is correctly written to disk. Storing data on a disk takes a bit longer when Verify is on. Setting Verify on is equivalent to using the /V parameter of the Copy command. MS-DOS assumes Verify is off unless you specify otherwise.

**verify on off**

*on* turns Verify on.

*off* turns Verify off.

If you enter a Verify command with no parameters (type just *verify*), MS-DOS displays the current status of Verify (*VERIFY is on* or *VERIFY is off*).

### Examples

To turn Verify on:

```
C:\>verify on
```

To display the status of Verify:

```
C:\>verify
```

MS-DOS responds:

```
VERIFY is on
```

or

```
VERIFY is off
```

## VOLUME (VOL)
## Display the Volume Label of a Disk

### Versions 2 and later

*Page 110*

The Volume command (vol) displays the volume label and, in versions 4 and later, the serial number of a disk.

**vol \<drive\>**

\<drive\> is the letter, followed by a colon, of the drive containing the disk whose volume label is to be displayed. If you omit \<drive\>, MS-DOS displays the volume label of the disk in the current drive.

### Example

To display the volume label of the disk in the current drive:

```
C:\>vol
```

If the disk's volume label is HARD DISK, MS-DOS responds as follows:

```
Volume in drive C is HARD DISK
Volume Serial Number is 1608-5A30
```

If the disk has no volume label, MS-DOS responds:

```
Volume in drive A has no label
Volume Serial Number is 3433-1BC6
```

## VSAFE
## Watch for Viruses

### Versions 6 and 6.2

*Page 222*

*See also* MS Anti-Virus (MSAV).

The Vsafe command loads the Vsafe program into memory, where it watches for activities that might signal the presence of a virus.

**vsafe /\<option\> /ne /nx /A\<key\> /C\<key\> /N /D /U**

<option> lets you customize the behavior of Vsafe. <option> is a number (from 1 through 8) followed by a plus sign (+) to turn on that option or a minus sign (−) to turn it off. You can include as many of these options as you want:

| Number | Default | Action |
|--------|---------|--------|
| 1 | On | Warns you when a hard disk is about to be formatted (completely erased) |
| 2 | Off | Warns you when a program tries to stay in memory |
| 3 | Off | Prevents any program from writing to any disk |
| 4 | On | Checks each executable file that MS-DOS opens |
| 5 | On | Checks the boot sectors of all disks for viruses |
| 6 | On | Warns you when a program tries to write to the boot sector or partition table of a hard disk |
| 7 | Off | Warns you when a program tries to write to the boot sector of a floppy disk |
| 8 | Off | Warns you when a program tries to modify an executable file |

/ne prevents Vsafe from loading itself into expanded memory.

/nx prevents Vsafe from loading itself into extended memory.

/A<key> and /C<key> specify the key combination that, when pressed, causes the Vsafe window to "pop up." <key> is the character that, together with the Alt key (/A) or the Ctrl key (/C), makes up the hot-key combination.

/N tells Vsafe to also watch for viruses on network drives.

/D tells Vsafe not to calculate checksums.

/U (for *unload*) removes Vsafe from memory.

## Examples

To start Vsafe with the default settings and enable protection of network drives:

```
C:\>vsafe /n
```

To start Vsafe and have it warn you if a program tries to write to the boot sector of a floppy disk but not check each executable file as MS-DOS opens it:

```
C:\>vsafe /7+ /4-
```

To unload Vsafe:

```
C:\>vsafe /u
```

# XCOPY
## Copy Files and Directories Selectively
### Versions 3.2 and later

*Page 172*

The Xcopy command lets you copy only files whose archive attribute is on or files that have changed since a particular date. You can also use the Xcopy command to copy files not only from the source directory but also from all the subdirectories it contains; if the corresponding subdirectories don't exist on the target disk or directory, the Xcopy command creates them. Xcopy is thus particularly useful in duplicating a directory structure from one disk to another.

**xcopy <source> <target> /A /M /E /P /S /V /W /D:<date>**

<source> is the name of the file to be copied. You can use wildcard characters to copy a set of files with similar file names or extensions. You must include <source>, specifying at least a drive letter.

<target> specifies where <source> is to be copied. You can include any combination of drive letter, path name, and file name.

/A copies only those files whose archive attribute is on but leaves the archive attribute unchanged.

/M copies only those files whose archive attribute is on, then turns off the archive attribute of the source files. Turning the archive attribute off is useful for backup procedures because it tells MS-DOS (or any other program, such as a backup utility) that the file hasn't been changed since it was last backed up and therefore doesn't need to be archived again.

/E creates subdirectories on <target> even if they are empty on <source>. If you use /E, you must also use /S.

/P prompts for confirmation before copying each file specified in <source>.

/S applies the Xcopy command to all subdirectories contained in <source> unless the subdirectories are empty. If you specify <source> as a drive letter or as the root directory of a disk, the Xcopy command is applied to every subdirectory on the disk.

/V verifies that the copy of the file on <target> was stored correctly. This option can slow the operation of the Xcopy command somewhat, but it's good insurance if you're copying critical data and must be certain that it was copied correctly.

/W waits and prompts you to press a key before the Xcopy command begins. This gives you a chance to put in the correct floppy disk before starting to copy files.

/D:<date> copies only files whose date of creation or last change (as displayed by the Directory command) is the same as or later than <date>.

### Examples

To copy all the files whose archive attribute is on from the directory C:\MKT\WP to the disk in drive A and turn off the archive attribute of the source files:

```
C:\>xcopy \mkt\wp a: /m
```

To copy all the files whose archive attribute is on from the directory C:\MKT\WP and all subdirectories that contain files to the disk in drive A and turn off the archive attribute of the source files:

```
C:\>xcopy \mkt\wp a: /s /m
```

To copy all the files that have changed since October 16, 1993, from the directory D:\MKT\WP and all subdirectories that contain files to the disk in the current drive, prompting for confirmation before each copy:

```
C:\>xcopy d:\mkt\wp /d:10-16-93 /s /p
```

To copy all the files and directories on the disk in drive A to the disk in drive B, including all empty subdirectories:

```
C:\>xcopy a:\ b:\ /s /e
```

# XMAEM.SYS
## Emulate IBM PS/2 80286 Expanded Memory Adapter
### Version 4

# XMA2EMS.SYS
## Manage Lotus-Intel-Microsoft Expanded Memory
### Version 4

XMAEM.SYS and XMA2EMS.SYS are device drivers that enable version 4 of MS-DOS to use memory beyond the normal maximum of 640 KB. Because these programs are for use by specific computer models and memory expansion boards, follow the instructions in the manual that came with your computer or memory expansion board when using these commands.

# Index

## Special Characters

@ (batch display-suppression operator), 341

: (batch file label operator), 345

% (batch replaceable parameter), 322–23

%% (batch replaceable parameter), 366–69, 504–5

\ (canceled command symbol), 29–30

/? (command help parameter), 68, 512

^ (control key symbol), 31

+ (Copy file-combining operator), 77

. (current directory marker), 139, 147–52

$T (Doskey command separator), 335

$ (Doskey replaceable parameter), 334, 478

* (Dosshell directory operator), 262

+ (Dosshell directory operator), 244, 262

– (Dosshell directory operator), 244, 262

% (Dosshell parameter), 271

… (Dosshell symbol), 250

.. (parent directory marker), 139, 147–52

\ (path name separator), 143

¦ (piping operator), 53, 310, 311–12, 516

$ (Prompt operator), 400–401, 558

< (redirection operator), 53, 301, 516

> (redirection operator), 54, 300, 311–12, 516

>> (redirection operator), 309, 516

\ (root directory marker), 139, 143

* (wildcard character), 45–46, 64–65, 347–48

? (wildcard character), 45–46, 65, 81–82

## A

accented characters, 132

access, file and directory. *See* attributes, file and directory

access, speeding disk. *See* disk buffers; disk caches; Fastopen command

adapter RAM/ROM memory, 117

Advanced Power Management (APM), 395

allocation units, 48, 99

Alt-255 keys, 350, 359

Alternate key (Alt), 31, 246

Alt-F1 keys, 285

Alt-F7 keys, 334

Alt-Minus keys, 285

Alt-Plus keys, 285

Alt-Tab keys, 265

ANSI.SYS device driver
command reference, 432
installing, 395, 465
Mode and, 120, 335, 360

anti-virus programs. *See* MS Anti-Virus program (msav); Vsafe program

APM (Advanced Power Management), 399

Append command, 165–66, 432–34

application programs, 4, 171–74, 221–22. *See also* program files

archive attributes, 174, 175–77, 183–86

archiving. *See* backing up files and directories

arrow keys. *See* direction keys

ASCII (American Standard Code for Information Interchange), 86, 254

Assign command, 434–35

## VAN WOLVERTON

A professional writer since 1963, Van Wolverton has had bylines as a newspaper reporter, editorial writer, political columnist, and technical writer. He wrote his first computer program—one that tabulated political polls—for the *Idaho State Journal* in Pocatello, Idaho, in 1965. His interests in computers and writing have been intertwined ever since. As a computer professional, Wolverton has worked at IBM and Intel and has written software documentation for national software companies, including Microsoft Corporation. He is the author of HARD DISK MANAGEMENT and MS-DOS COMMANDS, both Microsoft Press Quick Reference Guides, and SUPERCHARGING MS-DOS. He was also a contributor to THE MS-DOS ENCYCLOPEDIA. Wolverton and his wife, Jeanne, live in a twenty-first–century log cabin near Alberton, Montana.

The manuscript for this book was prepared and submitted to Microsoft Press in electronic form. Text files were processed and formatted using Microsoft Word.

Principal typographer:  Katherine Erickson
      Interior designer:  Kim Eggleston
      Illustrator, chapter opener art:  Mark Monlux
      Illustrator, interior art:  Lisa Sandburg
      Cover designer:  Rebecca Geisler-Johnson
      Photographer:  Karl Weatherly
      Cover color separator:  Color Service, Inc.
      Indexer:  Shane-Armstrong Information Systems

Text composition by Microsoft Press in New Baskerville with display type in Avant Garde Demi, using the Magna Composition system and the Linotronic 300 laser imagesetter.

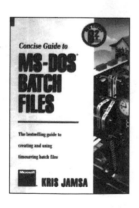

# Register Today!

Return the
*Running MS-DOS®*
registration card for:

✔ special book offers

✔ a Microsoft Press® catalog

Available in the U.S. and Canada only.
Fill in information below and mail postage-free.  Please mail only the bottom half of this page.

*Running MS-DOS*

_____
NAME

_____
COMPANY (if applicable)

_____
ADDRESS

_____

_____
CITY                                    STATE          ZIP

## *Your feedback is important to us.*

Include your daytime telephone number, and we may call to find out how you
use *Running MS-DOS* and what we can do to make future editions even more
useful. If we call you, we'll send you a **FREE GIFT** for your time!

(        )
_____
DAYTIME TELEPHONE NUMBER

# *For Desktop or Laptop*

**A Field Guide to MS-DOS® Commands**
*Seichert & Wood*
If you're new to the MS-DOS operating system, and want quick
answers to quick questions about MS-DOS commands, this handy
guide for you. It's arranged by task and orgaznized in easy-to-use,
easy-to-remember sections with rich cross-referencing for easy lookup.
Look for the friendly guy in the pith helmet, who leads you through
from start to finish. Covers MS-DOS through version 6.2.
**208 pages   $9.95 ($12.95 Canada)   ISBN 1-55615-560-3**
*Available February 1994*

NO POSTAGE
NECESSARY
IF MAILED
IN THE
UNITED STATES

## BUSINESS REPLY MAIL
FIRST-CLASS MAIL        PERMIT NO. 53        BOTHELL, WA

POSTAGE WILL BE PAID BY ADDRESSEE

**MICROSOFT PRESS REGISTRATION**
RUNNING MS-DOS
PO BOX 3019
BOTHELL  WA   98041-9910